History o

UNIVERSITY OF NEBRASKA PRESS
Lincoln and London

History of Nevada

Second Edition, Revised
By Russell R. Elliott
With the assistance of William D. Rowley

LINE DRAWINGS BY JACK BRODIE

The paper in this book meets the minimum
requirements of American National Standard
for Information Sciences—Permanence of
Paper for Printed Library Materials,
ANSI z39.48–1984.

Library of Congress Cataloging-in-Publication Data
Elliott, Russell R.
   History of Nevada.
   Bibliography: p.
   Includes index.
   1. Nevada—History.
I. Rowley, William D.
II. Title. F841.E43 1987   979.3   86–7064
ISBN 0-8032-1811-7
ISBN 0-8032-6715-0 (pbk.)

Second paperback printing: 1989

Dedicated to my wife, Annie, and my daughters, Patricia and Anne

Contents

A section of illustrations follows p. 210

Maps

Preface to the Second Edition

NEVADA, AS IT MOVES into the second half of the 1980s, exhibits much the same basic political, economic, and social patterns as it did in the previous two decades. Politically, although the players continually change, the state remains conservative, particularly in financial matters, its leaders facing the same questions that faced their predecessors: crowded schools, rising crime rates and over-crowded prisons, deteriorating transportation systems, air pollution, inadequate water supplies, and the numerous other problems caused by a population growing too rapidly. Economically, the state continues to place its main emphasis on gambling. Faith in that industry as a panacea for all ills, however, was weakened somewhat when the recession of the early 1980s destroyed the myth that gambling was recession proof. That realization sent Nevada's leaders hurrying to find ways to diversify the state's economy. The effort has had some success under Governor Bryan, but Nevada still has a long way to go before it can legitimately claim to have a diversified economy. Nevada's societal structure has changed little since the publication of the original edition of this work. The rather substantial movement of Hispanics into the state, however, and to a lesser degree the entrance of the Southeast Asians may modify the picture in the future. Ironically, the continuing stability of Nevada's gambling economy has made possible many cultural developments, particularly in the Las Vegas and Reno metropolitan areas.

A strong and continued interest in the history of the state has produced numerous articles and books and uncovered a number of important documents. Much of that research and writing is noted in the rather extensive addendum to the original bibliography. In order to keep abreast of that scholarship, important changes have been made throughout the text, particularly in chapter 3, where new material on Jedediah Smith definitely establishes the path of his journey eastward across the Great Basin in 1827, and in chapter 5, where Professor William C. Miller's discovery of the scrapbooks kept by Orion Clemens and the letters of Andrew J. Marsh adds new information to the story of Nevada Territory. More important are the changes in chapter 5 where new interpretations by David A. Johnson of the Constitutional Conventions of 1863 and 1864 have made obsolete earlier interpretations of those events. In order to complete the revision process and bring Nevada's political, economic, and social history through 1985, chapters 15, 16, and 17 have been completely rewritten. I wrote the first two of these and Professor William Rowley wrote chapter 17.

A revised edition also presents an excellent opportunity to correct mistakes, typographical and otherwise, in the original text. That task was made easier by students, teachers, and colleagues who brought to my attention typographical and factual errors. I am grateful for their suggestions. Special thanks are due to Professor Jerome Edwards for his many suggestions and particularly for his help with the bibliography and to Professor William Rowley for his rewriting of chapter 17. Errors, of course, are my responsibility.

RUSSELL R. ELLIOTT

Preface

NEVADA BECAME A STATE in 1864 when national and local leaders successfully took advantage of a combination of circumstances — the rapid growth following the discovery of the Comstock Lode and the Lincoln administration's political need for another free state. But economic stability was not so easily achieved. Before World War II the state passed through repeated cycles of boom and bust, its economy dominated by the fluctuations of the mining industry. Particularly in the periods of depression, attempts were made to broaden the state's economic base through federal aid, permissive state legislation, and various publicity schemes. These efforts met with little success, but after the war a transportation and recreation revolution and the pressure of population growth in the West brought a booming tourist industry to Nevada. The political and social institutions which developed from the mining economy blended easily into those required by an economy based on tourism. Thus, Nevada today is a strange combination of a sophisticated society and a mining frontier; while there have been liberal attitudes toward gambling, divorce, and prostitution, powerful conservative elements dominate the state's politics.

The decision to write a single-volume history of Nevada from its beginning to the present is complicated by the fact that there is so much basic research remaining to be done. Yet the need for such a study to serve as an introduction to Nevada for the college student as well as for the general reader overshadows the obvious danger of attempting a synthesis at this time. It is hoped that the present work will serve that need while filling some of the existing gaps in the history of the state.

My debts have accumulated over the many years spent in preparing this work. The extent of these debts is reflected somewhat in the essay on sources and in the footnotes. Besides the individuals noted therein I want to thank Professors Fred Peterson and David B. Slemmons for help with chapter one and Professor Kay Fowler and Dr. Donald Tuohy for similar aid with chapter two. Professors James Hulse and Wilbur Shepperson deserve special thanks for reading and critically evaluating the entire manuscript. Errors are, of course, my responsibility. Research for this study was aided by a grant from the Desert Research Institute's Committee for Research Planning in the Humanities.

RUSSELL R. ELLIOTT

CHAPTER 1

The Physical Environment

"It is a passive, imperturbable landscape, a sleeping grandeur laid in timeless space. It is a land that is older than history—the very blueprints of creation."—Richard G. Lillard, *Desert Challenge*.

THE PRESENT STATE of Nevada, except for its northeastern and southeastern corners, lies entirely within the region which John C. Frémont called the Great Basin in order to identify it as a land of interior drainage. Although the term is a colorful one and descriptive to a point, it also is misleading, for the so-called Great Basin is in fact a collection of some ninety basins separated from each other by more than 160 mountain ranges. The latter phenomenon is one of the Basin's most distinctive features. These isolated, nearly parallel mountain ranges and intervening plains, made for the most

1

THE GREAT BASIN

part of subaerial deposits of waste from the mountains, were described effectively years ago by the geographer C. E. Dutton as an "army of caterpillars crawling toward Mexico." The altitude of Nevada's mountain ranges and valleys generally increases to the northward and eastward across the state, although the highest point is Boundary Peak on its western border at an elevation of 13,145 feet. The lowest elevation, approximately 300 feet above sea level, is in Clark County in the southern part of Nevada. The mean elevation is approximately 5,500 feet. Nevada covers a land and water area of 110,540 square miles, ranking seventh among the fifty states in size. The great length of the state encompasses seven degrees of latitude, from the 35th to the 42d parallel.

Like other Great Basin states, Nevada had a violent geologic metamorphosis, undergoing continual erosion for a long period and experiencing earth movements which have been almost as continual, but vigorous only at infrequent intervals. As a result, most of the mountain ranges in the Great Basin are bounded by faults on either one or both sides. All of the major divisions of geologic time are represented by the rocks that form the mountains and valleys of Nevada, and from these the geologists have been able to construct a geologic history which dates to over one and one-half billion years ago.

The most significant phase of that history began about thirty million years ago when extensive block-faulting occurred. During this period, great fissures, generally with a north-south trend, broke the crust of the earth, and massive volcanoes covered most of the land with thousands of cubic miles of molten lava and volcanic ash. Along the fissures, blocks of the broken crust moved up or down in relation to the adjoining blocks, thus forming a series of elongated blocks tilted at various angles with the low sides forming the valleys and the high sides forming the mountains. It was during this period that the drainage to the prehistoric seas was disrupted, causing diversion of the streams into the interior basins and setting the basic structural outline of present Nevada. The outstanding event of the Pleistocene age in Nevada was the spread of the glaciers. A number of valley glaciers existed on the high mountain ranges in the region between the Sierra Nevada and the Rocky Mountains, and from the ends of these glaciers vigorous rivers swept into the valleys, forming large lakes.

PHYSIOGRAPHY OF NEVADA

The largest and most famous of the prehistoric lakes thus formed in the present state of Nevada was Lake Lahontan. Henry Engelmann, geologist for Captain James H. Simpson's exploration across the Great Basin in 1859, was the first to recognize the shore features of Lake Lahontan as evidence of an ancient deep lake. Clarence King, a prominent American geologist, named the lake in the 1870s in honor of Baron Louis Armand de Lahontan, a French explorer. Lake Lahontan dates from the last glaciation of North America, which ended about ten thousand years ago. It was never a solid body of water, but was broken by mountain ranges into a number of long arms. At its maximum it covered some 8,450 square miles and extended from the present Nevada-Oregon border on the north to the vicinity of present-day Hawthorne, about 250 miles to the south; it stretched from the Susanville-Honey Lake area of California on the west about 185 miles to the Stillwater Range in Nevada on the east, with one long arm reaching northeastward beyond the present town of Golconda. Stratigraphic detail indicates that the lake fluctuated greatly in water level, with two or perhaps three high-water marks and almost complete desiccation between. The drying-up process has continued since the last high-water stage, and all that remains now of the once great lake are two bodies of water, Pyramid and Walker lakes, and a number of playa, or dry-lake remnants, including the Humboldt and Carson sinks, the Smoke Creek, Granite Creek, and Black Rock deserts, and Winnemucca and Honey dry lakes.

The violent geologic history left Nevada with its interesting pattern of interior drainage. Of the four largest rivers in the state, the Truckee and Walker drain into Pyramid and Walker lakes, respectively, while the Humboldt and the Carson, at least until man began to interfere by constructing dams, drained into their respective sinks. Most of the lesser streams empty, generally, onto desiccated and cracked clay playa beds. The only exceptions to the pattern of interior drainage occur in the northeastern part of the state, where the Owyhee and Bruneau rivers and a few lesser streams eventually find their way to the Columbia River, and in the southeastern tip of Nevada, where the Muddy and Virgin rivers flow into the Colorado River.

The geologic changes which have been and are being noted by successive generations since the first white man entered that state

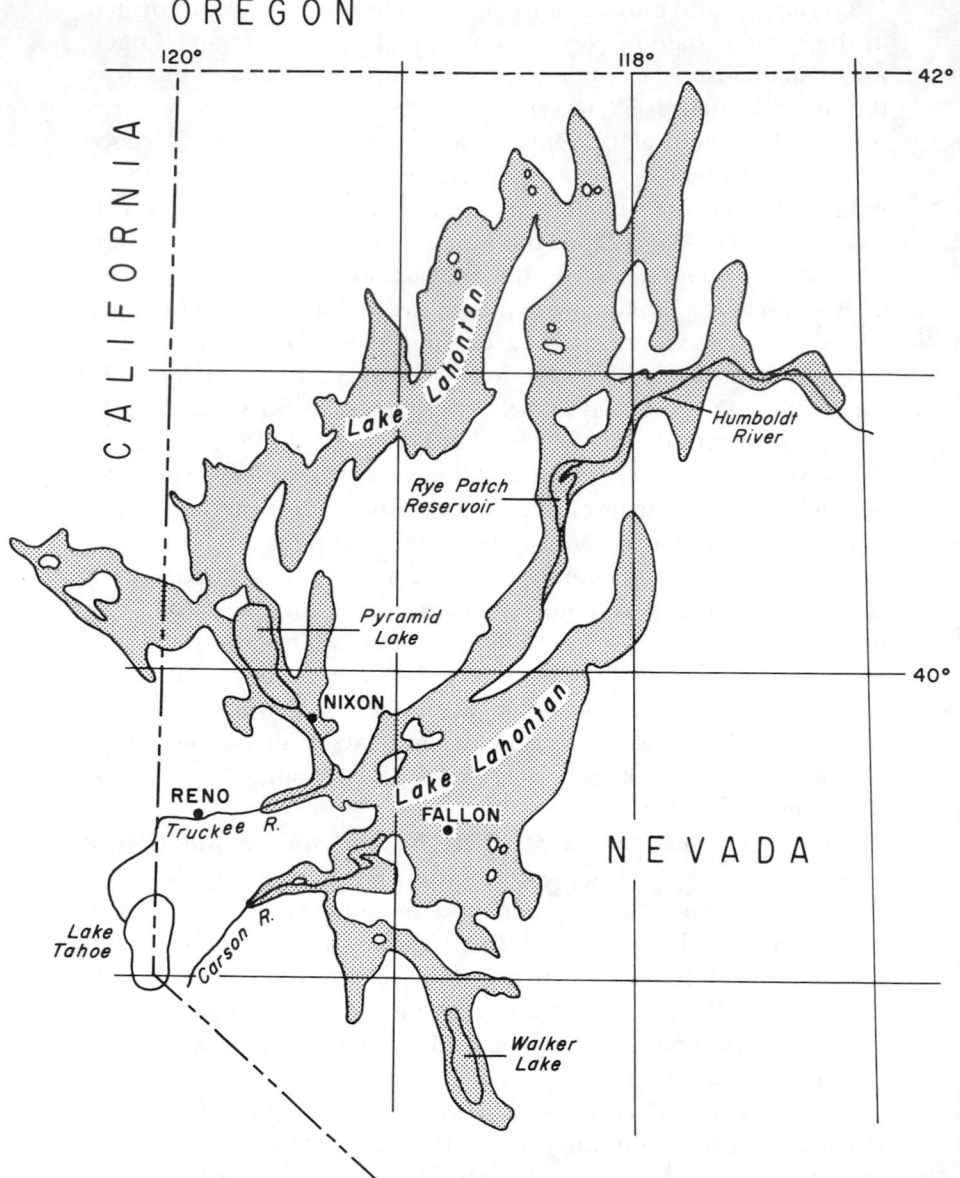

OREGON

CALIFORNIA

120° 118° 42°

Lake Lahontan

Humboldt
River

Rye Patch
Reservoir

Pyramid
Lake

40°

NIXON

Lake Lahontan

RENO
Truckee R. FALLON

NEVADA

Lake
Tahoe

Carson R.

Walker
Lake

PREHISTORIC LAKE LAHONTAN

are no doubt quite similar, though on a smaller and less violent scale, to those which occurred thousands of years ago. The theory of plate tectonics provides an interesting explanation of such changes and of the land forms seen in Nevada today. The idea that the earth is made up of crustal segments or plates that are continually moving and creating surface changes has focused new attention on the geologic history of Nevada. One expert suggests western Nevada as the focal point for possible major geological changes that will result from future movement of the plates.[1]

The Nevada climate is generally semiarid, but varies from small areas of arctic climate above timber line on the highest mountains to a genuine desert near sea level in the southern part of the state. The most striking climatic features are the bright sunshine, the small annual precipitation in the valleys and deserts, the heavy snowfall in the higher mountains, the dryness and purity of air, and the phenomenally wide daily ranges in temperature. Nevada's precipitation, mostly from snowfall, on the average is less than in any other state, and ranges from less than five inches in the arid regions to eighteen inches in Lamoille Canyon on the western side of the Ruby Mountains and to as much as twenty-eight inches at Marlette Lake in the most easterly range of the Sierra. Mountain snowfall forms the main source of water for streamflow.[2] Melting of the snowpack in the spring often causes some spring flooding; damaging floods, however, are rare. Temperatures in Nevada range from the coldest in the nation, often 30 to 40 degrees Fahrenheit below zero in the northeastern part of the state, to the hottest in the nation, at times reaching 115 to 120 degrees Fahrenheit in the southern tip of the state. The highest temperature on record is 122°F., observed at Overton in Clark County on June 23, 1954; the lowest recorded was -50°F, recorded at San Jacinto in Elko County on January 8, 1937. The range in temperature during a twenty-four-hour period, particularly in the late spring or early fall, some-

[1] John McPhee, *Basin and Range* (New York: Farrar, Strauss, Giroux, 1980).

[2] This fact lead a young University of Nevada humanities professor and member of the Sierra Club, J. E. Church, to conceive and develop a practical means of measuring the water content of winter snow and a method of evaluating the results in relation to the water supply. Dr. Church developed "snow-surveying" into a science which has become recognized throughout the world. An excellent article on "snow-surveying" appears in *Nevada Highways and Parks* (July–December 1952): 3–19.

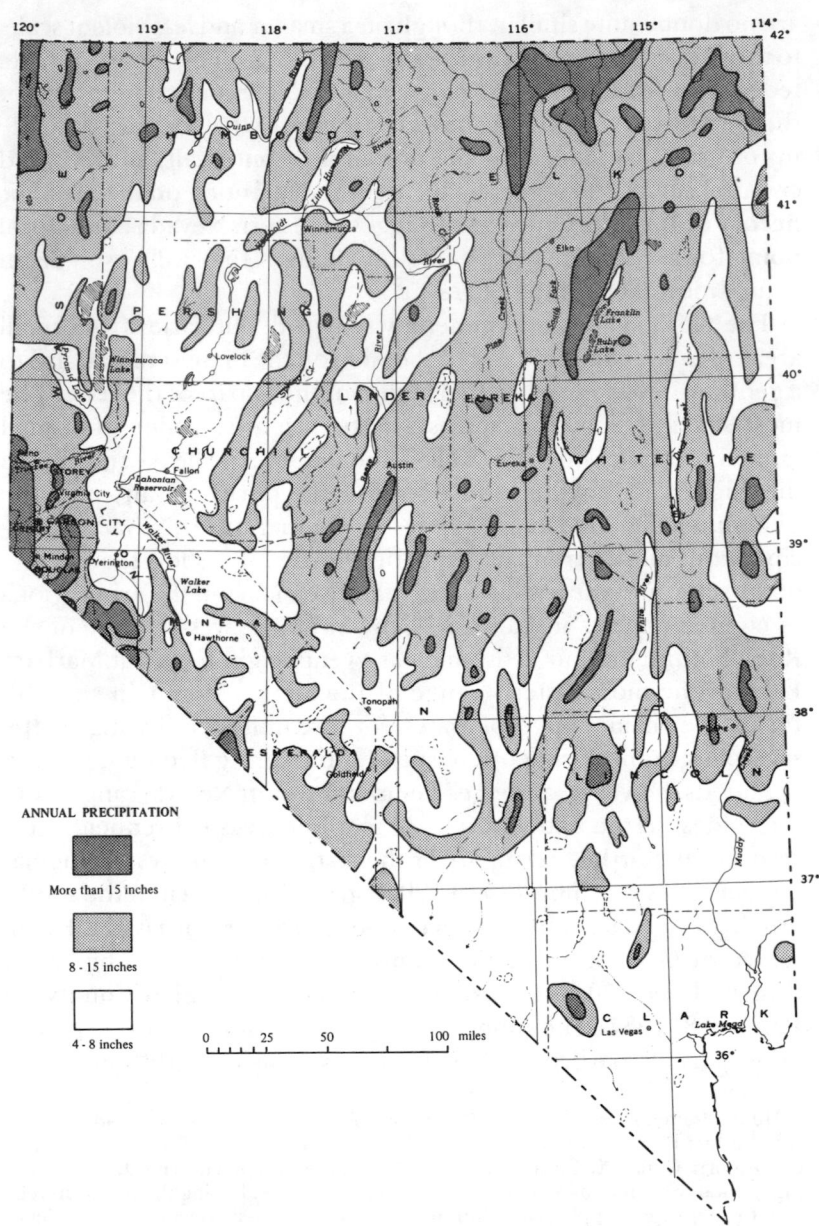

ANNUAL PRECIPITATION

More than 15 inches

8 - 15 inches

4 - 8 inches

0   25   50   100 miles

ASSUMED AVERAGE PRECIPITATION IN NEVADA

times reaches a variation of 50° or more. This wide diurnal range usually assures cool evenings in the heat of the summer and mild days in the cool of winter. The average mean temperature is 45° at Wells in the northeastern part of the state, 50.1° at Reno in the western part, and 67.8° at Overton in the southeast. Nevada's air is clear, dry, and generally pure, although mining centers in the state often did and some still do subject their citizens to varying degrees of air pollution. In addition, the state's two major urban areas, Las Vegas and Reno, are beginning to experience some air pollution during certain parts of the year. The average length of the growing season in Nevada varies from 103 days at Elko in the northeast to 155 days at Reno in the west, with 239 days at Las Vegas in the southern part of the state.

The soils of Nevada reflect the varied and typically harsh environments found throughout the state. The mountain-valley topography and the aridity of the climate are the overriding determinants of the type of vegetation and of the use of the land for crops, grazing, and forestry. The weathering processes peculiar to the high mountain ridges, the parched desert basins, the tablelands, and the wet meadows have led to the development of distinctive kinds of soils, composed of varying combinations of weathered and altered layers of parent geological materials. The parent materials, called soil horizons, determine the properties and uses of the different types of soils. Although some of Nevada's soils are classified as desert—shallow, raw, young, and rocky, hardly affected by the limited weathering supposed to occur in an arid climate—most are regularly moistened to moderate depths and weather at moderate rates. Large portions of the arid landscape date from glacial times and are mantled by strongly weathered soils which formed in those moister periods.

Except for limited areas of wet meadows, the soils of Nevada are characteristically dry through the summer and autumn and are moistened by winter rainfall. Two major kinds of surface soil horizons have formed under this environment of alternate moistness and dryness. At high elevations where precipitation is plentiful, a thick, dark-colored, organic-matter-rich surface horizon is found. Such soils, called Mollisols, are fertile, well structured, and resistant to erosion; they have a high water infiltration rate, and usually do not crust. Because of these qualities Mollisols offer a fair-to-good chance of success for rangeland reseeding and renovation projects. The most valuable rangelands in Nevada are on Mollisols occurring in a 50- to 100-mile-wide belt across the northern part of the state, and at higher elevations along most of the larger mountain ranges. In these regions, however, either the precipitation is too limited or the growing season too short for the production of any dryland crops such as small grains.

The second major type of surface soil horizon—light colored, with little organic matter, a weakly developed or no soil structure, and limited fertility—is typical of the Aridisols, Inceptisols, and Entisols which make up most of the more arid portions of the state. Although these soils are somewhat more difficult to bring into production than the Mollisols because of their slow water infiltration rates and lower fertility, they are potentially highly productive agricultural soils if irrigation water is made available. The gently sloping and level Aridisols and Entisols of the alluvial-fan piedmonts and basin fill plains are particularly well suited to mechanized and commercial agriculture. The greatest variety of economic crops could be grown in the basins of southern Nevada, where the growing season is longer and the temperatures are higher. The moderately sloping and steep Aridisols are useful only for extensive grazing and recreational purposes.

Salt- and alkali-affected soils are common in the valleys of Nevada. The soils of the mountains have been leached and salts from them carried in streams and ground water to the arid basins, where the water evaporates and salts accumulate. All degrees of salt-affected soils occur. The saltiest soils are found in areas with high water tables where ground water migrates to the soil surface and evaporates, leaving residual soluble salts. Some efforts to irrigate soils in Nevada have failed because they were located on such salt-affected soils. More commonly, the saltiness or alkali in irrigated soils is the result of high water tables created by overirrigation and lack of drainage.

Another kind of poorly drained soil occurs in Nevada where meandering streams flood during the spring snow-melt in the mountains. Native meadows of sedges and rushes occupy these wet bottom lands. The soils have thick, dark, organic-matter-rich surface horizons underlaid by dull gray or mottled mineral soil which reflects poor drainage. These soils, called Aquolls, are a wet type of

Mollisol. They may be salty, but ordinarily leached. Since these naturally irrigated meadow soils produce dependable, if small, yields of wild hay, they have been exceedingly important in the history of Nevada ranching and were vital to the emigrant parties crossing the Basin. About 90 percent of the state's irrigated land is devoted to forage crops, and wild meadow hay grown on Aquolls makes up a large proportion of that total. In recent years, the Agricultural Experiment Station has shown that wild hay production on these soils can be greatly increased by fertilization and control of water to prevent overirrigation.[3]

The desert soils in central and western Nevada at lower elevations support mainly shad scale, bud sage, greasewood, and saltbush, while at higher elevations sagebrush is dominant. In southern Nevada, large areas at lower elevations and with warmer climates are covered by creosote bush, mesquite bush, and the short, thicktrunked Joshua tree. This desert shrub-grass community comprises nearly 88 percent of the total area of the state. It was, and is, one of the most important determinants in deciding the roles to be played by men and animals in the desert environment.

Only about 12 percent of the total land in Nevada is forested, yet the state is so large that the small percentage represents some 8,650,000 acres, nearly one-third more land area than the state of Maryland. The forested lands, because of precipitation factors, are almost exclusively confined to the many mountain ranges. At the lower range level the Nevada forest land is dominated by singleleaf piñon and Utah juniper. The higher mountain ranges in various parts of the state show three zonal series.

In the western part of Nevada the Carson Range exhibits a Sierran sequence, with the Jeffrey, ponderosa, and sugar pines from 5,500 to 7,500 feet above sea level. Beyond that elevation, reaching to about 8,800 feet, the red fir, the western white pine, and the lodgepole pine are found. Between 8,800 feet and timberline at 10,500 feet, there is a subalpine forest with whitebark pine the actual timberline species, but with lodgepole pine and mountain hemlock also present.

In the central and southwestern part of the state the mountain

[3]I am indebted to Professor Frederick F. Peterson of the Soil Science, Plant, Soil, and Water Science Division of the University of Nevada, Reno, for help with the material on Nevada soils.

ranges have the simplified forest zones of the Great Basin, consisting of a low zone of piñon-juniper woodland reaching to between 7,500 and 8,500 feet. Above this and extending to 9,500 or 10,000 feet is a treeless zone of shrubs, mainly mountain mahogany and sagebrush. Beyond the treeless zone to 11,000 and 11,500 feet is a subalpine forest of limber pine and bristlecone pine, the latter species supposedly the oldest living plant. Either of these two may be the timberline species.

In the eastern part of the state the Rocky Mountain zonal series is found, with a ponderosa pine zone above the piñon-juniper forest, followed at higher elevations first by a Douglas fir–white fir zone and then by a subalpine forest of alpine fir, Engelmann's spruce, and sometimes limber pine and bristlecone pine. In all three zonal series, aspen, chokecherry, alder, water birch, willow, and cotton-wood trees border the mountain streams.

Nevada's early mining boom with its heavy demands for lumber cleared practically all of the virgin timber from the forest lands. Only 3 percent of the national forest in Nevada today contains timber which is considered harvestable on a commercial scale.

Nevada's vast open spaces harbor a surprising number of birds, animals, and fishes. The most common big game animal is the mule deer, with an estimated population of well over two hundred thousand spread throughout the state. In addition there are small herds of bighorn sheep, pronghorn antelope, and elk, the latter introduced into the state. Bighorn sheep in Nevada number about twenty-five hundred with some fifteen hundred of these (the Nevada desert or Nelson bighorn) protected within the Desert Game Range near Las Vegas. Antelope, numbering about three thousand, are found in White Pine County and in the Charles Sheldon National Antelope Refuge and Game Range in northwestern Nevada. Of some interest is the fact that the only federal area set aside in the United States for wild horses is a 435,000-acre refuge in southern Nevada.[4]

There are many small animals in Nevada; the most numerous are the rabbits. Others include the American mink, the muskrat, the

[4]Nevada's wild horse population, perhaps as many as one hundred thousand horses, has dwindled rapidly with the onslaught of civilization and the indiscriminate elimination of horses which followed the 1934 Taylor Grazing Act and the increasing demands for horse meat, coming especially from the manufacturers of food for pets. A fight to keep the animals from extinction has been led by a very interesting Nevadan, Mrs. Velma Johnston, more commonly known as "Wildhorse Annie."

beaver, the red fox, and the western badger, as well as coyotes, raccoons, porcupines, skunks, squirrels, chipmunks, and gophers. Nevada's desert environment also houses many varieties of reptiles, including rattlesnakes, gopher snakes, whip snakes, garter snakes, striped racers, and numerous varieties of lizards.

A number of upland game birds are native to Nevada, including the sage hen or sage grouse, the big blue grouse, and valley, mountain, and Gambel's quail. The chukar partridge and ring-necked pheasants are the most common of the bird species introduced into the state. All kinds of waterfowl inhabit Nevada waters, and one of the largest white pelican nesting colonies in North America is in Anaho Island National Wildlife Refuge in Pyramid Lake.

Nevada's most important game fish is the rainbow trout, found in many streams throughout the state, but particularly in the Truckee River. The only trout native to western Nevada is the famous Lahontan cutthroat, found mainly in Walker, Pyramid, Topaz, Catnip, and Summit lakes. Pyramid Lake also is the home of the rare cui-ui (kwee-wee), a type of sucker said to belong to an earlier geologic era. The state's only deep-water fish is the Mackinaw trout, found in Lake Tahoe.

Obviously, the geologic history and geographic setting have profoundly influenced the economic development of Nevada. The turbulent earth movements which lasted for millions of years created vast stores of mineral wealth which made Nevada in the nineteenth century the best example of a mining frontier state, and one of the best mineral producers in the nation today. Although substantial mineral discoveries have been made in nearly all of the state's seventeen counties, the great deposits of silver and gold occurred in the Comstock area in Storey County, at Aurora in present Mineral County, at Tonopah in Nye County, Goldfield in Esmeralda, Eureka in Eureka County, Pioche in Lincoln County, Austin in Lander County, and Hamilton in White Pine County. The largest copper deposits to date have been found in the Robinson district in White Pine County and at Weed Heights in Lyon County. Other important copper deposits have been found in the Mountain City area in Elko County and in the Copper Canyon—Copper Basin area in Lander County. Copper remained Nevada's leading metal producer until 1978 when the three leading producers in the state closed. In that year, stimulated by a number of low-grade gold mines, gold became the number one producer. In recent years, production of iron ores, manganese, tungsten, mercury, and nonmetallics such as gypsum, limestone, diatomaceous earth, magnesite, perlite and others have proved of great commercial importance to Nevada mining. Oil was discovered in Railroad Valley in eastern Nevada in 1954 and since that time the state's limited oil production has come from wells opened in that area, although a recent oil discovery in Eureka County, the first outside the Railroad Valley field, may alter that picture.

The same geological developments which gave Nevada ample mineral reserves made agriculture possible only in isolated areas where water resources were adequate. Only about 1.4 percent of Nevada's total land area of approximately 71 million acres is under cultivation, and that cultivation is dependent on irrigation. The production is mainly in hay and forage crops, but there are many other agricultural products grown in Nevada, from cantaloupes in the Fallon area to cotton in the Pahrump Valley of southern Nevada. The hay and forage crops and the extensive areas of desert grasses and edible shrubs throughout most of the state made possible a substantial cattle and sheep development. Ranching is Nevada's most important form of agriculture, with between 85 and 90 percent of the farm and ranch land in the state devoted to raising livestock. About three-fourths of the total value of all farm production sold in Nevada comes from the sale of cattle, calves, sheep, lambs, and wool. This is the highest proportion for any of the western states.

CHAPTER 2

Before the White Man

HOW AND WHEN man intruded upon the bleak, stark, and often beautiful land now known as Nevada cannot be answered with complete assurance. Scientists generally believe that man reached America from Asia via a land bridge across the present Bering Strait during the last deglaciation of western North America and passed into the High Plains through a corridor which opened between two great ice sheets. This took place probably between 11,000 and 13,000 years ago, a period which corresponds roughly to dates established at various archeological sites in the western United States. The story of his entrance into the Great Basin, and more specifically into the present Nevada, is gradually being pieced together by the combined efforts of geologists, archeologists, biologists, and paleoecologists.

15

PREHISTORIC PEOPLES

Perhaps the first written report of archeological remains in Nevada came in 1827 in a letter from the fur trader and mountain man Jedediah Smith to William Clark, superintendent of Indian affairs. The letter simply informed Clark of Smith's discovery of a flint knife and a pipe in a salt cave in a mountain near the Virgin River. The next description of possible archeological remains in Nevada came with the report of the Morgan Exploring Expedition in 1867. It was indicated by a correspondent of the *New York Tribune,* who summarized the report that the expedition when exploring in southern Nevada had found several salt works and a curious collection of rocks, mounds, and pillars that resembled an ancient city. Remnants of arches, with keystones still perfect and a number of small stone pillars constructed "with a peculiar kind of red mortar," were described.[1] A much more specific record of an archeological site was made in 1885 when Israel C. Russell published his classic geological study of Pleistocene Lake Lahontan. A spearhead found by W. J. McGee in the vicinity of Walker Lake was illustrated in the report. The spearhead, of human workmanship, was found associated with the bones of an extinct elephant, mammoth, or mastodon.[2]

From 1900 to 1920 there were sporadic reports of prehistoric remains in the southern tip of Nevada, but no systematic survey was made in that area during these years, probably because New World archeology was still in its infancy. However, an unusual archeological find made in 1911 in northwestern Nevada, near the present town of Lovelock, was the scene of the first scientific archeological excavation in Nevada. Archeological activity in Nevada increased in the 1920s with the discovery of what came to be known as the Lost City site, believed by many to be the ruins described by Morgan, and perhaps the most famous of all Nevada archeological

[1] The information about the Morgan Exploring Expedition is taken from Hubert H. Bancroft, *Native Races,* vol. 4, *Antiquities* (San Francisco: A L. Bancroft & Co., 1882), pp. 713–14. It should be noted, also, that in 1888 H. E. Boothby described some ancient canals located in the extreme southeastern tip of Nevada which supposedly had been seen in 1849 (H. E. Boothby, "Ancient Canals in Nevada," *American Antiquarian* 10 [1888]: 380–81).

[2] In 1889 McGee published his own account of the finding. W. J. McGee, "An Obsidian Implement from Pleistocene Deposits in Nevada," *American Anthropologist* 2 (1889): 301–12.

discoveries. Since then many additional sites have been explored in Nevada, and many others have been located for future excavations. The activities of the Nevada State Museum, the University of California at Berkeley, and the Desert Research Institute of the University of Nevada have been especially significant in recent years.

Although the excavations in Nevada, as elsewhere in the Great Basin, show extensive gaps in time, a story of man in Nevada has emerged from the scientific inquiries showing prehistoric peoples entering the Great Basin nearly 12,000 years ago as the pluvial lakes were beginning to recede. A number of sites have been found in Nevada which approximate this early date, but by far the most controversial and interesting is that at Tule Springs.

The Tule Springs site, located some fifteen miles northwest of Las Vegas at the foot of the Sheep Range, first attracted the attention of archeologists in 1933 when a field team from the American Museum of Natural History found evidences of man associated with extinct fauna—specifically, a concentration of charcoal with bones of extinct bison, camel, and horse. The particular evidence was a big bison skull with a large obsidian flake nearby. Three subsequent exploratory excavations were made in 1933, 1954, and 1956. Two charcoal samples subjected to radiocarbon dating showed rather surprising results: the one taken in 1954 showed a radiocarbon date of 23,800 years ago and the second, taken in 1956, showed a date of 28,000 years ago. Obviously, these figures intrigued scientists for if confirmed they would push back the known inhabitation of man in the Great Basin by thousands of years. The exploratory excavations had indicated that tremendous amounts of dirt would have to be moved before the Tule Springs site could be adequately explored, and because of the many difficulties involved it appeared that such an exploration would never be made. Yet, so many scientists were not satisfied with the conflicting testimony which came from the charcoal deposits and from the bones and artifacts, that an extensive excavation was made in late 1962 and early 1963. Two miles of trenches, twelve feet wide and up to thirty feet deep, were dug, enabling scientists to work out an elaborate stratigraphical detail. Animal bones were found in three main layers, with the oldest level showing bones of bison and predatory animals in a spring pit. Samples from this level showed a radiocarbon date of 40,000 years ago but no evidence of man. The next oldest level with animal bones present showed radiocarbon dates of 12,400 years ago, with some indications of man. However, these evidences are conjectural and will probably remain so. The bone objects in question may have been made and polished by man, but they may also have been polished by natural action of the spring. The third main channel bearing animal remains showed definite indications of man in association with Pleistocene elephants, camels, and horses. Objects in this channel were dated to about 11,000 years ago. In addition to these very early datings, a preceramic or lithic culture was uncovered, dating to 5,000 years ago.

The results of the extensive Tule Springs excavation, while inconclusive in some respects, did answer a number of questions which had puzzled researchers. For one thing, it was quite clear that the two earlier radiocarbon datings were erroneous: the first date of 23,800 years ago came from a sample that was an obvious mixture of deposits of different ages and was therefore meaningless; the other date of 28,000 years ago, taken from carbonized wood found at the site, could not in itself prove the existence of man at that time, and there was no other evidence found by the expedition of 1962–63. Although the very early date for Tule Springs has been discarded, the southern Nevada site shows definitely that man was in the area between 10,000 and 11,000 years ago. Evidence also suggests that he may have been in southern Nevada as early as 12,400 years ago. In any event these dates, roughly from 11,000 to 13,000 years ago, correlate with evidences of man at other sites in western North America and make the Tule Springs site still the most logical one to hold the honor of being man's earliest known home in present Nevada.[3]

A number of other sites in Nevada seem to corroborate the fact that early man lived in the region as early as 11,000 years ago. Perhaps the best known of these sites is Fishbone Cave, one of a series of caves discovered on the shores of the now dry lake Winnemucca in western Nevada. Excavations in 1952, 1953, and 1954 showed that Fishbone was one of a series of five caves, Crypt and Chimney at a slightly higher elevation, and Guano and Cowbone

[3] The excavation of the Tule Springs site, which lasted from October 1, 1962, through January 31, 1963, involved some two dozen scientists under the direction of Richard Shutler. Details of the excavation are given in H. M. Wormington and Dorothy Ellis, *Pleistocene Studies in Southern Nevada*, Nevada State Museum Anthropological Papers, no. 13 (Carson City, Nev., 1967).

at a lower elevation. Remains taken from the excavations indicate the association of man and horse in Crypt Cave and the association of man, horse, and camel in Fishbone. Reconstruction by the scientists indicates that man entered these caves as Lake Lahontan receded and that, in addition to hunting the now extinct horse and camel, he caught fish with nets. The earliest radiocarbon date is $11,555 \pm 500$ years B.P., but whether or not man was in the caves at that time has not been confirmed by the evidence presented to date. It appears from radiocarbon dates and other evidence that man occupied Fishbone Cave until about 6,000 years ago.

A few other sites in present Nevada correlate in time sequence to Fishbone Cave and suggest again that man may have been in these regions from 10,000 to 11,000 years ago. Of these, the best known are Falcon Hill on the western shore of Lake Winnemucca, with a date of 10,500 years ago; Leonard Rockshelter in the Humboldt basin, with a date of about 11,000 years ago, and Hidden Cave in the Carson Sink area near Fallon, with approximately the same dating.

Besides these sites, a number of Clovis points have been found in Nevada. The Clovis points are considered artifacts of a people who specialized in hunting mammoths. Radiocarbon dating of selected Clovis sites indicates a time of about 11,000 to 11,500 years ago, figures which also correspond to the culture that represents mammoth hunters. Isolated finds of Clovis points have been made near Tonopah, in Nye County, near Washoe Lake, in the Black Rock Desert, in Mineral County, and in Lincoln County.

One of the most controversial sites showing early man in Nevada is Gypsum Cave, located about twenty miles east of Las Vegas in a limestone spur of the Frenchman Mountains. Excavations in 1930 and 1931 revealed great beds of ground sloth dung in which were imbedded bones, horny claws, and the hair of the sloth. Beneath the sloth dung and hair, a number of atlatl points and parts of their wooden shafts were found. The finds were guess-dated at 8,500 B.C. on the assumption that man and sloth were coeval in the cave. Later, radiocarbon dating of dung samples confirmed the early date for the sloth. However, when a decorated atlatl shaft, thought to be the same age as the sloth dung, was dated in 1967 it showed only 950 B.C. Most archeologists now accept the dates of both the artifacts and the sloth dung as being valid, which, of course, would indicate that the artifacts found "under" the sloth dung were intrusive into that position.

In point of time-occupation by prehistoric peoples, the next important site is Lovelock Cave. Located twenty-two miles south of Lovelock, Nevada, on an intermediate shore line of ancient Lake Lahontan, this site first came to the attention of archeologists in 1911. At that time the cave was being mined commercially for guano, but so many artifacts and bones began to appear that the guano miners gave up and the archeologists moved in. Lovelock Cave was first explored in 1912 and again much more thoroughly in 1924. The many objects taken from it—human mummies, numerous artifacts, baskets (twined and coiled), flexible twined bags, matting, sandals, feather robes, rabbit and fish nets, remarkably lifelike painted and stuffed duck decoys, awls, sickles, and grass cutters made from bone and horn, knife handles, chipped flint knives and points, tubular pipes, scrapers, and hammers made from stone—indicated occupancy of the cave from about 2000 B.C. to the protohistoric period.[4] Unfortunately, private collectors got into the cave between the 1912 and 1924 excavations and not only took many of the important artifacts but made it difficult to excavate the cave properly. In spite of the vandalism, however, further excavations have been conducted there.

The Lovelock culture also has been identified in the majority of cave sites excavated in 1965 and 1966 in the Pyramid Lake area. The evidence accumulated from the many artifacts found indicates that, at the time of its apparent disappearance about 1400 A.D., the culture was a fairly complex one. The prehistoric peoples stored fish and other foods in cache pits, indicating that, had they chosen to do so, they were ready to move from a gathering and hunting society to a slightly more complex development. The aboriginal life, adapted to a lake-margin ecology, was not the "starving, miserable existence" the early explorers depicted for other parts of the Great Basin. The culture also showed a considerable development of the graphic and plastic arts, which probably stopped about 500 years ago for reasons as yet not clear to the archeologists. Perhaps a combination of pressures, from internal difficulties, from incoming

---

[4] Guano thrown out by the miners was screened during the late 1960s and artifacts of a late type were found, suggesting the occupancy of Lovelock Cave to the period just before the entrance of the whites.

groups (in this instance the Northern Paiutes), and from drought during the thirteenth century or other natural phenomena, caused the decline.[5]

Another interesting site in southern Nevada which shows a civilization roughly contemporary with that of Lovelock Cave is the Stuart Rockshelter, located about nine miles north of Moapa in Clark County. When the site was explored thoroughly in the late 1950s, many stone artifacts were found, including basin metates, projectile points, single and double blades, flake knives, and side and end scrapers. In addition, pottery remains showed the existence of three ceramic levels, the Paiute-Pueblo, the Pueblo, and Basketmaker. The many fire hearths located by the excavators indicated that the shelter in all of its cultural periods was used mainly as a campsite. According to the reconstruction, the first occupants of the shelter were hunters and gatherers—probably an eastward extension of the Pinto culture of the southern California desert. Radiocarbon dates placed this phase at 2094 B.C. The second culture period, the Basketmaker, is estimated to date from 300 to 700 A.D. The third phase was the Pueblo, typical of the culture of the Lost City, which lasted from 700 to 1100 A.D. The last occupants of the rockshelter in the prehistoric period were the mixed Paiute-Pueblo group, dating from 1100 A.D. to 1150 A.D. Various artifacts found in the rockshelter verify the fact that the Southern Paiutes penetrated into the southern Nevada cultural area before the departure of the Pueblos.

The most publicized of all the Nevada prehistoric sites is that of Lost City, the first center of population in what is now Nevada, as well as its first ghost town. Although the site was rediscovered in 1924, it did not receive national publicity until the 1930s, when it became apparent that the lake created by Boulder Dam would inundate the ancient site.

The work of excavation was begun in 1925 and 1926 and continued sporadically to 1938, when Lake Mead covered the area.

The site, called Pueblo Grande de Nevada by the excavator, encompassed a well-organized community of from ten to twenty thousand people who farmed, mined, hunted, and carried on exten-

---

[5] These excavations were under the leadership of Donald R. Tuohy of the Nevada State Museum, and although no official report has been issued to date, an interesting summary can be found in the *Nevada State Journal*, October 13, 1961, p. 41.

sive trading activity. Composed of pithouses, pueblo ruins, camp-
sites, rockshelters, salt mines, and caves, it covered both sides of
the lower sixteen miles of the Muddy River. Before Lake Mead
inundated the area, over 121 houses were wholly or partially excavated, the largest containing nearly 100 rooms.

The cultural sequence at Lost City as reconstructed divides the
history of the community into four phases. The first, or Moapa,
phase, dating from about 300 B.C. to approximately 500 A.D., was
a basketmaker culture, technically Basketmaker II. A number of
stones and many dartpoints were found at this level, but no arrow
points and no pottery. The second, or Muddy River, phase, dating
from 500 A.D. to 700 A.D., was that of Basketmaker III. During this
phase pottery was produced and salt was mined. In addition to earlier artifacts, slab and basin stones, blades, knives, and scrapers
were found. The third, or Lost City, phase lasted from 700 A.D.
to 1100 A.D. Most of the sites which were excavated belong to this
phase. Salt mining continued during the period and turquoise mining was initiated. Agriculture, probably with irrigation, thrived
during this stage in the history of Lost City. Much utility pottery,
many turquoise, shell, stone, and bone beads and pendants, and
coiled and twined baskets were found in these excavations. The
period was also very active in trading, with trade networks existing
to the north, south, east, and west. Turquoise was evidently one
of the big trade items. The villages of this period were combinations of pit and surface houses with many varieties of floor and
wall construction. The fourth, or Mesa House, phase was short-
lived, lasting only from 1100 A.D. to 1150 A.D. The sites from this
phase stood on the ridge of the valley high above its floor. The
center was the so-called Mesa House, which stood on a small mesa
some 120 feet above the valley, commanding an excellent view in
all directions. Artifacts from the period show the addition of articles
coming from the east, although the economy continued to be a
combination of trading, mining, and agriculture.

After 1150 A.D. the Mesa House and the few other houses occupied during this phase were abandoned—the exact cause can only be
guessed. There is no good evidence that drought forced out the
inhabitants; neither is there any indication of violent expulsion of
the Pueblo people. That they went eastward seems more certain;
the puebloid culture of western Utah and the Fremont culture of

eastern Utah and western Colorado are similar to the Pueblo culture of Lost City. There is positive evidence in the Lost City phase, 700 to 1100 A.D., of an intrusion of Southern Paiute peoples, but it is impossible to say with certainty where they came from. Southern Paiute brown ware sherds were found in almost all the Pueblo sites of the area and in both the Lost City and Mesa House stages. The pottery found is identical to pottery made in historic times by the Southern Paiutes. In addition, the Southern Paiutes have legends connecting them to the Pueblo people. Another interesting fact is that the Southern Paiutes were the only Great Basin Shoshoni people practicing agriculture when the white men first arrived in the region.

The economic development of the prehistoric people who inhabited Pueblo Grande is noteworthy. In view of the later history of the state, one is not surprised to find that mining was the chief economic activity. From the many salt caves excavated and the Pueblo pottery found, it is obvious that salt mining was a rather consistent vocation during the Pueblo period. The Southern Paiutes must have known of the existence of the salt mines before the arrival of the whites, but whether they worked them is questionable. The salt occurred mainly in veins in the native rock and was obtained by following the veins with tunnels and removing the salt with crude implements. Besides salt, these prehistoric people mined a low-grade turquoise which they used extensively in trade activities with their neighbors. They also mined magnesite, which was used for beads and in pottery making, and selenite, which was used for making charms and ornaments. Some copper ore was found at Lost City, but there is no evidence that these people knew about smelting techniques. Its use may have been for pottery and body paint.

Another interesting yet largely unexplained link with the past is the series of petroglyphs which are scattered widely throughout the state in sixteen of the seventeen counties. A recent work on Nevada's prehistoric rock art identified some ninety-nine sites.[6] The petroglyphs in Nevada have interested explorers, emigrants, miners, and sundry others for many years, and many conclusions have been drawn as to why they exist. Some consider the petroglyphs merely

[6] Robert F. Heizer and Martin A. Baumhoff, *Prehistoric Rock Art of Nevada and Eastern California* (Berkeley: University of California Press, 1962), p. 408.

"doodling," others think that they are writing and thus tell a story, and still others believe that they are art. Recent research seems to indicate that they are none of these, but are part of a magical or ritual aspect of taking large game. A point that reinforces this explanation is the fact that the petroglyphs rarely occur in Nevada except at springs or ambush spots along seasonal migration trails or where driven animals could be killed. Evidently only those who participated in the hunt could then participate in making petroglyphs.

Many of the petroglyphs are associated with important archeological sites, those for example at Hidden Cave, Lost City, and Leonard Rockshelter. The earliest dates are from 3000 to 5000 B.C. The petroglyphs appear to be the work of a prehistoric people who were forced out of Nevada or left sometime between 1200 and 1800 A.D. The end of the petroglyphs, roughly 1300 A.D., corresponds to the supplanting of the early inhabitants of Nevada by the present Shoshoni-speaking groups.

The story of prehistoric man in Nevada changes as new archeological sites are found and older ones investigated more fully. The picture is more meaningful as the historic period is approached. The evidence of the intrusion of the Southern Paiutes in the Pueblo and Mesa House periods of Lost City, and recent investigations of the Lovelock culture in the Pyramid Lake area are examples of such transitions. Sites explored during the past decade, particularly recent explorations on Mt. Jefferson in Central Nevada and a discovery in the Black Rock Desert in northwestern Nevada showing the possible association of man with a 13,000-year-old mammoth skeleton, add further evidence.

INDIANS OF NEVADA

Although some twenty-seven tribal groups existed at one time or another in Nevada, only four have been given much attention by scientists and historians—the Northern Paiutes, the Southern Paiutes, the Shoshones, and the Washos. Of these, the first three have been assigned by anthropologists to the Plateau Shoshonean subdivision of the Uto-Aztecan stock of languages. The fourth group, the Washos, speak a language related to others in North America that have been grouped together in the Hokan stock.

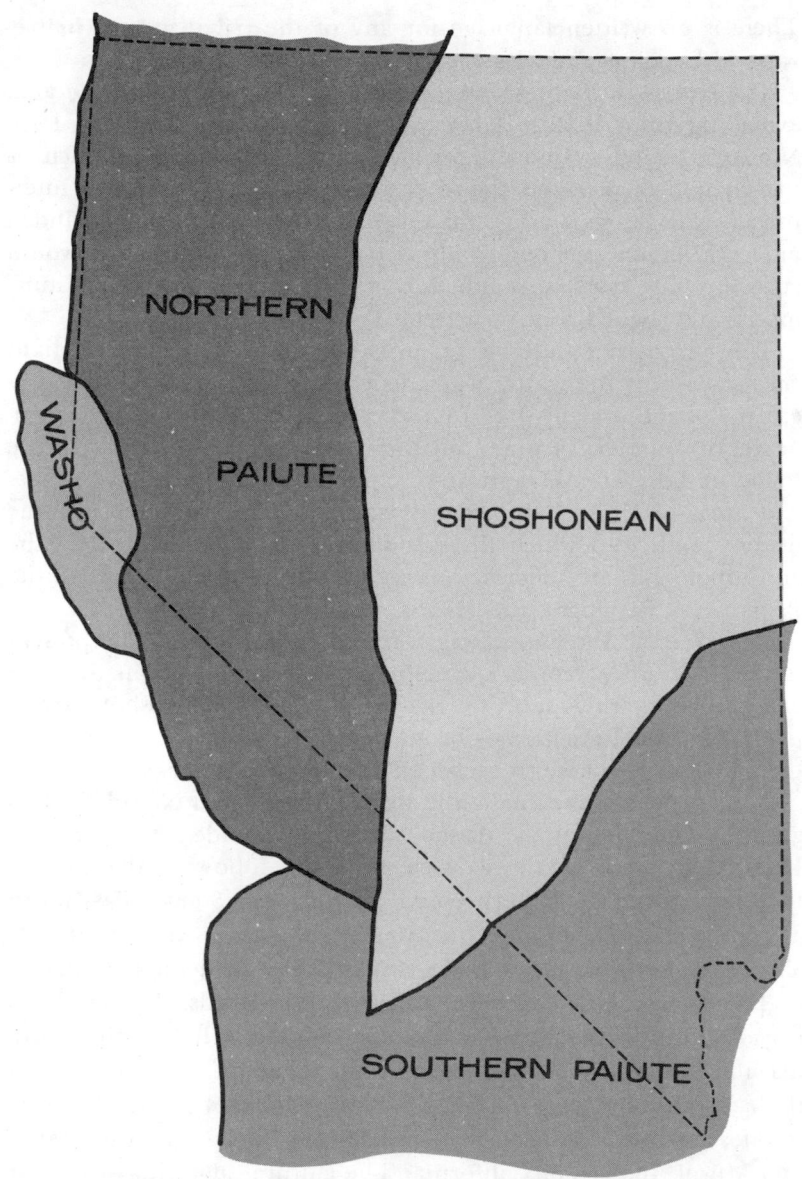

INDIANS OF NEVADA

There is no written language for any of the tribal groups in Nevada, although each had a vast oral tradition.

The Northern Paiutes were confined by early writers to the area extending from Walker Lake to Pyramid Lake. Today the term Northern Paiute is used to include other Indian groups such as the Oregon Snakes and the Western Bannocks. This latter interpretation indicates a range for the Northern Paiutes that included most of Nevada west of 117°30′ west longitude; such a line would cross the state north to south through the present town of Winnemucca and slightly west of present Tonopah.

The Southern Paiutes were probably the first Nevada Indians encountered by the whites when Jedediah Smith crossed the southern tip of the present state in 1826. As noted earlier, there is evidence of Southern Paiute intrusion into the prehistoric culture found at Lost City. Historically, the Southern Paiutes have inhabited areas of Utah, California, Arizona, and Nevada. Four of the fifteen bands into which these Indians have been divided by the anthropologists are identified as inhabiting southern Nevada: the Panaca, the Paranigat, the Moapa, and the Las Vegas.

The Western Shoshones ranged in the eastern half of the present state of Nevada to contact with the Northern Paiutes on the west and the Southern Paiutes on the south. Bands of Shoshones were likely the first Indians met by trappers, explorers, and later emigrants who moved westward along the Humboldt River.

The Washo was the smallest in number of the four Nevada Indian groups. The aboriginal Washo territory extended from Honey Lake to Sonora Pass, the western boundary following the crest of the Sierra while the eastern boundary ran from Sonora Pass north along the crest of the Pine Nut Mountains, passing west of Virginia City, then north to a few miles east of Reno, and then northwest to Honey Lake. The modern towns of Woodfords, Truckee, and Loyalton in California, and Reno, Carson City, Minden, and Gardnerville in Nevada belonged within the range of the Washos. On their eastern boundary the Washos were neighbors of the Northern Paiutes; on the west they were associated closely with the Maidu and Miwok Indians of California. The cultural affinities with their California neighbors are shown in the conical slab dwellings, in certain of their stone artifacts, in the use of acorns as food, and in the prominence of certain types of coiled basketry. Although the Great

Basin environment influenced the Washo culture, it is obvious that they were also influenced greatly by a second environment, the well-timbered and well-watered Sierra.

The Indians within the Basin Range province of Nevada, whether Northern Paiute, Southern Paiute, Shoshone, or Washo, were conditioned by that environment to a common material culture. There were, of course, some variations in the material well-being of the Nevada Indians; those bands which had established rights to districts where there were rivers and lakes stocked with fish fared better than others. In no case did Nevada Indians have an economy of abundance. The continuous search for food was the dominating fact of life. The economy was concerned primarily with the survival of the individual family, and this objective kept the Indians constantly on the move. They not only had to know when each plant was ready to be harvested, when birds were migrating, and when to hunt animals, but where to be in order to take the best advantage of every change of season. There was little leisure to develop a sophisticated culture; only industry and ingenuity brought success in the quest for survival in this hostile land. Their resourcefulness in maintaining life is shown in the unique and ingenious traps built to snare animals, the wooden and stuffed decoys used to attract migratory fowl, and the methods used to gather and store edible roots and seeds.

The Nevada Indians were basically hunters, fishermen, and gatherers. They hunted deer, antelope, and mountain sheep in the higher elevations; the Washos sometimes hunted the Sierra for bear (the "killing of a bear represented the ultimate in Washo bravery and the possession of the skin conferred extra powers on the owner").[7] At lower elevations they hunted rabbits, ground squirrels, gophers, badgers, and other small animals of the desert. The large animals were skinned and their meat either dried, pounded, and stored for later use, or boiled for immediate consumption. The smaller animals were generally eaten at once. Migratory waterfowl and other birds were important food supplies in the marshland and lake areas. Grasshoppers, fly larvae, lizards, ants, and all sorts of other small insects were gathered for food.

Some Nevada Indians were fortunate in having access to good

[7] John Andrew Price, *Washo Economy*, Nevada State Museum Anthropological Papers, no. 6 (June 1962), pp. 20–22.

fishing areas for at least part of each year; such, for example, were the Washos with Lake Tahoe and the Northern Paiutes with Pyramid Lake. They never developed the art of curing fish and thus were forced to a seasonal use of what might have become a supplement to their slender winter food resources.[8]

The food-gathering habits of the Nevada Indians matched their energy and ability in fishing and hunting. Wild berries such as raspberries, chokeberries, and elderberries were a delicacy. The edible roots of plants like the wild carrot, wild onion, bitterroot, trail potato, sego lily, wild caraway, camas, and white sage were used extensively. Seeds and desert grasses were gathered and either stored or made into a flour that was often baked, but more often used in making soup. Perhaps the most important of the seeds used was the pine nut, taken from the piñon pine, which grows in many areas of the Basin Range. The pine nut hunt was one of the most important of all the food-gathering activities of the Basin Indians. The harvest took place in the early fall when the Indians, usually in family groups, traveled to piñon groves within their basic food-gathering range. The pine nut harvests were uneven from year to year. In good years the pine nut crop ensured an adequate supply of food for the winter, but if the crop was poor the family had to make up the loss by increased activity in gathering other winter food supplies.

Nevada Indians had few rituals concerning food gathering and few food taboos; they simply could not afford them. Dogs and snakes were not usually eaten, and animals such as coyotes, foxes, skunks, certain lizards, and birds such as ravens, crows, owls, and hawks were eaten only in emergencies, which, one can imagine, came rather often in this barren land. The Washos appear to have had more religious elements connected with food gathering and eating than did the Paiutes or Shoshones.

Indians of Nevada did not develop agriculture to any extent before the coming of the white man, although there were isolated instances of harvesting maize. It is evident that the Indians could have developed more actively in agriculture, particularly in southern Nevada, where a definite agricultural development existed in prehistoric times. However, it is generally agreed by the experts that

[8] James F. Downs, *The Two Worlds of the Washo* (New York: Holt, Rinehart, & Winston, 1966), pp. 16–17.

the best solution to the problem of existence in the Great Basin environment was to turn to a food-gathering economy based on multiple sources. Nevada Indians also engaged in some trading activities, particularly with California tribes, for salt, fly larvae from Mono Lake, red ochre, and acorns.

Permanent homes were out of the question for a people whose economy forced them to follow the seasons and scour the land for a livelihood. Thus in the spring, summer, and early fall, the dwelling was likely to be a temporary structure of reeds, branches, or grass covering a framework of poles or boughs. For their winter homes, the Indians took a little more care in construction. They tried to be near sheltered valleys as winter approached so that they could take advantage of the terrain. Often a foundation two to three feet deep was dug and a framework of poles and branches erected over this opening. The framework was then covered by grasses and reeds, usually tied together in bunches and overlapped to cause proper runoff of rain and snow. The Shoshones and Washos also used bark as a covering for a winter home and, after the arrival of the whites, a covering of slabs. A hole was always left in the top of these structures for ventilation.

The scarcity of food in the Great Basin was duplicated to some extent in the lack of materials for clothing. There were not many large animals whose skins could be used for such purposes. Those that were available were used extensively for such items as moccasins, caps, and blankets. For the Washos, at least, the rabbit-skin blanket was the most prized article of apparel. The common sagebrush was also used for clothing. The inner bark was stripped, dampened, and pounded until a substance was formed which could be used for sandals, overshoes, twine, and skirts. Cattail reeds or tule were also used for skirts for the women. During the summer months, the Indians wore only the briefest costumes, a breechcloth for the men and a skirt for the women. In winter, buckskin shirts and rabbit-skin blankets were added.

Both men and women at times wore some ornamentation, generally necklaces and earrings fashioned from bird bones, deer hooves, and ocean shells. However, Nevada Indians did not usually indulge in elaborate costumes and ornamentation.

Because the culture was so dominantly a material one, the equipment made by Nevada Indians was first of all utilitarian. This fact did not, however, prevent a high degree of development in certain areas, notably basketry. Baskets were essential for gathering seeds, for separating seeds from the husks, for carrying food and water, and for cooking. Two methods, coiling and weaving, were used in making baskets. Willow formed the framework in either method, with reeds and grasses forming the body. All of the basic materials for basket making were found readily throughout the Great Basin. The use determined the size and shape of the various baskets. Conical baskets of all shapes and sizes were made for carrying burdens from one area to another. Winnowing trays for separating seeds and parching were developed, as were loosely woven baskets for use as sieves. Tightly woven and water-cured baskets were used for cooking and were able to hold boiling water without leaking. Stones were heated and immersed in the basket of water or soup until the proper temperature was reached. Ladles, tongs, and spoons were also fashioned from reeds. A very important basket for these nomadic peoples was the water container, a tightly woven basket treated with pitch on the outside and with a willow cover for use as a stopper. Water could be kept cool for days in these containers.

Baskets, although functional, were often elaborate in design. It is probable that ideas from other tribes who participated in trading activities were modified to become part of the basket-making tradition of the Nevada Indians. The Washos are generally considered the best basketmakers of all the Nevada Indians, and one of their members, Dat-so-la-lee, was the acknowledged master of her tribe in this respect. Many of her baskets have become prized possessions of private and public collectors.

The political and social organization of the Indians of Nevada before the white man were comparatively simple. In all three groups, the Paiutes, Shoshones, and Washos, life centered around the family, and the highest social unit in each appears to have been the band. There was no major tribal development in any of these units, although the Paiutes probably most closely approximated such development. It is suspected by some writers that the movement toward a single Northern Paiute chief (Winnemucca) was due mainly to the white man's desire to deal with a single authority. Among the Washos, the chief was mainly ceremonial, although they had a "rabbit" headman who organized the rabbit hunts. Each band within the large groupings had its own organization and generally tended to stay within a designated physical area.

Recreational activities of the Nevada Indians were limited by the long hours necessary to make a living. Nevertheless, their activity in this respect has often been minimized. Actually there were many occasions during the year when collective activity such as the pine nut harvest or the rabbit hunt brought families or even bands together for celebrations. At such affairs there was likely to be much dancing; circle dances accompanied by drums, rattles, and bowstrings were common. Physical contests of all kinds were popular. Numerous games such as "shinny," a type of hockey, were played by both men and women, and a form of football was played by the men. Various gambling games were enjoyed on these occasions. The Washos, particularly, liked to bet on any game, their wagers involving baskets, feathers, jewelry, buckskins, or even the prized rabbit-skin blanket.

The Nevada Indian lived in a world of spirits—spirits symbolized by the mountains, the lakes, the rivers, the moon, and the sun. Many legends and myths which have come down to the present show that the physical environment is the all-pervasive influence in religion as well as in material development. Death was of little consequence to a people whose daily existence was balanced so precariously. Their religion provided not only an explanation for their environment, but also a ritual system which sought to alleviate some of the dangers inherent in their hunting, fishing, and gathering. These were the peoples, then, wresting a precarious living from the barren land, who were soon to meet in the white man a greater threat to their civilization than the most terrible physical forces they had experienced.

CHAPTER 3

The Trailblazers

ALTHOUGH BY THE END of the eighteenth century the white man's search for furs, for mineral wealth, and for a water passage to India had taken him to many parts of North America, he seemed in no hurry to breach the Great Basin wasteland which lay between the Rockies and the Pacific Ocean. The first approaches to the area by the white man came from the south and the east as a result of Spanish attempts to develop an overland supply route from New Mexico to California and thus protect the latter against the threat of British and Russian encroachments. Two expeditions in the late eighteenth century were sent out with this purpose in mind, and although each barely touched the Great Basin, they had significance in the later successful opening of the area. The first of these was an outgrowth of the second expedition of Captain Juan Bautista de Anza, who had earlier marked a road from Tubac, near Tucson, to the Spanish missions in California. Seeking a more direct route from Santa Fe to Monterey, Father Francisco Garcés and two Indian guides left the Anza expedition near the present site of Yuma, Arizona, and passed through the general area of the southern tip of Nevada in the spring of 1776.

A second penetration of the Great Basin came later in 1776 when a party under the leadership of Fathers Francisco Atanasio Domínguez and Francisco Silvestre Vélez de Escalante, also exploring a route to Monterey, entered the region from the east. Leaving Santa Fe on July 29, the party traveled northwest as far as Utah Lake, then moved southwest to the Sevier River, which they reached on September 29. In the early part of October the leaders gave up the idea of going on Monterey and turned back east to Santa Fe. Although it is quite clear today that the Escalante party did not enter the present state of Nevada,[1] their mistaken assumption that the Green River—which they called the San Buenaventura—formed its own drainage system was magnified and perpetuated by mapmakers, affecting exploring expeditions into the Great Basin for the next seventy years.

An important result of the Spanish explorations in the Great Basin was the establishment of the eastern and western approaches to the Old Spanish Trail, a route inaugurated in its entirety in 1830–31 by George C. Yount and William Wolfskill. After 1776 the Spanish government took little interest in further official exploration of the area.

THE FUR TRAPPERS

A more important intrusion into the Great Basin came as the result of economic and, to a lesser degree, political rivalry between the British and the Americans in northwestern America. For ultimately it was the British and American trappers, tightening the circle of unknown fur areas, who unlocked the secrets of the Great Basin. The contest between the two groups reached the present state of Nevada when two fur trappers, Peter Skene Ogden of the British-

[1] See particularly Gloria Griffen Cline's *Exploring the Great Basin* (Norman: University of Oklahoma Press, 1963), pp. 46–49, and Gloria Griffen Cline's "Early Exploration Routes and Trails in Nevada" (M.A. thesis, University of Nevada, 1951), pp. 1–5.

owned Hudson's Bay Company and Jedediah Strong Smith of the American-owned Rocky Mountain Fur Company, penetrated opposite ends of the area in 1826. As they did so, both were seeking new beaver fields, both were looking for the mysterious San Buenaventura River, and both, when they entered present Nevada, were trespassing on Mexican soil. Mexico had gained her independence from Spain five years earlier.

Jedediah Smith, born in Jericho, New York, on January 6, 1799, entered the fur trade at St. Louis, Missouri, in 1822 with the formation of the Rocky Mountain Fur Company. He adapted so readily to the rather harsh demands of the trade that he was able, along with two other trappers, William Sublette and David Jackson, to purchase the Rocky Mountain Fur Company from General William Ashley in 1826. In the late summer of 1826, at the company's Cache Valley rendezvous north of the Great Salt Lake, it was decided that Smith would take a group of trappers and strike out across the unknown land to the southwest in the hope of opening additional fur areas and, at the same time, giving the Rocky Mountain Fur Company the much needed access to a sea outlet and a more direct connection with Canton, China, the world's chief fur-trading mart.

The expedition of fifteen men, including Smith as leader and Harrison G. Rogers as clerk, left Cache Valley on August 16. The group of trappers entered present-day Nevada near the site of Bunkerville and proceeded south along the Virgin River to its junction with the Colorado.[2] Continuing south along the latter river, Smith led his men to the Mohave Indian villages near the Needles and then struck directly west, arriving at Mission San Gabriel near Los Angeles on November 26. The Mexican civil authorities were understandably concerned about the reasons for the American intrusion on Mexican territory and ordered Smith to leave the same way he had entered. On January 18, 1827, Smith and his party started eastward but moved in that direction only far enough to allay the suspicions of the Mexicans. They then turned

[2] C. Hart Merriam, in an article in 1923, "Earliest Crossing of the Deserts of Utah and Nevada to Southern California: Route of Jedediah S. Smith in 1826," *California Historical Society Quarterly* 2 (October 1923): 228–36, insisted that Smith entered near present Panaca. However, the weight of evidence, particularly that suggested by Dale Morgan and Carl Wheat in *Jedediah Smith and His Maps of the American West* (San Francisco: California Historical Society, 1954), definitely favors the Mesquite-Bunkerville entry.

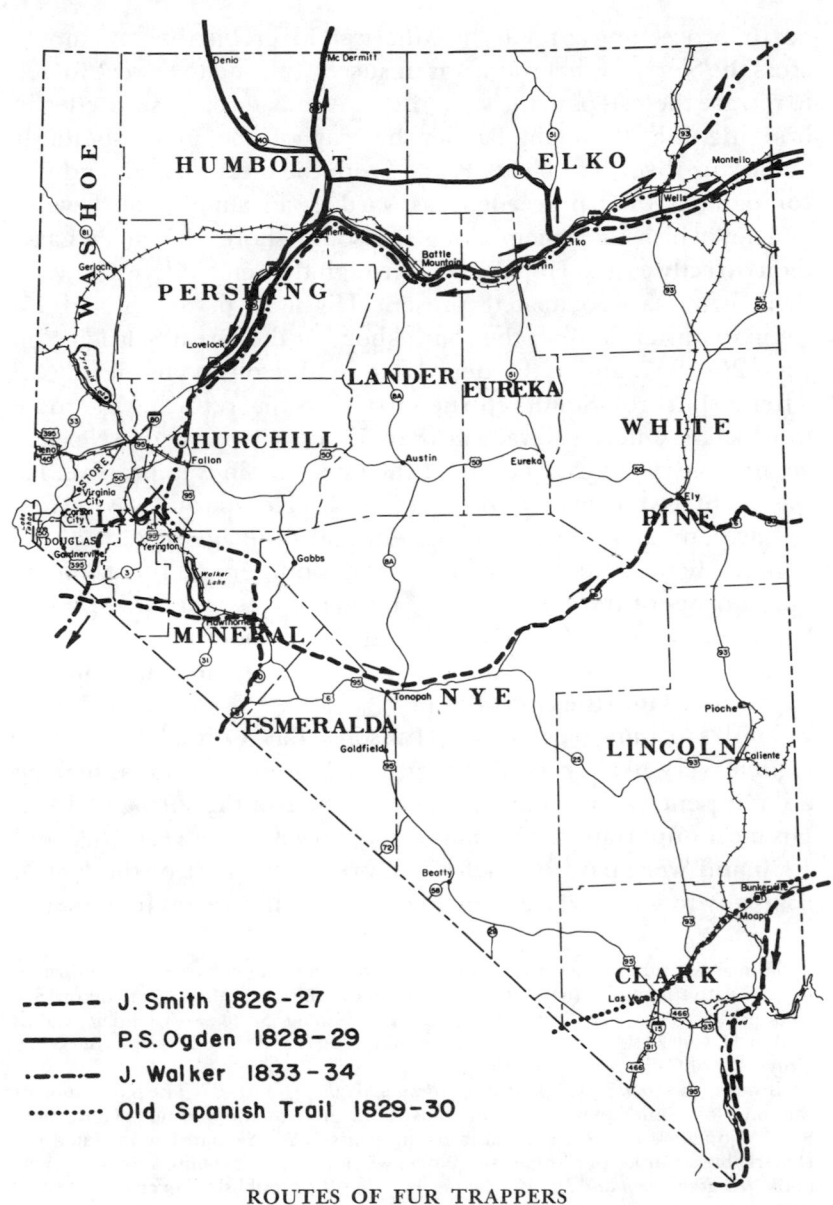

----- J. Smith 1826-27
——— P.S. Ogden 1828-29
-·-·- J. Walker 1833-34
········ Old Spanish Trail 1829-30

ROUTES OF FUR TRAPPERS

north, proceeding as far as the American River, but their attempt to cross the Sierra by that route was unsuccessful, and they were forced to retrace their steps to the valley floor. A smaller party succeeded in bridging the mountain barrier by way of the more southerly Stanislaus River, at Ebbetts Pass.[3] From the Sierra, Smith and two companions then proceeded eastward in an almost unbelievable journey which took them along the south shore of Walker Lake, then directly east to Hot Creek. Through the remainder of Nevada their route approximated present Highway 6. Smith and his companions arrived on the south shore of the Great Salt Lake on June 26, 1827, and at the Bear Lake rendezvous point on July 3.[4] After a short rest Smith returned to California, retracing the route by which he entered Nevada in 1826. He never returned to Nevada, yet his role in the exploration of the Great Basin is impressive. He was the first white man to cross present-day Nevada and was the first to have any awareness of the extent and drainage pattern of the region. He was also the first person to encounter and report on the native tribes of the area and the first to indicate that the supposed San Buenaventura River did not exist. It is obvious that others who followed, particularly John Frémont, owed a great deal to Smith's explorations into the Great Basin.[5]

Smith's counterpart in the Hudson's Bay Company, Peter S. Ogden, very likely preceded Smith into present Nevada, making a slight penetration in the northeast corner in the spring of 1826. His most important expeditions came, however, between 1828 and 1830 and were part of a definite move on the part of the British company to seek and trap out any fur-bearing streams to the south

[3]Francis Farquhar's view that the Smith crossing was at Ebbetts Pass was confirmed in 1977 with the publication of the lost journal of Smith's southwest expedition. See George R. Brooks, *The Southwest Expedition of Jedediah Smith* . . . (Glendale, Calif.: Arthur H. Clark, 1977); and Francis Farquhar, *History of the Sierra Nevada* (Berkeley: University of California Press, 1965).

[4]Brooks, *The Southwest Expedition of Jedediah Smith*, pp. 170–97. The publication of the long lost Smith journal not only answered most of the questions concerning Smith's journeys in the Great Basin in the years 1826–27 but demonstrated the remarkable accuracy of Morgan and Wheat when they traced Smith's routes in their book, *Jedediah Smith and His Maps of the American West*, published over twenty years earlier.

[5]Morgan and Wheat based their version of Smith's routes on a copy of the Frémont map of 1845, discovered by Wheat in 1953, which had notations in the handwriting of George Gibbs, a Frémont cartographer, showing references to the Smith journeys in the Great Basin.

in order to keep the Americans out of the Pacifiic Northwest. Leaving Fort Nez Percés on the Columbia River on September 22, 1828, Ogden entered Nevada near the present town of Denio[6] and proceeded south and southeast until he encountered the Humboldt, which he named the Unknown River, on November 9. Ogden and his party trapped westward along the river until the approaching winter forced a decision to move eastward to winter quarters northeast of the Great Salt Lake, where a supply of buffalo was assured. They left the Humboldt near the present town of Elko, crossed the Ruby Mountains at Secret Pass, swung around a spur of the East Humboldt Range, and passed eastward to Snow Water Lake, crossing the Pequop Range by way of Shafter Pass and moving northeast to enter present-day Utah a few miles northeast of Montello. With the coming of spring Ogden and his men retraced that route in basic detail to return to the Humboldt River, near the present site of Halleck. The party left the Humboldt River on April 16 and via Maggie Creek moved north to reach the south fork of the Owyhee River just south of the present site of Tuscarora. The trapping here was another disappointment, so the group, on May 2, moved westward to the Little Humboldt River via Willow Creek and Squaw Valley. On May 10 Ogden again reached the Humboldt near present Winnemucca and proceeded westward along that stream, reaching the Humboldt Sink on May 29.[7] The expedition left Nevada in early June by way of the Little Humboldt and Quinn rivers, probably near the present site of McDermit.

Ogden returned to Nevada in the fall of 1829, entering the state at McDermit and proceeding to the Humboldt Sink area. He then turned south to the present Walker Lake and continued in a southeasterly direction into California and ultimately back to the Hudson's Bay post at Walla Walla.[8] Ogden is generally credited with

[6] Most sources until recently have maintained that Ogden entered at McDermitt in 1828. Dr. Cline gives strong evidence for the Denio entry. See Cline, *Exploring the Great Basin*, pp. 112–25.

[7] I am indebted to Victor Goodwin of the U.S. Forest Service for information on Ogden's westward journey along the Humboldt in the spring of 1829. See his article on the Humboldt River in the *Elko* (Nevada) *Free Press*, October 17, 1964.

[8] Until recently historians assumed that the 1828–29 expedition was Ogden's last penetration of Nevada. The researches of Professor Cline, however, indicate that he returned to the Humboldt River and Nevada during his sixth and last Snake Country Expedition. See *Exploring the Great Basin*, pp. 126–27.

being the first white man to discover the Humboldt River and was the first to follow it from its source to its sink. He, too, demonstrated that the river San Buenaventura did not exist.

While Ogden and others were exploring and trapping the northern part of the Great Basin, a number of American fur traders operating out of Santa Fe had entered the southeastern tip of Nevada near the point Smith had crossed in 1826 and 1827. The activities of these men, beginning with Ewing Young in 1829 and continuing with Antonio Armijo in 1829–30 and William Wolfskill and George C. Yount in 1830–31, established a route which became known as the Old Spanish Trail and which provided the first charted track across the Great Basin.

Although it was clear by 1831 that neither the northern part of the present state of Nevada along the Humboldt River nor the southern part along the Virgin and Muddy rivers was important as a fur-trapping area, one additional major trapping expedition, the famous Walker-Bonneville party of 1833–34, crossed Nevada before the explorers and emigrants took over in the 1840s. In 1831 Benjamin Louis Eulalie de Bonneville, a captain in the United States Army, requested a leave in order to head a fur-trapping expedition to the Rocky Mountains. His motives have been the center of much controversy; adventure, curiosity, and economic gain have been suggested. As part of the overall expedition, Bonneville, in the summer of 1833, sent an exploring party under the leadership of Joseph Walker out to the southwest. Although it is quite clear that Bonneville's stated instructions to Walker were to explore the Great Salt Lake region, other evidence indicates that he intended to send Walker on a spying mission through Mexican territory to the Pacific coast and that some of those who went along knew this.[9] In any event, Walker did go to California.

Leaving the Green River Valley on July 24, the Walker party proceeded south to the Great Salt Lake and then west, probably north of Pilot Peak, until they reached Ogden's Unknown River,

[9] The best modern edition of Washington Irving's 1837 classic account of Captain Bonneville's activities in the Rocky Mountains is that by Edgeley W. Todd, ed., *The Adventures of Captain Bonneville, U.S.A., in the Rocky Mountains and the Far West* (Norman: University of Oklahoma Press, 1961). See the Editor's Introduction, pp. xvii–xlvii, and footnote 7, pp. 162–63, for a discussion of the reasons for Bonneville's expedition. See also Zenas Leonard, *Adventures of Zenas Leonard, Fur Trader*, ed. by John C. Ewers (Norman: University of Oklahoma Press, 1958).

which they followed to its sink. Increasing difficulties with the Indians led to an encounter there which cost the lives of thirty or more natives and laid the groundwork for later Indian animosity toward Walker in particular and whites in general. The expedition probably crossed the Sierra at the head of the East Walker River, somewhere west of Bridgeport Valley. The party tried to descend near the headwaters of the Tuolomne River but failed, so they moved to the Merced and followed it into the San Joaquin Valley and then north to San Francisco Bay, which they reached on November 12.[10] On November 25 the group arrived at the mission of San Juan Bautista, where they halted while Captain Walker went on to Monterey to get permission to remain for the winter.

On February 14, 1834, the Walker party left Monterey on the return journey. The expedition moved south through the San Joaquin Valley and passed over the Sierra at a low pass which was pointed out by the Indians and which today bears Walker's name. The party moved north up the Owens Valley and into the present state of Nevada, probably along the route later followed by the Carson and Colorado Railroad. Proceeding north to intercept the Humboldt River, the group nearly met disaster in the desert east of Walker Lake before turning west to the mountains and ultimately finding their trail of the previous year which led them to the Humboldt River. Instead of retracing their route to the Great Salt Lake, Walker led his party from the Humboldt, near the present town of Wells, to the northeast. Following Bishop Creek to Thousand Springs Valley, they went on to Goose Creek, to the Raft River, and finally, about mid-July, to a rendezvous with Captain Bonneville on the Bear River.

Walker's accomplishments in the journeys of 1833–34 were substantial. His was the first party of white men to make a round trip from the Great Salt Lake to the Pacific coast by way of the Humboldt River. He is credited with the discovery of the excellent pass from the Owens Valley into the San Joaquin Valley which now bears his name. Walker established the basic route connecting the Humboldt River at Wells to the Oregon Trail by way of Goose Creek and the Raft River. He is also credited by many with the discovery of the Yosemite Valley. His maps, although erroneous in

---

[10] There is much controversy over Walker's crossing of the Sierra and his discovery of Yosemite Valley. The account above generally follows that in Farquhar's *History of the Sierra Nevada*, pp. 33–38.

places, were a real contribution to the knowledge of the Great Basin and of interior California.

Although the Walker party supported the verdict of earlier trappers that the Great Basin had limited possibilities as a fur-trapping region, additional trapping parties were still to be found in the area as late as 1843.[11] And before the trappers were through and the first official explorers moved in, at least three different emigrant parties passed through the center of the Great Basin.

THE FIRST EMIGRANTS

The phenomenon of the westward migration of European peoples, first to the New World and then across the North American continent, is one of the most intriguing stories of mankind. Nowhere is the story more exciting than when this inexorable tide of humanity, held back briefly by the forbidding lands beyond the Mississippi River, jumped the barrier of the plains, desert, and mountains and began the settlement of the Pacific Coast.

The first of these parties was an unusual collection of individuals whose inexperience was exceeded only by their foolhardiness. The motivation for the trip came from a young school teacher named John Bidwell who accepted a teaching position in 1839 in Platte County, Missouri, in order to be closer to the frontier. Influenced by the stories of a mountain man, Antoine Robidoux, and letters from Dr. John Marsh, a large landholder in California, which were printed in a number of midwestern newspapers, Bidwell in 1840 helped organize the Western Emigration Society to obtain volunteers for a trip to California the following spring. Some five hundred persons signed for the expedition, but by May 9, 1841, the time set for the rendezvous, the number had slipped to Bidwell and a few others. During the next few days other westbound travelers, including John Bartleson, joined the small group, and after selecting Bartleson as captain and Bidwell as secretary and historian, the party started for California on May 12. The question of whether to follow the Santa Fe Trail or the more northerly fur-trader route to Fort Laramie was resolved with the arrival in camp of a party of

[11]The most important of the later trapping expeditions was that under the famous mountain man Bill Williams in 1843. After wintering in the Klamath Lake region of California, the party proceeded to Pyramid Lake and then trapped along the Truckee and the Humboldt. See William T. Hamilton's *My Sixty Years on the Plains* (Norman: University of Oklahoma Press, 1960), pp. 116–29.

three Jesuit priests under the leadership of Father Pierre Jean De Smet and guided by a capable trapper, Thomas ("Broken Hand") Fitzpatrick. The emigrants seized the opportunity to travel with Fitzpatrick and the missionaries, who were heading for Fort Hall. The trail experience with the De Smet party was instrumental in the survival of those members of the Bidwell-Bartleson group who left the missionary party at Soda Springs on the Bear River, in the southeastern corner of present-day Idaho, bound for California. From Soda Springs the party traveled south to the Great Salt Lake and then directly across the forbidding salt flats west of the lake. After crossing the rugged Ruby Mountains,[12] the Bidwell-Bartleson party followed the Humboldt River to its sink and then struck southwestward, crossing the Sierra, probably at Sonora Pass. On November 4, 1841, they arrived at their destination, the ranch of Dr. John Marsh at the foot of Mount Diablo, between the present cities of Stockton and Berkeley.[13]

Another emigrant group which penetrated the Great Basin before Frémont's expedition of late 1843 was that organized by Joseph B. Chiles, a member of the Bidwell-Bartleson party, which was guided from Fort Hall to California by Joseph Walker. The original party left the Missouri River for California in May, 1843. At Fort Hall, Chiles divided the party, sending the largest group with Walker, who then led his contingent over the route he and his men had discovered in returning from California in 1834, and thereby demonstrated the usefulness of the Goose Creek–Raft River connection between the Humboldt River and Fort Hall.

A more important emigrant party was that led by Elisha Stevens which left the Missouri River in May, 1844. Although this party did not precede Frémont into the present state of Nevada, it did blaze the trail over the Truckee or Donner Pass almost a year before the explorer managed the same feat, thus establishing an alternate route into California from the Humboldt Sink over the Sierra via the Truckee River.

[12] George R. Stewart, in *The California Trail* (New York: McGraw-Hill Book Co., 1962), p. 27, states that the group passed through the Ruby Mountains at Harrison Pass, although other researchers indicate that the passage was through the more northerly Secret Pass.

[13] It should be noted here that during the same year, 1841, a smaller party of emigrants under William Workman and John Rowland crossed the southern part of the Great Basin into California via the Old Spanish Trail. See Cline, *Exploring the Great Basin,* p. 186.

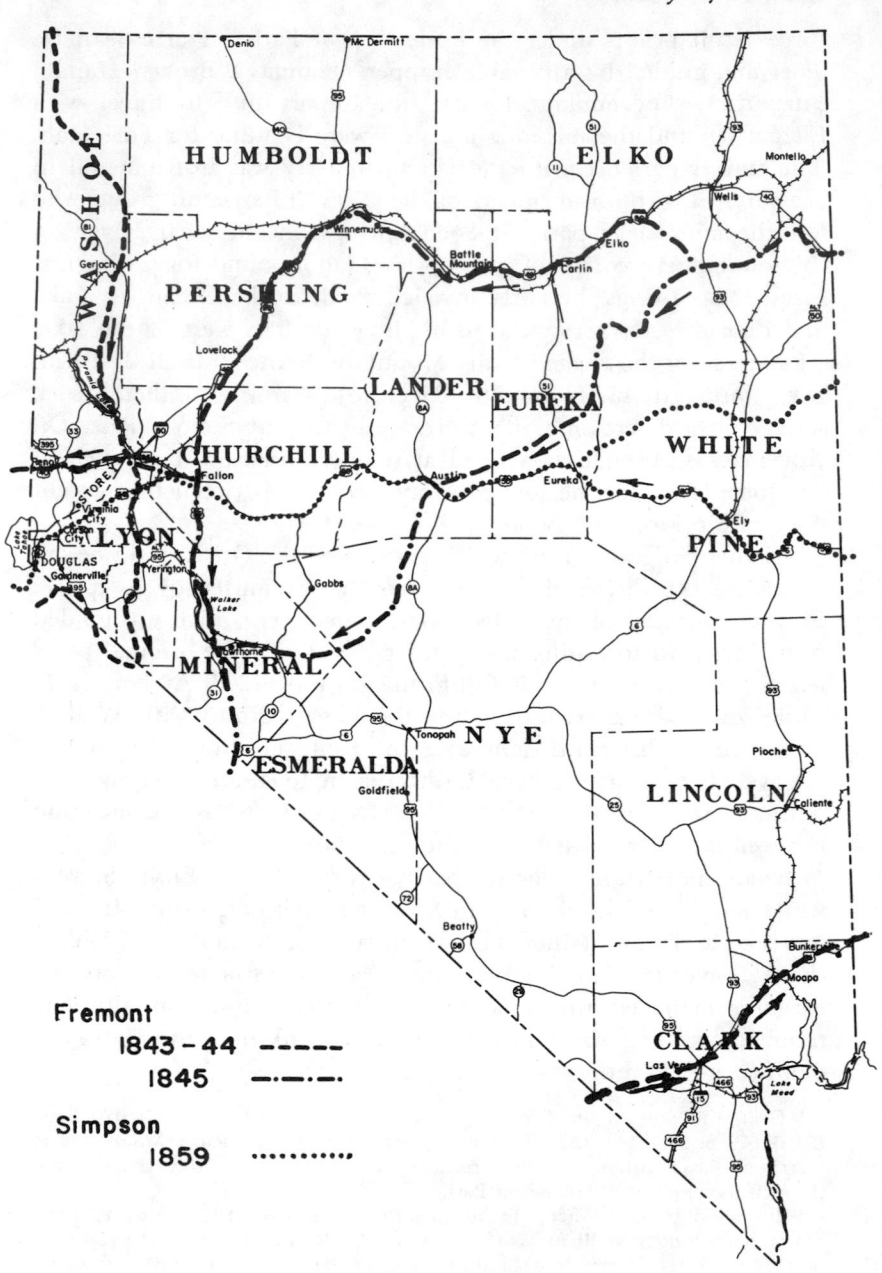

Fremont
    1843 – 44 - - - - -
        1845 - · - · -

Simpson
      1859 ············

ROUTES OF EXPLORERS

THE EXPLORERS

The climax in the exploration of the Great Basin came with the expeditions of Captain John Charles Frémont in the years from 1843 to 1853. These journeys must be considered in association with the rising tide of "manifest destiny" in the nation which ultimately brought the annexation of Texas in 1845 and the Mexican War from 1846 to 1848, giving the United States most of the present states of California, Nevada, Utah, Arizona, and New Mexico. Even before those territories were added to the Union, the United States Army had taken an active part in the exploration and mapping of the West. As a member of the Topographical Engineers, Frémont had gained valuable experience assisting the French explorer Joseph Nicollet. His selection to lead the expeditions was no doubt also influenced by his marriage to the daughter of the powerful expansionist senator from Missouri, Thomas Hart Benton.

Having successfully completed one mapping expedition of the Oregon Trail, Frémont was sent on a second, similar mission in 1843. On his return from Fort Vancouver, on the Columbia River, he took a southeasterly route, cutting into the northwestern part of Nevada in late December. Proceeding south, he discovered a large lake on January 10, 1844, and named it Pyramid Lake because a large rock formation jutting through the water reminded him of the great pyramid of Cheops. From there he followed the Truckee—which he called the Salmon Trout River—to present-day Wadsworth, then crossed to the Carson River and followed it to its sink. Instead of crossing the desert eastward Frémont turned back to the mountains and to California. Although it was now the middle of January and the Sierra was packed with snow, the Frémont party persisted, crossing the mountains near the present Carson Pass.[14] The party arrived at Sutter's Fort in early March and after resting for a number of days left that haven on March 22, to begin the return journey. Frémont now led his party south, then east, crossing the Sierra at Techachapi Pass and moving via the Old Spanish Trail into present Utah. Perhaps the most important result of the 1843–44 expedition was the excellent map done by Charles Preuss, the expedition's

[14] There are many summaries of the various Frémont expeditions. That by William Goetzmann, *Army Exploration in the American West, 1803–1863* (New Haven: Yale University Press, 1959), is brief and to the point. For more detail, see John Charles Frémont's *Narrative of Exploration and Adventure*, ed. by Allan Nevins (New York: Longmans, 1956).

official topographer, and Frémont's report, both of which gained wide circulation. The report was filed on March 1, 1845, the same day President Tyler signed the joint resolution annexing Texas to the United States. It was on Preuss's map and in his own report that Frémont for the first time identified the great unexplored land of interior drainage as the Great Basin. Frémont also gave their present names to a number of other important features, including the Humboldt River, which he named in honor of the great German geographer who never saw it;[15] the Walker River and Walker Lake; and the Carson River and Carson Pass.

In 1845 Frémont was placed in charge of another expedition into the Great Basin. Although the purpose of his party was ostensibly to discover a more feasible route from the Mississippi River to the Pacific, Frémont noted that "in arranging this expedition, the eventualities of war were taken into consideration." The 1845 party arrived at the Great Salt Lake on October 13 and spent the next few days exploring that body of salt water. Frémont then moved directly west across the salt flats, reaching Pilot Peak without too much difficulty. Continuing west, Frémont led his men through the Toana Range just south of the present Silver Zone Pass and camped at Mound Springs southwest of the present site of Shafter. At this point the party was divided in order to get a better mapping of the interior. One group, under the leadership of Theodore Talbot and guided by Joseph Walker, was to move to the northwest, follow the Humboldt River to its sink, and rendezvous with Frémont's group at Walker Lake. The latter party crossed the Ruby Mountains at Harrison Pass and then proceeded in a southwesterly direction toward the rendezvous point. This route led first into Diamond Valley and then south along the Toiyabe Range through Big Smoky Valley. Frémont and his small party arrived at Walker Lake on November 24 and were joined by the Talbot-Walker contingent three days later. At Walker Lake, Frémont again divided his party, sending the Talbot-Walker group southwestward into Owens Valley and to a second rendezvous point at Tulare Lake. Frémont and the smaller group moved north from Walker Lake, followed the Truckee River through the Meadows, and then passed over the

[15] Nevada's longest river, the Humboldt, was at various other times called the Unknown River, Ogden's River, Paul's River, Mary's River, Swampy River, and Barren River.

Sierra at what was later called Donner Pass. The party arrived at Sutter's Fort on December 9 and within a few days had made contact with the Talbot-Walker group.

Frémont crossed Nevada again in 1853, entering near the site of Pioche and leaving near present-day Beatty, but his reputation as an explorer rests upon the explorations of 1843–44 and of 1845. Although his part in the exploration of the Great Basin has been overemphasized, nevertheless, as Professor William Goetzmann points out, Frémont's report remains important for its comprehensiveness, its findings, and for the "relative trustworthiness of the authority upon which it rested."[16] Certainly, the maps drawn by various members of the Frémont expeditions and the reports were of inestimable importance in obtaining a proper knowledge of the Great Basin, both for use by official sources and by those moving westward to seek new homes.

THE HUMBOLDT TRAIL

A few emigrant parties crossed Nevada in the years between 1841 and 1845; after the latter date, however, the trickle of emigrants to California became a stream. Most of the parties found the route which followed the Humboldt River a useful, if at times difficult, cutoff enabling them to arrive in California without suffering a major disaster.

Not so fortunate was the Donner party, which started from Independence, Missouri, on May 5, 1846, as part of a larger group made up of the Colonel William Russell and the Edwin Bryant parties. The large wagon train split up at Fort Laramie with the Donner party falling behind the others. At Fort Bridger the Donners decided to follow a cutoff recommended by a young adventurer named Lansford Hastings which cut directly west from Fort Bridger to the Great Salt Lake and then across the salt desert.[17] The decision to follow the Hastings cutoff proved disastrous to the party, already tired and behind schedule. The group reached the Humboldt in

---

[16] Goetzmann, *Army Exploration in the American West,* pp. 103–4.

[17] Lansford Hastings had gone overland to Oregon in 1842 and then on to California. In 1844 he went east by sea and land across Mexico. The next year he published *The Emigrants' Guide to Oregon and California* . . . (Cincinnati: G. Conelin, 1845), and returned overland to California. In 1846 he moved eastward along the California trail encouraging emigrants to take his cutoff. The Donners were one of the few parties who did.

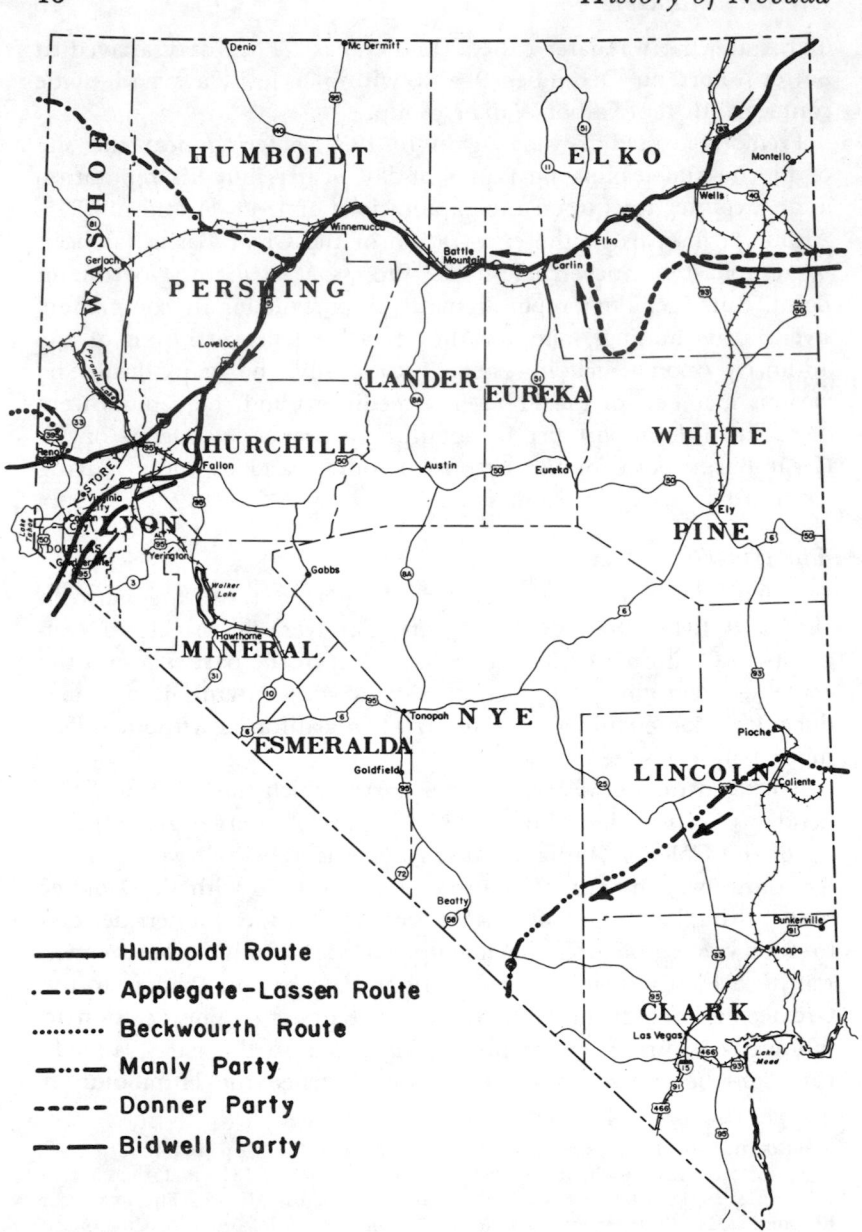

ROUTES OF EMIGRANT PARTIES

September and the Truckee Meadows a month later. As they crossed the Dog Valley grade and were nearing the shores of Donner Lake, heavy snowfall obliterated the trail, and within hours the passes were closed, making all efforts to cross futile. By the time relief parties reached the stricken wagon train some forty of the total membership of eighty-seven had died.[18]

The misfortunes of the Donner party placed a stigma on travel to California by the Truckee route that lasted until 1848. In that year two events occurred which sent thousands of emigrants across the Great Basin unmindful of the hardships to be faced or of the tragedies of earlier days. In January, 1848, James Marshall discovered gold in California; a month later the United States Senate accepted the Treaty of Guadalupe-Hidalgo which ended the war with Mexico and provided for the cession of all Mexican territory north of the Gila River to the United States.

As they neared the California cutoffs from the Oregon Trail, the emigrants to the new Eldorado found a number of fairly well defined routes open to them—trails which had been blazed by trappers, explorers, and early emigrant trains in the 1820s, '30s, and '40s. By far the most widely known and soon to become the most important route into California was the cutoff from the Oregon Trail at Fort Hall. This route, blazed by Joseph Walker and generally referred to as the Humboldt Trail, led the emigrants to the Raft River and into northeastern Nevada via Goose Creek and Thousand Springs Valley to the Humboldt River. The Humboldt itself became the lifeline for travelers across the Great Basin, although it failed by some forty miles to provide a fresh-water link for the California-bound emigrant. The intervening desert, from where the Humboldt ran into the ground until fresh water was reached at either the Truckee River or the Carson River, was thought by some to be the worst part of their overland journey. If the Truckee River route was chosen after crossing the "forty-mile" desert, the emigrant usually crossed the Sierra at Donner Pass. Variations were available, however, such as the route across Henness Pass, or the more northerly Beckwourth Pass which was discovered in 1851 by Jim Beckwourth, one of the few black trappers to appear

---

[18]There are many books on the Donner party. One of the best is George Stewart's *Ordeal by Hunger: The Story of the Donner Party* (New York: Henry Holt & Co., 1936). A new edition was published in 1960 by Houghton Mifflin and reprinted by the University of Nebraska Press in 1986.

in the American West. If the Carson River route was chosen, the emigrant usually traveled over Carson Pass or, after 1850, over Johnson Pass and into Placerville.[19]

A number of trails to California turned from the Humboldt River before reaching its sink. The earliest of these was the Applegate cutoff to Oregon, established in 1846 by Jesse Applegate, which, with some variations into California, became the Lassen Road in 1848. The terminus of the Applegate-Lassen Road was too far north to suit the goldseekers. Consequently, the Nobles Road was established in 1851 by William Nobles to cut from the Lassen route at Black Rock and to proceed directly west into the Honey Lake region of California and on to Shasta City; it became a more popular route. A few parties crossed into California during the gold rush period via the Old Spanish Trail, but like its counterpart to the north, the Lassen Road, this route placed the goldseeker much too far from his immediate goal.

[19] In 1968 a group of local enthusiasts from Reno, Sparks, and Fallon began to mark the emigrant trail across both the Carson and the Truckee routes. By 1970 this project had completed the marking of the "forty-mile" desert and was then enlarged to include, ultimately, the marking of the entire emigrant trail across the Great Basin.

CHAPTER 4

The First Settlements

IT WAS INEVITABLE, as the wagons rolled westward with the emigrants, that temporary and then permanent supply centers would be established along the trail, for the great need of the travelers as they neared the end of the journey was food and supplies. The condition of many of the emigrant trains as they approached the California border was known to many residents of Sacramento and San Francisco because early arrivals brought news from those they had passed along the way. Items in the newspapers in those towns and others near the border carried information about the progress of the year's overland emigration and often detailed the most important needs of specific wagon trains.[1] Thus relief trains

---

[1] The *San Francisco Daily Alta California* newspaper is very useful for such information. See particularly the issue of September 7, 1850, p. 2.

reached out from Sacramento, Placerville, and other points, some no doubt stimulated by feelings of brotherhood and good will, but many others by the simple economics of the situation.

Although available sources do not give a clear picture of the trading activity along the emigrant trail through the Great Basin until the year 1850, it is possible that some traders, particularly the type who sold goods from a canvas tent or cloth-house packed to the scene on the back of a mule, may have stationed themselves along the trail in 1849.

The first substantial trading post of record was established at present-day Genoa in Carson Valley by a party led by Captain Joseph DeMont and with Hampton S. Beatie as clerk. The group left Salt Lake City on April 18, 1850, and arrived at the site of Genoa sometime in June of that year.[2] The original motive of the group, to mine in California and return to Salt Lake City, was soon discarded when it became apparent that the location on the Carson River would make an excellent trading post to take advantage of the westward migration of that year. A temporary log structure was erected and the post was supplied with goods brought from California.[3] With the approach of winter the trading season closed. The DeMont-Beatie group sold out to a Mr. Moore and then split up, some returning to Salt Lake City while others crossed the Sierra to California.

The California-bound emigrants of 1850 not only supported the first trading activities in what was to become Nevada; one of them discovered gold in a ravine about forty miles east of the California border. On May 15, 1850, William Prouse, a member of the Thomas Orr emigrant train, panned some earth which showed a few specks of gold.[4] Although the discovery of gold was not sufficient to stay

[2] Most Nevada historians until recently accepted April 18, 1849, as the date of departure and June, 1849, as the date of arrival since Beatie in an interview many years later noted his arrival in Carson Valley as June, 1849. Recent research supports the 1850 date. See Russell R. Elliott, "Nevada's First Trading Post: A Study in Historiography," *Nevada Historical Society Quarterly* 13 (Winter 1970): 3–11.

[3] Hubert Howe Bancroft, *History of Nevada, Colorado and Wyoming, 1540–1888* (San Francisco: History Co., 1890), p. 68; Juanita Brooks, "The Mormons in Carson County, Utah Territory," *Nevada Historical Quarterly* 8 (Spring 1965): 11; *San Francisco Daily Alta California*, September 7, 1850, p. 2.

[4] Grant H. Smith, in *The History of the Comstock Lode, 1850–1920*, University of Nevada Geology and Mining Series, no. 37 (July 1, 1943), pp. 1–3, gives some attention to the 1850 discoveries. For the Prouse claim, the best detail

the progress of the wagon train, the news was significant enough to pass back along the trail. It was this discovery, no doubt, which was reported in the *Sacramento Transcript* and reprinted in the *California Courier* of July 8, 1850. The discovery also attracted a number of miners from California who journeyed back to the Gold Canyon area in the fall of 1850 to prospect for gold. At least one, probably others, returned the following year and were in the district when John Reese and his party arrived at the old DeMont-Beatie cabin.

Reese had arrived in Salt Lake City from the Midwest as part of the western migration of 1849. Soon after his arrival he and his brother Enoch established a general store, and it was there Hampton Beatie was employed after his return from Carson Valley in the fall of 1850. Encouraged by Beatie's stories about the region, Reese outfitted ten wagons with supplies to sell and a variety of seeds to plant and on April 5, 1851, left Salt Lake City for the Carson Valley area.[5] Arriving with his wagon train on June 4, Reese soon after purchased the trading post from Moore and proceeded to construct a more permanent building, some fifty yards from the old Beatie cabin. This was the first permanent structure in the present state of Nevada. Reese's success in the summer and fall attracted others, and by the time the trading season was over, additional settlers had moved into the neighboring Eagle and Jack's valleys and a few more miners had joined those already in Gold Canyon.

All of these individuals—miners, traders, farmers—legally were within the territory of Utah which had been created by the Compromise of 1850. The legislation was the result of more than two years of debate over how to provide political organization for the Mexican Cession lands and at the same time satisfy the opposing views of slavery and antislavery forces. By its terms California was to be admitted as a free state, and the remaining area was divided into the territories of New Mexico and Utah with a proviso that when they became states they could do so with or without slavery, as their constitutions indicated.

---

is found in Eliot Lord, *Comstock Mining and Miners*, U.S. Geological Survey Monographs, vol. 4 (Washington, D.C.: GPO, 1883), pp. 9–14. See particularly the footnotes on page 11.

[5]John Reese, "Mormon Station," *Nevada Historical Society Papers* 1 (1913–16): 186–90. In spite of certain discrepancies in his story, the Reese memoir is vital for this early period.

Utah Territory as organized included all of the present Utah, all but the southern tip of Nevada, the western third of Colorado, and a small corner of southwestern Wyoming. The territorial legislature located the seat of government at Fillmore City, about 150 miles south of the Great Salt Lake. However, its inaccessibility soon caused the permanent location of the territorial capital at Salt Lake City. Mormon control of the region was assured when President Fillmore appointed the Mormon leader, Brigham Young, as territorial governor.

The Young government was so involved in establishing an effective central government for Utah Territory that it paid little attention to the outlying parts. As a result the settlers in Carson Valley, unwilling to wait for the Mormon government to provide for their basic political needs, initiated a series of squatter meetings to establish local law and government in order to minimize criminal activity and protect those who had appropriated land. In so doing the Carson settlers were reenacting a role initiated in the year 1620 by their colonial ancestors and repeated over and over again during the westward movement in the United States when individuals found themselves in need of law, but outside the boundaries of effective government.

POLITICAL CONFUSION, 1850–55

In three successive meetings, held November 12, 19, and 20, 1851, over one hundred settlers meeting at Reese's Mormon Station established the framework of local control. Three important actions were taken. Eleven regulations concerning the survey, acquisition, and disposal of land were adopted; officers were elected and rules adopted to govern the community; and a petition was addressed to the Congress of the United States requesting "a distinct Territorial Government" for the western part of Utah Territory.[6]

The 1851 squatter movements in Carson Valley stimulated the Utah territorial government to pass a measure on March 3, 1852, extending county government throughout the territory. Of the twelve counties organized in 1852, seven—Weber, Desert, Tooele, Juab, Millard, Iron, and Washington—covered the area which is now Nevada. However, the organization was in name only since

[6] Myron Angel, ed., *History of Nevada* (Oakland, Calif.: Thompson and West, 1881), p. 33. This "Mug" history is the most useful history for this period. Details found here can be found nowhere else.

the seven counties were simply extension of counties in Utah, and officials appointed did not attempt to exert their authority in the western part of their counties. Continued inaction from Utah brought additional squatter meetings. In February, 1853, forty-three Carson Valley residents met and petitioned the California legislature for annexation to California for judicial purposes until Congress could act to create a separate territory for them. The prospect of losing its western territory to California stirred the Utah government to further action. On January 17, 1854, the territorial government brought Carson County into being, made up of the western parts of Tooele, Juab, Millard, and Iron counties. Again it was a paper creation only, for the Utah officials made no attempt to translate the legislation into action. Their failure to do so led to another approach by the settlers.

In the summer of 1854, a group of leading citizens in Carson County, fearful that the continued growth of population would soon overburden the squatter government, employed an attorney, William A. Cornwall, to draft a constitution to be presented to the people of Carson County. The preamble to the document indicated quite clearly that the action was taken because neither California nor Utah Territory had acted, and that the government which they proposed to establish was to be a temporary one.

Whereas the authorities of the State of California and the Territory of Utah have hitherto exercised no jurisdiction over the people residing in the colony of Carson's Valley, and the adjacent habitable country, lying between the populated districts of California and Utah; and whereas the boundary between said State and Territory, so far as we know, is unmarked and undefined; and whereas, by reason of the failure of government to cause the said line to be run, as well as on account of their isolated geographical position, the people of said colony have not hitherto participated in the local election of said State or Territory, and are unrepresented in their State and Territorial Legislatures. Now, therefore, as the people of Carson's Valley, in order to secure the blessings of tranquility and of free government, do ordain and establish this constitution for the colony of Carson's Valley, until provision is made for our government and protection by other proper authorities.

The draft of the constitution vested the powers in a president, a secretary, a sheriff, and a court of conciliation consisting of three members; all of these officers were to be elected by the people. Provision was made in the document for the collection of revenue to be spent for the esablishment of schools, for the construction of a prison, and for protection of the inhabitants against invasion and from the Indians. Cornwall concluded his document with the simple statement, "This constitution, of course, possesses no validity; it is a simple compact made by a people subject to the law and constitution of the United States."[7]

We know little about Cornwall's document, and there seems to be no evidence that it was ever presented for a vote. Coming as it did in the fall of the year, it may have sparked the next move by the Utah government. On January 19, 1855, the Utah territorial government established Carson County as the Third United States Judicial District of the territory and appointed George P. Styles as the territorial judge. At the same time the county was granted one representative in the Utah territorial assembly, and Orson Hyde, one of the twelve apostles, or governing officials, of the Mormon church, was appointed as probate and county judge to organize the county. Hyde, Styles, J. L. Haywood, the U. S. marshall, and thirty-six Mormon colonizers left Salt Lake City for Carson Valley on May 17, 1855.

The decision to send church members to Carson County was part of a much larger scheme to dispatch missionaries to different parts of the West. At a church conference held in Salt Lake City in April, 1855, a number of such missions were proposed. Besides the Mormons who were sent to Carson Valley, another group was to establish a mission in the area which later became Clark County in the state of Nevada. The second party, under the leadership of William Bringhurst, left Salt Lake City on May 10 and arrived at Las Vegas Spring, then in the territory of New Mexico, on June 14, 1855.[8] It was hoped that the settlement would thrive and thus act as a supply station for travelers between Salt Lake City and Los Angeles. Within a year the tiny settlement took on the appearance of permanency and might well have developed into a thriving community except for an unfortunate series of events which began with the discovery of lead in the nearby Spring Mountain Range in 1856.

[7] *San Francisco Daily Alta California,* October 27, 1854, p. 2.

[8] The site was discovered and named by the Spaniards, probably in the early nineteenth century, although it may have been as early as 1776 during the Garcés expedition.

The attempt to develop the Potosi mine, as it came to be called, proved too much for the slender resources of the small outpost. The colony was disintegrating of its own internal weaknesses when Young announced early in 1857 that the church members assigned to Las Vegas were released from their mission. The site was acquired by O. D. Gass and developed into the Las Vegas ranch. It was to be some time before the area became politically important to Nevada.[9]

EFFECTIVE MORMON CONTROL, 1855–57

The Hyde party, meanwhile, had arrived at Mormon Station on June 15, and its members proceeded immediately to establish land holdings in Carson and Washoe valleys. There was some question, posed mainly by anti-Mormon elements, that Mormon Station was in the state of California. Consequently, before he attempted to organize the county for Utah Territory, Hyde requested that Gov. John Bigler of California authorize a boundary survey. The survey which followed, conducted by George H. Goddard, showed that the interesecting line, an oblique line drawn north from the point where the 35th parallel crossed the Colorado River, met the intersection of the 120th meridian and the 39th parallel in the southeastern part of Lake Tahoe. Thus Carson County was definitely in Utah Territory, and Hyde proceeded to call for county elections to be held at Mormon Station, September 20, 1855. Enough Mormons were in the county by that time to ensure the election of all Mormons except one, Charles D. Daggett, who was elected to the office of prosecuting attorney.

The domination by the Mormons, completed almost exactly five years after passage of the Utah Territorial Act, increased the discontent of the Gentiles in the area. On November 23, 1855, a group of these non-Mormons petitioned the California legislature for the annexation of Carson County to California.[10] This time the petition was well received, and a resolution was passed by the California legislature urging the Congress of the United States to extend the boundaries of California east to the 118th meridian. No action was

---

[9] An excellent account of the mission is found in Andrew Jensen, "History of the Las Vegas Mission," *Nevada Historical Society Papers* 5 (1925–26): 115–284.

[10] Beulah Hershiser, "The Adjustment of the Boundaries of Nevada," *Nevada Historical Society Report* 1 (1907–1908): 123.

taken in Congress when opposition developed to increasing the size of the state, thought by some to be already too large. There was sentiment in Congress that the solution to the problems of Carson County would come with the improvement of the government of Utah Territory.

The continued agitation by the Gentiles in Carson County encouraged the church to send additional colonizing missions from Salt Lake City. New arrivals in the spring of 1856 spread through Carson, Eagle, Washoe, Jack's, and Pleasant valleys, bringing cattle and other livestock with them. Hyde's work was typical of the activity of the settlers: he surveyed Mormon Station in the spring of 1856 and renamed it Genoa; he established the new community of Franktown in Washoe Valley; and he constructed a sawmill to provide better homes and farm buildings for the newcomers. By the middle of 1856 Carson County was organized politically, economically, and socially in the firm and able hands of the Mormons.

Within a few months, however, Mormon control was weakened, and by mid-1857 was as ineffective as it had been from 1850 to 1855. In July, after a long period of misunderstanding and ill feeling between the federal and Utah governments, President Buchanan appointed new officials for Utah Territory and dispatched a military force to Utah for their protection and, as he explained it, to aid in the enforcement of federal law. Brigham Young, regarding this action as an invasion, issued a call for all Mormons to return to Salt Lake City to help in the defense of the community in the event of war.

The Mormon exodus from Carson Valley really started before the official call came from Young. Orson Hyde left Carson Valley on November 6, 1856, and a much larger contingent of sixty-four Mormons under the leadership of P. G. Sessions left for Salt Lake City on July 16 the following year. Such a large party, if not formally called back by Young, must have had his permission to return.

The official call from the church was received by the Mormons of Carson Valley in early September, 1857. Express riders were sent from Salt Lake City to the settlements on the Green River, at San Bernardino, and at Carson County. These messengers arrived at Genoa on September 5 and proceeded to alert the various Mormon families to the call to return. The settlers were told to bring as much ammunition as possible and to hurry. They were also counseled to say as little as possible about the matter. Nevertheless, word got out about the departure, and to allay suspicion the newspapers were told that the destination of the Mormons was the Salmon River in what was then Washington Territory.[11] The train, made up of 123 wagons and about 450 persons, left Carson Valley on September 26, 1857, and arrived at Salt Lake on November 2, 1857.[12]

The departure of the Mormons left approximately two hundred persons in Carson Valley. Many of them were engaged in placer mining in Gold Canyon. However, a number of individuals remained in the various valleys and continued to farm and raise livestock. Some of these were Mormons, like John Reese, who did not heed the official call at this time; still others were Gentiles who took advantage of the Mormon exodus to acquire their holdings, either at a minimal cost or simply by taking them.

Anticipating trouble, the Utah legislature had rescinded the action making Carson County a separate judicial district on January 14, 1857, and had attached it to Great Salt Lake County for election, revenue, and judicial purposes in order to forestall complete loss of political control over the area. As a result, the records of the probate and county courts were sent to Salt Lake City and the county lost its representative in the territorial legislature.

POLITICAL CHAOS, 1857–61

The Mormon withdrawal also led to another series of squatter meetings which were initiated when a group of leaders met at Gilbert's Saloon at Genoa on August 3, 1857, and appointed a committee to arrange for a mass meeting to be held five days later.[13] John Reese presided at the August 8 meeting in Genoa. In attendance were representatives from Honey Lake in California, Eagle Valley, Carson Valley, Willow Town, Ragton, Twenty-six-Mile Desert, Humboldt River Valley, Hope Valley, and Lake Valley. Three main actions were taken. The first was the drafting of a memorial to Congress requesting separate territorial status for western Utah, since the withdrawal of the courts to Salt Lake had

[11] *San Francisco Daily Alta California*, October 8, 1857, p. 2 (editorial).

[12] Brooks, "Mormons in Carson County," pp. 20–23.

[13] A good source for this period with excellent maps showing the changes in political status is Secretary of State (Nevada), *Political History of Nevada*, 5th ed. (Carson City, Nev.: State Printing office, 1965). This pamphlet is often referred to as John Koontz, *Political History of Nevada*.

left Carson County without effective law. The territory was to be
called Columbus, with its capital at Genoa. The second action was
the selection of James M. Crane, a native of Virginia, as the delegate to Congress to present the memorial for territorial status. The
third major business attended to by the 1857 squatter meeting was
the appointment of a committee of twenty-eight "to manage and
superintend all matters necessary and proper in the premises." The
committee included representatives from Honey Lake, California.
There is no record of effective action by the committee of twenty-
eight.

The petition Crane carried to Washington had the endorsement
of the California legislature, of Gov. John B. Welles of California,
and of many California newspapers. In addition, it came before
Congress at a time when federal relations with the Mormon government were at their lowest ebb. Crane, noting this, addressed a letter
to his constituents in February, 1858, predicting early passage of
the territorial bill as a war measure "to compress the limits of the
Mormons and defeat their efforts to corrupt and confederate with
the Indian tribes." The bill establishing territorial government for
Nevada was reported favorably by the Committee on Territories
on May 12, 1858. However, when William Smith of Virginia, a
friend of Crane's, introduced the bill in the House that same day,
he was unable to get action, and on May 14 the House adjourned
without acting on the Nevada bill. The settlement of the Mormon
question and the increasing sectional tensions had combined to
prevent the addition of another territory at that time.

Meanwhile, conditions within Carson County deteriorated when
the committee of twenty-eight proved incapable of action. Again
residents of Carson Valley met in mass meeting in March, 1858, but
this time to establish a vigilante committee to deal with the criminal
elements. A number of persons were tried and sentenced by this
tribunal, and at least one person, William ("Lucky Bill") Thorring-
ton, was hanged for his alleged participation in a murder.[14]

The attempts by the Utah territorial government to regain control in Carson County added to the confusion in the years between
1857 and 1861. Alfred Cumming, a non-Mormon who had replaced
Brigham Young as territorial governor of Utah on July 11, 1858,
initiated these moves when he appointed a Carson Valley resident,

[14] See Angel, *History of Nevada,* pp. 49–51.

John S. Child, as probate judge of Carson County. Child called elections in October, 1858, but the results only gave further evidence of the difficulty inherent in a situation which included Mormons, Gentiles who wanted no part of "Mormon law," and politicians who were eager to take advantage of any circumstance to press for separate territorial status. The returns in four of the six precincts were thrown out because of alleged voting frauds. According to contemporary writers, the anti-Mormon faction entered charges of fraud in order to prevent the local government from falling into Mormon control, since it was thought that pro-Mormon candidates would have been elected to most of the offices. In a second move to reassert its authority, the territorial legislature on January 17, 1859, restored Carson County as a legal entity, attaching St. Mary's and Humboldt counties to it as the Second Judicial District and assigning the Honorable John Cradlebaugh as judge.

The actions of the Utah government seemed to encourage dissidents in Carson County who wanted law and order but wanted it under their own control and not that of Utah Territory. Consequently, on June 6, 1859, another mass meeting was held in Carson City at which Carson County was divided into voting precincts and July 14 set as the date for an election to choose a representative to Washington and fifty delegates to a constitutional convention. The July election returned James M. Crane as the Washington representative and duly selected the membership of the constitutional convention, which opened in Genoa on July 18 with John Musser presiding. The constitution framed by the convention borrowed liberally from that of California and included a Declaration of Cause for separation which charged, among other things, that the Mormon government had violated the organic act establishing Utah Territory by provoking the Indians to depredations against the Gentiles, by failing to provide proper justice, and by attempting to exercise an absolute spiritual despotism.

The constitution was submitted to the voters of Carson County on September 7, and at the same time an election was held to fill the offices created by the document. No election returns have been found; however, John Musser certified that the constitution was adopted by a substantial majority and that Isaac Roop was elected governor. A great deal of secrecy, doubt, and confusion surrounded the election results, no doubt in part because Musser's certificate of election was not issued until December 12, some three months after the election. It is probable that besides Roop, A. D. Dorsey was elected secretary of state, John D. Winters auditor, and B. L. King treasurer, but only Roop attempted to serve. Either at the same time or at a later date, not recorded, delegates were elected to the legislature, which was to meet in December.

Meanwhile, John Cradlebaugh, judge of the Second Judicial District, arrived in Genoa in the summer of 1859 and immediately called a federal grand jury. Its report, issued in September, was mainly political in tone and listed the familiar grievances of the Gentiles against the Mormon government but failed to issue any indictments.

In the autumn of 1859, Judge Child of the probate court again tried to restore the authority of the Utah government, first by convening a session of the probate court on September 12 and then by calling an election for October 8. However, the court soon adjourned for lack of business and the second election was no more successful than the previous one. Although only three of the ten precincts opened their polls, Child and Governor Cumming were so eager to reestablish Utah Control that they issued commissions to those elected. However, none of the candidates were willing to take the oath of office under the uncertain conditions.

The provisional legislature met in Genoa on December 15 at the home of J. B. Blake and, after listening to an address by Governor Roop, adjourned for lack of a quorum. Although it was supposed to meet again in July, 1860, it was never reconvened. But if the provisional government was thwarted at home, its delegate to Washington continued to press for congressional action. Judge Crane, who had been reelected in July, died in September of 1859. John Musser was chosen at a special election on November 12 to replace him and left for Washington one month later. However, the short session of Congress to which Musser directed his efforts was a turbulent one because of sectional tensions occasioned by the approaching party conventions and presidential election. Consequently, he was unable to obtain legislation for separate territorial status for the Carson County residents in 1860.

On August 6, 1860, an election called by Judge Child of the probate court succeeded in filling the offices of selectmen, sheriff, treasurer, surveyor, and member of the territorial legislature. Judge

Child, on September 3, opened the first session of county court in three years. He continued to act as probate and county judge until the Nevada territorial government took over in 1861.

A final complication was injected into the government of Carson County in October, 1860, when President Buchanan appointed a new judge for the Second Judicial District, R. P. Flenniken, to succeed John Cradlebaugh. The latter refused to give up his post, claiming that the president had no legal right to remove a federal territorial judge. As a result, until the establishment of Nevada Territory six months later, there were two federal judges, both claiming to represent federal authority, in Carson County.[15] Obviously, under such circumstances the authority of the federal court was limited.

Most of the population of western Utah in the months from June, 1859, to the end of 1860 cared little about any of the three governments then attempting to exert authority over the area. The sudden lack of interest in political affairs, blamed by Roop in his message for the poor attendance at the legislative session in December, resulted from the discovery of a fabulously rich body of ore in June, 1859, on the eastern slope of Sun Mountain, thirty miles north of Genoa. The demands of the Carson Valley residents for law, order, and effective government now were pushed aside by the mad rush of people to the discovery site. However, these pressures quickly returned as the mining excitement increased in intensity and added new problems of control to the earlier and unsolved political problems of Carson Valley. The political development which resulted from the 1859 mineral discovery cannot be understood properly without a brief summary of the events leading to the opening of one of the great mining developments in history.

THE COMSTOCK DISCOVERY

From the discoveries of gold in 1850 until the major mineral find in 1859, the Gold Canyon area supported between 100 and 180 miners who took from their claims an estimated total of $642,000.

---

[15] Effie M. Mack, *Nevada: A History of the State from the Earliest Times through the Civil War* (Glendale, Calif.: Arthur H. Clark, 1936), pp. 188–89. Dr. Mack states that Stewart forced Flenniken to recognize Cradlebaugh's authority and that Flenniken then abandoned his post. However, John North noted in a letter to his wife that Flenniken was in Carson City when he, North, arrived in June, 1861. See the North Papers, Huntington Library, San Marino, Calif.

According to Eliot Lord, the best year was 1855, when some 180 miners recovered a total of $118,400. The miners during this period took practically all of the half-million dollars from gold placers found in the canyons; they threw away black sand (later proven to be silver ore) which interfered with their search for gold.[16]

An exception to the general practice of mining in placers was the activity of the Grosh brothers, Ethan Allan and Hosea. The brothers, like most of the Gold Canyon miners, worked in the California gold fields during the winter months and came to Carson Valley in the summer. Their first attempt to work the Gold Canyon placers came in 1853, although they may have visited the area earlier. In subsequent years they returned to Carson Valley but, unlike most of the other miners, began to prospect for silver along with their search for gold. Within a short time they had uncovered a ledge of silver ore, which they called the "monster ledge." Some historians claim this was the Comstock Lode, but it would appear more accurately to have been the Silver City branch of the Comstock Lode, a ledge of low-grade ore that was never profitable, although later developed by a number of companies. It is possible that the two brothers, had they lived, might have discovered the Comstock Lode. However, tragedy struck twice in 1857—first when Hosea struck a pick in his foot on August 19 and died from the injury on September 2, and again when Allan, in company with a friend, Richard M. Bucke, ran into heavy snows in the Sierra as they were attempting to return to California. When they were rescued in December, both had badly frozen legs. Allan refused to allow amputation and died on December 19; his friend Bucke had one foot and part of the other amputated, but survived. The tragic story of the Grosh brothers has, no doubt, romanticized their activities in the Gold Canyon area. It is quite clear that they did not discover the Comstock Lode; they were, however, the first to prospect intelligently for silver.[17]

Although the placers at Gold Canyon had declined in importance by1857, a number of prospectors continued to work that canyon and its neighbor to the north, Six-Mile Canyon. Their efforts were rewarded twice in the year 1859 with discoveries which, although

[16] A good source for the very early mining activities in Gold Canyon is Lord, *Comstock Mining and Miners,* pp. 24, 63.

[17] Smith, *History of the Comstock Lode,* p. 4, gives a careful analysis of the part played by the Grosh brothers.

widely separated, proved to be part of the same mammoth ledge. The first discovery came when four men, James ("Old Virginny") Finney, Alec Henderson, Jack Yount, and John Bishop on January 28 located what later proved to be the Gold Hill end of the Comstock Lode. The discovery created some excitement and within a few days a number of locations were made in an area which was called Gold Hill to distinguish it from the Gold Canyon placers. Winter stopped further activity and it wasn't until March or April, when weather permitted, that Finney and his associates uncovered, at about ten feet from the surface, what came to be known as the Old Red Ledge. The ore at this point was mostly gold; the rich silver ore bodies were located a few months later farther to the north.

The second discovery of 1859 came from the activities of the miners in Six-Mile Canyon. A number of them, including "Old Virginny" and his friends, had worked the placers in Six-Mile Canyon but had become discouraged in the summer of 1858. At that time they were within a few feet of the rich black sand which a year later heralded the "effective" discovery of the Comstock Lode. Credit for the find must go to Patrick McLaughlin and Peter O'Riley. In the early days of June, while attempting to increase the flow of a spring at the head of Six-Mile Canyon, they discovered gold in the sand from the spring. Further digging brought them to a solid ledge which proved ultimately to be part of the mammoth Comstock Lode; the discovery of the ledge was probably on June 11. Almost at once questions of ownership arose. The first to question O'Riley and McLaughlin's right to the find was Henry Paige Comstock. Comstock had been in the Gold Canyon area for a number of years, but had gained little except a reputation for laziness. He was called a "loud-spoken trickster" and "half-mad." Half-mad he may have been, but he was sane enough to come forward after the discovery and point out that the spring belonged to him and Emanuel Penrod and that a number of other miners had claimed the land earlier. After Comstock and Penrod's claims were clarified, an agreement was reached whereby O'Riley and McLaughlin agreed to a four-way partnership. After further exploration work, the claim, at the insistence of Penrod, was located as a quartz vein, thus giving the four men some 1,500 feet along the vein rather than the 50 feet each would have received had the ground been located as a placer claim. Two additional partners were taken in on June 22, when John D. Winters, Jr., and J. A. Osborn were given a one-third interest in the claim in return for building two arrastras in which to crush the ore.

The O'Riley-McLaughlin discovery did not create an immediate rush to the district; it did attract the attention of J. F. Stone, a former Grass Valley miner and, at the time of the discovery, a partner in the Stone and Gates trading post on the Truckee River, near the present site of Glendale. Stone obtained samples of the ore and sent these to J. J. Ott of Nevada City for assay. Additional samples were given on June 27 by Judge James Walsh, a prominent mill and mine owner of Grass Valley, to Melville Atwood of Grass Valley for the same purpose. The results of both assays indicated a rich find. The Atwood assay was particularly significant, since it showed a result of $3,876 in gold and silver per ton at a time when any gold and silver ore which assayed over $100 per ton was considered a good mining prospect. This knowledge was sufficient to send Walsh and his partner, Joseph Woodworth, hurrying to the Washoe discovery. It was impossible to keep the results of the assays secret, and close on the heels of Walsh came dozens of others from the Nevada City–Grass Valley area, eager to get in on the new find.

The first newspaper report of the discovery, appearing July 1, 1859, in the *Nevada Journal*, published at Nevada City, California, was reserved in its enthusiasm. The description was brief and gave no indication that a major mineral discovery had been made.[18] The rush to Washoe began in a mild way in the late summer and fall of 1859, stopped as winter closed the mountain passes, and swelled into a massive wave of humanity, in the spring and summer of 1860.

The same "madness" which had caused them to leave their homes and sometimes their families and to rush across thousands of miles of plains, mountains, and deserts to reach the "pot of gold" now seized these "new Californians" and shot them back over the mountains in what came to be known as the "rush to Washoe." They came from every walk of life and by any mode of conveyance available: by wagon, by mule, by horse, on foot, and sometimes pushing wheelbarrows before them. Along with the miners came people with sup-

---

[18] California newspapers by this time were disillusioned by many "false" boom notices. The editor of the paper at this point no doubt knew only about the Ott assay.

plies of all kinds, including herds of sheep, hogs, and cattle, who had learned from other mining rushes that wealth often came more easily from above ground than below it. Soon rough communities—Gold Hill, Virginia City, and Silver City—began to form near the areas of greatest activity as the hordes, dazzled by a dream of easy riches, rushed happily and recklessly to exploit the wealth buried in Sun Mountain, blithely unaware of the tremendous political, economic, and social changes their activity would spawn.

The Comstock discovery had the immediate political effects of complicating the already confused situation then existing in western Utah Territory and disrupting the attempt to form a provisional government; these efforts had been initiated almost exactly at the time O'Riley and McLaughlin made their discovery. Within the next few months the center of population shifted so strongly from Genoa to the villages on Sun Mountain that, when the provisional legislature met on December 15, 1859, only four members appeared and the meeting was adjourned for lack of a quorum.

However, the shift of population to the Comstock Lode area did not bring with it a solution to the political disorders which had characterized events in Carson County in the years after 1857. On the contrary, the confusion and lawlessness were intensified by the mining boom, in spite of the fact that the California miners brought with them a political device known as the mining district.

The mining district was a product of the California gold rush, when thousands of miners found themselves outside the boundaries of effective government and with no legal means of taking and holding mineral claims. To correct this, impromptu meetings were held at which officials were elected and rules established for securing mineral titles. Within a few years the mining district meeting had become a necessary part of each new mining rush, and the codes therein developed were accepted as legal by the California courts. Thus, by the time the Comstock was discovered, the district type of organization had been used enough in California to prove its worth in protecting and legalizing mining claims and transfers. However, there were neither national nor Utah territorial laws governing mineral claims when O'Riley and McLaughlin made their discovery at the head of Six-Mile Canyon. Whether or not the California mining codes, or local adaptations of them, would be accepted by the Utah territorial courts was, of course, a moot point in Jan-

uary, 1858, when the first mining district was established in Carson
County, Utah Territory.

The Columbia Quartz District was formed at Johntown by a
number of Gold Canyon miners. Included within its boundaries
were what later became the Virginia, Gold Hill, Flowery, and Silver
City districts. The man elected as district recorder, William H.
Dolman, noted afterward that there wasn't even a blank book in
Johntown and that a makeshift "Book of Laws and Records" was
made by sewing together a "few quires of letter papers." Apparently, a number of claims were recorded by Dolman; however, the
records of the Columbia District were lost or destroyed and did not
become part of the legal record of Carson County.[19]

The inactivity of the Columbia District and the prospecting activity of Finney and others at Gold Hill brought into being a
second and more important unit, the Gold Hill Mining District,
which was organized on June 11, 1859. The miners who organized
it were quite well aware of the lack of political and legal control
in western Utah and intended to do something about it, as the
preamble to the minutes indicates:

Whereas, the isolated position we occupy, far from all legal tribunals, and
cut off from those fountains of justice which every American citizen should
enjoy, renders it necessary that we organize in body politic for our mutual protection against the lawless, and for meting out justice between man
and man; therefore, we, citizens of Gold Hill, do hereby agree to adopt
the following rules and laws for our government.

The organizers, considering themselves citizens as well as miners,
proceeded on the one hand to lay down rules and regulations governing social conduct and to elect officials to maintain political
control, while on the other hand they specified the usual rules governing the location, recording, transfer, and sale of mining claims.
Included in the former were regulations setting the punishment for
homicide (death by hanging); robbery, theft, and assault and bat-
tery (as the jury might determine); and banking games, or gambling
(final banishment from the district). A justice of the peace and a
constable were elected to enforce these rules and a recorder chosen to
record the mining claims. In neither instance was effective control

[19] Interesting sidelights of this district are told in Austin E. Hutcheson, ed.,
"Before the Comstock, 1857–1858: Memoirs of William Hickman Dolman,"
New Mexico Historical Review 22 (July 1947): 205–46.

achieved, mainly because of the magnitude of the rush that soon frustrated these feeble efforts.

Particularly unfortunate, in the light of subsequent mining development, was the inability of the mining district to make and keep proper records and to enforce its own regulations. The regulation concerning the record of claims was quite clear:

> The duty of the Recorder shall be to keep in a well-bound book a record of all claims which may be presented for record, with the names of the parties locating or purchasing, the number of feet, where situated, and the date of location or purchase; also to return a certificate for such claim or claims.

V. A. Houseworth, the first recorder of the district, allowed the book of records to be kept at a saloon, on a shelf behind the bar, where individual miners could consult it whenever they wished. The result was that the book soon showed erasures and irregular additions which made its value as a legal document questionable and ensured the rise of numerous court battles.[20]

The miners at Gold Hill had no intention of establishing a substitute for the provisional government which was forming at Genoa. On the contrary, the mining district sent five delegates to a meeting on June 20 at Carson City to nominate candidates for election to the constitutent assembly which was to meet on July 18. The Gold Hill Mining District regulations were simply meant to take care of the local situation on Sun Mountain.

Regardless of intent, the political effect of the Comstock discovery and the subsequent formation of the Gold Hill Mining District added further confusion to the already chaotic conditions then existing and magnified the lack of authority present in western Utah Territory. From the exodus of the Mormons in the fall of 1857 until March, 1861, when Nevada became a territory, the various attempts to exert political control in Carson County—the squatter governments, the Utah territorial government under Judge Child, the efforts of the federal government through Judge Cradlebaugh and

---

[20] These two works—Lord, *Comstock Mining and Miners,* pp. 41–55, and William Wright [Dan De Quille], *The Big Bonanza* (New York: A. A. Knopf, 1947), pp. 34–37—are indispensable to any study of the Comstock Lode, for as contemporaries to its developments the authors used sources that are no longer available to us, for example, many files of the *Territorial Enterprise* in its early years.

the territorial courts, and the Gold Hill Mining District—all failed to establish the minimal authority necessary.

Territorial Status, March, 1861

By the end of 1860 it was quite clear that the citizens in Carson County wanted a government of their own, free from Utah control. Nevertheless, in January, 1861, the Utah territorial government initiated a number of reforms for Carson County in a last-minute effort to save the area. The two most important of these were an act which moved the county seat from Genoa to the more populous Carson City, and an act providing for the incorporation of Virginia City. The latter act was especially significant in that it gave a great deal of self-government to the citizens of Virginia City, recognizing that this burgeoning village held the key to effective control of the area.

The efforts were months too late. John Musser, the delegate of the provisional government, was in Washington when the 36th Congress opened its first session in December, 1860. The chance for territorial status for western Utah was enhanced by the impending secession of the southern states, who had been responsible for much of the congressional opposition to the creation of a Nevada Territory in 1859 and 1860, since such an event would strengthen anti-slavery forces. True to its threat to withdraw from the Union if Lincoln was elected, South Carolina seceded on December, 1860, and was followed in this action by six other southern states in the next few weeks. Bills to establish Nevada Territory, sponsored by Senators William Gwin and Milton Latham of California, were introduced in the Senate after the Confederate States of America was formed on February 8, 1861. It soon became evident that some sort of territorial bill for Nevada would be passed by Congress, and on February 26 a bill written by Senator James S. Green of Missouri passed the Senate. A companion bill passed the House on March 2 and was signed by President Buchanan the same day. Thus, after a decade of effort, the citizens of western Utah Territory achieved separate territorial status, aided in great part by two events—the discovery of the Comstock Lode in 1859, which furnished the population pressure for a new government, and the secession of the southern states from the Union in 1860 and 1861, which removed a major obstacle to the formation of additional free territories.

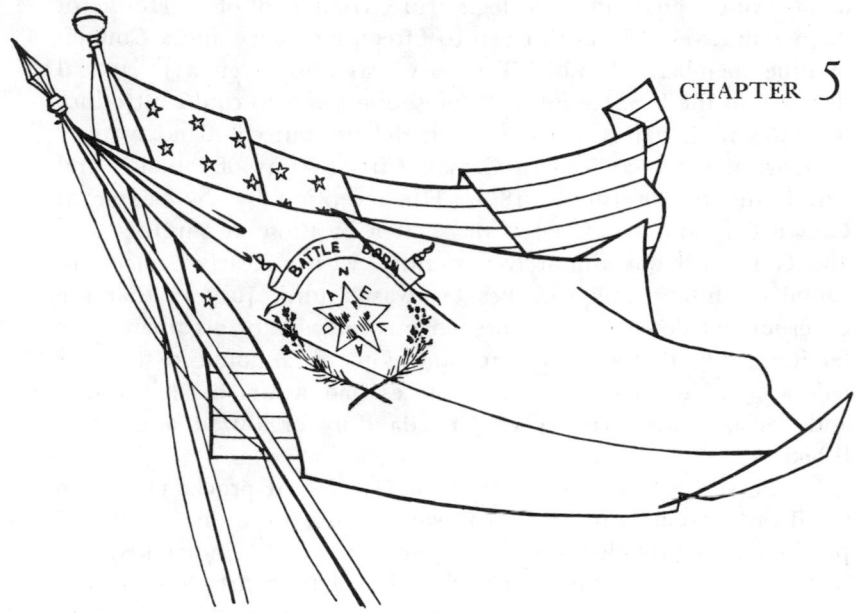

Territory to Statehood, 1861–64

THE APPOINTMENTS to the new territory devolved on President Lincoln, who named a native of New York, James Warren Nye, as governor. It is obvious that Nye's appointment was influenced greatly by his friendship with Secretary of State Seward and by his work in New York for the election of the Republican ticket in 1860. Orion Clemens was appointed as territorial secretary and Gordon Mott, Horatio M. Jones, and George Turner were named as territorial judges. Many of the appointments to lesser territorial offices were also political, suggesting that patronage figured strongly in the organization of Nevada Territory as it had in earlier territorial movements.

In accordance with procedures laid down originally in the Northwest Ordinance of 1787, the Nevada Organic Act made it possible for Nevada to enter at once the second stage of territorial development, which guaranteed a legislature composed of a House of Representatives of from thirteen to fifteen members, and a Council of nine members. Nevada Territory was also given a territorial delegate to the U.S. House of Representatives who could introduce measures in Congress, participate in debate, but could not vote.

Governor Nye arrived in Carson City, by way of Panama and San Francisco, on July 7, 1861. His reception by the people at Carson City and again, a few days later, by those at Virginia City and Gold Hill was almost too friendly, with a nearly continuous round of dinners and speeches. It wasn't until July 11 that the governor got down to the more serious business of organizing the territory. On that day, by proclamation, he announced that the federal appointees to territorial offices had assumed their duties and declared the territory of Nevada duly organized and established.

In the succeeding weeks, Governor Nye issued proclamations in rapid order, completing the basic work of organization. A July 17 proclamation provided for the organization of a judicial system including a supreme court, district and probate courts, and justices of the peace. The three federally appointed justices—Mott, Turner, and Jones—constituted the supreme court, which was given both original and appellate jurisdiction. Each of the supreme court justices was assigned individually to one of the three district courts. Until an election could be held, Governor Nye appointed officials to the lower courts.

A third proclamation, issued by Nye on July 24, provided for a census of the territory, the election of a delegate to Congress, and selection of members for the territorial legislature. Although the decennial census of the United States had just been completed, it was necessary, under the Organic Act, to take a new census as a preliminary to the first election. The governor named Dr. Henry DeGroot to conduct the census and divided the territory into twelve electoral districts for this purpose, including the Honey Lake region of California in Nevada Territory in his division. The census as reported to Governor Nye on August 5 showed a population of 16,374 persons exclusive of Indians and emigrants, which, when contrasted with the 1860 census figure for Carson County of

6,857 persons, shows the remarkable growth occasioned by the discovery of the Comstock Lode. For a more accurate figure the 1861 total should be reduced by approximately 1,000 for the electoral district which included the Honey Lake residents, who had been counted as Californians in the 1860 census.

On August 8 Nye issued a call for an election to be held throughout the territory on August 31 to elect nine members to the Council and fifteen members to the House of Representatives and a delegate to the U.S. Congress. He also set the date for the first meeting of the territorial legislature as the first Tuesday in October (October 1), and the place as Carson City. In designating Carson City as the meeting place for the territorial legislature, Nye ensured that town an advantage in the race for capitol site when the territory moved toward statehood. The choice may well have been the result of successful maneuvering on the part of a number of Carson City citizens, including William M. Stewart, Major William Ormsby, and Abraham Curry. The fact that a number of small counties were subsequently established in western Nevada, insuring county seat status to many of Carson City's rivals, points to that conclusion. However, the county seat of Carson County had been moved from Genoa to Carson City by act of the Utah territorial legislature on January 18, 1861, and Nye's choice may simply have been a carryover of this action.

The territorial legislature, which met a total of three times—in 1861, 1862, and 1864—held its first session from October 1 to November 29, 1861, in the upper story of Abe Curry's Hotel, now the site of the Nevada State Prison. J. L. VanBokkelen presided over the Council and Miles Mitchell served as speaker of the House; both men were from Virginia City. The Honey Lake residents were represented in the Council by Isaac Roop and in the House of Representatives by John C. Wright. The legislature, after organization, proceeded to pass the myriad of laws necessary to make the transition to a properly organized territory. As a first step, it adopted the Common Law of England. The transfer of the authority from Utah Territory was made by legalizing acts passed by the Utah Territorial legislature prior to the establishment of Nevada Territory. In succeeding days the legislature defined in more detail various civil and criminal codes, some of which, in the light of subsequent events in Nevada, appear quite interesting. For example, the law governing the Sabbath prohibited the operation of theaters, race tracks, and cockpits and "engaging in any noisy amusement." Another act prohibited games of chance; violators were subject to imprisonment as felons for a maximum of two years and a fine of $500 or both. The gambling act had been suggested by Governor Nye in the following words:

I particularly recommend that you pass stringent laws to prevent gambling. Of all the seductive vices extant, I regard that of gambling as the worst. It holds out allurements hard to be resisted. It captivates and ensnares the young, blunts all the moral sensibilities and ends in utter ruin. The thousand monuments that are reared along this pathway of ruin, demand at your hands all the protection the law can give.[1]

The matter of revenue to operate the territorial government created some discussion and may well have laid the groundwork for the later argument over mine taxation. According to the Organic Act, the salaries of the federal officials in the territory and the expenses of the territorial legislature would be borne by the federal government, but other territorial expenses and the costs of county and local government would have to be met by taxation.[2] The principal source of wealth was, of course, the mines, and it occasioned little surprise, but a great deal of opposition, when Governor Nye suggested that the gross proceeds of the mines should be taxed. The House Committee on Mining did not agree, and recommended instead a tax on "the net profits arising from the mines." The revenue act, as finally adopted on the last day of the session, placed an ad valorem tax of forty cents per $100 of assessed valuation on all property in the territory and authorized each county to levy and collect a tax not exceeding sixty cents per $100 of assessed valuation of county property. In addition, a poll tax of $2 on each male inhabitant between the ages of twenty-one and fifty and a number of license taxes were provided to obtain additional revenue for territorial and county purposes. However, terri-

[1] This quote is taken from Governor Nye's address to the First Territorial Legislature on October 2, 1861. It is printed in the *Journal of the Council of the First Legislative Assembly of the Territory of Nevada* (San Francisco: Commercial Steam Printing, 1862), pp. 14–27.

[2] The difficulty of getting anything from the federal treasury comes to life in a fascinating letter from Orion Clements, territorial secretary, to the acting comptroller of the treasury, Washington, D.C., published in the *Nevada Historical Society Quarterly* 6 (Spring 1963).

torial expenses increased more rapidly than did revenues, and the territorial debt on October 30, 1864, the day before the granting of statehood, was $264,110.74. This sum included some $60,000 owed to Abraham Curry for construction of a prison, which was deemed absolutely essential for the territory.

In his address to the legislative assembly, Governor Nye emphasized the importance of establishing a system of common schools, noting that "the public have an interest in the instruction of every child within our borders, and as a matter of economy, I entertain no doubt that it is much cheaper to furnish school-houses and teachers than prisons and keepers."[3] The legislature, by act of November 29, 1861, created the offices of territorial superintendent of public instruction and of county superintendent of county schools, and provided the necessary administrative machinery for organizing and maintaining the schools. Although the Organic Act provided that sections 16 and 36 in each township were to be reserved and dedicated to the use of the common schools, this land could not be sold by the territory. Consequently, the burden of school support rested on the territory and the counties. County commissioners were required by law to reserve 10 percent of all monies paid into the county treasury from property taxes for "the hire of school teachers in the several school districts." Income from fines for breaches of the penal laws was also to be used for school purposes, as was also $.75 of the extra dollar collected on delinquent poll taxes.

To ensure the benefits of government to outlying districts and provide a means for their orderly development, the legislature divided the territory into nine counties with county seats as follows: Esmeralda, Aurora; Douglas, Genoa; Ormsby, Carson City; Washoe, Washoe City; Storey, Virginia City; Churchill, Buckland's; Humboldt, Unionville; Lake, no county seat named; Lyon, Dayton. Each county was to have a county clerk and ex officio auditor, a sheriff, tax collector, assessor, treasurer, recorder, county surveyor, county school superintendent, and three county commissioners. In addition, for each township, a justice of the peace and ex officio coroner and a constable were provided. The county governments were made operative when the legislative assembly nominated for each county three commissioners, who were then commissioned by

---

[3] *Journal of the Council of the First Legislative Assembly* . . . , p. 23.

the governor, and charged them with the duty of apportioning their counties into election districts for an election on January 14, 1862, of other county officials. The nomination by the governor and approval by the legislature of district attorneys and probate judges completed the work of providing at least the most basic elements of law and order throughout the territory.

BOUNDARY ADJUSTMENTS

The establishment of Lake County, renamed Roop on December 5, 1862, ultimately precipitated a boundary dispute with California, variously called the Roop County War, the War of Injunctions, and the Sagebrush War. The dispute was the result of a peculiar boundary provision in the Organic Act which invited controversy with California, and the fact that geography united the Honey Lake residents with Carson Valley.

Instead of providing that the new territory's western boundary would be the eastern boundary of California, the Nevada Organic Act specified that the boundary between California and the proposed territory would be the "dividing ridge separating the waters of Carson Valley from those that flow into the Pacific," or the crest of the Sierra Nevada. However, the stipulation was added that "so much of the Territory within the present limits of the state of California, shall not be included within this Territory until the State of California, shall assent to the same by an act irrevocable without the consent of the United States."[4] Needless to say, California never assented to the dividing ridge as a boundary, although Nye led a delegation to petition the California legislature to cede the area east of the ridge to its "weaker neighbor." There appeared to be some support within the California legislature for such a move, but it apparently was overruled by the fact that the mineral discoveries at Aurora in Esmeralda County, Nevada Territory, might lie in California, and the latter did not wish to lose the possible tax revenues from this area.

The boundary dispute moved from discussion to action early in 1863 when officials from Roop County, Nevada Territory, and officials from Plumas County, California, attempted to exercise jurisdiction over the same area. From injunctions issued and ar-

---

[4] Secretary of State (Nevada), *Political History of Nevada*, 5th ed. (Carson City, Nev.: State Printing Office, 1965), p. 67.

rests made by each side upon the other, the dispute soon degenerated into physical violence between the supporters of the Roop County officials and the sheriff of Plumas County and a posse comitatus which he had brought with him to enforce the decrees of the Plumas County courts. One or two people were wounded in the ensuing conflict, but before major damage could be done an armistice was agreed upon and a procedure worked out whereby each side was to seek the aid of its respective governor to effect a settlement of the dispute.

The result was the appointment of a joint boundary survey, with Surveyor-general Houghton acting for California and Butler Ives, the territory of Nevada. The completed survey report, accepted by California on April 4, 1864, and by Nevada on February 7, 1865, indicated definitely that the Honey Lake area was in California; consequently, the political ties which had connected those residents with Carson Valley since the 1850s were broken, although their economic ties continued. The report just as definitely concluded that Aurora was in Nevada, but not before that community, the county seat of both Mono County, California, and Esmeralda County, Nevada Territory, carried out the unique political trick of holding two elections covering different jurisdictions on the same day. Thus, citizens of Aurora voted in one election for California officials and in another for Nevada territorial officials; the coincidence stretched further when a citizen of Aurora, Thomas Machin, became presiding officer of the California Assembly and another Aurora citizen, Dr. John Pugh, became president of the Nevada Territorial Council.

Although the territory of Nevada was thwarted in its attempt to gain additional lands in the west, it did expand eastward at the expense of Utah Territory. The territorial delegate, John Cradlebaugh, had presented a memorial to Congress from Governor Nye and the legislative assembly requesting the extension; on July 14, 1862, Congress approved the act adding the area which, under Utah Territory, had been St. Mary County. The reasons for the request and for congressional action are not clear at this late date, although it was apparent that if Nevada wished to expand, the obvious direction in which to do so was to the east, where appeals to prejudices against the Mormon territory of Utah could be used to advantage.

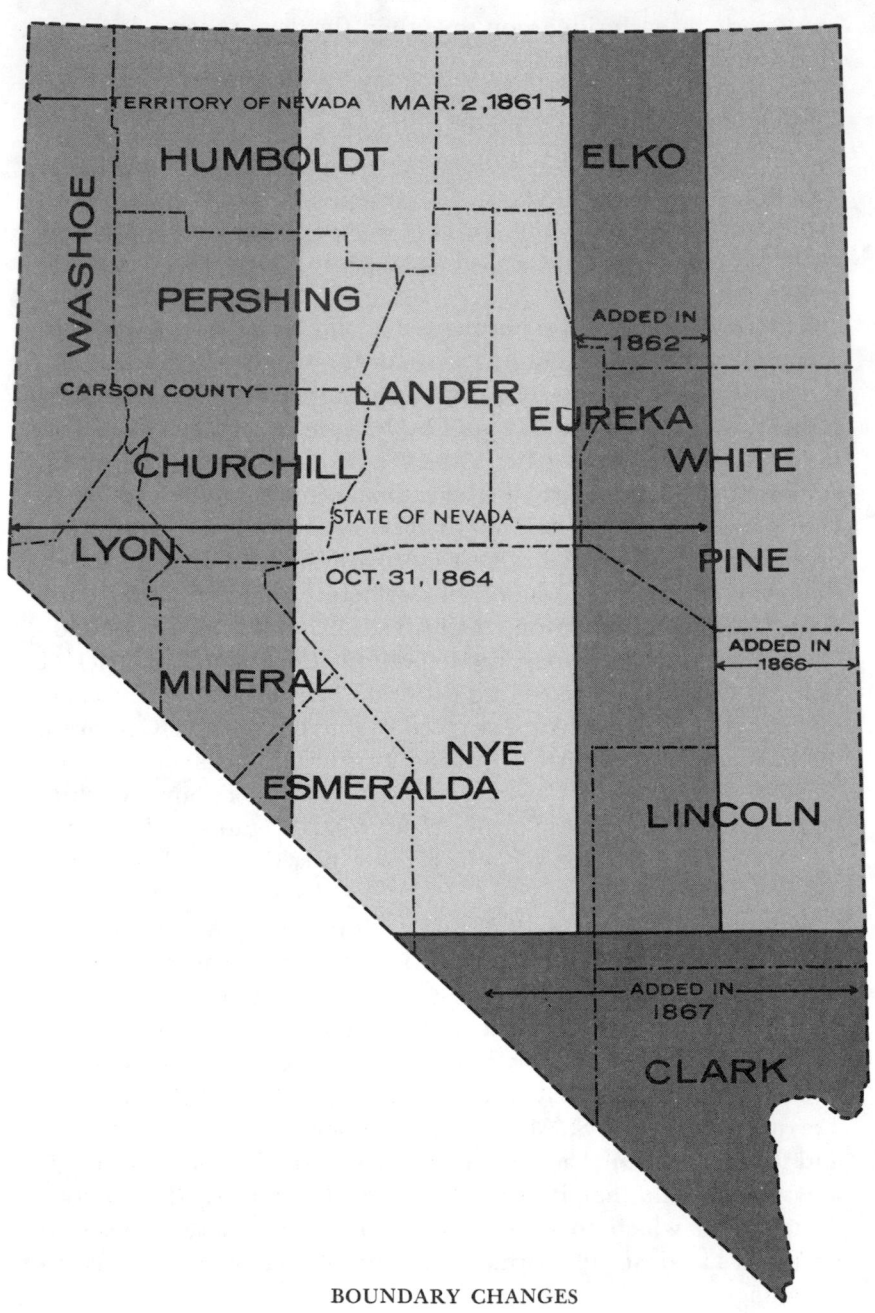

BOUNDARY CHANGES

The territorial legislature, in its first session, took cognizance of the transportation problem by granting six toll-road franchises. Toll roads, particularly where emigrant roads crossed streams or negotiated difficult passes, had been an integral part of the transportation system during the 1850s, and the territorial legislature, in most of these instances, simply affirmed rights which already were being exercised. Succeeding territorial legislatures were much more liberal in the granting of such franchises: the legislature of 1862 granted twenty-three, and that of 1864, twenty-eight. The first legislature also granted a number of railroad franchises, none of which were used.

The 1861 legislative assembly did not provide incorporation charters for any municipalities, although in certain other acts it did recognize Carson City, Gold Hill, and Virginia City as being in that category. However, in the legislative session of 1862 incorporation acts were passed for Gold Hill on December 17 and for Virginia City two days later; the legislature of 1864 incorporated the towns of Aurora, Star City, and Austin. The 1861 legislature ratified Nye's choice of Carson City as the territorial capital by an act on November 25, 1861.

Perhaps the most important single action taken by the legislature, other than the measures to organize the territory, was an act approved December 20, 1862, "to frame a Constitution and State Government for the State of Washoe." The act combined a provision for an election, to be held in September, 1863, to determine sentiment for and against the organization of a state government, with a provision for a constitutional convention to be held at Carson City on the first Tuesday in November if voter sentiment was favorable in the September election. The act provided, also, that those who voted, whether for or against a state government, might also vote by ballot for thirty-nine delegates to the constitutional convention. At the election on September 2, 6,660 votes were cast in favor of a state government and only 1,502 against it; at the same time the membership of the constitutional convention was selected.

THE 1863 CONSTITUTIONAL CONVENTION

It is quite clear that the only authority for the convention was the above-mentioned act of the territorial legislature. There was no enabling act passed by Congress at this time, although a major effort was made to obtain one; Nye even visited Washington, D.C., in the spring of 1863 with this objective in mind. Bills to enable Nevada, Colorado, Montana, and Nebraska to frame constitutions were introduced into the United States Senate in the early months of 1863. Although some opposition was voiced at once to the Nevada bill, it was successfully overcome through the efforts of Senators William Latham of California and Thomas B. Wade of Ohio; the Nevada bill was passed by the Senate on March 3, 1863, by a vote of twenty-four to sixteen. However, a move to suspend the rules in the House of Representatives in order to take a vote on the Colorado and Nevada state bills was unsuccessful, and the attempt to win an enabling act was lost for that session.[5]

The attitude of the residents of Nevada territory in rushing into a demand for statehood even before territorial organization had been completed was in keeping with historical precedents since the adoption of the Northwest Ordinance of 1787. The people of frontier areas in the United States had not been content with what was considered second-class citizenship, and there always seemed to be enough ambitious individuals in each new territory who were willing and able to direct such feelings into demands for statehood. The fact that Congress had been unwilling to grant an enabling act in 1863 did not disrupt the procedures established by the territorial legislature in December, 1862, for those who wanted statehood were quite willing to act with or without prior congressional approval. Consequently, on November 2, 1863, the elected delegates met to frame a constitution for the "State of Washoe."

On December 11, after thirty-two days of deliberation, the convention produced a constitution which, although defeated by the voters, was an important document and served as the basis for the successful constitution of 1864. Of the thirty-nine delegates, thirty-five had come directly to Nevada Territory from California, but the states of New York, Pennsylvania, and Ohio, in that order, were most often cited as place of birth. Only four of the delegates could date their arrival in the territory before the opening of the Com-

[5] U.S., Congress, House, *Congressional Globe,* 37th Cong., 3d sess., 1862–63, pt. 2: 1510–12, 1543, and 1549. Dr. Effie M. Mack states that "the congress passed the Enabling Act for the State of Nevada on March 3, 1863" (Effie M. Mack, *Nevada: A History of the State from the Earliest Times through the Civil War* [Glendale, Calif.: Arthur H. Clark, 1936], p. 250). This is a mistake since neither the records of debate nor the U.S. statutes shows evidence of the passage of such an act.

stock Lode in June, 1859. Five were foreign born. The delegates, representing a range of professions, included eight lawyers, four miners, two farmers, five merchants, a banker, doctor, notary public, sign painter, coach-maker, hotel keeper, civil engineer, and lumber dealer; a number of delegates had no profession listed. Many were outstanding men: J. Neely Johnson had served a term as governor of California and was to serve later on the Nevada Supreme Court; John W. North, appointed surveyor-general of Nevada Territory in 1861, was serving as a territorial judge at the time of the convention; William Stewart was to become one of Nevada's most prominent United States senators; John Kinkead later became Nevada's third governor; C. N. Noteware became the state's first secretary of state; and C. M. Brosnan became a justice of the Nevada Supreme Court. John W. North was chosen as president of the convention.

The delegates began their deliberations with an argument over a name for the proposed state. The legislative act of 1862 had called it Washoe, but many were not satisfied and offered Humboldt, Esmeralda, and Nevada as possible alternatives. On November 6 the name Nevada was decided upon.[6]

The most controversial issue to arise during the debates was that of mine taxation. It was obvious that, as the territory moved away from the protective support of the federal government, additional funds would be necessary to organize a state government; and since mining was the basic industry of the territory, it was just as obvious that it would get special attention in this respect. One group, led by John North, supported the idea that mines should be taxed exactly as other property. A second group, led by the prominent and powerful attorney William M. Stewart, favored taxing only the net proceeds of the mines. The convention, by a rather substantial margin of twenty-one votes to ten, ultimately decided in favor of the North forces by giving the legislature power to "provide by law for uniform and equal rate of assessment and taxation and [to] prescribe such regulations as shall secure a just valuation for taxation of all property, both real and personal including mines, and mining property."[7]

---

[6]*Virginia Evening Bulletin*, November 7, 1863.

[7]Ibid., December 1, 1863. Invaluable for the 1863 constitution is William C. Miller and Eleanore Bushnell, eds., *Reports of the 1863 Constitutional Convention of the Territory of Nevada as Written for the "Territorial Enterprise" by Andrew J. Marsh and Samuel L. Clemens and for the "Virginia Daily Union" by Amos Bowman* (Carson City, Nev.: Legislative Counsel Bureau, State of Nevada, 1972).

Other debates centered around provisions aimed against secessionists and states' rightists, but these were handled without difficulty and the convention adjourned at 10 P.M. on December 11, when the members who were in attendance "pledged themselves to work for the adoption of the Constitution. Patriotic speeches were made, and three cheers for the State of Nevada were given."[8]

The contest for ratification of the constitution began immediately. The forces favoring adoption appeared unbeatable. They included: the San Francisco-controlled, large-company mining interests and their spokesman, William Morris Stewart; all of the important Comstock newspapers (one later switched sides) and all but three of the nine papers in the territory; and strong Union sympathizers like John W. North, who wanted another "free" state added. The opposition, which consisted in the beginning of small-company mining interests; agriculturists; and states' rightists, particularly the so-called secession element, at first were ineffective. Public meetings held throughout the territory, however, stimulated important debates on various constitutional issues and gave the antiratification element an opportunity to focus on two major weaknesses of the 1863 document: the taxation clause, which did not give mining the preferential "net proceeds" tax it wanted; and the election provision, which asked the people to vote for adoption of the constitution and at the same time choose officers to serve under it. William M. Stewart's position on those two issues made it appear that a vote in favor of the constitution would be a vote in favor of control of the new state government by the large mining companies that Stewart represented.

Although Stewart had favored a net proceeds tax during the constitutional convention, he found the lack of such a provision no bar to ratification of the 1863 document.[9] Shortly after the ratification debates began, Stewart and his supporters promoted the idea that a net proceeds tax could be achieved by legislation. Such an argument drove a wedge between the mining interests on the

---

[8]Ibid., December 12, 1863.

[9]Stewart's role in the ratification of the 1863 constitution has been misinterpreted by historians for nearly a century. The record was set straight in an excellent article by David A. Johnson, "A Case of Mistaken Identity: William M. Stewart and the Rejection of Nevada's First Constitution," *Nevada Historical Society Quarterly* 22 (Fall 1979): 186–98.

Comstock, since the representatives of small mining companies, who generally favored the multiple-ledge theory of the Lode, demanded that any net proceeds tax be constitutionally guaranteed. Their opposition to the constitution was not assuaged by the Stewart position. On the contrary, their antagonism to Stewart and ratification was increased since it was clear that control of the state government would be necessary to obtain such a legislative tax measure. The prospect of having a state dominated by William M. Stewart and San Francisco capitalists united various groups against ratification. Thus, the fight for adoption of the 1863 constitution became a contest for economic and political control of the Comstock Lode.

The Stewart forces were quick to see the Union party as a key to the control of the proposed state. Standing in the way of such dominance was John W. North, for not only did he oppose the single ledge theory advocated by Stewart, North had also decided to enter the contest for governor. That move placed him in direct conflict with Stewart and the large mining interests, who could not afford to have a chief executive who favored ideas and procedures so directly opposed to their own plans for exploitation of the lode. The initial stage in the fight for control of the Union party came when the Storey County convention met at Virginia City the last week of December, 1863. The Stewart faction dominated the proceedings, naming not only their own delegates, including Stewart, to the state convention but their slate of candidates as well. Not content with the omission of North's name from the Storey County slate of candidates, Stewart pushed through a resolution that pledged the Storey county delegates to oppose North's nomination at the state convention.[10]

Although snubbed by Storey County, North still had sufficient support in a number of smaller counties to be nominated for governor. However, when the state convention met at Carson City on December 31, the Stewart forces dominated the proceedings, and their choice for governor, Miles N. Mitchell, a member of the territorial House of Representatives, received twenty-nine to twenty-two for North.

[10]*Gold Hill Daily News*, December 28, 1863, p. 2, col. 3; December 29, 1863, p. 2, col. 2; Johnson, "A Case of Mistaken Identity," p. 193.

The victory of the Stewart forces in the nominating conventions set the stage for the defeat of the 1863 constitution, for the show of power by the victors in eliminating Judge North from the Union party slate of candidates made it clear that a favorable vote on the constitution would bring to power those candidates supported by Stewart and company.

Almost at once the opposition press adopted an anti-Stewart position and began to portray the ratification fight as one between the monopolists who wanted statehood under the 1863 document and the people who opposed statehood under that banner. The *Virginia Daily Union,* an earlier supporter of the constitution, now began an unrelenting fight to defeat it by focusing on the figure of William M. Stewart. The newspaper's position, that adoption of the constitution would place the new state government in the hands of California speculators and their local agent, Stewart, was fortified by a number of mass meetings sponsored by those in opposition to the constitution. Stewart's continuing attempts to discredit North as a judge added weight to a growing conviction that the Stewart forces wanted nothing less than complete control of any state government and economic dominance of the Comstock Lode.

The contest for ratification, in the newspapers, in mass meetings, in the saloons, and on the streets, became a bitter fight between Stewart and anti-Stewart forces that continued to the day of the election. On that day, January 19, 1864, however, a carnival-like mood swept the Comstock as voters went to the polls to record a major defeat for the 1863 constitution, with only 2,157 votes in favor and 8,851 opposed.[11]

Many theories have been offered to explain how a vote of more than four to one for statehood in September, 1863, could be changed by January, 1864, into a vote of nearly four to one against the state constitution. Included among such reasons were: the taxation clause, which failed to give mining interests the preference they demanded;[12] the dual election procedure, which not only was a bad technical arrangement but tied a favorable vote on the constitution

---

[11]Bushnell, *Nevada Constitution,* p. 50.

[12]See particularly, Andrew Marsh, *Official Report of the Debates and Proceedings in the Constitutional Convention of the State of Nevada . . . , July 4, 1864. . . .* (San Francisco: F. Eastman, 1866), pp. 325, 411.

to a vote of approval for the Union party's slate of candidates dominated by the Stewart interests;[13] the strong pro-Union provision that alienated states' rightists; and the opposition of property owners, particularly agriculturists, who opposed statehood because it would bring additional taxes.

Although the taxation clause and the dual election procedure themselves might have brought defeat to the constitution, it seems apparent that the tremendous outpouring of opposition to the 1863 document resulted from a clever campaign by anticonstitution groups to portray William Morris Stewart as an unholy symbol of a group of unscrupulous individuals who wanted to take possession of the new government for their own selfish purposes. The charges against Stewart were not without foundation.[14]

The defeat of the 1863 constitution was so decisive that one might well have assumed that the statehood movement in Nevada Territory had been killed. Such might have been the case had not national pressures intruded to give the citizens of the territory another opportunity to adopt a constitution and enter the Union as a state. Apparently there were at least three different, but related, national circumstances which pointed to this end. In the first place, Lincoln needed additional votes in Congress to ensure passage of the antislavery amendment and there was a real question whether or not he could muster the required two-thirds vote in each house; an additional Republican state also would help in ratification of such an amendment if passed by Congress. Second, it has been held by some that Congress supported Nevada statehood in order to secure additional votes to help ward off presidential reconstruction.[15] A third possible reason is that many national political leaders felt that the 1864 election would be a very close one and might well be thrown into the House of Representatives, where another Republican vote could prove decisive. Both of the latter reasons might appeal to

[13]*Virginia Evening Bulletin,* editorial, January 20, 1864.

[14]David A. Johnson states categorically that Nevadans rejected statehood in 1863 because they "feared and distrusted William M. Stewart" and thought that he was the instrument through which San Francisco capitalists would gain control of the state government.

[15]Edward S. Dodson, "A History of Nevada during the Civil War." (M.A. thesis, University of Oregon, 1947), pp. 92—93.

Lincoln as well as to the radical Republicans in Congress.[16] Pressure for Nevada statehood was found not only on the national scene; ambitious local politicians could see real advantages to statehood, and no doubt many Nevadans supported statehood because of considerations of prestige. Citizenship in a state, after all, was a higher status than territorial citizenship.

THE STATEHOOD MOVEMENT SUCCEEDS, 1864

It appears that national pressures were responsible for the introduction of a bill by Senator James R. Doolittle of Wisconsin, on February 8, 1864, to enable the people of Nevada to form a constitution and a state government. On this occasion, under conditions quite different from those which had defeated the 1863 bill, there was little opposition in Congress and the Nevada Enabling Act passed both houses. It was signed by President Lincoln on March 21, 1864.

The Enabling Act for Nevada set certain conditions which had to be satisfied in the constitution before statehood could be obtained: (1) the constitution must be republican in nature and not repugnant to the federal constitution nor to the principles of the Declaration of Independence; (2) there was to be no slavery or involuntary servitude other than punishment for crimes; (3) the constitutional convention must disclaim all right to unappropriated public lands in Nevada, and allow these lands to remain at the disposition of the United States; (4) all lands belonging to American citizens residing outside of Nevada should never be taxed at a higher rate than those belonging to Nevada residents; (5) toleration of religious sentiment and worship must be guaranteed; and (6) there was to be no taxation of federal property by the state of Nevada. In an exception to the general rule that Congress was to approve state constitutions after ratification by the people, the president was authorized to accept the document and to declare Nevada a state if in his opinion it satisfied all the provisions of the Enabling Act.

---

[16]A thoughtful summary of the continued pressure for statehood is found in Bushnell, *The Nevada Constitution*, 2d ed. rev., pp. 35–36. For additional information on Lincoln's attitude, see Frederick Lauriston Bullard, "Abraham Lincoln and the Statehood of Nevada," *American Bar Association Journal* 26 (March and April, 1940): 210, 313.

Governor Nye, on May 2, 1864, issued a proclamation calling for an election on June 6 to select delegates to frame a state constitution in accordance with the Enabling Act. The delegates—thirty-nine were elected but only thirty-five served—met from July 4 through July 27, to produce Nevada's second constitution within a year. J. Neely Johnson, a former governor of California, was chosen president of the convention, William M. Gillespie was named as secretary, and Andrew J. Marsh was selected as the official reporter.

In a general way the makeup of the 1864 constitutional convention was similar to that of 1863. Ten of the delegates, including the presiding officer, had participated in the 1863 deliberations. As in the earlier convention, most of the delegates had come to Nevada from California; and again, lawyers and those directly concerned with mining dominated the professions represented. All but one of the delegates, Francis Proctor from Nye County, were listed as members of the Union party; Proctor was registered Democrat. The two most prominent members of the 1863 convention, John W. North and William M. Stewart, were not present in 1864.

The convention opened on a rather pessimistic note with one delegate wondering what could be accomplished since the voters had so recently and decisively voted against statehood. It was soon agreed, however, that a fresh attempt should be made, using the 1863 constitution as the basis for a new document. Again, although seemingly settled by the earlier convention, an argument arose over the naming of the state. Some were still dissatisfied with "Nevada," mainly because of prior usage in Nevada City and Nevada County, California, and the names Washoe, Humboldt, and Esmeralda were suggested as substitutes. The debate over the naming of the state came to an abrupt halt when J. Neely Johnson noted that

Congress has provided that a State called the State of "Nevada" shall be admitted after certain proceedings have been had, and the President is authorized to declare by proclamation the admission of the State of "Nevada" into the Union; and I conceive that no other name would comply with the terms under which we are to be admitted. It is true that the late Constitutional Convention did override the act of the Legislature by substituting the name of "Nevada" for "Washoe"; but that cannot be regarded as a precedent because the Convention was held entirely without authority having previously been given by Congress. . . . In that Enabling Act, as I conceive, Congress has specifically prescribed our name. . . . Now the child is named; it had been baptized by the name of Nevada, and nothing short of an act of Congress can change that name.[17]

The fact that the 1864 convention used the 1863 document upon which to base its proceedings did not prevent the delegates from engaging in long and sometimes rather heated debate, particularly on the subjects of taxation, education, a proposed railroad subsidy, and the question of loyalty to the Union. In spite of the numerous arguments, however, the 1864 constitution, as signed by thirty of the delegates on July 28, 1864, was very similar to that defeated by the voters in January. The most important change, at least from the standpoint of later ratification, involved the taxing of mines. While the 1863 constitution had provided for the taxation of mines on an equal basis with other property, the 1864 document excepted mines and mining claims, "the proceeds alone of which shall be assessed and taxed."[18] A second possible source of opposition to the 1864 constitution was removed when it was decided to hold the election of state officers separately from the vote on the constitution. The removal of those two potential obstacles to ratification made it possible for supporters of the 1864 document to wage a positive campaign for adoption by emphasizing two major benefits that statehood would bring the territory, the end of the economic depression on the Comstock and the end of the "corrupt" judiciary.

The depression, which had started in the spring, deepened in the summer and fall of 1864 and added to an already confused economic and political situation. Stewart and his supporters took advantage of the circumstances to mount a strong, positive campaign to convince the voters that statehood would end the depression.[19] The argument was strengthened when it was tied to charges that the mining crisis was due to the inability of the judges to clear the court dockets of large amounts of litigation. The "corrupt" judiciary thus became a do-nothing one responsible for the decline of mining activity in the territory.

[17]Marsh, *Debates*, pp. 34–35.
[18]By far the best discussion of the debates in the Second Constitutional Convention is found in Bushnell, *The Nevada Constitution*, 2d ed. rev., pp. 36–56. Dr. Bushnell's work also offers an excellent, up-to-date summary and evaluation of the constitution itself.
[19]David A. Johnson, "Industry and the Individual on the Far Western Frontier: A Case Study of Politics and Social Change in Early Nevada," *Pacific Historical Review* 51 (August 1982): 243–64.

The attack against the territorial judiciary had strong political motivations for it gave the Stewart forces an opportunity to mask their own intentions, which were what they had been earlier, to gain control of the state government and of the congressional delegation. It also gave Stewart an opportunity to eliminate a potential political rival, Judge John North.

The feud that had developed between Stewart and Judge North, which apparently had originated in political differences, was intensified when North, on May 5, 1864, ruled against the Chollar company and in favor of the Potosi company in a suit which had dragged on for months. The crux of the matter was a disagreement about the geological characteristics of the Comstock Lode. From the date of North's decision until August 22, when North and the other two judges, Locke and Turner, resigned, Stewart and his supporters waged an unrelenting campaign to remove the territorial judiciary, charging them with bribery and corruption.

Even the most cursory examination of the circumstances surrounding the Chollar-Potosi case indicates that the action of all three justices, but particularly of Locke, were highly irregular; that they were also corrupt has never been proved. As a matter of fact, Judge North, the only one of the three judges to try to clear his name, was later vindicated in court. North and his supporters claimed that he resigned in August specifically to bring charges against Stewart and the owners of the *Territorial Enterprise*. Thus two suits, one for slander against Stewart and one against J. T. Goodman and D. E. McCarthy, editor and publisher of the *Territorial Enterprise*, were filed by North on December 6, 1864, in the Fourth District Court of the State of Nevada. By mutual consent the cases were taken from the court and submitted to three arbitral referees. Their report, dated September 6, 1865, held generally in favor of Judge North, noting that the evidence showed the character of John W. North "free from each and every imputation cast upon it by the accusations of the defendant, William M. Stewart." It stated further that the evidence did not support any acts of corruption on the part of North and that William M. Stewart was guilty of the slanderous charges averred against him in the plaintiff's complaint.[20]

[20]Clipping from *Washoe Times* of September 21, 1865, North Papers #80.

Nevada's territorial judges were placed in untenable positions, called on as they were, to decide complex issues of mining law involving millions of dollars and control of the Comstock Lode itself. Their actions in the Chollar-Potosi case, however, were so irregular as to invite attacks. Stewart saw an opportunity to eliminate the entire territorial court and initiated a campaign in the newspapers and in public meetings to accomplish that end. Its success was evident when North resigned shortly after the Supreme Court opened its August 22 session. Stewart and followers forced the resignation of the other two judges the same day.

The resignation of the judges made it appear that the charges of bribery and corruption were true. The pro-Stewart newspapers portrayed the resignations in that light insisting that the only cure for the judicial problems was statehood. Such a conclusion echoed the statement of Nevada's second Attorney-General, Robert M. Clarke, when he remarked on May 13, 1867, "Nevada became a State to escape the deadfall of her Territorial courts."[21]

Those few who opposed the constitution in the election on September 7 were motivated, no doubt, by fear of increases in taxation and by a belief that statehood was not needed at the time. One of the major opponents of the 1863 constitution, W. J. Forbes, editor of the *Humboldt Register,* continued his opposition to any statehood movement in a forceful editorial on July 23, 1864:

DON'T WANT ANY CONSTITUTION—That's what's the matter. The Humboldt world is dead-set against engaging to help support any more lunk-heads till times get better. . . . If we have a State Government we'll have more fat-headed officers to support; and if we undertake to support them without taxing the mines, we'll run hopelessly into debt. If we do tax them, we'll stop the development of them.

Such opposition was minimal and the constitution was ratified with 10,375 votes in favor and only 1,284 against, no doubt reflecting a feeling that statehood would bring economic and judicial stability. Another positive factor influencing the vote was the opportunity to place Nevada in the ranks behind Abraham Lincoln.

As soon as the vote was officially counted and tabulated, the entire

[21]*Nevada Reports,* vol. 3, p. 17.

constitution was sent by wire to Washington, D.C., at a cost of $3,416.77. Lincoln proclaimed Nevada a state on October 31, 1864, in plenty of time for its citizens to participate in the November election. The strategy of the Republican Congress and president in pushing statehood for Nevada was justified by the results of the November 8 election. Although the Democrats and Republicans both ran full slates of candidates, the Republican party was victorious in every contest in the state. H. C. Worthington of Lander County was elected Nevada's first representative to Congress; H. G. Blasdel was chosen as the state's first governor; and Republicans dominated both houses of the state legislature, thus assuring the selection of Republican senators.

Nevada's first state legislature met December 12, 1864, listened to Governor Blasdel's message on the fourteenth, and the next day began the balloting which ultimately chose William M. Stewart and James W. Nye as Nevada's first two United States senators. Stewart was elected on the first ballot, convincing proof that his rather rough tactics against North and other potential opponents had paid off. The selection of the second post soon turned into a contest between John Cradlebaugh, Charles DeLong, and James W. Nye. A number of ballots were taken without a choice being made. A persistent story, told first in a contemporary account, suggests that Cradlebaugh could have won the seat had he been willing to give his patronage to Stewart, but upon his refusal, Stewart swung his support to Nye, who was selected on the first ballot taken on December 16.[22] Both senators hurried to Washington in time to vote in favor of the resolution calling for the Thirteenth Amendment, and the Nevada legislature ratified the amendment on February 16, 1865. Thus, by helping to abolish slavery, Nevada paid the initial installment of its debt to Lincoln and Congress.

[22]Angel, *History of Nevada,* p. 88.

CHAPTER 6

Early Statehood:
The Economic Foundations

WHILE THE STATE MAKERS at Carson City were engaged in establishing an effective government, a few miles to the northeast on the slopes of Sun Mountain members of the mining fraternity were just as busy trying to unravel the mysteries of the new and unusual mineral discovery. Their success in devising methods to extract and refine the silver-gold ores efficiently meant that the Comstock would dominate the whole life of the state—economically, politically, and socially—for the next two decades. In fact, from 1859 to 1880 the history of the Comstock is the history of Nevada, for economic growth and settlement within the state were directly stimulated by the Comstock activity. But, since certain events on the Comstock are best understood in the context of state-wide developments such as the building of the Central Pacific Railroad through Nevada, we shall, after a brief discussion of the foundations of the Comstock mining industry, consider happenings elsewhere in the state, returning in the next chapter for a comprehensive look at the Comstock.

The first arrivals lacked the experience, the money, and the discipline necessary to develop a silver mine. Most were seeking a quick ride to fame and fortune, and when it didn't come through surface placers they turned to indiscriminate location of claims, hoping to gain by speculation the fortune closed to them by their own ignorance of mining. Fortunately, a few of those who came in the first "rush to Washoe" were experienced quartz miners from California who were able within a short time and by extremely crude methods to uncover the ore body for some three hundred feet through the Ophir, Mexican, and Central claims. The first shipments of ore to San Francisco, in August and early November before snow storms shut down operations for 1859, demonstrated very clearly that while selected ore from the Comstock was rich enough to overcome heavy reduction and transportation costs, additional capital and better organization would be necessary to exploit the ore body properly.[1]

In the spring of 1860 when weather conditions permitted the resumption of mining operations, the informal associations which had taken over from the original claimants the previous year passed the challenge in turn to more sophisticated organizations, the incorporated stock companies. The initial development in this direction came when Judge James Walsh and other early purchasers sold their interest to San Francisco capitalists, who organized the Ophir Silver Mining Company with 16,800 shares, that is, 12 shares for each of the 1,400 feet of the claim. The shares, at the time of incorporation, had a par value of $300 each, giving the Ophir company a stock market value of $5,040,000. Within a short time most of the better claims along the lode were formed into similar stock companies.

---

[1] In August, 1859, thirty-eight tons of selected ore sent to San Francisco for reduction yielded a net of $91,424 after transportation and reduction charges of $20,576 were subtracted.

The stock company organization brought with it many advantages, perhaps the most important being the broader capital base which it provided. In addition, the actual work of mine development and plant operation was placed in the hands of a competent superintendent, who could be held responsible for efficient operation. The establishment of the incorporated companies reflected a change in philosophy from the get-rich-quick idea of the first locators. It was a tacit recognition by the new owners that the Comstock would not give up its riches easily and that substantial amounts of money and effort would have to be expended in order to overcome the problems of transportation, mining, and reduction.

Eighteen-sixty began with a surge of excitement as the thousands who had waited for the opening of the Sierra passes poured into the district. It has been estimated that about ten thousand persons came to the Comstock that year, but nearly half of them returned at once to California; the best claims were already taken, and the outbreak of the so-called Pyramid Lake War caused a near panic in the area.

THE PYRAMID LAKE WAR, 1860

Minor difficulties between whites and Indians had taken place almost from the beginning of the white man's penetration into the present state of Nevada. The trappers and explorers posed little threat to the Indian economy, based as it was on hunting, fishing, and food gathering; but the farmer and the miner, by intruding into the Indian domains to take up permanent land holdings, disrupted the Indian's social and economic life and provided no acceptable substitute. Indian raids against the emigrant trains in the late 1840s and throughout the 1850s had neither slowed down the white man nor provided any major economic relief to the Indian. The Carson Valley settlements, with between five hundred and one thousand persons, were no real threat to the Indians. The discovery of the Comstock Lode in the summer of 1859, however, brought thousands of people to that area and caused the Paiutes and some of their Bannock allies to gather at Pyramid Lake in the spring of 1860, evidently to determine what to do about the encroachments of the white men. The conference was interrupted by the news that a group of Bannocks had killed three whites and burned William's Station on May 7, apparently in retaliation for the capture of two Indian women.

The reaction of the miners and settlers was immediate and generally irrational. Rumors magnified both the number of whites killed and the number of Indians who were thought to be ready to move against the white settlements. Hasty and ill-conceived plans were made, and volunteers were formed into military companies, but without proper equipment and mounts, and under no single authority. To most of the recruits, ridding the area of the Indians would be not only a simple but an enjoyable task. Little thought was given to the possibility that the Indians might have had just cause for the William's Station incident. The Indians, meanwhile, prepared their forces more carefully, although many of the young leaders were just as eager for combat as were the whites. Contact between the two groups came on May 12 a few miles from Pyramid Lake when the Indians led the motley group of volunteers into a well-prepared ambush. The results of the ill-advised action by the whites, although predictable, were nonetheless frightening. Of the 105 men who participated in this first encounter, 76 were killed and many of the remaining 29 were wounded. When news of the defeat reached the Comstock settlements the residents began to panic. Immediate efforts were made to defend the towns against the expected attacks. These included sensible provision to take care of women and children and a number of not so sensible reactions, such as the attempt by citizens of Silver City to construct a wooden cannon. Fortunately for any potential operators, it was never fired. More important were the measures taken to provide troops and ammunition. Ultimately, a force of 549 volunteers was organized under the command of Colonel Jack Hays. In addition, 207 regular army men, under Captain Joseph Stewart, were sent from California. The two groups joined on May 31 at the big bend of the Truckee, where Wadsworth now stands, and proceeded cautiously toward the mouth of the river. The ensuing battle was short but decisive. Now outnumbered, the Indians were dispersed to the north and to the west. When it was evident that the Indians had been routed, the volunteer army returned to Virginia City and disbanded. The regulars constructed a temporary post at Pyramid Lake, which Stewart called Fort Haven. Stewart's troops occupied it until the middle of July, when they moved to a site on the Carson River which became Fort Churchill on August 7.

The Pyramid Lake war of 1860 was the signal for a series of

Indian raids throughout the territory, aimed mainly at the Pony Express and stage stations. During the next decade many stations were overrun, their stock driven off, and some station agents killed. To meet the threat, the government established more than two dozen military posts throughout Nevada to protect the main travel routes and the important settlements, yet difficulties with the Indians continued into the 1870s.[2]

TECHNICAL PROBLEMS AND SOLUTIONS

Mining activity on the Comstock practically ceased during the Indian uprising and continued to be slow for the remainder of the summer. Those who arrived in the district during that time were generally disappointed to find that development was centered in only two places: at Gold Hill, where men such as Joe Plato and Sandy Bowers had uncovered a rich vein of gold ore, and at the Ophir mine, where it was evident that the ore body widened as operations went deeper. Furthermore, their experience in the California placers had conditioned the gold seekers to a mining environment totally different from the one they now encountered on the Comstock. Not having the patience, money, or experience necessary to exploit the lode, they found it easy to belittle the Washoe diggings and either return to California or drift to other likely mineral prospects in western Utah Territory. For those miners and owners who remained, 1860 proved to be a year when the first great challenges of the Comstock Lode were met and successfully overcome through two developments—the *Washoe pan process* of reduction and the invention of *square-set timbering*.

Fortunately, the Comstock ore was predominantly silver and gold with very few of the base metals which later caused so much difficulty in other silver areas of the Far West. The heavy penetration of gold in the ore, particularly at the beginning of operations, made possible early profits which were necessary for continued developments: not only was the ore sent to San Francisco in 1859 rich enough to sustain good profits in spite of heavy reduction and transportation costs, but a great deal of ore taken in the early months of operation was shipped all the way to England to be smelted. It was evident to the experienced miners, however, that

[2]For the story of the military posts in Nevada, see Colonel George Ruhlen, "Early Nevada Forts," *Nevada Historical Society Quarterly* 7 (1964): 7–63.

such shipments could not continue for long and that a cheap method of reduction was necessary for continued operations.

The California miners and millmen had little to guide them in the search for a process to reduce the silver ores. Crushing the ore was speeded by the introduction of the so-called California stamp mill, which by 1860 was sufficiently developed to serve as a basic model for the Comstock. Actual reduction of the ores was another matter; the only real help came from two processes, the patio and the cazo (kettle), which had been used for years by the Mexicans. In the former process the crushed ore, quicksilver, salt, and copper sulphate were spread over a paved area, or patio, and stirred by driving mules or horses through the mixture, with the sun supplying the necessary heat; in the latter, the ore and other ingredients were boiled in a large kettle. Both of these processes were effective if the ores were simple and if time and labor costs were not considered important. But the Americans couldn't wait and almost immediately began experiments which they hoped would lead to a mechanized version of the older processes.

So many people participated in developing the milling improvements which ultimately led to the famous Washoe pan process that it is difficult and perhaps somewhat unfair to single out any individual. However, most historians of the Comstock era have pointed to Almarin B. Paul as the man who perfected the process which became one of the Comstock's great technical achievements. Paul, a friend of George Hearst, was an experienced quartz miner and the owner of a quartz mill in Nevada City, California. Paul visited the Washoe mines in the autumn of 1859, took ore samples from the Ophir and Mexican mines, and returned to his mill to experiment during the winter months. His experiments proved so successful that he decided to erect a twenty-four-stamp mill in Gold Canyon, and in March, 1860, with the help of a few friends, he organzied the Washoe Gold and Silver Mining Company No. 1. After signing contracts with mill owners whereby he guaranteed to have the mill operating within sixty days, Paul proceeded with its construction and was able to complete it on August 12, the last day of the contract. In spite of this speed, Paul's mill went into operation just a few hours before a similar but smaller eight-stamp mill, built by Charles S. Coover and Elias B. Harris, was completed. Both mills proved successful and within a short time a number of additional mills were built. These new mills used iron pans to mix the crushed ore and the chemicals; iron mullers were soon added to grind the mixture. Hot air at first provided the heat, but steam was found later to be more satisfactory.

Paul was quick to acknowledge that he and other Comstock millmen knew nothing about milling silver ores in 1860, but with continued experimentation, by 1862 they perfected what came to be known as the Washoe pan process, or Washoe pan amalgamation. Although it was never completely satisfactory, particularly with silver, the method was soon employed by most of the mills on the Comstock and within a short time had spread to mining camps throughout the United States.

The success of Paul's mill led to a veritable mill-building craze that mirrored the same pressures and illogical development which had resulted in the indiscriminate location of claims in 1859 and 1860. By 1863 there were nineteen mills in Virginia City and in Six- and Seven-Mile canyons; Gold Canyon had thirty-five mills stretching from Gold Hill to Dayton; between Empire and Dayton, on the Carson River, were twelve more; and in Washoe Valley an additional nine.

Just as important as the milling problem and much more direct was the mining challenge which was presented when the Ophir shaft moved beyond the 50-foot level. At that point the ore body was 10 to 12 feet wide and could be mined without difficulty. However, it steadily increased in width as the tunnel went deeper, until at the 180-foot level it was 40 to 50 feet wide and so soft and crumbling that the usual method of timbering was ineffective. The immediate danger to the miners was so great that mining could not be continued until a safe and efficient method could be found for removing the ore. Confronted by this dilemma, one of the directors of the Ophir company, a San Franciscan named W. F. Babcock, called in from California a young German engineer, Philipp Deide-sheimer. Arriving on the Comstock in November, 1860, Deide-sheimer worked out a basic idea within a few weeks which was developed into the famous square-set timbering. With this system timbers were framed in rectangular sets which could be joined to-gether in interlocking cubes and extended in any direction. Thus ore could be taken from above, ahead, or from either side, and the cubes could be filled with waste rock to form a solid pillar of wood and rock, or covered with planks to make a floor. The solution was at once simple and effective and became standard throughout the Comstock mines. Probably no single development on the lode was as widely copied elsewhere, and certainly, without it the great mineral deposits could not have been so thoroughly and quickly exploited. The invention of the square-set was much more the work of a single person than the Washoe pan process, yet Deidesheimer never had his invention patented and lost the opportunity to profit by it.

Thus, the first two major technical problems were overcome with simple and effective solutions. In succeeding years as the mines went deeper, the problems increased in number and complexity and taxed the ingenuity, patience, and resources of the miners, employers, and engineers. The most persistent underground difficulties after 1860 were those connected with ventilation, fire, heat, and water. They were never satisfactorily solved, but until the mines reached great depths they were controlled sufficiently to allow fairly efficient mining of the ore body.

Ventilation became a problem as soon as the tunnels were a few feet into the mountain, and as the mines reached deeper, excessive heat added to the basic difficulty of poor air circulation. Root blowers were introduced in 1865 but were not much help. Conditions were improved when Burleigh mechanical drills, using compressed air, were introduced in 1872. The compressed air not only ran the drills and other underground equipment but helped ventilate the mines and run additional blowers; however, the unsystematic operations underground in the first few years did not allow for the most efficient development of shafts and drifts for ventilation purposes, and it was some time before connections were established systematically to allow fresh air to flow from one shaft to another. Working underground with such conditions became a real test of stamina. Employers had to work their miners in double shifts, sometimes not longer than fifteen minutes at a time, in order to prevent illness and even death. The miners consumed huge amounts of ice water; Eliot Lord, the mining historian, estimates that ninety-five pounds of ice per man were used in an eight-hour shift in 1878. In some instances the heat became so unbearable that work was halted temporarily while cooler air was introduced from the blower tubes or while air shafts were cut to adjoining tunnels.

A combination of water and heat presented a further problem. The heated water which collected in pools was a constant danger, and a number of lives were lost in the early days when miners fell into these pools or when they inadvertently punctured a hidden reservoir and the heated water literally exploded in their faces. Water alone caused difficulties when flooding began to interfere seriously with mine production. Pumps were introduced during the first few months of operation, and as the problem worsened, huge Cornish pumps were employed with varying success.

Many other mechanical and technical improvements were made as the demands of the Comstock continued. Mine owners were willing to borrow ideas from other areas and to experiment and devise new methods. Thus they hurried to introduce into their mines the compressed-air drill and diamond-studded rotary drill, both invented in France, and dynamite, invented by Alfred Nobel. They were equally eager to adopt the flat, woven-wire hoisting cable invented by A. S. Hallidie of San Francisco specifically to meet the needs of the Comstock mines.[3] The huge expenditures of money for these improvements in some cases were extravagant and wasteful, but they brought results and made the Comstock the showplace of western mining. Moreover, the application of these technological innovations outside the Comstock facilitated the development of less easily exploited mineral areas elsewhere in the state.

MINING DEVELOPMENT OUTSIDE THE COMSTOCK

From 1859 through 1880, the Comstock produced $308,894,721 of a total state production of $447,330,536. Thus, all of Nevada's other mines accounted for a production of $138,435,815 during that period. The production outside the Comstock was widely scattered over the state, and the yield of an individual district was not always consistent with the area's reputation at the time or indicative of its importance to the state. Of the dozens of mineral strikes which resulted directly or indirectly from the great Comstock boom, Austin, Aurora, Belmont, Candelaria, Eureka, Hamilton, Pioche, Tuscarora, and Unionville became fairly significant producers. The importance of each of these districts cannot be measured by mineral production alone, for no one of them was a heavy and steady pro-

---

[3] Hallidie is much more famous for designing San Francisco's cable cars.

ducer for any length of time; yet each in its day was the center of a boom, attracting people in numbers all out of proportion to the value of the minerals hidden in the mountains. Each mining boom set up a chain reaction, for invariably by the time the strike became known to the outside world, the best property was taken and newcomers then overflowed into the surrounding areas. Thus, in opening the state to mineral exploration, these successive mining booms, if nothing else, stimulated agricultural and livestock development and provided the basis for territorial and then state political divisions.

The boom mining camp itself was an ephemeral thing. Born to instant glory, its present was a thousand nights of never ending pleasure, its future hidden in the earth which gave it birth. The story was always one of discovery, boom, and bust—one mining camp differed from another mainly in the rapidity of its passage through the three stages. Some boomed, prospered for a few years, and started to decline, but were saved from oblivion because they were county seats or were located strategically on major transportation routes where they could function as supply centers for surrounding agricultural or mining areas. Others were thriving towns with thousands of people one day and literally none the next, as ore bodies expected "to last forever" suddenly petered out. Often such boom camps were aided in their rush to "ghost" status by a major flood, or more often by a devastating fire.

The immediate problems encountered by the prospectors in these booms were in many ways greater than those on the Comstock. Almost without exception the other mineral areas were poorer than the Comstock, not only in the quality and quantity of the ore, but also in water, timber, and other resources. The ore from many of the districts was much more complex, requiring expensive treatment by smelting. In addition, most of the camps were much more isolated than the Comstock. As the Comstock developed, it served as a supply center for camps as far east as Austin, but it could offer little help to those like Eureka, Hamilton, and Pioche at the other end of the state. Cheap transportation became a necessity for such mining districts, particularly where the ore was complex, as at Eureka. Eureka is a good example, too, of the problem of lack of available wood. The timber resources of the Comstock were munificent indeed in comparison with those of most of the smaller strikes of this era, and a camp such as Eureka had to have an extra supply of wood for the production of the charcoal used in smelting.

The first important mining discovery outside the Comstock was made at Aurora, some ninety miles southeast of Virginia City and only about four miles from the California border, by J. M. Cory, James M. Braly, and E. R. Hicks in the fall of 1860. The first two had reached the Comstock Lode during the main rush in the spring of that year but were prevented from prospecting there by the outbreak of the Paiute War. On August 25 they located four claims in the Wassuck Range which formed the basis of the Esmeralda Mining District, organized on August 30. Although the area was extremely isolated, hundreds of prospectors rushed to the new strike, and within a short time the town of Aurora was laid out, beginning the usual cycle of boom and bust.

Aurora's boom was short but productive. In a period of less than ten years her mines produced $29,366,968 and only two million dollars more during the next eighty years. The boom lasted long enough for the construction of eighteen mills of various sizes, and although always overshadowed by the Comstock, Aurora played an interesting and important role in the territorial and early statehood years of Nevada. The political importance of the new boom area led to the bitter, if at times somewhat funny, jurisdictional dispute between Nevada Territory and California which was finally settled by the Kidder-Ives boundary survey. However, Aurora's decline was so rapid that her position as the seat of Esmeralda County was lost to Hawthorne in 1883.[4]

About the same time that prospectors from the Comstock were finding new mineral areas to the southeast, others were probing the mountains to the east along the old Emigrant Trail. Early in the spring of 1860 two Frenchmen, Louis Barbeau and A. Gintz, who kept a trading post on the Overland route, reported a rich mineral find. The news attracted enough of the overflow from the Comstock to found Humboldt City on the west side of the West Humboldt Range. However, results were not encouraging and prospectors began to move to the east side of the range, led, according to contemporary writers, by Indians who carried rich mineral specimens which they said were found in the canyons on the eastern

[4] Hawthorne, at the southern end of Walker Lake, came into existence in 1881 as a division headquarters of the Carson & Colorado Railway. The town was built strategically where the Bodie wagon-road met the new railroad.

side of the mountains. In any event, on May 12, 1861, Hugo Pfers-
dorff and J. C. Hannan found rich silver ore in a canyon which
they called Buena Vista. A short time later, two other prospectors,
Isaac Miller and Joe Thacker, found excellent ore in Star Canyon,
a few miles to the north. The two discoveries attracted hundreds
of persons to the area and resulted in the establishment of Unionville in Buena Vista Canyon and Star City in Star Canyon.

Unionville, platted as a townsite early in July, soon became the
center of the new mineral district. The town grew rapidly enough
to warrant being named the county seat of Humboldt County when
the territorial legislature divided Nevada Territory into counties in
November, 1861. There is no way of knowing accurately how many
residents were in the community at that time, although the territorial census taken in July, as the boom on the east side of the
West Humboldt Range was just beginning, showed 469 residents
for the entire county. The big boom at Unionville appears to have
occurred between 1863 and 1870, when at one point the town was
reported to have as many as 1,500 persons. The decline began
soon afterwards when it was apparent there was little rich ore in
the district, and was speeded by the completion of the Central
Pacific Railroad through the Humboldt valley and the establishment of Winnemucca as its major trading and shipping center.[5]

The Reese River District, the third mineral area to develop in
Nevada Territory outside the Comstock, was the most remote from
the western settlements, and in certain respects the most important,
The discovery was made by William Talcott on May 2, 1862, in a
canyon about 174 miles east of Virginia City on the old Pony
Express route. A former Pony Express rider, Talcott was employed
at the time of the discovery in hauling wood for the Overland
Stage station at Jacob's Station (Jacob's Well).[6] The actual mineral
find was made in Pony Canyon, a short distance east of the station.
The ore, assayed at Virginia City, proved very rich, and a new boom
was on. The Reese River Mining District was organized on May 10,
1862, with Talcott as its first recorder. Enough people had entered
the area by the fall of that year to bring pressure for the organization of a new county, and the territorial legislature finally acted on
December 19, creating Lander County from the eastern portions of

---

[5] Unionville in 1870 had a population of 470 people.

[6] Due to the Civil War the Overland Stage moved its route to the central
passage across Nevada, a trail blazed by Howard Egan in 1854.

Humboldt and Churchill counties. Jacob's Well, or Jacobsville, was made the first county seat.

Additional mineral finds in Pony Canyon in the winter of 1862 brought a stream of people eastward from the Comstock and resulted in the establishment of three small camps in the canyon— Clifton near the valley floor, and Austin and Houston farther up the canyon. The contest for survival among the small communities was won by Austin when that community was designated the new seat of Lander County on September 21, 1863. The inhabitants of Jacobsville moved most of the town's buildings with them to the new county center. Austin completed its political victory by becoming an incorporated city on February 20, 1864. By that time California newspapers were giving the Reese River area almost as much attention as the Comstock, and when the first minor depression hit the Comstock region, the rush to Austin was stimulated further. Within a short time the town had its share of stone and brick buildings, churches, schools, and saloons. The ore body was sufficient to attract outside capital, and soon dozens of mills were built in an effort to reduce the very heavy costs of production and transportation. From the standpoint of production, however, Austin proved to be one of the most overrated booms in Nevada history, producing only about $20 million from 1862 through 1940.[7] But in spite of its rather weak production record in the 1860s and 1870s, Austin was able to obtain a narrow-gauge railroad, the Nevada Central, which was completed February 9, 1880.

Austin's real claim to fame came not from its production record but from its role as a "mother camp" to many other discoveries in eastern Nevada and from the development of the Reese River process for treating silver ore. Once Austin had established supply routes to the Comstock, it served as the base for prospectors moving out in every direction to open up the surrounding area; and since it was the first and for many years the only supply center in central Nevada, its position in this respect was emphasized. Not only was Austin responsible in this way for the discovery of numerous strikes, but in many instances these new discoveries led to the creation of additional counties in central and eastern Nevada. Thus, when their respective counties were organized, Ione became the county

[7] Production from 1865 through 1940 was $18,494,209. No firm figures can be obtained for Austin's production from its discovery in 1862 to 1865, although it probably was not more than $2,000,000.

seat of Nye County in February, 1864; Hamilton of White Pine County in 1869; and Eureka, of Eureka County in 1873.

The ores found in the Reese River District were more complex than the free-milling ores of the Comstock and needed roasting to eliminate the arsenic and antimony before amalgamation could take place. Various types of reverberatory furnaces were used in treating the Reese River ores during the early years, but they were all costly in time and labor. In 1870 a furnace designed by Carl A. Stetefeldt was put in operation at the Murphy mine in Ophir Canyon near Austin. It proved so successful in reducing costs that within a few years it had replaced other types of roasting furnaces in the district.[8]

The next mining boom in Nevada, in a remote area about 110 miles east of Austin, was probably the shortest, most wasteful, and most intense rush in the history of the American West. It began when a party of prospectors from Austin entered the White Pine Mountains in eastern Nevada and discovered enough low-grade silver ore to warrant the formation of the White Pine Mining District on October 10, 1865. The Monte Cristo Mining Company was organized in 1866 and a small mill constructed the following year. However, no major development of the area took place until the fall of 1867, when a discovery was made on Treasure Hill by A. J. Leathers, the blacksmith of the Monte Cristo company. According to persistent stories, Leathers was led to the ore by an Indian named Napias Jim who thus returned an earlier favor on Leathers's part.

It was impossible to keep the find a secret, and before the snows of winter had closed the area hundreds of claims had been staked. Some of the ore uncovered was rich beyond belief, assaying as much as $27,000 per ton. The real rush to the district began in the spring of 1868, continued throughout 1869, and began to subside by 1870. While it lasted, the district mining recorder had to hire four assistants to help him record thirteen thousand claims in a

---

[8] The Stetefeldt furnace was a shaft roasting furnace in which finely ground silver ore and salt passed down a shaft against a current of hot air. The result was a 90 percent chloridized product ready to be amalgamized. The addition of the Stetefeldt furnace to the earlier processes used in the Reese River district gave the Nevada mineral industry two successful processes for the treatment of silver ores: the Washoe pan process for docile or free-milling ores and the Reese River process with the Stetefeldt furnace for rebellious ores. See Ernest Oberbillig, "Development of Washoe and Reese River Silver Processes," *Nevada Historical Society Quarterly* 10 (Summer 1967): 43.

period of two years. Within a year and a half the population of the district was estimated at thirty thousand people, centering in five towns which sprang into existence literally overnight. The largest, and the center of the new district, was Hamilton, boomed by the newspapers as a city of some twenty thousand. Over a thousand feet higher, near the crest of Treasure Hill, stood Treasure City, the second important town of the district, boasting a population of five thousand persons. The three other communities, ranging in size from a few hundred to a few thousand people, were Shermantown, Eberhardt, and Swansea. Other towns, such as Pocotillo and White Pine City, became ghost towns before they had an opportunity to be real ones.[9]

The White Pine rush led to an orgy of speculation that far exceeded any other in Nevada history. Between February and April of 1869, capitalization of White Pine companies incorporated in California jumped from $62,000,000 to $246,884,000, the latter figure representing some 170 firms. Both sums were far beyond the real wealth of the mines. Actual working capital moved more slowly into the new district, and as early as 1870, California capitalists were becoming disillusioned about the quality of the ore body. However, British capitalists moved in to take their place. The entrance of British capital into Nevada mining was part of a major flow of investments from Great Britain to the United States in the post–Civil War era. The British had not participated to any real extent in the capitalization of the Comstock mines, and perhaps their failure to take advantage of the Comstock wealth made them a little too eager to invest in Nevada mining ventures outside the Comstock. In any event, it was British capital which kept the White Pine District alive into the early 1890s, long after it was apparent that the rich ore was not to be found at depth.

If the boom had not collapsed so suddenly, a railroad probably would have been built. As it was, Hamilton became the center of a very extensive stage and express system. The best production year was 1870 when $2,137,801 was recorded; by 1876 production was down to $38,268. The total production of the district from 1866 through 1940 was only $10,675,388. People left the White Pine District almost as rapidly as they had entered. Estimates of population during the boom period of 1868 and 1869 were obviously

[9] These were examples of the "paper town"—speculative ventures that were platted but never built.

optimistic. The census of 1870, the first official check during the boom, showed only 7,189 people in the county, with 3,913 at Hamilton, 1,920 at Treasure City, and 932 at Shermantown. By 1880 the county's population had dropped to 2,682 with just 203 in the once prosperous town of Hamilton and only 44 left in Treasure City. Hamilton lost its last chance for survival when the county seat was moved to Ely in 1887 after a disastrous fire destroyed the county courthouse.

Perhaps the final word about the White Pine rush should come from the great naturalist John Muir, who visited the area and described the great waste: "Many of [the mines] do not represent any good accomplishment and have no right to be. They are monuments of fraud and ignorance—sins against science. The drifts and tunnels in the rocks may be regarded as the prayers of the prospectors offered for the wealth he so earnestly craves; but like prayers of any kind not in harmony with nature, they are unanswered."[10]

Two other districts, Eureka and Pioche, were organized prior to the White Pine district, but neither boomed until 1869. The first of these, about seventy miles east of Austin, was located by a group of prospectors from that camp, W. O. Arnold, W. R. Tannehill, G. T. Tannehill, J. W. Stotts, and Moses Wilson, on September 19, 1864. The discovery met with only mild excitement because of the early acknowledgement of the complexity of the ores due to heavy intrusions of lead. This was the first major strike of silver-lead in the United States, and it was soon evident that the locators had uncovered a mineral deposit which was beyond their limited knowledge and capital means to develop. Not until Major W. W. McCoy, who had acquired one of the important mineral claims in the district, employed two experienced Welsh smeltermen, R. P. Jones and John Williams, was any real progress made. The two men modified Stetefeldt's furnace so that by July of 1869 the successful smelting of Eureka ores was possible. Additional small furnaces were soon constructed copying the adaptations made by Jones and Williams, and with about the same results, which were not exceptional but sufficient to attract outside capital in the form of two well-financed and well-organized companies.

[10] John Muir, *Steep Trails*, ed. William F. Bade (Boston: Houghton Mifflin, 1918), p. 203.

The Eureka Consolidated Mining Company, incorporated by San Francisco capitalists, took over one important group of claims, while the Richmond Consolidated Mining Company with London capitalists in charge took over another in 1871, setting the stage for important new developments. It was quite clear to the owners that more efficient smelting procedures had to be developed if the district was to be exploited properly. Consequently, the Eureka Consolidated Company hired W. S. Keyes, known for his competence in engineering and metallurgy, as general manager. Aided by Albert Arents, an experienced metallurgist, he introduced major improvements in the smelting of silver-lead ores that ensured a bright future for Eureka.

The production of the Eureka mines, which had been only $5,932 in 1869, jumped to slightly over $2 million in 1872 and continued near or above that mark for each of the years through 1885. Although experts disagree on the total production, it is apparent that Eureka was by far the most productive mineral district outside the Comstock area in the years from 1859 through 1881.[11] The mineral activity attracted a sizable population, making Eureka the most important city in central Nevada, and on March 1, 1873, the state legislature split up Lander County to establish Eureka County, with Eureka as the county seat. The usual exaggerations jumped the population estimates to anywhere from ten to twenty-five thousand people, yet the stability of the town was indicated when the 1880 census showed an official tabulation of 4,207 people. The district was prosperous enough to win a narrow-gauge railroad, completed from Eureka to Palisade on the Central Pacific in 1875.

As a town and as a mining district, Eureka has clung tenaciously to life. Although her mines still hold within them valuable ore deposits, excessive water in the tunnels presents a problem which has not been solved. From time to time technical improvements in mining and reduction have made possible short bursts of activity, as in the decade from 1900 to 1910, when a production of $838,423

[11] The U.S. Geological Survey estimated a production of $60,000,000 in the years through 1881. However, Couch and Carpenter list Eureka with $52,288,024 from 1866 through 1940. See Bertrand Couch and Jay Carpenter, *Nevada's Metal and Mineral Production (1859–1940, Inclusive)*, University of Nevada Geology and Mining Series, no. 38, (November 1, 1943), pp. 59–60; Rodman Paul, *Mining Frontiers of the Far West, 1848–1880* (New York: Holt, Rinehart & Winston, 1963), p. 104.

was listed for the year 1909; again in the 1920s, when production reached a peak of $962,403 for 1926; and in the years before and during World War II, when the town and district were moderately prosperous. However, in spite of the repeated but short revivals, the latest as recent as the late 1950s, it appears that Eureka's future as a town will depend mainly on its being a county seat on a main interstate highway, and on whether it will continue to act as a supply center for livestock and mining interests in the surrounding areas.

Pioche, the next mining district to boom, was located in western Utah Territory at the time of its organization. Named after F. L. A. Pioche, the San Francisco financier who helped to develop its resources, the town and district came into existence as the result of an ore discovery by William Hamblin, a Mormon missionary who had been living in southern Utah Territory. The most persistent story is that an Indian showed Hamblin samples of silver-bearing rocks which he said came from the mountains to the west. In the spring of 1864, Hamblin led a number of prospectors into the region described by the Indian and on March 15 or 16 located a number of claims at the present site of Pioche. Enough miners were present to organize the Meadow Valley Mining District on March 18.

In May, 1864, Francis Lee, a Mormon missionary acting under orders from Brigham Young, established a colony a few miles to the south of the mining district at the present site of Panaca. Their arrival marked a renewal of the missionary activity which had been interrupted by the outbreak of the Mormon War in 1857, and again Mormon colonization in an area where mineral discoveries were soon to become important precipitated Mormon-Gentile conflict not unlike that which had occurred earlier in Carson County, Utah Territory.

The situation moved toward a climax as Mormons from Panaca organized another church ward in 1865 at Eagle Valley, a few miles to the northeast and Brigham Young sent additional missionary and trading parties into western Utah Territory and northwestern Arizona Territory. The first of these, under the leadership of Anson Call, established Callville on the Colorado River in December, 1864, as a potential warehouse and shipping center to facilitate the movement of goods along the Mormon Trail between Salt Lake

City and Los Angeles. When Arizona formed Pah-Ute County in 1865, Callville became the county seat. Other missions were established along the Muddy River at Saint Thomas, Saint Joseph, Moapa, West Point, and Overton.

In the meantime, the first Nevada legislature passed and sent to Congress, on December 27, 1864, a joint resolution asking that an additional degree of territory be added to Nevada on its eastern border. While this request was being debated in Congress, a number of important mineral strikes were made in March, 1865, in the Pahranagat Valley approximately sixty miles southwest of Pioche, by T. X. W. Sayles, John H. Ely, David Sanderson, Samuel S. Strutt, William McCluskey, and Ira Hatch. Within a short time the town of Hiko came into existence, and the ensuing rush to the district emphasized its extreme isolation. As the demand for county organization grew, the Nevada legislature passed an act which was signed by Governor H. G. Blasdel on February 26, 1866, authorizing the creation of a county whenever three hundred persons signed a petition requesting such a government. Evidently motivated in part at least by an interest in the new mineral districts, the governor personally took charge of the movement to obtain the necessary signatures. In attempting to reach the Pahranagat mines from the west, he was forced to lead his party over some of the most desolate and barren country in Nevada. Before the journey was completed one man died of starvation and the entire party narrowly escaped a similar fate. The trip proved to be doubly disappointing, because there were not enough people to warrant the establishment of a county, and because of the poor mineral showings.

At this point, Nevada's request for a boundary extension to the east and the matter of the Pahranagat mines became inseparably mixed. A bill to annex the additional territory to Nevada passed the Senate in 1865 but failed in the House of Representatives. However, the following year, on May 5, in spite of intense opposition from representatives of Utah and Arizona territories, Congress granted Nevada an additional degree of territory to the east and the triangle below the 37th parallel in the south, the latter subject to the approval of the Nevada legislature, and on January 18, 1867, the state legislature accepted the grant. During the debate in Congress, the principal argument used to back Nevada's request was that the desired territory was valuable for its mining, and since Nevada was a mining state, the interests of the two sections were identical. Proponents of the measure conveniently ignored the fact that the Pahranagat mines already were inside Nevada.

The congressional action ensured support for another attempt to organize a county in eastern Nevada, and in its 1867 session the state legislature created Lincoln County with Hiko as the county seat. The new county included within its boundaries not only the mineral districts of the Pioche and Pahranagat areas but also the Mormon communities at Panaca and Eagle Valley and in the triangle along the Colorado, Virgin, and Muddy rivers. However, when Lincoln County authorities attempted to collect taxes from the Mormon settlements, they found the settlers paying their taxes to either the Utah or the Arizona territorial government. The situation was not clarified until Congress appropriated $17,000 for an official survey of the Nevada-Utah boundary. The survey, which was completed in the winter of 1870–71, showed definitely that the communities were in Nevada. Most of the inhabitants of the Muddy River settlements returned to Utah; those Mormons who remained in Lincoln County, mainly at Panaca and benefiting from the Pioche mines, then acknowledged Nevada's political sovereignty, ending another conflict between Mormons and Gentiles.

The original ore discoveries at Pioche, although fairly rich, did not bring an immediate rush to the district. One reason for this was the belief that smelting was necessary to reduce the ores properly. However, when smelters were built in 1868 and 1869 they failed to produce satisfactory results. It was not until mills employing the basic Washoe pan process were constructed in 1870 that Pioche began to boom. In that year two different companies concluded that chemical processing of the ore was the answer to the dilemma. The Meadow Valley Company, formed by a group of San Francisco capitalists including F. L. A. Pioche, put a mill into operation in Dry Valley, about six miles southeast of the mines, in July. The other company, the Raymond and Ely, organized by William Raymond and John Ely, who had been prominent among the early miners in the Pahranagat area, also began milling operations in 1870 with a five-stamp mill which they moved from their Pahranagat property. The success of the two mills inaugurated the Pioche boom. The production of the district, which had been

$2,821 in 1869, increased to $1,629,339 in 1870 and reached a peak of $5,462,572 in 1872.

Pioche production began to move upward just as the rush to Hamilton, some one hundred miles to the northeast, was subsiding. By July of 1870, Pioche had a population of 1,141 persons, mostly men and nearly half of them foreign-born. The camp soon came to be known as one of the rowdiest and most lawless in Nevada. It was also one of the most isolated, which might help account for its reputation. The closest railroad connection was Toano, nearly 260 miles away, on the Central Pacific. Hamilton was the nearest Nevada town of any size. The seat of state government at Carson City was about 430 miles away, accessible only by an indirect route which necessitated going first to Hamilton, or in later years to Ely, and then across the entire state. Pioche did not receive a direct railroad connection until 1907, when a branch line from Pioche to Caliente connected with the Union Pacific, which had been built into Nevada in 1905.

Pioche's production was substantial in the period from 1870 through 1875, showing a total of $16,998,732 for that six-year period. However, it declined rapidly and fell by 1880 to $7,654 and by 1884 to only $4,073. Like Eureka, Pioche had many ups and downs. Substantial booms during World Wars I and II and again during the Korean conflict pushed the total production of the camp well above $100 million.

THE CENTRAL PACIFIC RAILROAD

Although later Nevadans were to criticize the railroad for using their state as a bridge between Salt Lake City and San Francisco, the building of the Central Pacific through Nevada in the 1860s and its continued operation in the following decades was of primary importance to the economic development of the state. It provided a promise of markets for ore and agricultural goods produced in Nevada and at the same time distributed supplies from a wide variety of sources to aid the booming communities. In addition it founded or was the cause for the founding of a number of railroad communities from the western border of the state to the Utah line, communities that often boomed as riotously as the mining towns but generally lasted longer. In a number of instances these railroad towns, like their mining counterparts, brought pressure to bear to become county seats if a county government was already organized, or demanded a new county government if that was the only way to obtain the coveted county seat status. Thus Reno, at the western end of the state, literally took the county seat from Washoe City after a rather bitter fight; Winnemucca took county seat status away from Unionville, while Elko in the northeastern part of the state was instrumental in the establishment of Elko County from Lander County in 1869. During the halcyon days of construction of the Central Pacific and immediately thereafter the railroad builders were considered great benefactors, but a few years later vast disillusionment set in as the public became convinced that the railroad was discriminating against Nevada interests. Yet through prosperity and depression the railroad was one of the few stable economic forces in the state; and although it may not have paid what it should in taxes, the revenue obtained from it helped to keep county governments alive and its operation sustained a number of communities.

The idea of a transcontinental railroad dates to many years before the Civil War and no doubt the building of one would have started sooner had sectional controversy not thwarted such efforts. Five different routes were surveyed under the War Department in 1853–54 and the results, published in 1855, showed the feasibility of four, two northern and two southern. A decision on a single route was made possible by the secession of the Southern states in 1861, but it was not until the next year that a group of California promoters, led by Theodore D. Judah, obtained congressional authorization to build their Central Pacific Railroad from San Francisco to the state border, where it would connect with the Union Pacific, building west from the Missouri River. Both roads were granted federal help in the form of right-of-ways, liberal land donations, and substantial government loans.

While Nevada was still a territory, railroad interests made their first attempt to gain economic advantages from the area through which a proposed railroad might be built. The unsuccessful Nevada constitution of 1863 included a provision which allowed the legislature to give $3 million in bonds to the first company to connect Nevada by rail with navigable waters. When the second constitutional convention met in July of 1864, railroad interests were again in evidence. During the numerous debates over the question of a

railroad subsidy various proposals were submitted which in one
way or another would allow Nevada to aid the building of a railroad through the state. The president of the Central Pacific,
Leland Stanford, appeared before the convention on July 13 to
present his views. He made it quite clear that he favored a railroad
subsidy, but only one which would specifically name the Central
Pacific; any provision like that in the earlier constitution obviously
would encourage competitors. Supporters of Stanford and the Central Pacific were able to prevent the granting of bonds to the first
railroad into Nevada but were unable to get a specific subsidy for
the Central Pacific. The final version of the constitution simply
provided that "the State shall not donate or loan money or its
credit, subscribe to or be interested in the stock of any company,
association, or corporation, except corporations formed for educational or charitable purposes."

A large loan from the state of California enabled the Central
Pacific to start building in 1863, many months ahead of the Union
Pacific. However, progress was very slow because of the difficult
terrain and the instability of the labor force. The latter problem
was solved by the hiring of thousands of Chinese; the former was
not overcome until the railroad crossed the California-Nevada
boundary on December 13, 1867. By that time the Central Pacific
officials had, with the aid of a number of friendly legislators, obtained congressional authorization to build the Central Pacific
tracks across Nevada "until they shall meet and connect with the
Union Pacific Railroad." This act stimulated a race so competitive
that the two railroads, obsessed with gaining additional government
land and money, began to survey past each other and were brought
back to reality only when Washington officials reminded them that
the 1862 act had envisioned a single transcontinental line, and decreed that the roads were to join at Promontory, Utah.

Before the Central Pacific reached that rendezvous it passed over
hundreds of miles of Nevada and brought into being a number of
communities. The first of these rose as the track crews reached the
Truckee Meadows. This area was well known to emigrants for its
water, game, and grass, features which had attracted permanent
settlers in the 1850s. One of them, C. W. Fuller, built a rude bridge
across the river and a half-dugout, half-log shelter on the south side;
the site soon became known as Fuller's Crossing. The property was

sold in 1861 to Myron C. Lake, who improved the bridge and established a hotel and trading post. By the time the Central Pacific was ready to cross into Nevada, Lake had a strong claim to a large section of land directly in the path of the oncoming railroad. He soon struck a bargain with Charles Crocker, superintendent of construction for the Central Pacific, whereby Lake donated land north of the river to the Central Pacific for a townsite and Crocker agreed to build a station there. On May 9, 1868, an agent of the railroad conducted a well-attended auction of lots on the former Lake property, marking the birth of a community which Crocker named Reno in honor of General Jesse L. Reno, a Union officer killed at the battle of South Mountain, Maryland, in 1862. The wisdom of selecting Reno as a station site was evident as soon as regular railroad traffic from Sacramento made the new town a major supply center for the Comstock, a position which was made more secure when the Virginia and Truckee Railroad was extended to Reno in 1872.

The railroad builders pushed rapidly on east to build a division point on the Truckee River at a place formerly known as Lower Emigrant Crossing and now named Wadsworth after General James S. Wadsworth, another Civil War general.[12] It took the Central Pacific builders five and one-half years to reach Wadsworth; it took just nine months and twenty days more to lay over five hundred miles of track to Promontory, Utah. Additional railroad towns sprang into existence as the builders extended the iron rails across Nevada. Some ninety miles from Reno, in an area referred to as the Big Meadows by the emigrants, a small station was built at George Lovelock's trading post. A more substantial station point came into being at the site where early traders had maintained a post at first called French Ford and then French Bridge, and by the time the first train entered on September 16, 1868, a small town, named Winnemucca after the Paiute chief, was already in existence.

Charles Crocker's desire to call one of the stations Argenta was finally gratified when that name was given to the station about

---

[12]By the middle of July, 1868, trains were running daily except Sunday from Sacramento to Wadsworth. The latter camp was replaced as a division center in 1903 when the Southern Pacific officials began moving shops and facilities to a point a few miles east of Reno which was named Sparks after the governor of Nevada at the time.

sixty miles east of Winnemucca. However, the town was soon over-shadowed by Battle Mountain, a lustier neighbor a few miles to the west, which was located more advantageously to gain the trade of the mining districts in the Battle Mountain Range. More successful sites were chosen by the builders at Carlin and Elko. Surveyors were in both locations laying out lots in December, 1868. The former town was named after General William P. Carlin, a Union officer during the Civil War who had seen some service at Camp Floyd, Utah Territory, in the late 1850s. Carlin was assured of some permanence when railroad officials designated it as the eastern terminus of the Humboldt division, and it gained further stability from its location as a supply center for the mining camps of Austin, Eureka, and Hamilton. Twenty-five miles to the east Carlin surveyors started laying out lots for the future town of Elko on December 29, 1868, although the railroad did not offer them for sale until January 15, 1869. The name of the new town brought another interruption in the procession of railroad towns named after Civil War veterans. At this late date no theory about the origin of the name Elko appears very satisfactory, but the most likely story is that Charles Crocker named it after the elk and simply added the *o* for a more pleasant sound.[13] Mineral discoveries and livestock developments soon made Elko the center of a thriving trade activity.

The last railroad division point in Nevada was Toano, which the railroad builders reached in the middle of March, 1869. Like Carlin and Elko, the new town found immediate prosperity in a freight tieup to the north with Boise and southwestern Idaho and to the south with Pioche, Hamilton, and other eastern Nevada towns. In 1904 Toano was eliminated as a railroad division point, and in 1906 the completion of the Nevada Northern Railroad from Ely to Cobre, a new station on the Southern Pacific, removed its potential as a supply center for the White Pine towns. Toano declined rapidly thereafter and soon took its place among the many other ghost towns of Nevada.

With its completion the Central Pacific became a vast magnet

[13] The naming of Elko and dozens of other details concerning Elko County and the development of agriculture in the northeastern part of Nevada can be found in a work by Edna B. Patterson, Louise A. Ulph, and Victor Goodwin, *Nevada's Northeast Frontier* (Sparks, Nevada: Western Printing & Publishing Co., 1969).

attracting farmer, miner, and merchant. Like a large river gathering the waters of its tributaries, it became the focal point for every mining boom and for the many agricultural developments in the nearby valleys, for it was readily apparent that linkage to the transcontinental railroad might well mean the difference between success and failure, stability and decay.

AGRICULTURAL AND LIVESTOCK DEVELOPMENT DURING THE COMSTOCK ERA

The mineral strikes in Nevada after 1859 and the building of the Central Pacific across the state had the important effect of stimulating agricultural and livestock development. The successive mining booms advertised Nevada and brought to many different parts of the state thousands of persons, most of whom would not have come to this semidesert land in the first place and would not have undergone the hardships they did without the promise of gold and silver to lure them on. Yet, whatever their reasons for entering the state, once within its boundaries they had to be fed; and in a number of instances this necessity led to agricultural, and particularly livestock, development in the lands adjacent to the mining areas. This is not to imply that mining always preceded agricultural development, for agriculture developed originally in Nevada as part of the emigrant movement to California and existed independently of mining in a few isolated instances.

The white man began farming in the land that is now Nevada when John Reese and his party from Salt Lake City arrived in the Carson Valley in June of 1851 and planted wheat, barley, corn, turnips, and watermelons, which they later sold to emigrants on the way to California. Reese's success brought additional ranches and trading posts into Carson Valley, and before the end of the year over one hundred persons were living in the vicinity of Reese's settlement, by that time more commonly referred to as Mormon Station. In December, 1851, a party of settlers moved into the next valley to the north and established Eagle Ranch. Farming in the Carson and Eagle valleys paralleled the increased mining activity in nearby Gold Canyon during the early 1850s. However, it was only after the arrival of Orson Hyde's party in the summer of 1855 and the subsequent movement of large numbers of Mormons into the area in the next two years that the first real farming development took place. Under Hyde's leadership the Mormons established additional farms in Carson, Eagle, and Washoe valleys, built irrigation canals and flour mills, and were well on the way to developing a stable agricultural society when the official call for their return to Salt Lake came from Brigham Young in 1857. Although the withdrawal of the Mormons caused a temporary setback in agricultural development in Carson County, by 1859 most of the Mormon farms were again in production, having been either purchased from the retreating Mormons or appropriated after their departure.

The year 1851 also marked the beginning of a permanent livestock development in Nevada. The first livestock brought into the present state by white men came with the fur trappers. Smith and Ogden brought horses and mules in 1826–28, and cattle entered for the first time when Joseph Walker took forty-seven head from California on his return trip to the Great Salt Lake in 1834. However, the first cattle to winter in what is now Nevada were those belonging to John Reese and a few dairy cattle brought into Carson Valley in the same year by Captain H. A. Parker, a wagonmaster for Ben Holladay. Like farming in Carson County, the livestock industry got its first real impetus when the official missionary groups were sent from Salt Lake in the period from 1855 to 1857. Almost every Mormon family brought three or four head of cattle and some drove as many as forty head. The Mormons were also responsible for the introduction of cattle into present southern Nevada when the Mormon party led by William Bringhurst established the Las Vegas Mission in 1855. Thus, although the Mormon dominance in both areas was short-lived, it was important to the farming and livestock developments in those regions.

In 1858 another phase of the state's cattle industry opened when California cattlemen began to drive their herds into Nevada to winter in the Carson and Eagle valleys and in the Truckee Meadows. This practice increased until in the 1870s and 1880s the presence of foreign cattle on Nevada rangeland became a major threat to local interests.

On the eve of the discovery of the Comstock Lode, the foundations of three important ranching developments were laid. One was initiated by N. H. A. ("Hock") Mason, who had first entered Nevada in 1854 on the way to California. He returned in 1859 with a herd of cattle and wintered them in a valley of the Walker River which has since been known as Mason Valley. His success led him to establish a permanent herd of cattle in the valley, and from this beginning he became one of the most important livestock men in Nevada during the Comstock era. In August of 1859 four cattlemen from Stanislaus County, California—R. B. Smith, T. B. Smith, S. Baldwin, and J. A. Rogers—crossed the Sierra with a herd and located on the West Walker River, just west of Mason Valley in an area which was soon designated Smith Valley. A third ranching development initiated in the 1850s was that of Henry Fred Dangberg, who settled in the Carson Valley in 1855 and within a few years had established the foundations of one of the most important ranching empires in western Nevada.

Probably the first sheep to enter Nevada were the 150 head taken across the southern tip of the present state in 1841 by John Workman and William Rowland's emigrant party. Although other bands may have entered with emigrant parties during the 1840s the next clear evidence of sheep in the state indicates those brought into southern Nevada by Captain Lorenzo Sitgreaves in 1851 as part of his food supply while his crew surveyed the 35th parallel. The first permanent band of sheep in Nevada was the few hundred Spanish Merinos brought into the Carson Valley in 1852 by C. D. Jones, who evidently continued to raise sheep there during the 1850s but did not prosper because of the lack of a market.

The future state played a role in the development of the sheep industry in the western United States in the 1850s, but it was a passive role as a bridge to California. The gold rush had by 1852 created a demand for foodstuffs, particularly meat, which could not be met by local producers. Since sheep could be purchased in New Mexico for less than $1 per head and sold in Sacramento for $5 to $12 per head, a number of large sheep drives were made from New Mexico to California via the Humboldt River route. The first of these was led by Richens Lacy ("Uncle Dick") Wootton in 1852. Wootton purchased some 9,000 sheep at Taos, New Mexico, hired fourteen New Mexican sheepherders and seven former soldiers to act as guards and brought along eight trail-trained goats to lead the sheep, as well as a number of sheep dogs. The drive was very successful. Wootton arrived in Sacramento with 8,900 sheep, which he sold for a profit of over $50,000. The next year Kit Carson, the famous Frémont scout, and his partner, Lucien B. Maxwell, purchased about 13,000 sheep near Santa Fe, trailed them through Nevada to Sacramento, and sold them for a handsome profit. The success of these early drives encouraged many others; it is estimated that between 1852 and 1860 over half a million sheep crossed Nevada on the way to the California market.

The 1850s brought little in the way of a permanent agricultural or livestock development. Agricultural statistics for 1860 place the total farm value at that time at $302,340, representing only a few farms and just 14,132 acres of improved land. The agricultural products sold that year brought in only $2,225, while the value of all livestock amounted to $177,638 and of all animals slaughtered, $9,385.

The discovery of the Comstock Lode in the summer of 1859 ushered in a new stage in the development of Nevada agriculture, as the same economic factors which had created a market in California for cattle and sheep in the 1850s now worked to bring thousands of these animals from California to the Comstock and stimulated the development of permanent farms and ranches throughout western Nevada. The thousands of people who poured into the Comstock area during the early 1860s needed food of all kinds, and farmers and ranchers in Carson, Eagle, Washoe, Mason, and Smith valleys put additional acreage into production to meet the demands for potatoes, flour, butter, cheese, and milk, as well as for livestock feed. As the Comstock towns moved from rough frontier communities to cosmopolitan cities the demand for fresh vegetables and fruits induced Nevada farmers to raise strawberries, raspberries, and gooseberries and to plant apple and peach orchards.

Livestock developments such as those initiated in Carson Valley by Fred Dangberg and in Mason and Smith valleys by Hock Mason and the Smith brothers prospered as a result of the Comstock boom. Ranching spread into other valleys of the state during this period, partly because of the Comstock demand, but more often as a result of mineral discoveries made in nearby areas. The booms at Aurora, Austin, Unionville, Eureka, Pioche, Hamilton, and elsewhere, like the Comstock boom, created demands for agricultural products. Thus the Mason and Smith valley ranching developments were aided further by the mining boom at Aurora. The Austin boom stimulated settlements in Reese River and Smoky valleys in the early 1860s. The mineral discoveries at Unionville and Star City in Humboldt County led directly to the settlement of Paradise Valley by W. C. Gregg in 1864 and the establishment of Paradise City in 1866 by the C. A. Nichols family. The Humboldt County strikes also prompted one of the strangest schemes in Nevada history when J. Ginacca in 1862 organized the Humboldt Canal Company to construct an irrigation canal on the Humboldt River. The canal, which was to run from present Golconda to Mill City, the proposed milling and reduction center for all the mines in the district, would also furnish motive power for the mills.

In much the same manner, the agricultural developments in Nye County, particularly the settlement of Monitor Valley by Jacob and Samuel Steinenger in 1866, followed the discovery of minerals at Ione in 1863 and Belmont in 1865. Mining in the county or in neighboring areas appears to have been responsible for many agricultural developments in White Pine County. Newark Valley was settled in 1866 by E. Orser and James and Samuel Gilson, partly as a result of the mining activities at Eureka and Hamilton. Steptoe Valley, farther to the east, was settled in 1868 as a result of the mineral strikes in the Robinson District.

It is quite apparent that ranching increased during the 1860s largely because of the expanded market provided in the population jump from 6,857 in 1860 to 42,491 in 1870, and that this population growth was due mainly to the Comstock and other mining rushes during that period. It would be incorrect, however, to infer that mining was the only factor involved. The missionary activity of the Mormons in the 1850s in Carson County and the Las Vegas area, and again in the 1860s in the Lincoln County area, was important in establishing agriculture and livestock raising in those regions. In addition, the cattle and sheep drives across Nevada in the 1850s and the use of certain areas in the state by California and Utah stockmen as temporary feeding areas for their cattle demonstrated the excellent grazing potential of this seeming desert land.

It would appear, too, that many of the first livestock developments in Elko County had origins outside of mining. For example, Peter Haws established one of the first ranches along the Humboldt River in the early 1850s in order to take advantage of emigrant trains passing through the area. (The Haws family gained notoriety for allegedly inciting Indian raids on emigrant trains and then gathering the cattle which had been driven off by the Indians.) More important, the land itself attracted a number of ranchers who settled in present Elko County during the 1860s and 1870s: George and Edward Seitz in Pleasant Valley in the early 1860s; Captain G. A. Thurstin, Lieutenant Toles, and Dr. John W. Long in Clover Valley in 1865; John P. Walker and Thomas H. Watterman in Lamoille Valley in 1865; W. M. Kennedy in Mound Valley in 1866, followed shortly by L. R. Bradley and his son, John R. Bradley; and Pedro Altube of the Spanish Ranch in Independence Valley in 1871.

Ruby Valley, Elko County, is a good example of agricultural development due, in the beginning at least, to the freighting and stage business. Throughout the late 1850s the valley had been used extensively as a holding area for cattle destined for California, Utah, or mining areas in Nevada, and an early but very minor beginning was made in 1859 when William ("Uncle Billy") Rogers, commissioned by the Bureau of Indian Affairs to select a reservation site for the Shoshone Indians, chose Ruby Valley. Although the selection was vetoed by the government, Rogers planted grain and vegetables in a successful attempt to prove the productivity of the region. The Overland Mail Company made the first permanent development in the Ruby Valley when it established a large farm a few miles north of Rogers's in 1863 to escape the exorbitant feed prices demanded by the Mormons in Utah. The operation was so successful that by the second year it was supplying nearly all the needs of the thousands of horses and mules and hundreds of drivers. When the completion of the Central Pacific in 1869 brought the Overland Mail to an end, the farm was broken into smaller holdings which continued operations. Another agricultural development in Ruby Valley, initiated about the same time as the Overland farm but of more lasting importance, was the large ranch of Colonel Jeremiah B. Moore, who had become impressed with the agricultural potential of the region during his tenure as commander of Camp Ruby in 1863–64.

The 1860s saw the beginning of four other important cattle and sheep empires. In 1862, Lewis Rice Bradley, destined to become the state's second governor, drove a herd of longhorns into Nevada to help supply the Comstock's demand for beef. After locating for a short time in Mason Valley and then moving to Lander County, in 1866 he shifted operations into Mound Valley in Elko County, where he established a large ranch in the vicinity of Deeth. John Sparks, a Texan, moved into Elko County in 1868 and with Jasper Harrell founded a major cattle empire that included a number of ranches in Oregon and Utah. One of the first cattlemen to switch to sheep, Daniel C. Wheeler brought sheep into the Truckee Meadows from Oregon in 1867 and established the most extensive permanent sheep development in Nevada in that decade. An important eastern Nevada sheep ranch began operations in 1865 when William McCurdy, a Civil War veteran, bought out Bob Chin's band in Antelope Valley. In partnership with a man named Chapman, McCurdy built up a sizable outfit of several thousand head which used the Antelope Range and Antelope Valley for summer and winter range.

The continuing boom on the Comstock and the discovery and development of additional mineral areas throughout the state, the increase in Nevada's population from 42,491 in 1870 to 62,266 in 1880, and the completion of the Central Pacific in 1869 made the decade of the seventies a period of remarkable growth for the livestock industry in Nevada even though it was overshadowed by the tremendous mineral production of those years. Between 1870 and 1880 the number of cattle in the state increased from 72,000 to 250,000 head, of sheep from 33,000 to 259,000, of horses from 8,000 to 34,000, and of hogs from 4,000 to 12,000.

Since the railroad roughly paralleled the Humboldt, it encouraged the development along that river and its tributaries of ranches which produced hay and commanded neighboring valleys for summer range. In addition, the railroad made outside markets for Nevada livestock profitable. By the middle of the 1870s, for example, San Francisco was obtaining half of its beef supply from Nevada, and both sheep and cattle were being shipped to eastern markets. Those ranches, many established in 1868 and 1869, which were within driving distance of the railroad, expanded rapidly; and others initiated in the 1850s and 1860s blossomed into major operations. This was particularly true for Fred Dangberg in Carson Valley; Hock Mason, who in 1871 enlarged his holdings to include range along the Quinn River in Humboldt County; and John Sparks in Elko County. The seventies also saw the establishment

of ranches by Abner C. Cleveland in Spring Valley, White Pine
County, and by Jewett Adams in the Belmont area of Nye County.
Both of these men later became major livestock producers. Thus
by 1880, just as the Comstock depression set in, Nevada's agricultural and livestock developments were expanding, but they were
not able to maintain the Nevada economy at the level reached
during the 1870s.

CHAPTER 7

The Comstock

THE COMSTOCK went through various economic phases, from initial conditions of chaos when thousands staked out claims and disposed of them without much rhyme or reason, to rather sophisticated monopolies of financial and industrial wealth which were brothers in spirit to the huge combinations then developing in the industrial east.

The early confusion in ownership was due in large part to the idea of indiscriminate location and the lack of specific legal regulations governing mining titles. Some sixteen thousand claims were recorded in the various mining districts on the lode, most under district rules that permitted a miner to locate a vein for two hundred feet and to follow it into the earth "with all of its dips, spurs, and angles." The locator was allowed the full width of the vein, which on the Comstock might be as much as one thousand feet. A claim located by a group was divided equally, with the discoverer receiving an additional two hundred feet. These rules and others prescribing the conditions under which claims could be worked and transferred were based on local usage in the California mining districts; accepted by the California legislature and courts, they became a sort of common law throughout the western mining areas. The adoption of the National Mining Law in 1866, mainly the work of Nevada's Senator William M. Stewart, not only gave sanction to the miners' trespassing on the public domain, but made the local customs binding. Unfortunately, those rules were generally badly phrased, loosely interpreted, and poorly enforced. Added to the careless manner in which the records were often kept and innumerable instances of claim jumping, these abuses resulted in an orgy of litigation which persisted throughout most of the history of the lode and brought power and wealth to many of the important attorneys like Stewart.

The question of the legal ownership of the original claims took on new importance as a dispute arose early over whether the Comstock was a series of parallel quartz veins separated by belts of porphyry and sheets of clay, or a single, well-defined ledge. Separate, often conflicting claims had been made for the several veins which appeared on the surface of the Comstock. If these veins came together in one lode, the original locations, particularly the Ophir claims, would be of major significance. Consequently, the court fight between the advocates of the single-ledge theory and the many-ledge theory soon became a bitter and ruthless battle. Stewart had won a number of legal battles advocating the single-ledge theory. However, John North's appointment to the territorial judiciary in the fall of 1863 disrupted Stewart's victories as the new justice began ruling in favor of the multiple-ledge theory. North, unsure of his interpretation, appointed a respected attorney, John Nugent, to referee the suit of the Gould and Curry against the North Potosi. His report in August, 1864, favored the single-ledge theory making "Stewart and Company" the ultimate victors. It has been estimated that litigation on the Comstock during the first five years cost between nine and ten million dollars and involved well over two hundred cases, most of which were unimportant but costly.

DOMINATION BY THE "BANK CROWD"

In spite of the problems which arose from indiscriminate location and loosely defined mining regulations, a primitive form of corporate ownership had emerged by 1864 which had succeeded in achieving a certain fundamental exploitation of the lode. Under the guidance of the numerous companies formed during this period, dozens of mills were built and basic problems of extraction and reduction were solved. The structure of the Comstock Lode was much more complex than at first suspected, and without adequate guides the miners simply struck out in every direction hoping for a bonanza. The fact that only sixteen important ore bodies were found in a lode that ran for nearly three miles along the base of the Virginia Range is indicative of the problems faced. The early bonanzas—the Ophir, the Gould and Curry, the Savage, the Chollar-Potosi, the Yellow Jacket, and the original Gold Hill mines—which had been opened between 1859 and 1863, seemed to have been depleted by the end of 1864, and the Comstock entered its first depression period. It was this period of depression which made possible the transition from independent ownership to a monopolistic control by the Bank of California.

The Bank of California was founded in June, 1864, by William C. Ralston, with a capital of $2 million and strong backing from a group of financiers including D. O. Mills, who became its first president. Ralston, whose contact with the Comstock Lode dated back to 1860, immediately established a branch of his bank at Virginia City with William Sharon as the manager.

A native of Ohio, Sharon had joined the rush to California in 1849 when he was twenty-eight years old. After a brief and unsuccessful merchandising career at Sacramento, he established a real estate office in San Francisco and accumulated a small fortune which he soon lost in mining stock speculation. When Ralston asked him to become manager of the branch bank at Virginia City, Sharon was ready and eager to assume the responsibility. Described as shrewd, cold, cynical, and ruthless, he soon initiated policies which gave the Bank of California economic control of the Comstock from 1867 to 1875 and brought him a reputation as the dominant figure on the lode during those years, assuming the role that William M. Stewart had played during the period when litigation was more important than mining.

Sharon and the Bank of California reached the Comstock at an opportune moment, for the mine and mill owners needed money to carry them through the depression. Sharon had the money to loan and was willing to loan it at 2 percent, undercutting other loan agencies, which charged 5 percent. When the depression continued through 1865, many of the owners were unable to repay their loans. Thus, a number of mills which had been held as security passed into the bank's possession. Obviously, Sharon and the directors of the Bank of California took calculated risks in loaning money so freely when the initial ore bodies seemed depleted. No one at the time the loans were made could do more than guess that additional rich deposits would be found, for the first report on the geology of the Comstock, written by the German geologist and geographer Ferdinand von Richthofen, was published late in November, 1865. The work was an amazing prophecy of the Comstock development, and while it may well have influenced the thinking of Sharon in moving toward a mill monopoly, it could not have had anything to do with the original loans. In any event, the Bank of California had seven mills on its hands by the spring of 1867, and at Sharon's suggestion the directors agreed in June of that year to form a subsidiary, the Union Milling and Mining Company, which then took over the control and management of all the mills held by the bank.

The milling monopoly by the Bank Crowd was soon fortified by control of the leading mines and strengthened further by the building of the Virginia and Truckee Railroad. Although the transportation demands of the Comstock by the spring of 1860 had brought into existence an extensive freighting system which at its height employed about two thousand men and used from twelve to fifteen thousand mules and horses, the disadvantage of freighting resulted in pressure for the early building of a railroad. Nothing came of the four railroad franchises granted by the territorial legislature; and the Virginia and Truckee River Railroad Company, which was granted a charter in 1865 by the state legislature, failed to win sufficient financial support to begin construction. William Sharon entered the picture two years later by incorporating the Virginia and Truckee Railroad Company to build from Gold Hill through Virginia City to a point on the Truckee River about ten miles east of present Reno. The route was surveyed in September, but almost at once citizens of Eagle and Washoe valleys protested at being bypassed. Sharon was amenable to changing the route when delegations from Ormsby and Storey counties petitioned the legislature to authorize those counties to help finance the road. The company was reorganized on March 5, 1868, with Sharon, Ralston, and Mills as three of the directors, and with a charter to build from Virginia City to Carson City. Sharon may have chosen the earlier route deliberately in order to win support for the latter and more sensible route which was ultimately followed. Actually, only a route which led directly from the Comstock to the mills on the Carson River would eliminate the most costly part of the wagon route.

The route for the proposed railroad was surveyed by Isaac James, a prominent Comstock engineer. His most immediate problem was how to get the railroad from the Comstock Mines to the Carson River mills, a drop of 1,575 feet, and yet maintain a satisfactory grade. By means of trestles, tunnels, and curves, James literally "wrapped the railroad around the mountain" and brought it to the river with a maximum grade of 2.2 percent. Ground for the road was broken in February, 1869, and work was pursued so diligently that the twenty-one miles from Virginia City to Carson City were completed in January, 1870. There was an immediate, if not completely satisfactory, reduction in freight rates; the price of cordwood dropped from $15 to $11.50 a cord, and the cost of transporting ore from the Comstock mines to the Carson River mills fell from $3.50 to $2.00 per ton. By the close of 1870 a general reduction of 27 percent in the cost of hauling mining materials had been effected. Perhaps as important for the mine owners was the opening of the U.S. Mint at Carson City in January, 1870. With the mint and the railroad in operation, the bullion from the mills could be shipped directly to Carson City, eliminating an expensive haul to San Francisco.

The main objective of the V & T Railroad was achieved when it reached Carson City, but the new community of Reno on the Central Pacific soon became important as a railroad connection for freight to and from Virginia City via the Geiger Grade. Before the Virginia and Truckee Railroad reached Carson City, Reno citizens were pressing for an extension of the line to Reno. However, Sharon and the Bank Crowd were in no hurry to build such an extension, and it wasn't until a potential competitor obtained a franchise for one from the Nevada legislature in 1871 that the owners of the V & T got busy and started construction of their Carson City—Reno line, which was finished the next year.

Completing its monopoly of the Comstock with the purchase of vast timber resources in the Tahoe Basin, ownership of a fluming company, and control of the principal water company on the lode, the Bank of California was often ruthless but generally effective in its operations. Sharon, through a combination of shrewd manipulation and just plain luck, was able to take advantage of his opponents' mistakes and somehow to benefit when on occasion his organization was defeated. During the period of its dominance, the Bank Crowd was challenged successfully only twice. The first such occurrence was in 1869 when the newly formed association of John Mackay, James Fair, James Flood, and William O'Brien gained control of the Hale and Norcross mine, establishing the basis for their rival Bonanza firm. The mine had produced well in 1866 and 1867, but in 1868 the stock fell rapidly. Fair, who had been involved for a short time in 1867 in the management of the mine, was convinced that it was a worthwhile venture. The partners began buying up stock and at the annual election in March, 1869, took control of the mine from Sharon and the Bank of California. Although the loss of the Hale and Norcross was of no major importance at the moment, dividends from the mine's successful operation made possible the purchase of milling facilities and eventually cost the Bank of California its control of the Comstock.

A much more immediate threat to the bank's domination was a challenge from within its own membership. Late in 1870 John P. Jones, the superintendent of the Crown Point Mine, one of the many properties controlled by the Bank Crowd, reported a discovery on the 1,100-foot level. Jones may or may not have discussed the new find with the principal owners. If he did, only one, Alvinza Hayward, a key man in the formation of the Bank of California, took him seriously and, representing Jones and himself, bought as much Crown Point stock as possible. By the time Sharon realized what had happened it was too late; Jones and Hayward had gained effective control of the mine. The question now facing Sharon was whether to enter a long, costly fight, which he would probably lose, or make some concessions. Sharon chose the latter course, but made a fortunate move when he offered to sell Hayward and Jones his

Crown Point stock if they would relinquish their stock in the neighboring Belcher mine to the Bank of California. Jones and Hayward immediately proceeded to increase their independence from the bank by establishing their own milling company and shifting their banking business to a rival firm. In spite of this seeming defeat, the Bank Crowd benefited a great deal from the transaction, for Sharon's belief that the Crown Point bonanza would extend into the Belcher proved correct, and the Belcher ultimately produced more than the Crown Point and paid more dividends. As a matter of fact, the operations of the Bank of California on the Comstock were so critical in 1870 that it is very likely that the institution would have collapsed if the 1871 bonanza had not occurred.

The greatest potential threat to the Bank of California's dominance of the lode was the Sutro Tunnel. The idea of a deep-level drain for the Comstock mines went back to the early 1860s, and one firm, the Gold Hill and Virginia Tunnel and Mining Company, in the summer of 1863 actually started construction of a tunnel from the west side of Gold Canyon that would have cut the lode at the 800-foot level. Workmen had progressed approximately 840 feet into the mountain when the mining depression in the summer of 1864 halted construction. Perhaps it was just as well that the work stopped when it did, since a tunnel at that level would have done little to alleviate the problem of water in the mines.

It is impossible to indicate with any degree of accuracy when Adolph Sutro became interested in a drainage tunnel for the Comstock. A Prussian immigrant, Sutro was just thirty years of age when he visited the Comstock for the first time in 1860. He had previously owned a thriving merchandising business in San Francisco and had joined the gold rush to the Fraser River in 1858 in an unsuccessful attempt to establish a store at Victoria. He returned to the Comstock with much the same purpose in mind, but once there he was so intrigued by the problem of ore reduction that he sold his stores in San Francisco and built a small stamp mill near Dayton in 1861. It is quite possible that the idea for his tunnel began to take form while he was operating the mill, a task which meant almost daily trips by horseback through Six-Mile Canyon to the ore bodies on the lode. The destruction of the mill by fire in 1863 released his immense energy for the undertaking which was to keep him busy for the next fifteen years.

When the Nevada legislature met in 1865, Sutro approached its members with what must have seemed to them a wild scheme to construct a tunnel about four miles long directly into Mount Davidson to serve as a deep-level drain for the mines, provide better ventilation, and act as a two-way funnel whereby ore could be taken out and supplies and men taken in. The unanimous vote in the legislature, on February 4, to grant Sutro and his associates an exclusive franchise was a tribute to his persuasive ability.

The initial reaction of the important mining and financial figures on the Comstock was enthusiastic. When the Sutro Tunnel Company was formed in July of 1865, its trustees included William M. Stewart, Louis Janin, Jr., Henry K. Mitchell, and D. E. Avery, in addition to Sutro himself. The choice of Stewart as first president indicated not only that the Bank Crowd approved the idea but that success seemed assured. The mine superintendents, who by this time were important figures in the Comstock hierarchy, were harder to convince, but after months of hard work Sutro was able to announce in April of 1866 that twenty-three of the leading companies on the lode had entered a contract to pay him a fee of $2 on each ton of ore extracted after the tunnel reached their mines. This charge was for drainage and ventilation; additional services were made available on an optional basis at a charge of 25¢ per mile for each ton of ore removed through the tunnel, 25¢ per mile for each ton of supplies taken through the tunnel to the mines, and 25¢ per person for each individual entering or leaving the tunnel.

With the support of dozens of prominent officials and with a congressional act of July 25, 1866, granting his company a right of way and other privileges, Sutro optimistically approached New York capitalists for funds. Here he met his first major rebuff, for the eastern financiers wanted some tangible evidence of financial support from the West Coast before pledging their monies. By the time Sutro arrived back on the Comstock, opposition, led by William Sharon and the Bank Crowd, had developed. Such opposition was inevitable as soon as Sharon realized that Sutro was aiming at nothing less than domination of the Comstock. Sutro was his own worst enemy in this respect, for in September, 1866, he published and distributed a persuasive pamphlet which showed how the tunnel would move the center of political and economic control from Gold Hill and Virginia City to the new town of Sutro which was planned at the mouth of the tunnel.

The opposition of the Bank Crowd made it apparent by the end of 1867 that Sutro would have difficulty obtaining funds in the United States, so he turned to Europe and in the latter part of that year made the first of many trips to European financial centers seeking aid for his tunnel project. His reception in Europe was friendly but otherwise unrewarding. Returning to the United States in December, he again presented a request to Congress for government aid. But the Bank of California forces were too powerful and Sutro was blocked in Congress as he had been elsewhere in the United States.

A disastrous fire in the Yellow Jacket mine on April 7, 1869, which cost the lives of thirty-seven men gave Sutro opportunity to present his case to the miners. Arguing that such a fire would have been prevented if the tunnel had been in operation, Sutro was able to obtain a pledge of $50,000 from the Virginia and the Gold Hill miners' unions. With this money Sutro started work on the tunnel in October of 1869. He still had no major funds pledged, and it wasn't until 1871 that his European trips began to pay off with the first of a number of loans from the McCalmont Brothers and Company of London. On July 8, 1878, nearly nine years after the initial groundbreaking, the tunnel was completed, a tremendous feat of engineering as well as a monument to the dogged perseverance of Adolph Sutro. It stretched 20,484 feet from the mouth to the first connection with the lode at the 1,650-foot level of the Savage mine. The cost of construction was approximately $3½ million.

Completion of the tunnel did not end Sutro's troubles with the mine owners, for they now refused to enter into new agreements with him, expecting to take advantage of the tunnel without any expenditures on their part. Finally, after months of negotiations, new contracts were signed in March, 1879, whereby the mine owners agreed to pay $2 a ton on ore valued at more than $40 a ton and $1 a ton on ore worth less than that. The other provisions concerning supplies and passengers remained the same as in the original contracts.

The tunnel was completed ten years too late for the Comstock Lode, if not for Adolph Sutro. By the time connection was made with the Savage shaft, the great mines on Mount Davidson had begun a decline that was never reversed. In addition several shafts were below the level of the tunnel when it reached the lode, and it failed to provide the benefits of better ventilation which Sutro claimed for it. Needless to say, the tunnel did not pay for itself, and the McCalmont firm and lesser investors suffered large losses. The venture did, however, set Sutro on the road to a fortune, for that genius had quietly unloaded his stock soon after completion of the tunnel. While he did not make the five million dollars usually credited for the sale, he did manage to pocket a profit of nearly a million dollars which he invested in enough San Francisco real estate to make him a millionnaire many times over.[1]

THE BONANZA FIRM TAKES CONTROL

The Bank Crowd successfully fought Sutro and forestalled completion of the tunnel until it was no longer a major threat. Although they were forced to share control of the Comstock with Jones and Hayward after 1871, it wasn't until 1875 that they were pushed into a position of secondary importance. A series of circumstances which coupled the failure of the mother bank because of Ralston's unfortunate investments with the rise of the Bonanza group was responsible for driving Sharon and the Bank Crowd from the position of power which they had held since 1867.

The last power combine to control the Comstock, the Bonanza associates were two miners, John W. Mackay and James G. Fair, and two stockbrokers, James C. Flood and William S. O'Brien. All of them were Irish and all had been in California since the early days of the gold rush, with indifferent success. Mackay, who arrived on the Comstock in 1859, and Fair, who arrived the following year, each worked his way from miner to superintendent independently of the other. Fair's most important position before the partnership was formed was the superintendency of the Ophir mine. Mackay, through hard work and shrewd investment, became a partner in the Kentuck mine and by 1868 had amassed a small fortune. After combining forces to wrest control of the Hale and Norcross from Sharon and develop it into a very profitable investment, the Bonanza partners undertook two mining ventures which were complete failures. Then they decided to gamble on the possibility that rich ore would be found in a section of the lode between the Gould and Curry

---

[1] Sutro became a prominent figure in San Francisco, spending large sums of money in projects such as the Sutro Baths, Sutro Heights Park, and the Sutro Library. He was elected mayor of San Francisco on the Populist ticket in 1894.

mine and the original Ophir holdings, an area which to that time had been considered completely worthless. The land in question was controlled by the Consolidated-Virginia Company until the Bonanza firm acquired it in 1871. However, it was two years before their effort began to pay off with the gradual opening of a deposit whose richness could only be guessed, but which entitled it to be known then and forever after as the "Big Bonanza." In order to ensure that no part of the find was lost, the Bonanza firm reorganized the California Mining Company, made up of a number of claims adjacent to the Consolidated-Virginia, in December, 1873. The exploitation of the deposit continued slowly and cautiously into the spring of 1874, but by the time the first dividend was paid in May, 1874, it was quite clear to everyone that the lode was once again "in bonanza." Stock in the Consolidated-Virginia which sold for $1 in July, 1870, slowly moved forward to $15 in June of 1872, and leaped to $700 per share in 1875. Stock in the California mine which had reached no higher than $37 per share as late as September, 1874, jumped to $780 in January of 1875. The production of the Big Bonanza is almost unbelievable; in nine years, from 1873 to 1882, these two mines produced $105,157,490 and paid dividends of $74,250,000.

The Bonanza firm lost little time in translating their new wealth into economic dominance of the Comstock. One of their first moves was to establish a milling monopoly by incorporating the Pacific Mill and Mining Company in the fall of 1874. By this device, which had been employed so successfully by the Bank Crowd, the Bonanza group, in effect, made exclusive and very liberal contracts with themselves to mill the ore from the Big Bonanza. They next moved to obtain financial independence by organizing the Nevada Bank of San Francisco with a main branch in Virginia City. Their entrance into the Virginia and Gold Hill Water Company in 1871 gave them the base for ultimate control over the Comstock's major water supply, and through the formation of the Pacific Wood, Lumber, and Fluming Company in 1875 they secured an independent lumber supply. The only important part of the economic machinery of the Comstock which the Bonanza firm was unable to control was the Virginia and Truckee Railroad. A competing line would have been very costly to the new Comstock kings and they knew it, but the constant threat to build such a line, even to sending surveyors into the field, was sufficient to force the Bank Crowd to make rate concessions.

Although the Big Bonanza lasted only a few years, the firm monopolized the Comstock for twenty years, from 1875 until Mackay sold his interests to San Francisco stockbrokers in 1895. The decline of the lode was very rapid with the exhaustion of this great ore body. In 1876 production reached a high of $38,048,145; five years later it was down to $1,414,308. The Big Bonanza proved to be the last great ore body of the lode. Although the partners continued expensive exploratory work in the California and the Consolidated-Virginia and spent millions of dollars sinking shafts in various mines to below 3,000 feet, no important new ore bodies were discovered. Mackay was the last of the four Bonanza kings to leave the Comstock; O'Brien died in 1878, Fair withdrew in 1881, and Flood died in 1889. In spite of many harsh words written about them, the Bonanza firm brought to the Comstock not only a much more efficient operation of the mines and the mills but a much fairer financial control than their predecessors in the Bank Crowd.

The production summary of the Comstock Lode in the years from 1859 to 1882 shows many interesting but frustrating results. During that period a total of $292,726,310 was produced. Out of this amount, $125,335,925 was paid in dividends, over half from the property of the Bonanza firm. The dividends tell only part of the story, for $73,929,355 was levied by various Comstock mines in assessments. Only a few Comstock mines paid more in dividends than they levied in assessments. The Consolidated-Virginia and the California, which levied only $762,499 in assessments and paid nearly $75,000,000 in dividends, were outstanding in this respect. The more typical Comstock producers levied more assessments than they paid in dividends. This was true even of excellent producers such as the Savage mine, which yielded $15.7 million, paid $4.2 million in dividends, and levied $5.4 million in assessments; and the Ophir, which produced approximately $11 million, paid dividends of $1.5 million, and levied assessments of $3.1 million. At the other extreme were those properties which produced nothing, paid nothing in dividends, and levied millions of dollars in assessments. The best example of this type of mine was the Bullion, which levied $3.8 million in assessments while producing nothing. Obviously, millions of dollars of stockholders' monies were spent in needless excavation in order to maintain mines with a superintendent and officers, thus supporting mill rings, politicians, and stock manipulators.

A fundamental part of the rather sordid financial history of the Comstock era was the speculation which accompanied it. Beginning early in the history of the lode and continuing long after the last bonanza was found, speculation dominated the public's interest. The center for Comstock investment was the San Francisco Stock Exchange, established in 1862 as a result of the first boom. No one, from janitors and scrubwomen to merchants and bankers and from the lowest-paid miner to the richest mine owners, seemed immune to the desire to gamble in stocks. The bankers and mine owners had one major advantage over the general public; they knew when a discovery had been made, often maintaining secrecy by keeping the miners underground, and they knew when the rich ore was petering out. Each successive boom period was marked by the formation of more companies, capitalized beyond reason, and the successive advance of nearly all of the stock market offerings, regardless of whether or not they were in production. A good example of this pattern in the early years occurred in 1867, when of some 400 companies organized, only three—the Ophir, the Gould and Curry, and the Savage—were paying dividends.

The speculation craze of 1867 was dwarfed by that of 1872 which resulted from the bonanzas in the Crown Point and the Belcher. Stock in those two mines advanced to nearly $300 per share in the second half of 1871; there was no stock boom, however, during this period. Then in January, 1872, Alvinza Hayward launched an artificial stock boom by starting a rumor of a rich find in the Savage mine, which the new firm of Hayward and Jones now owned. The rumor was followed by Hayward's order to buy Savage stock and by the well-worn trick of confining the miners underground and refusing entrance to the mine. The ruse succeeded and Savage stock rose from $62 a share in January to $725 a share on April 25, although no new ore body had been found. Other stocks followed the lead of Savage: Belcher went to $1,525 per share on April 25 and Crown Point reached $1,825 on May 5. The San Francisco Mining Exchange listing of 150 stocks moved from a total value of $17 million in January to $81 million on May 5. It was obvious that the market could not hold up under such flimsy circumstances.

The inevitable crash was hastened by a rumor from the opposition. William Sharon, who was running against Jones for the U.S. Senate, and who had many other reasons for wanting revenge against Jones and Hayward, circulated a story that Jones had been involved in starting the Yellow Jacket fire in April, 1869. Although the rumor was as baseless as was Hayward's, it was sufficient to start an immediate downward trend in stocks which created a financial panic in San Francisco and ruined thousands of small investors.

The discovery of the Big Bonanza ultimately brought on a third major speculative boom. Contrary to earlier practices on the Comstock, the Bonanza firm did not attempt to initiate a stock boom on the basis of the new discovery, but were satisfied, for the moment at least, to allow the market to move forward by itself. William Sharon, however, was eager to participate in the new development and realized the only way he could do so was by speculation. The mine he chose was the Ophir, which lay to the north of the Big Bonanza, and which at the time was controlled by E. J. ("Lucky") Baldwin. Sharon began to buy Ophir stock at $20 per share and after some negotiations with Baldwin gained control of the property. His manipulations were successful; by January 7, 1875, Ophir stock was at $315 per share. The rest of the market went along, Consolidated-Virginia reaching $710 and California $780 per share on the same day. The market value of the thirty-one leading mines on the Comstock on January 7 was $262,669,940, and the value of three mines alone—the California, the Consolidated-Virginia, and the Ophir—was $193,808,000, over three million dollars more than the entire assessed value of real estate in San Francisco!

The market began to break on January 8 with the usual disastrous results. Within a month Consolidated-Virginia fell to $50 per share, California to $250, and Ophir to $65. The general public again were the real losers, while a number of stock manipulators made handsome profits. Although the Bonanza firm itself did not participate actively in the speculative boom of 1875, it did so on a number of occasions after the Comstock had started its last decline, leading Grant Smith to write, "Flood and his partners guessed the market wrong at every important period. . . . Flood's undoubted talent for stock-market operations was not profitable in the end, and brought only a world of cares. It was his misfortune to be supporting a failing bonanza and a declining stock market. Both Mackay and Flood, in later years, often expressed regret that they had not confined themselves to mining."[2]

Speculation in Comstock Lode stocks became more persistent as the mines continued to decline, and most of it, after the 1875 boom, was based on rumor and wishful thinking. Two of the many manipulations which ultimately ruined the reputation of Nevada mining stocks on the California exchanges deserve special mention.

The first occurred in 1878, just as the Big Bonanza was ending. This manipulation, known as the "Sierra Nevada Deal," was based on the premise that additional bonanzas would be found at the north end of the lode. Consequently, when the Sierra Nevada ran into a very small pocket of ore, speculators got busy and Sierra Nevada stock was jumped from $90 per share on September 4 to $280 per share on September 27. Only a few manipulators benefitted when the market broke, sending Sierra Nevada stock to $65 on November 20.

Another deal occurred in 1886 when James L. Flood, son of James C., deliberately manipulated Consolidated-Virginia and California stock from $4.50 on October 31 to $62 on December 4. This operation was completely speculative, for both of these mines at that time were operating on low-grade ore. As usual, however, many small investors bought stocks, and when the market broke and stocks declined in value, they were wiped out.

WATER AND WOOD

The Comstock could not have reached the level of development it attained without adequate sources of water and wood. Water, except in the mines where it wasn't wanted, was scarce almost from the beginning. The supply from underground springs in the area adjacent to the mines was not sufficient to meet the needs of a growing community and the demands of the mine owners. By 1870 the problem of an adequate water supply was so critical that new sources had to be found at once if development was to continue. Two main possibilities were the use of the Carson River, which would entail an expensive system of pumping from the valley floor to the mines, and the Sierra, also a costly prospect, but it was considered a better plan and was the ultimate choice.

[2] Grant H. Smith, *The History of the Comstock Lode, 1850–1920,* University of Nevada Geology and Mining Series, no. 37 (July 1, 1943), p. 210.

In order to tap this latter source, the Virginia and Gold Hill Water Company, controlled by the Bank Crowd, was reorganized in 1871 to include the new Bonanza firm. The new directors called upon a German engineer, Hermann Schussler, to solve the difficulty of carrying water from the Sierra to the summit of the nearby Virginia Range. The distance was not a problem, but the pipe was to be laid in the form of an inverted siphon, with the source of water at Hobart Creek in the Sierra, which was at a higher elevation than Virginia City. Thus, gravity was to do the work, but the depressed curve of the siphon which crossed the southern end of Washoe Valley would subject the pipe to a vertical pressure of 1,720 feet, and there was a question whether or not the pipe then available would withstand that kind of pressure.

Schussler had supervised the installation of a similar but smaller system at Butte County, California, where the vertical pressure was 910 feet, and was convinced that San Francisco foundries could provide pipe capable of withstanding the pressure to be met where the line crossed Washoe Valley. The pipe sections were ordered in 1872 and installation began in the early summer of 1873. The first water flowed through the pipe in July, but there were so many leaks that it wasn't until August that an uninterrupted flow began. The new supply not only gave the Comstock communities sufficient water for the first time, but also made possible the increased exploitation of the mines created by the discovery of the Big Bonanza in 1873.[3]

Just as interesting as the inverted siphon, which solved the water problem, was the invention of the *V-flume*, a device which came into existence as a direct result of the unusual Comstock demand for timber—for fuel, for the construction of mine buildings and commercial and residential establishments, and especially for the square-set timbering in the mines, which was adopted universally after 1860. Eliot Lord in his *Comstock Mining and Miners* estimates that some 600 million board feet of lumber went into the mines alone. The Virginia Range, in which the lode was situated, had little timber except for the piñon pine, useful for fuel but for little else. Fortunately for the exploiters, adequate timber sources were found

[3] The demands of the Comstock for water following the discovery of the Big Bonanza were such that a second pipeline was laid across Washoe Lake and additional water sources made available in the Sierra Nevada above Lake Tahoe.

in the nearby Sierra Nevada. The less heavily timbered eastern slope, from the Truckee River, north of Reno, to the head of the East Carson River in Alpine County, California, and the heavily timbered areas on the western slope around Lake Tahoe, bore the brunt of the logging activity which ensued as a result of the Comstock demand. As the loggers moved from the valley floor to the slopes and over the mountains, the cost of hauling the logs and the construction and repair of mountain wood roads became greater. A cheaper method of getting the lumber down the slopes was called for, and the V-flume was the result.

J. W. Haines is generally credited with the invention of the V-flume, although there was enough question about the origin of the device to lead to a costly suit which Haines brought against William Sharon for infringement of patent. Although Haines lost the suit because the court held that the device had been in common use for two years prior to filing for a patent, it is quite clear from the facts brought out in the case that Haines was the first to use the V-flume idea. The flume Haines constructed in 1867 was as simple as it was effective. Two boards were joined together at their lower edges at an angle of ninety degrees. The resulting trough, resting on trestles of varying height to provide the proper grade, and partially filled with water, was capable of carrying sawed lumber up to forty feet in length and sixteen inches square over canyons and around hills quickly and cheaply. Within a short time the V-flume had become indispensable to the exploitation of the Comstock Lode, and large lumber and fluming companies with ample capital were brought into the operation.

Probably the most important was the Carson and Tahoe Lumber and Fluming Company, formed in 1873 and controlled by the Bank of California as part of their Comstock monopoly. The operation centered around fifty thousand acres of timberland on the shores of Lake Tahoe and in Lake Valley at the southern end of the lake. Timber cut along the lake shore or brought to the water by logging trains was towed by barge to Glenbrook, where three mills were situated. From the mills at Glenbrook the lumber was taken by a narrow-gauge railroad to Spooner Summit and placed on a twelve-mile-long V-flume which emptied into a large lumberyard where spur tracks made connection with the Virginia and Truckee Railroad. A large staging area was constructed on Spooner's, called

Summit Camp, which became the receiving end for feeder flumes bringing additional lumber as well as the water necessary to supply the large flume from the summit to Carson City.

A second major company, the Sierra Nevada Wood and Lumber Company, operated a complex arrangement which included a narrow-gauge railroad, rafting on Lake Tahoe, and an interesting tramway system and V-flume. The lumber for this operation came from the northern part of Lake Tahoe and was brought to the mill at Incline by rafting and by the railroad. From Incline a tramway was constructed which was operated by a hoist at the upper end. The lumber, after being hoisted to the summit, was placed on a V-flume which passed first through a tunnel, built originally by the Virginia and Gold Hill Water Company to augment its supply of water from the Sierra Nevada, and then down Lakeview Hill to a storage yard which was served by a spur track from the Virginia and Truckee Railroad.

The Pacific Wood, Lumber, and Fluming Company, the third important fluming operation, was established in 1875 by the Bonanza firm as part of their successful attempt to supplant the Bank Crowd as the key monopoly on the Comstock. The lumber source in this instance was twelve thousand acres of timberland on the eastern slope of the Sierra Nevada. The V-flume, when completed, was fifteen miles long, extending from Huffaker's station on the Virginia and Truckee Railroad to the head of Hunter's Creek on Mount Rose. Two sawmills were built at the staging area and about two hundred miles of road were constructed in the mountains to bring the logs to the mills. In the first complete season's run in 1876, some fifteen million board feet of lumber and seventy-five thousand cords of wood were delivered at Huffaker's. This particular flume received unusual publicity when on its completion Fair and Flood of the Bonanza firm decided to initiate the structure by riding two improvize boats, referred to by one as a "pig trough with one end knocked out," over the fifteen-mile length. Reluctant additions to the passenger list on the initial trip were John B. Hereford, who had superintended its construction, H. J. Ramsdell, a reporter for the *New York Tribune*, and an unidentified carpenter "yanked aboard as an afterthought." Long before it was over, the five riders wished fervently that the crazy trip would end, but once under way the boats could not be stopped. As Ramsdell later reported, "You have nothing to hold to; you have only to sit still, take all the water that comes—drenching you like a plunge through the surf—and wait for eternity." When the two boats finally arrived at the end of the flume, the men jumped clear at the first opportunity. Each had something to say about the hectic thirty-minute ride, but all at the moment could agree with Hereford when he stated that he wished he had never built the flume.[4]

ORGANIZED LABOR

With all its technological innovations and improvements, the Comstock would not have been exploited so readily if large numbers of skilled miners had not been available. The California rush in 1849 and after had brought thousands of Cornish and Irish miners to the area and a decade later they, like their employers, turned eastward to the Comstock. Also like the engineers and superintendents, the miners had little to guide them from their California experience; it was enough, however, to carry them through the first months of operation, and the Comstock then became their teacher. When the rush from California began to taper off, a growing supply of immigrants provided the necessary labor force. During most of the Comstock era, foreign-born laborers dominated the labor market. This was true in 1860 as development was beginning, and was still the case in 1870 when Virginia City had developed into a cosmopolitan city. In that year the foreign-born not only dominated the labor market, but outnumbered the native-born in the entire population. As late as 1880, when the Comstock mines were definitely on a decline, there were only 770 native-born in a labor force of 2,770, although by that time American-born citizens outnumbered the foreign-born in the general population. The immigrant domination of the labor force on the Comstock gave to Virginia City and Gold Hill an appearance similar to that of eastern industrial communities of the same era. Miners on the Comstock, first at Gold Hill and later at Virginia City, were the first in the West to form miners' unions. The constitution of the Gold Hill Union became a model for miners' unions throughout the West.

The first attempt at labor organization was made on May 30, 1863, when a Miner's Protective Association was formed to maintain a

[4]For an amusing summary of this ride based on the newspaper report by Ramsdell, see Bert Goldrath, "River in a Box," *Argosy* 352 (March 1961): 34–39, 104–5.

$4-per-day wage for all underground work. The formal organization was not completed at that time and might well never have been had not some mine owners reduced the wage to $3.50 per day. On July 31, 1864, the miners held a parade at which they shouted the watchword, "$4 a day." The following day about one hundred miners visited various mines and mills in a formal appeal to the owners to maintain the higher wage. Shortly thereafter, on August 6, the miners completed the organization initiated the previous year by forming the Miner's League of Storey County. After adopting a constitution and bylaws and electing officers, the members pledged never to work in Storey County for less that $4 per day in gold and silver coin. The league soon realized that such a pledge backed by their small membership was ineffective; consequently, on September 18 it passed a resolution authorizing a committee of the organization to notify employers that no person except members of the league should be permitted to work in the mines and mills after Tuesday, September 27. The resolution was a tactical error, for the league neither had the membership nor the money to sustain such a position in the face of a growing depression on the Comstock. The officers of the league acknowledged their mistake when they withdrew the resolution four days later. The league died a slow death as employers gradually dropped its members and hired miners not in the league to replace them. By the spring of 1865 most mine owners had adopted the $3.50 wage and union labor at Virginia City seemed to have suffered a critical blow.

The 1864–65 setback was temporary and apparently more the result of hard times than of any antilabor sentiment among the owners. New and more important organizations came into being with the formation of the Gold Hill Miners' Union, December 8, 1866, and the Virginia City Miners' Union on July 4, 1867. With the Gold Hill Miners' Union leading the way, the two unions forced the establishment of a $4-a-day wage for underground workers and a restriction against the employment of nonunion miners. This time the union was strong enough to make both the wage and employment restrictions effective until long after the Comstock had begun its final decline in the 1880s. The companies not only came to recognize the union as a powerful bargaining voice, but in many instances helped it by deducting the $2 monthly dues from the miners' pay checks. It became almost automatic for a miner to enroll as a union member at the same time that he was employed by a company. The activities and development of the Virginia City Miner's Union were mirrored in a similar development by the Gold Hill Miner's Union, the two usually setting parallel programs.

In May of 1869 the threat of Chinese labor on the Comstock brought the two unions together in a formal appeal to the working-men of Nevada to send delegates to a workingmen's convention to be held in Virginia City in July. The object of the proposed meeting was to maintain wages at a satisfactory standard and "prevent the firm seating of Chinese labor in our midst." The convention never met, although the threat of Chinese labor continued and ultimately brought about a demonstration by 350 miners against the Chinese laborers being used by William Sharon to construct the Virginia and Truckee Railroad. The union's opposition was sufficient to force Sharon to sign an agreement guaranteeing that no Chinese would be employed within the limits of Virginia City and Gold Hill.

The achievements of the Virginia City and Gold Hill Miner's unions in maintaining wages and controlling the camp without a major labor strike are rather outstanding when one remembers that labor organizations were just getting a foothold on the national level at this time. In trying to explain this success one must consider the richness of the ore, the difficulty of obtaining skilled miners, the need for a stable working force (which high wages guaranteed) to exploit the mines properly, the high living costs when the $4 wage was first introduced, and the moderation of the miners in their demands. Then, too, it seems apparent that both operators and miners took pride in the fact that the Comstock was the model for western mining. It was the richest mineral area in the United States and it contained the best machinery and the best engineers— why not the best and highest paid miners? The operators saw another advantage of a strong union membership; the union, with some company help, cared for the sick and disabled miners and helped to take care of the family of any miner who met death by accident.

The $4-per-day wage, considered very high at the time, seems little enough for the risks that the miner faced from the moment he entered the cage to go underground until he left it at the end of the shift. In spite of the invention of square-set timbering and constant improvements in hoisting machinery, the danger from caving earth, fire, falling timbers, faulty cables, and defective machinery was continuous throughout the history of the Comstock Lode. Sudden death was never very far away, as for instance on December 2, 1879, when the hoist engineer pulled the wrong lever and sent the skip containing seventeen men to the top of the forty-foot gallows frame, killing two men and seriously injuring most of the others; or on that April morning in 1869, when fire on the eight-hundred-foot level of the Yellow Jacket mine killed thirty-seven men; or on the day when a miner named William Jenkins fell into the sump of the Julia mine shaft and was scalded to death. But as Eliot Lord states in his *Comstock Mining and Miners,* "To describe in detail the manifold ways in which men have lost their lives in these mines would be a needless catalogue of horrors." A summary for the year 1878 shows twenty-six fatal accidents: four from caving, four from premature explosion of powder, six from falls unconnected with hoisting machinery, one from being crushed by a cage in motion, three from defective machinery in shaft works, six from heat, and two from hoisting machinery. It seems superfluous to note that the Comstock mines lacked even the most primitive type of safety inspection system or a program of accident prevention. The fatalistic attitude of miners and owners toward accidents is shown in the fact that the state of Nevada did not establish the position of state inspector of mines until 1909.

QUEEN CITY OF THE COMSTOCK

The rush of Californians across the Sierra to the "Washoe diggings" in 1859 and 1860 brought into existence three small towns, Silver City, Gold Hill, and Virginia Town, roughly marking the line of the Comstock Lode from south to north along Mount Davidson. Officially named at a miner's meeting in September, 1859, Virginia Town (City) soon came to dominate life on the Comstock. Like all mining towns, its existence was based entirely on the ore bodies which had given it life. But because the Comstock Lode was of such magnitude, Virginia City acquired a permanency and a significance in the history of Nevada and the West which far surpassed that of most mining camps. Its first appearance as a community in 1860 was colorful, if not inviting, as thousands came pouring into the area after the winter and spring storms had subsided. Among the newcomers was J. Ross Browne, a noted traveler and reporter, who left a word picture of Virginia City as he saw it in March, 1860, that has rarely been equalled:

On a slope of mountain speckled with snow, sagebushes, and mounds of upturned earth, without any apparent beginning or end, congruity or regard for the eternal fitness of things, lay outspread the wondrous city of Virginia. Frame shanties, pitched together as if by accident; tents of canvas, or blankets, of brush, of potato-sacks and old shirts with empty whisky-barrels for chimneys; smoky hovels of mud and stone; coyote holes in the mountain side forcibly seized and held by men; pits and shafts with smoke issuing from every crevice; piles of goods and rubbish on craggy points, in the hollows, on the rocks, in the mud, in the snow, everywhere, scattered broadcast in pell-mell confusion, as if the clouds had suddenly burst overhead and rained down the dregs of all the flimsy, rickety, filthy little hovels and rubbish of merchandise that had ever undergone the process of evaporation from the earth since the days of Noah. The intervals of space, which may or may not have been streets, were dotted over with human beings of such sort, variety, and numbers, that the famous ant-hills of Africa were as nothing in comparison.[5]

The center of activity during the day was the thousands of claims which had been located on every possible foot of ground from Silver City to Virginia and up and down each canyon and ravine on Mount Davidson. In the evenings attention centered in the canvas shacks which enterprising merchants had turned into saloons, dispensing whisky as fast as supplies could be carted over the mountains. There wasn't much in this shapeless city, with its incessant noise, its drunkards and desperadoes, to attract one such as Browne, and as his writing indicated in rather strong language, he was happy to rid himself of the place.

Yet the face of Virginia City changed rapidly as the early confusion gave way to stable mining operations and the rude, temporary shelters of canvas and miscellaneous material were replaced by wood cabins and business houses. While the town was still in the boom stage, brick buildings began to dot the landscape and gas and sewer pipes were laid on the principal streets. Browne, revisiting the mines in 1863, grudgingly admitted,

[5] J. Ross Browne, *A Peep at Washoe and Washoe Revisited* (Balboa Island, Calif.: Paisano Press, 1959), p. 64–65.

The business part of the town has been built up with astonishing rapidity. In the spring of 1860 there was nothing of it save a few frame shanties and canvas tents, and one or two rough stone cabins. It now presents some of the distinguishing features of a metropolitan city. Large and substantial brick houses, three or four stories high, with ornamental fronts, have filled up most of the gaps, and many more are still in progress of erection. The oddity of the plan, and variety of its architecture—combining most of the styles known to the ancients, and some but little known to the modern—give this famous city a grotesque, if not picturesque, appearance, which is rather increased upon a close inspection.[6]

As the control of mining moved from dozens of independent companies to domination by "fortified" monopolies, such as the Bank of California and the Bonanza firm, the town grew into a city by adding first-class restaurants and hotels, opera houses and theaters, churches, schools, and newspapers. By 1870 Virginia compared favorably with eastern cities its size or larger in having lighted streets, municipal gas, water, sewerage, four daily and four weekly newspapers, rail and stage terminals, and other accouterments of civilization. By that time it had become a curious combination of industrial city and frontier town.

The complex of mine and mill buildings, railroad yards, and foundries; the large well-organized labor force, dominated by foreign-born; the specialized equipment so necessary to support the underground network of shafts and tunnels; the problems of water, finance, and government; and the heterogeneous population of twenty thousand persons—all pointed to an industry-dominated type of community like so many in the eastern states in the post–Civil War period.[7] Yet this comparison should not be overemphasized, for throughout its history, from discovery to boom to bust, Virginia City remained in many respects a frontier mining town. The numerous saloons, gambling houses, pool rooms, and the extensive red-light district where prostitution flourished openly, gave to the city

[6] Ibid., p. 181.

[7] One of the first to describe the industrial aspects of Virginia City was Eliot Lord in his *Comstock Mining and Miners,* U.S. Geological Survey Monographs, vol. 4 (Washington, D.C.: GPO, 1883). Robert Merrifield enlarged the theme in his doctoral dissertation, "Nevada, 1859–1881: The Impact of an Advanced Technological Society upon a Frontier Area" (Ph.D. diss., University of Chicago, 1957). More recently Rodman Paul has emphasized the same point in the chapter on the Comstock found in his work *Mining Frontiers of the Far West, 1848–1880* (New York: Holt, Rinehart & Winston, 1963).

at night an atmosphere more reminiscent of gaudy carnival than of a stable industrial community.

And in back of the carnival city was another community of churches, schools, fraternal organizations, and homes, where family life was probably not much different from that experienced in communities of similar size elsewhere in the United States.[8] The people who were the foundation of the "other" side of Virginia City seemingly had little to do with the public image of that community. The married miner with family, in particular, was likely to lead a life far removed from the many pleasures available to the single man. Family picnics to Sutro, the Carson River, Steamboat Springs, and Bowers Mansion, or hikes to the top of Mount Davidson, or participation in Fourth of July celebrations, or enjoying the Christmas and New Year's holidays, were likely to consume most of the limited leisure time available.

It is difficult to categorize Virginia City in its heyday, for its social patterns varied from day to day and from morning to night, but whatever else might be said about it, the city became one of the wonders of western America, a place that had to be seen to be believed. One can only hazard a guess as to the number of individuals who became believers by visiting Virginia City on their way either to or from San Francisco. The many visitors to the "Queen of the Comstock" included some of the most prominent persons in the United States at the time: three former presidents—Benjamin Harrison, Rutherford B. Hayes, and Ulysses S. Grant—politicians like James G. Blaine and Schuyler Colfax, Civil War generals Phillip Sheridan and W. T. Sherman, the financier Baron Rothschild, the inventor Thomas A. Edison, the famous preacher Henry Ward Beecher and the equally famous agnostic Robert Ingersoll, the latter remarking after a visit underground that there might be a hell after all, humorists such as Artemus Ward and Mark Twain, and prominent women of the era such as Susan B. Anthony, Tennessee Claflin, a leading advocate of free love, and Mrs. Maggie Van Cott, cited as the first woman ever licensed by the Methodist Episcopal Church to preach in the United States. Besides these, nearly every important stage or theatrical troupe during the 1860s and 1870s had Virginia City on its itinerary.

[8]The two faces of Nevada towns continue to be emphasized today, with many residents of Las Vegas and Reno, particularly, insisting on separating the gambling city from the stable city of schools, homes, and churches.

That the mining frontier was often a vast mixture of nationalities was nowhere more apparent than in Virginia City during its boom period. Aside from their sheer numbers, the importance of the foreign-born in the management, engineering, and political fields was attested to by the names of such persons as John Mackay and James Fair, both born in Ireland, Adolph Sutro, Philipp Deidesheimer, and Hermann Schussler, all born in Germany, and John P. Jones, who claimed Wales as his birthplace.

The immigrant influence spread as well through the whole societal structure of the Comstock. Thus a number of groups, the German Catholics, German Lutherans, French and French-Canadians, and Welsh, held religious services in their native languages. There were German bands, a Cornish orchestra, Irish bands, an English choral society, and a Scottish bagpipe band. Songs in English, French, German, Spanish and Italian were offered in productions at the opera house. Actually, much of the professional entertainment on the Comstock was designed to appeal to the foreign-born population, particularly the Irish, who constituted the largest foreign-born group on the Comstock.

Besides having their own saloons and restaurants, most of the foreign-born organized at least one distinctive national society. The Irish led the way in this respect with the formation of three military companies, the Emmet Guard, the Sweeney Guard, and the Scarsfield Guard, and chapters of the Fenian Society and the Ancient Order of Hibernians. In addition to their musical organizations, Germans were reminded of their homeland by the Turnverein societies which held Sunday evening socials at Von Bokkelen's Beer Gardens and by three short-lived German-language newspapers, the *Nevada Pionier*, the *Nevada Staats-Zeitung*, and the *Deutsche Union*. The Scots had a Caledonian Society which sponsored a "Gathering of the Clans" in August of each year, and they customarily celebrated the birthdays of Robert Burns in January and of Walter Scott in August. The Italian Benevolent Society was quite active with its sponsorship of picnics and balls.

Other national groups such as the Mexicans and Chinese celebrated various holidays, the former with parades marking their independence day and their defeat of the French, and the latter with a big parade and celebration at the beginning of the Chinese New Year. During the bonanza period it was unusual for a week to pass without a parade, ball, picnic, or other social event sponsored by one of the many Comstock societies of foreign-born.

The Mexicans and Chinese along with the Indians and the blacks formed the lowest rungs of the social ladder on the Comstock. The Indians, shorn of their native livelihood, clustered on the outskirts of the towns and performed whatever menial tasks were given them. The blacks, for a time at least, developed some institutions of their own. For example, a Masonic lodge, St. Johns Lodge, No. 13, was organized at Carson City under the jurisdiction of the Sovereign Grand Lodge of California in 1875. In addition, two churches were established, a Baptist church by the Reverend Mr. Satchell in 1863, which at the time of organization had one white member, and the African Methodist Episcopal Church, established in June, 1875. The former was discontinued in 1866 and the African Methodist Church seems to have disappeared after 1880. Some attempts were made, beginning in January, 1866, to establish schools for black children, but apparently these were unsuccessful because of the small black population in Nevada at the time. By 1880 black children as well as some Chinese and a few Indians were being educated in the public schools.

It is quite clear that Virginia City's numerous foreign-born gave the community an unusual cosmopolitan atmosphere. Whether or not the peculiar mixture of industrial and frontier characteristics of society on the Comstock speeded assimilation of these divergent groups is a debatable point.

Virginia City passed through several stages of local government in its rise to fame. From its founding in the summer of 1859 and throughout 1860, the booming town had no effective political control, although the Gold Hill Mining District at its first meeting in June of 1859 had recognized the need by electing a justice of the peace and a constable and by establishing certain rules of conduct. However, such rules were almost totally ignored during the early months. The situation was helped when the Utah territorial legislature passed an act on January 18, 1861, incorporating the town of Virginia. Under its provisions the corporate powers and duties were vested in a board of five trustees who were to hold office for one year. After the organization of Nevada Territory, a new act of incorporation was passed on December 19, 1862, which was superseded by a more elaborate one approved by the legislature on

February 19, 1864. The 1864 act established a mayor-council type of government control and in some detail outlined its duties and powers. After Nevada became a state, a new incorporation act for Virginia City was approved by the legislature on March 4, 1865. It provided for the election, for one-year terms, of a mayor, a board of aldermen (one from each of four wards), a recorder, a treasurer, an assessor, and a chief of police who was also ex-officio street inspector. The board of aldermen had the power to create additional offices such as those of city clerk, city attorney, and city tax collector. It also was given power to levy and collect city taxes and to fix license fees on such things as circuses, billiard tables, and saloons.

Although very little has been written about the actual governing procedures of the Comstock towns, it seems apparent from the duties and responsibilities listed in the incorporation acts that these local governments faced the same basic problems of police and fire protection, street and sewer maintenance, water supply, sanitation, abatement of nuisances, schools, and finance that are faced by any modern-day Nevada community. The support of the city government must have been costly to the taxpayers, for the movement to disincorporate followed quickly on the heels of the decline of the Big Bonanza. By an act of the legislature, approved February 26 and effective as of May 2, 1881, Virginia City was disincorporated, and control of the area passed into the hands of the county commissioners.

Of all the problems faced by the community, perhaps none was handled so ineffectively as that of fire protection. This was true in most mining camps and the reasons were generally the same: little or no attention was paid to fire prevention; the buildings for the most part were wooden construction and bunched together; the water supply was never entirely adequate; and the city depended entirely upon volunteer fire fighters. Added to these problems at Virginia City was the fact that for a good part of each year one could be certain that stiff winds, sometimes called "Washoe zephyrs," would fan any spark into a blazing inferno within minutes.

Virginia City had its share of fires, but it wasn't until the city was at the height of its glory that real disaster struck. In the early morning of October 26, 1875, a fire started in a small lodging house and within minutes had engulfed the main business section. The strong wind blowing from the west ensured the spread of the conflagration, and when efforts to contain the many blazes centering in the main part of the community proved futile, attention focused on the necessity of keeping the fire from the mine buildings, and more particularly, of keeping it from moving down the shafts. These efforts were generally successful in stopping the fire at the mouth of the shafts, although it did burn four hundred feet down the Ophir shaft before it was contained. Attempts to save the mine buildings were not so successful and the hoisting works of the Ophir and the Consolidated-Virginia were destroyed, as was the new Consolidated-Virginia mill.

Before the ashes had cooled, residents could see that the center of the city was destroyed, with damage estimated at between five and ten million dollars. Even more immediately disastrous, three important producing mines, the Consolidated-Virginia, the California, and the Ophir, were shut down temporarily. In spite of their losses, the mine owners and businessmen moved at once to rebuild. Within a few months new business houses and mine buildings had replaced those destroyed by fire. In addition, a second water line was constructed from the Sierra to Virginia City and a better system of pipelines and hydrants was provided for that community. Although Virginia City was rebuilt, its days as an important western metropolis were numbered. Production fell rapidly from a peak of $36,799,791 in 1876 to $1,247,732 in 1881. The population, which probably peaked during the heyday of the Big Bonanza in 1875 or 1876, declined from 10,917 in 1880 to 2,695 in 1900. The vibrant, aggressive city which once dreamed of becoming the Queen of the West became instead an aging dowager interested only in survival.

Comstock Era Politics

THE DOMINANCE OF THE COMSTOCK in Nevada's economy was paralleled by its dominance of the political scene. As would be expected from the events leading to Nevada's statehood, the influence of the Republican party was strong throughout the Comstock era, especially in respect to the Nevada congressional delegation. Until the rise of the Silver party in Nevada in 1892, the Democrats were able to elect only one United States senator for a single term and two members of the House, both for two terms. In state politics the Democrats did somewhat better, holding control of the governorship for twelve of the twenty-seven years through 1891. Within the state during the main producing years of the Comstock, the major political issues centered around the problems of revenue, particularly mining revenue, the assessment and rates of the Central Pacific and other railroads, and Chinese immigration.

THE BULLION TAX FIGHT

The first governor of Nevada, H. G. Blasdel, met the questions of revenue head-on when, in his first message to the legislature, he asked for an act that would erase the territorial debt of $264,000 and at the same time provide an operating revenue for the state. In answer, the legislature passed a tax bill on March 9, 1865, which included a property tax specifically favoring the mining interests. The act authorized a levy of $2.75 for each $100 of assessed valuation; $1.50 of this amount was marked for the county and $1.25 for the state. However, Section 99 of the act limited the levy on the proceeds of the mines to $1 for each $100 of assessed valuation, one-half for the county and one-half for the state. In addition, the law provided that $20 per ton was to be deducted for working the ore and that only three-fourths of the remainder would be taxed. Thus the mine owners got a three-way benefit in taxation, first in the state constitution, which specified that mines and mining claims were to be assessed on net proceeds only, and then in the revenue act of 1865, which allowed the deduction for working the ore and then taxed only a portion of the remainder.

The discriminatory aspects of the revenue act had been argued during and after passage, but not until the spring of 1867 was the act tested in the courts. In February, 1867, an action was brought before the court of Judge S. H. Wright of the Second Judicial District charging that Section 99 was discriminatory. From the district court the case was appealed to the Nevada Supreme Court which in April declared that section unconstitutional.[1] However, the court action meant little because a special session of the legislature had been called by Governor Blasdel in March to consider additional sources of revenue, since funds from the 1865 act had not been sufficient. The legislature passed two measures which

[1] The Nevada Supreme Court, in *State of Nevada* v. *Daniel E. Eastabrook,* 3 Nevada 173 (1867), stated that the legislature can make the tax on the products of mines neither greater nor less than on other property. The court also acknowledged "that the mines which constitute the greater part of the wealth of the state have for the last two years almost entirely escaped taxation, is true."

more than made up for the loss of Section 99 of the revenue act of 1865. The first provided for a deduction of $18 per ton on free ores and an exemption of $40 per ton on ores that required roasting or smelting; the second limited the bullion tax in Storey County to 25¢ on each $100 for county purposes, just one-half of what it had been under the 1865 act. The power of the Bank of California crowd was evident in these proceedings since Storey County was the only county so benefited.

The Bank Crowd acted again in 1871 after the discovery of rich ore in the Crown Point and Belcher mines indicated the need for further mining exemptions. Under a new bill passed in February of that year deductions were to be based on the value of the ore as follows: 90 percent of the cost of extraction for ore yielding $12 per ton or less; 80 percent for ore yielding between $12 and $30 per ton; 60 percent for ore yielding between $30 and $100; and 50 percent for ore yielding more than $100. An additional $15 per ton could be subtracted for ore that needed roasting.[2]

Opposition to the favored tax position of mining grew steadily in the years after 1867, and in 1875 the opposition, aided by a governor with livestock rather than mining interests, finally gained passage of a more equitable act. The 1875 measure ended the industry's special position by setting the county's share of the state tax on property, including mining property, at $1.50 per $100 of assessed valuation. An interesting aspect of the law was its sponsorship by John Piper, state senator from Storey County, an indication that even citizens of the Comstock were tired of Bank Crowd control. The new kings of the Comstock, the Bonanza firm, had neglected their political chores in allowing the tax law to pass without a legislative struggle, and they were now faced with a much heavier bullion tax than the Bank of California crowd paid during their control of the Comstock. Declaring the new law unconstitutional and refusing to pay taxes, the Bonanza group thus began the famous bullion tax fight that was carried on in the courts and the legislature from 1875 until a settlement was finally reached in 1883.

[2] A detailed explanation of the various mining revenue acts, including a table showing specifically how each revenue act affected mining property and proceeds, is included in Myron Angel, ed., *History of Nevada* (Oakland, Calif.: Thompson & West, 1881), pp. 123–30.

The Bonanza firm's refusal to pay their taxes brought political repercussions when the party conventions met the next year. Public pressure was such that both political parties placed resolutions in their platforms opposing changes that would favor mining property. In addition each candidate for the legislature, except in White Pine County, was asked to pledge himself not to vote for a reduction of the bullion tax. The attitude of the parties forced the Bonanza firm to take a more active part in the legislative session which met in January, 1877, and to seek the help of certain members of the Bank Crowd who were far more adept at influencing state legislatures.[3]

As a result of the mining industry's lobbying, a compromise bill was introduced before the senate during the 1877 session which in effect would reduce bullion tax by more than 30 percent. In spite of their pledges during the election campaign, enough legislators in both the senate and the assembly switched opinions to allow the measure to pass both houses. Governor L. R. Bradley vetoed the bill, on March 1st, strongly protesting against vested interests and asserting support of the people's concerns. Some of its advocates had suggested that approval of the measure would ensure the payment of back taxes by the owners of the Consolidated-Virginia and the California mines. Governor Bradley replied to that idea in the following words:

My answer is, that it does not become the dignity of a State to be dictated to by a couple of non-resident corporations, nor does experience teach us that a submission to the demands of wealth today will prevent it from doubling its demands tomorrow. If this Legislature, pledged as it is to the whole people of the State to protect them against the release of these foreign corporations from the payment of taxes upon their profits, choose to go back upon their pledges, and turn over the States, bound hand and foot, to these companies, I cannot help it, but no part of the crime shall rest upon my shoulders.

[3] Yerington Papers, Bancroft Library, University of California, Berkeley. In a letter to D. O. Mills, August 23, 1876, Henry M. Yerington, general manager of the V & T Railroad, wrote that John Mackay of the Bonanza firm had "finally made up his mind that he can't figure things to any extent in the Legislature without our assistance." In a later letter, February 10, 1877, Yerington indicated that one of the V & T lobbyists, A. C. Cleveland, would manage James G. Fair's fight against the bullion tax.

Bradley also pointed out that the measure violated the constitutional provision calling for a uniform and equal rate of assessment and taxation, and that the Nevada Supreme Court had held earlier that net proceeds of mines were subject to the same ad valorem taxation as other property. The veto message noted further the stand taken in both party platforms and a number of county conventions supporting equal taxation of mining property. The senate sustained Bradley's veto.[4]

The Comstock newspapers were unanimous in their bitter reaction to the governor's action. The *Virginia Evening Chronicle* called Bradley "Our Boss Lunatic" and went on to say, "We move for commission *de lunatico enquirendo* in his case, and that pending the inquiry pen and paper be carefully kept out of his way. In his hands they are as dangerous as a razor in the hands of a maniac." The *Territorial Enterprise* added, "He is old and decrepit, and it would be cowardice to abuse or insult him. . . . But would to God that he was a young man that we might publish how much we wish that he was dead." On the other hand, the *Eureka Republican* which had consistently opposed Bradley, stated, "Governor Bradley deserves well of the people of this State. We are always glad to do justice to a political opponent, and on this occasion we tender the Governor our hearty thanks for his action. He has, we believe, saved the already overburdened tax-payers . . . from the imposition of additional and unjust burdens." Bradley may well have had the support of the people, but not enough to re-elect him in 1878 to a third term; and the mine owners seemed to have won the battle when their candidate, John Kinkead, took over the governorship in 1879.[5]

[4] Bradley, a rancher by profession, in his veto message expressed many ideas that soon were put forward by the Populists. Nevada, *Journal of the Senate*, 8th Session, 1877, pp. 315–19.

[5] The Bonanza firm, while the legislative battle was proceeding, made an interesting attempt to avoid paying their mining taxes by arguing that the property belonged to the U.S. government and was not subject to state taxation. In *Forbes* v. *Gracey*, 94 U.S. 762 (1877), the United States Supreme Court, on May 7, 1877, held that "the moment mineral ore becomes detached from the soil of the public lands in which it is embedded, it becomes personal property, the ownership of which is in the man whose labor, capital and skill has discovered and developed the mine and extracted the ore." Thus the Bonanza group was thwarted from another direction in their attempt to avoid payment of taxes.

In spite of Bradley's defeat, it was soon apparent that the Bonanza firm would not be able to obtain legislation reducing the tax assessment. Consequently, in the early part of 1879 they paid their back taxes amounting to $290,275.72 and then sought legislative exemption from the penalties of $77,578.22 which had accrued from their failure to pay their taxes. A bill to effect such a compromise was introduced in the state senate in February, 1879, and passed that house and the assembly without difficulty. It was signed into law by the governor the next month but was challenged almost at once by the attorney general and was held unconstitutional by the Nevada Supreme Court as a special act. When the court in November, 1880, ordered the companies to pay the accrued penalties, the Bonanza firm decided to carry their appeal to the federal courts, even though the United States Supreme Court had held against them in the matter of their back taxes. Meanwhile, the mine owners made another effort to get legislative relief. In January, 1881, a new bill to exempt the Bonanza firm from the penalties was introduced in the state senate and again it passed both houses. This time, however, Governor Kinkead vetoed the bill because the earlier act had been found unconstitutional by the Nevada Supreme Court. Shortly thereafter the United States Supreme Court ruled against the company and ordered payment of the penalties. The Bonanza firm finally paid its taxes and penalties in 1883. In spite of their final victory over the Bonanza firm, it is clear that Storey County and the state of Nevada were denied a major source of revenue during these years by virtue of the political control exerted on the legislature by the mining interests.

RAILROADS AND NEVADA POLITICS

The railroad owners and their lobbyists were much more effective than the Bonanza firm in keeping a watchful eye on the Nevada legislature. Although the Central Pacific did not obtain a subsidy from the state, it did not lose interest in Nevada politics, nor did Nevadans lose sight of this railroad monopoly which discriminated against the state so blatantly throughout the Comstock era and into the twentieth century.

The Central Pacific Railroad gained and held a strong hand in Nevada politics by means of a resident agent or lobbyist, by control of the United States senators from Nevada, and by economic coercion. The Central Pacific often inadvertently received additional aid in the Nevada legislature through the activities of Henry M. Yerington, general manager of the V & T Railroad, who labored long and conscientiously to ensure that each Nevada legislature would be favorably disposed toward the interests of the railroad.

The basic grievances of Nevadans against the Central Pacific and the short line railroads within the state were similar to those which were then being expressed in other parts of the United States and which, in the 1880s, led to national regulatory legislation. The two most consistent sources of protest against the railroads were the nefarious long- and short-haul practice whereby goods from New York or Chicago to Reno were charged for as though the articles were routed to San Francisco and back to Reno, and the matter of equitable assessment and taxation of railroad property in the various counties of the state. The evidence against the Central Pacific on these counts was substantial. Rollin Daggett, Nevada's representative to Congress from 1879 to 1881, in a famous speech before Congress just before the end of the 1881 session, lashed out against the unfair discrimination of the Central Pacific, citing a number of specific instances to prove his case.[6] Another bitter protest against the railroad came from Governor Kinkead, who in his last message to the legislature stated:

The discriminations of the Central Pacific Railroad Company against Nevada continue unchanged and unabated. We are the victims of an injustice in the matter of transportation charges by this railroad company which is well nigh intolerable. The energies of our people have been fettered, the growth of the State retarded, and the development of its resources hampered by the outrageous exactions imposed upon us by this corporation. Thus far appeals to the merciless autocracy directing its policy have been without effect. Neither have the oft-repeated memorials

[6] Daggett pointed out, for example, that the railroad charged Nevadans the traffic for goods shipped from New York to San Francisco and then, additionally, from San Francisco to the Nevada points, although the goods were left off as the train passed through Nevada on the way to San Francisco. Thus a carload of coal oil would cost $300 from New York to San Francisco, $536 from New York to Reno, and $716 from New York to Winnemucca. Daggett suggested that the railroad had overcharged Nevadans about $30 million in ten years. "Railroad Wrongs in Nevada," U.S., Congress, House, *Congressional Record*, 46th Cong., 3d sess., 2, pt. 3, Appendix, pp. 181–90.

sent to the National Congress proved thus far effectual. We are bound hand and foot; our industries languish, and the State which should be prosperous, is struggling on the verge of retrogression. In other States and Territories concessions and reductions in transportation rates have been made by railroad corporations to meet the public demand. In some, such concessions have been compelled; in others, policy has dictated fair treatment. In Nevada, neither justice nor policy have given relief. I commend this matter to your earnest consideration.[7]

In spite of the continuing protest against the Central Pacific and the Nevada short lines, however, the state legislature made no serious effort to extend its regulatory powers over the railroads during the Comstock era. Some attempts were made to change the assessment procedures, but where such laws were passed the railroads were successful in gaining their repeal and in fighting assessments in court. The Central Pacific also threatened and on occasion carried out economic coercion against Nevada counties which tried to establish a more equitable assessment or to obtain additional taxes from the railroads. The usual practice was to raise freight rates in that county or to drop the rate on competing items from California until the Nevada producers were forced to drop their action.

The activities of the Central Pacific's lobbyists in Nevada were, no doubt, of some importance in keeping the state legislature from passing unfriendly legislation. It is clear from the Yerington correspondence that the Central Pacific agent, Stephen Gage, cooperated with Yerington to some extent at least in trying to elect the "right" people to the Nevada legislature and in helping to defeat antirailroad legislation if and when it arose in either house. However, the Central Pacific was much more concerned about national legislation and relied upon the Virginia and Truckee Railroad lobbyists to take care of Nevada developments, assuming correctly that the latter would fight any legislative proposals to control railroads in the state. The attitude of the Central Pacific officials infuriated Yerington and on occasion he sent them stinging rebukes. One such letter, which is also one of the most revealing documents about railroad action in Nevada, pointed out that

---

[7] "Second Biennial Message of Governor John H. Kinkead," in *Appendix to Journals of Senate and Assembly, 1883* (Carson City, Nev., 1883), 1: 12.

during every Nevada Legislature since 1869 bills have been introduced to
regulate freight and fares and many other matters connected with the
working of railroads in this state, most of them have been of a blackmailing
character requiring *Coin* to prevent them from being introduced or to get
them out of the road after introduction. This Co. has put up the Coin
in large sums every session and the result has been not one bill inimical
to railroads has been passed during all these years and I have yet to learn
that your Co. has advanced one cent to assist in beating them. . . . Then
in order to have friends at Court we have spent thousands at every
primary and Elections and have always succeeded in placing good honest
men in the Legislature on whom our Co. could rely when threatened with
outrageous blackmailing legislation. I am not aware that your Co. spent a
dollar in these fights or taken any necessary action or part in them for the
reason, as we have been advised by the leading officers of your Co., that
they did not care a cent for any actions that might be taken by the
Legislature of Nevada so far as the C. P. RR was concerned that Congress
was the only power recognized and the consequence was we were obliged
to bear it without complaint although it was rough, for we found the
Legislature had power to regulate certain matters on *all* roads within the
borders of the state such as taxation, forcing Co.s to fence their roads, to
maintain a number of crossings, to put in cattle guards at each crossing,
etc., etc. . . . we "stood in" with our forces and assisted Mr. Gage to
defeat those bills solely and wholly for a/c of your Co.[8]

Yerington later noted that Gage had agreed to share some of the
expenses of the legislature, and there is further indication from
Yerington that he received some help from the Central Pacific. It
appears that direct involvement of the Central Pacific in activities
of the Nevada Legislature increased in the 1880s and 1890s, particularly after C. C. Wallace replaced Gage as their Nevada agent.[9]

The part played by Yerington and the Bank Crowd in preventing
the Nevada legislature from passing laws to control the railroads
appears to have been quite effective, particularly from the early
1870s to the late 1890s. Yerington looked upon himself as a master

[8] Yerington, to A. N. Towne, San Francisco, January 11, 1879, Yerington
Papers, vol. 2.
[9] Stephen Gage moved to Virginia City from California in 1862 and almost
at once became associated with the railroad interests in Nevada. He proved so
valuable to the Central Pacific that he was called to California to assist the
railroad in its political machinations. In the 1880s he was replaced by a
Eureka, Nevada, politician, Charles C. Wallace, commonly referred to as "Black"
Wallace because of his unyielding stand for the Republican party.

lobbyist and in his correspondence constantly boasted about his accomplishments in such statements as the following:

I have looked over the returns [1876] and honestly believe the next legislature will be composed of men far more friendly to the V & T RR than any we have had for years. . . . our man Boardman, has a majority of nearly 200! we carried the Assembly, Sheriff, County Commissioners, Treasury, etc. *all friendly to us* (and God knows they ought to be) and so we have Washoe in the hollow of our hand for many a year to come if desirable. The fact is with Washoe, Ormsby, Douglas, and Esmeralda under our control no legislature could really get away with us.[10]

He continued his lobbying almost until his death in 1910, although the silver question so dominated Nevada politics in the 1890s that antirailroad legislation was pushed into the background.

Yerington and the railroad interests were able to maintain their dominance by a number of devices. First, they literally bought legislators who promised to work for the railroad interest. The V & T had agents in a number of counties to help in this work. During the 1870s and 1880s Yerington tended to supervise the western counties of Nevada and employed A. C. Cleveland to "take care of" the eastern counties. Second, Yerington attempted to control the delegates to the county and then the state political convention (Republican) and attended the convention meetings to use his influence in obtaining favorable platforms. Third, the railroad maintained control of the legislature, once it had convened, by means of lobbying and additional money if necessary and by liberal use of railroad passes. Here again the services of A. C. Cleveland were important. Just how much money the V & T spent in such activities probably never will be known, but it must have been substantial, for Yerington notes in letters that Cleveland alone was paid $3,000 in 1876 to help state senators sympathetic to the V & T in Eureka and White Pine counties.[11] The results must have warranted the effort and the expediture, otherwise hard-headed business men like Mills and Sharon, presumably, would not have continued these practices.

[10] Yerington to D. O. Mills, Nov. 6, 1876, Yerington Papers, vol. 11.
[11] Yerington to D. O. Mills, Sept. 5, 1876, Yerington Papers, vol. 10. The Yerington correspondence is very revealing of methods used by the railroad lobbyists.

In keeping with their greater concern with the national situation, the Central Pacific was much more interested in controlling Nevada's representatives to Congress, particularly the two senators. The owners of the railroad apparently made overtures to both Nye and Stewart shortly after their selection to represent Nevada in the United States Senate. Stewart received many favors from the railroad during his first ten years in the Senate and was generally considered favorable to railroad interests from that time forward. Some attention was given to cultivating Nye's friendship, but he apparently didn't wear well with the Central Pacific officials and they made little or no effort to have him reelected when his first six-year term was over in 1872.

Nye's record during his eight years in the United States Senate had not been spectacular. He had made a number of speeches which were well received, but he had not sponsored any major legislation, and as his term drew to a close it became apparent that he was becoming somewhat senile. Without money of his own and without major sources of financial support, Nye appeared to have almost no chance of reelection. Consequently, two Comstock millionaires, William Sharon of the Bank Crowd and John P. Jones, former superintendent of the Crown Point mine, decided to try for the Senate post.

As the election campaign got under way it was clear that Sharon could not match Jones's popularity with the people, nor did he have the support of the important newspapers, particularly the *Territorial Enterprise,* which, under the editorship of Joe Goodman, came out strongly for Jones. Consequently, he attempted to discredit Jones by implicating him in a purported attempt to manipulate the stock market by starting the Yellow Jacket fire. When these efforts failed, Sharon withdrew from the race, leaving Nye the field against Jones. It was an uneven contest from the start, for Nye had no money and Jones had a great deal and was willing to use it. When the legislature met in Carson City in January, 1873, Jones received fifty-three votes to seventeen for the nearest competitor, Major W. W. McCoy. Nye's name was never introduced. Jones is reported to have spent between five and eight hundred thousand dollars buying candidates who, if elected, would support him for the Senate post. The results in the legislative voting attested to the success of such procedures and opened

the door to others with money who also might have political ambitions.

Jones presented something of a problem to the owners of the
Central Pacific since he had entered the Senate as an antimonopolist
and, unlike Stewart and Nye, was independently rich so the methods
used to control the first two senators obviously wouldn't work in the
case of Jones. Central Pacific officials gave some thought to a scheme
to show how Jones had purchased his Senate seat. It was hoped that
any such disclosure at the time when the Grant scandals were
becoming public and when the liberal Republican movement was
strong would force Jones into political exile. But if the Central
Pacific management had any such intentions, they waited too long to
put them into effect.[12]

Sharon received a second chance for the United States Senate in
1874 when William M. Stewart announced that he was leaving the
Senate to engage in a number of mining ventures and to reenter law
practice, and he moved quickly to establish himself as a strong
candidate. In February of 1874 he purchased the *Territorial Enterprise* and replaced the editor, Goodman, with Rollin M. Daggett.
Almost at once the *Enterprise* changed its tone of hostility and, from a
man "feared, hated and despised," Sharon turned into one who "by
his sagacity, energy and nerve . . . has amassed a fortune."

Sharon's entrance into the Senate race immediately drew Adolph
Sutro as an opponent because Sutro could not afford to have
Sharon in the Senate to continue his efforts to block completion
of the Sutro tunnel. Sutro did not have funds to equal Sharon's,
but he was a persuasive speaker and endowed with tremendous energy. He helped found and gave financial support to a newspaper,
the *Daily Independent,* and ran under the banner of a new party,
officially called the Independents, but more commonly known as
the "Dolly Vardens." He took his lantern slide lecture to just about
every community in the state. However, his cause was in vain, for
he could not match Sharon's lavish expenditure of money to purchase seats in the Nevada legislature. The election of 1874 did not
return a single Independent candidate; consequently, when the
legislature met in January, 1875, Sutro's name was not presented.
Sharon was selected by a vote of forty-nine to twenty-one over his

[12]Huntington, later was able to do a favor for Jones and thus won his support.

nearest opponent, although before the vote was taken, a resolution was introduced in both houses to the effect that "it is a notorious and indisputable fact that William Sharon, candidate for senator, now is, and for more than three years past has been residing with his family, at his only and permanent family residence on Sutter Street in the City of San Francisco." The resolution was ruled out of order in the assembly and tabled by a vote of sixteen to nine in the senate. Sharon was reported to have spent at least as much in 1874 as Jones had in 1872 in supporting proper candidates for the legislature.

Sharon's record in the United States Senate is one of the worst in the history of that legislative body. His record of inaction is unbelieveable. He was seated at only five sessions and was recorded on less than 1 percent of all roll calls. He never introduced a bill and if he spoke on one it is not recorded. More important to Nevadans, he was absent from Washington during the important discussions on the silver question. His absences from Washington were exceeded only by those from the state he was supposed to represent; his only visits to Nevada during his incumbency in the Senate came while passing through the state on his way to or from the east.

Such a record was an open invitation to his political opponents. The Democrats, who had never elected a United States Senator from Nevada, now saw an opportunity to do so. The candidate considered most available—mainly because of his money—was another Comstock millionaire, James G. Fair. The circumstances surrounding Fair's choice were summed up by a well-known Comstock historian: "Fair did not seek the office; it was wished on him by the hungry Democratic politicans who had never had a 'sack' at their disposal in a senatorial campaign. His well known lack of every qualification for that high office was scarcely considered. . . . He had taken so little interest in politics that he 'hardly knew which party he belonged to,' as he admitted later."[13]

Fair may have lacked initial interest in the post and he certainly lacked political experience, but he had money, the essential ingredient for victory, and he was willing to spend it. Sharon made some efforts to indicate his availability for reelection, but even he

[13] "The Mackay Story," Grant Smith Papers, vol. 1D, pp. 604–6, Bancroft Library, University of California, Berkeley.

was unwilling to spend money on an obviously futile cause. In spite of Sharon's reluctance to wage an expensive campaign, the Fair forces could not be certain of victory unless they could reverse the Nevada tradition of Republican-dominated legislatures. To achieve this Fair and his supporters used the device which had proven so successful for his predecessors. Personal representatives with seemingly unlimited funds, commonly referred to as "sack bearers," were sent into each county of the state. H. M. Yerington, a Republican stalwart, noted pessimistically that "Fair spent about $40,000 in Washoe and Eureka counties" and that in White Pine County "his people freely offered from $40 to $80 for a vote and of course that knocked [A.C.] Cleveland clear out of time." Yerington pointed to another useful vote-getting device that the Fair crowd appropriated from the Republicans when he wrote that the Democrats are "naturalizing the French, Italians and general floating population who are always willing to sell their votes— heretofore they have voted Republican and through them the party has won—there are large numbers in Washoe, Ormsby, and Douglas counties and Fair is busy taking them in, hence it now looks as if we would lose all these counties and all but Eureka in the East."[14]

As it turned out, Yerington was too optimistic, for when the election returns were in the Democrats had carried all the counties except Ormsby. It appeared that Fair's selection would be no more than a formality. However, just before the session opened, the perennial Senate hopeful Adolph Sutro appeared, rented rooms in the Ormsby House, and indicated he had unlimited funds to capture some of the Fair men and assure his own election. When asked why he had not contested Fair during the election for legislative seats, he replied that he had sent a man to Nevada but that Fair had silenced him with money. At one point Sutro allegedly had thirty-five members of the legislature willing to renege on their pledges to Fair if some legitimate reason for doing so could be found. A scheme was developed by the Sutro forces whereby certain legislators, pledged to Fair, would be accused of buying votes for their election. The supposition was that if warrants for the arrest

[14] Yerington to D. O. Mills, Nov. 4, 1880, and October 21, 1880, Yerington Papers, vol. 13.

of these men could be sworn it would result in the collapse of the Fair candidacy. Before the trap could be sprung, Fair found out about the scheme and was able to thwart efforts to obtain the proper warrants.

Neither Sharon's name nor Sutro's appeared before the legislature when it met in 1881. Fair was easily elected, receiving fifty-two votes to twenty for his nearest competitor, Thomas Wren; Rollin Daggett received one vote.[15] Fair's activities in the United States Senate beginning in 1881 were not much higher in quality than those of his predecessor, although he did attend a little more regularly.

THE CHINESE QUESTION

Another consistent state political issue of the Comstock era resulted from the completion of the Central Pacific Railroad in May of 1869. That event threw thousands of Chinese on the labor market in Nevada, adding to the antagonism toward that race which had developed shortly after their arrival in the state.[16]

The first major display of that antagonism broke out when William Sharon in 1869 employed a number of Chinese to help build the Virginia and Truckee Railroad. By that time labor on the Comstock had become fairly well organized and Sharon was allowed to proceed only after he had signed a pledge not to employ Chinese within the limits of Virginia City and Gold Hill. It should be recalled that when the Virginia City Miner's Union attempted in 1869 to form a state workingmen's association, one of its primary purposes was "to prevent the firm seating of Chinese labor in our midst." Although a state labor organization was not formed at that time, union strength on the Comstock and elsewhere in Nevada forced a legislative resolution in 1871 against the use of Chinese labor on public grounds in the state.

For the next few years anti-Chinese sentiment in Nevada seemed

---

[15] After two unsuccessful tries, Sutro was content to leave Nevada politics and confine himself to California affairs. Sharon returned to San Francisco and almost at once got involved in one of the most lurid divorce cases in the history of California. See Brooks W. MacCracken, "Althea and the Judges," *American Heritage* 18 (June 1967): 60–63:.

[16] Although the first Chinese were brought to Nevada in the 1850s by Reese and other Mormons to help construct water ditches for irrigation, it wasn't until they posed an economic threat to the miners that opposition developed.

to be disappearing. In 1875, however, a good indication that it was still alive came when a concurrent resolution was passed by the Nevada legislature appealing to Nevada's representatives in Congress to use their efforts to modify the Burlingame Treaty to prevent the importation of contractual Chinese labor.[17] From this date until the passage of the Chinese Exclusion Act in 1882, anti-Chinese agitation in Nevada continued to recur.

Between 1876 and 1878 anti-Chinese societies were formed in towns from Tuscarora in the east to Reno and Carson City in the west, and a number of anti-Chinese riots occurred throughout the state. Typical of these was the demonstration which erupted on August 4, 1878, when Reno citizens attempted to take advantage of a fire which had broken out in Chinatown by ordering the Chinese to leave the city within forty-eight hours. Rioting followed the issuance of the ultimatum but finally order was restored and the Chinese were allowed to stay.

The popular outcry against the Chinese in these years was soon reflected on the political scene. Governor Bradley took several pages of his 1877 biennial message to the legislature to list the grievances against the Chinese, pointing out that "in every instance where public opinion has permitted the Chinese to labor, they have driven out and supplanted white labor, both male and female." By 1878 agitation against the Chinese was sufficient to cause both the Republicans and the Democrats to include anti-Chinese planks in their platforms. The Republican statement was particularly strong, not only opposing Asiatic immigration, but advocating the use of "just and peaceful" methods to deport the Chinese already in Nevada. Senator John P. Jones, up for re-election to the Senate, recognized the strength of the anti-Chinese feeling by delivering a speech in Carson City in November 1878, in which he summarized the evils of Oriental immigration, paying particular attention to the Chinese threat to American industry and labor.

Anti-Chinese sentiment in Nevada increased in intensity with the mining decline which began on the Comstock in 1878 and

[17] The Burlingame Treaty of 1868 assured most-favored-nation treatment of Chinese residing or visiting in the United States. The demands for cheap labor on the Pacific Coast at that time brought thousands of Chinese to the United States.

was reflected statewide the next year with a mineral production of approximately 50 percent of the 1878 total. The 1879 legislature took cognizance of the problem by passing several acts which, in one way or another, were aimed against the Chinese. The first provided for the voters to express their opinion on Chinese immigration on the 1880 general election ballot. A second act attempted to prohibit Chinese immigration into Nevada on the ground that all the Chinese who had entered Nevada had done so under labor contracts which were tantamount to slavery and involuntary servitude and thus contrary to state laws. It also prohibited companies from paying wages to persons defined by the act, that is, those in slavery or involuntary servitude. A third act authorized aliens and nonresidents to own and control real estate in Nevada, but made a specific exception of subjects of the Chinese Empire. A fourth act prohibited the employment of Mongolians or Chinese in or about buildings or grounds belonging to the state and stipulated that companies seeking contracts for state public works or railroad fanchises must agree not to employ Mongolians or Chinese. In addition, the 1879 legislature passed a number of anti-Chinese resolutions. One of these asked the Nevada representatives in Congress to vote for the passage of anti-Chinese legislation which was then before that body. Another congratulated James G. Blaine for his stand against Chinese immigration, and a joint memorial to President Hayes asked him to approve the Chinese Immigration Act of 1879.

When Hayes's veto prevented a national solution to the problem in 1879, it was apparent that the issue was far from dead, either locally or nationally. In 1880 both national party platforms included anti-Chinese planks, the Republicans stating that they would seek to restrain and limit Chinese immigration and the Democrats guaranteeing that they would amend the Burlingame Treaty to restrict Chinese. On the state level the two major parties tried to outdo each other in expressing anti-Chinese feeling. That the parties had judged the political winds correctly in Nevada was apparent when the 1880 general election results were tabulated. Of 17,442 votes cast on the resolution regarding Chinese immigration, only 183 favored allowing Chinese to enter the United States.

The 1881 session of the Nevada legislature sent another resolution to Congress asking for national legislation to restrict Chinese immigration. As a result of continuing pressure from California, Nevada, and other western states, Congress passed a Chinese exclusion act in 1882. Contrary to general expectations, the new law did not eliminate the Chinese question as a political issue in Nevada, although it may have helped to change the focus of action from the state to the local political arena. Both political parties continued to incorporate anti-Chinese planks in their platforms, and anti-Chinese agitation continued throughout the 1880s in the form of riots and boycotts. The boycotts, which increased after 1885, illustrated a change in the anti-Chinese fight from the political to the economic area. Feeling against the Chinese in Nevada declined rapidly as the decrease in Chinese population in the state lessened the threat to white labor.

CHAPTER 9

The Depression Period, 1880–1900

FROM THE DECLINE of the Comstock Lode until the Tonopah mineral discoveries in 1900, Nevada suffered a severe economic depression—the price paid for an almost total dependence on the mining industry. In view of the resources of the state, it was inevitable that mining would play an important role in the economy, yet a more enlightened political leadership might have attempted to broaden the economic base before the need was made obvious by the depression. As it was, the live-for-today philosophy engendered by the mining frontier cycle of discovery, boom, and bust so permeated the Nevada atmosphere that it seemed only normal to exploit each new mineral find as quickly as possible before moving on to the next one. And although Nevadans were quick to blame the Comstock exploiters who financed banks, railroads, and telegraph and other companies in California and elsewhere, it should be remembered that investment opportunities in Nevada at that time were limited, to say the least. The Comstock itself gave Nevadans a false sense of security, for each successive depression on the lode from 1864 to 1878 was followed by a bonanza greater than the previous one. When the looked-for bonanza did not materialize on the Comstock after 1878, Nevadans sought a return to prosperity by a widespread search for new mineral areas and a belated attempt to increase agricultural, particularly livestock, production.

Many Nevadans chose to blame the Central Pacific Railroad for the depression, maintaining that discriminatory rates and other abuses had retarded the growth of the state. Throughout the two decades of the depression there was almost continuous pressure in the state legislature to lower railroad rates and levy fairer assessments. It is difficult to evaluate the strength of that pressure since many such efforts no doubt were what H. M. Yerington, lobbyist for the V & T, referred to as "blackmailing" schemes, for with one or two minor exceptions, legislative attempts to control the railroads during this period were unsuccessful.

Ultimately, the failure to find new and important mineral areas, the inability to increase agricultural production, and the impossibility of achieving meaningful changes in railroad rates led state officials to seek economic recovery for Nevada by joining two national political movements, the irrigation-conservation campaign and the fight for remonetization of silver. The story of the various attempts to regain prosperity follows.

Mining Developments, 1880–1900

The search for new mineral areas to replace the dying Comstock Lode proved extremely frustrating during the 1880s, for not only were no important mining discoveries made, but many promising areas which had been opened in the sixties and seventies declined rapidly in the eighties. This was particularly true of Austin, overrated from the beginning, where production fell to $94,596 in 1890, and of Pioche, whose production plummeted to $4,073 in 1884 and never really recovered until the beginning of World War I. Even Eureka, which had produced over $30,000,000 in the 1870s and appeared to be the most likely successor to the Comstock, suffered a marked decline after 1885 and in the decade of the 1890s produced only $2,468,299.

Two other old camps, Candelaria and Tuscarora, raised high hopes when their mineral production began to jump in the later 1870s. Candelaria, located in Mineral County in southwestern Nevada, was discovered by a group of Mexicans in 1864. Little was heard about it until 1876, when it produced nearly a million and a half dollars. A production of approximately $5,000,000 in the four years from 1880 through 1883 caused the camp to be hailed as another Comstock Lode, but a yield of only $26,616 the following year returned its boosters to reality. Although Candelaria had a slight revival between 1885 and 1891, it sank to near oblivion after that. Tuscarora, located in Elko County in northeastern Nevada, dated from a placer discovery made in 1867 by John and Steve Beard. The camp's first recorded production of $7,000 in 1875 was not impressive, but when the figure jumped to over $1,000,000 in 1878 the familiar cry of "another Comstock" was heard. Again, however, the cry was premature; Tuscarora was not destined to become even another Eureka or another Austin. Its annual production, which never again reached $1,000,000, fell to $41,396 in 1895.

Thus, as Nevada entered the decade of the nineties, not only was the Comstock continuing to decline, but the other mineral areas which had taken up some of the slack in the 1880s, were petering out. Annual production, which had ranged near the eight-million-dollar mark throughout that decade, reached a low of $1,995,830 in 1894. It would have dropped even more except for the discovery of gold at Delamar in Lincoln County.

The Delamar boom was initiated in 1891 when John E. Ferguson and Joseph Sharp found gold approximately forty miles southwest of Pioche. The first rush to the district established the town of Golden City, a mining community whose few weeks of life marked a record in decline even among Nevada ghost towns. Golden City gave way to a new town, Helene, a short distance to the south, but the development of the mines proved premature and by the end of 1892 Helene was also on the decline. The entrance of Captain J. R. DeLamar into the district in 1894 brought about the first real exploitation of the mines and the establishment of the new town of Delamar. Coming as it did when Nevada mining had reached an all-time low, the discovery brought thousands of people to the district and launched once again the familiar pattern of discovery, boom, and bust. Delamar produced very well from 1895 through 1900—a total of nearly $9 million for those years—and the district was, during that period, the main sustenance of mining in Nevada. It wasn't enough, however, and as the decade closed, the Nevada mining industry was still looking for that "other Comstock."

AGRICULTURAL DEVELOPMENTS, 1880–1900

The declining fortunes of the mining industry led many Nevadans in the 1880s to take a fresh look at the agricultural possibilities of the state. It had been demonstrated during the seventies that Nevada had large amounts of land suitable for the grazing of cattle, sheep, and horses. A spectacular rise in the number of livestock on Nevada ranges in the first five years of the 1880s supported the hope that further agricultural, particularly livestock, development might revive the lagging economy. Although the number of livestock continued to rise, however, the price per head fluctuated sharply: in 1874, the 135,000 head of cattle in the state were worth $3,261,000, yet in 1895, 255,000 head were worth only $2,783,000. By 1899, on the eve of the second great mining boom, the total valuation of cattle in Nevada reached $6,429,000, a figure less than the annual mineral production as late as 1890. The total value of sheep and horses added little to the total for cattle; in 1900, the best year of the period, the total value of sheep was only $2,018,400 and of horses, $1,264,000.[1] It was quite obvious by the middle of the 1880s that agriculture would never replace mining in the state's economy unless additional water could be obtained.

THE FIGHT FOR MORE WATER

Nevada's surveyor general in his first annual report in 1865 recognized the need for additional water when he wrote, "Many millions of acres of land in this state now comparatively worthless, would be valuable if irrigated." In fact, it had been evident from prehistoric times, when the pueblo dwellers in the southern part of the state practiced a crude type of irrigation, to the first white settlements along the Carson, Truckee, Humboldt, Muddy, and

[1] There were 351,000 cattle, 696,000 sheep, and 79,000 horses in Nevada in 1900. A competent history of Nevada agriculture is long overdue.

Virgin rivers, that agriculture in Nevada was virtually impossible without irrigation. Although the need for state aid was recognized at an early date, there was no great pressure toward that end until the mining decline in the 1880s focused attention on the necessity to diversify the economy.

Beginning in 1885 attempts were made to obtain legislation in support of irrigation and reclamation projects for Nevada. However, nothing of significance occurred until 1889, when the legislature passed two laws which at least gave some encouragement to such developments.[2] The first recognized public ownership of unappropriated water of natural springs and allowed that water to be used by builders of irrigation projects. The second established a Board of Reclamation and Internal Improvements and authorized it to divide the state into reclamation districts, appoint district superintendents and supervise the survey and construction of reservoirs and canals. The measure also appropriated $100,000 for the construction of such works.

At the national level, Senator William M. Stewart, who had been reelected to the United States Senate in 1887 after a twelve-year retirement, quickly became a leader in the fight for irrigation of desert lands. An expert at interpreting the political winds, Stewart, in his victory address, reviewed the problem of arid lands and set forth his solution, which included extensive hydrographic and topographical surveys of streams usable for irrigation and either direct financial aid to the states or the surrender of public lands to states for reclamation purposes. In the Senate, Stewart proposed the creation of a Senate Committee on Irrigation and was named chairman of it. He also supported an act authorizing hydrographic investigations under the direction of John Wesley Powell, head of the U.S. Geological Survey.

The Senate Committee on Irrigation, accompanied by Powell as an advisor, toured the arid states of the West in the summer of 1889, holding hearings in a number of cities including Nevada's state capital. The State Board of Reclamation and Internal Improvements met with the committee and presented a report which

[2] In 1885 Governor Adams asked the legislature for a hydrographic survey. The legislature did not act on the suggestion but passed a law establishing a State Agricultural Society. In 1887 the legislature provided for a State Bureau of Immigration to encourage colonization in the state.

asked, among other items, for government aid for Nevada "at a time in its history when its needs are more pressing than at any period since its organization as a state." The report closed on a plaintive plea that recognized the state's impotency: "Can the General Government refuse to render assistance or will it allow one of its sovereign states to languish?"

Although the Board of Reclamation did little else and went out of existence when the 1891 legislature repealed the act which had established it, the irrigation issue was not dead. Helping to keep it alive during the 1890s was a series of National Irrigation Congresses held annually in various western cities from 1891 through 1900, with the exception of 1892. These meetings introduced a new political figure, Francis G. Newlands, to Nevada politics and to the national movement to reclaim the arid West.

Born in Mississippi in 1848, Newlands moved to the West after completing his education at Yale and the Columbia Law School. He was admitted to the California bar in 1870 and began practicing law in San Francisco. His marriage to Senator Sharon's daughter brought his first contacts with Nevada, although he didn't become deeply involved in state affairs until 1886, when he was appointed a trustee of the Sharon estate. For the next two years this position brought him to Nevada on numerous occasions and in 1888 he decided to make the state his permanent home.[3] Politically ambitious, he recognized immediately that irrigation and silver were the main political issues before the Nevada voters and proceeded to become a recognized expert in each field.

In an interview for a Reno newspaper in February, 1889, Newlands suggested the need for the planning and construction of

[3] Newlands had campaigned for the United States Senate in California in 1886 against George Hearst. After his defeat he left California in order to continue the *Sharon* v. *Althea Hill* case in federal court under diversity of citizenship since he had lost all the cases against Miss Hill in the California courts. This unusual case had started when Sarah Althea Hill produced a paper which she claimed was a declaration of marriage signed by William Sharon. She sued for a divorce and after Sharon's death demanded her share of his estate. Newlands had first entered the case as Sharon's son-in-law and continued it, first from New York City and then from Nevada, as one of the executors of the estate. His decision to take up residence in Nevada probably was encouraged by Senator Stewart, at whose Carson City home Newlands and his second wife spent Christmas of 1888. The material on Newlands in this chapter comes mainly from William Lilley III, *The Early Career of Francis G. Newlands*, (Ann Arbor, Mich.: University Microfilms, 1967).

reservoirs and for extensive surveys of water resources and water usage. He recommended that Congress act on water problems impossible of solution by the states and that the national government cede lands within the arid states which could be reclaimed. His concern with the subject was rewarded by his selection as a Nevada delegate to the first irrigation congress, which was held at Salt Lake City in September, 1891.[4]

The first two irrigation congresses (the second was held at Los Angeles in 1893) supported the idea of the cession of arid federal lands to the states, but with the states controlling reclamation projects within their borders. Congress answered the pressure for such legislation in 1894, with the passage of the Carey Act authorizing the secretary of the interior to donate areas not to exceed one million acres to any of the arid states, provided that those states irrigate, reclaim, and occupy the tracts. Most of the western states, including Nevada, were in no financial position to take advantage of the act, however, and in the first five years of its operation only Wyoming actually developed lands under its provisions. Nevada did try to implement the Carey Act by the passage of a bill in 1897 which was designed to stimulate immigration, create additional taxable property, and promote the development of agriculture and mining. Under its terms the state would act as agent for individuals who filed claims through the office of the State Land Register upon proof of compliance with the provisions of the Carey Act. Technicalities in the Carey Act and in the Nevada law prevented the processing of all but a few such claims.

Although the irrigation congresses continued to meet during the 1890s, the national depression and the opposition of easterners to any program which would add to the farm surplus made it impossible to achieve any worthwhile legislation. The chances for a workable reclamation program for the arid West seemed quite remote at the turn of the century. Both national political parties in 1900 favored reclamation, but opposition in Congress was still powerful and President McKinley refused to support legislation for federal reclamation projects. An assassin's bullet on September 6, 1901, brought to the presidency Theodore Roosevelt, whose

[4] Stewart had invited Newlands to tour through Montana, Idaho, Washington, and Oregon with the Congressional Committee on Irrigation and Reclamation in 1889 and Newlands no doubt benefited from the contacts he made then.

help was important, perhaps even vital, in securing congressional action. In his message to Congress in December, 1901, he recommended the construction of great storage works to equalize the flow of streams and to save flood waters, pointing out that the undertaking was too great for private efforts and was a proper national function. He also suggested that lands reclaimed should be reserved for actual settlers and the cost of the dams and reservoirs should be repaid by the land reclaimed. These ideas and others had been formulated by congressional reclamation leaders at a meeting at Newlands's home and were incorporated in the so-called Newlands bill. Introduced in the House by Newlands and in the Senate by Senator Henry C. Hansbrough of North Dakota, it became law on June 17, 1902.

Nevada's fight for more water during the eighties and nineties was largely an exercise in futility until sufficient pressure was built up to bring about a national approach to the problem. The campaign was started much too late to aid the state's lagging economy before 1900; however, there is little reason to believe, on the basis of the later fight for reclamation, that Nevadans could have achieved any signficant increase of their agricultural resources had they initiated the movement earlier.

SILVER POLITICS, 1880–1900

The depression in Nevada's mining industry placed the spotlight on another political issue which began to attract national attention in the late 1870s. The so-called silver question originated in the passage by Congress of the Mint Act of 1873, more commonly known as the "crime of '73." The act, ostensibly at least, was intended to revise and update the United States monetary system. In its final form it made no provision for the coinage of silver dollars. However, early versions of the bill did provide for a silver dollar, and silverites later charged Senator John Sherman of Ohio, its sponsor, with conspiring with national and international bankers to put the United States on a gold standard. According to this reasoning, demonetization of silver would increase the demand for gold and the purchasing value of the gold dollar would rise, to the advantage of creditors and the disadvantage of the debtor class—the common man—as well as to the detriment of the silver industry. In spite of the conspiracy charge by the silverites, recent research indicates that the basic motivation of Sherman and others in sponsoring silver demonetization was to protect the public credit.[5]

In any event, it appears that during the bill's long history of debate, amendment, referral to committee, and reintroduction, the section concerning the coinage of the silver dollar was manipulated in such a way as to cause misunderstanding and that the manner of adoption was well planned to take advantage of the silver senators. A number of them, including Stewart of Nevada, failed to speak in opposition to it; they later blamed the confusion created by Sherman's procedure for their inaction. Nevertheless, the bill without the silver dollar was reported in the Senate on December 16, 1872, but was not passed by that body until January 17 and by the House until January 21 and did not become law until February 12, 1873. Certainly this was enough time to discover the omission of the silver dollar, as demonstrated when a Virginia City assayer wrote in a letter to the *Territorial Enterprise* of February 4, 1873, that "Senatorial stupidity" had caused the substitution of the trade dollar for the money dollar.[6]

The Mint Act received only token opposition at the time of its passage, partly because few but treasury and congressional policy makers anticipated the decline of silver. In addition, the act was passed the same year the Big Bonanza was discovered, and far from experiencing a depression, the Comstock reached its highest production in the ensuing five years. While not affecting production on the Comstock, the price of silver declined substantially after 1873, reaching a depreciation of 21 percent by the middle of 1876. By

[5] Allen Weinstein, "Was there a 'Crime of 1873'?: The Case of the Demonetized Dollar," *Journal of American History* 54 (September 1967): 307–27. Weinstein argues that Senator John Sherman, Secretary of the Treasury George L. Boutwell, and others did not act to demonetize silver for corrupt private gain, but did so in order to eliminate silver as a monetary standard before the expected flood of depreciated silver made it attractive to monetary inflationists. He points out that "although they were not self-interested rascals, as advocates of the 'Crime of 1873' later charged, neither were they economic innocents, as most historians have portrayed them, caught without warning by a sudden and fatal decline in the silver market" (p. 312). See also Walter T. K. Nugent, *The Money Question during Reconstruction* (New York: W. W. Norton & Co., 1967).

[6] An earlier issue of the *Territorial Enterprise*, December 18, 1872, p. 2, indicated that the editor of the paper was quite disturbed that Stewart and other western senators didn't seem to know what was going on.

that time the silver supporters were laying the entire blame for the deteriorating silver market at the door of the Mint Act. While this was a satisfying, even necessary, political explanation for the silverites, it was much too simple for the complex series of events involved in the decline of silver. Yet the very simplicity of the argument that the depression was due to the demonetization of silver led to an equally simple solution: repeal the 1873 act, re-monetize silver, and thus restore prosperity.

Richard P. ("Silver Dick") Bland of Missouri made the first attempt in 1876 when he introduced a bill in the House of Representatives providing for the free and unlimited coinage of silver at the ratio of sixteen to one, that is, sixteen units of silver would be legally equivalent to one unit of gold. The bill received little support and Bland had to be satisfied with a small additional issue of subsidiary silver coin and the establishment of a silver commission to consist of three members from each house of Congress and no more than three "experts" to study the silver question with a view to the "restoration of the double standard in this country."

The Silver Commission, which included in its membership Bland and Senator John P. Jones of Nevada, reported to a special session of Congress in the fall of 1877 favoring free coinage of silver and warning that the economic depression and the increase in unemployment would intensify if the policy of chaining industry and commerce to a single standard was continued. A minority report, signed by three of the eight members, strongly opposed the use of a double standard and noted that it was "an illusion and an impossibility." Soon after, Bland introduced in the House a new measure calling for the free coinage of silver. Although the House passed the bill, it was emasculated in the Senate by an amendment offered by Senator William B. Allison of Iowa which eliminated free coinage and substituted the purchase of not less than $2 million nor more than $4 million of silver monthly. Bland, realizing the futility of opposing the Senate and President Hayes, accepted the modified bill as a "step in the right direction" but vowed he would continue the fight for the restoration of silver. The Bland-Allison Act was vetoed by the president but passed over his veto to become law on February 28, 1878.

In the initial fight for free silver, Senator Jones was the most active member of Nevada's congressional delegation.[7] Senator Sharon's absenteeism kept him from giving any real support to the silverites, and Thomas Wren, Nevada's lone representative in the House, supported Bland, but not actively. Except for Jones, Nevada's important political figures simply were not greatly concerned about the silver question until after 1878 when the decline of the Comstock became more apparent.

Silver became a political issue in Nevada during the governorship of Jewett W. Adams, from 1883 to 1887. Adams, who had served as lieutenant governor in the two preceding administrations, warned Nevadans in his inaugural address of the "threatened dissolution which would result from the demonetization of silver." The first legislative session under Adams, in 1883, sent three memorials to Congress on the subject of silver. Two sought relief for silver by the passage of protective tariff laws, of doubtful benefit at best since domestic producers were already flooding the market at home and abroad; the other demanded the free (unlimited) coinage of silver.

Agitation for free silver continued in Nevada during the remainder of the 1880s, but the issue found little support in Washington after Grover Cleveland, an avowed gold-standard man, became president in 1885. In that year Nevadans demonstrated their support of free silver by joining other western states at a National Silver Convention and by attempting to form a state silver organization. The Nevada Silver Association met only once, however, and accomplished little more than drawing further attention to the silver issue. A further rallying cry was raised when Cleveland, by executive order, suspended coinage at the Carson mint in April of 1885. The combination of these and other events in 1885 forced both Nevada political parties to carry planks in their 1886 platforms calling for the free coinage of silver.

The activities in Nevada and other western mining states during the 1880s emphasized the fact that no real accomplishments would occur in the fight to restore free silver until the national political parties became more receptive to the idea of bimetallism.

---

[7] See the recently published work by Allen Weinstein, *Prelude to Populism: Origins of the Silver Issue, 1867–1878* (New Haven: Yale University Press, 1970), for an excellent summary of Senator Jones's activity during the initial fight in Congress for silver remonetization.

Such a change appeared likely in 1888 when the Republican party platform condemned the Democratic administration for its efforts to demonetize silver and when Republican campaigners promised to aid the the silver interests. They were able to honor this pledge in 1890 with the adoption of the Sherman Silver Purchase Act, made possible by a series of political maneuvers.

The road to the passage of that act was tortuous, although it was clear during the initial weeks of the Congress of 1889–90 that some sort of silver bill would be passed. A National Silver Convention was held in November, 1889, to promote legislation for the free coinage of silver; and additional pressure for a new silver bill came from agrarian groups such as the farmer alliances. Southern and western farmers were experiencing a severe depression and as a debtor group stood to benefit from the remonetization of silver and resulting devaluation of money. It was expected that the achievement of statehood in 1889 and 1890 for North Dakota, South Dakota, Montana, Washington, Idaho, and Wyoming—all agricultural or mining states—would add substantially to the clamor for free silver.

After the free coinage of silver, favored by the Senate, was twice voted down in the House, a conference committee worked out a compromise bill, adopted as the Sherman Silver Purchase Act. It called for the purchase by the Treasury Department of four and a half million ounces of silver per month at the market price. In obtaining the passage of the act, the silverites had shown that they constituted an important political force, particularly in the Senate. However, their success was due to a fortuitous circumstance whereby they were able to trade their support of a high tariff measure for Republican backing for the silver purchase bill. The prospects of continuing such an alignment with the Republican party were not good.

Nevada political leaders, reflecting the increasing pressures within the state for bimetallism, played a more important role in the fight for the Sherman act than they had in events leading to the passage of the Bland-Allison measure; and the legislative battle brought two of them, Francis G. Newlands and William M. Stewart, into the national limelight.

Newlands's activities on behalf of free silver started with his entrance into the state's political picture in 1888. He attended the

National Silver Convention in 1889 as a delegate from Nevada and
won appointment to the National Silver Committee.[8] In Washington, Newlands worked to get the Republican majority in Congress
to back remonetization and met with President Harrison as a representative of the silver committee. He gave a major speech at Salt
Lake City on June 21, 1890, urging the formation of a bimetallic
league to correspond with similar societies in Europe, and in a
July 4 address at Virginia City he made an able defense of the free-
silver movement. During the next two years he continued to campaign for silver, climaxing his work with a speech before the House
Committee on Coinage on February 8, 1892, which was cited by
the *Territorial Enterprise* of March 20 as "the most thorough and
convincing free coinage argument ever presented to Congress." Although Newlands held no political office in Nevada until 1893, his
activities in support of free silver in 1889 and 1890 were important
in forcing federal action.

As noted earlier, Stewart had retired from the Senate and Nevada
politics in 1875 to devote his time to a number of mining schemes
and to resume the practice of law. The failure of his mining plans,
the almost total ineptness of his successors in the Senate, and pressure from Nevada and California mining and railroad interests,
brought Stewart back to Nevada in 1885 in an obvious move to
regain his former seat in the Senate. There were major obstacles
to his return to Congress, for the very connections, mining and railroad, which drew him back to Nevada worked against him in many
parts of the state. In addition, by 1886 the overriding issue in Nevada politics was that of free silver and Stewart's actions during the
passage of the "Crime of '73" had been suspect, to say the least.
To complicate matters James Fair, the incumbent, desired a second
term and it was obvious that he could make it difficult for anyone
to displace him if he wanted to spend enough money to maintain
the Democratic majority in the state legislature. It was rumored
also that Senator Jones might support another Republican, C. C.
Powning, a state senator from Washoe County, for the post, although ultimately he swung behind Stewart. John Mackay turned
against Fair, his old partner, because of his treatment of Mrs. Fair.
Her divorce from the senator in 1883 on grounds of habitual adul-

[8] It appears that Newlands obtained his appointment on the National Silver
Committee through Stewart's influence. See Lilley, *Francis G. Newlands*, p. 215.

tery brought nationwide publicity and alienated many of his followers besides Mackay. The threat from Fair was completely eliminated by a Republican victory in the November election. The rumored "rough fight within the party over Stewart" did not materialize, probably because of his powerful supporters—the Central Pacific Railroad, Senator Jones, and John Mackay. When the legislature met in 1887 Stewart was reelected to the post he had left in 1875.

Stewart immediately began a campaign for the remonetization of silver which he continued until he became convinced of its futility on McKinley's second election in 1900. In December, 1887, he introduced a bill in the Senate to reestablish the bimetallic standard. It was referred to the Committee on Finance under the chairmanship of John Sherman and remained there for the rest of the session. Stewart took a prominent part in the debates leading to the passage of the free silver amendment to the party-supported silver bill in 1890 and by that time was recognized, along with Senator Jones of Nevada and Senator Henry Teller of Colorado, as a leader of the Senate silver bloc. After his return to the Senate, he never lost a chance to reiterate his charge that John Sherman had used deception in pushing the Mint Act of 1873 through Congress.

Nevadans had followed events in Congress very closely throughout the 1880s, only to see their hopes founder on the compromise Sherman Silver Purchase Act. Stronger state action appeared necessary in order to put additional pressure for silver reform on the federal government. The initial move in this direction was made by a silver convention at Carson City in May, 1890. The meeting attracted delegates from every county in the state with the exception of Churchill and Lincoln. Although it did not advocate a separate political party, it did create a central committee with the power to call another convention. Newspaper editors throughout the state added to the clamor for silver reform by calling for the formation of silver clubs to support candidates pledged unequivocally to free silver.

One of the early leaders in the silver club movement was George Nixon, who had come to Nevada in the early 1880s as a telegrapher. In 1886, while still in his twenties, he organized the First National Bank of Winnemucca. Young and politically ambitious, Nixon took up the silver cause and through the pages of his *Silver State* news-paper became its strongest supporter in Humboldt County. It was on his initiative that a group of silverites met at Winnemucca on April 10, 1892, to organize the first silver club in Nevada and to elect Nixon its chairman. The same week a silver club of some eight hundred members was organized at Eureka with Thomas Wren as chairman and Reinhold Sadler as vice chairman. The Winnemucca and Eureka clubs were the beginning of a statewide campaign for action to ensure the free and unlimited coinage of silver. When such action was not forthcoming from the two major parties, a third-party movement was inevitable. The Democratic and Republican state conventions of 1892 prepared the way.

The Democrats met early in June and instructed their delegates to the national convention to strive for the adoption of a platform emphasizing bimetallism. The naming of presidential electors brought the local Democrats face to face with their own peculiar dilemma, for Grover Cleveland, certain to be the presidential nom-inee, was a strong gold-standard man. Rather than risk a fight be-tween the Cleveland supporters and the silverites, convention leaders decided to leave the naming of presidential electors to a nominating committee. But when the nominating committee gave its support to the silver candidates, the Democratic Central Commit-tee condemned its choice and named a new set of candidates friendly to Cleveland. Thus the Democrats in Nevada tried to go both ways with a platform pledged to silver but with electors pledged to Cleve-land. The Democratic National Convention aggravated the local Nevada situation by adopting a platform which called for the repeal of the Sherman Silver Purchase Act.

The silver issue also began to drive a wedge into the state Re-publican party. Silverites within the party wanted a strong stand for bimetallism, but the so-called straight-outs, who felt that any-thing less than full support of the national platform would disrupt the party locally, named their own nominees and pledged loyalty to the administration. On the national level the Republican party refused, as did the Democrats, to take a strong stand on the silver issue. President Harrison, in his message to Congress in December, 1891, had defended the silver purchase act but opposed free coinage and stated that further international conferences on silver were useless.

Dissatisfied with the action of the Democratic state convention and holding no hope that the Republicans would support a silver stand, members of the silver clubs throughout Nevada met in Reno during the last week of June to form a separate Silver party. The convention adopted a platform which called for the remonetization of silver at the ratio of sixteen to one and pledged their nominees for presidential electors to support no candidate who did not favor free silver. The new Silver League—it would be incorrect to call it a party at this time—was interested only in the national offices. Since the Republicans nationally had already nominated Benjamin Harrison and the Democrats were in the process of nominating Cleveland, it seemed clear that the Silver League's electors would be pledged to the candidates of the new third party which was to hold its convention at Omaha on July 4.

The People's, or Populist, party was born from over a decade of dissatisfaction, particularly among the southern and western agricultural sectors, with the failure of the two major parties to act upon the numerous grievances of the farmers. The platform they adopted demanded, among many other items, the free and unlimited coinage of silver. In supporting a silver plank the Populist gave the new Silver party in Nevada a national forum to pursue its fight for remonetization.

Because its first convention did not meet the requirement of a Nevada election law that electors on the ballot be nominees of a certified party, the Silver League held a second convention in Winnemucca in September. At that time silver candidates were nominated for all state offices except justice of the supreme court and the nominees for electors were instructed to support the People's party candidates for president and vice-president. The Silverites nominated Newlands for the House of Representatives and supported William M. Stewart in his bid for another term in the Senate. Thus the Silver party was born in Nevada.

Stewart had followed the events in Nevada in 1890 and 1891 with an ear cocked for their political significance. Although he opposed a third-party movement as late as March, 1892, he hurried to participate in the organization of the Silver party when he became convinced that silver would be the major issue in Nevada politics in the election year. Later, with his campaign manager, C. C. Wallace, he toured the state helping to organize silver clubs and, along with Thomas Wren, drew up the petitions to the Secretary of State to have the Silver party appear on the November ballot. In August, on the day after General James B. Weaver, the Populist candidate for president, and Mary Lease a foremost Populist campaigner, spoke at Virginia City, both Stewart and Newlands joined the Silver League. It was something of an anticlimax, then, when Stewart announced at the September convention that he was switching his party affiliation from Republican to Silver.

On the surface it might appear that Stewart's move to join the Silverites would cost him the support of the Central Pacific Railroad, for certainly the objectives of the Silver party in Nevada and the Populist party, which the Silverites supported nationally, had little in common with those of Collis P. Huntington and the other railroad officials. However, the railroad not only did not oppose Stewart's move, but encouraged and helped to promote it through C. C. Wallace, who continued to act as Stewart's campaign manager while at the same time serving as the Central Pacific's main lobbyist in Nevada. It seems apparent that the railroad's support of the Silver party in Nevada was a practical way to assure control of the state.

That both Newlands and Stewart had gauged the political winds correctly was demonstrated in the November election. Newlands received over three times as many votes as his nearest competitor. The Silver party's electorial candidates also won substantial majorities, as did a majority of its candidates for the legislature, thus assuring Stewart's selection as United States Senator.

Although a number of prominent Republicans—William M. Stewart, Francis G. Newlands, and C. C. Wallace, to name only a few—were active in the formation of the Silver party, the results of the 1892 election indicate quite clearly that the Silver victory, although it hurt the Republicans, nearly ruined the local Democrats. This was most apparent in the race for Congress: in 1890 the Democratic candidate had polled 5,736 votes to the Republican's 6,610; in the 1892 election the Democratic candidate received 345 votes to 2,295 for the Republican candidate and 7,171 for Newlands and the Silver party. While the election of 1892 did not bring the Silverites complete control in Nevada, they elected three national officers and gained control of the assembly. The Republicans maintained control of the senate, but two Republican senators voted with the Silverites to give them a working majority.

Some observers feared that the Silver party–dominated legislature would be more radical than previous ones. H. M. Yerington had no such fears; writing to D. O. Mills, president of the Bank of California, he stated rather smugly, "am satisfied that we are all OK—Stewart and Newlands are our friends in Congress and the Democrats and Silver men here are the same *in and out* of the Legislature, which I believe to be a good one and which I am sure we can control with ease. . . . so local matters have all gone our way most beautifully and we are on the top *as usual* which delights me exceedingly."[9]

Yerington had reason for his optimism. The 1891 legislature, at the request of Governor R. K. Colcord and under pressure of agricultural and small property owners generally, had established a state board of assessors and equalization. It consisted of the governor, state controller, secretary of state, attorney general, and state treasurer and was charged with assessing the railroads throughout the state and equalizing the valuation of taxable property in the different counties. Its action had raised the total valuation of property in the state from $24.6 million in 1890 to $31 million in 1892, increasing the total state revenues by over $67,000 in that biennium even though the 1891 legislature had reduced the tax rate. The new assessment and the heavier taxes fell most heavily on the railroad interests and abolishment of the board of equalization became their number one priority as the 1893 legislative session got under way.

The act creating the board had obvious flaws which made it an easy target for the railroad lobbyists. The board members had no particular training for the job of assessment and equalization and did not have adequate technical assistance to ensure proper decisions. Some mistakes, such as the horizontal rise in assessments by counties, brought reaction from those areas where property already was assessed high enough. Such opposition was used adroitly by the lobbyists to bring about the repeal of the law. Governor Colcord later expressed concern over the action, pointing out that the assessed valuation of railroads by the county boards was in

[9] H. M. Yerington to D. O. Mills, December 14, 1892, Yerington Papers, vol. 18, Bancroft Library, University of California, Berkeley.

every instance lower than that of the state board and that in the case of the Central Pacific the difference amounted to about $2,640 per mile.

While the legislative session was proving that Silver party lawmakers were just as susceptible to railroad pressure as were those bearing other party labels, national events began moving toward a showdown on the money question. The collapse of the stock market in the first week of May signaled the beginning of the panic of 1893. President Cleveland, convinced that the Sherman Silver Purchase Act was responsible for the depression, called a special session of Congress for August 7. He recommended immediate repeal of the silver purchase law and in a direct bid for Republican support, described the matter as "above the plane of party politics." The repeal bill passed the House on August 28 by a vote of 239 to 108 after a number of free-coinage amendments were decisively beaten. It faced a more decided opposition in the Senate and the issue was in doubt until Cleveland used the patronage "club" to beat reluctant Democrats into line. Both Nevada senators made heroic efforts to defeat the bill: Stewart spoke for three days and Senator Jones for seven (his speech was 463 pages long). Finally, on October 30 the repeal bill passed the Senate by a vote of 43 to 32. The fight in Congress over repeal of the Sherman act demonstrated again the potential strength of the silverites, but more than that, Cleveland's action drove a deep wedge into his own party on the national level, reflecting the antagonism of the silver West and South toward the industrial and gold-standard East. Furthermore, the repeal act heightened the movement in Nevada and other mining states for free and unlimited coinage of silver at a ratio of sixteen to one. By 1894 each of the four parties entering the Nevada elections supported the remonetization of silver.

In the months before the meeting of the various state conventions, Nevadans experienced the low point in the depression which had plagued their state since the decline of the Comstock.[10] During that time many who lived along the Central Pacific Railroad were able to observe, some even to participate in, two events which related the nationwide depression to their own particular problems. "Coxey's Army" and the Pullman Railroad strike, both originating

---

[10] See Appendix, table 2.

thousands of miles from Nevada, gave Nevada silverites additional reasons for demanding a change in political leadership.

"General" Jacob Coxey, a wealthy citizen of Ohio, had proposed a scheme for creating jobs and easing unemployment with public works. When Congress failed to act on his proposals, he called on a "ragamuffin army" of unemployed to gather from all parts of the United States to present a "petition of boots" in Washington, D.C. Actually, it was not so much a single army as a number of contingents under self-styled lieutenants. Although the alarm created throughout the country was all out of proportion to any threatened danger, the prospect of having hundreds of unemployed men move into a community on the way to join Coxey's Army disturbed hundreds of city officials in California and Nevada during the spring of 1894. Officials in Reno, Nevada, came face to face with the problem when the *Reno Evening Gazette* reported on April 6, 1894, that a thousand men were moving toward Reno on their way to join Coxey.

The reaction in Reno was similar to that in other cities through which these armies were scheduled to pass; that is, get them through the town and on to the next with a maximum of speed and a minimum of cost and effort. Allen C. Bragg, editor of the *Gazette,* seemed to be particularly worried at the prospect of having the "Industrial Army" in Reno. In a telegram to Governor Colcord on April 6, he inquired, "What can you do to stop them at State line, or what idea have you regarding their disposition? Answer immediately." The governor's reply, while immediate, was of no comfort to Bragg: "We have no law preventing their coming. It would be madness for such an army to subsist while marching this sparsely settled State. If the railroad company dumps them here they will be compelled by force of circumstances to take them through the State."[11]

There was little for Reno citizens to fear. The superintendent of the Reno-Sacramento division of the Central Pacific rushed the special train of twenty-three cattle cars and one thousand men through Reno and on through Nevada the next day. The problem was then one for Utah authorities.

The Industrial Army continued to haunt western Nevada, for

[11] A copy of the telegram to Colcord and his reply were published in the *Reno Evening Gazette,* April 6, 1894.

a number of recruits, hoping to join the train in Reno, had been left behind. Their continued presence in the community, spotlighted by parades on April 9 to gain additional members, brought a public meeting to end the recruiting. Much more effective than the public meeting was the action of the sheriff, who ordered the leaders of the Industrial Army to be out of town by noon of April 10 or face arrest. With their exit the estimated three hundred recruits began to leave Reno by hopping rides on the freight trains. The whole fabric of the Nevada contingent of Coxey's Army fell to pieces with the arrest of Coxey on May 1 in Washington, D.C., for marching on the White House lawn.[12]

The Central Pacific hardly had time to clear its line of the stragglers from Coxey's Army before it became involved in the nationwide Pullman railway strike. The strike against the Pullman Company in the latter part of June became a nationwide boycott against all trains pulling pullman cars when the American Railway Union, under the leadership of Eugene V. Debs, took up the cause of the Pullman employees. President Cleveland ordered federal troops to protect the railroads and prevent "holding up the mails." In Nevada the presence of such troops provoked mob attacks against train crews, the dynamiting of tracks and bridges, and finally a petition to Governor Colcord asking him to use his good office to have the soldiers removed. The governor replied that Cleveland had acted legally and that any protest would be useless and unwise.

The use of federal troops was decisive in breaking the Pullman boycott, but it was clear that the attitude of railroad officials and government leaders would have political repercussions in the coming elections on both the national and the state level. Nevada newspapers took the occasion to renew criticism of railroads in general and the Central Pacific in particular; one editor went so far as to suggest that public ownership of railroads would prevent incidents such as the Pullman strike. He severely criticized Colcord and stated flatly that the state needed a new governor.

The issue of free silver was tied closely in Nevada to both the Coxey's Army episode and the Pullman strike. Parades in Reno in connection with the Industrial Army had featured banners demanding the free coinage of silver, and local newspapers empha-

---

[12]These events can be followed in detail from the files of the *Reno Evening Gazette* from March 27 through April 12, 1894.

sized that the plight of the unemployed should be laid at the door of President Cleveland and the gold standard. The tie-up between the Silverites and the Pullman strike was even clearer. Throughout the strike the Silverite press supported the American Railway Union and when its members were brought to trial in Carson City on charges of obstructing the mails, Thomas Wren and S. J. Bonnifield, two prominent silver attorneys, defended them.[13]

The year 1894 gave the newly formed Silver party of Nevada its first opportunity to compete for the entire slate of state offices, and it was apparent as the summer wore on that divisions within the two major parties, on both the national and the state level, made it the odds-on favorite to win the election. The Republican party opened and closed its state convention in Reno on August 25 with the so-called straight-outs in control. The inroads of the Silver party were evident from the fact that three counties sent no delegates, a marked change from 1890 when the Republicans had captured every state office. The platform called for the free coinage of silver at the ratio of sixteen to one, but emphasized that the fight for silver should be waged within the major parties. In a direct reference to the part played by C. C. Wallace in the organization of the Silver party, the Republicans charged the Silverites with subservience to the Central Pacific and went on record as favoring a second transcontinental line through Nevada. A. C. Cleveland, a leading figure in the politics of the eastern part of the state, won the nomination for governor and Horace Bartine, who had served two terms in Congress, from 1889 to 1893, was nominated for the House of Representatives.

The Silver party was next to hold its convention, its members assembling the first week of September at Carson City. The major plank, of course, was that demanding the remonetization of silver at the ratio of sixteen to one. However, the platform mirrored the Populist influence in its demand for government ownership of railroads and telegraph lines, compulsory arbitration of labor disputes, and the direct election of Senators. Besides Francis G. Newlands, who was renominated for Congress, the nominees included two prominent Silverites from the eastern part of the state: John

---

[13]For a much more detailed account of the silver question in Nevada politics, see Mary Ellen Glass, *Silver and Politics in Nevada: 1892—1902* (Reno: University of Nevada Press, 1969).

E. Jones, Nevada surveyor general from 1887 to 1894, for governor, and Reinhold Sadler for lieutenant governor. Both came into state politics from earlier political activities in Eureka County.

The plank in the Silver party's platform calling for government control of the railroads brought into relief the peculiar role played in Nevada politics by the Central Pacific and its agent, C. C. Wallace. During the convention Newlands came out in opposition to government ownership of railroads. His position troubled a number of delegates, including Wallace, who cautioned him to abandon such a stand. It was obvious that the Central Pacific officials recognized the strong antirailroad bias of the mass of Nevada voters and did not want it to affect the success of the party which they controlled. Newlands later went along with the entire platform.

A third party convention, not originally scheduled, resulted from an attempt to have the Silver party become affiliated with the national People's party, with an approporiate change in name. When the motion to accomplish this was tabled, its supporters withdrew and held a People's party convention, nominating James C. Doughty for Congress and George E. Peckam for governor, and pledging allegiance to the national People's party. The local platform, among other items, called for silver at sixteen to one, repeal of the National Banking Act, the use of unemployed in reclamation projects, the prohibition of Chinese and Japanese immigration, direct election of senators, and mandatory disclosure of campaign expenditures. The explanation of the organizers that they acted in order to have a local unit of the People's party ready for the election of 1896 and because they objected to control of the Silver party by the railroad was convincing; yet the formation of the new party in the face of a Silver party platform that was extremely Populist in tone couldn't help but raise questions as to the motives involved.

The fourth Nevada party to qualify candidates for the election, the Democrats, holding their convention the second week in September, demonstrated again the dichotomy of their position. Actually, there were two Democratic conventions, a splinter group which met first and nominated Robert Keating for governor and J. E. Gignoux for Congress, and the regular group which met under the leadership of John H. Dennis, chairman of the state central committee, and nominated B. F. Riley for Congress, Theodore M.

Winters for governor, and a number of other candidates to fill the slate. The latter were certified as the Democratic party nominees. The Democratic platform, like the others in 1894, called for the free coinage of silver at sixteen to one. However, the local organization nullified that plank by endorsing the administration of the gold-standard Grover Cleveland.

The Prohibition party, meeting later, did not qualify any candidates for the general election but did adopt a platform statement which, except for the plank condemning strong spirits, was quite similar to those of the Silver party and the People's party. It called for free silver at sixteen to one, favored woman suffrage and restriction of immigration, supported government ownership of "natural monopolies," and called for elections free of corruption and for reclamation of western lands.

Although all of the Nevada parties in the election of 1894 supported the remonetization of silver, the Republicans and the Democrats were handicapped on this issue by the attitudes and actions of their national parties. This was particularly true of the Democrats with the blame for the repeal of the Sherman Silver Purchase Act laid at their door. The Republicans were scarcely any better off in Nevada, for it was clear that the repeal would not have been possible without strong Republican support. Furthermore, it had been evident for years that the Republican party nationally was moving toward all-out support of the gold standard.

As the campaign got under way it appeared that the Silver party had all the advantages. Its leadership, culled from the best politicians in each of the two major parties, was superior, and it had less internal dissension than either of the other parties. What was more important, it had popular support as well as the backing of important mining interests and the Central Pacific Railroad. Why the railroad should support a party whose platform called for government ownership of railroads completely baffled the straight-out Republican lobbyist, H. M. Yerington. In a letter to A. N. Towne, vice-president of the Southern Pacific, he wrote:

Recently I have on several occasions earnestly begged Col. Crocker and Mr. H. E. Huntington to help me protect the property holders of this State and of course that of the C. P. RR Co., by and through their powerful influence and the election of *good reliable men* for State and County Officers, for some incomprehensible reason, my appeals have been ignored and I now see your Company's agent, C. C. Wallace, backing up one Jones for Governor who in July last signed a petition to Gov. Colcord *demanding* the immediate withdrawal of the U.S. soldiers from Reno, Wadsworth, etc, which, if done, would probably . . . have destroyed the C.P. RR.

Yerington went on to note that Wallace was supporting all the "wrong" men, "wrong," that is, from the standpoint of favoring the railroads.[14] He never forgave Wallace and other former Republicans for leaving the Grand Old Party during the 1890s. Yet the railroad's position was unusual. Perhaps the answer to this marriage of convenience was the obvious fact, proved on many earlier occasions and much to the disgust of Yerington, that the officials of the Central Pacific were much more interested in the control of Congress than the Nevada legislature. Thus it made sense to help organize and support a state party which would ensure the election of United States senators friendly to the railroads. While his statement may be an oversimplification, Professor Gilman Ostrander probably came very close to the heart of the matter when he wrote, "Huntington was a practical man. Nevada got its Silver Party, and Huntington got its Silver senators."[15]

Nevada voters gave the Silver party a landslide victory in 1894. Silverite candidates won every contest they entered, and by substantial margins. The Republicans, as in 1892, ran second, while the Democrats and the People's party vied for third place. The damage wrought on the Democrats by the Silver party was nowhere better demonstrated than in the four-way race for representative where B. F. Riley, the Democratic candidate, came in fourth, gaining but 217 votes to 4,581 for Newlands, the Silver party candidate. The election also swept Silverites into power in both houses of the Nevada legislature.

The 1895 Silver legislature with its strong Populist overtones accomplished little effective reform legislation, with the possible exception of a "purity of elections" law which required the disclosure of campaign expenditures. It did pass two interesting resolutions. One calling for woman suffrage was approved after much activity

[14] Yerington to A. N. Towne, October 17, 1894, Yerington Papers, vol. 25, pp. 288–90.

[15] Gilman M. Ostrander, *Nevada: The Great Rotten Borough, 1859–1964* (New York: Alfred A. Knopf, 1966), p. 116.

by suffragettes and a speech to lawmakers by Mila Tupper Maynard, a national leader of the movement. However, this was only the first step in a complicated procedure necessary to amend the state constitution and the second step, passage of the resolution by the 1897 legislature, was never taken. The second resolution demanded the collection of the debts of the Pacific Coast railroads, and was aimed against the so-called Reilly funding bill, then in Congress, which provided for the issuance of government bonds to pay the railroad debts. After a number of heated debates, it passed both houses in spite of open lobbying against it by railroad interests.

Although the Silver party had won a smashing victory in Nevada, it was apparent to party leaders and other Silverites throughout the West that their main objective, the remonetization of silver, would not be accomplished without stronger support on the national level. The Bimetallic Union, intended to give national direction to the fight for free silver, was a near failure by 1896, and some silver leaders felt its place should be taken by a national Silver party. Both Senator Stewart and Congressman Newlands played a leading part in the attempt to form such a party. Committees were organized in major cities to work for the fusion of local silver forces, to raise money, and to publicize the cause. A proposed national Silver party convention was scheduled for July, 1896, but before it could take place, action taken by the Democrats in their national convention doomed the national Silver party to an early death.

Prominent Silver Democrats such as Richard Bland and William Jennings Bryan, although sorely tried during the administration of Grover Cleveland, had resisted all pressures to join the Populist party. Their decision paid off when the Democrats met in July of 1896. Supporters of the gold standard stood helpless as the Silverites took control of the convention, wrote a platform emphasizing the free and unlimited coinage of silver at sixteen to one, and nominated Bryan, the young orator from Nebraska, as their candidate for the presidency. The Democrats had stolen the Populist's platform and their most likely candidate, so when the People's party met later in July it could do little but ratify the choice of Bryan. It refused, however, to back Arthur Sewall for the vice-presidency and named Tom Watson of Georgia instead. The na-

tional Silver party "died aborning." Meeting on the same day
as the People's party, under the temporary chairmanship of Francis
G. Newlands, the delegates hurried to endorse the nominees of the
Democrats and adjourned, never to meet again.

The Republican party had held its national convention in June.
Silver Republicans were outnumbered and outmaneuvered; and
when the convention nominated William McKinley for president
and adopted a strong gold plank, the silver delegates, led by Senator Henry Teller of Colorado, bolted the convention. Senator
Teller then made an unsuccessful move to unite the silver forces
behind him as a candidate for the presidency.

Monetary policy dominated the national political conventions
of 1896 and it was obvious that the campaign would be fought
on that issue. The election, in giving voters a clear-cut contest
between gold and silver and between control of the government
by the industrial East or by the agrarian interests of the South
and West, was not only of extreme national importance but significant, also, in redirecting Nevada politics.

The Democratic and Republican national conventions in 1896
rescued Nevada's Democratic party, which had been dying a slow
death since the organization of the Silver party in 1892, and confronted the state's Republicans with a dilemma which pushed them
out of political contention for over a decade. By adopting a free
silver platform, the national Democratic party gave Nevada Democrats a chance to merge with the Silverites, with only one possible
result since the Silver party had no national organization. The
Republican national convention, on the other hand, by adopting a
gold standard, forced Nevada Republicans either to denounce the
national party or to repudiate the free silver issue. To oppose free
silver in Nevada at that time was political suicide; thus former
Republicans in the Silver party found themselves actively allied
with the national Democratic party.

In the weeks between the last national convention in July and
the first state convention in September, efforts were made to unite
locally the three parties supporting the remonetization of silver
on the national level. Such a unification, on the surface quite
logical, was not easy to effect. Part of the difficulty lay in the
beginning of a power struggle between the Stewart-Wallace forces
on the one hand and the Newlands-Sharon group on the other for

control of the Silver party, a prize which would give the winner political dominance of the state. Then, too, some Republicans in the Silver party hesitated to merge with Democrats and a few Democrats and many Populists felt that a merger with the Silverites would eliminate their parties. The various supporters of silver met during the latter part of August to attempt to find a workable solution to the problems of fusion. Evidently the Stewart and Newlands factions of the Silver party and representatives of the Democrats and of the People's party, realizing the solid advantages, agreed to some sort of unification. The fusionists, as the supporters of the merger were generally called, then moved to control their respective party conventions.

The People's party, meeting the first week of September, voted against merging with the Democrats and the Silver party. Their action was a reversal from earlier informal discussions and came only after hours of debate. The party named James C. Doughty for Congress and endorsed free silver and other reforms demanded by their national party.

The attempt to bring the Silver and the Democratic parties together was both more important and more successful. The Democratic state central committee gave the initial impetus to complete fusion when it decided, in effect, to support the Silver party candidates and to nominate only presidential electors in order to preserve their party's legal status.

The Democrats and the Silverites, by prearrangement, held their conventions in the same town and on the same date. Fusionists controlled both conventions, although not without some difficulty in the case of the Silver party. Certain former Republicans resented joint action with the Democrats, and one of the outstanding opponents of fusion, Thomas Wren, an organizer of the Nevada Silver party, refused nomination as a presidential elector, stating that he didn't propose to be shoved into the Democratic party.

The fusion platform supported the aims of the National Silver party and its nominees, William Jennings Bryan and Arthur Sewall. The main issue, of course, was silver; however, other resolutions favored collection of debts of the Pacific Coast railroads, government ownership of the telegraph lines and railroads, compulsory arbitration of labor disputes, and popular election of United States senators. The fusionists also endorsed the candidacy of John P.

Jones for senator[16] and nominated Francis G. Newlands for Congress. The combined parties also nominated C. H. E. Hardin for lieutenant governor, assuming that a vacancy existed in that office since Reinhold Sadler had moved up to acting governor on the death of John E. Jones.[17]

The Republican state convention, now in the same uncomfortable position that the Democrats were in when Cleveland was president, tried to go both ways by endorsing the nomination of McKinley for president and at the same time supporting free coinage of silver at sixteen to one. Republicans hedged the latter endorsement, adding "by international agreement" to show their local allegiance to the silver question while maintaining their position within the national organization. Their platform also supported the high tariff, the "purity of elections" law, and woman suffrage. A full slate of candidates was named, more in the hope of keeping the party alive than in any prospect of victory.

The Silver-Democrats, as they were listed on the ballots, proved a formidable combination, winning every office by overwhelming majorities. In the case of the presidential electors and the race for Congress the fusion candidates received three times as many votes as their combined opponents. Thus, the 1896 election continued the Silverite domination of Nevada's legislative and administrative machinery.

With the fusion candidates in firm control, it seemed reasonable to assume that Senator John P. Jones would have no opposition when the legislature met to choose a United States senator. However, just a few days before the 1897 legislative session was to begin, George Nixon, a powerful leader within the ranks of the Silver party, declared that he would be a candidate for the Senate post. The surprise announcement created little enthusiasm, as Nixon was given no chance to defeat the venerable senator. The gesture was not a political whim, however, but part of the continuing struggle for control of the state's political machinery.

[16]Jones had switched allegiance to the Silverites in 1894 when it was apparent that such action was necessary if he wished to run for the Senate in 1896.

[17]Sadler insisted that there was no vacancy in the office of lieutenant Governor and refused to issue a certificate of election. The Nevada Supreme Court upheld him in *State of Nevada, Ex. Rel. C. H. E. Hardin, Relator v. Reinhold Sadler, Governor of the State of Nevada, Respondent,* 23 *Nevada Reports* 356 (1897).

It was obvious to the Stewart-Wallace faction that Newlands was behind Nixon in his attempt to gain the Senate seat; consequently, they threw their support to Jones. Another factor in their rush to aid Jones was the fact that the Nixon forces were basing their campaign on the issue of "home rule." It was not a new issue in Nevada politics, for almost from the beginning of statehood Nevada's senators had made a practice of living in California while maintaining a token residence in Nevada. Jones had abused the residence requirement and certainly was vulnerable on that point, particularly at a time when the direct election of senators had become a national issue. However, if Jones was vulnerable, so was Stewart, and with his own election coming up in two years, it behooved him to do all he could to help reelect Jones.

Nixon's move also presented an opportunity to the V & T interests to trade support to Jones for his aid on tariff matters. The go-between here was the general manager of the V & T, H. M. Yerington. He wrote to his boss, D. O. Mills, explaining that Nixon's announcement for the Senate would "oblige Mr. Jones to look after his fence from now up to the sitting of the legislature," and further suggested that Jones be helped, "provided he stands in and aids our Borax-Soda tariff and other matters in which we are interested."[18] Yerington's opposition to Nixon evidently led him into some difficulty with Newlands, who was closely associated with D. O. Mills and the V & T interests. He wrote a long letter to Newlands trying to explain his position and noting that he didn't know that Newlands was supporting Nixon. The latter point contradicts an earlier letter, dated December 28, 1896, in which Yerington wrote to Mills, "This little Nixon escapade is likely to get many people by the ears—he is Mr. Newlands' protege and very close to him."

Nixon's candidacy didn't have a chance in the face of the Stewart-Wallace opposition and the popularity of Senator Jones. When the legislature met on January 19, Jones won a decisive victory with a vote of thirty-five to three. The skirmish had ended in favor of the Stewart followers, but the battle for power within the Silver-Democratic, or fusion, party was just getting started.

[18] Yerington to D. O. Mills, December 28, 1896, Yerington Papers, vol. 19, pp. 40–42.

The 1897 Nevada legislature, again heavily dominated by Silverites, made little contribution to solving the state's pressing financial problems. Acting Governor Reinhold Sadler asked that the State Board of Equalization be reinstituted as a means of gaining higher assessed valuations and urged the legislators to observe strict economy in appropriations. The lawmakers answered the governor's request for additional revenue measures by passing a bill to license prize fights.

As it finally was passed into law, the act called for a licensing fee of $1,000, one-tenth of which went to the county where the fight was held and nine-tenths to the state's general fund. Health examinations were required of the fighters and bouts were to be held inside enclosures to exclude the view of the general public. As negotiations were begun immediately for a match between James J. Corbett and Bob Fitzsimmons, the new law drew national attention, most of it uncomplimentary. Nevada's first attempt to attract the tourist dollar was received in much the same way as were the later ones emphasizing "easy divorce" and gambling—defensively by Nevadans and with a sense of outrage by citizens outside the state. The battle for the heavyweight championship (ending in victory for Fitzsimmons in the fourteenth round) was incidental to the fact that the prizefight had proven its worth as a promotional scheme.

The legislators did not perform in such a positive manner on a much more important measure. The resolution to amend the constitution to permit woman suffrage was pending when the legislature met in January. It passed the senate but was defeated in the assembly by a tie vote, which meant that the procedure had to start over again from the beginning. Undaunted, its supporters resolved to double their efforts.

When the legislative session ended, politicians directed their attention to the election of 1898; with all the state offices, a congressional seat, and a Senate seat open, it would present an excellent test of the continued vitality of the silver issue in Nevada politics. Interest centered on the offices of governor and United States Senator. Reinhold Sadler, who had become acting governor in 1895 on the death of John E. Jones, had by 1898 defined his stand, either by word or by action, on most public issues and was satisfied that the voters would recognize his service to the state by electing him governor. However, his administration had not been outstanding and a number of people, including some within his own party, considered him vulnerable.

The fight for Stewart's seat in the United States Senate was expected to be the most interesting contest. Stewart had indicated that he wished to be returned to the Senate, and even his enemies recognized that he was a formidable candidate. By 1898 he had succeeded in erasing the stigma of having voted for the Mint Act of 1873. He was one of the early sponsors of the Silver party in Nevada, going so far as to leave the Republicans to join the Populists in 1892 when they came out for free silver. He had further aided the cause of free silver by helping to finance and publish a Silverite paper, the *Silver Knight-Watchman*. In addition, Stewart had the support of the Central Pacific Railroad, which meant also the able help of their Nevada agent, C. C. Wallace, who had acted as his campaign manager since his return to Nevada in 1886.

Yet strong opposition to Stewart had developed and his supporters were worried about the divisions within the Silver party. Whether or not Stewart was a legal resident of Nevada was open to question, and of course his switch to the Populists had alienated many old-line Republicans. What really worried the Stewart-Wallace faction, however, was the fact that Francis G. Newlands was the opposition. As a potential candidate for the United States Senate, Newlands had many fine qualifications. His support for silver, first as a private citizen and later as a member of the House of Representatives, was hardly less substantial than that of Stewart, and he had literally stolen leadership of the reclamation and irrigation issue from Stewart. Much more important, however, Newlands had money. The fact that money bought votes and legislators was a lesson learned early and well by the Stewart-Wallace faction.

Newlands's possible candidacy was looked upon as a mistake by his good friend George Nixon, who warned that opposition to Stewart and Wallace at this time would split the party. Nixon suggested that Newlands wait until 1902 and contest John P. Jones; but his advice seemed to fall on deaf ears and as the convention drew near, it was more and more evident that Newlands would challenge Stewart.

The Democratic party held the first state convention in 1898.

At once a fight broke out between delegates from the western counties who wanted fusion with the Silver party and delegates from eastern Nevada who opposed merger. A motion to appoint a committee on fusion failed, and a platform statement that the Silver party of Nevada, in serving the political interests of but a few men, was detrimental to the cause of silver boded ill for further attempts at fusion. Otherwise the platform adopted by the convention duplicated the 1896 Democratic national platform in every detail. Candidates were nominated for all offices except representative and attorney general.

The Silver party opened its convention the day after the Democrats. The interparty rivalry between the Newlands-Sharon and the Stewart-Wallace factions flared for a moment when Newlands indicated he would like the party's endorsement for the Senate seat held by Stewart. Apparently an agreement was reached whereby the convention would back Stewart for the Senate, but if Stewart men failed to be elected to the legislature, Newlands would not be obliged further to support the junior Senator. When efforts by the party leaders to effect fusion with the Democrats failed, the Silverites nominated a full slate of candidates, including Sadler for the post of governor. The platform, of course, emphasized the silver issue, but included planks endorsing Newlands's attempts to obtain reclamation legislation and urging further strengthening of the powers of the ICC.

The Republicans had difficulty obtaining a quorum to open their convention. Once under way, it adopted a platform which supported bimetallism and emphasized the role of the party in the defeat of the Spanish and the acquisition of a colonial empire. William McMillan's name was placed on the ticket for governor and nominations were made for all other offices except that of congressman.

The People's party convention adopted a platform which, like those of the other three parties, supported silver. However, the Populists made condemnation of the railroad their major theme in both their platform and the campaign. They did not list a complete set of candidates, but did nominate J. B. McCullough for governor and Thomas Wren for Congress. Wren provided the only opposition to Newlands, whose forces had managed things so adroitly that he received the nomination of the Silver party and endorsement by the central committee of the Democratic party, and had confused the issue among the Republicans so that they failed to nominate for that office.

The failure of the Democrats and the Silverites to fuse in 1898 almost proved a disaster to the interests of many politically ambitious individuals. The Republicans came within twenty-two votes of placing McMillan in the office of governor, but a recount showed that Sadler had won by sixty-three votes. Although the Silver party captured every office except that of superintendent of public instruction, the contests were close in most cases. Again it was apparent that the Democrats as a party suffered most from the failure to fuse; in every race they entered they came in third behind the Silverites and the Republicans.

The election also raised a question about Senator Stewart's future. The Newlands forces and some neutral observers immediately noted that the Stewart forces had not won enough legislative seats to ensure the Senator's selection in January, 1899. The reason was obviously the failure to effect fusion between the Silverites and the Democrats, for which Wallace blamed Newlands. Newlands stood to benefit from such a situation; his own victory in the House race seemed assured and a split vote for Stewart men in the legislative races would release him from his convention pledge. Although it cannot be documented, Newlands may well have been the main instrument keeping the Silverites and Democrats apart in 1898.

But Newlands was not the only important enemy facing Stewart. Both A. C. Cleveland and H. M. Yerington, former supporters of the senator, were now openly opposing him, probably for the same basic reasons. Newlands was associated closely with the William Sharon interests, which meant, of course, the Virginia & Truckee Railroad and other elements of the old Bank of California monopoly. Cleveland had worked as a lobbyist for those forces for many years and Yerington had held a number of positions within the old empire, including the general managership of the V & T. In any event, both began active opposition to Stewart in October preceeding the election. Cleveland announced his candidacy for Stewart's position and began a campaign in his own behalf. About the same time Yerington, in letters to his boss, D. O. Mills, began to strike out against his former friend, calling him "a bull-dozing, foul-mouthed, ungrateful rascal," and expressing the hope that he would be "thoroughly beaten."[19] Later he told Mills that Wallace had asked him to support Stewart but that he had refused, "telling him we were Republicans and in fact out of politics, and proposed staying out."[20]

The argument over whether or not pro-Stewart men had carried the legislative election became academic on December 6 when Newlands announced that he planned to contest Stewart for the Senate seat. The struggle within the Silver party between the Newlands and Stewart factions, which had been smoldering for nearly two years, was at last in the open. Newlands and his supporters, including a number of newspapers, were convinced that the Stewart forces had lost the legislature and that Newlands was therefore justified in declaring for the Senate, while Stewart and his followers were just as convinced that they had won the legislature. Stewart was outraged by Newlands's action. In a letter to a supporter, he wrote: "Mr. Newlands is giving out interviews declaring that I am defeated, and that he will be elected. If his treachery does not disgust the people of Nevada I shall be very much disappointed."[21] His campaign manager was more realistic. In noting that Nixon had "sold out" and turned his paper loose for Newlands, Wallace wrote to Stewart:

The election is over and it is votes that we want and not newspapers. I leave tonight for Nevada and expect to go over the whole field and investigate. I have waited so as to let the Enemy go over the field first and then follow at their heels—if we can't win the fight we must not let Newlands win it. It will be simply a monied fight, if there was no money in the fight you would win by a two-third vote—but with money in the fight it simply makes mercenaries of nearly all of [the legislators].[22]

Between the November election and the meeting of the legislature in January, the contest between Stewart and Newlands was waged on many levels. In the newspapers, candidates were praised or vilified according to the political complexion of the editors.

[19] Yerington to D. O. Mills, October 27, 1898, Yerington Papers, vol. 19, pp. 448–49.

[20] Yerington to D. O. Mills, November 26, 1898, Yerington Papers, vol. 19.

[21] W. M. Stewart to General J. C. Hagerman, December 7, 1898, W. M. Stewart Papers, Nevada State Historical Society, Letter Book, vol. 24, p. 613.

[22] C. C. Wallace to W. M. Stewart, December 6, 1898, Stewart Papers.

Much more important were the contests to control, first, the Silver party's central committee and, second, the legislature.

Wallace's political talents were never put to a more severe test than in those weeks in 1899 before the legislature selected a senator, nor were they ever better displayed. While others were busy elsewhere, Wallace had managed to obtain the proxies of a majority of the Silver party central committee. When that body met at Carson City on January 12 with an attendance of only fifteen of the membership of fifty-one, the proxies became all-important. Nevertheless, action on resolutions by the Stewart faction to force William Sharon's resignation as chairman of the committee and to condemn Francis G. Newlands was postponed a week when Sharon's friends protested strongly. The untimely opposition was referred to by one of the Stewart men as "very annoying . . . ; however, next week will probably go different."[23]

Go differently it did. At the second meeting of the Silver party central committee, Newlands was censured and Sharon removed as chairman, both by a vote of thirty-one to thirteen. Before the Newlands men left the committee meeting, Sharon made a bitter speech in which he condemned the "railroad faction" of the party and its leaders, Wallace and Stewart. Wallace had won the first round, but the importance of the initial victory could only be tested by the legislative ballot.

The battle was not yet completely lost for Newlands. A test vote on a parliamentary maneuver the day before the actual vote was to take place indicated that the result in the assembly might well be a tie. The Stewart forces controlled the senate; however, if the two houses could not agree on a candidate by a majority vote in each house, the selection would go to a joint meeting of the two bodies where each vote was of equal weight. Balloting began on January 24 in the state senate, and as expected, Stewart received nine votes to six votes for his combined opponents. When the assembly met later the same day, it was discovered on roll call that W. A. Gillespie, assemblyman from Storey County, was absent.[24] After efforts

[23] M. Scheeline to W. M. Stewart, January 13, 1899, Stewart Papers, Letter Box J.

[24] W. A. Gillespie, during the subsequent investigation, stated that he had gone home when it was apparent that his own Republican party could not elect anyone. Another more colorful version is that which appears in Samuel P. Davis, ed., *The History of Nevada*, vol. 1 (Reno, Nevada: Elms Publishing

to find him failed, the Newlands forces tried to adjourn the meeting, but without success. In the voting which followed, Stewart received fifteen votes to his opponents' fourteen. Newlands's name was not presented in either house, apparently on the premise that to do so before Stewart was definitely blocked would jeopardize his political future.

The next day a joint session of the senate and assembly formally elected Stewart to the United States Senate. The Central Pacific had succeeded again in controlling the Nevada legislature. The main cog in the operation had been C. C. Wallace, but the railroad had sent in other "friends" to aid in the fight: Stephen Gage, whose reputation as a lobbyist of the Central Pacific before the Nevada legislature won him a similar post to defend the railroad's interest at Sacramento; Colonel Jack Chinn, formerly of Kentucky, who asserted that he was in Nevada as a representative of the national Democratic central committee to investigate Newlands's alleged treachery to the party, but who in reality was an employee of the Central Pacific; and Dave Neagle, famous by this time as the killer of Judge David Terry in the Terry-Field affair.[25] Rival newspapermen called the group a body of "hired gunmen" and it was suggested that the citizens of Carson City organize a vigilance committee to protect themselves against such characters. Regardless of their reputation, they had overcome the money advantage possessed, in the beginning at least, by the Newlands forces. They had done so, first, by eliminating Sharon and Newlands from the Silver central committee, and second, by controlling a majority of the

Co., 1913), p. 432. Sam Davis, who was very close to state politics, wrote that Gillespie had been asked by friends if he wanted a ride to the capitol. Instead of the capitol the friends took him to Empire and he was "locked up" in the house of State Senator Warren W. Williams, where he remained a prisoner for two days. Davis stated that the invitation to take the ride came from Sam Jones, brother of Senator John P. Jones, and that Gillespie was paid $1,800 for his absence from the assembly.

[25] This famous affair grew out of the legal proceedings which started as *Sharon* v. *Althea Hill* (see footnote 3). In its continuation after Sharon's death it involved David Terry first as an attorney for Miss Hill and later as her husband. Justice Stephen J. Field ruled against Althea Hill, an action which so angered Terry that he threatened Field's life. As a result of these threats a deputy United States marshal, Dave Neagle, was assigned to protect Field; in the performance of this duty he later killed Terry when he thought Terry was preparing to murder Justice Field.

legislators, even to the extent of "kidnapping" one member when his presence in the assembly threatened to cause a tie vote.

A complete and accurate history of the 1898 election and the subsequent action of the Nevada legislature in choosing a senator no doubt can never be written; the record suggests, however, that both sides used money liberally in the attempt to ensure a legislative majority. Gillespie's absence and charges of corruption brought a special assembly investigating committee, which held, after brief hearings, that the charges of corruption against Gillespie and George Leidy, assemblyman from Esmeralda County, were unfounded. Typical of newspaper reaction was an editorial in the *Territorial Enterprise* of February 4, 1899:

The very school children here should be taught to avoid the man Gillespie, who sold us into six more years of bondage. . . . The Hon. Leidy is also worthy of a passing notice. His picture in one of the San Francisco dailies labeled sell out Assembly-man from Nevada would fill a niche in the rogue's gallery with honor, and be excellent for future reference. In conclusion let me ask you which is the most dangerous—one bribe-giver or the hundreds that are willing to accept bribes?

All but four of the legislators involved in the 1899 affair—one senator and three assemblymen—were defeated by the voters the next time they stood for election. Apparently, the citizens generally had no such faith in the lawmakers as had Stewart, who noted in a letter to a friend that Newlands "with all his money" had not captured a single vote in the legislature and that "this speaks very highly for the honesty of Nevada legislatures."[26]

Any action by the 1899 legislative session had to be anticlimatic after the selection of the senator, although two rather opposite acts of that session are of interest, and both, oddly enough, probably were due to the activities surrounding the Senate election. The first repealed the "purity of elections" law, recognizing the futility of such legislation in the face of the political campaign of 1898. The second went in the other direction by trying to provide the state with a system for election of United States senators which, by placing the names of senatorial candidates on the regular ballot, would give the voters an opportunity to indicate their preference for that office. The legislators would be morally but not legally bound to

[26] Stewart to E. D. Stableman, February 9, 1899, Stewart Papers, Letter Box, vol. 24, pp. 723–24.

support the choice of the people. The act also prohibited the payment of money or reward to any elector in return for his vote.[27]

As plans for the 1900 state conventions got under way, the question of fusion was the most important matter to be resolved by the Democrats and Silverites. The failure of the two groups to merge had been disastrous to the Democrats in the election of 1898; consequently, Democratic party leaders were anxious to effect some kind of fusion. The Silver party was divided over the issue. Newlands and his supporters saw fusion as the only way to ensure his reelection to the House and to strengthen his chances to replace Jones in the Senate in 1903. On the other hand, the Stewart-Wallace faction of the Silver party opposed fusion, not only because it would help Newlands, but also because they were convinced that the Silver party would lose its identity to the Democrats, and Wallace wanted to use the Silver party for one more election.

As in 1898, the issue of fusion was decided within the Silver party central committee. It appeared at the outset of their April meeting that Wallace and his supporters were in control and would prevent merger. However, a parliamentary struggle developed, and when it was over the Newlands forces had managed to put through one resolution appointing a conference committee to meet with the Democrats and another setting the Silver party convention at the same time and in the same town as the Democratic. These two resolutions practically ensured fusion and virtually ended control of the Silver party by the Wallace faction.

The action of the national party conventions in the summer of 1900 made certain the ultimate take-over of the Silver party by the Democrats. The Republicans nominated William McKinley and Theodore Roosevelt for president and vice-president and adopted a platform endorsing the gold standard and imperialism. The Democrats, after a brief debate over the silver issue, adopted a platform calling for the free and unlimited coinage of silver at a ratio of sixteen to one and condemning imperialism. Bryan won the nomination for president and Adlai Stevenson for vice-president.

The Republican National Convention again left Nevada Republicans with nowhere to go on the financial issue. Their state convention endorsed the national ticket and platform, but attempted to modify the gold standard plank by calling for the larg-

[27] *Nevada Statutes* (1899), chap. 71, pp. 86–87.

est possible use of silver as money. The major Republican candidate was E. S. Farrington, who was selected by Wallace supporters to oppose Newlands for the House of Representatives. His nomination was a clear indication that Wallace had already moved to carry out one of his earlier remarks to Stewart that when the Silver party collapsed they would have to move to organize the Repubican party in Nevada "or be left out in the cold."

Although the two parties had agreed to meet at the same time and in the same city, when the Democrats and Silverites opened their conventions it was obvious that fusion would not be automatic. The first attempts at merger were defeated because the Democrats balked at what they considered Wallace's undue influence in the ranks of the Silverites. The Silverites had been weakened by the defection of a number of its earlier supporters, including Senator William M. Stewart, who had returned to the Republican Party in the late summer of 1900. Unable to stand alone in Nevada without a national organization to back them, they were, in effect, forced to join the Democrats or concede the election to the Republicans. Consequently, the Silver party accepted the merger report submitted by the Democrats and then adopted a platform which nearly duplicated that accepted by the Democratic convention. Before the Silverites adjourned to meet jointly with the Democrats, they passed two additional resolutions: one denounced Stewart for his defection and demanded that he resign as senator, and the second rescinded the action of the state central committee in 1899 which had deposed William Sharon from the chairmanship of the committee and had read Newlands and Sharon out of the party.

The election of 1900 proved that the silver question was still a major issue in Nevada politics even though it had ceased to be so on the national level. The Silver-Democrats won every position by a substantial margin. Newlands defeated Farrington by a majority of 1,785 votes in spite of strong opposition from Wallace and Stewart, who had made a number of speeches supporting Farrington and trying to convince Nevadans that the silver issue was dead. When the election proved him wrong, he immediately started a movement to try to prevent Newlands from replacing Jones for the Senate in 1902. The story of that campaign marks the beginning of a new era in Nevada politics.

CHAPTER 10

Twentieth-Century Boom:
Copper Becomes King

THE YEAR 1900 not only opened a new century to Nevadans, it also presented them with a second great mining boom which in a few years pulled the state out of its twenty-year depression. The new discoveries were due collectively to the hundreds of prospectors who continued to roam the vast Nevada deserts and mountains not only blithely unaware of the political ramifications of the depression, but confident that the next piece of ore they found would lead to the dreamed-about bonanza.

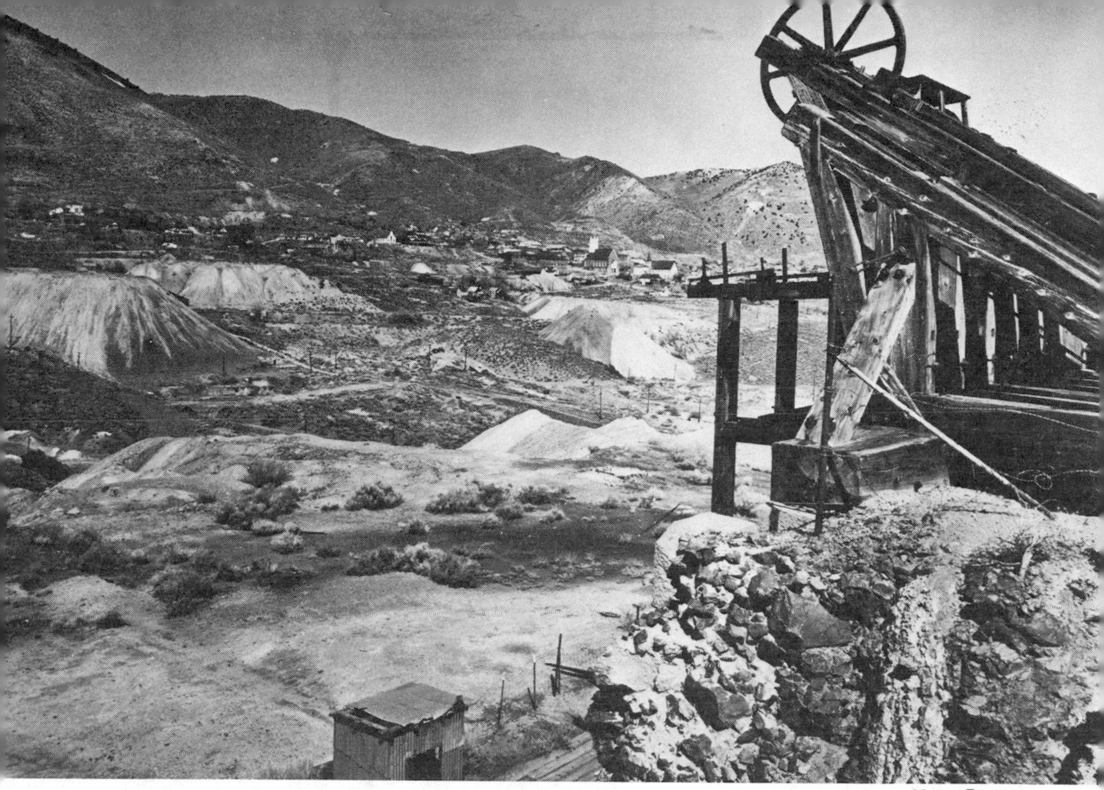

Reno News Bureau

Virginia City as it appeared in the 1960s

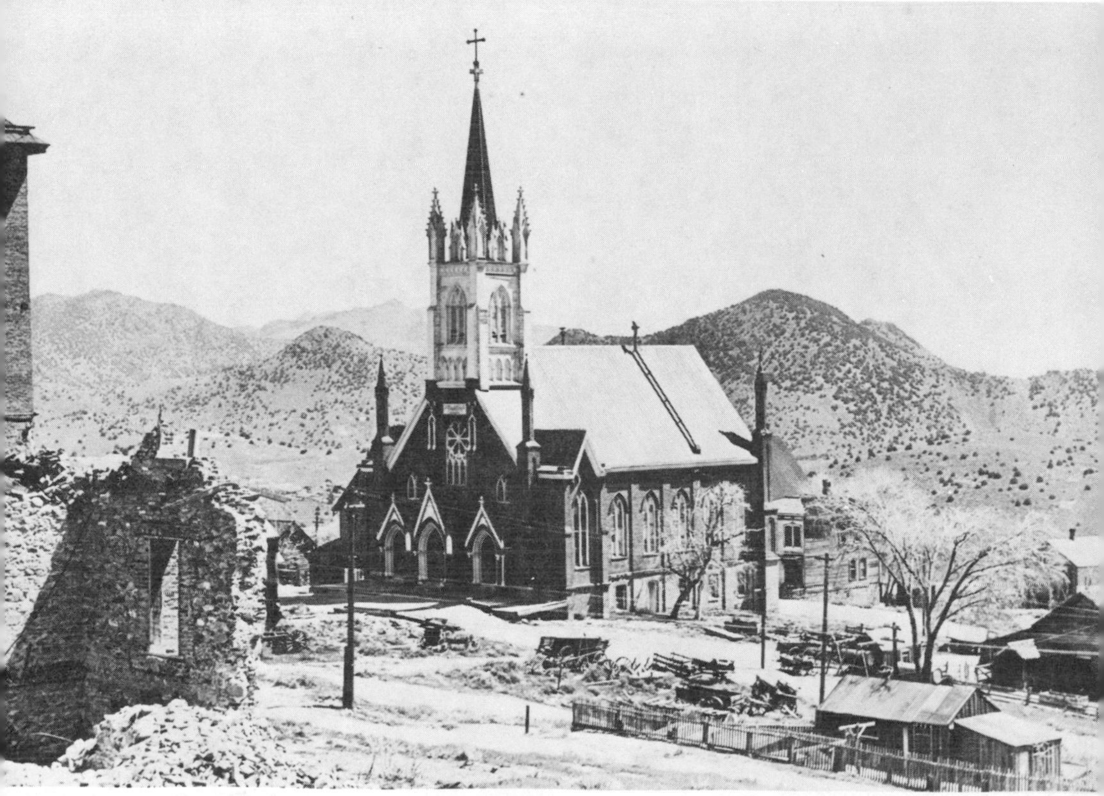

Nevada State Historical Society

St. Mary's Catholic Church, Virginia City

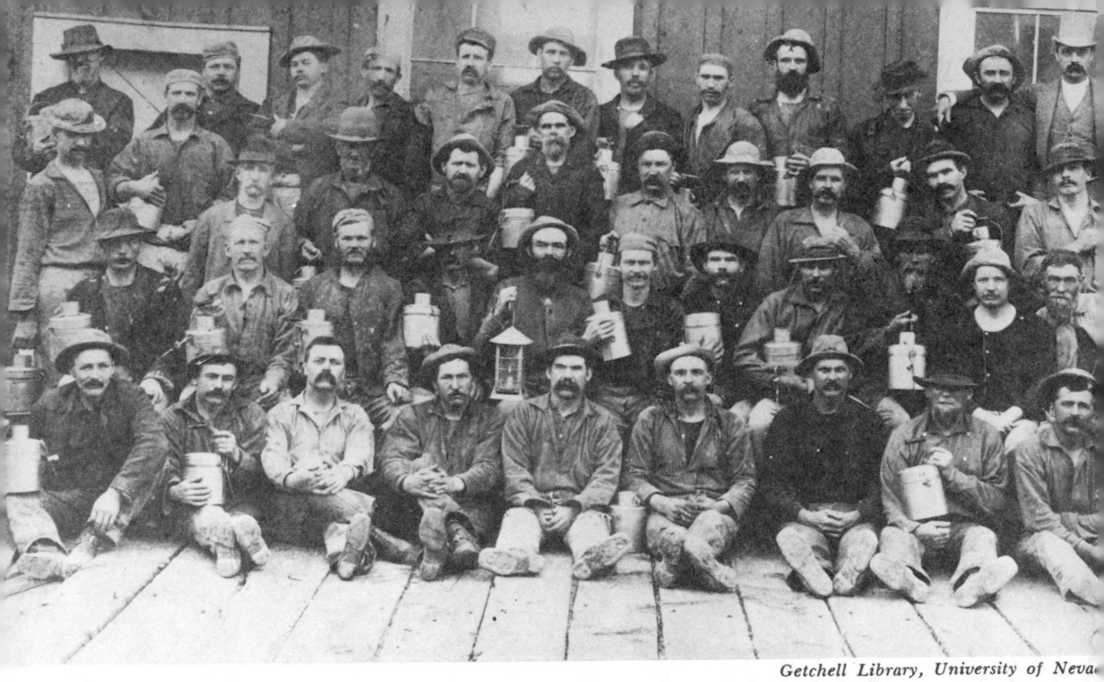

Getchell Library, University of Neva

Gould and Curry miners, Virginia City, about 1875

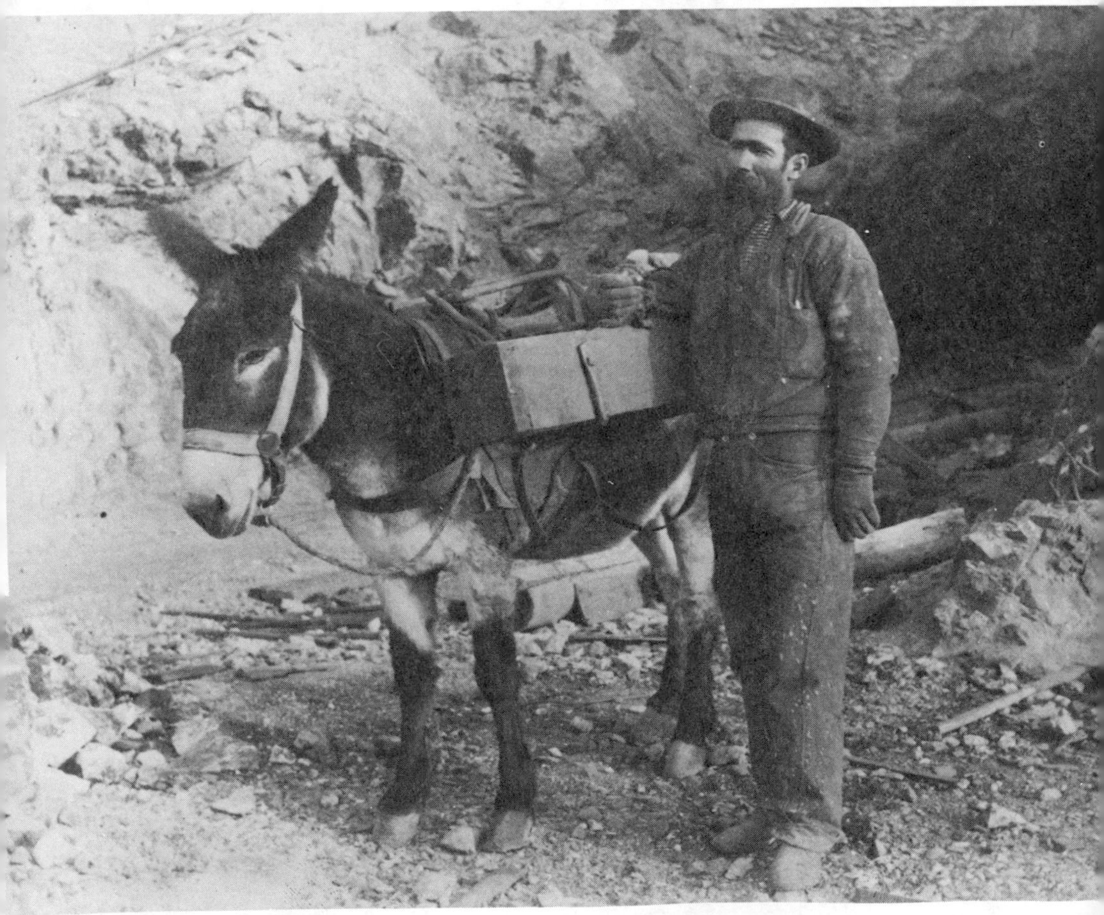

Getchell Library, University of Neva

"Steady, Jack"

Comstock ore wagons

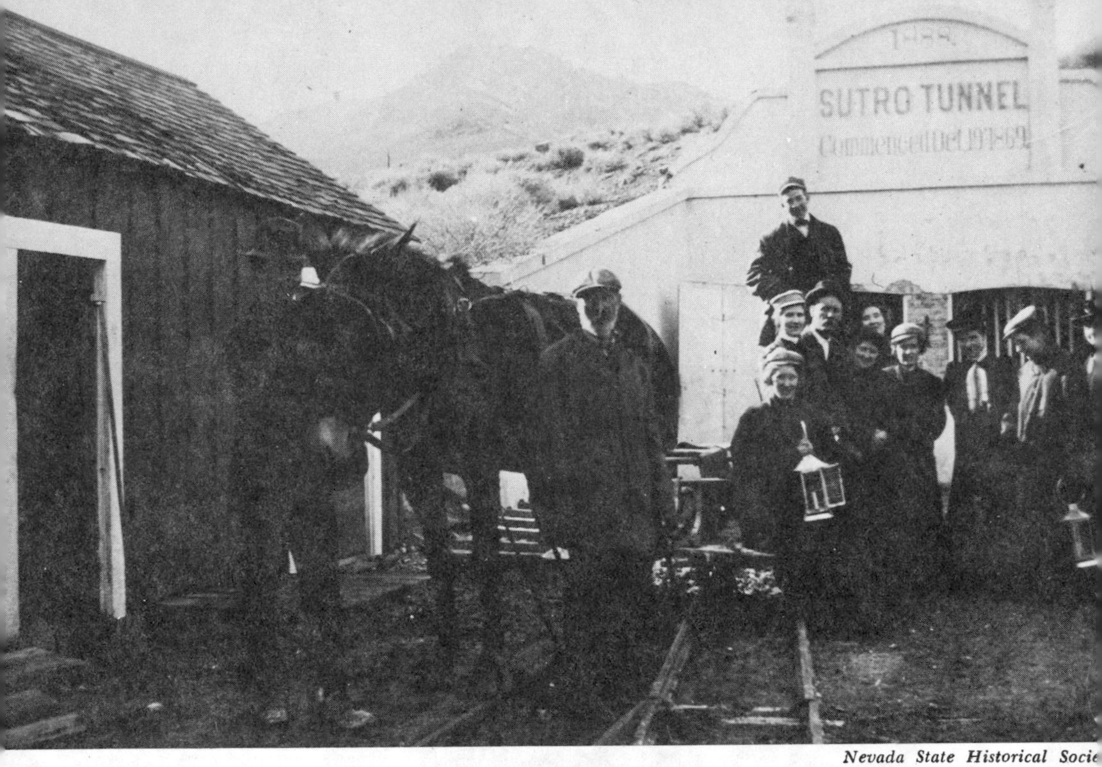

Nevada State Historical Soci

Sutro Tunnel portal

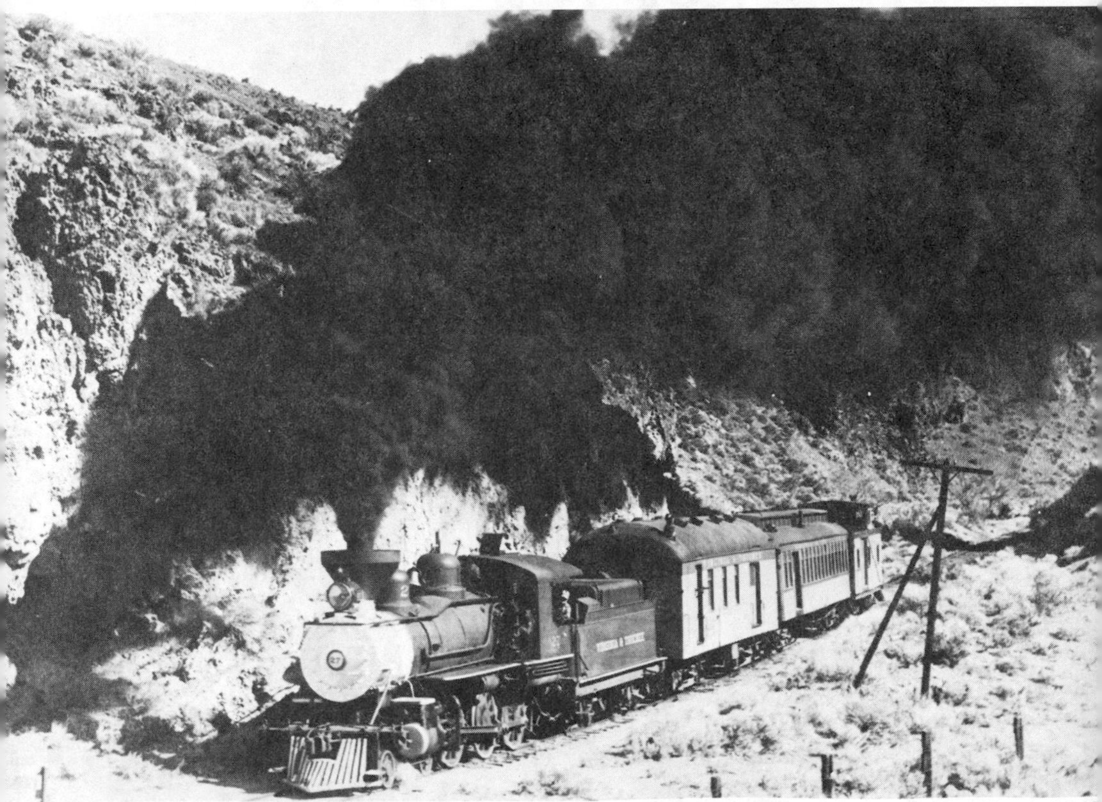

Nevada State Historical Soci

Virginia and Truckee Railroad

Nevada State Historical Society

Black Rock Desert, a remnant of prehistoric Lake Lahontan

Reno News Bureau

Pyramid Lake, once a part of Lake Lahontan

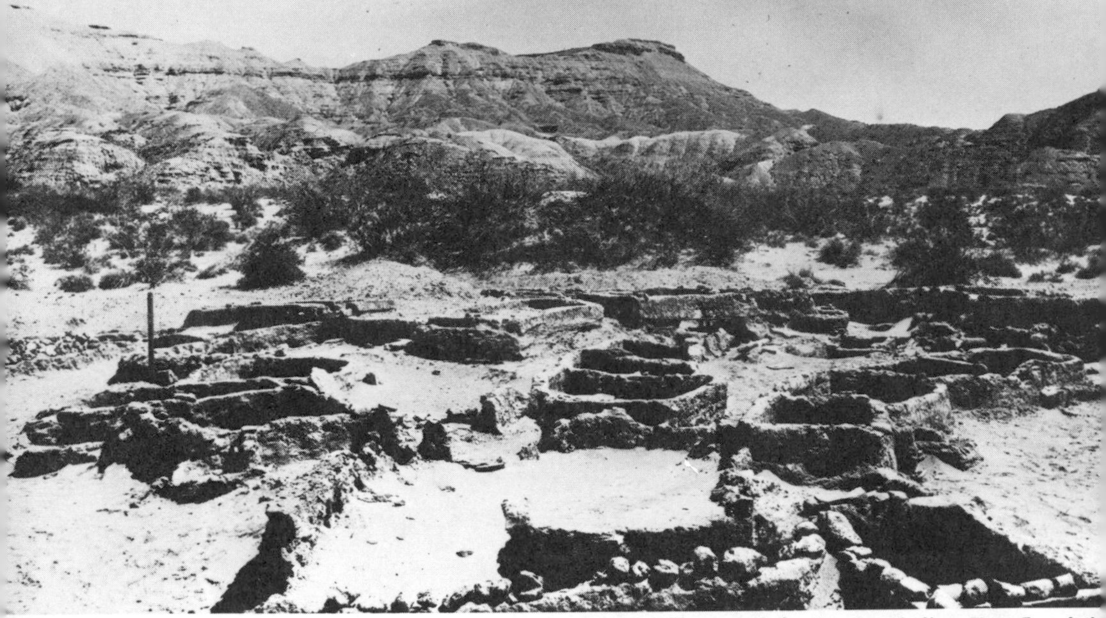

Museum of the American Indian, Heye Foundatic

Pueblo Grande (Lost City)

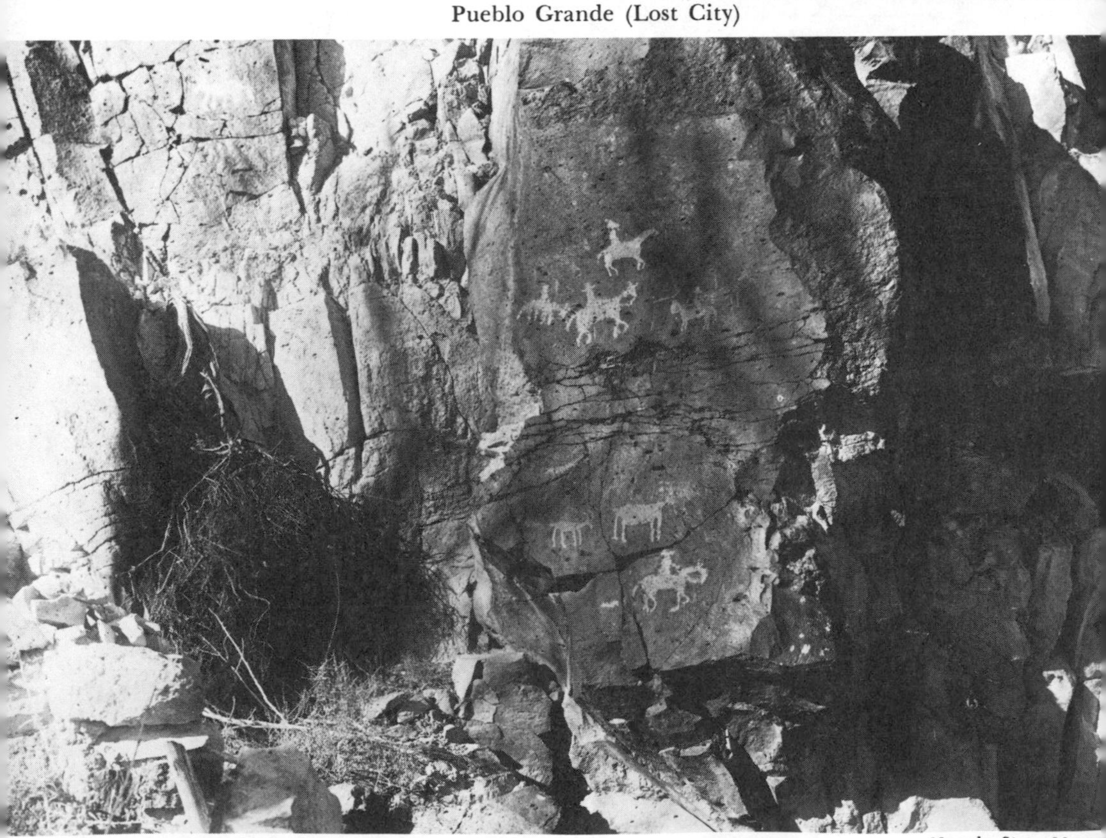

Nevada State Museu

Petroglyphs, southern Nevada

Paiute house at Walker Lake

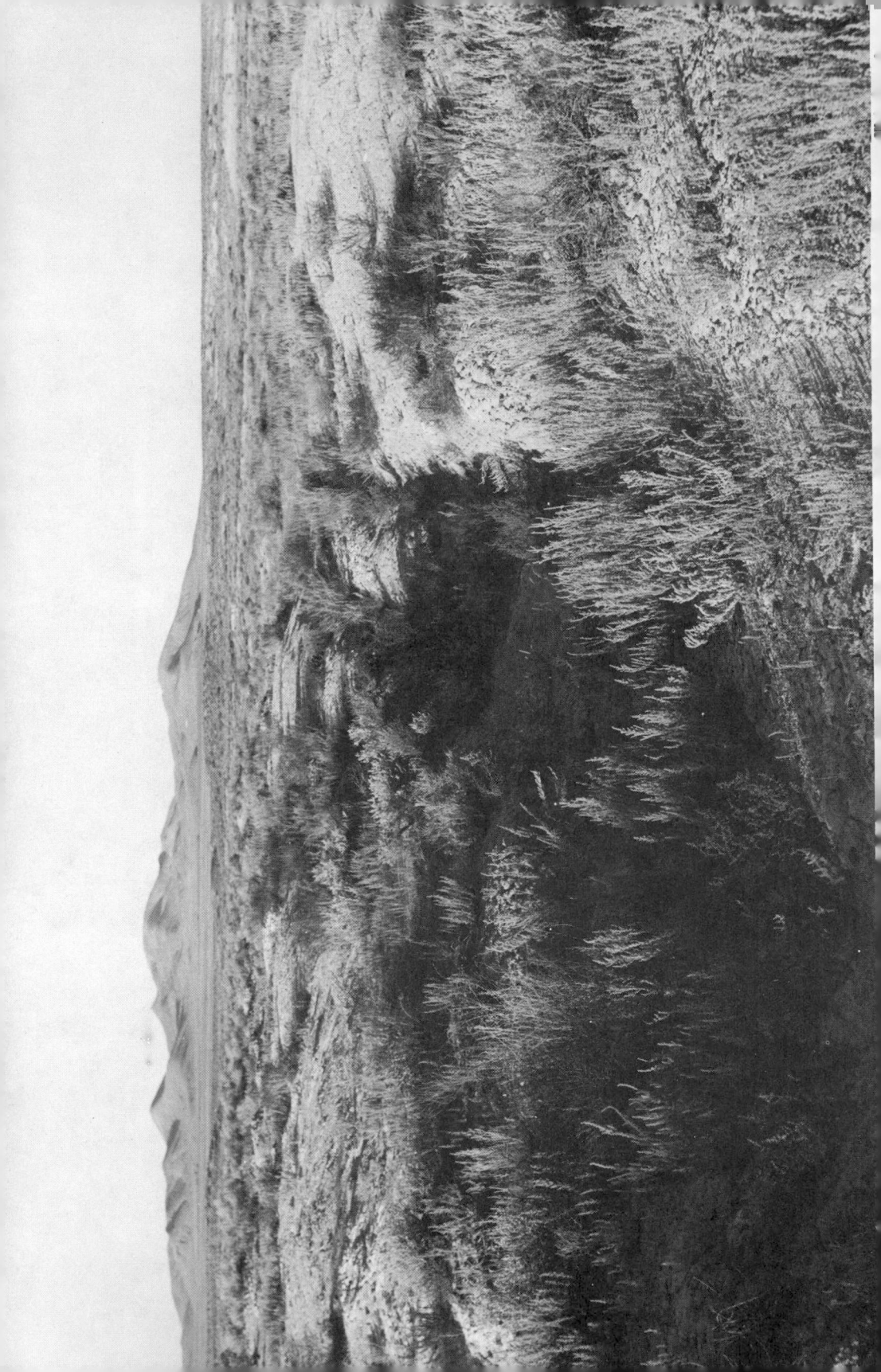

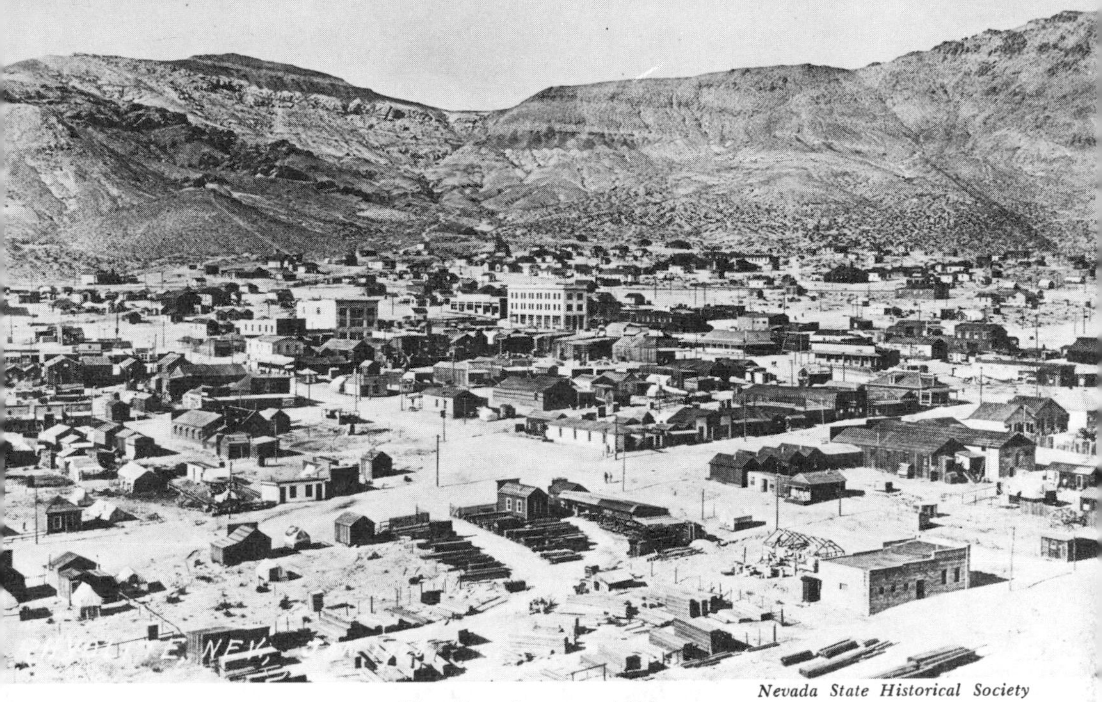

Nevada State Historical Society

Rhyolite, January, 1908

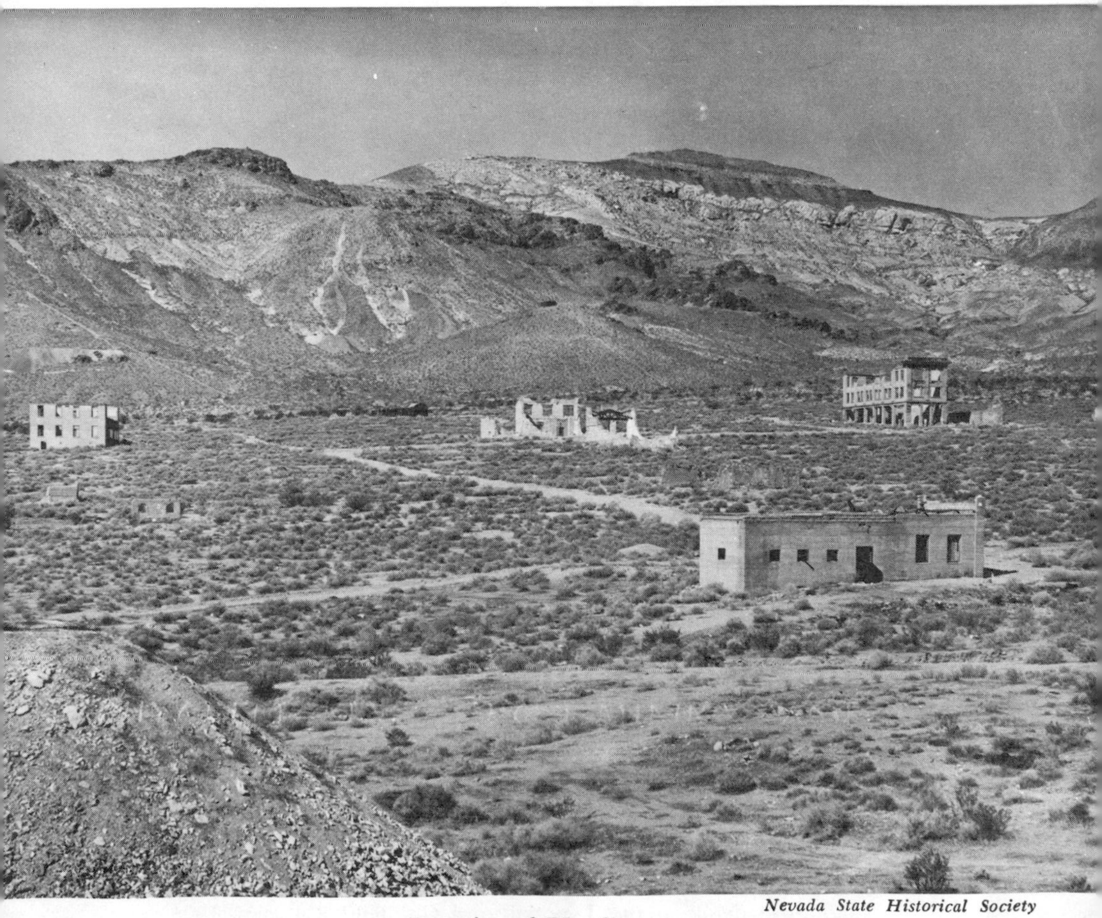

Nevada State Historical Society

Remains of Rhyolite

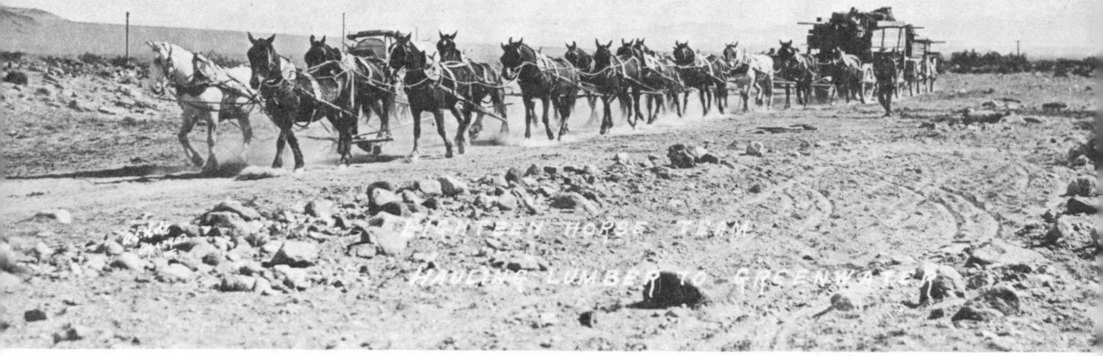

Nevada State Historical Societ

Eighteen-horse team hauling lumber, early 1900s

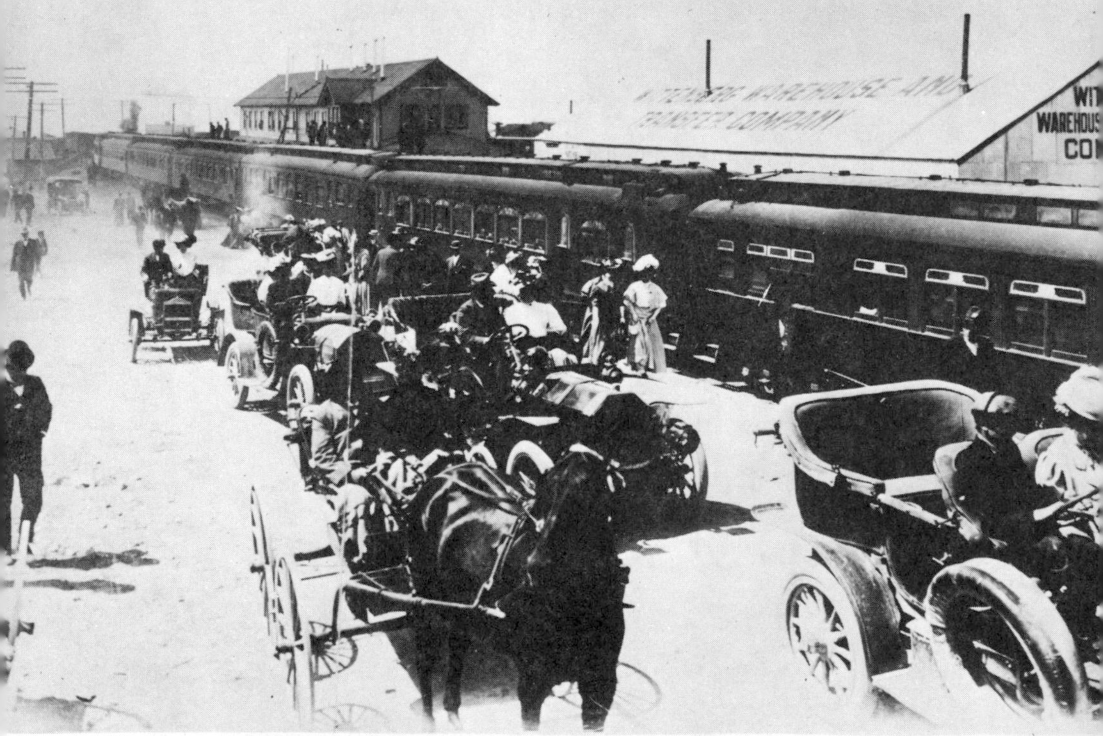

Nevada State Historical Society

Tonopah depot of the Tonopah and Goldfield Railroad, 1906

Fourth of July drilling contest, Goldfield, 1907

Governor Sparks and party leaving Goldfield for the Bullfrog District, 1906

D. O. Mills

Senator William Sharon

Senator James G. Fair

John Mackay

Senator William M. Stewart

Senator John P. Jones

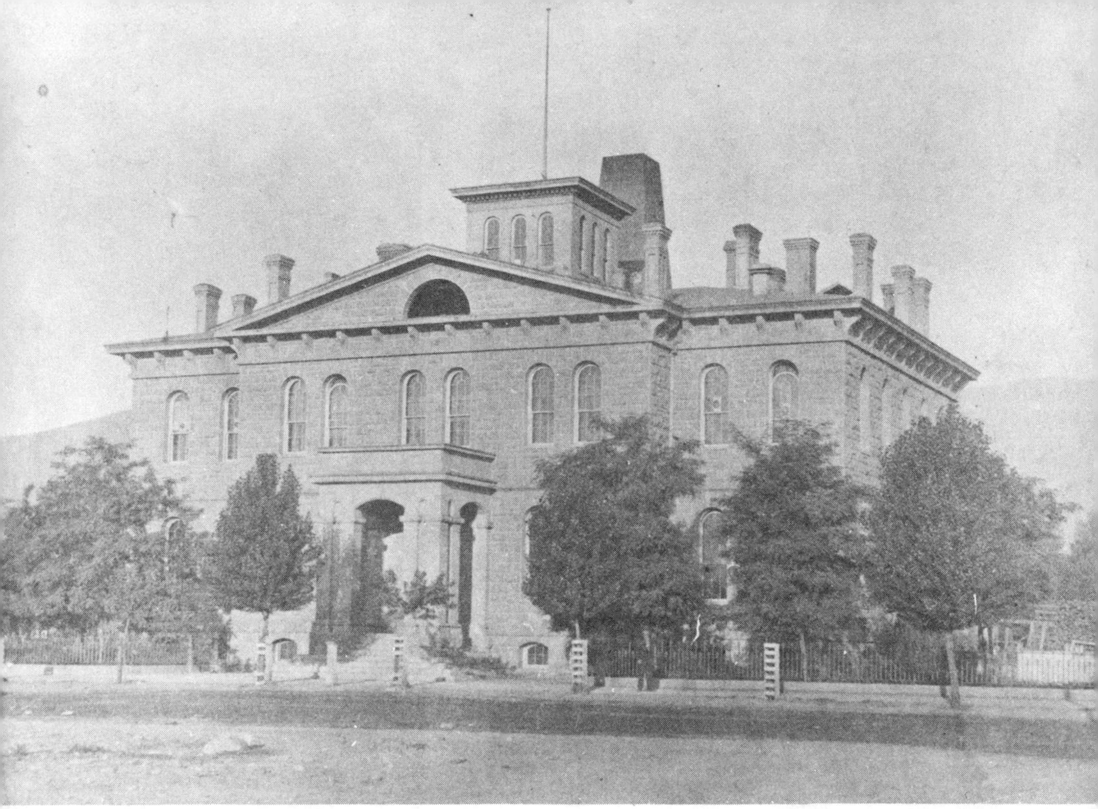

Nevada State Museum

The Carson City Mint in the mid-1870s (now part of the Nevada State Museum)

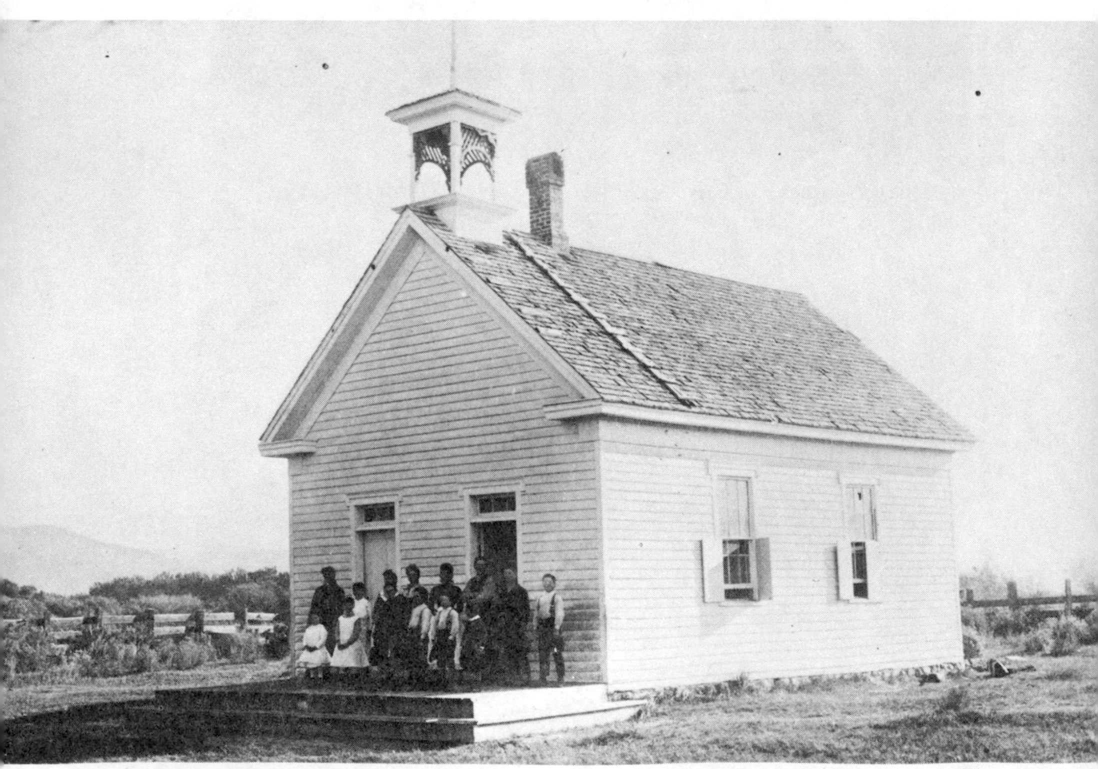

Nevada State Historical Societ

Glendale School, the earliest in the Truckee Meadows

Goldfield, 1903. Two years later Goldfield was a teeming city of 25,000.

Prospectors setting out from Goldfield, 1903

Civilian Conservation Corps camp at Berry Creek, near McGill

Hoover (Boulder) Dam

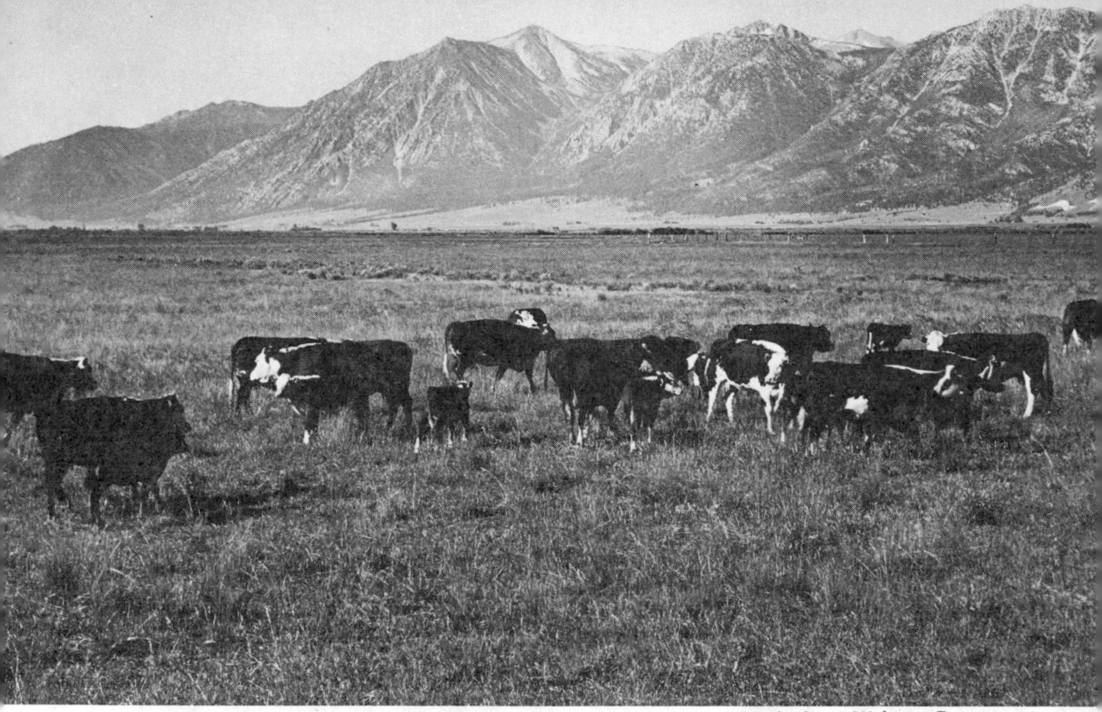

Nevada State Highway Department

Cattle grazing, Carson Valley

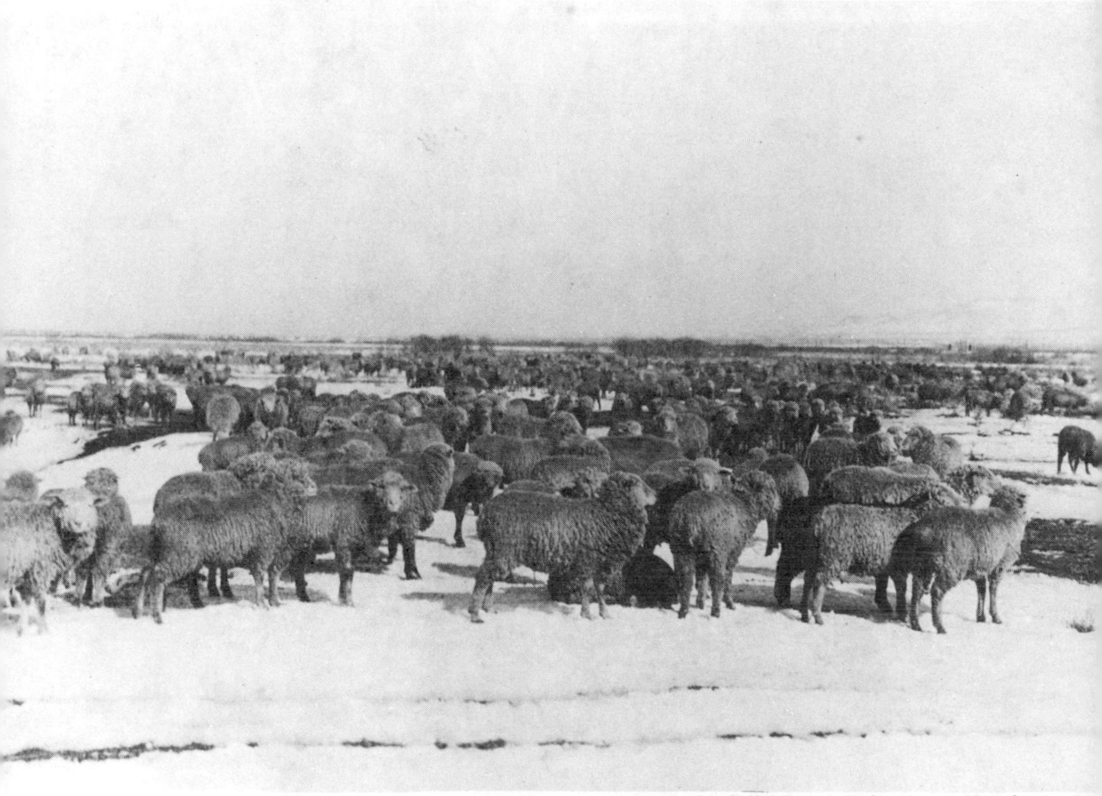

Getchell Library, University of Nevada

Sheep on their winter range

Copper reduction plant, McGill

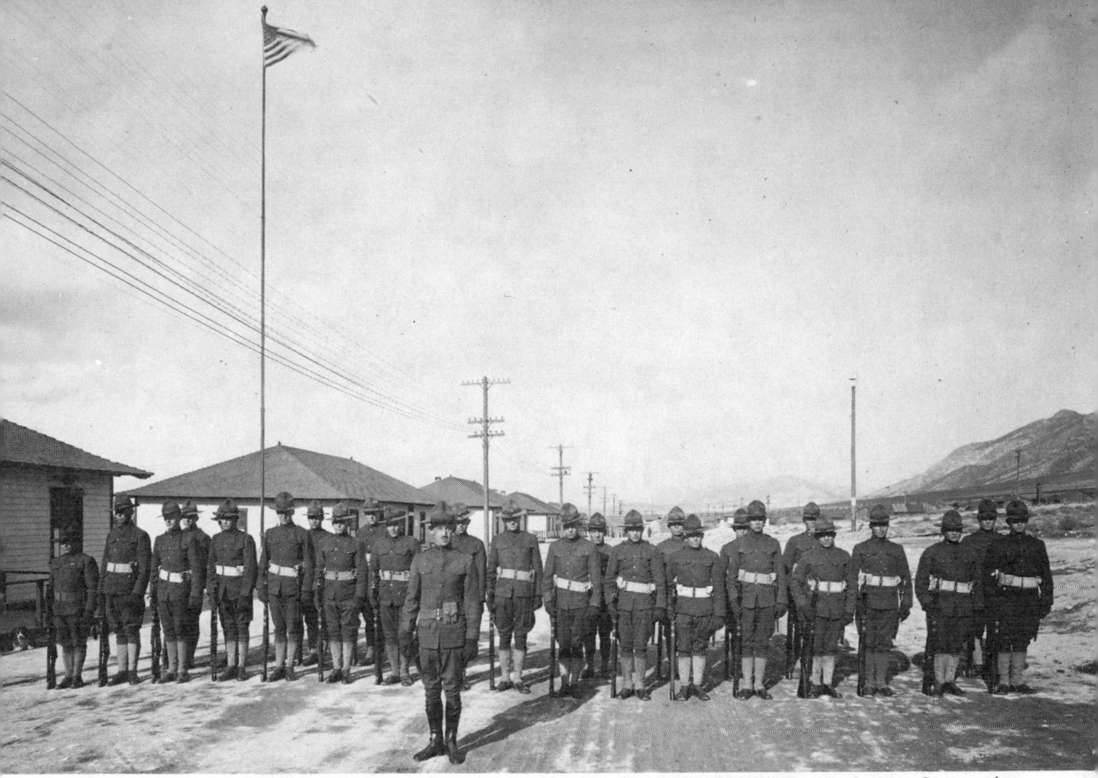

Nevada Mines Division, Kennecott Copper Corporation

Troops sent to guard the McGill copper reduction plant during World War I

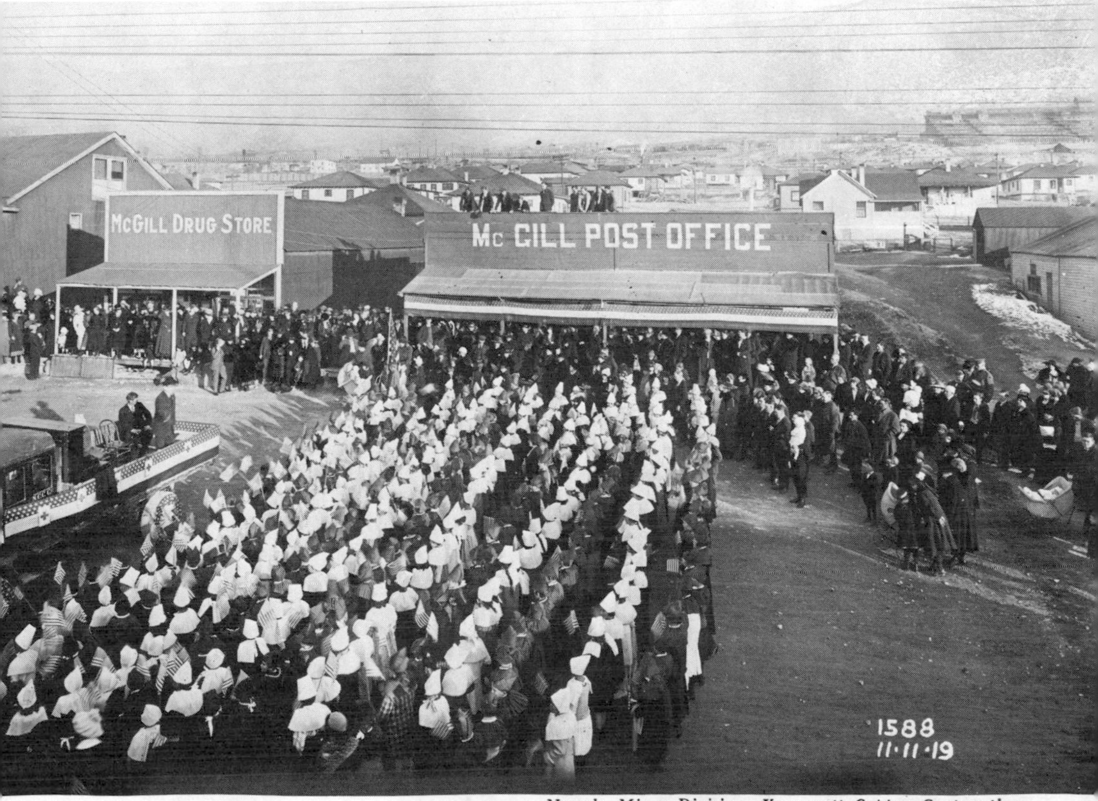

Nevada Mines Division, Kennecott Copper Corporation

Armistice celebration at McGill, 1919

Anne Martin, Nevada's first woman candidate for the United States Senate, 1918

George Nixon

Senator Francis G. Newlands

Senator Key Pittman

Senator Pat McCarran

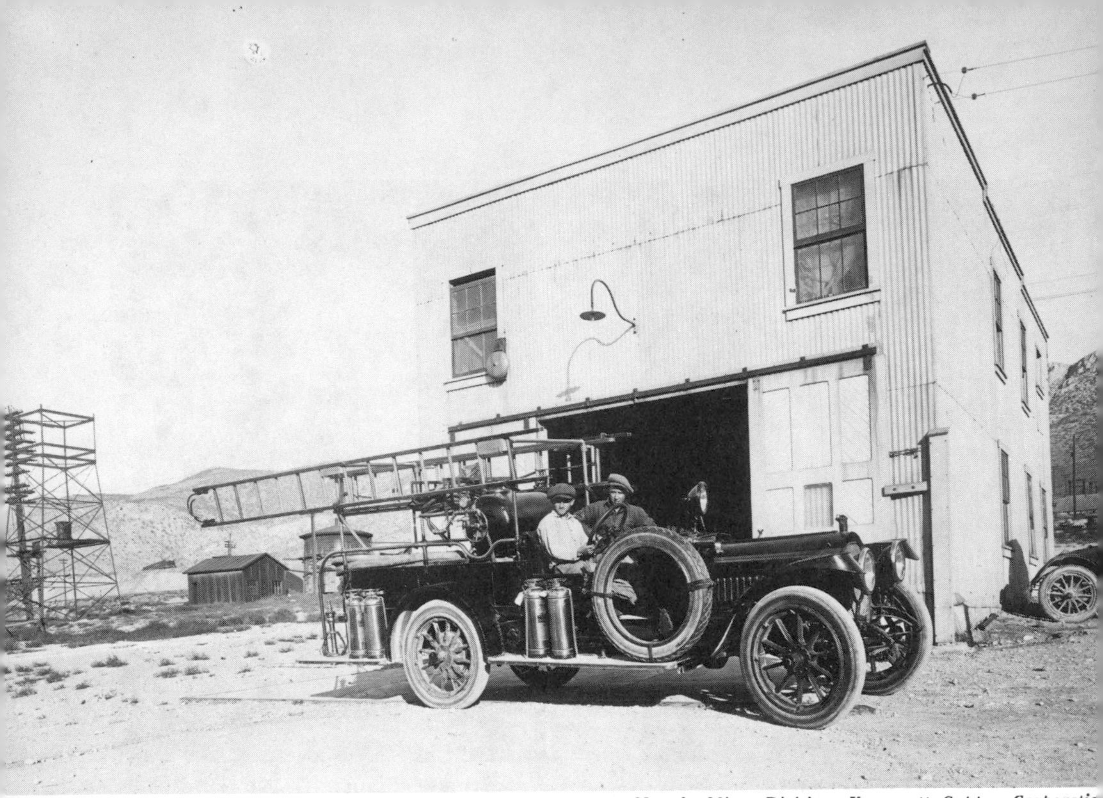

McGill's fire engine, 1920

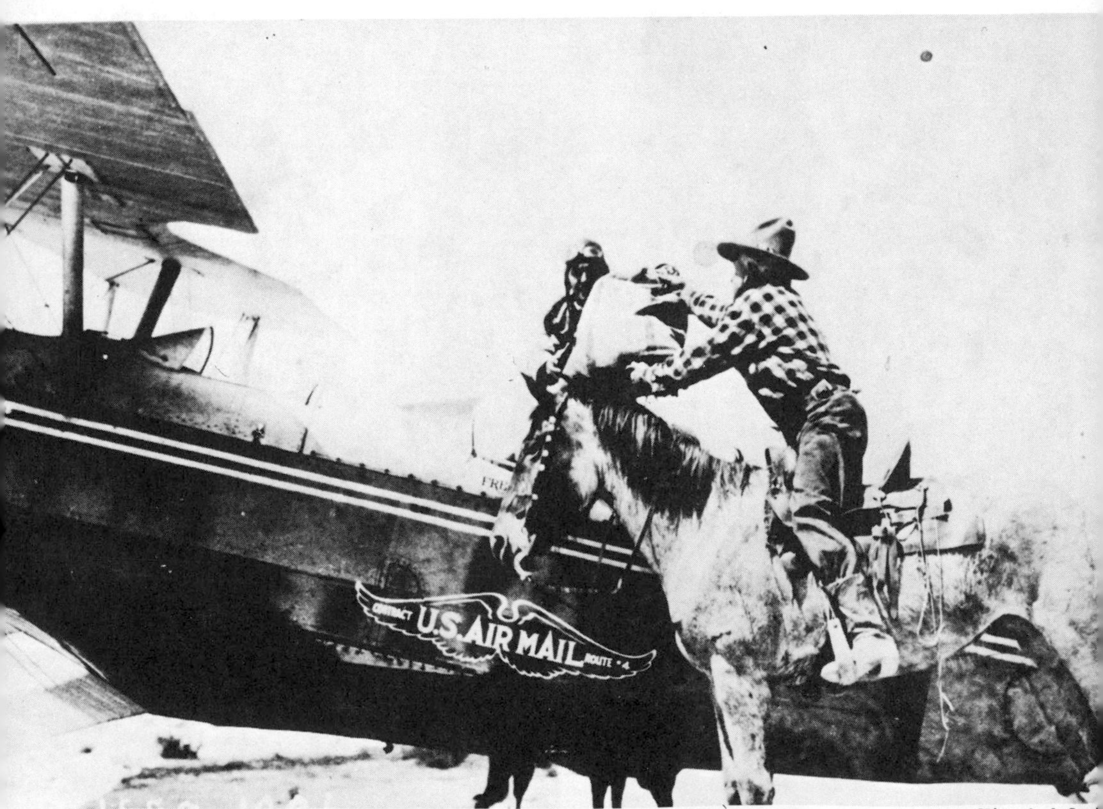

U.S. AIR MAIL ROUTE 4

United States airmail, Las Vegas, 1921

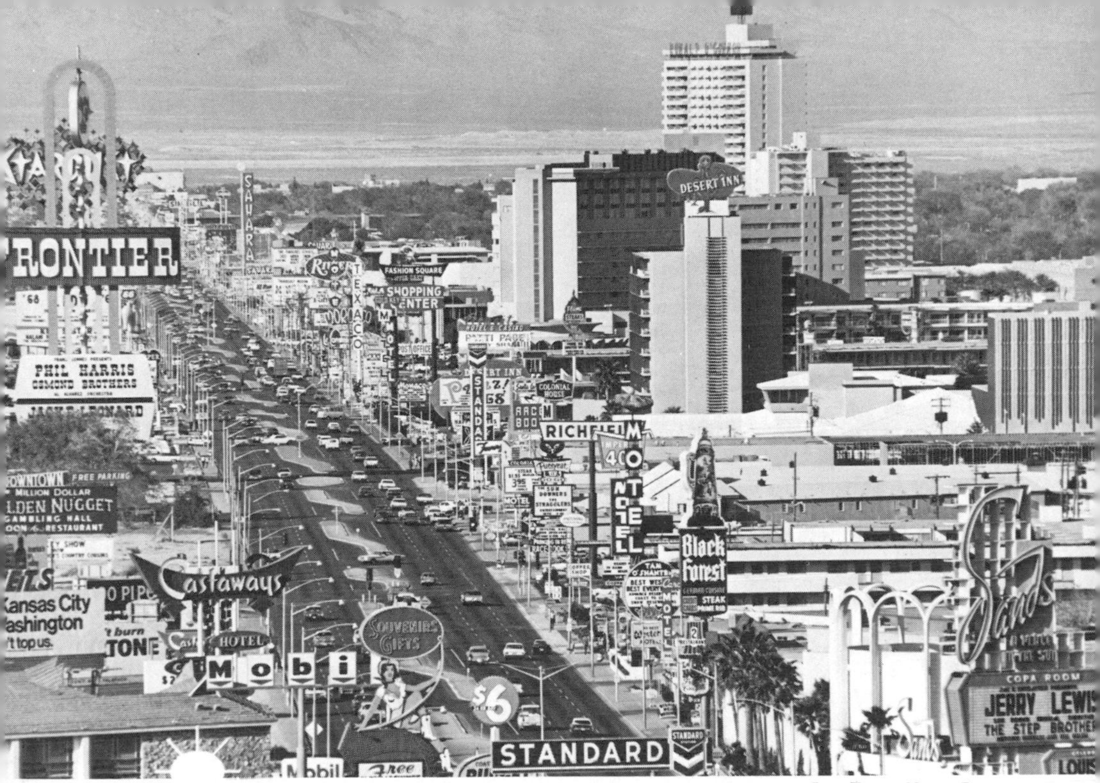

Las Vegas News Bureau

Hotel-casinos along the Las Vegas Strip

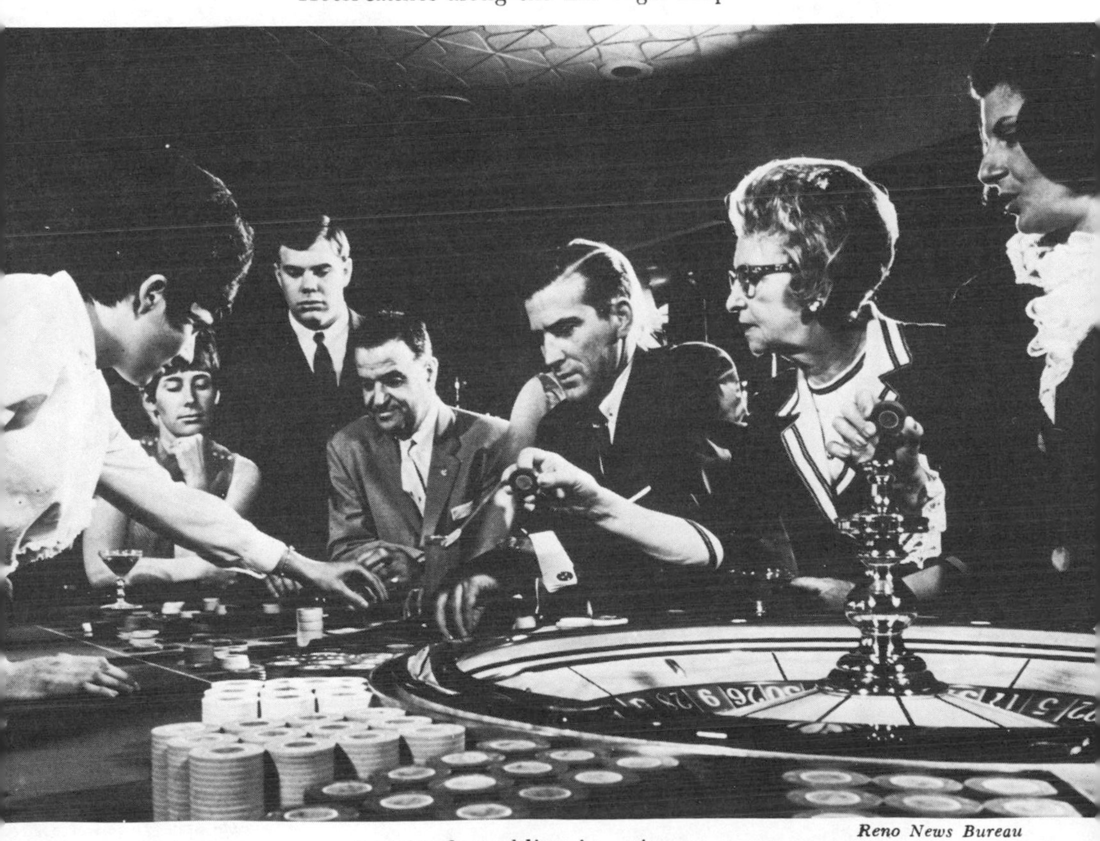

Reno News Bureau

Legalized gambling in action

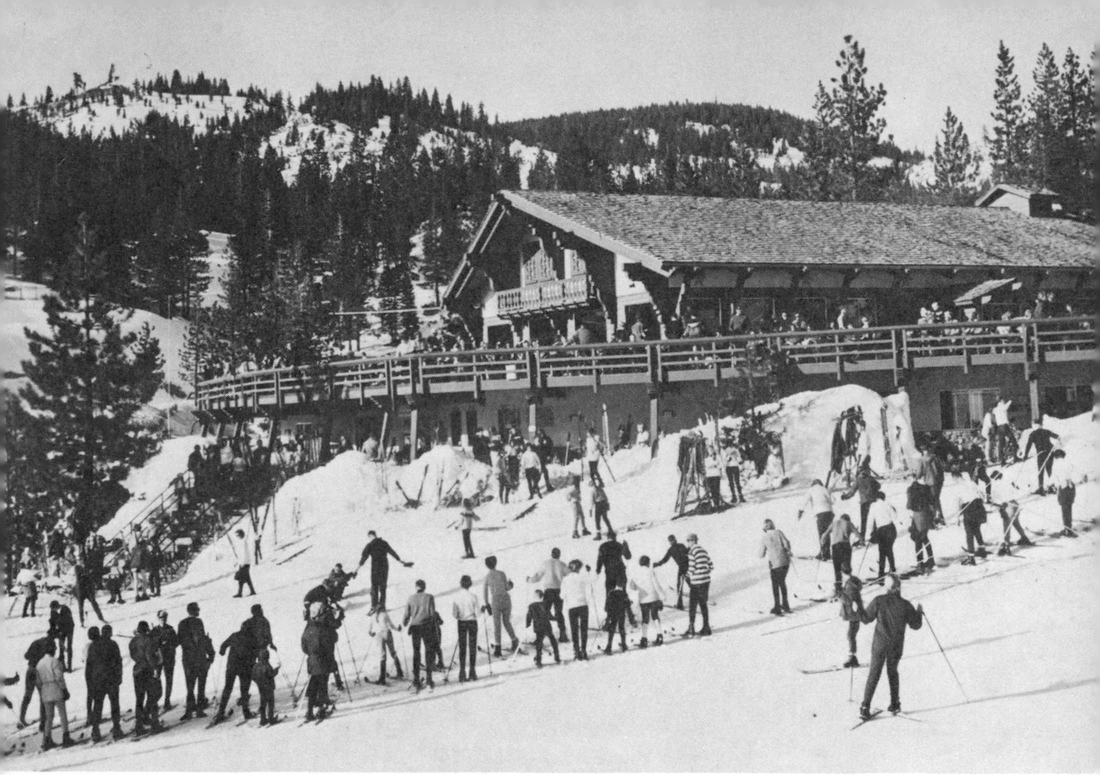

Reno News Bureau

One of the many ski resorts in western Nevada

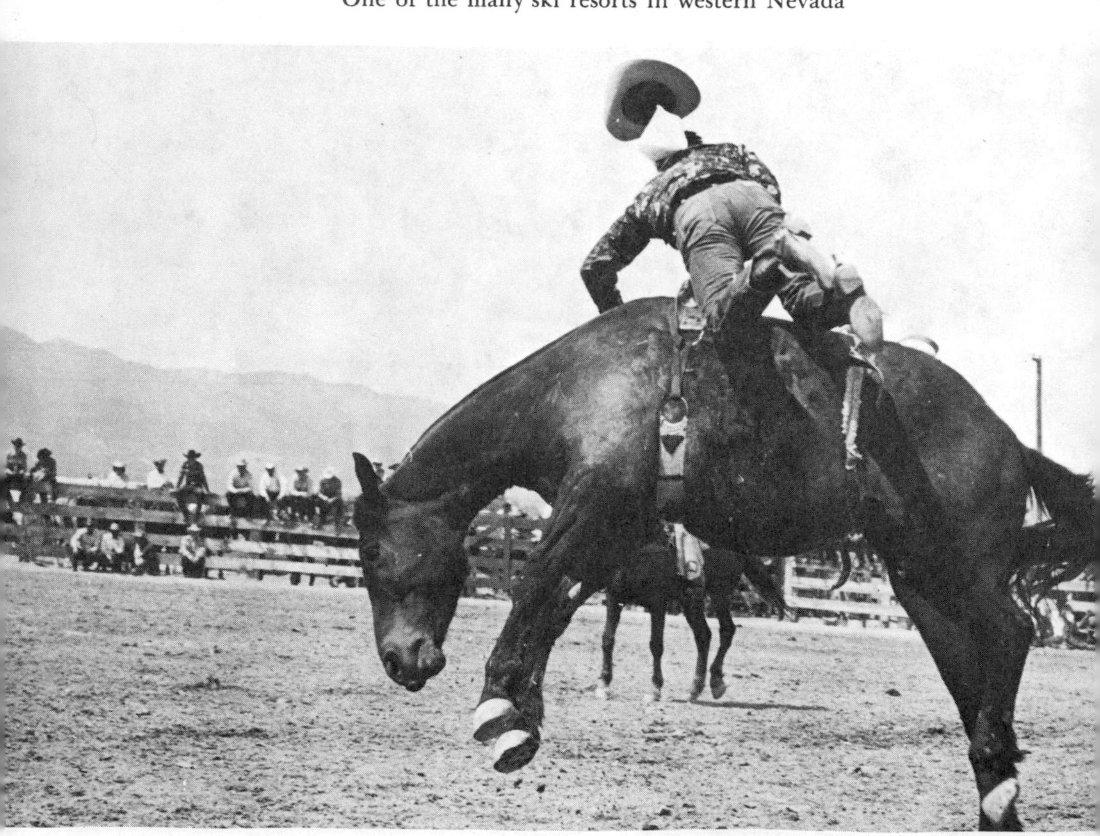

Nevada State Historical Society

Lovelock rodeo

Lake Tahoe

State capitol building, Carson City

Nevada State Highway Department

Reno News Bureau

Atmospherium-planetarium, Desert Research Institute, University of Nevada System, Reno

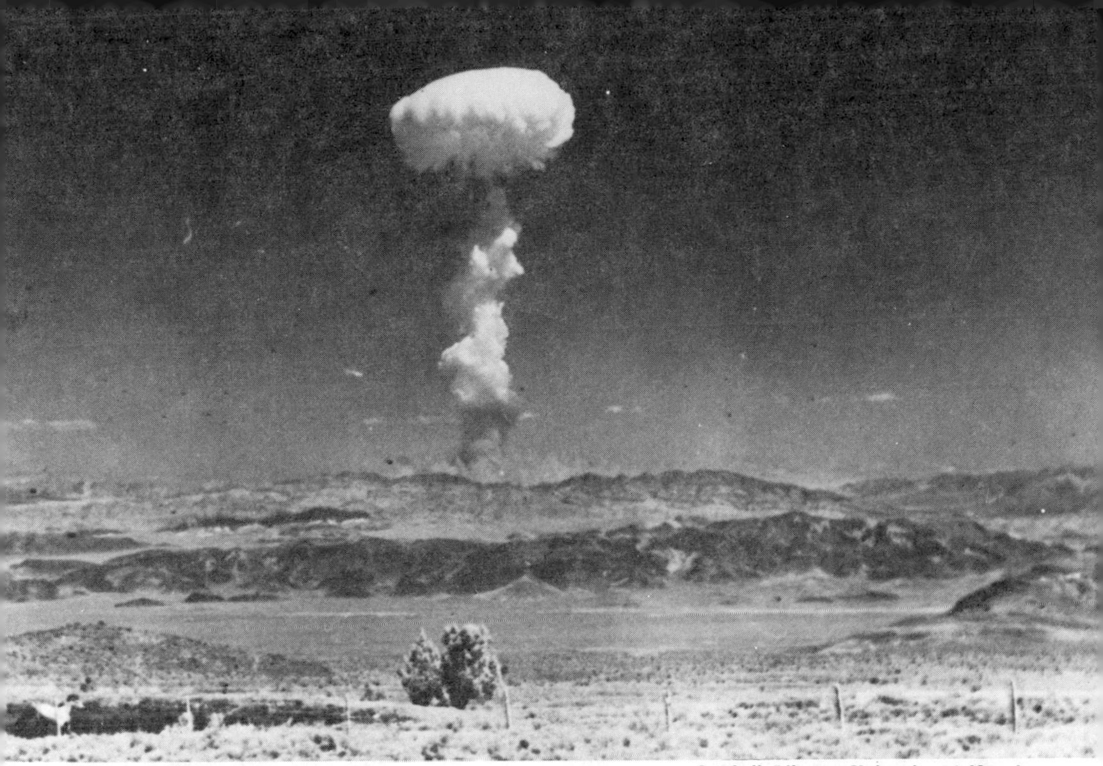

Getchell Library, University of Nevada

Operation Big Shot atomic blast, Yucca Flat

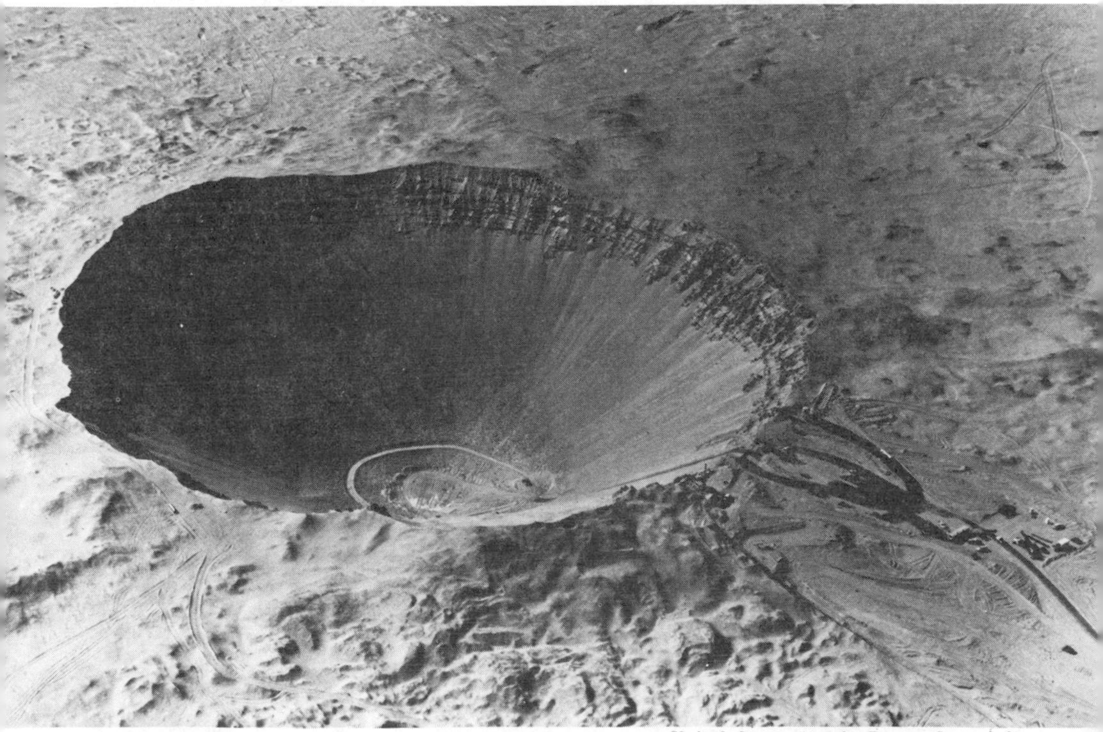

United States Atomic Energy Commission

Crater formed northwest of Las Vegas by Project Sedan, part of the Plowshare Program to develop civilian uses for nuclear explosives. Approximately twelve million tons of earth was lifted, forming an excavation 635 feet deep and 1,280 feet in diameter.

Governors of Nevada

Nevada State Highway Department

Senator Charles B. Henderson

Senator George W. Malone

Senator Alan Bible

Senator Howard Cannon

Representative Walter S. Baring

Governor Mike O'Callaghan

Office of James D. Santini

Representative
James D. Santini

Office of Senator Chic Hecht

Senator Chic Hecht

Nevada State Historical Society

Representative David Towell

Office of Representative Harry Reid

Representative Harry Reid

Office of Governor Richard Bryan

Governor Richard H. Bryan

Office of Representative Barbara Vucanovich

Representative
Barbara F. Vucanovich

Nevada State Historical Society

Governor Robert List

Office of Senator Paul Laxalt

Senator Paul Laxalt

NEW DISCOVERIES OF SILVER AND GOLD

The boom got under way slowly and haphazardly on May 19, 1900 when a sometime miner by the name of Jim Butler, while roaming the hills of southwestern Nevada, came across the outcroppings which led ultimately to the formation of the Tonopah Mining District. Butler's funds were so limited that he could not afford the necessary assays and had to turn to a young attorney friend, Tasker L. Oddie, for assistance. A native of Brooklyn, New York, Oddie had come to Nevada in 1898 to investigate business interests for his employer, Anson Phelps Stokes. He was so impressed with the area that he decided to remain in Nevada and opened a law office in the old mining camp of Austin.

Oddie's finances at the time of the discovery were little better than Butler's, but he was able to get a science teacher, Walter Gayhart, to perform the necessary assays in return for a share of Oddie's part interest in the still unlocated claim. The Gayhart assays, dated June 18, showed 640 ounces in silver and a value of $200 in gold per ton. Oddie and Gayhart, understandably excited, wanted to locate claims immediately; not so Butler, who had office duties to attend to and hay to harvest. It was not until August 25 that he returned to the discovery site to locate and record the necessary claims.

The problems faced by the first locators in the district were, in many respects, greater than those met by their earlier counterparts on the Comstock. Tonopah, as the camp which grew up around the discovery site was called, was situated in one of the most inaccessible regions in Nevada.[1] The lack of water, timber, and capital for development added to the problems of transportation and communication. Using picks and shovels and a hand windlass, Butler and his associates obtained two tons of ore, which was hauled by wagon to Austin for shipment to Salt Lake City. The $500 check that they received for the ore not only demonstrated the high costs of transportation and reduction—it publicized the new campsite.

The Tonopah discovery closed the door on the long depression which had plagued Nevada mining since the decline of the Comstock. Within months dozens of new discoveries were made in the southern part of the state. Two of them became producers and,

[1] Tonopah is an Indian word meaning brush springs.

with Tonopah, formed the nucleus of Nevada's second great silvergold boom.

Harry Stimler and William Marsh, prospectors who were grub-staked from Tonopah by Tom Kendall and Jim Butler,[2] made the first of these discoveries on Columbia Mountain, about thirty miles south of Tonopah, on December 4, 1902. The first locations attracted little attention, but additional locations in the summer of 1903 and a rich gold strike in January, 1904, set the stage for a mining rush reminiscent of earlier days on the Comstock. As at Tonopah, newcomers to the new Goldfield Mining District found the best ground located and pressed on to the south. Their activity resulted in a third strike, made on August 9, 1904, by Frank ("Shorty") Harris and Ernest Cross, seventy miles south of Gold-field in a desolate region of southern Nye County just a few miles east of Death Valley, California. The new discovery was in a region even less accessible than Tonopah, and although the first samples from the new district, called Bullfrog because of the coloring of the ore, were very rich it was some time before development could begin. One hundred or more mineral discoveries resulted from Butler's first locations in 1900. To avoid repetition, the three districts cited above will be used to illustrate the story of this twentieth-century silvergold boom.

DEVELOPMENT OF MINING COMPANIES

Exploitation of the new areas was delayed by the cloud of suspicion which surrounded Nevada mining as a result of the speculative frauds of the Comstock era. San Francisco capitalists, hurt most by these speculative failures, were particularly wary of Nevada mining investments. Shut off from the most likely financial support, yet reluctant to dispose of their claims, Butler and his associates turned to the leasing system as the only possible way to prove the value of their holdings and at the same time gain additional capital for later development.

Butler granted the first leases in December, 1900, and the idea proved immediately popular and practical. The leases, all oral,

---

[2]Grubstake contracts were an essential part of the mining frontier. By this device an investor supplied a prospector with supplies in return for a share in his discoveries. Thus, large areas of Nevada were prospected with a minimum of investment.

granted 100-foot lengths along the vein and 50 feet on each side. The owners received 25 percent of the production after operating costs were subtracted. The lessees, anxious to get as much ore from the ground as possible, publicized the camp throughout the mining world and within a short time attracted a number of prospective capitalists. Among them was Oscar A. Turner, a mining promoter from Grass Valley, California, who represented a group of Philadelphia financiers including John Woodside, John Andersen, and Arthur Brock.[3] Turner negotiated a deal whereby Butler and his associates were paid $336,000 for their Tonopah holdings. Incorporation of the property as the Tonopah Mining Company in July, 1901, heralded the end of the leasing stage of development, although at Butler's insistence the lessees were allowed to work their ground until January 1, 1902.

Gradually the Philadelphia capitalists who made the initial investments at Tonopah gained financial control of the mining district. By 1905, led by the Brock family, they controlled the most important mines in the district, the Tonopah Mining Company, the Tonopah-Belmont Company, the Tonopah and Goldfield Railroad, and the Bullfrog-Goldfield Railroad. John Brock was president of all four companies. The addition of milling companies, water companies, and banking interests gave the Philadelphians an economic control of the Tonopah area which, while not as colorful as the control of the Comstock by the Bank Crowd, no doubt was just as efficient.

The leasing system was also used at Goldfield to develop and publicize that camp. The most famous lease there, the Hayes-Monette, uncovered an unbelievably rich body of ore, including one carload which, when sent to a smelter near San Francisco, returned the owners a check for $574,958.39. The leasing system at Goldfield led at first to the formation of over 100 separate mining companies and then to a major consolidation by George Nixon and George Wingfield. Nixon, a native Californian who started his career in Nevada as a telegraph operator on the Carson and Colorado Railroad, and Wingfield, a native of Fort Smith, Arkansas, who had joined the rush to Tonopah in 1901, began the move to corporate control of the area in 1906 by purchasing the Jumbo, Red Top, and

[3] This group also included Charles Miller, former governor of Delaware.

Mohawk properties. With these as a nucleus, they incorporated the Goldfield Consolidated Mines Company with a capitalization of $50 million. Additional purchases in January, 1907, gave them control of all but one of the operating mines at Goldfield.

By the time the Bullfrog district was opened to exploitation the reluctance of investors to enter the Nevada mining field had disappeared and thus leasing did not gain a foothold. The most prominent of the companies organized in the new district was the Montgomery-Shoshone, incorporated in 1905 by E. A. Montgomery and purchased soon after by Charles Schwab, president of the U.S. Steel Corporation. Neither that company nor the many others formed here justified the faith of the organizers, for the Bullfrog was the first district to fail.

The formation of mining companies in each of the new districts brought a corresponding growth and development of the water and power systems which in turn made large-scale mining and milling possible. The early water supply systems were built by private concerns more interested in bringing water to the business houses and residences than to the mines. Mining companies found it necessary to purchase these companies and to seek additional sources of water in order to keep pace with the increasing demands from the mines and mills. Power development followed much the same pattern initially, with numerous small companies organized throughout southern Nevada. Ultimately, most of them were absorbed into the Nevada-California Power Company, which by 1912 had three hydoelectric plants generating 16,500 horsepower, and 350 miles of transmission lines reaching to Tonopah, Goldfield, Rhyolite, Beatty, Manhattan, Gold Center, Lida, and numerous other, smaller camps in Nevada and California.

With adequate water and power, the mining companies were able to move from experimental mills to rather sophisticated operations that employed the latest milling techniques and ensured an efficiency of operation quite superior to that achieved during the Comstock era. During the developmental period there was much discussion about the advantages and disadvantages of smelting as opposed to milling in the extraction of local ores. Experimental mills, first constructed at Tonopah in 1903 and at Goldfield in 1904, demonstrated by 1906 that practically all the ores from these districts could be handled more profitably by milling than by smelting processes.

The first large mill at Tonopah was constructed by the owners of the Tonopah Mining Company, who followed Comstock precedents in forming a separate milling organization, known as the Desert Power and Milling Company. The new mill, a 100-stamp cyanide plant, was built at Millers, a station on the Tonopah and Goldfield Railroad approximately thirteen miles west of Tonopah. It was in full operation by the end of 1907 and immediately proved itself with a consistent extraction of approximately 90 percent. Its completion set the stage for the construction of additional mills which made possible efficient exploitation of the Tonopah district's low-grade ores.

The mill-building period in the Goldfield District, initiated in 1904 with the construction of a number of small, experimental mills, climaxed in 1908 with the completion of the 100-stamp Consolidated Mill. Designed by Francis L. Bosqui and John B. Fleming, it was of the "all-sliming" variety employing a combination of crushing, amalgamation, concentration, and cyaniding. Under the management of George Wingfield the mill became a model of efficiency and safety. The average recovery rate reached as high as 93 percent in 1912 and the cost per ton was reduced to $2.50.

Adequate water and power made possible large-scale mining and milling operations; adequate capital had been assured by the formation of the mining companies as eastern capitalists moved into the districts. It was left for the railroads to complete the circle of potential exploitation by solving the basic transportation problems.

TRANSPORTATION DEVELOPMENT

Railroads became a necessity once the leasing system demonstrated the existence of large deposits at both Tonopah and Goldfield, but before capital became available for the building of railroads an extensive freighting system developed between each of the new towns and the nearest railroad. The first major freight route was established between Tonopah and Sodaville, a small station on the Carson and Colorado Railroad. The huge wagons, often carrying a twenty-ton load and pulled by twenty- or twenty-two-horse teams, were a common sight on the road between those points before the arrival of the railroad forced the horses, mules, and wagons to other developing areas.

Once it reached Tonopah, the freighting system expanded easily into each new camp. From Goldfield the freighters discovered a direct route to Candelaria, another station on the Carson and Colorado Railroad, which was approximately the same length as that between Sodaville and Tonopah. When the Bullfrog strike was made, freighters from Goldfield soon established a flourishing trade with the new district. Later a more extensive freighting system developed between the Bullfrog mines and Las Vegas, the new town in the southern tip of the state, built in 1905 as a result of the completion of the San Pedro, Los Angeles, and Salt Lake Railroad.[4]

From the beginning, freighters were unable to keep pace with development in the new mineral districts. Tons of sacked ore soon accumulated at the mines ready for shipment to the smelters, while mining equipment, timber for the mines, lumber for homes and business houses, and household goods were piled high along the tracks at Reno, Sodaville, and Candelaria, awaiting transportation to the new towns. Proposals to alleviate the transportation bottleneck by construction of railroads were made as early as 1901, but it was not until the spring of 1903 that realistic efforts were initiated to bring railroad connections to Tonopah. In that year the Brock interests supported the reorganization of the Tonopah Railroad Company, and a narrow-gauge line connecting Tonopah with the Carson and Colorado Railroad was completed in July, 1904. The weight of traffic forced the owners to broad-gauge both of these lines. Meanwhile, construction of the Goldfield Railroad was started. Upon its completion in September, 1905, the newspapers advertised that Goldfield now had broad-gauge connections with San Francisco. In November of 1905 the Tonopah and Goldfield lines were consolidated as the Tonopah and Goldfield Railroad.

The railroad builders shifted their interest to the Bullfrog district with the formation of the Bullfrog and Goldfield Railroad, which was incorporated in August, 1905, but didn't reach Beatty and Rhyolite until a year and a half later. While the Bullfrog-Goldfield railroad was moving slowly southward, two other short-line railroads entered the southern Nevada mining districts from the south, both sponsored by capitalists who wished to share in the profits of the new mining rush but found entrance to the new districts blocked

[4] C. O. Wittemore, representing the Clark railroad interests, auctioned the first lots on May 15, 1905, marking the formal beginning of the town of Las Vegas.

in the north by the Brock monopoly. The first of these, the Tonopah and Tidewater, was the brainchild of Francis M. ("Borax") Smith, president of the Pacific Coast Borax Company, who saw an opportunity to build a railroad which not only would tap the mineral resources of the boom area but would also provide an outlet for his extensive borax deposits in and near Death Valley. The other line, the Las Vegas and Tonopah, was proposed initially by Senator William A. Clark of Montana as a feeder line for his San Pedro, Los Angeles, and Salt Lake Railroad, which had been opened for business across the southern tip of Nevada in May, 1905. After some difficulties with Senator Clark over a Las Vegas site, Smith began his line at Ludlow, California. It was completed to Beatty in October, 1907. Smith then leased the Bullfrog-Goldfield Railroad to connect with the northern camps. The Las Vegas–Tonopah was completed from Las Vegas to Beatty in October, 1906, and to Goldfield approximately one year later.

While these new railroads did bring Los Angeles into the picture as a supply area for the Nevada mining camps, they were never able to compete with the Tonopah and Goldfield Railroad in total freight and passengers carried. The railroads which were completed to the new area numbered but a small proportion of the dozens which were proposed but never built. In many cases only time and circumstances saved the waste and extravagance which would have resulted from their building, although a line connecting the Tonopah-Goldfield area with the copper mines near Ely would have made sense. Such a railroad might have tied together the two major mineral-producing areas in Nevada and in so doing have redirected the entire economic structure of the state.

Transportation development in the new boom camps was marked also by the introduction of the automobile, first as an object of curiosity and later as an aid to prospecting, as a passsenger conveyance, and as a sign of social distinction. Automobiles were not used extensively around the mines until after 1913, when trucks came into limited use for hauling. Cars, on the other hand, moved quickly into competition with the railroads and stage lines for passenger and mail service over short distances. Within a short time auto companies were formed to connect Tonopah with Goldfield, Reno, and Ely, and Rhyolite with Goldfield and Las Vegas. Roads during the early years of development were practically nonexistent, and traveling in the Nevada desert often was extremely hazardous.

The increased use of automobiles soon brought regulation from the town governments. At both Tonopah and Goldfield ordinances were passed establishing a speed limit (four miles per hour in Tonopah, six miles per hour in Goldfield) and requiring that all vehicles have lights and mufflers. Lest the citizen get the impression that cars were here to stay, a Goldfield ordinance pointed out that "vehicles drawn by horse, at all times, have the right of way." Licenses were not required by the state until 1913 when the legislature set a minimum fee at $1.88 and stipulated that thereafter it was to be based on the horsepower of the automobile. For tax purposes, a minimum horsepower of twenty was designated, to be charged for at the rate of twelve and one-half cents per horsepower.

THE BOOM TOWNS

The new mining camps followed the usual pattern of birth, boom, and decay, differing only in the speed and intensity of their development and decline. Thus Tonopah, based on a solid silver-gold ore body, had a moderate boom and a slow decline; Goldfield, with a rich gold ore body, had a rapid rise, an intense boom, and a quick decline; while Rhyolite, based on a rich but shallow body of ore, rose rapidly but declined even faster.

Although the discoveries were made in the early part of the twentieth century, the extreme isolation of the camps forced them to face many of the same challenges and to experience a political and social development similar to that of the Comstock era. Compelled to solve their immediate problems outside the effective range of county and state government, the residents turned again to the squatter meeting. However, the new camps did have access to a governmental device, the town board system, which had been created in order to dispense with the constant incorporation and disincorporation of cities so prevalent during the Comstock period. An 1881 act authorized the establishment of town governments directly under the authority of the county commissioners, making possible quick, inexpensive, but effective local government for the boom camp which might have five residents on one day and five thousand a week later. In effect, the county commissioners were asked to perform for the towns all the functions normally served by a city council and mayor in an incorporated community. All three of the major camps in the southern boom areas achieved town board status, Tonopah and Goldfield in July, 1905, and Rhyolite two years later.

These three communities with a similar political evolution faced the same basic problems of sanitation, police protection, light and water supply, fire protection and control, regulation of prostitution, street maintenance, and finances. Schools, although at first bound closely to town affairs, were later looked upon as a county or district responsibility and the town boards paid little attention to them. The experiences of these communities under the town board plan demonstrated that while the system was far from the ideal predicted, it did provide basic services with a minimum outlay of tax funds. At least one of the purported advantages, that of bringing adequate government to a new mining community without delay, simply did not materialize; experiences in all three communities indicated that county commissioners were extremely slow to act even when the need was great. The situation improved with the achievement of county seat status by Tonopah in May, 1905, when it wrested the Nye County seat from Belmont, and by Goldfield two years later when it won the Esmeralda County seat from Hawthorne.

In spite of the slow and often weak political development of the new camps, civilization soon caught up with them and within a short time Tonopah and Goldfield could boast of hotels and restaurants comparable to those in San Francisco. And although forty years had passed since the Comstock boom, the social face of the new mining towns differed little from that of the earlier communities.

PUBLICITY AND SPECULATION

A characteristic aspect of the boom in southern Nevada was the wild speculation which accompanied it. At Goldfield the amazing richness of the ore stimulated an undue amount of publicity, opening the door to excessive speculation in mining stocks and to more than a few outright fraudulent schemes. The greatest individual publicists of these camps were the stock promoters and the speculators, for they needed the widest publicity to attract suckers to their schemes. Newspapers, magazines, championship boxing matches, rich ore shipments, and other means were used to attract attention to the southern Nevada mines. Promoters were aided by the almost complete lack of legal regulations to protect investors and by what one writer called "the veritable craze" of the public to invest in mining stock. No news seemed too absurd to be believed in the atmosphere of the time, and the most extravagant claims in mining advertisements and prospectuses were accepted at face value. Thousands of people throughout the United States pledged their modest means to back various promotional schemes without giving a thought to the most cursory investigation.

The huge demand for Nevada mining stock invited the operations of unprincipled speculators who promoted mining claims against all the rules of mining law, mining custom, and accepted promotional methods. They appropriated mineral ground before making the discovery of a vein or lode within the limits of the claim, made false claims of ore values, used false advertising, and resorted to all the tricks of mine salting which were known to their particular breed of men.

The most notorious of these so-called wildcat promoters was George Graham Rice. Born in New York in 1870 as Jacob S. Herzig, he already had a prison record when he arrived at Goldfield in 1904. He immediately established an advertising bureau there which was expanded the next year into the L. M. Sullivan Trust Company to promote mining stock. In partnership with Tex Rickard, he was successful in promoting a championship fight between Joe Gans and Oscar ("Battling") Nelson in September, 1906; this brought him thousands of subscribers and made him one of Goldfield's most important citizens. His respectability was short-lived, for the Sullivan Company failed in December, 1906, in turn causing the collapse of the State Bank and Trust Company of Goldfield. Rice promised to meet all his obligations—an idle pledge, as his immediate flight to Reno proved.

From Reno, Rice helped to launch a new speculative scheme which surpassed any of his Goldfield activities. With his old friend Rickard and Nat C. Goodwin, a prominent New York stage actor, he took advantage of the 1907 depression and the Goldfield labor difficulties to promote an entire town. Rawhide, the district chosen, was established in December, 1906, but its mineral potential was limited from the beginning and its speculative possibilities unknown until Rice and his partners began their promotional campaign in the spring of 1908 under the name of the Nat C. Goodwin Company.

Not content with the usual publicity stories about the great mineral possibilities of the district, the trio convinced Elinor Glyn, author of the best-selling novel *Three Weeks,* that she should visit the camp of Rawhide. Her every move through the town's dusty streets was chronicled in minute detail. Not content with taking advantage of Mrs. Glyn's wide popularity, the promoters went a step further and used the death at Rawhide of a well-known race track gambler, Riley Grannan, to stage a lavish funeral. An itinerant preacher, W. H. Knickerbocker, delivered the oration, which was recorded in shorthand by a California newspaper reporter. A strange mixture of quotations from the Bible, Shakespeare, and Omar Khayyam, it was published in pamphlet form and widely distributed. Thus even the solemn occasion of death was turned into a promotional vehicle. The exposure of Rice's connection with the Nat C. Goodwin Company by the editor of the *Mining and Scientific Press* ruined the speculative attempt, and a fire on September 4, 1908, practically destroyed the town. Its end marked the close of the speculative boom in southern Nevada.

LABOR DISPUTES AND THE BEGINNING OF THE DECLINE

By 1900 revolutions in industrial production and distribution had transformed the face of America while bringing fundamental and lasting changes in the economic, social, and political patterns of the society. Industrial expansion led to business monopoly and in so doing fostered the growth of organized labor. This development was reflected in the western mining camps by the organization of the Western Federation of Miners in the early 1890s and the adoption of a new radicalism when that group joined others to form the Industrial Workers of the World in the fall of 1905. The mining boom in southern Nevada provided the occasion for a major showdown between the forces of the new militant labor and the Goldfield mining monopoly, for it was at Goldfield in the years 1906–1908 that the IWW made the first real test of its theory of revolutionary industrial unionism.

Union labor came to Goldfield in 1904 with the establishment of two American Federation of Labor affiliates and a local of the Western Federation of Miners. Relations between union members and management were excellent until the end of 1906, but a continuing influx of miners and operators from the strife-ridden Cripple Creek district of Colorado and the growing influence of the IWW combined to spark a major labor quarrel which, when finally settled in 1908, effectively eliminated union labor from Goldfield.

A new series of severe labor disputes broke out in 1907, including a jurisdictional controversy which led to the killing of an antiunion restaurant owner and a comic-opera affair involving the "change-room" system.[5] The trouble came to a climax on November 27 in a major strike, ostensibly brought about by the financial panic, when union members refused to accept the operators' paper scrip in lieu of money. The mine operators' association chose the occasion to eliminate the Western Federation of Miners from Goldfield. Their plan needed the support of Governor John Sparks, who cooperated by wiring President Theodore Roosevelt to send in federal troops since "there does now exist domestic violence and unlawful combinations and conspiracies . . . and the constituted authorities of the State of Nevada are now and continue to be unable to protect the people in such right."[6] The troops arrived from the Presidio in San Francisco on December 6, and the following day the operators published a lengthy statement in the newspapers justifying their actions. On December 9 the operators lowered the wage scale a dollar per day and adopted the use of the card system, which was similar to the more familiar yellow-dog contract. When the miners refused to return to work under the new rules, the operators recruited nonunion workers from neighboring states. Under the protection of federal troops, the mines reopened early in January, 1908.

The advisability of using federal troops to quell a local labor disturbance troubled President Roosevelt enough to send a commission to investigate the Nevada situation. Their report, dated December 30, 1907, was a strong indictment of the methods em-

[5] As the name suggests, change rooms were simply rooms where the miners changed from street clothes to work clothes and vice versa under the eyes of company guards. The device was an attempt to eliminate "high-grading," an abuse whereby literally millions of dollars worth of high-grade ore was stolen by miners who concealed it in their clothing and carried it out of the mines.

[6] Most of the material on the Goldfield labor troubles, including the specific quotes, comes from the report of the Roosevelt commission appointed to investigate the troubles. See U.S., Department of State, *Report of Special Commission on Labor Troubles at Goldfield, Nevada* . . . , 60th Cong., 1st sess., 1908, House Ex. Doc. 607.

ployed by the mine operators and the governor of the state. It emphasized a weakness of the federal system of government when it noted:

There is absolutely no question that if the State of Nevada and the County of Esmeralda exercise the powers at their disposal they can maintain satisfactory order in Goldfield; that so far these authorities have done nothing, but are relying upon Federal aid, and their attitude now is expressly that of refusing to do anything and desiring to throw their own burdens upon the Federal Government for the maintenance of those elementary conditions for which they and they only are responsible.

The report had absolutely no effect upon the Goldfield labor difficulties, but it did bring an ultimatum from the president to Governor Sparks that the federal troops would be withdrawn immediately unless a special session of the Nevada legislature was called to establish a state police force. Sparks accordingly called the session for January 14, 1908, and on the twenty-seventh a state police bill was passed. By March 7 the federal troops had been replaced by the new state police force and within a month the union voted to return to work.

The Goldfield labor disturbances signaled the end of boom conditions in southern Nevada. The period which followed was marked by a more efficient exploitation of the mines as business combinations such as the Brock interests at Tonopah and the Wingfield-Nixon partnership at Goldfield solved transportation, power, water, milling, and financial problems, increasing the production of the mines and bringing new stability to the towns. The many well-constructed brick, stone, and wooden homes and public buildings of the new era contrasted sharply with the dugouts, tents, and shanties of the boom period. Theaters like the Nevada, the Pavilion, the Idora, and the Butler at Tonopah, and the Gem, the Hippodrome, and the Lyric at Goldfield now competed with the gambling houses and dance halls as entertainment for a quieter society. The towns, like Virginia City earlier, became, in effect, industrial communities.

Meanwhile, Rhyolite began a short but rapid journey into oblivion. Production from the Bullfrog district had practically ceased by 1911, and Rhyolite, with an estimated population of from five to eight thousand in 1908, had but fourteen people in 1920. By then Goldfield was definitely declining and no doubt would have shared

Rhyolite's fate except that it was on a main north-south highway and it remained a county seat. Tonopah, the first of the new boom camps, was the last to decline. A number of factors kept mineral production at a substantial level into the late 1920s and by the time the mines were no longer productive the town had discovered other interests which kept it alive, if not always prosperous, into the 1970s.

World War I created a sufficient demand for silver to raise the price from 60¢ to over $1 per ounce. The war was also responsible for the Pittman Silver Act, passed by Congress in 1918 in answer to an appeal from the British government, which had exhausted its supply of silver and needed additional sources to meet its overseas obligations. The law in effect guaranteed silver producers a minimum price of $1 per ounce until the British loan was repaid. It wasn't until 1920 that the world price of silver fell below $1 and thus brought the Pittman Act into operation. From that time until after July, 1923, when the amount of silver sold to Great Britain had been replaced, the act was a real boon to American silver producers, enabling districts such as Tonopah to maintain a high production for approximately three years after the collapse of the world silver price. The end of the government subsidy in 1923, the decreasing value of the ore, and the rising cost brought Tonopah's great production era to a close and with it the last phase of the mining boom initiated by Jim Butler's discovery in the spring of 1900.

BEGINNINGS OF THE COPPER BOOM

While evidences of decline were closing the door on Nevada's age of silver, a huge deposit of copper in the eastern part of the state opened the way to a mineral production destined to eclipse that from the great Comstock Lode. Copper ore had been discovered in the Robinson District in White Pine County in the early 1870s but its low-grade character, the lack of demand for copper, and the expense of transportation and reduction had combined to discourage development of the ore body. In 1900, the same year the Tonopah boom got underway, copper was rediscovered in the district, but the problems associated with the exploitation of the ore were so much greater than those of putting silver and gold mines into operation that it took nearly eight years of development before real production began.

Two young men, Edwin Gray and Dave Bartley, entered the district in the fall of 1900, optioned two copper claims, and immediately began a tunnel into the mountain to define the limits of the ore body. The tunnel, surrounded on every side by copper ore, soon attracted a number of engineers and prospective buyers. One of them, Mark Requa, son of a prominent Comstock engineer, became interested in the area as a potential feeder to the nearly defunct Eureka and Palisade Railroad, which his father had given him to manage. Requa optioned the Gray-Bartley claims in October, 1902, for $150,000 and the following year, with the financial help of some of his father's friends, organized the White Pine Copper Company. When he was satisfied that reduction and transportation posed no difficult technical problems, Requa went east to obtain funds for constructing the reduction plant and the railroad.

An unexpected windfall came his way when he discovered that the New York and Nevada Copper Company, which owned a large amount of land next to his, was bankrupt. Without too much difficulty he was able to unite these holdings with his own into the Nevada Consolidated Copper Company, incorporated in November, 1904. The new company had a tremendous ore reserve but no cash for development. It was, perhaps, inevitable that Requa's search for funds would lead to contact with the Guggenheim family, who were then beginning to consolidate their control of many of the great copper deposits in the world.

GUGGENHEIM CONTROL

In the 1890s the Guggenheims had taken over the Utah Copper Corporation with a huge low-grade deposit at Bingham, Utah. Eager to add a second large porphyry copper holding but moving cautiously as usual, they helped Requa organize the Nevada Northern Railroad in May, 1905. Rather than risk extensive funds in an outright purchase, the Guggenheims organized another firm, the Cumberland-Ely Copper Company, which immediately gained control of the best water rights in the district and a site for the proposed reduction works. In January, 1906, the Guggenheim family tried to effect a merger of their company with Requa's. Requa opposed the merger, but in October he reached a compromise with the

Guggenheims to form a new company, jointly owned, which would construct and operate the proposed reduction works. As an additional price for the agreement, the Guggenheims insisted that the Cumberland-Ely Company be allowed to purchase one-half interest in Requa's Nevada Northern Railroad. The compromise soon proved to be an illusion, and within a short time Requa was removed as general manager of the Nevada Consolidated Copper Company. Thus the man whose vision uncovered the immense copper deposits in White Pine County was ushered aside in the interest of monopoly control. He did have the satisfaction of driving the last spike on the Nevada Northern Railroad on September 29, 1906, bringing to a successful conclusion a work he had started two years earlier when he first sent survey teams into the field. It was somewhat ironic that the new railroad ran directly north from the copper deposits through Steptoe Valley to connect with the Southern Pacific at Cobre, since Requa had entered the district in the first instance to find a feeder for the Eureka-Palisade Railroad.

In August, 1908, the first shipment of blister copper from the district marked the completion of the reduction plant. Nearly eight years had elapsed since the Gray-Bartley discovery, a period which saw a recorded production of only $420 and an expenditure of over $4,000,000 by the Guggenheim family.[7] The cost was high but the reward proved the far-sightedness of the exploiters. Production jumped from $622,470 in 1908 to $6,561,787 in 1909 and continued to rise steadily in the ensuing years, making Robinson the richest mineral district in the history of Nevada.

COPPER BOOM TOWNS

The boom which followed in the wake of the copper discovery was one of the few in the state to occur near an established town. Ely, the county seat of White Pine County, was only seven miles from the huge copper ore body that formed the nucleus of the Robinson Mining District. The town, named after Smith Ely, an absentee mine owner of the early days, had a precarious existence from 1878, when a post office was established there, until 1887, when it became the county seat. It survived until the beginning of the copper boom because of that political plum. The very fact of Ely's

[7] Production from the Robinson District had been less than $65,000 for the decade of the 1890s.

status as a county seat modified the intensity of the boom when it finally got underway. Before it was over, it had made Ely into a modern community and brought a political development which led first to town board government in 1903 and then to incorporation in 1907.

The housing decisions which company officials made set the pattern for town development throughout the rest of the copper district. The planners first favored a housing program whereby supervisory personnel would be furnished residences near the mines and the reduction plant and the mass of laborers would live outside the industrial area. Consequently, a number of real estate promotions blossomed in the years before 1908 and one, the Ely Townsite Company, seemed to have the blessing of the Guggenheims. Its proposal for a new town, unfortunately called Ely City, was approved by the White Pine County Commissioners in November, 1906. The community seemed assured of permanency when it was designated as headquarters for the Nevada Northern Railroad. The sale of lots was brisk throughout 1907 and the early months of 1908, but the bubble burst when company officials reversed their early position and began building houses at McGill. Their decision brought into being the company towns and caused the rise of a number of parasitic fringe communities.

Four company towns, designed primarily to maintain a stable work force, were established in the copper district. Of these, the two largest were built by the Nevada Consolidated Copper Company, Ruth at the mine area and McGill some twenty-one miles to the north. Another company town, Veteran, grew up around the Veteran shaft of the Cumberland-Ely Copper Company, but it did not survive the closing of the shaft in 1914. The fourth community, Kimberly, was established by the Consolidated Copper Company near its holdings in the western part of the district. McGill was by far the largest and most important of the company towns. Located at the site of the huge reduction works, it was named for W. N. McGill, who had owned a nearby ranch.

In the early stages, the company town in the copper district differed little in appearance from any boom mining camp. However, within a short time company control was exerted to change both the external and internal makeup of the communities. The external differences were obvious in the general pattern of the town: the row upon row of well-constructed houses, all looking confusingly alike; the rather broad and generally well-kept streets; the lack of hotels and the scarcity of saloons along the main street; and the fact that there was no restricted district in the town. There were subtle differences, too, which did not appear on the surface. The company town, regardless of the wishes of its citizens, had no local government of its own. Company control derived basically from company ownership of all the property on which the town was built. Private businesses operated only with the consent of the company and its policy was to allow only a limited number of each type of operation.

Such control had definite effects upon the social life of the residents. A policy limiting gambling and the sale of hard liquor to certain establishments and prohibiting hotels, dance halls, and red-light districts within the city limits in effect drove the miners into the saloons and pool halls authorized by the company or to the fringe areas. Most of the single men and a substantial number of married men spent a large part of their free time and a sizable amount of their semimonthly checks in the authorized establishments. Such spending was made easy by a simple procedure which enabled the employee to sign over his check to the pool hall or saloon and thus carry a debt approximately equal to his income after deductions. The system provided a convenient service for the employees, guaranteed the proprietor ultimate payment, and, most important, furthered the company's goal of a stable work force by binding the individual to the establishment and to the town.

Another important factor in obtaining and keeping an adequate labor supply was the company policy regarding housing and town services. To most residents of the towns, the company was a benevolent although slow-moving landlord, renting houses for a very small sum per room (generally $3 per month for "whites" and $1.50 for "foreigners"), providing all the supplies necessary to keep the houses in good condition, and making repairs when needed. Electricity, wood, and coal were sold to employees at about half the price charged elsewhere in the district. Water, garbage collection, and police and fire protection were furnished free, since the residents paid no town taxes.

In addition, company officials, in their efforts to create conditions which would make for a peaceful, stable community, encouraged various recreational activities and subsidized sports such as tennis, baseball, football, and bowling. In 1915 a clubhouse was completed at McGill which included a small swimming pool, two bowling alleys, a library, a billiard table, and a combination recreation, dancing, and athletic hall.

The company also provided excellent medical facilities for its employees. Emergency hospitals with doctors on call were established at McGill and Ruth and a large modern hospital was built at East Ely to supplement the emergency facilities. Each employee paid a fixed and quite nominal monthly fee entitling him to such medical care as he needed, including surgery and hospitalization. Although the charge did not include services for members of the employees' families, they usually received free medical care from the company doctors at Ruth and McGill.

Criticisms were, of course, leveled against company officials and the manner in which they controlled the towns. Some of the complaints concerned the economic aspects of company domination, but many more were aimed at the political aspects of company rule. Residents of company towns had to live within limits prescribed by company officials rather than elected officers; economic security was gained at the expense of political freedom.

An unusual problem developed in the company towns when large numbers of immigrants, mostly Greeks, Austro-Hungarians, Serbs, and Japanese, were brought in to provide a cheap labor supply for the mines and smelter. These immigrants, part of the so-called new immigration from southern and eastern Europe in contrast to the earlier immigration from western Europe and the British Isles, were at first greeted with open hostility by all groups except the company officials. Individuals from southern and eastern Europe were labeled "foreigners" immediately upon arrival in the copper towns while their English or Scandinavian counterparts moved at once into the charmed circle of "whites."

Generally, the "foreigners" were separated from the other inhabitants economically, socially, and geographically. The economic distinction stemmed mainly from the company policy of employing the men in unskilled jobs at wages lower than those paid to others for similar services. The social barriers resulted not only from the economic distinction but also from language and cultural differences. Both the economic and social barriers were emphasized and perpetuated by the geographic separation imposed by the company in order to alleviate the early antagonisms among the different groups. The result, particularly at McGill, was the development of a number of communities along ethnic and economic lines and marked by strong social distinctions.[8]

Although the town was segregated, the public schools were not; and soon many Serbians, Greeks, and other so-called foreigners obtained a grade school and high school education and thus were able to move from unskilled to skilled labor. The process of assimilation was speeded by activities where common participation was encouraged without regard to race, social position, or economic status, particularly athletic contests, both those sponsored by the company and those held within the school systems, and holiday events such as the footraces and other contests during the Fourth of July and Labor Day celebrations. By the 1930s numerous second-generation "foreigners" were being apprenticed as carpenters, plumbers, electricians, and bricklayers. Once the economic barrier was breached and after years of integration in the public schools, the last social barriers, including those against intermarriage, were broken.

The social controls that characterized the company towns were almost completely lacking in the fringe communities which they spawned. Places like Ragdump, Smelterville, and Steptoe City on the outskirts of McGill, and Riepetown, strategically located between Ruth and Kimberly, provided the entertainment unobtainable in the company towns. Company officials thus shifted responsibility for control of prostitution, drinking, and gambling to the already overburdened county commissioners, who took action only when public pressure forced them to.

LABOR TROUBLES

The benevolent paternalism in the company towns did not prevent the outbreak of serious labor difficulties in the period before World War I.[9] In the fall of 1912 there was a major strike

---

[8] Thus six different "towns" were established based on economic and ethnic segregation. Jap town occupied the lowest rung of the social ladder, followed by Greek town and Austrian town. Then in order came the three "white" sections—lower town, upper town, and middle town. The "Circle," made up of some seven large homes, was reserved for the highest supervisory personnel and stood at the top of the social ladder.

[9] A wildcat strike in 1902, before the Nevada Consolidated Copper Company was organized, cost the lives of three union members and cast a dark shadow over union activities in the district for the next three or four years. Additional labor disputes broke out between 1902 and 1912, but none of them were serious.

against the properties of the Nevada Consolidated Company at Ruth and McGill. Basically, it was a sympathy strike called by Charles Moyer, president of the Western Federation of Miners, against all Guggenheim properties for alleged unsatisfactory working conditions at Bingham, Utah. In an attempt to break it, the company employed thirty armed guards (strikebreakers, the union officials called them). After two workers were killed and another wounded, Governor Tasker L. Oddie, who had been called to the strike area the day before, declared martial law. The strike was settled with the union winning a small wage increase, but an attempt to obtain an indictment for the killing of the strikers failed when the grand jury found no true bill against the alleged slayers. No further labor difficulties disturbed the copper camps until 1919, when postwar problems brought strikes in nearly all Nevada mining properties.

SPECULATION

The only major speculative venture in the history of the Robinson district occurred in 1909 and involved an old firm, the Ely Central Copper Company, which was incorporated in 1906 but showed no production for the next three years. Then in 1909 the stock suddenly began to rise because of manipulations by the well-known speculator George Graham Rice. It moved from 87¢ per share in September to $4.25 on November 6. On that day, the *Engineering and Mining Journal* carried a story, entitled "A New Scheme to Hook Suckers," about Rice's manipulations, bringing the scheme to an untimely end. The final act in the drama came in September, 1910, when federal officers made simultaneous raids on Rice's home office in New York and its branches in other large cities. Within a week Rice and other officials of his company were arrested for mail fraud, operating a "bucket" shop, and making false quotations and charging interest on false securities. Rice claimed that he was a victim of a conspiracy on the part of the Guggenheims and while awaiting trial he wrote a series of articles, later published in book form, appropriately titled *My Adventures with Your Money*. Rice's speculative career in Nevada came to an end in 1912, when he was sentenced to a year in a federal penitentiary.

THE EFFECTS OF THE TWENTIETH-CENTURY MINING BOOM

Nevada's second great mining boom dominated the state's economic, political, and social life in much the same way as the Comstock era had. The new discoveries revived mining in Nevada and other western states and brought about the development of supporting industries, opening up areas of the state which hitherto had been neglected. The boom did not succeed in welding the state into an economic unit, for the southern mining districts found their markets and supply centers in California while the eastern copper regions looked to Salt Lake City and other eastern points. Fortunately, the decline of the southern mining camps did not seriously effect the state's economy as had the Comstock decline in the earlier period. This was due partly to the continuation of copper production in the eastern part of the state; to the Pittman Act of 1918, which gave Tonopah a few extra years of life; and to the action of George Wingfield in investing much of the fortune he obtained from the Goldfield mines in Nevada hotels, banks, real estate, and extensive livestock interests.

CHAPTER 11

Politics of the Progressive Era

CENTERS OF THE MINING INDUSTRY in Nevada generally have dominated the politics of the state. That was the case during the Comstock era, and soon after their discovery the new mining areas of southern Nevada began to exert a similar although less dramatic influence, first dominating the state government and then controlling the Nevada delegation to Congress. The contrasts, however, between these two political eras were much greater than their likeness in both being oriented to mining. The Tonopah-Goldfield rush ushered in a new era in Nevada politics. Less beholden economically to California, the new boom towns were less responsive politically to California banking and railroad interests and more responsive to local institutions; thus the Bank Crowd and the Southern Pacific

233

political bureau of the Comstock era gave way to Nevada-oriented politicians. Moreover, the center of political activity shifted before the boom was over from the mining towns of Tonopah and Gold-field to the non-mining community of Reno. Mining continued to dominate the state's economy, but the decline of the southern silver camps, coupled with the almost complete lack of interest in Nevada politics by the exploiters of the White Pine copper mines, pushed Reno into a position of prominence. Equally important, the first two decades of the twentieth century saw the emergence in Nevada of major reform movements, first progressivism and then socialism.

The first person associated with the southern Nevada mining boom to gain national political prominence was George Nixon. Although his role in the boom was mainly that of absentee landholder, his election to the United States Senate in 1904, replacing the venerable William M. Stewart, symbolized the new mining era supplanting the old. Nixon, one of the founders of the state Silver party in the 1890s, was an early example of the new breed of Nevada politician who had earned a fortune in Nevada, invested it in Nevada, and then chose to maintain his permanent residence there. It is quite unlikely that Nixon and others who followed could have succeeded politically in the new atmosphere of reform had they not remained loyal Nevadans in every respect.

The most important national political figure to come directly from the Tonopah-Goldfield rush was Key Pittman. Pittman arrived in Tonopah in the spring of 1902 after a brief participation in the Klondike rush, established a law practice, and entered politics almost simultaneously. He was so successful at both that within a few years he had accumulated a small fortune and in 1910 was prominent enough in the Democratic party to challenge George Nixon for his post in the United States Senate. Although defeated, Pittman was back in 1912 to contest a number of candidates for the unexpired term of Nixon, who died in June of that year. This time he was successful in the preferential ballot of the voters, and was selected by the legislature to fill the vacant Senate seat. He was reelected five times, the last occasion on November 5, 1940, just five days before his death. Pittman's early and continued activity on behalf of silver legislation has blinded many to the fact that he supported Wilson's reform program almost without exception. It was politically expedient for him to do so, for it gave him status as an administration Democrat and thus assured him a great deal of local patronage. His motives were little different from those of the majority of his brother senators, however; like most of them, he was a politican, not a statesman.

In this respect he differed considerably from Nevada's senior senator during the early 1900s, Francis G. Newlands. Newlands, as we have seen, was a product of the Comstock political era, yet he was able to make the transition into the new period of Nevada politics through his independent financial position, which gave him control of the state Democratic central committee. Moreover, his theory and practice of government fitted into the atmosphere of Progressive reform. It is impossible to tell for certain, but it is reasonable to assume that his advocacy of certain reforms gained him as much support from labor and other dissident groups as he lost to conservative forces within the state.

Newlands's ideas of the political process, enlightened by any standard, seem doubly so when placed against the Comstock political environment which gave him his first political success. Long before Herbert Croly developed the idea of a "New Nationalism," Newlands believed that the federal government should be a positive force in the economic and social welfare of the people. Some of his proposals, such as his plan for a bureau of industry, the use of a corporation tax to control trusts, and a national railroad incorporation law to effect unified control of railroads, were quite radical when first presented and consequently received little legislative support. In fact, the only major Progressive measure to bear his name was the Newlands Reclamation Act of 1902.[1] In his support of it, Newlands demonstrated a national outlook on economic issues which became central to his political beliefs and which set him apart from many, if not most, of his contemporaries in the Congress. But his conservation program was not intended to end with the Reclamation Act. In 1907 he introduced a bill calling for a revolving fund of $50 million to finance the multipurpose development of the nation's rivers. The bill died in Congress mainly because it re-

---

[1] William Lilley III, *The Early Career of Francis G. Newlands* (Ann Arbor, Mich.: University Microfilms, 1967). In his biographical study of Newlands, Lilley points out that handwritten drafts show Newlands's participation in shaping the Federal Trade Commission Act and that other handwritten drafts show him to be the author of the 1917 U.S. Railroad Administration Act.

quired an administrative body of experts, free from congressional interference, to allocate funds.

Although Newlands's reputation rests almost entirely on the Reclamation Act, his was an important voice within the Democratic party in the early years of the twentieth century advocating a move from states' rights to strong government interference in behalf of the general welfare of its citizens. The Newlands Act was of direct economic benefit to many Nevadans, bringing thousands of acres of desert into production and adding two small communities—Fernley and Fallon—to Nevada's population, but voters did not always appreciate his efforts along national lines.

Newlands's first attempt at national office in 1892 was successful mainly because he had sensed the importance of the silver issue and realized the potential of the state Silver party. His consistent support of silver was sufficient to get him reelected to the House of Representatives four times. He survived an intraparty quarrel in the Silver-Democratic ranks in 1898, emerging in 1902 as the strongest Democratic candidate to replace John P. Jones in the Senate. His money was influential in assuring his selection by the state legislature.

Newlands's continued popularity was evidenced in 1908 when Nevada voters, as a result of a pledge by both parties to support the person receiving the highest number of votes on a preference ballot, gave him a substantial majority over his Republican and Socialist opponents. The political situation changed dramatically after 1908, and by 1914 Newlands found himself fighting for his political life. Although his Republican opponent, a young Reno attorney named Samuel Platt, waged a vigorous campaign against him, the greatest challenge to Newlands came from the intrusion of a strong Socialist party in the election.

SOCIALISTS IN NEVADA

The Socialist party entered Nevada politics for the first time in the 1906 election, just as the Democrat-Silver fusion party was breaking up. It posed no threat to Newlands in the 1908 contest, but the use of federal troops by a Democratic administration during the Goldfield labor troubles and of state troops at McGill a few years later by a Republican administration drove thousands of miners into the new party. The growing popularity of the Socialists was shown in 1912 when it placed one of its members in each of the two houses of the Nevada legislature. In 1914 the Socialist candidate for the Senate, Grant Miller, received over 20 percent of the vote and brought Newlands within forty votes of defeat by his Republican opponent. Election results from 1906 through 1914 indicate clearly that the Socialist party gained strength from the Democrats rather than from the Republicans. If World War I had not intruded, the Socialist party might well have forced a fusion with the Democrats similar to that of the earlier Silver-Democratic merger.

Before the 1916 election socialism in Nevada gained further strength from the founding of a socialist colony. The community was located in Churchill County on land reclaimed by the Newlands project, which had been inaugurated under the Newlands Reclamation Act and by 1916 had resulted in the reclamation of thousands of acres of desert land. The headquarters, Nevada City was four miles east of Fallon. Founded upon the philosophy of the Danish-American socialist Laurence Gronlund,[2] the colony was to provide the center from which first Nevada and then the West would be won for socialism. Two of its leaders, Job Harriman, an unsuccessful candidate for vice-president of the United States in 1900, and C. V. Eggleston, his financial adviser, saw in the Nevada City experiment a means to add five thousand new socialist votes in Nevada and thus swing the state for socialism. The idea seemed eminently workable in 1916. At that time hundreds of socialists throughout the country were discouraged by the outbreak of the European war and by the lack of unified antiwar policy within their own ranks. Many of them joined the colony because its physical isolation appeared to make it the only place where certain socialist policies, particularly the antiwar stand, could be preserved. The election of 1916 did little to dim Harriman and Eggleston's dreams

---

[2] Wilbur S. Shepperson, *Retreat to Nevada: A Socialist Colony of World War I* (Reno: University of Nevada Press, 1966), pp. 36–37. Laurence Gronlund, born in Denmark in 1846, emigrated to the United States in 1867. His interest in social questions led him to an active career as a socialist leader and writer. In 1884 he published his most important work, *The Coming Revolution: Its Principles,* in which he forecast inevitable breakdown of the wage system. Since it was the first comprehensive work on socialism published in the United States in the English language, it was widely read and enhanced Gronlund's position as a leader in socialist thought in the United States.

that Nevada could be won for socialism. The Socialist candidate for the Senate, Grant Miller, running against Samuel Platt, Republican, and Key Pittman, Democrat, polled over 28 percent of the votes cast, with 9,507 against 10,618 for Platt and 12,765 for the popular Pittman.

The strong antiwar position of the socialist colony, until the election of 1916, fit in well with the Democratic party's attitude ("He Kept Us Out of War") and if anything had helped the group politically in Nevada. However, the colony's persistence in continuing and even increasing its antimilitarism in the face of the country's growing involvement in the war ultimately led to its downfall and the decline of the Socialist party in Nevada. Throughout the early months of 1917 and even after the United States entered the war on April 6, the colony's newspaper cried out against it and recommended Nevada, with its deserts and mountains, as a safe refuge. It seemed to be that until the early part of 1918, when the draft board listed one of the colony's members, Paul Walters, as a draft evader and ordered Sheriff Mark Wildes of Churchill County to arrest him. The sheriff was killed while attempting to do so. In the resulting public outcry, a posse of seventy-five men, strengthened by the addition of many "bounty hunters," ferreted out the frightened boy and killed him. The antagonism created toward the colony created a threat so powerful as to cause most of the residents to leave. Only a few families remained at Nevada City on November 11, 1918, when the war ended; the next year the colony property passed into the hands of the receiver.

The decline of socialism in Nevada was reflected in succeeding elections. In 1918 the Socialist candidate for senator received only 710 votes out of 25,563 cast, and in 1920, the last election the Socialists entered as a party, they polled but 494 votes out of 27,427 cast. The demise of the Nevada City colony and the Socialist party was due not only to public reaction to the antimilitaristic stand but also to the fact that when the United States entered World War I, many socialists found patriotism a stronger bond than socialism. Thus several members of the colony left to join the army while others, such as Grant Miller, who became a member of the Nevada Council of National Defense, took governmental positions. In any event, it was quite clear by 1920 that Harriman's plan of using the colony as a means of winning Nevada to socialism was defeated by a combination of outside pressures and internal dissension.

PROGRESSIVISM IN NEVADA

The unlikely role of Nevada as the center of a movement to win the West for socialism was paralleled somewhat by its role in the multipronged Progressive movement which swept the United States in the first years of the twentieth century. This is not to suggest that Nevada was a leading western Progressive state, but it should be noted that between 1900 and 1920 the state passed a substantial number of laws which reflected the Progressives' concern to make government a responsive and effective instrument in relieving the social and economic distress of the people. Of course, the shoddy political record of Nevada from its inception as a state until the first rumblings of reform in the 1890s was an open invitation to those who wished to restore government to the voters. With the record of corrupt control by the Comstock mining companies and the Central Pacific Railroad in mind, it is reasonable to question why the reform movement in Nevada did not extend further than it did.

One of the first instances of the involvement of Nevadans in Progressive legislation came, as noted earlier, as a result of the need for irrigation. State political leaders, with the possible exception of Newlands, were in effect forced into the conservation fight, not through any idealistic urge to save the nation's natural resources, but because irrigation projects appeared to offer a way out of a deep economic depression. Much more closely allied with the later Progressive measures which aimed at reforming politics and restoring voter prestige were two laws passed in the early 1890s. An 1891 act provided for the use of the secret, or Australian, ballot, established a new method of counting ballots, and specified the duties of election officials. A Purity of Election Law, passed in 1895, required every politician candidate to form a committee to receive, expend, and audit campaign funds. Both the candidate and the committee had to file itemized statements of expenditures; the act listed in great detail items for which money could not be spent. It proved so cumbersome to enforce that it was repealed in 1899.

A more important political reform got under way in 1885 when Governor Jewett Adams suggested that the Nevada legislature memorialize Congress for a constitutional amendment for the direct election of United States senators. No action was taken at that time, but in 1893 the legislature requested a referendum on the direct election of senators. The results of the vote—7,208 for and 443 against—were sent to the president and Congress, as were legislative resolutions for such an amendment in 1895, 1897, 1899, and 1901. In 1899 the Nevada legislature passed an act providing that candidates for senators might be nominated in the same manner as that specified for the nomination of state officers. The original bill stipulated that state senators and assemblymen must vote for the senatorial candidate receiving the most votes; failure to do so constituted a felony. In the final version the latter provision was eliminated and compliance was made voluntary.

In the 1902 senatorial race, the first after the passage of the senator preference act, the incumbent, Senator Jones, indicated that he would not be a candidate for a sixth term. His most likely successor was Congressman Francis G. Newlands, who had lost a dramatic contest to Stewart in 1898. It had been known for some time that Newlands was interested in Jones's Senate seat, and that knowledge had disturbed a number of prominent Republicans. In fact, it may well have been the threat of a costly political fight with Newlands that persuaded John P. Jones to retire from the Senate. Nevada's other senator, William M. Stewart, presented the strongest opposition to Newlands. Although not politically threatened at this time himself, he had never forgiven Newlands for his part in the election of 1898. Shortly after Newlands's fifth election to Congress in 1900, Stewart began a campaign to thwart the congressman's known ambition to win a Senate seat by encouraging prominent Republicans to run against him. His first choice was a well-known mining figure, Captain J. R. DeLamar, who was responsible for the development of the Lincoln County gold district which bears his name. In a series of letters to DeLamar in November and December, 1900, Stewart pressed him to announce for the Senate, assuring his success: "If you would like to go to the Senate the way is clear, and with proper effort the result is certain." Stewart even guaranteed the support of the railroads: "I have seen the railroad people and they would be very pleased if you would become a candidate. You can safely rely on their friendly offices." Stewart was convinced that DeLamar would have no difficulty obtaining newspaper support as well, noting, "You can have the *Reno Journal* and all other papers in the state which you want for 50 cents on the dollar of what it will cost Newlands."[3] Stewart's letters to DeLamar leave no doubt that his main object was to keep Newlands out of the Senate. When DeLamar refused to enter the race, Stewart swung behind the candidacy of Judge Thomas P. Hawley.

Hawley had served in the Nevada Supreme Court from 1872 until 1890, when he resigned in order to accept an appointment to the United States Circuit Court. While serving in the circuit court he had issued a ruling in favor of the Central Pacific in its suit against the state board of equalization. An act of 1901 had established the board, made up of fourteen county assessors, whose main duty was to set a uniform state-wide valuation for certain classes of property. When the board increased the valuation of the Central Pacific Railroad properties in Nevada by some $5 million, the railroad brought suit against the assessors and the case was heard before Judge Hawley. After lengthy testimony, Hawley granted the railroad's request for an injunction against the assessors. Although the Central Pacific won the case, its officials recognized the need for some adjustment and agreed to a $2 million increase. It appears that railroad officials also recognized the potential value of Judge Hawley in the United States Senate. Hawley was seventy-two years of age when he announced his candidacy; it is unlikely that he would have forsaken the security of the federal bench unless he had been assured of significant support by the railroads and other interests.

Stewart's antagonism toward Newlands continued to shine forth in his correspondence with Hawley and others in support of Hawley's candidacy. In one letter he wrote that the "President and others indicate a better irrigation bill would have come out if Newlands had not been in Congress. Newlands is a drowning man catching at a straw." In another he set aside criticism of Hawley's age with malicious remarks about Newlands:

No man is old while he is in full vigor of both body and mind. If measured with Mr. Newlands in these respects Judge Hawley is at least thirty years his junior. . . . I never heard of Mr. Newlands being well a week at a time; it is either rheumatism, gout from English high living,

[3] Much of the information and the direct quotations in this and following paragraphs are taken from the Stewart Papers, Nevada State Historical Society, Reno, Nev.

bladder trouble, headache, indigestion, or all these combined, . . . and any person who will examine the Congressional record of Mr. Newlands will be unable to determine from anything they find there whether he has been dead or alive at any time since the 4th of March, 1893.

Stewart's support was considered by some to be as much of a hindrance as a help since his return to the Republican party after the 1898 election had alienated Silverites throughout Nevada.

Newlands realized that a victory in 1902 would depend upon how successful he was in maintaining the fusion of the Democrats and the Silver party. He and his manager, William E. Sharon, used their subsidized press to publicize the need for fusion, insisted on calling the Silver-Democrats the Fusion party, and to assure support at the local level, organized Fusion clubs in the various counties. Such a merger received a temporary setback when the Democrats met in convention in Reno in the latter part of August. Two Silverites, Reinhold Sadler and Lem Allen, had announced for governor before the convention opened. Then John Sparks, a prominent cattle owner, decided to enter the race, Sparks was very popular throughout the state, but he had been a gold standard man, which made him anathema to the Silverites. For a time it appeared that Sadler, with strong Silver party support, might block Sparks's candidacy and in so doing ruin the chances of fusion. However, when former governor Sadler took the gavel as chairman of the Silver party convention he announced that he was willing to give up his own ambitions for the cause of fusion. After a meeting of the leading members of both the Silver and the Democratic party gave additional support to fusion plans, the two separate conventions proceeded to name candidates, agreed upon earlier by the fusion committees of each party, and to adopt a platform. Then meeting jointly, the two parties ratified their nominations and endorsed Newlands for the Senate. The action of the joint convention in supporting the Democratic choices of Sparks for governor and Van Duzer for congressman indicates clearly that the Democrats were now in control of the so-called fusion party. Newlands, always an astute political observer, decided to stand for the Senate as a Democrat.

The successful fusion of the Democrats and the Silverites was an accomplished fact when the Republicans met to choose candidates and write a platform. Their nominee for governor was A. C. Cleveland, a prominent politician who had been closely associated with the Bank of California crowd during an earlier era. For congressional representative the Republicans turned again to Edward S. Farrington, a prominent attorney who had been defeated by Newlands in 1900 in a fairly close race. The convention gave formal endorsement to Thomas Hawley for senator and approved a platform which, among other items, gave the credit for the Reclamation Act of 1902 to Theodore Roosevelt and the Republicans and again tried to go both ways on the money question.

The campaign of 1902 was generally colorless. The Republicans tried to make much of the fact that Newlands's supporters, either through carelessness or by intention, had failed to have his name certified to appear on the November ballot as provided by the senator preference law. Thus only Hawley's name appeared, but Newlands forces were not worried since they had distributed campaign funds liberally. The Silver-Democrats won all of the state offices except those of superintendent of schools, which they lost by 11 votes, and secretary of state, lost by 166 votes. When the legislature met in January, 1903, Newlands was selected without difficulty, in one of the most remarkable political recoveries in Nevada history. In 1899, the Newlands forces were in complete rout, for not only had the congressman been defeated in his attempt to move up to the Senate, he had also been ignominiously read out of the Silver party, which he had helped to organize. It appeared that he was through in Nevada politics. Yet by astute maneuvering within the Silver party, he not only kept alive the idea of fusion but wrested control of the party's central committee from the Stewart-Wallace faction in time to ensure his reelection to Congress in 1900. Senator Stewart's return to the Republican party shortly after his election by the Silverite legislature no doubt made possible Newlands's victories; by that one action the senior senator became a "perfidious traitor" to the silver cause and his influence in Nevada politics diminished rapidly. The death of C. C. Wallace, Stewart's campaign manager, in 1901 removed another important block to Newlands's control of the silver forces in Nevada. Patience, perseverance, a great deal of luck, and an independent fortune had combined to bring the congressman the senate post he had sought for so long. It was a fortunate development for Nevada, the West, and the United States, for Newlands "proved to be an able and diligent public officer, perhaps the most useful Nevada ever had."[4]

Although fusion of the Silver and the Democratic parties continued in 1904 and 1906, it was clear by 1902 that the formerly powerful combination was on the wane in Nevada politics. In the campaigns of 1904 and 1906 the name of the combined parties was changed from Silver-Democrat to Democrat-Silver, and after 1906 the Silver party ceased to exist. It had lasted less than fifteen years, yet its appeal had been so powerful that no politician could expect to win an election in Nevada unless he became a member. Politics at the national level ultimately forced a union of the Silverites and the Democrats, thus saving the Democratic party in Nevada and giving it the impetus to become the majority party during the decade which followed collapse of fusion. When the Silver party came into existence, state politics were dominated by the Comstock, the railroads, and the Republicans. By the time the party went out of power the last of the Comstock senators, Stewart and Jones, were gone and men much more oriented to Nevada and its needs had taken their places; the railroad had passed from the hands of Henry E. Huntington into those of Edward H. Harriman, who was not interested in controlling Nevada's Senate delegation; and the Democrats were in control of state politics.

The issue of direct election of senators continued to be a lively one. In 1903, 1905, and 1907 the Nevada legislature petitioned Congress to initiate the procedures necessary to obtain a constitutional amendment for the direct election of senators. In 1908 the issue was strong enough to bring about a mutual agreement by the Democratic and Republican state conventions that each would pledge its legislative candidates to support the person receiving the most votes for senator, regardless of political affiliation. Thus the 1908 election saw the first popular preference vote for senator in Nevada history. Newlands received 12,473 votes to 8,972 for P. L. Flanigan, his Republican opponent, and 1,939 votes for T. C. Lutz, the Socialist candidate. Not surprisingly, the heavily Democratic state legislature honored the preference vote.

A much more significant popular preference for senator took place in 1910 when Key Pittman contested the incumbent, George Nixon. The 1910 general election was the first after the passage of

[4] Grant Smith Papers, Collection no. 229, Box 1, Getchell Library, University of Nevada, Reno.

the Direct Primary Law by the 1909 Nevada legislature. The act provided that candidates for the United States Senate were to be nominated in the same manner as candidates for state offices and stipulated that candidates for the legislature agree either to abide by the results of the popular vote for senator or to regard the vote as a recommendation. Pittman and Nixon went one step further and made a gentlemen's agreement whereby the candidate receiving the smaller number of votes would withdraw and prohibit the presentation of his name before the legislature. Nixon received 9,779 votes to Pittman's 8,624, but the new legislature was in Democratic hands and the Republicans had some bad moments before Pittman announced that he would honor his pledge. The Republican minority in the legislature in an action suggesting a basic distrust of any political accommodation, passed a resolution that "our thanks and congratulations be extended with a hearty good-will to the Democratic members for the honorable way in which they have accepted the result of the last election and bowed to the will of the people as expressed by the popular vote."

Pittman made it into the senate after another preference ballot in the 1912 election gave him a slim margin of eighty-nine votes over W. A. Massey, his Republican opponent, and the Democratic legislature ratified the popular preference. One wonders whether or not Pittman would have stepped down again had he not received the popular vote. The question of a popular preference became academic when the Seventeenth Amendment, providing for the direct election of senators, was ratified in 1913, but Nevada's attempt to obtain a popular preference demonstrates an early desire to keep pace with the reform movement.

Between 1904 and 1912 Nevada adopted three other political reforms that were considered fundamental by Progressive reformers, who felt the best way to cure the ills of democracy was with more democracy: the referendum, the initiative, and the recall. All were accepted by constitutional amendment, a process which required passage by two successive legislatures and the favorable vote of the people. A legislative resolution to establish the referendum, whereby 10 percent of the voters by petition could demand that any law or resolution passed by the legislature be submitted to the voters, was approved for the first time in 1901, passed its second legislative test in 1903, and was ratified by the voters in 1904. It appears that a move was made at the same time to obtain an initiative measure, but somewhere along the legislative trail the initiative was dropped from the bill, but not from the title. Thus when the article was made a part of the constitution in 1905 it carried the title "Initiative and Referendum," but only the latter measure was included. A second attempt to obtain the initiative passed the 1903 legislature but failed to pass in 1905. Success finally came in 1912 after the legislatures of 1909 and 1911 endorsed the initiative measure and the voters by a whopping majority made it a part of the constitution. The provision for the recall of public officers, a process also initiated by voter petition, was approved by the voters in 1912 after acceptance by the 1909 and 1911 legislatures.

Nevada's record in labor legislation during the Progressive years was a solid if unspectacular one. Beginning in 1903 with a law to prohibit the card system, the legislature in 1903 and 1908 passed a number of separate acts guaranteeing the eight-hour day in specified occupations, and in 1911 passed a workmen's compensation act. The establishment of the post of mine inspector in 1909 culminated efforts to ensure better safety standards in Nevada's main industry. However, the state government alienated labor by bringing federal troops into the Goldfield labor dispute in 1907, the passage of a state police bill in 1908, and the use of state police in the labor troubles at McGill in 1912. After 1908 Nevada labor turned increasingly toward the Socialist party.

Nevada's role in the woman suffrage movement was significant only as part of the general trend toward equal voting rights, since Nevada, along with Montana, was one of the last western states to give women the franchise, doing so in 1914. The state suffrage movement got under way in 1869 when the Honorable Curtis J. Hillyer of Storey County delivered a rather remarkable speech to the Nevada assembly in which he chided his fellow legislators for depriving half of the community of participation in government. Hillyer's efforts were in vain, for a resolution to strike the word "male" from the suffrage article of the constitution was defeated in the legislature. The same fate awaited similar efforts in 1883, 1885, 1887, and 1889. In 1895 a major campaign on the part of Nevada suffragettes achieved partial success when the state legislature approved a resolution to amend the constitution to allow woman suffrage. In spite of spirited activities between 1895 and 1897, including a woman suffrage convention, the establishment of the Nevada Equal Suffrage Association, and visits to the state by national figures such as Susan B. Anthony, Anna H. Shaw, and Emma Smith DeVoe, the resolution was defeated by the 1897 legislature and the amending process had to begin over again. For some unexplained reason the movement for woman suffrage in Nevada came to a halt between 1897 and 1911. In the latter year, Professor Jeanne E. Wier had organized the Nevada Equal Franchise Society, which lobbied successfully to resurrect a resolution for woman suffrage which had been defeated earlier in the session by both houses. By that time Progressive reforms had paved the way for woman suffrage. In addition, in 1912 a remarkable woman, Anne Martin, took over the presidency of the Equal Franchise Society, and immediately launched a campaign to establish equal suffrage organizations in every county. With Miss Martin leading the way, the society attempted to reach all the legislative candidates in order to ensure a legislature sympathetic to woman suffrage. Their task was made easier when Governor Tasker L. Oddie in his biennial address to the lgislature recommended that women be granted the vote. The assembly approved the woman suffrage resolution by a vote of forty-nine to three and the senate by a vote of nineteen to three. In 1913 and 1914 the suffragists intensified their activities, only this time the object of their pressure was the voter. The forty-five-year struggle for woman suffrage ended in success in the election of 1914, when 10,936 votes were counted in favor of the amendment and 7,258 against.

Nevada followed the lead of other Progressive states in these years by setting up a number of regulatory boards and commissions. Thus in 1907 a Board of Bank Commissioners was established and the office of bank examiner created. In the same year a Railroad Commission of three members was established to regulate railroad and telegraph and telephone companies and other common carriers. The act was quite specific, particularly in listing maximum rates for general freight and for ores according to their value. By an act of 1911 the Railroad Commission became ex officio a public service commission when public utilities including heat, light, power, water, and sewerage companies were placed under its jurisdiction. Two years later the Nevada Tax Commission was established, in part, at least, in answer to criticism leveled against the assessment of railroad property. The chairman of the Railroad Commission automatically became one of the three members of the new commission.

Reformers also succeeded in putting a halt to an amusement which had grown up with the state; on October 1, 1910, gambling became illegal in Nevada. The fight against gambling went back to Nevada's first governor, H. G. Blasdel, who came out strongly against it in 1867 when he vetoed an act legalizing gambling. In 1869 the legislature legalized gambling over the governor's veto. From time to time reformers returned to attack gambling, but without real success until the early 1900s when it became a target of Progressive reformers. The 1911 legislature made certain card games such as poker legal again, but another act in 1913 outlawed all gambling. The restriction once more proved too much for the citizens of Nevada and the 1915 legislature legalized card games where the deal alternated. It was well known that illegal gambling thrived in most Nevada communities during these years.

Divorce was still another target of Progressive reformers in Nevada. The state began to attract attention as a divorce mecca in the early 1900s, and by 1909 its reputation for easy divorce was so widespread and the attendant publicity often so bawdy that reformers could not ignore the social implications. Acting governor Denver S. Dickerson in 1909 came out for a stronger divorce law, but the legislature did not follow his recommendation. However, when Governor Oddie recommended in 1913 that the six-months law be changed, the legislature complied with the adoption of an act requiring a year's bona fide residence before divorce could be granted. The reform failed to outlast the Progressive era as local businessmen, more concerned about economics than morals, lobbied successfully in 1915 to restore the six-months residence law.

The 1910 election in Nevada was unusual in bringing face to face in the contest for governor two avowed Progressive candidates. Denver S. Dickerson, who had become acting governor upon the death of Governor John Sparks in 1908, had demonstrated strong Progressive principles in a remarkable message to the 1909 legislature. He had recommended reform in the state prison system and the state hospital for mental diseases, strengthening the State Railroad Commission by giving it full power to fix passenger and freight rates, strengthening the banking laws to protect the investor, creation of the office of state mine inspector, prohibition of wildcat stock promotions, the direct election of United States senators, a strong antilobby act, a more stringent divorce law, establishment of a state conservation commission, and provision for the initiative and the recall. Although not all of his suggestions were carried out by that legislature, enough had been accomplished to mark Dickerson as a progressive Democrat.

His opponent, Tasker L. Oddie, had entered Nevada politics in 1904 when he succeeded in winning a seat in the state senate. In the 1906 campaign he was the preconvention favorite of the Repubicans for governor, but declined to run. Any plans he may have had for 1908 or later years seemed to evaporate with his fortune as a result of the panic of 1907 and a number of unprofitable mining investments. However, in June of 1910 Oddie surprised many people by announcing his candidacy for governor. This decision pitted him against Judge W. A. Massey, who had been elected to the supreme court years earlier as a Silver-Democrat. Oddie's announcement was accompanied by a blast against the Southern Pacific's domination of state politics and against boss control of the Republican party. He insisted that he was a "Progressive Republican" and that he stood "for the rights of the people and intend[ed] to represent them at all times."[5] Although he had little money with which to finance his campaign and was opposing the state Republican machine, Oddie managed to win a narrow victory over Massey, beating him by 159 votes.

Oddie's campaign must rank as one of the most unusual in the state's history. His insistence on remaining financially independent imposed severe austerity on him. His lack of money was balanced by a strenuous, almost evangelical effort, which included an automobile tour of the entire state over almost impassable roads, with gasoline furnished by supporters at each stop. The campaign paid off in November when Oddie won a substantial victory over Dickerson.

Oddie took office as governor at a time when Progressive forces within the national Republican party were making a concerted effort to gain control of the party in 1912. Oddie supported the movement; in a letter to Jonathan Bourne of the National Progressive Republican League he wrote, "Many of your views I am in

[5] The material on Oddie is taken mainly from the Oddie Papers, Huntington Library, San Marino, California.

hearty accord with as I believe in progressive principles which will mean the upbuilding and strengthening of the Republican party in the future." His messages to both the 1911 and the 1913 legislatures included a variety of Progressive proposals, and although he should not be given all the credit for the result, a solid body of Progressive legislation was passed during his four-year term from 1911 to 1915.

Oddie's relationship with the Roosevelt Progressive party of 1912 is interesting. In the preconvention skirmishes between the Taft and Roosevelt factions it was clear that Oddie supported Teddy Roosevelt. In a letter to a friend he stated, "I have come out good and strong for Roosevelt and have gotten myself in hot water with the Taft men in this state but I cannot help that as I am following my own conscience and think I am right." However, after the Progressives broke with the main wing of the Republicans and formed their own party in August, Oddie deliberately avoided joining it. He wrote to a friend, "A third party has been started here but I have purposely been laying low and not taking part in things as yet." H. B. Lind, the state chairman of the Progressive, or Bull Moose, party, tried to force his hand in September but Oddie was able to avoid a definite commitment since he was not a candidate in 1912. It is interesting to note that George Wingfield, in a letter to Oddie in September, warned him that appearing on stage in favor of Bull Moose candidates would be a mistake.

Oddie's role in the 1912 campaign, while not a very positive one, enabled him to maintain the support of the Republicans when he ran for reelection in 1914. In his campaign for reelection he continued to emphasize Progressive legislation, and when he was defeated by the Democratic candidate, Emmett D. Boyle, Oddie blamed the result on his opposition to a return to open gambling and his support of the one-year residency for divorce. Although the Progressive party in Nevada held a state convention in 1914 and named candidates for attorney general, superintendent of state printing, and the board of regents, they admitted their weakness as a party by endorsing all the Republican nominees who were not specifically opposed by Progressives. Nevada's role in the Progressive movement was pretty much over by the end of 1914. While there had been much legislative accomplishment, there had been no effective Progressive leadership with a firm program.

CHAPTER 12

World War I and the 1920s

WHEN WORLD WAR I broke out in Europe in August, 1914, Nevadans were in the midst of a primary election campaign, but for a short period the war pushed the election news from the front pages of the more important state newspapers. Advertisements in papers in towns like Ruth, McGill, and Tonopah called upon citizens of Austria and Serbia to return to fight for their country; for hundreds of immigrants they were unwelcome reminders of recent allegiances.

There was a feeling among some of the state's leaders that the war would accelerate the depression already noticeable in the United States before Austria declared war on Serbia. George Wingfield, the most powerful economic figure in Nevada, expressed a contrary opinion in an interview in the *Nevada State Journal* of August 7:

This European war should give Nevada a gilt-edged market for all her products as soon as trans-Atlantic shipping is resumed, and that will be within a short time, according to present indications. There will be a big demand for mutton and beef from our ranges, and also a strong market for horses, which will give us a chance to work off our less desirable stock into the war for re-stocking with a better quality of animals. Our mines are going to go ahead and I am thoroughly optimistic that Nevada will not only not suffer from the European war, but will ultimately be benefitted, as will the United States in general.

His prediction was correct, as Nevada's mining industry experienced a boom which centered in the great copper deposits in eastern Nevada. War demands for copper shot production from $7 million in 1914 to $25 million in 1916 and the following two years, and mines were developed in Lyon County, near Yerington. The copper production was only part of a general mineral revival in which old silver-lead camps such as Pioche, Goodsprings, and Eureka made comebacks. Newer camps such as Tonopah and Goldfield, which had started to show the first signs of decay as the war broke out, were able to continue at substantial levels during the war and the immediate postwar period. The state's total mineral production in 1918 was $48,635,168, nearly two million dollars more than the peak during the Comstock period.

The war also stimulated agriculture in Nevada, particularly the livestock industry. Encouraged by congressional appropriations, state livestock men increased their flocks and herds, and farmers brought into use all lands subject to irrigation, as well as much submarginal land. Sugar beet raising and beekeeping became profitable in western Nevada because of greater demands for sugar and honey. Prices for all food items were high enough, in spite of growing production costs, to bring Nevada agriculturalists real prosperity.

Before the United States entered World War I, Nevada's participation in military activities was limited by the small population of the state, its geographic isolation, and its lack of a functioning state militia. A state guard had been mobilized during the Spanish-American War, but after that it was allowed to deteriorate and was officially disbanded in 1906. A militia had seemed unnecessary, particularly since the state legislature had passed a state police act in 1908 to supplement the authority of county and local officials, but Governor Emmet Boyle was obviously embarassed in early 1916 when President Woodrow Wilson requested National Guard troops from several states for service on the Mexican border. In a telegram to the secretary of war, Boyle offered to provide six hundred volunteers from Nevada in order to honor the request; the offer was declined. Then on June 3, 1916, Congress passed the National Defense Act; among other things, the law placed the National Guard under federal authority and specified that participating states must have an organized guard of not less than six hundred men by July 1, 1917. Governor Boyle made a number of efforts to organize such a force in the latter months of 1916 but without success. He blamed his difficulties on the antagonism of labor and asked the legislature to draft a constitutional amendment exempting the National Guard from strike service. The lawmakers did not comply, but even if they had voted to amend the constitution, the process requires a minimum of three years. Thus, on the eve of World War I, Nevada had no National Guard, but only a unit of ROTC, established at the University in the autumn of 1916, and nine "Government Civilian Rifle Clubs," sponsored by the War Department, to show for its contribution to national defense.

Although events in 1917 were moving the United States closer to involvement in the war, the state legislators seemed not unduly concerned. However, they did appropriate $25,000 to be expended under the direction of the governor, "for the sole purpose of meeting any military demands which may be made upon the State of Nevada by the President or the Government of the United States." Ultimately the money was used to establish the Nevada State Council of Defense, which, while it had no formal grant of legal powers from the state, had the support of the administration and of the people. Through it and the regional councils which were set up in every county and school district, Nevada served, in effect, as an administrative unit of the federal government in regard to defense measures. The state council became an agency to transmit governmental orders and requests, publicized many necessary wartime projects, and aided such defense-related organizations as the Red Cross, the Liberty Loan Committee, and the fuel and food administrations.

The Selective Service Act of 1917 also depended greatly on cooperation by the states and their local units, placing the responsibility for the draft on local boards established within each county. All males between twenty-one and thirty-one were to register on June 5, a day on which demonstrations of patriotism were held across the nation in order to forestall violent protests similar to those which met the Civil War draft. In Nevada, Governor Boyle declared registration day an official state holiday and in most towns all businesses were closed except the banks, which remained open to sell Liberty Bonds. A number of communities had patriotic observances on the eve of registration and parades were held the next day. Apart from the opposition encountered at the Socialist colony near Fallon, Nevadans experienced little difficulty with the draft machinery. Total registration in the state under the 1917 act was 30,808 persons, including 3,600 aliens; 3,384 Nevadans were inducted. Most of them were sent to Camp Lewis in Washington and became part of the Ninety-first Division which reached France in July, 1918, and became actively engaged almost at once on the front line. In addition to the draftees, Nevada sent 1,447 volunteers into the regular army, proportionately one of the highest involvements in the nation.[1]

When the United States entered World War I, Nevada was still basically an immigrant state. The largest foreign-born group in 1910 were the Italians, with 2,831 of a total of 19,691 immigrants in the state. Following in order were the Germans, with 1,916; the English, 1,793; the Irish, 1,702; and the Greeks, 1,051. Although there were 822 Austrians listed as residing in Nevada, it seems that most were not Teutonic and probably were opposed to the Central Powers during the war. While Nevada's foreign-born population appeared to be heavily weighted in favor of the allies, state leaders were concerned about the concentrations of immigrants from the Austro-Hungarian Empire living in the Ruth-McGill area and at Tonopah, and the pocket of German-born in Douglas County.

The United States entered World War I in the spring of 1917 without a full understanding of the nature of the European struggle and how it was perceived by the nation's foreign-born population. A strong feeling persisted throughout the war that the immigrants had not been assimilated and that many continued their allegiance to their native land. In his efforts to overcome this difficulty, President Wilson interpreted the nation's entry into the war in moral

[1] Much of the material for this chapter comes from state publications such as the *Appendices to the Journals of the Senate and Assembly*.

terms: in the right was pure democracy, represented by the Allies; in the wrong was the militaristic authoritarianism of the Central Powers. To ensure that the public recognized American involvement as a moral issue, Wilson created the Committee on Public Information, with George Creel, a journalist, as its head. The Creel committee proceeded to sell the war to the American people, emphasizing always the idealistic crusade of the Allies "to make the world safe for democracy" as against the menace of the Hun, who was out to ravish Europe and then extend control over the Western Hemisphere. Soon anyone who opposed the entrance of the United States into the war or the activities of the Allies, or who might have been associated in any way with the Central Powers, became the uneasy target of the many volunteer security and protective organizations which were springing up all over the country. The fear-oriented propaganda pouring forth from the Allies and from the Creel Committee stimulated a hysterical outburst of narrow nationalism aimed mainly against all things German, but also against peace groups, radical labor organizations such as the IWW and socialists.

In Nevada, German-Americans of Douglas County were suspect during much of the war, although some of the most prominent citizens, such as C. O. Dangberg and George Hussman, served on the county council of defense and participated actively in wartime activities. Under pressure of the war hysteria in 1918, the Lutheran Church at Minden gave up conducting religious service in the German language on alternate Sundays, and the teaching of German in the high school there was discontinued by the school board at the request of the student body. The Germans of Douglas County were fortunate, however, in that they were a strong minority group with roots deep in Nevada. Much more harassed were individual German families scattered in communities throughout the state who had to suffer personal indignities and social ostracism along with the persistent suspicions of their loyalty.

The large number of people from central and southern Europe in the eastern Nevada copper communties experienced somewhat different problems. Among the former subjects of the Austro-Hungarian Empire there were many with divided loyalties, and newspaper reporters and others tended to lump indiscriminately under the label of Austro-Hungarians all those who had come from central and southern Europe. The Serbians and the Greeks reacted strongly, even going so far as to organize loyalty parades in Ruth, Ely, and McGill. Speakers at these gatherings vowed their loyalty to the United States, denounced autocracy, the Hapsburg empire in particular, and pledged their lives and fortunes to the service of the United States. Later in the year the Serbian Benevolent Society of the Ely district sent a resolution to President Wilson denouncing Austria-Hungary and pledging loyalty to America. Evidently the Serbians succeeded in dissociating themselves from the Austro-Hungarian label; in June, 1918, forty-two of them were recruited by the Serbian army for service on the Balkan front, whereupon the Nevada Consolidated Company gave them a big farewell and asked them to return to the community and to company employ after the war.

Across the country, civilians participated in numerous activities connected with the war effort. In Nevada, they listened to the Four-Minute Men (volunteer speakers enlisted by the Committee of Public Information) addressing large audiences in the local theaters to spearhead the war loan drives; helped to collect tin foil; tried to observe Food Administrator Herbert Hoover's wheatless Mondays and Wednesdays, meatless Tuesdays, and porkless Thursdays and Saturdays; took part in Red Cross drives; and sent their sons to induction centers amid bursts of patriotism which in some cases nearly overwhelmed the draftees. Typical was the celebration at Ely when the first contingent of troops left for Camp Lewis, Washington. First the group was taken to a movie, then entertained at a dance which lasted until midnight. At that hour each of the sixty-five "boys" was presented with a "comfort bag" which had been prepared by the ladies of the Red Cross and the sewing class of the local high school. The next morning the band appeared on the main street at five-thirty and played patriotic music for half an hour before leading the procession which escorted the draftees to the depot. The newspapers noted that the "sidewalks were a mass of humanity." The inductees than boarded the train, obviously relieved to get out of the hands of their many well-wishers. Civilians continued to give draftees enthusiastic send-offs in most communities throughout the war.

Another patriotic gesture was the flag-placing ceremony. Nearly every community in the state during the initial months of American participation in the war planted a flag, usually on some prominent nearby hill. At McGill, for example, a flag measuring 20 by 32 feet was unfurled atop a 100-foot steel pole placed at the summit of Lakenan Peak. The flagpole was constructed in sections of standard pipe and packed to the top of the peak by a combination of mules and block and tackle. The total weight of the pole was 2,150 pounds, causing some uneasiness as it was placed in a hole prepared in the solid rock, cemented, and secured with guy lines. The ceremony at the spot included a salute by the school children, the firing of shots by a detachment of the Nevada State Police, and patriotic addresses by public officials. Electric lights placed at the base of the pole beamed skyward so that "Old Glory could be seen day and night." National holidays, especially July 4 and Memorial Day, provided further opportunities for civilian expression of wartime emotion. Patriotism was the only theme as bands played, veterans and high school and university cadets marched, and orators filled the air with fervent speeches which generally echoed the themes publicized by the Committee on Public Information.

Advocates of liquor prohibition found the war an excellent opportunity to push their reform program. After years of effort and little progress, the movement gained support as soon as the United States entered the war. A spectacular victory came on the national level when prohibitionist pressure led to the addition of an anti-liquor rider to the Lever Act of 1917. Under this provision, which forbade the use of foodstuffs in the manufacture of distilled beverages, Wilson ordered breweries throughout the United States closed in October, 1918. From that point it was a short step to national prohibition, declared under the Eighteenth amendment to the Constitution in 1919. Nevada voters brought prohibition to their state on November 5, 1918, using for the first time the initiative procedure which had been established by constitutional amendment in 1912. By a vote of 13,248 to 9,060 they approved a measure to prohibit the manufacture and sale of all intoxicating drinks. The act was so inclusive in defining what constituted intoxicating liquors that the legislature felt it necessary to pass an act several months later exempting vanilla, lemon, and similar extracts and perfumes and other such items used for toilet purposes. Near-beer and similar beverages were not prohibited.

Attention to the war effort was diverted briefly in Nevada and elsewhere in the United States while the processes of democracy ground slowly forward in the election of 1918. Major statewide contests developed between Governor Boyle and former governor Tasker L. Oddie for the governorship and between four candidates vying for the United States Senate seat left vacant by the death of Senator Newlands in December, 1917. Charles B. Henderson, a prominent Democrat from Elko county whom Boyle had appointed to fill the vacancy temporarily, appeared to have the best chance to complete the unexpired term. However, a lively contest was ensured when Congressman E. E. Roberts was nominated by the Republicans and when Anne Martin, a tireless worker on behalf of women's rights, qualified to run on the Independent ticket. Although her candidacy was opposed by many powerful and vocal interests, including such influential newspapers as the *Carson Appeal,* Miss Martin carried her campaign to the people of the state and received a substantial vote, probably pulling more from the Socialists than from either the Democrats or Republicans. Henderson easily won the election, with a vote of 12,197 to 8,053 for Roberts, 4,603 for Miss Martin, and 710 for M. J. Scanlan, the Socialist candidate. The decline in the Socialists' strength from 1916, when A. Grant Miller polled 9,057 votes in the Senate race, was largely due to the party's earlier pacifism and to the internal conflict which led many of its leaders, including Miller, to move with the tide of national patriotism. The race for governor was much closer, but Boyle defeated Oddie by over a thousand votes. The Democrats won all of the other state offices except that of inspector of mines and for the first time in years, Nevada sent a solid Democratic delegation to Washington, even though a national swing to the Republicans brought them into power in Congress.

Shortly before the war ended, an epidemic of Spanish influenza moved across the United States, ultimately costing many more lives than were lost in battle. When it reached Nevada in October, 1918, many schools, churches, and movie theaters were closed, and scheduled public meetings were canceled or postponed as state and county health officials tried to halt the spread of the deadly disease. Some county authorities required the wearing of gauze face masks in public, a precaution of dubious value, like many of the home remedies employed. The so-called flu bans were not removed in some counties until late in December. When they were lifted, the following advertisement appeared: "The Grand Theatre reminds Renoites the flu ban is off, that all showhouses have been fumigated, and it is now showing Big Bill Russell in 'Hobbs in a Hurry'." Before the disease had run its course in Nevada it had touched every community and had caused many deaths.

The influenza epidemic limited celebrations of the armistice on November 11, but most communities responded with spontaneous outbursts in the streets, ringing bells, or marching in parades. A few months later, returning soldiers were welcomed back to their home communities; close on their heels, various army groups came to Nevada towns and dozens of American communities elsewhere to demonstrate new weapons of war and to push subscriptions for the Victory Loan drive. Usually the displays featured the tank, described as the ultimate weapon of destruction. People watched as they rumbled through old sheds, uninhabited wooden shacks—anything that stood in their way. After each demonstration one of the members of the crew stood on top of the tank and made a patriotic appeal for support in the bond drive. Later in the same year an army motor convoy of 72 vehicles and 300 men passed through Nevada on its way to San Francisco and the men were feted at overnight stops along the way. Typical was the celebration at Ely, where the soldiers were served a huge buffet dinner, followed by a dance in their honor. Before the dance the band which accompanied the convoy played wartime songs on the courthouse lawn. Many local veterans and other townspeople listened, hummed, or sang along as the band played songs like "K-K-K Katy," "We're All Going Calling on the Kaiser," "Keep the Home Fires Burning," "Beautiful Ohio," "We'll Knock the Heligo into Heligo out of Heligoland," and "Keep Your Head Down, Fritzie Boy."

POSTWAR LABOR TROUBLES

The war was over, but serious numerous labor troubles were beginning in various Nevada communities early in 1919. In his message to the 1919 legislature Governor Boyle warned that economic readjustments would be necessary because of curtailment in metal production and sharp declines in the prices for livestock and other agricultural products. He pointed out that the "great problem" in the state in the next few years would be unemployment, and with it, said Boyle, will come the danger to harmonious relations between employer and employee; danger of the absorption by idle and discouraged groups of false philosophies and increasing danger to the state of the recurrence of the intense and bitter industrial disputes which at one time served to write disgraceful pages in the history of the intermountain country. The I.W.W. ism with its faults and brutal philosophy has not been and will not be successfully combatted by mob rule or by methods which do not lie wholly within the law, and it lives and thrives on the petty autocracy manifested in the inconsiderate acts of capital.

Boyle praised the self-restraint of Nevada labor during World War I and suggested that the legislature study the advisability of enacting some kind of conciliation act to help ease the threat of industrial disturbances.

However, in Nevada and elsewhere in the United States, the patriotism which had been directed toward winning the war began to move in ever narrower paths of unthinking nationalism; the new target, particularly in the western mining areas, was radical labor. There had been many incidents in the state during the war growing out of animosity toward the IWW, and after the war this antagonism became evident in the legislature. The most specific result of the reaction was the Criminal Syndicalism Act, passed in February, 1919. Aimed directly against the IWW, the law made criminal syndicalism—any "doctrine which advocates or teaches crime, sabotage, violence or unlawful methods of terrorism as a means of accomplishing industrial or political reform"—a felony punishable by not more than ten years in prison or a $5,000 fine, or both. In Nevada the act was not utilized the way a similar measure was used in California, to arrest hundreds of individuals suspected of subversive activities, but it was brought directly into the Tonopah labor dispute of 1919.

As Governor Boyle had predicted, labor disturbances began to break out soon after the war ended. Most stemmed from sharp cutbacks in metal production which were demanded by stockholders interested in reducing costs in order to continue dividend payments. Glutted inventories caused further decreases in production and wages without corresponding reductions in living costs. Besides, labor had been promised many times during the war, particularly when strikes seemed imminent, that their wage grievances would be settled after the war. Under these circumstances, clashes between employees and employers in mineral camps throughout Nevada were inevitable, and solutions were complicated by the wave of antilabor feeling sweeping the United States. The animosity toward the IWW which had led to the passage of the Criminal Syndicalism Law now resulted in an indiscriminate labeling, usually inaccurate, of all strikes as IWW-directed movements. This was the case in the first major postwar labor disturbance in Nevada. In January, 1919, 150 men refused to go to work in the copper mines at Ruth, demanding raises to make up for the high living costs of the wartime period. Almost at once the walkout was branded the work of the IWW, a charge that was easily accepted by the public since the headquarters for union activity in the district was at nearby Riepetown. But it was really an insignificant wildcat strike, like most of the others in the state in 1919; the leaders were old members of the Western Federation of Mines, an organization whose earlier ties with the IWW were conveniently used in these years to deny the legitimate goals of union labor.

A much more important strike was called at McGill in July, 1919, to obtain higher wages and additional benefits. Negotiations began immediately, with Governor Boyle and federal mediator J. Lord attempting to work out a compromise, and settlement was reached August 29. Meanwhile, in August a second major disturbance broke out at Tonopah. The district had escaped major labor difficulties during the very bitter troubles which had rocked her sister camp, Goldfield, in the years from 1906 to 1908. Many grievances developed during the war but again the "no strike" pledge was observed. However, as soon as the war ended, it became clear that adjustments would have to be made. As months dragged on without action from the employers, the workers were left in a receptive mood for a small group of IWW agitators who arrived at Tonopah on August 17. When operators refused union demands for raises, the unions went out on strike. Little headway was made in negotiating an agreement until the arrival of Governor Boyle, Nevada Labor Commissioner R. F. Cole, and J. Lord, the federal mediator. On September 13 a plan for settlement was submitted to the miners. A secret ballot was used in order to isolate IWW influence and the referendum showed a heavy majority in favor of settlement, but the IWW refused to return to work and other union members honored its pickets. Finally, the mine operators persuaded the craft unions to withdraw support of the miner's strike. A new organization, the Tono-pah-Divide Mine and Millmen's Union, was then formed in October as the result of numerous conferences held between the operators, led by George Wingfield, and representatives of the craft unions. The new union promptly voted to accept the operators' original offer, and the strike was declared officially over by Governor Boyle.

But, when IWW members still refused to abide by the agreement, the Governor obtained a temporary injunction, later made perma-nent, against the strike committee on the basis of the Criminal Syndicalism Law. On November 8, the Tonopah strike was finally settled with an agreement which provided that the operators would establish a commissary for employees, that they would sell coal to employees at cost and grant a bonus of fifty cents per day to all workers, retroactive to October 4, and continue the bonus inde-finitely unless the commissary reduced living cost sufficiently to eliminate it.

The radical labor movement in Nevada had suffered severe blows in the earlier strikes at Goldfield and McGill, and after the 1919 strikes it was reduced to impotency. Organized labor in general was unable to divorce itself from the IWW in the eyes of the public and suffered a major decline in the state.

Governor Boyle was much more successful in negotiating labor troubles than he was in obtaining approval for his legislative program. In 1919 he advocated a major tax reform to broaden and equalize the tax base, condemning Nevada's tax laws as the most cumbersome and inequitable of any state in the Union. He even went so far as to suggest that the "net proceeds" provision for the taxing of mines be abolished, noting that it overtaxed the small producers and undertaxed the large ones. A mining engineer himself, the gov-ernor gained the animosity of the mining fraternity by insisting that the mining industry of the state had never paid its fair share of taxes. However, the 1919 legislature ignored both Boyle's suggested tax reform and his other recommendations.

ECONOMIC DEVELOPMENT IN THE 1920s

Nevada began the decade of the twenties on a pessimistic note. Mineral production, which had declined sharply in the first year after the war, dropped another $6½ million, making the output for 1920 less than one-half the total for 1918. Agricultural production decreased along with prices for farm products. To emphasize the decline, census figures for 1920 indicated that Nevada had but 77,407 persons, 4,468 less than in 1910. Although mineral production dropped still further in the nationwide depression of 1921, the heavy industrial demands in the United States, particularly for copper, ensured prosperity for most of Nevada's small population during the remainder of the decade.

Adding to the state's economy in the twenties was a substantial expenditure of federal and state funds for the construction of highways. The American people were rapidly becoming a nation on wheels, spending more than a billion dollars annually for road building in that period. In the construction of the nation's highway network Nevada played basically the same role as it had during the exploration of the West and the building of the railroads: that of a bridge to get somewhere else, usually California. But whatever the purpose behind Nevada's road system, the transportation revolution brought with it a new business interest, the road builders.

Governor R. K. Colcord had been the first Nevada governor to recognize the importance of good highways. In 1895 he told the legislature that "good roads are the most hearty invitations that can be extended to induce immigration. . . . national legislation should be advocated for the construction and maintenance of good interstate roads." Colcord's message went unheeded until 1911, when Governor Tasker L. Oddie, who had campaigned all over the vast state of Nevada by automobile, appealed for the establishment of good highways as a source of revenue from tourist travel and suggested that convict labor might be employed to reduce costs. The 1911 legislature did pass an act authorizing the use of convicts to build public roads and highways and provided $20,000 for the program, which was placed under the supervision of the state engineer. Some construction was completed between Carson City and Reno, but the experiment was so unsatisfactory that the 1913 legislature refused to provide funds to continue the program. A major reason for the reversal was the state prison warden's biennial report, pointing out that less than six miles of road had been built by prison labor at a cost of $63,933.55, not including the rewards for escaped prisoners. His conclusion was that "better roads could have been built for less money with free labor." In spite of this setback, Governor Oddie continued to press for a better highway system. Since the condition of the state treasury precluded help from that source, he suggested that the counties, as the chief beneficiaries of the roads, should be allowed to let bonds for road construction. The legislature responded with an act which created boards of county highway commissioners, established a county road supervisor, and authorized counties to issue bonds after approval by public vote. The act shifted responsibility for road building to the counties, but they had no money either; it was clear that there would be little real achievement in road building in Nevada unless the United States government appropriated the funds.

Federal help became available in 1916 with the passage of the Federal-Aid Road Act, which introduced a dollar-matching plan. States were required to have highway departments in order to receive funds under the provisions of the law, and since Nevada lacked such an agency, Governor Boyle recommended that the legislature take the necessary action to establish one. In March, 1917, a comprehensive general highway act was passed which not only provided for a department of highways but also created the office of state highway engineer, designated four original routes in Nevada to compose the state highway system, and provided a tax to raise funds to meet the requirements of the federal act.

While Nevada's highway system received its initial impetus from the 1916 act, it gained additional benefits in 1921 under new federal legislation. The law included a matching formula which gave an advantage to states where the unappropriated and unreserved public domain exceeded 5 percent of the total area. Thus Nevada, with a high proportion of public lands (over 80 percent), benefited greatly in having to supply only 16.32 cents of each dollar spent on joint construction. The state's highway program picked up momentum between 1922 and 1926, aided substantially by the new formula and by the imposition in 1923 of a state gasoline tax.

By 1926 approximately $10 million had been expended on Nevada highways, the state's contribution representing Nevada's largest expenditure for any single purpose in the postwar years. Nevada joined with other states that year in celebrating the completion of the main transcontinental road through the state, the so-called Lincoln Highway. The 1925 legislature had appropriated funds for a Nevada Transcontinental Exposition to be held in Reno when the highway was finished. A "permanent" symbol of this event was the state building, completed in 1926 from those funds, intended to house a temporary exhibit in honor of the completion of the highway and to provide permanent quarters for the Nevada State Historical Society after the celebration.[2] By the end of the decade, the Nevada highway system as defined in 1917 was virtually completed, but with gravel surface for a great deal of its length. The major task of oiling and paving the surface was left until the next decade.

The pressure for better roads forced the state legislature to double the gasoline tax, and in 1929 all the revenues from it were placed in the state highway fund. (An amendment to the state constitution in 1940 stipulated that all license and registration fees and the proceeds of excise taxes on gasoline and other motor vehicle fuel must be used exclusively for the construction, maintenance, and repair of the state's public highways.) With the gasoline tax, license tax, and state property levy of five cents, Nevada appropriated about one million dollars annually for road building and maintenance purposes in the 1920s. When one considers all of the auxiliary services brought into play by such projects, it is evident that road building played a significant role in the state's economy during the twenties.

Politics in the Twenties

The Republican party returned to power in Nevada in the twenties, although its progress toward political control was slow and not really complete until 1926. It began by upsetting the Democrats in 1920 in the contests for United States Senate and for the one seat in the House of Representatives. And for the first time since Teddy Roosevelt's election in 1904, Nevada was won for the Republican presidential candidate.

The Republican primary election reflected the belief that 1920 would be a Republican year. No less than five men sought the Senate seat then held by Democrat Charles B. Henderson, including former governor Tasker L. Oddie; A. Grant Miller, who twice had been a candidate for the Senate on the Socialist ticket; Sardis Summerfield, who had run in 1912 on the Progressive ticket; Brewster Adams, a Reno clergyman who had been prominent in the Progressive movement; and Charles E. Wharton of Reno. Conservative

---

[2] The "permanent" state building was torn down in 1966 to make way for the present Pioneer Auditorium.

Republicans were given little choice in the primary, since three of the leading candidates had been associated in one way or another with the Roosevelt Progressive party and a fourth had been a Socialist. From the beginning Oddie's campaign had the support of the so-called Wingfield machine, but Adams and Miller were both popular and the regulars feared that the large number of candidates might splinter the vote and one or the other might be nominated. Oddie managed to win by a comfortable, if not overwhelming, margin, and in the general election he ran against Henderson, who had no primary opposition. Anne Martin, running again on the Independent ticket, received nearly 5,000 votes and may well have cost Senator Henderson the election: Oddie won by 1,148 votes. Republican Samuel Arentz defeated the incumbent Democrat, Charles R. Evans, for Congress.

In spite of the 1920 Republican victories, Nevada remained predominantly Democratic for the next few years. This was clearly demonstrated in the 1922 election as all the major state offices and two national posts were contested. Many Republicans were particularly interested in unseating Key Pittman in the Senate, and on the basis of their victory in 1920 the task did not appear impossible. Republicans entering the primary contest included Congressman Arentz; Charles S. Chandler, a prominent attorney from White Pine County and speaker of the state assembly in 1921; Samuel Platt, a Reno attorney who had come within 41 votes of unseating Senator Newlands in 1914; Peter Buol, a well-known Clark County Republican and former mayor of Las Vegas; and Lydia Adams-Williams. The race was closely contested, with Chandler receiving 2,540 votes; Arentz, 2,225; Platt, 2,143, Buol, 1,403; and Adams-Williams, 447.

In the general election, Chandler was no match for the experienced Pittman, who had became adept at serving local interests, making certain that Nevadans knew that he was in Washington on their behalf. He campaigned for reelection carefully and strenuously with the tacit support of the Wingfield machine. The result was a landslide victory over Chandler with a total of 18,201 out of 28,971 votes cast.

Pittman's success led a statewide victory for the Democrats, who won all the offices contested except that of inspector of mines. The Republicans had looked upon their success in 1920 as indication that the political pendulum had started to swing their way, but it seems that national issues played little part in these mid-term elections and Nevada voters were not yet disillusioned with the Democrats on the state and local level. Governor Boyle's prestige may have played a part also, particularly since the winning candidate for governor, James G. Scrugham, was looked upon as handpicked by Boyle.

The Democrats were unable to maintain their strength during the 1924 campaign. Not only did they lose the only important race, in which Samuel S. Arentz won the congressional seat by a narrow margin over C. L. Richards, but they came in last in the three-way race for presidential electors. The LaFollette Progressive party attracted liberals of both the Democratic and Republican parties, making a surprisingly strong showing. Also, the personal appearance of President Calvin Coolidge in Nevada undoubtedly aided the Republican cause. On the other hand, William Jennings Bryan's appearance in Carson City in support of the Davis-Bryan ticket did little for the Democrats. (He did take occasion to praise the Nevada electorate when he exclaimed, "If all the people of the country had known as much as you, I'd have been President long ago.") Even the strong support of Key Pittman apparently had little effect in bringing votes to the Democratic presidential nominee, John W. Davis, although that race in Nevada might well have taken a different turn had Pittman accepted Davis's bid to become his running mate.

The Democratic dominance of the state offices was finally broken in 1926 when the Republicans, besides returning Oddie to the Senate and Arentz to the House of Representatives, elected the governor, lieutenant governor, and four of the other seven state positions. The Democratic state convention endorsed the record of Governor Scrugham; his prestige throughout the state and his party's support were sufficient to forestall a primary contest for governor. The Republican state convention did not endorse a candidate for that office. Before and during the convention, a great deal of pressure was applied by some Republicans to get George Wingfield to run for governor, but he resisted all such efforts—including the publication of a list of prominent Republicans supporting the movement to draft him—and stayed in the political background. Wingfield's continued refusal brought forth a number of possible candidates including Fred B. Balzar, who was then serving a second term as state chairman of the Republican central committee. In the days following the state convention it became increasingly evident that Balzar was the choice of the Republican stalwarts, including George Wingfield, particularly when Balzar's announcement of candidacy frightened off other pretenders, thus avoiding a primary fight. The situation prompted an accusation by the editor of the Democratic *Nevada State Journal* that a small group of Republicans—an obvious reference to the Wingfield machine—were undermining the objectives of the direct primary by choosing the candidates for the Republican party.

Fred Balzar proved to be one of the most popular campaigners in Nevada history. His warm, outgoing personality attracted friendly crowds wherever he went and with the support of Wingfield it was soon apparent that he would be a formidable threat to Scrugham in the general election. The governor campaigned mostly on the basis of his considerable achievements while in office, including completion of over one thousand miles of highways and the establishment of a number of recreation grounds and game refuges. Scrugham was the first Nevada governor to ask the legislature for authority to set aside such areas within the forest reserves. It was granted in 1923 and the governor designated fifteen recreation areas within the state to be administered under the State Game and Fish Commission. His actions marked the beginning of the development of the Nevada State Park system. Particularly noteworthy were Scrugham's efforts to preserve prehistoric sites such as Lost City, which was first investigated during his administration, and a major investigation of Lovelock Cave in 1924 by Drs. L. L. Loud and Mark Harrington. However, even the compliment from Secretary of Commerce Herbert Hoover that Scrugham was the "outstanding executive in the Western states" could not stem the tide of Balzar's popularity and the growing strength of Republicanism throughout the United States which was reflected in Nevada. Scrugham was defeated by a margin of 1,853 out of 30,895 votes cast.

The race for the United States Senate post held by Oddie attracted a number of candidates, forcing primary battles within each party. The most prominent of the four Democrats who entered the contest were Ray T. Baker and Patrick A. McCarran. Baker had been the director of the United States Mint under Woodrow Wilson and had the support of the oldline Democrats as well as the strong personal endorsement of his friend Key Pittman, who had fought McCarran relentlessly since the latter had tried to defeat him in 1916. Baker was the victor in a fairly close race.

The Republican senatorial primary threatened to split the party wide open. Both candidates, the incumbent senator T. L. Oddie and his opponent, former congressman E. E. Roberts, had announced for the Senate before the Republican state convention met in June. As a result the convention became a battleground between the two forces, each trying to get party endorsement. A split was prevented when George Wingfield, national committeeman, sat down with a three-member contingent from each faction and worked out a compromise whereby Balzar was to continue as state chairman until after the primaries and the state central committee pledged to remain neutral in the contest between Roberts and Oddie. Actually, the truce was a victory for Oddie, for he entered the state convention with a minority of votes and came out of it on equal terms with Roberts. This result was no doubt due to Wingfield's influence, and the advisors around Oddie were obviously Wingfield men, including the latter's good friend Noble Getchell. Roberts obtained much of his support from the more liberal Republicans, including the former Socialist Grant Miller and the former Progressive Sardis Summerfield. In the primary Oddie made a surprisingly strong showing, defeating his opponent by 4,610 out of 12,414 votes cast. One immediate effect of Oddie's victory was a revamping of the Republican platform, which originally opposed American participation in the World Court while Oddie favored it. Since it was necessary for the party to hold a second convention to replace Balzar as state chairman, they took advantage of the occasion to eliminate the plank against U.S. participation in the court in order not to embarrass Oddie. In the general election, Oddie had little difficulty in defeating Baker by a vote of 17,430 to 13, 273.

Prohibition was an interesting side issue in the 1926 election. Although Nevadans had favored state prohibition by a substantial margin in 1918 and had quickly ratified the Eighteenth Amendment in 1919, a strong wet movement began to develop in the early twenties and by 1926 had gained enough strength to place two antiprohibition measures on the November ballot. The first was a petition to Congress to call a constitutional convention to eliminate prohibition; the second called for endorsement of a simple legislative resolution opposing constitutional prohibition. Both measures received overwhelming approval from the Nevada voters.

The 1926 election also brought into focus the position of George Wingfield in Nevada politics. There is little doubt that Wingfield played an increasingly important role within the Republican party from about 1908 until the failure of the Wingfield banks in 1932. He generally preferred the role of a kingmaker, always operating behind the scenes. This was demonstrated clearly in 1912 when he refused Governor Oddie's appointment to the United States Senate seat left vacant by the death of his former partner, George Nixon, and again in 1926 when he refused to accept a draft for the Republican nomination for the governorship. His influence in first bringing harmony to a badly split 1926 convention and then victory at the polls demonstrates not only his prestige but also his strong determination to maintain unity within the Republican ranks.

Not so clearly defined within the Wingfield political operation is the phenomenon usually labeled the bipartisan machine, which Wingfield presumably controlled. The general thesis of Nevada bipartisanship is that the two major parties agreed to keep one Republican and one Democratic senator in Washington in order to ensure proper patronage and representation for the state no matter which party was in power in Congress. The machine was supposed to operate on the local level by supporting candidates for the Nevada legislature from each party who could be depended upon to vote for the establishment. Thus, no matter who controlled the legislature, business interests such as those represented by Wingfield would benefit.

The evidence for such a machine is sketchy but pertinent. In actual fact Nevada was represented in the Senate by one Republican and one Democrat during most of the period when the Wingfield power was supposed to be strongest. Whether this was coincidence or the result of a fixed policy of a small group of political leaders of both parties controlled by Wingfield is difficult to determine. Newspaper articles, particularly during the 1920s, often referred to the Wingfield-controlled "bipartisan machine," and a number of historians have acknowledged its existence. Certainly there was a strong belief in Nevada during these years that such a machine existed. The best specific evidence for bipartisanship on the national level is the strong support Wingfield, a Republican, gave Democrat Key Pittman in his numerous races for the United States Senate.

Wingfield's prestige and political power were tested shortly after the 1926 election when a scandal rocked the state government at Carson City. The issue involved the state treasurer, Ed. Malley, former state controller George A. Cole, and H. C. Clapp, cashier of the Carson Valley Bank, and became public in May, 1927, when the Ormsby County grand jury returned seven indictments against the three men, charging, among other things, embezzlement and collusion to defraud the state of $516,322.16 over the years since 1919.[3] The embezzlement struck personally at George Wingfield since his Nevada Surety and Bonding Company held Malley's bond and the Carson Valley Bank was one of the Wingfield chain. The disclosure of the shortage placed the bank in an extremely vulnerable position as it did not have sufficient funds to cover the loss. Wingfield immediately placed a $500,000 deposit with the bank to forestall any difficulties which might arise from publication of the grand jury indictments. He then asked Governor Balzar to call a special session and place the matter before the legislature. Balzar did call the lawmakers together in January, 1928, and although he listed a number of items on the agenda, it was obvious that the major reason for the session was to reach some kind of compromise with Wingfield. In a letter to the governor on November 26, 1927, Wingfield explained his position. He emphasized that two innocent parties, the Carson Valley Bank and the state of Nevada, had been the victims of the criminal acts of their servants. The responsibilities of the bonding company were not defined by Wingfield, although he did point out that

the major portion of any loss which may be sustained by the Carson Valley Bank in the event the State is successful in its claims must of necessity fall upon me personally. You are aware that the total capital and surplus of the Carson Valley Bank is but $90,000 and that except for my voluntary deposit of $500,000 the bank could not pay the amount of the State's claim and the State and all depositors of the Carson Valley Bank would suffer a tremendous loss.

During the hearings which followed, a number of legislators questioned whether or not the state could collect the entire $516,-322.16 from the bondsmen. Meanwhile, Wingfield offered a com-

[3] *Ex Parte Malley, Nevada Reports* 248 (1927).

promise whereby he would pay $124,000 cash for release of all bonds-
men and settlement in full of the state's claim against the Carson
Valley Bank. When it was suggested that Wingfield might withdraw
his earlier deposit of $500,000 and thus prevent collection from the
bank, his statement during the Malley-Cole trial was read into the
record as follows:

Pending such investigations I have personally deposited in the Carson
Valley Bank the full amount of money involved, to be there held to meet
and liquidate whatever liability may be legally imposed on the bank. I
am taking this course in order to guarantee to the people of the State of
Nevada that whatever shortage in the funds of the State legally chargeable
against the bank will be paid without a cent of loss to anyone, other than
to myself.

Reassured by this testimonial to Wingfield's public responsibility,
the legislature passed an act providing for a board of compromise
and adjustment to settle all claims of indebtedness to the state
against any corporation, association, or person, and to release or
adjust such claims after hearing upon such terms and conditions as
should appear just and equitable. The board could not accept less
than 30 percent of the claim in each case.

A compromise settlement of $154,896.65, based on the above
formula, was accepted by the state and the question of whether the
entire amount could have been recovered, as the attorney general
insisted, became a moot point. The state tax levy was raised to
offset the loss occasioned by the compromise settlement, which cost
the state $361,425.51 directly and $52,000 indirectly because of the
extra session, additional audits and attorneys, and incidental costs.
One might well question the purpose of bonding of state officials, in
view of the settlement.

The Republicans continued to show strength in the presidential
election year of 1928, supporting Hoover electors by a wide margin,
reelecting Arentz to Congress, and supporting George Russell for
the post of state treasurer left vacant with the resignation of Ed.
Malley. However, the perennial Republican senatorial candidate
Sam Platt was decisively beaten by Key Pittman, who again received
bipartisan support to win reelection to the Senate. George Wingfield
was elected to the board of regents of the University of Nevada in his
first and only attempt at public office. The Republicans also continued in control of the state legislature.

MEMBER

WE DO OUR PART

CHAPTER 13

The Depression and the New Deal

GOVERNOR FRED BALZAR'S MESSAGE to the 1929 legislature was filled with optimism concerning Nevada's economic future: mineral production, the backbone of the state's economy since entering the union, had by 1928 recovered from the 1921 decline; the state treasury in 1929 received a welcome windfall of nearly $600 thousand ($600,000) in settlement of the state's claim against the federal government for monies loaned during the Civil War; and Congress had authorized the building of a naval munitions storage depot in the vicinity of Hawthorne, in southwestern Nevada, with an appropriation of $3½ million, and the erection of a dam on the Colorado River at an estimated cost of $125 million. The bright outlook was dimmed but slightly by news of the stock market crash in October, 1929. The

Nevada State Journal of October 25 carried the story of the previous day's disaster on its front page, but Nevada was far removed, both physically and in spirit, from the financial centers of the East and the next issue highlighted the annual University of Nevada homecoming on the front page, relegating news of the financial crisis to page 2.

It wasn't until 1930, when mineral production dropped by almost half from the previous year, that Nevadans began to feel some effects of the crash. However, there was little real economic distress at that time and voters went to the polls in November little aware that the nation was entering the worst of all its depressions. Governor Balzar, seeking reelection, remarked at one point that there were no real issues in Nevada; and the election held no surprises. Republicans retained their control of most of the state posts, losing only those of secretary of state, attorney general, and superintendent of state printing, although Balzar's victory over former congressman Charles L. Richards was very narrow, as was that of Samuel Arentz, who was reelected to Congress for the fourth time, defeating Maurice Sullivan by slightly more than 3,000 votes out of over 33,000 cast.

The same lack of concern over the economic crisis was evident in Governor Balzar's condition of the state message to the Nevada legislature in January, 1931:

Most fortunately, the existing Nation-wide condition of financial stress is but lightly felt within our own borders, when comparisons are made with conditions prevailing in other States, and this is partly due to our solid financial standing and partly due to the large Federal expenditures which have heretofore been made within the State, or those authorized to be made.

The Governor soon regretted his remarks about Nevada's solid financial standing, but he was certainly right in crediting federal aid —particularly in the form of highway construction and building of the naval munitions depot and Boulder Dam—for helping to sustain the state's economy in the early years of the depression.

As noted earlier, Nevada had taken advantage of the Federal Aid Act of 1916 and its subsequent amendments to develop, especially in the 1920s, a state-wide network of graveled highways. In the 1930s the state moved to bring this network into the category of oiled or paved roads. Federal aid for Nevada highway construction increased substantially during this decade, partly because of additional sums allotted as part of the New Deal recovery program and partly because of appropriations authorized under the Oddie-Colton bill of 1930. Under that act the federal government assumed the entire cost of federal roads which traversed unappropriated public land and Indian reservations. The combined federal aid to Nevada highways in the 1930s was $29,971,258.63, compared to a total of $9,672,411 expended in the twenties.

The commissioning of the Naval Ammunition Depot at Hawthorne opened a new era in state-federal relations in Nevada. The depot, ultimately covering some three hundred square miles of desert wasteland, showed the way to an effective use of part of Nevada's sparsely settled, wide-open spaces and established a precedent for future federal programs during and after World War II. The installation brought about five million dollars into the economy from construction alone, since it required its own sewer system, fire department, water system, over five hundred miles of oiled roads, and the employment of hundreds of vehicles to serve its transportation needs. Later, the small town of Babbitt was established by the Navy to house the personnel working at the base. Although the depot is not on the state tax rolls, its buildings and maintenance not only gave an immediate boost to the area but provided the state an economic crutch to help it through the depression.

Boulder Canyon Project

An even more important stimulus to the Nevada economy in the 1930s and one of the most important long-range developments in Nevada history was the construction of Boulder Dam. Although it was not until December 21, 1928, that President Coolidge approved the Boulder Canyon Project Act, at least a decade of conferences and controversy had preceded its passage, and one can only guess how much earlier man had dreamed of harnessing the waters of the mighty Colorado. Certainly the gigantic flood of 1905 showed the devastation which could result from unusually heavy spring runoffs from the river's major tributaries.[1] In subsequent years a number

[1] Henry C. Schmidt, a prominent Tonopah businessman in 1909 considered the possibility of building a dam at Boulder Canyon but there was little support for such a project at that time. Before Schmidt, Arthur Powell Davis in 1904 conceived a plan for controlling the Colorado by means of a dam of unprecedented size. For the latter story see Malcolm T. Thompson, "To Tame a Giant," *Nevada Highways and Parks* 29 (Winter 1969): 9–16.

of states in the Colorado River drainage area attempted to survey or assess their particular roles within the drainage basin, but only when the Federal Water Power Commission in 1920 claimed full jurisdiction of the Colorado River did the states concerned awaken to the challenge. Governor Boyle, following the suggestion of the state engineer, appointed an informal committee in 1920 to study ways of safeguarding the interests of the state and on the basis of their report recommended the establishment of a Colorado River Development Commission. The 1921 legislature created such a commission to determine Nevada's claims to waters of the Colorado. By that time pressures in Congress had brought about legislation which authorized compact negotiations among the states of the Colorado River drainage system and set a deadline of January 1, 1923, for completion of a compact.

An interstate commission was formed with representatives from the federal government and the states of Arizona, California, Colorado, Nevada, New Mexico, Utah, and Wyoming. Herbert Hoover, secretary of commerce, was elected permanent chairman of the group. A compact for division of the waters of the Colorado was signed by the delegates in November of 1922, but it had to be ratified by the legislatures of all seven states to become effective. By the time Nevada approved the compact two months later, a quarrel had broken out between California and Arizona over disposition of water under its terms, and Arizona refused to sign. An attempt was then made to waive the unanimity requirement and although the Nevada legislature did so in 1925, it wasn't until 1928 that six states agreed to the compact and Congress followed with passage of the Boulder Canyon Project Act.

The 1928 law appropriated $250,000 for investigation and preliminary work, to be available in June, 1929. Approximately one year later, Congress appropriated $10,600,000 for preliminary construction, including the building of 22.6 miles of railroad from a point on the Union Pacific some seven miles west of Las Vegas to the top of the dam site. The road was completed in the early part of 1931, and in addition, an electrical transmission line was brought 222 miles from San Bernardino, California, paved highways were built from Las Vegas to the construction site, and miscellaneous machine shops, garages, warehouses, a gravel screening plant, and two concrete mixing plants were built in preparation for the major task of erecting the dam. The contract for the construction of the dam, first called Hoover, then Boulder, and again Hoover Dam was let in March, 1931, to Six Companies, Incorporated, the lowest bidder at $48,890,999. The dam, when completed, was 727 feet high and 660 feet thick by 1,244 feet long at the base.

Construction attracted thousands of workers, and since the nearest town, Las Vegas, was nearly 30 miles away, many of them preferred to live near the site in tents or other temporary buildings. Health and sanitation considerations demanded better living conditions, so the Bureau of Reclamation spent over 2 million to build a town on a high plateau seven miles southwest of the dam site. During its initial stages, the new town of Boulder City was a construction camp made up of houses, dormitories, cafeterias, and a general store operated by the Six Companies, and government buildings constructed and operated by the Bureau of Reclamation. At the height of building activity, the city reached an estimated population of eight thousand, but the figure declined rapidly after the completion of the dam.

The Boulder Canyon Project provided important economic benefits to the state which were particularly welcome in the months before the heavy New Deal spending became effective. The employment of between three and five thousand persons, many of them Nevadans, with a monthly payroll of over $750,000, gave a strong impetus to the economy of southern Nevada during the depression. The permanent effects of the project could only be guessed at in 1936, but it was quite evident that Boulder City would be a permanent addition to the region, that the huge lake created by impounding the waters of the Colorado would become an important recreation area, and that Nevada's allotment of power and water from the project would bring additional benefits.

Gambling and Divorce

As we have seen, Balzar's address to the 1931 legislature was generally optimistic and fairly prophetic concerning future of state-federal relations. Part of his message, however, wherein he boasted of Nevada's excellent financial condition, proved not only to be premature, but based on supposition rather than upon fact. Although the governor did not specifically request such action, the legislature in 1931 passed two acts which were directed, at least in part, toward increasing the state's economic potential. The first of these, signed into law in March, returned legalized gambling to Nevada after an absence of over twenty years, while the second, which went into effect on May 1, lowered the divorce residency from three months to six weeks.

It has been assumed by many that the legalization of gambling was due to the depression and the need for additional revenues. This is a great oversimplification, based more on the later effects of the legislation than upon the immediate economic prospects. There is no doubt that economic factors were considered in passing the law, but certainly dissatisfaction with control during the period when gambling was illegal also was a major factor.

The true origin of the 1931 gambling bill is still something of a mystery. Its sponsor in the assembly, Phil Tobin, at the time a freshman assemblyman from Humboldt County, maintained in a 1964 interview that the bill was his idea and his idea alone,[2] and that it was intended to keep for Nevada revenue which was being diverted outside the state through illegal gambling. There is evidence, however, that others had been thinking of a gambling bill before Tobin introduced his measure. The *Reno Evening Gazette* on January 24, 1931, stated that "no one will admit having been approached to offer such a bill, but all of the legislators profess a lively interest in one. None of the Clark County delegation has an idea in mind of introducing a gambling bill, although the latest agitation for such legislation started in that county." In later issues the newspaper noted that no one could be found to sponsor the bill and that at least two assemblymen had carried copies around to study them but no decision had been reached about the sponsorship. On February 12 the *Gazette* published the text of the proposed gambling bill and said it would be offered the next day. The following day it announced that Tobin had introduced the measure but that he had been the fourth or fifth man to have had the bill.

After introduction, the bill received wide backing and seemed assured of passage. The only real opposition came from a vocal minority made up mainly of religious leaders and members of various women's organizations. Their attack was sharp but hopeless, and the

---

[2] This interview was with Frank Johnson who reported the events in an article in the *Nevada Centennial Magazine* (1964) titled, "The Man Who Brought Gambling to Nevada."

bill moved through the assembly and senate without major difficulty and was signed by Governor Balzar on March 19, the same day that he signed the six-weeks divorce bill.

Legalized gambling was welcomed eagerly in most Nevada towns; particularly at Reno, where work crews had been employed to enlarge the city's biggest casino, the Bank Club, and to remodel others in order to ready them for gambling. Many such clubs had been operating as speakeasies, with gambling carried on illegally behind closed doors. It was no secret to most officials or to the public generally that such activities had been going on since gambling had been prohibited in 1910. Numerous editorials in state newspapers pointed out that the gambling bill of 1931 simply meant that what had been done previously in secret could now be done openly, that it had moved operations out of obscure second-floor or back-room hideaways into ground-floor quarters on the busiest streets. The crowds which gathered at the Bank Club in Reno on the first night of legalized gambling indicated, however, that there were many interested in legal gambling who might never have participated otherwise. It was obvious that many of the visitors were from California, attracted by the publicity which preceded the passage of the act. Activity continued at a high pitch, reaching a climax when the Easter weekend brought an estimated five thousand visitors to Reno. Most of them were attracted by gambling, although it should not be forgotten that Nevada had easy marriage and divorce laws which some of the visitors were in the state to take advantage of. Railroad and automobile associations reduced their rates to encourage travel during these weeks. Out of force of habit most of the Reno clubs at first continued to operate on a peephole basis of entry. Counties and cities were caught without proper licensing authority when the gambling act, which placed licensing in the hands of local officials, was passed. Thus, until they had an opportunity to meet and provide the proper ordinances, gambling existed without legal authority—a factor which may have been responsible for the continued secretiveness in the clubs.

At Las Vegas, then a city of a little over five thousand, legalized gambling started more slowly than at Reno. Local newspapers were much more interested in the Boulder Canyon Project which was just then getting under way. The *Las Vegas Evening Review-Journal* pointed out on March 19 that open gambling could not be effective there until April 9 since it would take some time to prepare and pass the necessary city ordinances; but two days later it reported that city officials had declared a moratorium on city licenses until ordinances were passed and county officials were allowing operation without licenses if proper license deposits were made. The editor of the paper was quite pessimistic about prospects for gambling in Nevada. His words appear very strange indeed in the lights of events which have occurred in southern Nevada in the past two decades:

Nevada should not become unduly excited over the prospects of luminaries from all over the world coming to the state to establish the gambling casinos made possible under the new regulatory law passed by the recent session of the legislature. . . . People should not get overly excited over the effects of the new gambling bill—conditions will be little different than they are at the present time, except that some things will be done openly that have previously been done in secret. The same resorts will do business in the same way, only somewhat more liberally and above-board.

He did add, however, that crowds might be attracted, as suggested by the bill's proponents, but that it would take some time for legalized gambling to become popular.

Not all Nevada towns welcomed back legal gambling. At Elko the district attorney dealt a major blow when he ruled that slot machines were illegal in drugstores, grocery stores, and other such establishments that minors frequently visited, and at Sparks the city officials assessed a heavy fee—$100 per month for each gambling device and $50 per month for each slot machine—in an obvious attempt to discourage gambling.

In spite of the immediate and occasionally noisy welcome in some cities, legalized gambling made no startling gains during the 1930s. For one thing, city officials at both Reno and Las Vegas were cautious in the issuance of licenses. The editor of the *Las Vegas Evening Review-Journal* noted on March 26, 1931, that Las Vegas could support only a limited number of gaming halls:

Any more than that number means crooked games, cheating the law at every turn, and extreme difficulty in enforcement. . . . We are unalterably opposed to the granting of any further city licenses at this time, and from a careful survey of the community we are prepared to state that the sentiment of a great majority of residents is in absolute accord.

Reno officials were momentarily blinded by the onslaught of visitors following the passage of the gambling law, but they too soon adopted a policy of restrictive licensing. The caution in both cities no doubt was due to many factors, not the least being the fear that unbridled licensing would lead to abuse and to repeal. The latent antagonism based on moral grounds remained to haunt local and state officials as well as the gamblers themselves from that time forward.

The return to legalized gambling in Nevada was met by a flood of unfavorable publicity throughout the United States. Shortly after its passage, the law was attacked by religious groups in several eastern cities, and a Methodist conference in Washington, D.C., demanded federal intervention. The idea of such intervention, not given much thought at that point, later became the most persistent fear of Nevada gamblers. In addition to outside criticism there was obvious potential opposition within the state. The editor of the *Carson City Daily Appeal* no doubt mirrored the thoughts of many when he wrote, "The passing of the six weeks divorce law and the gambling law is nothing to be proud of. Both measures could have been forgotten and the state would have been better off from a moral standpoint."

In spite of the fear that gambling might get out of hand and again be prohibited, the state took few precautions to ensure effective control. Little realizing the open invitation such an act gave to the gambling syndicates, the legislature placed licensing in the hands of the counties. Five-man boards composed of the three county commissioners, the sheriff, and the district attorney were to be established in each county. In incorporated cities additional licenses were required by the city councils. Fees collected by the counties were to be distributed as follows: one-quarter to the general state fund and three-quarters to the county general fund. In the case of incorporated cities, one-quarter of the fees collected went to the state, one-quarter to the county, and two-quarters to the city. Revenue from gambling was of little importance to the state during the 1930s, producing, for example, approximately $69,000 in 1933. Cities such as Reno and Las Vegas benefited more, the former in the same year receiving about $50,000. City and county officials were unaware of the potential danger in the lack of specific controls. The words of the Reno sheriff when told Al Capone was in California and might be interested in moving into Nevada rang with the assurance of the old West and the foolhardiness of ignorance: "Al Capone is welcome in Reno as long as he behaves himself."[3]

Although gambling was not a large producer of revenue in the 1930s, nevertheless it was in that decade that the foundation was laid for developments which ultimately made gambling the state's prime industry. Of the few new clubs which were established in Reno during the thirties, two were to become particularly important. The first of these was a small casino on Virginia Street opened in 1936 by Harold Smith, which for a brief period of time featured roulette played with live mice. Mice-roulette was a passing fancy; the Smiths were not, and within a decade they had revolutionized gambling in Nevada. The little casino grew very slowly for the next five years; then the entrance of the United States into World War II provided the opportunity for expansion of gambling in Nevada. Until the arrival of the Smith family on the scene, Nevada gamblers took the view that no publicity was good publicity. The attitude was probably due to the fact that gambling traditionally had been relegated to the back rooms. The suspicion persisted that advertising would be the surest way to bring the moralists running to do battle for its elimination. The Smiths sensed a changed atmosphere brought about by the war and began an advertising campaign which took their now familiar covered wagon sign with "Harold's Club or BUST" blazoned on the side throughout the world.[4] Thus the Smith family began the task of taking gambling from the back rooms and putting it before the world as a legitimate business. The success of Harolds Club persuaded others to follow the same philosophy, that is, that gambling is legal in Nevada and should be advertised like any other business. In order to make their advertising more sophisticated and at the same time erase the stigma attached to all things associated with gambling, the Smiths initiated an advertising program to make Harolds Club in particular, and the gambling industry in general, not only a functioning part of Nevada's social and economic life, but an acceptable part as well. Included in the campaign was a program to place huge Harolds Club signs at historical landmarks throughout the state.

[3]*Las Vegas Review-Journal,* April 4, 1931.
[4]Club officials, perhaps with tongue in cheek, asked permission of NASA to have the Harolds Club sign placed on the moon during the first lunar landing.

These signs as well as brief stories appearing as newspaper advertisements throughout Nevada were researched and drawn by a professional advertising agency in Reno. The short "Pioneer Nevada" stories later were published by the club in book form and not only furthered its advertising but brought enjoyment to thousands of western history buffs. The publicity was so effective in the next few years that the building which housed the club had to be continuously expanded. By the end of the war approximately five thousand persons visited Harolds daily and by the end of the decade of the forties this number had increased to over twenty thousand a day.

A second major stimulus to gambling in Reno came in 1939 when William Harrah opened Harrah's Tango Club on Douglas Alley. The tango or bingo club proved popular and expansion brought it a Virginia Street entrance. In 1942 Harrah entered the casino business, opening the Blackout Bar on North Virginia. From a modest beginning with one twenty-one game, a crap table, and a few slot machines, Harrah soon expanded and occupied larger quarters, obviously benefiting at first, because of the similarity of their names and location, from the extensive Harolds Club advertising. It was clear by the close of the 1940s that William Harrah was a figure to be reckoned with in Nevada's gambling industry.

While men like Harold Smith and William Harrah were taking Reno's gambling from Commercial Row and Center Street to a more fashionable development on Virginia Street, Las Vegas began to move cautiously to establish itself as a gambling center. At the time gambling was legalized in Nevada, Las Vegas was not quite a third as large as Reno in population, and was much less concerned at the moment than Reno with the economic possibilities of the new gambling act. At that time, and contrary to later attitudes, the southern Nevada city was more cautious than its northern neighbor in allowing the expansion of gambling. The city council initially limited the number of licenses to six but subsequently raised the number to ten. Las Vegas officials saw the city's future as tied to Boulder Dam, and certainly its construction created a temporary boom and ensured crowds in the clubs which made "every Saturday a New Year's Eve." It was during the building of the dam that Las Vegas received its first real night club, The Meadows. Strategic-ally located on the outskirts of town near the road leading to Boulder City, The Meadows was built and operated by Tony Cornero and his brothers Frankie and Louie. It included a large gambling casino with armed lookouts stationed around the room and a night club which presented one of the first floor shows in Nevada. The Meadows prospered for a few years but like a number of such establishments could not survive the loss of business occasioned by the completion of the Boulder Dam.

One of the more important of the original licenses in Las Vegas was J. Kell Houssels, who had first entered the state in 1923 as an employee of the Nevada Consolidated Copper Company in White Pine County. For the next few years he moved in and out of the state with various interests in mining and gambling. When construction of the dam started, he purchased the Old Smoke Shop, a poolhall and saloon near the railroad depot, and in 1931 he acquired the Las Vegas Club on Fremont Street.[5] Houssels was one of a few operators in the city who were able to bridge the economic gap between the boom of the Boulder Dam construction era and the increased prosperity of World War II. By 1940, on the eve of that conflict, Las Vegas had grown to 8,422 people, a 63 percent increase from the previous census, and had started, slowly at first, to overtake Reno, which in the same years showed only a 15 percent increase. As Reno had demonstrated its attraction to visitors from the San Francisco area, Las Vegas in the 1930s showed that its source of customers would basically be Los Angeles and other southern California cities.

Although the gambling bill ultimately was of much greater importance to the state, the six-weeks divorce bill was of more immediate economic benefit. Nevada, and particularly Reno, had entered the picture of easy divorce in the early 1900s, aided, first, by a California requirement of a one-year waiting period before the final decree and the right to remarry and, second, by the Corey divorce case. The Corey case had all the elements of a popular scandal: a famous name, William Ellis Corey, at the time of the divorce one of the most prominent young industrialists in the United States, having become president of the United States Steel Corporation before his fortieth birthday; a dutiful wife, who had borne him a

[5]Houssels gradually built a successful operation which in 1950 included the El Cortez Hotel in downtown Las Vegas and in 1957 the Tropicana Hotel and the Showboat on the Strip.

son and lived faithfully with him for over twenty years; and the other woman, a young actress named Mabelle Gilman. The combination attracted worldwide publicity when Mrs. Corey sued for divorce in Reno in July, 1906. Further attention was drawn to Nevada as a divorce mecca when the well-known actress Mary Pickford obtained a divorce in 1920 from her film-star husband, Owen Moore. Although there was no moral scandal involved, the case was played up in the press. Nevada's divorce trade flourished when the legislature in 1927 reduced the required residency to three months. However, three years later Idaho and Arkansas reduced their residency requirments to a similar period and other states threatened to do likewise. Nevada lawmakers needed little urging to push through a measure further reducing the residency to six weeks, assuring the state a lucrative divorce trade throughout the 1930s.

It would be difficult, if not impossible, to arrive at a figure to represent accurately the value of the divorce trade to Nevada's economy during the thirties. Estimates range from $1 million to $5 million annually, but these are no more than guesses based on the number of divorces multiplied by the estimated amount of expenditure for each divorce. It is nevertheless clear that the several thousand persons who came to the state annually to obtain divorces left substantial sums of money, particularly in Reno and Las Vegas, which aided materially in easing the effects of the depression.[6]

Although the divorce business received a great deal more notoriety, Nevada was also building a reputation as a marriage center. Actually, marriages consistently outnumbered divorces in both Reno and Las Vegas during the twenties and thirties, and still do. However, since those attracted to the state to take advantage of its lax marriage laws stayed only a fraction of the time spent by those seeking divorce, the total economic benefit to the state was considerably less.

BANK FAILURE

Nevadans were shocked on November 1, 1932, to learn that Acting Governor Morley Griswold had declared a two-week banking

[6] Richard Lillard has an excellent summary of the divorce and marriage businesses in Nevada and details the various ways each affected the economy in the 1930s. His estimate that the divorce trade brought Nevada $5 million annually is, perhaps, too high (*Desert Challenge: An Interpretation of Nevada* [New York: Knopf, 1942], pp. 335–76).

holiday. Very few people, other than several state and banking officials, had any inkling of financial trouble within the state. The blow was multiplied when it became known that the banks had been closed in an attempt to save the Wingfield banking chain. To many individuals, it seemed impossible that the man whose name had become synonymous with Nevada's prosperity should now be in financial distress. Yet there had been warning signals for those who cared to heed them. At almost the same time that Governor Balzar boasted before the legislature of Nevada's "solid financial standing," the first in a series of bank failures occurred in Nevada. By June 30, 1932, the date of the state bank examiner's report, four state banks had failed, and in addition, one of the twelve-bank Wingfield chain, the Reno National Bank, was in deep trouble. Wingfield requested and received a loan of $4,800,000 from the newly created Reconstruction Finance Corporation (RFC) to try to stabilize his banks. Evidently most of this money went to the Crocker National Bank in San Francisco in payment of a loan owed by the Wingfield interests and thus did little to help the Nevada banks. By the end of October it was obvious that the entire chain would collapse if additional help was not forthcoming. It was this emergency which sent Governor Balzar hurrying to Washington to plead personally for an additional RFC loan to save the Wingfield banks. Before leaving the state, the governor had made arrangements for his lieutenant governor to call a banking holiday if he could not obtain the loan; thus the action of Acting Governor Griswold was pre-arranged, but this fact did not lessen the impact of the closure on the people of Nevada.

It was soon evident that the Wingfield banks would not be able to open at the end of the two-week holiday and there was increasing concern over whether or not they would ever reopen. Consequently, the governor extended the holiday to December 18 for those banks which wished to remain closed, but before that deadline was reached the state bank examiner officially took possession of the Wingfield chain.

Almost as soon as the bank holiday was declared, a fight developed within the Wingfield group over whether or not individual banks should be allowed to open if they could satisfy the bank examiner of their stability. Nevada law did not require a stronger bank within a chain to bear the burden of a weaker one, so legal authorities counseled that individual members should be allowed to open on their own merits. George Wingfield had other ideas and fought for the next three years on the principle that the banks should stand or fall together. Forcing the issue, the depositors of one of the stronger banks in the chain, the United Nevada Bank, in January, 1933, indicated that they were ready to present a plan of reorganization so that the United Nevada could open independently. Wingfield, however, refused to release his stock and no action could be taken. That some of the other banks could have opened independently was revealed in the bank hearings of February, 1933, when Roy Frisch, cashier of the Riverside Bank in Reno, testified that his organization would not have closed had it not been part of the Wingfield chain.[7] The bank hearings were brought to a close in November, 1933, with Judge Guild ordering the Wingfield banks into receivership.

Additional details concerning the operation of the Wingfield chain were disclosed in a series of hearings before a joint legislative commission established to investigate the closed banks. The state had a major interest in the reopening of the banks since $572,000 of its funds were tied up in them. The joint committee's report showed many deficiencies in the operations of the state bank examiner and the state board of finance. For example, the examiner had not made bank examinations as required by law and one examiner had known for some time that the cash reserves of the Wingfield banks were below the legal limit but had failed to take action against them. The report revealed further that the state board of finance was almost totally ignorant of the activities of the Wingfield chain and that the two laymen on the board were seldom notified of its meetings. The dereliction of both the examiner and the board seems inconceivable, and it remains a mystery whether their inaction was

[7] Frisch later disappeared under mysterious circumstances. On March 22, 1934, he left his home on Court Street to go to a movie a few blocks away. He was never seen again and his disappearance remains a mystery, although there is strong suspicion that he was eliminated by Baby Face Nelson. Frisch at the time of his disappearance was receiver for the Riverside Bank and assistant state bank examiner. He was due to testify in New York against McKay, Graham, and others in a federal trial which started on July 4, 1934. See the articles by Art Suverkrup in the *Nevada State Journal*, March 23, and March 30, 1969.

due to fear of the Wingfield machine or faith in Wingfield's ability to correct the situation.[8]

It was also brought out in the legislative hearings that most of the state officials were bonded by the Nevada Surety and Bonding Company, which was owned and operated by the Wingfield interests. More important, the company held certain worthless stock as a major asset and nearly every responsible public official in Nevada had known about the uncertain financial condition of the bonding company but had done nothing about it. The report was also critical of state officials for refusing to file suit for recovery of state funds as soon as the banks were closed. A series of articles published in the *Sacramento Bee* early in 1934—which won for the paper and the author, Arthur B. Waugh, a Pulitzer Prize—brought to light additional facts concerning the bank scandal and the operation of the Wingfield interests in Nevada. The series apparently was undertaken when the Wingfield interests, through the Nevada delegation in Congress and particularly Key Pittman, attempted to get federal court appointments for two persons whose careers were closely linked to the Wingfield machine. Such appointments would place Wingfield men in judgment of the merits of any bankruptcy proceedings by Mr. Wingfield—proceeding which appeared inevitable at the time—and protests from Nevada citizens were strong enough to prevent a favorable recommendation from the Senate Judiciary Committee and to cause both names to be withdrawn.[9]

Even without the accompanying publicity it was clear that improper auditing and investigative procedures had combined with questionable banking practices to create a financial crisis in the state. The involvement of the powerful Wingfield interests as possible beneficiaries of this lack of control, the fact that most Nevada public officials were bonded by a Wingfield firm, and the seeming attempt to get friendly judges appointed to key court posts brought strong

[8] It is quite clear from the transcript of hearings before the senate investigating committee that state officials, including the bank examiner, E. J. Seaborn, and Governor Balzar himself, did not have clear knowledge of the banking situation in the state in 1932. The domination by Wingfield officials, particularly his attorney George Thatcher, is obvious throughout the hearings. In the case of Seaborn it is evident that he took Wingfield's word and opinion on matters concerning the Wingfield banks rather than exercising his own judgment.

[9] It should be noted that Senator McCarran opposed both of the appointments and his opposition was important in their defeat.

public reaction against Wingfield. His insistence on reopening his banks as a chain or not at all intensified the animosity among many who had belonged to the machine. Later indications that much of the financial difficulty of the Wingfield chain resulted from loans to save the Nevada livestock industry did little to lessen public resentment toward Wingfield during the remainder of the decade. Wingfield was forced into bankruptcy in 1935, and although he later recovered financially to amass another small fortune, his economic and political dominance in the state came to an end. The loss of his political power was demonstrated in 1938 when he was defeated for reelection to the University of Nevada Board of Regents by a margin of 9,573 votes; he had won ten years earlier without opposition. The Wingfield banks never reopened, although depositors recovered varying percentages of their monies according to the strength of the individual banks.

THE DEPRESSION AND THE LIVESTOCK INDUSTRY

The failure of the Wingfield banks not only made thousands of Nevadans painfully aware of the depression but also spotlighted the precarious condition of the state's livestock industry, which had been declining steadily throughout the closing years of the twenties. Gross income from crops and livestock fell from $22.1 million in 1928 to $6.4 million in 1932. Governor Balzar had noted this problem in August, 1931, by appointing a State Agricultural Relief Committee with Cecil Creel as executive secretary. The committee secured freight rate reductions on feed sent into Nevada and on livestock which had to be moved to feeding areas, and in addition received some 12,488,172 pounds of wheat, valued at $200,000, from the Federal Farm Board for distribution to stockmen. Such actions, although helpful, were not adequate. Consequently, in August, 1932, Governor Balzar established the State Emergency Relief and Construction Committee by enlarging the Agricultural Relief Committee so that Nevada might receive federal relief funds from the Reconstruction Finance Corporation. The move from state to federal responsibility in agricultural relief was typical of similar action taken later in other areas of the economy.

The failure of the Wingfield banks forced many stockmen into bankruptcy, and much agricultural property was taken over by Pacific Coast and eastern capitalists, thus giving a new direction to the state's livestock industry. As federal policies increasingly directed agricultural recovery after 1933, state agencies were created to act as clearing houses for federal programs. Thus the Nevada Livestock Production Credit Association was formed to assist farmers and ranchers in refinancing their operations, and the State Emergency Relief Committee became a unit of the federal Civil Works Administration, which gave large sums to agricultural relief. State and county extension agents and the director of agricultural extension at the University of Nevada played key roles in the administration of early New Deal programs to aid farmers and stockmen.

However, before the New Deal programs could do much toward permanent recovery in Nevada, a severe drought in 1934 demanded the immediate attention of federal and state agencies. The federal government provided approximately one-half million dollars to pump water from Lake Tahoe into the Truckee River in order to save crops in the Truckee Meadows and the Wadsworth-Fernley area. In addition, over two million dollars was spent in drilling wells, installing windmills, and developing springs on the public domain, particularly in Eureka, Esmeralda, Lander, Mineral, Nye, and White Pine counties. Federal funds were used to purchase thousands of inferior cattle and sheep from ranchers in the drought area for relief purposes throughout the United States.

Most farmers and livestockmen in Nevada suffered extreme hardship in the period from 1930 through 1934. From the latter year until the outbreak of World War II, New Deal programs such as the first and second Agricultural Adjustment Administrations, the Rural Rehabilitation Administration, and the Soil Conservation Service gradually stimulated the rural economy, although it wasn't until the United States entered the war that annual production of crops and livestock equaled the best years of the 1920s. A total farm income of $8,000,000 in 1932 marked the low point of the agricultural depression in Nevada. By 1935 federal programs and gradual recovery brought that figure to $12,400,000 and the European war helped to raise production to $16,000,000 in 1940.

The Taylor Grazing Act of 1934 in effect eliminated homesteading but, more important to Nevada livestock interests, it restricted grazing on public lands in an attempt to conserve their forage resources. Although it was bitterly criticized in the beginning, its basic purpose of conservation has been realized, if not completely, at least sufficiently to have won grudging support from livestock men.[10]

THE SILVER ISSUE AGAIN

Mining in Nevada did not immediately reflect the stock market crash, but when it did, because it was the leading industry, the ultimate effect was more severe than the agricultural decline. The low point in mineral production during the depression came in 1932, when the gross yield from the state's mines was only about one-seventh of the 1929 production. Nevada's senators, Tasker L. Oddie and Key Pittman, pushed for federal support to the mining industry. Oddie, although aiding Pittman's fight for silver, put more effort in an attempt to secure a duty on copper. Since the latter metal was by this time much more important in the state's economy than either silver or gold, Oddie's effort made sense. However, he was unsuccessful while Pittman, fighting a more traditional battle for the restoration of silver, succeeded in obtaining federal action.

Pittman's continuing struggle for silver, stymied temporarily by a failure in 1925 to extend the 1918 Pittman Act, received a new impetus when the stock market crash of 1929 emphasized that a depression had been developing in the silver market since 1926. In that year India began a program to demonetize silver, triggering a decline in the price of the metal which was furthered two years later when a number of European nations released large amounts of silver bullion on the world market. By 1932, with the price of silver at 25¢ an ounce, down from 73¢ before the Indian demonetization began, unemployment was widespread among Nevada miners and production severely curtailed. As early as 1929 Pittman had introduced an amendment to the tariff bill calling for a duty on imported silver. It passed the Senate the next year, but was defeated in the House. While continuing to press for a silver tariff, he proposed, in April, 1930, the establishment of a Senate Foreign Relations subcommittee to study American commerce and trade with China, the only major power still on the silver standard and the nation Pittman saw as the key to increased world silver prices. His resolu-

[10] Alton E. Glass, *The Life of Alton Glass*, Oral History Project, Center for Western North American Studies (Reno: Desert Research Institute, University of Nevada, 1966).

tion passed, and Pittman was appointed chairman of the subcommittee. His objective—the improvement of commercial relations with China in order to raise the price of silver in the United States—was mirrored in his final report in February, 1931, which concluded, despite much evidence to the contrary, that the decline of American exports to China in 1929 and 1930 was due to the unprecedented drop in the price of silver. The remedy was suggested in two resolutions: that the president call an international conference to secure agreement on the status of silver as money, and that he consider loaning silver to China and melting dollars in the United States Treasury for that purpose. The second recommendation could not muster sufficient support in the Foreign Relations Committee to receive a favorable report, even after Pittman spent more than a month in China promoting his scheme.

The proposal for an international conference, on the other hand, gained support as the depression worsened in 1931 and early 1932, and in 1933, President Franklin D. Roosevelt, on the advice of Raymond Moley, assistant secretary of state, asked Key Pittman to serve as a delegate to the World Monetary and Economic Conference in London.[11] Although Pittman has been criticized strongly for his narrow attention to the silver issue during the conference, it must be admitted that his dogged determination won concessions from delegates who were not very much interested in the question of silver. What he achieved specifically was a resolution by eight nations that each would replace low-valued paper money with silver coins, would refrain from legislation which might depress the world price of silver, and would stop melting and bebasing coins. By additional agreements the United States committed itself to share with Mexico, Peru, Canada, and Australia the obligation of purchasing annually not less than 35,000,000 ounces of silver. Since the United States' share was 24,421,410 ounces, Pittman in effect won a pledge

---

[11] Moley is one of the few administration leaders who has spoken and written favorably about Key Pittman during the New Deal years. He states that one of the reasons he wanted Pittman along at the conference was "the wide knowledge of national issues generally and the experience he had enjoyed." Moley also notes that Pittman was a valued supporter of FDR and helped write the speeches he used in his 1932 campaign on public power and the tariff. See Raymond Moley, *The First New Deal* (New York: Harcourt, Brace & World, 1966), pp. 368–71.

by the United States to a purchase for four years of all but about 1 percent of the nation's total annual silver production.

However, since the agreement still had to be ratified by the eight nations by April 1, 1934, Pittman's next move was to try to persuade President Roosevelt to accept it by proclamation, insisting that it was not a treaty and did not require Senate endorsement. The president was not anxious to make the silver pact effective at a time when he was initiating large purchases of gold to raise commodity prices, but when it became clear that the sixteen-to-one advocates in Congress, led by Burton K. Wheeler of Montana, would obtain passage of a remonetization act, he compromised and put the London resolution into effect by proclamation. Thus, in December 1933, he ordered the secretary of the treasury to purchase the United States' allotment at 64½¢ an ounce, which was 21½¢ higher than the prevailing market price but a good deal lower than the 80¢ that Pittman had requested, and authorized the mint to buy the yearly output of American silver until December 31, 1937. It was no wonder that Nevadans and other silver producers were overjoyed at the president's action, which had the effect of extending presidential power by implementing an international agreement without congressional approval.

The president's efforts to thwart cheap-money advocates played into Pittman's hands again in 1934. Senator Wheeler and his supporters, still out to use silver to induce inflation and raise farm prices, introduced an amendment to the gold reserve bill providing for a huge increase in the government's purchase of silver. It was defeated by the narrow margin of forty-three to forty-five. Although Pittman had supported the amendment on the floor—to do otherwise would have hurt him politically in Nevada—he was not in favor of such a radical approach and very soon afterward approached treasury officials with a plan to have the president, by proclamation but under powers granted earlier by Congress, buy silver until 30 percent of the American currency was silver. This would bring the ratio of currency backed by silver to the 1900 level. Secretary of the Treasury Henry Morgenthau did not approve the plan, so Pittman took the issue to Congress and emerged with the Silver Purchase Act of 1934, which incorporated the basic points he had proposed to Morgenthau. Once again he had been able to achieve his aim by acting as a broker between the administration and the silver inflationists. He succeeded only because of the administration's fear that if they did not accept Pittman's act Congress might pass a far more radical measure, placed before it by Representative Martin Dies of Texas, to sell American agricultural surplus to foreign purchasers for silver and guarantee up to 25 percent over the world market price for it.

Pittman's bill, signed by Roosevelt in June, 1934, was the largest silver purchase act in world history, calling for a continuing government purchase of the metal in order to maintain United States monetary reserve at 25 percent silver to 75 percent gold. With its passage the future of American silver producers looked bright indeed. Nevada's silver production increased by 166 percent from 1933 through 1934 and continued at a high level for the next few years. The price paid by the government for domestic silver rose steadily from 64.5¢ in 1933 to 77.57¢ in 1937, the importance of government purchase emphasized by the foreign silver price of 44.8¢ in that year.

Pittman's role as the watchdog of the silver interests was called into play many times from the passage of the 1934 act until his death in November, 1940. During those years he continued to act as a conciliator between the radical silver forces and the administration, demonstrating time and again that he was more interested in mining silver than in the theory of bimetallism. However, he was quick to react to critics who tried to modify the 1934 Silver Purchase Act, and when members of the National Committee on Monetary Policy petitioned Congress to repeal all silver legislation, he advised them to stay with their texts and classrooms and leave the silver issue to him.

In order to thwart investigation of the Treasury Department's handling of the 1934 Silver Act by the radical silverites, Pittman, at Morgenthau's suggestion, proposed a senatorial inquiry committee and was appointed chairman. Pittman saw to it that the committee did not meet until February, 1939, and did so then only because congressional and other critics threatened to topple the government's entire silver program. Pittman's resolve to keep the Silver Purchase Act alive led him to use his position as chairman of the Senate Foreign Relations Committee to successfully link the administration's neutrality to the silver issue. The result was the passage of a new act in July, 1939, which continued the government's power to purchase foreign silver but gave silverites more political security by making the purchase of newly mined domestic silver a matter of law rather than of presidential prerogative and setting its price at 71.11¢ an ounce (short of the $1.16 demanded by Pittman). Thus silverites again won a government subsidy by a combination of parliamentary maneuvering and political pressure which had changed a temporary program into one guaranteed by law. In spite of the subsidy, however, silver producers in Nevada were unable to bring production of that metal to its earlier importance, although old silver camps like Pioche in Lincoln County, Eureka in Eureka County, Tonopah in Nye County, and a few others made substantial production gains in the years from 1934 to 1940.[12]

Despite the political success of Pittman's efforts in behalf of silver, it was clear from the beginning of the depression that Nevada's return to prosperity would be much more closely tied to recovery in the copper industry, since that metal was the backbone of Nevada's mineral production and therefore of the state's economy. Attempts to stabilize the copper market and raise the price of copper came with the passage of the National Industrial Recovery Act (NIRA) in June, 1933. As originally written, the act tried to guarantee a reasonable work week and income to labor through the adoption of codes for industry and business drawn up by committees representing management, labor, government, and the public. The process of code making proved to be a complex and generally lengthy one, and it wasn't until April, 1934, that the copper code was adopted.[13]

Meanwhile, to achieve the most important objectives of the NIRA without delay, employers were invited to subscribe to the president's reemployment agreement of July 27, 1933, which established a maximum work week and minimum wage and prohibited child labor. To encourage compliance with the recovery measures, Hugh S. Johnson, the National Recovery Administration (NRA) head, launched a tremendous publicity campaign. Employers who signed either the agreement or the code for their industry were entitled

[12] Fred L. Israel, *Nevada's Key Pittman* (Lincoln: University of Nebraska Press, 1963), pp. 113–20.

[13] The copper district newspapers kept a close watch on the copper code-making procedures. See particularly the *Ely Record*, April 27, 1934.

to display the Blue Eagle flag, adopted as the NRA symbol. Blue
Eagle parades were held throughout the nation and many other
devices were used to make conformity with NRA objectives appear
to be a patriotic duty. In Nevada, the Blue Eagle parade held at Ely
in August, 1933, under the sponsorship of a local unit of the Patriotic
Volunteers of Americans with Vail Pittman as the county chairman,
was typical. The group also sponsored a campaign to secure the
full cooperation of local businessmen with the NRA program which
included an NRA Sunday observed in all the local churches, a
series of talks by Four-Minute-Men throughout the local communities, and cooperation with local committees in charge of the
Labor Day celebration. The latter event featured a parade of some
eight hundred union workers with a huge NRA Blue Eagle banner
at its head.

Possibly because of its industrial code, conditions in the Nevada
copper industry improved slightly in 1934. Nevada Consolidated
(now Kennecott), the state's largest copper producer, operated 201
days that year for an average of 16.75 days per month, as compared
to 168 days of operation in 1933 with an average of 14 days per
month. Copper production from the Ely district, which had dropped
to $2,033,882 in 1932, increased to $3,369,239 in 1934 and to $7,224,-
585 in 1935.

Although the NIRA came crashing to the ground when a Supreme
Court decision in May, 1935, declared it unconstitutional, economic
conditions throughout the United States continued to improve during the next two years. Nevada's copper production followed the
general pattern, increasing to $15,333,826 in 1937, approximately
equal to the 1927 output. Total mineral production in the state
for that year was $34,039,068, a figure higher than the best year
of the 1920s and one which reflected the recovery not only in copper
but also in silver. Again following the general economic trend in
the United States, Nevada copper production began to taper off
in the latter half of 1937 and by the end of 1938 was down by more
than one-third from the previous year. The situation was so serious
that the Nevada Consolidated Company suspended operations from
June 16 to August 1. When it resumed production, it did so under
the provisions of the Fair Labor Standards Act, which had been
signed by the President in June, 1938. That act and additional
pump priming by the Works Progress Administration (WPA) and

the Public Works Administration (PWA) in 1938 improved economic conditions in Nevada's mining industry, provided support until growing United States commitments in foreign affairs brought a marked increase in the demand for copper and other metals.

Gauged by mineral production, Nevada's depression was over by the end of 1939, when the output reached over $31 million. The approaching war in Europe brought heavy demands for copper. That metal has, in the United States, been something of a barometer of increasing world tensions. In Nevada, copper represented only 39 percent of the total metal production in 1939; it constituted 51 percent in 1940.

THE NEW DEAL IN NEVADA

There is little doubt that the many federal spending programs initiated during the New Deal were of substantial help in maintaining the state's economy. Per capita expenditures of selected New Deal agencies from 1933 to 1939 were greater for Nevada than for any other state. Not only was Nevada first in total per capita expenditures, but first, also, per capita in loans, Civil Works Administration (CWA) and Civilian Conservation Corps (CCC) funds, and funds for public roads.[14] The reasons for the exceptional expenditures are not entirely clear, although the state's small population and powerful congressional delegation may have been contributing factors. Nevada's political leaders seemed more interested in obtaining as much federal money as possible than in establishing "little New Deal" programs in the state.[15]

Generally speaking, President Roosevelt, in the beginning of his administration, followed Hoover's policies in regard to public works and indirect relief but was more imaginative in his attempts to take care of the unemployed. For example, in Nevada, the CCC, from its establishment in April, 1933, to the end of June, 1939, employed nearly four thousand young men in twenty-four camps ranging

[14] Leonard Arrington, "The New Deal in the West: A Preliminary Statistical Inquiry," *Pacific Historical Review* 38 (August 1969): 311–17. Very little research has been done on the effects of the New Deal in Nevada. A doctoral dissertation on this subject is in the process of completion at the University of Nevada, Reno.

[15] See James T. Patterson, *The New Deal and the States: Federalism in Transition* (Princeton, N.J.: Princeton University Press, 1969), for an excellent summary of this subject.

from the comparatively luxurious one in Idlewild Park on the Truckee River in Reno to the desolate and isolated post at Westgate on Highway 50. The CCC enrollees built secondary roads, dug canals and irrigation ditches, planted trees, and in many ways aided conservation. No matter where located, the camps had a beneficial, if somewhat limited, effect on the economy of the nearest towns.

Much more important to Nevada and to the nation was the Civilian Works Administration, created by the president in November, 1933, with Harry Hopkins as administrator. In Nevada, Cecil Creel, who had been head of the Nevada Emergency Relief Administration, was appointed to head the CWA. Creel had approximately two weeks to put into operation a program which would ensure that the unemployed would receive their first checks before Thanksgiving. The CWA was an emergency program, lasting for only a few months; yet in that short time it gave jobs to thousands of Nevadans who participated in programs such as labeling street signs, painting barns and schoolhouses, improving roads, drilling wells, and erecting historical markers.

The termination of CWA funding in the spring of 1934 placed the burden of relief back on the Federal Emergency Relief Act for the remainder of the year and generally has been cited as an indication of a conservative trend on the part of the administration. If it was a conservative move it was soon reversed by radical pressures which in effect forced the administration to undertake a new spending program. The emergency Relief Appropriation Act of April, 1935, provided nearly $5 billion for the fiscal year 1935–36 and was implemented by the establishment of the Works Progress Administration (WPA) and allied agencies. The WPA, administered at the national level by Harry Hopkins and in Nevada first by Cecil Creel but later by Gilbert Ross, soon became the largest employer in the state. It engaged in all kinds of activities; for the first time during the depression, for example, it was recognized that artists, musicians, writers, and other professional people, as well as laborers, needed financial aid to survive. Thus allotments were granted for the establishment of city bands, for artists to paint pictures and murals for public buildings, and for writers to produce surveys of county archives and an excellent historical guide to the state.

Besides the economic benefits accruing from the New Deal, another important result of federal legislation in the thirties was the tremendous impetus it gave to organized labor. Labor unions in Nevada had suffered badly from the generally unsuccessful strikes throughout the state in 1919. They lost additional prestige, particularly in the White Pine copper areas, when the "welfare capitalism" of the company towns in the twenties succeeded sufficiently to cause a sharp decline in union activity. Organized labor made a strong comeback in Nevada, as elsewhere in the United States, with the passage of the NIRA, which specifically guaranteed the right to organize and bargain collectively, and employees at Ruth and McGill formed local affiliates of the International Union of Mine, Mill and Smelter Workers, essentially the old Western Federation of Miners under a new name. When the NIRA was declared unconstitutional in 1935, the rights it granted to labor were continued in other federal legislation passed in subsequent years.

POLITICS IN THE THIRTIES

The advent of the New Deal brought an end to the short-lived Republican control of Nevada politics which had started with the election of 1924. The 1932 election swept Nevada Republicans from national office, and for the remainder of the decade the Democrats gained control of the state posts as well. The 1932 election was surprisingly quiet for one occurring in the midst of a major depression. There was no clamor for change within either of the two major parties in Nevada; in fact, there was only one statewide primary contest, that in the Democratic party between James G. Scrugham and Maurice J. Sullivan for the House of Representatives. The political inactivity may well have been a further indication that Nevada at the time was not suffering unduly from the depression.

The 1932 Republican state convention endorsed Hoover, praised Senator Oddie and Congressman Arentz for their record, and supported their reelection. It showed little concern in its platform for the extension of federal aid to counteract the depression. The Democrats made their strongest plank the repeal of Prohibition and called for additional federal aid to the unemployed and for the extension of old-age benefits. The Democrats also showed an awareness of the competition for jobs by demanding that restrictions on immigration be continued and that precedence be given Nevada residents in employment on state construction projects. Only one challenger, Patrick McCarran, entered the race against Republican Tasker L. Oddie for the Senate post he had held since 1920.

McCarran, as a potential candidate, certainly was not invincible at the time. Born near Reno in 1876, he had gained some statewide fame as a politician when he was elected to the assembly from Washoe County in 1903. Shortly thereafter he moved to the Tonopah-Goldfield boom area, and in 1905 was elected to a two-year term as Nye County district attorney. He continued to press for recognition in the Democratic party and was rewarded in 1912 with a six-year term on the state supreme court, but before it was over, he made the mistake of contesting Key Pittman in 1916 for the Democratic nomination for the Senate. There were no primary elections that year, but Pittman easily won the party's endorsement at the state convention.[16] McCarran was no more successful in 1926 when he lost the primary race for Senator to Ray T. Baker. In 1932, although he was unopposed, McCarran lacked the support of both the old-guard Democrats, who were controlled by Pittman, and the Wingfield bipartisan machine, which supported Oddie. The Pittman forces may very well have underestimated McCarran and by a similar token overestimated the popularity of his opponent; they unquestionably underrated the forces of change which were then sweeping the country. Oddie had made a rather unimpressive record in his twelve years in the Senate. Upstaged constantly on the silver issue by his colleague, Pittman, he had had to content himself with the minor legislative role, although he did obtain substantial highway aid for Nevada and other public-land states through the Oddie-Colton Act of 1927 and had made good use of his position on the Senate Appropriations Committee to get Nevada the Naval Ammunition Depot at Hawthorne. Oddie was defeated by 1,692 votes. His personal popularity and support of the Wingfield machine could not overcome the forces working for McCarran: the failure of the Wingfield banks just days before the election; the Great Depression; and strong support for McCarran in heavily Democratic Clark County.

[16]A movement in the 1915 legislature against the direct primary as a nominating device succeeded in winning repeal of Nevada's primary law and the substitution of a system whereby each party would send delegates to a state convention which in turn would nominate. The system was used just once, in 1916. Opposition against party boss control brought a new direct primary law when the legislature met in 1917.

Samuel Arentz, Sr., who had served five terms in the House of Representatives, was soundly defeated by former governor James G. Scrugham; and Democratic presidential electors won an overwhelming victory, with more than twice as many votes as their Republican opponents.

The Eighteenth Amendment had been under fire, particularly from the Democrats, almost from its passage. The huge Democratic majority in the 1932 national election brought sufficient pressure on the lame-duck Congress for passage of a resolution to repeal Prohibition; and on September 5, 1933, thirty-nine delegates from Nevada's seventeen counties met at Carson City and voted unanimously for ratification of the Twenty-first Amendment, which was certified as part of the United States Constitution three months later.[17]

McCarran's victory over Oddie was the most important political event of the 1932 election in Nevada. After struggling so long for such recognition and finally achieving it by a very narrow margin, McCarran, once in the Senate, set out to make certain that he would not be dispossessed. He seemed determined, further, to replace Key Pittman as Nevada's leading national statesman. Working at first without the backing of the party regulars, who were controlled by Pittman until his death in 1940, McCarran gained national notice almost immediately by becoming one of the few Democrats to oppose the president's policies—at a time when it appeared political suicide to do so. It was apparent to McCarran that he had little chance to steal the mantle of silver leadership from Pittman and that as a "me-too" junior senator from Nevada he would attract little attention; however, he correctly guessed that by making known his disagreement with certain New Deal policies he would garner publicity out of proportion to his status as a newcomer. Thus, just a few days after being sworn in as a senator he rose to speak out against an administration bill. Yet before he showed his hand publicly, he was clever enough to use the president and the Democratic party to win seats on the powerful Judiciary and Appropriations committees, having campaigned with a slogan that linked his name with those of Roosevelt and John Nance Garner to bring a "New

[17] "Proceedings of the Nevada Repeal Convention, September 5, 1933," in *Appendices to the Journals of the Senate and Assembly,* 37th sess. (1933), pp. 1–15.

Deal for Nevada." Once assured of his committee assignments, McCarran began to oppose FDR on many important measures, although it should be recognized that his opposition to the New Deal has frequently been overemphasized.[18] McCarran also imitated a practice of his erstwhile political enemy Key Pittman when he began to find jobs in Washington for students who wished to complete their law schooling. Most of these able young attorneys later returned to Nevada and gave McCarran the core of political support which, after Key Pittman's death, brought him control of Nevada politics.

The 1932 election revitalized the Democratic party in Nevada, and long before the 1934 state convention dozens of ambitious Democrats had indicated that they wished to enter the primaries in order to have an opportunity to recapture the state offices which the Republicans had gained in 1930. The death of Governor Fred Balzar in March of 1934 eliminated one of the best Republican vote getters and increased the possibility of a Democratic victory. Six prominent Democrats entered the gubernatorial primary. After a strenuous campaign Richard Kirman, Sr., won a close victory from Harley A. Harmon of Las Vegas by less than 500 votes out of 18,672 cast. Kirman had little political experience, but his reputation as a businessman, gained mainly from the fact that he had been president of the only Reno bank to weather the 1932–33 bank depression, won him strong support. Key Pittman successfully gained nomination for a fourth consecutive term in the Senate by defeating H. R. Cooke of Reno by over 9,000 votes. Congressman Scrugham was uncontested for the House seat.

The Republicans had only one major primary contest, that for senator, which George Malone, former state engineer, won by defeating August Frolich and Clyde Souter by a substantial margin. Morley Griswold, who had become acting governor on Balzar's death, had no primary opposition, nor did George Russell, former state treasurer, now seeking the Republican nomination for the House of Representatives.

The Democratic sweep which followed in the general election

[18] A recent work on the New Deal notes that McCarran was not among the top one-third of Senators most consistently opposed to Roosevelt. See James T. Patterson, *Congressional Conservatism and the New Deal* (Lexington: University of Kentucky Press, 1967), p. 348.

was even more decisive than the party's victory in 1932. Pittman won nearly twice as many votes as George Malone, while Scrugham defeated Russell by an even greater margin. The contest between Richard Kirman and Morley Griswold for the governorship had appeared to be the only one in doubt when the voters went to the polls on November 6. Griswold was considered a strong candidate, particularly since he appeared to have the backing of the Wingfield machine and his opponent had neither great political experience nor charm as a campaigner. However, the continuing depression, Kirman's reputation as a solid, honest businessman, and the defection of many anti-Wingfield Republicans brought Kirman a solid victory. The Democrats took every state office and control of both houses of the state legislature.

The presidential election of 1936 gave Nevada Democrats another decisive victory. There were no state primary contests that year since the only national office contested was that of congressman, and James Scrugham appeared unbeatable. That assessment was verified in November when he received twice as many votes as his nearest opponent. Roosevelt electors received over twenty thousand votes more than their Republican opponents. The only real sign of life demonstrated by the Republicans in 1936 was their capture of the state senate.[19] A number of important measures were voted upon in the election, including an initiative old-age pension act which was defeated by a large majority and a constitutional amendment which was passed, setting a tax limit on assessed valuation. A special election held later, in March, 1937, amended the state constitution to enable Nevada residents to participate in federal programs of old-age assistance and to implement a law passed by the 1937 legislature which, in effect, acknowledged federal-state rather than the county responsibility for the care of the indigent.

The elections of 1932, 1934, and 1936 thoroughly demoralized the Republicans and convinced many Democrats that Nevada had become a one-party state. Evidence of this feeling became apparent as the 1938 election preliminaries got under way. While the Republicans held a primary contest for only one of the twelve offices open, all but four of the Democratic office seekers had to go through

[19] Republican control of the senate in 1936 initiated a precedence lasting until 1966 whereby the Democrats controlled the assembly and the Republicans the senate.

primaries. Those who were able to escape preliminary contests were Congressman James Scrugham, Attorney General Gray Mashburn, Superintendent of State Printing Joe Farnsworth, and State Treasurer Dan Franks, who faced a Democratic opponent in the general election since no Republican filed for the office. The most important primary races pitted Albert Hilliard, a well-known Reno attorney, against McCarran for the Senate, and Harley A. Harmon against E. P. Carville for the governorship. It was rumored that President Roosevelt had marked McCarran as one of the Democrats he wanted defeated in the primaries. McCarran's opposition to certain New Deal policies had climaxed in 1937 when he took a prominent part in the defeat of Roosevelt's so-called Supreme Court–packing plan. In June, 1938, FDR denounced the copperheads within the Democratic party before setting off on a campaign tour of the country. But if he planned to speak out against McCarran in Nevada there was no such indication as the presidential party crossed the state.[20] McCarran's opponent found it almost impossible to get his campaign off the ground and was badly defeated.

McCarran's victory placed him against former governor and former senator Tasker L. Oddie, and although he was elected by a handsome margin, his majority was smaller than either that of Congressman Scrugham, who buried his opponent, H. E. Stewart, under a mass of votes, 30,156 to 15,285, or Carville, who won the governorship by 28,528 votes to 17,586. It is possible that McCarran could have been defeated had the Pittman forces worked more actively against him. The senior senator's animosity toward him was well known, but he did not announce his feelings publicly or make any move either within or outside the party to defeat McCarran. Moreover, McCarran's opposition to FDR's court plan and his strong isolationist bias were approved by many Nevadans who saw no inconsistency in voting in a president by an overwhelming margin and two years later applauding one of his critics.

In the 1940 election Nevadans showed that their support of McCarran in 1938 had in no way affected their admiration for Key Pittman. Pittman escaped a primary fight, although it was rumored that the

[20] According to William Leuchtenburg in his *Franklin D. Roosevelt and the New Deal* (New York: Harper & Row, 1963) and James T. Patterson in *Congressional Conservatism and the New Deal*, Roosevelt made no serious attempt to unseat McCarran in 1938.

McCarran forces were trying to persuade Governor Carville to enter the contest against the senior senator. Certainly it was clear as the election campaign got under way that the old Pittman-McCarran hostility was still alive. It had been exacerbated by a bitter contest between the two over the appointment of the United States District Attorney for Nevada and by McCarran's attempt in 1939 to delay Pittman's measure, ultimately vetoed by the president, to establish a park in the Lake Mead area. Pittman's proposal was an obvious attempt to ensure votes for the coming election and McCarran's opposition was just as obviously an attempt to embarrass Pittman and weaken his Nevada support. That others thought Pittman was vulnerable was shown when four Republicans entered the primary contest—the only statewide contest held that year—vying for the chance to unseat the incumbent. It was won by Samuel Platt, an old hand at winning Republican primaries and losing general election contests to the Democrats, as his record in three previous elections had demonstrated.[21]

Throughout the campaign it was apparent that Pittman's excessive drinking had taken its toll and that he was a very sick man. However, his position as chairman of the Senate Foreign Relations Committee underscored the importance of his seniority and the magic of the Pittman name brought him a sweeping victory on November 5, the sixth time Nevada voters had chosen him for the Senate. Five days after the election Pittman died in a Reno hospital.

Many rumors surrounded the possible action of Governor Carville in naming a successor to Pittman. Some political observers were certain he would resign and have Lieutenant governor M. J. Sullivan, also a Democrat, appoint him to the Senate. It came as a surprise, therefore, when he appointed Berkeley L. Bunker to the position. Bunker, a Democrat from the southern part of the state, had much less political experience than several other Democrats ignored by Carville.

The riddle was solved when Pete Petersen, Reno postmaster at the time and a strong McCarran supporter, later stated that the decision to nominate Bunker was the result of a series of meetings between Governor Carville, Senator McCarran, and himself. Congressman

---

[21]Platt had been defeated in 1914 by Newlands by only 40 votes, in 1916 by Pittman by 2,147 votes and in 1928, again by Pittman, by 6,101 votes.

Scrugham had been one of the first to be considered by the group, but his name was passed over since the November election had brought him his fifth consecutive term in Congress, and if he resigned from that post to accept a Senate nomination, a special election would be necessary to fill the two-year term. Governor Carville then became the number one candidate but eliminated himself from consideration because of personal reasons. Peterson then suggested Bunker. The fact that Bunker was from Las Vegas and was a prominent member of the L. D. S. Church, the latter a powerful force in southern Nevada, may well have influenced the final selection.[22]

Pittman's death brought Pat McCarran at long last to control of the Democratic party machinery in Nevada. It was not to be all clear sailing, as events in the early 1940s were to demonstrate, but with Pittman out of the political picture the former ugly duckling of the party could look forward with some optimism to a McCarran era in Nevada politics.

[22]Peter C. Petersen, *Reminiscences of My Work in Nevada Labor, Politics, Post Office, and Gaming Control* (Reno, Nev.: Oral History Project, 1970), pp. 42–43.

CHAPTER 14

Nevada and World War II

WORLD WAR II as much as any other event shaped the present economy of Nevada. It was not the first time Nevada had benefited from a national or international crisis. Its very existence as a territory and then as a state was due to discovery of great mineral wealth on the Comstock at a time when political and economic factors decreed the establishment of another state. It is unlikely that Nevada would have become a state when it did without the Civil War. Again, in World War I the demands for copper and silver almost doubled the state's mineral production between 1914 and 1918. Similarly, the outbreak of the European war in 1939 and the growing commitment of the United States to aid its friends stimulated the state's economy by placing heavy demands on copper

307

and other minerals. These wartime requirements caused Nevada's mineral production to rise from $24,945,376 in 1938 to $43,864,107 in 1940. The continuing involvment of the United States in both the Far East and Europe, culminating with the Pearl Harbor attack on December 7, 1941, and the American entrance into a multifront war initiated a sequence of events which set the pattern of Nevada's economic development in the postwar years.

The growing threat of war in Europe and Asia seemed remote to Nevadans even in the last half of the decade of the thirties, for most residents had little quarrel with the policies of protectionism and isolationism which had dominated the nation's foreign policy during the 1920s. Generally, Nevadans seemed to favor the strong isolationist stand taken by their two senators during the 1930s and readily made that isolationism synonymous with nationalism. Senator Pittman's position as chairman of the Senate Foreign Relations Committee ultimately forced him into a conflict between state and national interests. He continually cried out for American neutrality in the early 1930s, yet as the picture of aggression became clearer and American economic support was urgently needed by Great Britain and France, he found himself in the uncomfortable position of being pushed by the administration to move faster and further than he was prepared to. Pittman's attitude changed, as did that of many others, under the growing threat of war. By the summer of 1939 he was asserting emphatically that the United States had to take part in world affairs, and a short time later, during the Senate fight over the 1939 Neutrality Act, he openly admitted that he had been mistaken two years earlier when he asked for an arms embargo. However, he continued to believe that United States help should stop short of entering the war and that helping the democracies to rearm was the surest way of keeping the nation out. It is likely that the cautious moves by Pittman to amend the neutrality laws and his outspoken references to the threat of European war in the later 1930s both reflected the mood of his constituency.

In September, 1940, Congress passed the first peacetime draft law in the history of the nation. It called for one year's service in the armed forces within the United States for approximately 900,000 men between the ages of twenty-one and thirty-six. As in World War I, national registration day, October 16 was declared a legal holiday in Nevada by the governor. Patriotic demonstrations again were made part of the registration process, but they were on a much smaller scale than those held before the Great War. The Veterans of Foreign Wars and the American Legion sponsored defense parades in a number of communities, and most businesses closed on registration day, although those engaged directly in defense production, such as the Nevada Consolidated Copper Corporation at Ruth and McGill, continued to operate, allowing employees time off to register. The draft board setup in Nevada was very similar to that in World War I as local communities again became convenient administrative units to carry out the orders of the burgeoning bureaucracy which accompanied the American preparedness movement. In November, the first peacetime draftees entered the armed forces expecting to be home in a year. Events in Europe and Asia in the spring and summer of 1941, however, brought a reevaluation of the draft plan, and in August, 1941, Congress passed by a very close margin a six-months extension of the draft. The 1940 draftees were able to enjoy only a couple of weeks of civilian life before the Pearl Harbor attack and the United States' entrance into the war, which necessitated the call-up of all trained personnel.

There were many evidences throughout Nevada, as elsewhere in the United States, of increasing defense activity by the federal government in 1941. The most noticeable from an economic standpoint was the growing demand for copper which boosted pay for Nevada Consolidated employees in the eastern part of the state in early 1941. United States defense bonds were placed on sale at about the same time. County defense councils, formed in Nevada shortly after the Council of National Defense was established by Congress in May, 1940, began their programs with a state-wide scrap-aluminum drive in July. Such drives became common during the war, emphasizing the critical shortage of rubber and aluminum, iron, and other metals. Schoolyards often gave the impression of junkyards rather than playgrounds as the students joined adults in the collection of scrap materials. That some Nevadans were further along the road to war than the national administration was demonstrated in July of 1941 when a state convention of the Veterans of Foreign Wars called for immediate war against Germany and Italy, for extension of the draft law, and for giving the president the authority to send troops wherever they were needed.

BASIC MAGNESIUM, INC.

Perhaps the most important defense program initiated in Nevada before the Japanese attack on Pearl Harbor was the building of the Basic Magnesium plant, authorized by the federal government in July, 1941, in the southern part of the state near Las Vegas. Construction of the $150-million plant was begun in September and completed within a few months. Under a contract with the Defense Plant Corporation, Basic Magnesium, a subsidiary of Basic Refractories, which was based in Ohio and owned extensive brucite and magnesite deposits in Gabbs Valley, Nye County, agreed to furnish 112 million pounds of magnesium per year. With power available from Boulder Dam, the plant utilized a process developed by an English firm for the manufacture of the metal. Federal approval of the project had not been immediately forthcoming, but defense needs for magnesium were great, and Nevada's congressional delegation, particularly Senator McCarran, successfully sponsored the proposal. The plant operated until November, 1944, when the government closed it because large stockpiles of magnesium had built up and further mining, an expensive procedure, seemed unnecessary. Its production justified its construction; more important to Nevada, however, it stimulated the economy of the southern part of the state. The successful operation of the huge industrial complex, using power from Boulder Dam, suggested to many Nevadans the peacetime possibilities of the area. The millions of dollars spent in construction, the thousands of workers employed at the plant, and the rise of the new community of Henderson all contributed to a boom which foreshadowed the state's future economic and political development, and the plant's potential importance led shortly to a request from Nevada leaders that the installation not be dismantled as originally planned.

ANTI-JAPANESE SENTIMENT

Before the Basic Magnesium plant was completed, the Japanese attack at Pearl Harbor focused the attention of Nevadans on the few hundred Japanese residing in the state. The heaviest concentration was at the copper camps of Ruth and McGill, where nearly one hundred Japanese, mostly either bachelors or married men with families in Japan, were employed. In both communities they had been segregated by the companies almost from the time of their arrival. Antagonism toward them stemmed from their accepting lower wages and a longer working day than the white workers. The years between the entrance of Japanese into the district in 1908 and the attack on Pearl Harbor saw the easing of hostility, but the bombing quickly revived many of the earlier animosities. On December 8 a group of white employees at Ruth asked the company to keep the Japanese from their jobs to prevent sabotage. Copies of the request were sent to the White Pine County Defense Council, Governor E. P. Carville, and the FBI office in Salt Lake City. An FBI official advised the company at Ruth to keep the Japanese confined to quarters, and two Japanese bosses at Ruth and McGill were taken into custody and held for immigration authorities. The Nevada Consolidated Copper Company dismissed most of its Japanese employees on December 14. In the next few weeks the Japanese nationals at both Ruth and McGill were taken from the district to Salt Lake City, Utah. The policy took its toll: two Japanese committed suicide as a result of this dislocation. Most of the immediate reaction in the copper district apparently was due to the fear of sabotage based on the fact that most of the Japanese there were aliens. In other areas of the state the first reaction to the Japanese after Pearl Harbor was one of toleration. Newspapers in widely separated areas—Las Vegas, Fallon, Sparks, and Caliente—cautioned against blaming all Japanese for the attack. The commander of the Nevada American Legion appealed to members to aid local authorities in preventing sabotage and subversion but warned against allowing patriotism to cloud their judgment in regard to loyal Japanese-Americans. In a similar vein, Governor Carville in a state-of-emergency speech pleaded with Nevadans not to cause strife by persecuting loyal naturalized or natural-born citizens.

The mood of toleration soon disappeared in the growing climate of fear and suspicion which engulfed the West Coast in the early part of 1942. The decision by the government in February, 1942, to evacuate all Japanese from certain areas of California, Oregon, Washington, and Arizona gave rise to a rumor that thousands of

Japanese were to be sent to Nevada. Governor Carville was concerned enough to ask that, if Japanese were sent to Nevada, they be placed in concentration camps. It was suggested that all Nevada Japanese be interned within the state, and Carville announced that he would consent to such a plan but that Nevada was not going to become a dumping ground for the aliens of neighboring states. When it became apparent that federal officials had no such plans, antagonism toward the Japanese cooled and before the war was over a number of Japanese-Americans from the relocation center at Topaz, Utah, were allowed to enter Nevada to work on farms and ranches.[1] The few Japanese-American families living in towns like Elko, Ely, Winnemucca, Sparks, Reno, and Las Vegas managed to survive the war with a minimum of hostility and harassment.

Although no significant research has been done concerning German and Italian aliens in Nevada during World War II, it appears that they suffered very few restrictions and little antagonism in comparison with the war aliens of World War I. As aliens they had to register in accordance with the law and were required to turn in to county and state officials all arms and short-wave radios in their possession, but otherwise their normal activities were interfered with very little. Certainly Nevadans, like Americans generally, were much more sophisticated in their emotional reaction to European aliens in World War II than they had been from 1914 to 1918.

ECONOMIC IMPACT OF WORLD WAR II ON NEVADA

The Pacific Coast soon became a great staging arena for the shipment of troops and supplies to battle stations in the Far East, and within a short time several military bases were established in Nevada, with pronounced effects on the economic life of nearby communities. Nellis Air Force Base near Las Vegas was founded in 1941 as an Army Air Corps gunnery school and Stead Air Force Base, north of Reno, was established in 1942 to train signal companies, later becoming a center for radio and navigation schools.

[1] The Governor Carville Papers, in the Nevada Archives, Carson City, Nevada, contains a sizable amount of material on the Japanese problem in Nevada during World War II. The correspondence demonstrates that Governor Carville opposed the relocation of Japanese in Nevada and for some time refused to take any state responsibility for their protection.

Fallon was selected for a naval air station and an army air base was located at Tonopah. In addition, the war activity at the naval ammunition depot near Hawthorne increased tremendously. Peak civilian employment was reached there in December, 1944, with 2,620 civilian employees and 2,495 military personnel. The highest total was reached in August, 1945, with 1,736 civilians employed and 3,889 military stationed at the depot.

Legalized gambling, easy liquor sales, and red-light districts—at least at the beginning of the war—made Nevada towns very attractive to soldiers on pass looking for amusement. Small towns in the eastern part of the state, such as Elko and Ely, outdrew Salt Lake City as overnight designations for the thousands of soldiers who were stationed at the huge Wendover Air Base on the Nevada-Utah border. Such communities were literally deluged at times with soldiers. Reno and Las Vegas, more easily accessible and able to offer more varied entertainment, attracted even more soldiers from the many military and naval bases in California.

The large number of servicemen visiting Nevada soon caused the official elimination, at least for the war's duration, of one of the frontier's oldest institutions, the red-light district. By the middle of 1943 military authorities and representatives of the Federal Security Agency put pressure on local authorities to close all houses of prostitution.[2] Although there was some grumbling about federal interference, the economic benefits derived from military spending plus the desire to cooperate in the war effort caused local officials to bring about effective restriction. But at the same time many local police officials insisted that such closures simply drove the prostitutes into cheap hotels and rooming houses.

Soldier visitors were only part of the thousands who flocked to Nevada during the war to take advantage of its wide-open atmosphere. The large influx to the Pacific Coast, particularly California, of people attracted by the opportunities in the many defense plants located there and perhaps answering the same siren's call which pulled John Bidwell west in 1841 caused the population of Nevada to jump from 110,247 in 1940 to 160,083 in 1950. The numerical

---

[2] There are a number of letters from military officials to Governor Carville complaining about the sale of liquor to military personnel and warning against the threat of venereal disease (Carville Papers, Nevada Archives).

gain was comparatively small and would have been ignored in the growth of, say, Los Angeles, yet it represented an increase of 45.2 percent for the state of Nevada. Over half of this total gain went to two cities: Las Vegas, which grew from 8,422 in 1940 to 24,624 in 1950, a gain of 192.4 percent, and Reno, which increased from 21,317 in 1940 to 32,492 in 1950, a gain of 52.4 percent. In 1940, 39.3 percent of Nevada's population was listed as urban; in 1950 that percentage had jumped to 57.2, and it continued upward throughout the 1950s.

Many of the new westerners visited Nevada during the war years to take advantage of the recreational activities, including skiing, which had started to develop in the Reno area just before the outbreak of the war, or of the liberal marriage or divorce laws. World War II had a definite impact on the divorce trade in Nevada. For example, divorces performed in the Washoe District Court in Reno jumped from 2,300 in 1940 to 7,022 in 1944 and to 11,082 in 1946. Most of the visitors to the state, however, were attracted by its gambling.

By the time of the Pearl Harbor attack, Nevada had completed a decade of legalized gambling without any startling changes in either its economy or its societal structure. Nearly every community in the state had gambling in one form or another by 1941. However, only two, Reno and Las Vegas, had benefited economically to any extent from gambling, although Elko gave some indications that it was ready to take advantage of the growing surge of visitors to the state. Although all three were on main highway and railroad routes, Reno and Las Vegas had the additional advantage of a major California metropolitan area to support its gambling and recreational activities. Nevertheless, it was Elko which introduced Nevada gambling to what has become one of its biggest publicity gimmicks, the big-name entertainment show. The idea came from Newton Crumley, Jr., who surprised casino owners throughout the state by paying $12,000 to Ted Lewis and his orchestra for an eight-day engagement at the Commercial Hotel. The crowds which gathered each night of the performance proved the soundness of the plan, and Crumley followed Lewis with many other well-known names such as Paul Whiteman, Tommy and Jimmy Dorsey, the Andrews Sisters, and Chico Marx. Wartime travel restrictions no doubt helped to slow down the traffic to the Commercial Hotel, but the real reason Elko lost its initial advantage in the race for gambling customers was that Reno and Las Vegas, with better positions geographically, were quick to imitate Crumley's innovation and as new casinos were opened there in the 1940s a major feature was the big name chosen to open the entertainment.

Reno on the eve of World War II had a few night clubs, like the Willows, mostly on the outskirts of the city; some old-line gambling casinos like the Palace Club and the Bank Club, located mainly on Center Street and Commercial Row; and two newer ventures, Harolds Club and Harrah's Tango Club.

The situation was much the same in Las Vegas, although the building of the Basic Magnesium plant and the defense activities in nearby southern California had stimulated the construction industry and created a general boom in Clark County. The El Cortez Hotel opened in Las Vegas in November, 1941, and while its 91 rooms and $325,000 cost might look like a minor addition to one of the later Strip hotels, its opening was an important event for the city then. It was not the only one. The flow of visitors between southern California and Las Vegas led a California hotel owner, Thomas E. Hull, to construct a tourist court, the Hotel El Rancho Vegas, on the road leading south from the city. With its swimming pool, guest cottages, bars, and gambling casino, it became the first resort hotel outside the city limits in an area which has become famous as the Strip, but it was not overly successful until after the United States entered the war. The successful operation of El Rancho Vegas soon drew a second large hotel to the Strip, the Hotel Last Frontier, built by a Texas theater owner, R. E. Griffith. More elaborate than its neighbor, it may well have been, as its publicity claimed, "the most magnificent gambling hall Nevada has ever seen." The two resorts, borrowing Crumley's big-name entertainment idea, hired entertainment directors and tried to outdo each other in the magnificence of their floor shows, all, of course, with a view to luring customers to the gaming tables. Although the two Strip hotels were quite successful, the real center of gambling in Las Vegas during the war continued to be the city's main thoroughfare, Fremont Street. Such clubs as the Pioneer, the El Cortez, the Frontier, the Golden Nugget, and the Mint changed it from the main street of a small railroad town of approximately 8,500 people in 1940 to a glittering, neon-lighted hub of activity in a city which by 1946 had an estimated population of 20,000 people, with hundreds more entering the area each day. By 1946 it was obvious that the war had created new economic patterns in Nevada and that most of them favored Las Vegas and the southern part of the state.

During the period of rapid growth in the gaming industry in the early 1940s, control of gambling was unwisely left in the hands of county and city officials where it had been placed by the 1931 act. In 1945, the Nevada legislature finally imposed stricter controls by requiring applicants for gambling licenses first to obtain a license from the State Tax Commission, which at the time was composed of the governor; the chairman of the State Public Service Commission, an appointee of the governor; and five additional members appointed by the governor on a bipartisan basis and for staggered terms. The five members were, by law, to represent the mining, agriculture, banking, business, and livestock industries. At the same time the state levied a 1 percent tax on the gross earnings from gambling, and the gambling tax soon became an easy source of revenue. In 1947 the legislature raised it to 2 percent and added a system of table fees which brought additional funds into the state treasury. Gambling tax receipts totaled only $215,754.72 for the fiscal year 1945–46, but reached $1,211,194.08 for the year 1949–50. There was constant pressure to raise the table fees and the tax as population growth created demands for additional state services.

That state control of gambling may have come too late to be really effective was indicated dramatically when the well-known gambler Benjamin ("Bugsy") Siegel was killed, the victim of a gangland-style murder, in 1947. His death focused national attention on Las Vegas and Nevada gambling and caused some writers to mark it as the beginning of big-time gambling in southern Nevada.[3] Siegel had entered the Las Vegas area in 1942 to establish and control the racing wire services in that city. Although many Nevadans knew of his connection with Chicago and Los Angeles gangsters—he had been named by the Los Angeles police as that city's number one

[3]See particularly Dean Jennings, "The Hood Who Invented Las Vegas," *True Magazine* 48 (August 1967): 23–25, 89–103; and John Cahlan, *Reminiscences* (Reno, Nev.: Oral History Project, 1970), pp. 121–24.

gangster—he moved freely in Las Vegas and purchased interests in the Golden Nugget and Frontier clubs. He had no difficulty obtaining a license to build a gambling casino on the Strip, the Flamingo Hotel, since at the time no investigation was required by the state. Completed in 1946, it was by far the most lavish resort in Nevada's history. When it opened, old-time Nevadans found themselves rubbing elbows with movie stars and gangsters, either not recognizing the latter or not caring about their background in the rosy glow of prosperity which the opening presaged. Yet neither Siegel's assassination nor other evidences of gangster infiltration were sufficient to snap Nevada officials out of their lethargy. Soon after the killing Harry Sherwood was shot in his Lake Tahoe resort by a man identified as Louis Strauss. First accounts of the shooting in local newspapers treated it as just another local homicide, until it was revealed that Sherwood was a one-time partner of Tony Stralla, a well-known West Coast gambling figure, and Strauss was the notorious "Russian Louie" of eastern gangland fame. In 1949 hidden assailants cut down but did not kill Lincoln Fitzgerald, then co-owner of the Nevada Club in Reno and a former Detroit mob figure. So little effect did these events have on knowledgeable Nevadans that one of the state's most distinguished newspapermen, Joseph F. McDonald, wrote in 1950: "There is probably no other state in the United States that could successfully control gambling. . . . There are no bosses and no political organization to deal out favors. The people will not tolerate such things, and they are close enough to the picture because they are few enough to know and understand what is going on."[4] His statement reflected blind optimism, but it was several years before Nevadans recognized their responsibility and attempted to establish effective control over gambling. By 1950 it was clear that gambling not only had become a major economic force in the state but a permanent one as well. Whether or not it could be effectively regulated was open to question.

Gambling was not the only industry in Nevada to benefit from World War II and the westward movement of population which it stimulated. The war had an immediate and important effect on Nevada mining generally but especially for certain metals such

---

[4] Joseph F. McDonald, "Gambling in Nevada," *Annals of the American Academy of Political and Social Science* 269 (May 1950): 30–34.

as copper, tungsten, zinc, and lead. In 1943 the state's mines produced a record $56,525,000. Although mineral production fell after the war, the beginning of the cold war and subsequent increased demands pushed the output in 1949 to $37,376,000, a figure greater than for any of the boom years of the 1920s. Agriculture also benefited from wartime and postwar demands, and farm production jumped to record figures. Total farm income increased from $16,000,000 in 1940 to $32,900,000 in 1945 and $52,300,000 in 1950, when it exceeded the year's mineral production by almost $4 million.

Particularly interesting are the changes which took place in the 1940s in the industrial sources of income in Nevada. Mining, traditionally the state's leading industry, dropped from 16.5 to 4.8 percent of the 1950 total between 1940 and 1950, while agriculture increased from 10.1 to 13.3 percent. Construction, following wartime demands for military construction and postwar requirements for housing, moved from 5.1 to 8.8 percent during those years. More important as an augury of future economic growth was the change in the category services. Mirroring the impact of gambling, it rose from 13.9 to 20.9 percent. These changes take on added significance in view of the threefold increase in total civilan income, from $79,000,000 to $249,000,000.[5]

POLITICS IN THE 1940s

The decade of the forties marked a new high of factionalism within the Democratic party which on numerous occasions benefited the minority Republicans. Difficulties began for the Democrats with the election of 1942. It was an important one because not only were all state officials to be selected but also a senator to complete Key Pittman's term. It was thought at the time that Carville appointed Berkeley L. Bunker to the senatorial position left vacant that he himself was preparing for an attempt to gain the Senate seat at a later date. If that was his plan, it began to go awry when James G. Scrugham, a five-term congressman and one of the prominent Democrats ignored by Carville when he made the 1940 ap-

[5] See Appendix, table 3, for mining, agricultural, and gambling statistics. For the total production statistics, see Department of Economic Development, *Nevada Manufacturers and Population Centers, with Basic Economic Data* (Carson City, Nev., 1956).

pointment, challenged Bunker in the primary and won a very close contest. Scrugham went on to defeat the Republican contender, Cecil W. Creel, in the general election by a sizable margin. As had been the case in Nevada elections since 1934, the Democrats won all the important state offices. Carville, running for a second term as governor, waged his campaign almost entirely on the basis of his record as a war governor, and defeated his Republican opponent, A. V. Tallman, without difficulty. Vail Pittman, Key's younger brother, won the lieutenant governorship with more than twice the vote cast for his Republican opponent, Mark Bradshaw. The weakness of the Republican party in 1942 was shown by its failure to enter candidates in four of the nine state contests open.

The 1944 election saw a split in the Democratic party that not only threatened its future in Nevada but prepared the way for the 1946 Republican victory, their first since 1930. For years Key Pittman's opposition had helped thwart McCarran's bid for the Senate, and the antagonism between the two men continued after McCarran was finally elected senator. McCarran's growing political domination of the Democratic party machinery in Nevada following Pittman's death was threatened when Vail Pittman, trading on his brother's name, announced for the primary in 1944. McCarran pulled out all stops to defeat him, and the bitter campaign that ensued dealt deep wounds to the party which were not healed until after McCarran's death in 1954. McCarran defeated Vail Pittman by a vote of 11,152 to 9,911, with strong support from the important political powers Norman Biltz and John Mueller and vital backing from Senator Scrugham, who had not been particularly friendly to McCarran before the 1944 election.[6] McCarran's stress on his senior-

---

[6]An extremely fascinating political memoir is that of Thomas Miller, who was active politically in Nevada during these years and apparently was friendly to both Pittman and Scrugham. He indicates that he was placed on the spot when Scrugham asked him to act as his personal emissary to McCarran to promise McCarran his support in 1944. Obviously Scrugham was willing to support McCarran in return for the latter's support in 1946 (Thomas W. Miller, *Memoirs of Thomas Woodnutt Miller,* Oral History Project, Center for Western North American Studies [Reno: Desert Research Institute, University of Nevada, 1965], pp. 175–77). The bitterness of the campaign is noted, also, in a letter from William S. Boyle to Vail Pittman in which he wrote, "I owe McCarran nothing but abuse and political defeat if I can assist in doing it" (William S. Boyle to Vail Pittman, May 1, 1944, Sp. B no. 33, Vail Pittman Papers, Getchell Library, University of Nevada, Reno.

ity in the Senate and the instances in which it had been important
to Nevada no doubt contributed to his victory. He had little trouble
defeating George Malone, the Republican candidate, in the general
election. Berkeley Bunker, defeated in the 1942 primary, showed
he still had great political strength by decisively winning over Rex
Bell for representative.

The peculiar workings of the Nevada Democratic party were
underscored again in 1946 when wounds opened in the 1944 campaign were deepened. The senatorial primary pitted Berkeley Bunker against former governor Carville, who, on Scrugham's death in
1945, had resigned and had Lieutnant Governor Vail Pittman appoint him to the Senate post. Most political observers in Nevada assumed that Carville's appointment would ensure him the party nomination in 1946. Thus, Bunker's action in announcing for the Senate,
against the man who had appointed him to the same post in 1940,
caught many by surprise and angered Carville's supporters. Yet,
it was still felt the Carville's prestige would win him the victory.
A new element was injected when it became apparent that McCarran
was supporting Bunker, not Carville. There had been suspicions
of such help but no verification until political advertisements linked
Bunker's name with McCarran's. Since McCarran had been quite
friendly with Carville, it came as something of a shock. The initial
break between McCarran and Carville apparently stemmed from
events just before the 1944 primary. At that time a group of Carville's supporters tried to remove Ed Clark, a southern Nevadan,
as national committeeman and at the same time leveled an attack
against Senator McCarran. Vail Pittman's entrance into the race
shortly thereafter made it appear that the move to dump Clark
was an attempt by the Carville-Pittman forces to defeat McCarran,[7]
and McCarran reacted as though that were so. Carville later asserted
that he was ill and out of the state when these events took place,

---

[7] There is evidence in the Carville Papers, Nevada Archives, that Carville
and McCarran had started to draw apart earlier, mainly because Carville resented McCarran's attempt to use the governor and his office for patronage.
Numerous letters show the extent of McCarran's effort to put his own men
in state positions. McCarran's daughter states that the break came because
Carville resigned the governorship and placed Vail Pittman in that sensitive
post (Sister Margaret Patricia McCarran, "Patrick Anthony McCarran," *Nevada Historical Society Quarterly* 12 [Spring 1969]: 37). No doubt all of these
factors were involved in the split between the two men.

but McCarran seemingly paid little attention to his explanation. McCarran's support for Bunker was obviously important, and when the ballots were counted Bunker had defeated Carville 13,354 votes to 10,826. Another, sometimes forgotten, factor in Carville's primary defeat was that labor strongly opposed him because of his veto of bills they supported.

The antagonism created by the primary caused thousands of Democrats, particularly Carville's supporters, to vote for the Republican nominee in the general election. As a result, George Malone, who had run unsuccessfully against McCarran in 1944, was elected to the Senate, beating Bunker by a vote of 27,801 to 22,553. There is no doubt that the postwar reaction against the Democrats, which saw Republican Charles Russell win Nevada's lone congressional seat and helped give the Republican party control of Congress for the first time since 1930, also aided Malone. Nevertheless, it is highly unlikely that he could have captured the Senate post against a politician of Bunker's stature without the help of many Carville and Pittman Democrats. The Democrats carried every state office in the 1946 election.

Republicans in Nevada, as elsewhere in the United States, went into the 1948 election campaign feeling certain that Thomas E. Dewey would be the next president of the United States. Henry Wallace's Progressive party qualified under Nevada laws and knowledgeable state politicians were convinced that the third party would take enough votes from Harry S. Truman to give Dewey Nevada's three electoral votes. The Wallace vote, as it turned out, 1,469 ballots, or 2.37 percent, was not sufficient to override the heavy Democratic registration in the state and the Truman electors won a close victory with a plurality of 1,934 votes out of 62,117 cast. Walter Baring, a young Reno Democrat running for national office for the first time after some success in local politics, defeated the incumbent congressman, Charles Russell. Baring made the most of Russell's vote for the Taft-Hartley Act, which labor violently opposed, and that, probably more than anything else, brought him victory by the narrow margin of 761 votes.

It was clear by the end of the 1940s that a new political machine controlled Nevada politics and that Senator McCarran stood at its center. He had succeeded in erecting a personal political organization quite unlike that of any previous Nevada politician. There is little evidence that he was controlled by monied interests like those which had kept William M. Stewart in the Senate during and after the Comstock Era; nor did he have a personal fortune like John P. Jones or Francis G. Newlands to ensure his election and reelection, or the powerful bipartisan machine of Wingfield behind him as had Tasker L. Oddie and Key Pittman. Yet the Wingfield machine may well have created McCarran as a political force by ignoring the threat he posed in 1932. After that election the so-called Wingfield bipartisan machine slowly disintegrated as its leader was forced into bankruptcy following the collapse of his banking chain in 1932. Some political observers saw a new bipartisan machine forming from the ashes of the old, but this time controlled by Senator McCarran, Norman Biltz, and John Mueller.

Norman Biltz had become a powerful figure in Nevada's economic and political life by taking advantage of the depression and subsequent New Deal taxing programs and the lack of taxes in Nevada to promote the state as a haven for the wealthy. The promotion worked and Biltz became rich in the process of bringing millionaires to Nevada. Somewhere along the line John Mueller, who had been an assistant state engineer, joined Biltz and became extremely useful as a lobbyist for his interests.[8] Biltz and Mueller did not become a functioning part of the new political alignment until the 1944 senatorial campaign, although they had supported the senator in his 1938 race. Biltz's main contribution centered on campaign funding. Pete Petersen, a McCarran stalwart, called Biltz "a sort of finance chairman." John Mueller added his extensive knowledge of Nevada politics and politicians. The combination produced a formidable team, master-minded always by Pat McCarran.[9]

Probably no one person or group of persons controlled McCarran

---

[8]Thomas Miller in his *Memoirs,* p. 213, states, "Johnny Mueller was perhaps the premier of all legislative lobbyists that it has ever been my good fortune to know and work with."

[9]Petersen, *Reminiscences,* pp. 54–55; Norman Biltz, *Memoirs of "The Duke of Nevada,"* (Reno, Nev.: Oral History Project, 1969), pp. 133, 166–67; Jerome E. Edwards, *Pat McCarran, Political Boss of Nevada* (Reno: University of Nevada Press, 1982), pp. 112–13, 182–84; Freeman Lincoln, "Norman Biltz, Duke of Nevada," *Fortune* (September 1954), pp. 140–44.

during his senatorial career. McCarran understood power and was not afraid to use it ruthlessly and effectively, as he demonstrated many times in his committee chairmanships. He was also a shrewd politician who never forgot his constituency. No senator from Nevada ever took more pains to make each citizen believe that he was promoting that person's interests in Washington. He neglected no Nevadan, giving letters from the poorest constituents the same personal attention that he gave those from the rich. Every county in the state could boast of many items of federal aid which came its way because of McCarran. He saw to it, through effective use of his power, that Nevada got more than its fair share of federal largess.[10] And he did all this while often opposing the national leaders of his own party and for the last two years of his life while a Republican administration was in power. McCarran was criticized unmercifully by liberals who saw in him one of the best examples of a legislator who placed state interests ahead of national ones, but he was always able to convince Nevadans that the issues he favored were not only in their best interests but those of the United States as a whole. In his campaigns for reelection he cleverly made his position appear to be the national one. Thus in 1944 when he was in a bitter primary fight with Vail Pittman, the avowed isolationist McCarran appeared in political advertisements as one of the strongest advocates of a United Nations. Quotations from his speeches were placed alongside items from the 1944 Dumbarton Oaks Conference, which laid the ground work for the permanent United Nations, to show "the almost exact similarity in thinking between Pat McCarran and the views of the Roosevelt Administration, in which allied peace leaders concur."[11]

McCarran evoked strong emotional reactions from all with whom he had contact. Those who liked him and what he was doing were extremely loyal to him, none more so than the group of young attorneys he helped through law school and into law practice in

[10] A "McCarran Day" was held in Reno to mark the McCarrans' fiftieth wedding anniversary. A model of the state of Nevada was formed as a representative from each county added that county's scale model in bronze, at the same time listing "work done, benefits procurred and progress stimulated" through the efforts of Senator McCarran (Sister Margaret Patricia McCarran, "Patrick Anthony McCarran," *Nevada Historical Society Quarterly* 12 [Spring 1969]: 50).

[11] *Nevada State Journal*, August 25, 1944.

various parts of the state. He was not the first senator to do this, but he made excellent choices, including Alan Bible, who won election to the Senate after McCarran's death, and Grant Sawyer, two-term governor of Nevada (1958–66). Such men aided him substantially in maintaining control of Nevada politics. Entering the Senate in 1932 with the Wingfield machine opposing him, McCarran, the lone wolf, in a few years became the king of Nevada politics.

It is interesting, however, that in spite of his party control, McCarran was never as popular at the polls as was his arch rival Key Pittman. In the four senatorial elections from 1922 to 1940 Pittman received successively 63, 59.3, 65.9 and 60.5 percent of the two-party vote, while in the four elections between 1932 and 1950 McCarran received 52.1, 59, 58.4, and 58 percent of the vote.[12]

[12] Elmer Rusco, *Voting Behavior in Nevada* (Reno: University of Nevada Press, 1966), pp. 41, 43.

CHAPTER 15

Economic Development
since 1950

The key to Nevada's economic growth since 1950 will be found in that tremendous surge of population into western states, a movement that has made Nevada the nation's fastest-growing state and created a population increase from 160,083 in 1950 to 800,493 in 1980.[1] Las Vegas officially became Nevada's largest city in 1960, with a population of 64,405. Twenty years later its population reached 164,674 for the city proper and 442,464 for the metropolitan area. At the same time Reno's population was 100,756 for the city and 171,054 for its metropolitan area. More significant from an economic standpoint are the millions of people who moved to

---

[1]See Appendix, table 1, p. 404.

California. In the thirty years from 1950 through 1980, that state added 13,063,744 people to its population and each became a potential Nevada customer, as are the millions of residents of other western states such as Arizona, Oregon, Idaho, Washington, and even Utah.

LEGALIZED GAMBLING

Gambling is the magnet drawing millions of visitors annually to Nevada and making possible a developing economy able to support ever increasing numbers of permanent residents. The state's excellent recreation areas—Lake Tahoe, Lake Mead, Boulder Dam, Pyramid Lake, Walker Lake, Lehman Caves, Virginia City, and other old mining camps—also are a drawing card. These sites attract thousands of visitors to boat, hunt, fish, ski, hike, or just relax.[2] Nevertheless, legalized gambling stands in the center of a development which, for lack of a better term, has been labeled tourism by Nevadans.

It is a convenient and useful term, enabling the casinos, hotels, and others to emphasize the more acceptable tourist attractions in their advertisements and thus avoid federal regulations against gambling advertisements. Every tourist is a possible gambling patron and advertising is directed to that end. The best example of such promotion is the emphasis on big-name entertainment, which has led to the reputation of Las Vegas as the entertainment capital of the world. A number of national surveys have shown Las Vegas, Reno, and South Lake Tahoe high on the list of the most attractive vacation areas in the United States. It is reasonable to assume that gambling, with its accompanying entertainment, accounts for much of that image.

Gambling, although sometimes hidden in statistical tables under "tourism" or "the service sector," has become the number one industry in Nevada, forcing mining and agriculture into secondary roles. Its dominant position in the economy is shown dramatically in the statistics on employment, tax revenues, and total income

[2]Some claim that Nevada's tourism package includes prostitution. An article in *Time*, June 27, 1969, p. 54, reported there were thirty to forty brothels operating in fifteen of the seventeen counties where prostitution is permitted by local option. Although prostitution exists in many Nevada areas, no study has been published yet that might give a clue to its economic importance.

produced. In 1981, the service sector, which includes gambling and related areas, was responsible for some 41 percent of the state's total employment. In the same year, gambling taxes amounted to 45.9 percent of the state's total tax revenue. The gambling tax figure is only part of the picture, for gambling is responsible for 64 percent of the sales and use tax, 69 percent of the cigarette and alcoholic beverage taxes, 71 percent of the gasoline tax, and nearly all of the money from the room taxes.[3] It has been estimated that at least 80 percent of Nevada tourism is attributable to legalized gambling.

The growth of gambling in Nevada since 1950 has been phenomenal. In the fiscal year 1951–52, the total gross gambling income was $55.2 million, from which the state received $1.57 million in tax revenues. Thirty-five years later the gambling revenue stood at $3.20 billion, from which the state received $177.2 million in taxes. Since statewide gambling statistics have become available, each successive year has shown an increase in the gross revenue produced. Prosperity in the gambling industry, however, has been measured on the basis, not of any real loss or gain, but of the percentage of growth over the previous year. So consistent was that growth that Nevadans assumed the gambling industry was recession proof.[4] That attitude changed in the early 1980s as the continuing national recession began to affect the western states, particularly California, the source of most of Nevada's tourists. In addition, the introduction of legalized gambling in Atlantic City, New Jersey, no doubt helped to slow gambling activity in Nevada, although the extent is difficult to judge because of the national recession.[5]

[3]Thomas F. Cargill, "The Nevada Economy: Past, Present and Future," *Nevada Review of Business and Economics* (Winter 1982–83): 2–6; "Nevada Looks Ahead," *Reno Gazette-Journal*, special edition, March 7, 1983, p. 12; see Appendix, table 3, pp. 408–9.

[4]As early as 1979 an economics professor at the University of Nevada, Reno, warned that it was wrong to assume that Nevada was recession proof. See Thomas F. Cargill, "Is the Nevada Economy Recession Proof?" Bureau of Business and Economic Research, College of Business Administration, University of Nevada, Reno, paper no. 79-4, pp. 1–21.

[5]The growth of gambling in Atlantic City has been even more phenomenal than that in Las Vegas. The first casino opened there in 1978 and by the fall of 1982 there were nine casinos operating and a tenth on the drawing boad. Atlantic City casino winnings stood at $1.5 billion in 1982 compared to $1.56 billion for Las Vegas during the same period. See *Nevada State Journal*, September 5, 1982, p. 1F, cols. 2–5; September 6, 1982, pp. 7A and 8A; June 14, 1983, p. 1D, col. 2; *Reno Gazette Journal*, March 7, 1983, p. 6; William Eadington, "The Evolution of Corporate Gambling in Nevada," *Nevada Review of Business and Economics* (Spring 1982): 18–20.

The percentage of growth in Nevada gambling revenue declined rapidly from 14.9 in fiscal 1980 to 3.2 in fiscal 1983. This decline caused the closure of casinos in both Reno and Las Vegas and threatened the continued operation of some of the important hotel-casinos on the Las Vegas Strip. The 11.1 percent unemployment rate statewide and the 12-plus percent rate in Las Vegas, the potential state budget deficit brought about by declining tax revenues, and the financial condition of the state's major industry were clear indications that Nevada had not remained untouched by the national recession. Recognition of that fact sent Nevada political and economic leaders scurrying to find ways to diversify the economy. The search lost some of its immediacy when gambling revenue for fiscal 1984, with an 11.5 percent increase over the previous year, showed how quickly the industry had recovered from the recession.

GAMBLING CONTROL

The rapid increase in the relative importance of gambling in the economy and the need for additional revenue to accommodate the growing demands of school districts, cities, and counties combined in the 1950s to place the spotlight of publicity on the need for more effective control of the gambling industry if it was to survive. Unfortunately, by that time, many individuals associated with mob activities outside Nevada had gained entry into the state's legalized gambling industry and there appeared no simple way of getting them out.[6]

The problem began with the 1931 act that legalized gambling. Control was placed in the hands of the counties, probably the weakest link in the state's administrative structure. Most damaging was the practice, which started immediately after the passage of the act, whereby the county sheriff could issue a temporary license, the action to be ratified later by the five-member county board, of which

---

[6]*Nevada State Journal,* August 27, 1979, p. 14, cols. 1–4. The article notes that Bugsy Siegel had been licensed in the 1940s, that Meyer Lansky had become associated with the Thunderbird in 1948, that Moe Dalitz and five of his partners in Cleveland's Mayfield Road gang became part of the Desert Inn operation in 1950, and that Ray Patriarca, the alleged boss of Rhode Island's Mafia, was a backer of the Dunes Hotel-Casino when it opened in 1955. See also, Eadington, "Evolution of Legalized Gambling," pp. 16–17.

the sheriff was a member. The problem with that practice, as Robbins Cahill, the first chairman of the Nevada Gaming Control Board later noted, was that "it was too late, then, to reconsider and try to withhold it, or put conditions on it, or anything else."[7] Laws added in 1945 and 1947, although bringing state licensing, were basically revenue measures and did little to bring about better control. Often overlooked in the passage of these acts is the fact that the state's recognition of gambling as a major revenue producer made it a partner in the industry and obviously interested in its growth. The question became, therefore, one of how gambling could be controlled enough to preserve an image of respectability without hindering its economic growth, and the problem intensified as revenues increased and gambling more fully dominated Nevada's economy.[8]

Nevada authorities were brought face to face with reality by a number of events in the 1950s. The "mid-century crisis in gambling regulation," as one Nevada historian recently called it, started when the Senate Committee on Organized Crime held hearings in Las Vegas in 1950.[9] The hearings confirmed to a national audience rumors that had been circulating for some time that mobsters were operating in Nevada. The committee's conclusion that both major crime syndicates were then in Las Vegas raised the specter of what Nevada officials feared most: federal control of Nevada gambling. Unfortunately, Nevada officials paid little attention to the committee's findings, generally dismissing the hearings as publicity intended to further the political ambitions of its chairman, Estes Kefauver.

In 1954 a series of revelations in the *Las Vegas Sun* again focused attention on a potentially explosive situation in Las Vegas and emphasized that past measures to control gambling had not been

[7]Robbins E. Cahill, *Recollections of Work in State Poltics, Government, Taxation, Gaming Control, Clark County Administration, and the Nevada Resort Association* (Reno: University of Nevada Oral History Project, 1976), p. 291. The Cahill memoirs are very important for this period of Nevada history.

[8]Jerome H. Skolnick, *House of Cards: The Legalization and Control of Casino Gambling* (Boston: Little, Brown, 1978), pp. 98, 329. This very carefully researched volume is by far the best work on gambling control.

[9]Mary Ellen Glass, *Nevada's Turbulent '50s: Decade of Political and Economic Change* (Reno: University of Nevada Press, 1981), p. 25.

adequate. The articles, supported by evidence collected in a cloak-and-dagger operation, not only revealed gangster involvement in the Thunderbird Hotel-Casino, but also indicated that gambling interests were seeking to oust the secretary of the State Tax Commission, Robbins Cahill, whose removal would be accomplished more easily if Vail Pittman were to be elected governor. Although Pittman apparently knew nothing of the alleged movement to dump Robbins Cahill, there is little doubt that these events, coming shortly before the November election, helped to reelect Governor Charles Russell. Another indirect result of the *Sun's* revelations was the revocation of the Thunderbird's gambling license by the State Tax Commission early in 1955, an act that initiated a two-year contest in the state courts to determine the extent of the commission's power as a quasi-judicial body.

Governor Russell, meanwhile, took his reelection as a mandate for stricter gambling controls. In his message to the 1955 legislature he proposed a thorough reorganization of the administrative machinery. He urged that a gambling division be established under the State Tax Commission; he specifically requested that a three-member board, with its chairman acting as executive secretary, be given the responsibility of investigating all license applications and checking for cheating. The tax commission and the gambling board were to constitute a board of review on all gambling matters including the power to deny or revoke gambling licenses. The legislature followed the governor's recommendation by creating the Gaming Control Board to act as the enforcement and investigative arm of the tax commission. The new arrangement, although a major improvement in the supervision of gambling, still fell short of recognizing the problems inherent in leaving the control mechanism within the tax commission. Governor Russell lost an opportunity to further strengthen the regulation of gambling when he indicated that he would not support a suggestion by some legislators that a separate and independent agency be established to govern gambling matters.[10] Nevertheless, through its actions during the next few months, the Gaming Control Board demonstrated that the 1955 act introduced more effective gambling control in Nevada.

To that time there had been little overt evidence that gambling

[10]Ibid., p. 33.

interests might attempt to control the Nevada legislature as mining and railroad interests had done during and after the Comstock era. Then in the 1957 session a new gambling bill was introduced with strong support not only from many prominent state senators but also from a few important gambling interests in the state. Senate Bill 92 would have virtually destroyed the tax commission's role as an effective instrument for gaming control by nullifying its hearing powers in granting gamblers a "trial de novo" when faced with a commission closure ruling. Introduced in the senate on February 20, the bill passed that house two days later by a vote of fourteen to three, without hearings and without debate. The bill was held up temporarily in the assembly when Robert Vaughan, a Republican from Elko County, initiated a fight against the measure on the floor of the assembly. His opposition focused public attention on the bill but was not sufficient to keep it from passing by a vote of thirty-two to thirteen.[11]

On March 20 Governor Russell vetoed the bill, stressing that it would grant to gambling privileges not extended to other businesses and that it would weaken control of gambling by making it harder for the tax commission and the Gaming Control Board to police and supervise the industry. It took courage to veto the bill, particularly since it had passed both houses with such heavy majorities, and Russell was placing his political future on the line in doing so. Most observers assumed that the veto would be overridden without difficulty, so it came as a surprise when one Republican senator reversed his original vote and joined the five earlier opponents of the bill to sustain the veto by a vote of 11 to 6.[12] In retrospect, it appears that the governor, the six senators who sustained his veto, and Assemblyman Vaughan did the state and the gambling industry a real service in refusing to allow a weakening of gambling controls.

On May 3, 1957, shortly after the defeat of SB 92, the Nevada Supreme Court published its decision in *Tax Commission* v. *Hicks.* The case stemmed from the tax commission's revocation, two years

---

[11]The legislative details concerning passage of SB92 can be found in the *Journals of the Senate and Assembly* for the 1957 session. For the background story and continuing comment, the best sources are the newspapers.

[12]The changed vote came from Ralph Lattin from Churchill County. The original opponents of the bill, two of whom had voted with the majority in order to move for reconsideration, were: Newton Crumley, Charles Gallagher, Forrest Lovelock, Wilson McGowan and Fred Settelmeyer.

earlier, of the gambling licenses of the owners of the Thunderbird Hotel-Casino. At the trial in October, 1955, the district court had ruled in favor of the defendants, in effect granting them a trial de novo. In his decision, Charles Merrill, chief justice of the state supreme court, noted that the trial court had erred in receiving new evidence, for "if trial de novo is permitted here it would completely destroy the effectiveness of the tax commission as an expert investigative board." Trial de novo in effect could relegate the commission hearing to a meaningless, formal preliminary and place upon the courts the full administrative burden of factual determination. The supreme court concluded, however, that the so-called hidden interests that had brought about the revocation order concerned the building ꞓf the Thunderbird Hotel and not the operation of the casino, and the commission's order was therefore voided. Nevertheless, the tax commission had won a victory in the recognition of its right to close a club immediately and to prevent a trial de novo.[13]

Continued suspicion of underworld infiltration into Nevada gambling led the next governor, Grant Sawyer (1959–66), to recommend, in his first message to the legislature, the establishment of a gambling commission separate from the tax commission. The legislature complied by passing a new gambling control law that established a five-man Nevada Gaming Commission independent of the tax commission. The new agency was given policy-making functions and the power to pass regulations, issue licenses, and act as the ultimate authority on the regulation of gambling. The three-man Gaming Control Board was moved from the tax commission to become the investigative and enforcement arm of the new gaming commission. Under the new arrangement the governor was not a member of either body.

The Sawyer administration also introduced a new technique in gaming control when it listed leading underworld figures in a "black book" and advised gambling interests throughout the state not to associate with anyone so listed.[14] Although the "black book" has continued as part of the gambling control machinery, its effective-

[13]*Tax Commission* v. *Hicks,* 73 *Nevada Reports* 117 (1957).
[14]*Marshall* v. *Sawyer,* 365 F.2d 105 (1966).

ness is open to some question because of the problem of constitutionality.[15]

In 1961, the Nevada legislature added a Gaming Policy Board to its control machinery, to be chaired by the governor at his call. Although its use has varied widely according to the preference of individual governors, it does give the governor the opportunity to take an active part in establishing gambling policy, if so desired.

Nevada's efforts in the 1950s to erect an effective gambling control machinery did not prevent the federal government, under Attorney General Kennedy, from launching an attack against Nevada gambling. Kennedy's antagonism was stimulated by the questionable sources of income that entered the state in the 1950s and early 1960s. Particularly suspect was Jimmy Hoffa and the Teamsters' Central States Pension Fund, which in 1962 allocated 22 percent of its disbursements to Nevada operations, including loans to the Stardust, Fremont, Hacienda, Desert Inn, Dunes, Landmark, Four Queens, Aladdin, Circus-Circus and Caesar's Palace in Las Vegas; and Harolds Club and the Riverside in Reno.[16]

Kennedy's "war on Nevada," as it has been called by some, began in May, 1961, when officials of the Department of Justice asked the Nevada attorney general to deputize some sixty-five federal agents as his assistants in order to carry out raids on all major Nevada casinos. Action by Governor Sawyer averted the threatened raids, but it was soon clear that numerous federal agencies, particularly the FBI and the IRS, had turned their investigators loose on Nevada's gambling industry.[17]

The results of certain FBI activities in Las Vegas became known when a federal court case involving the Desert Inn revealed publicly in 1966 that the FBI had been using secret surveillance of Nevada casinos since 1963.[18] This disclosure was followed by newspaper

[15]*Nevada State Journal*, April 1, 1983, p. 1A, cols. 2–4. The Nevada Supreme Court on March 31, 1983, ruled that Anthony Spilotro's name had been listed in the book without proper basic facts to support the listing. The supreme court, however, did uphold the state's right to list individuals in such a book.

[16]Eadington, "Evolution of Corporate Gambling," pp. 16–17. See also, Peter Wiley and Robert Gottlieb. *Empires in the Sun: The Rise of the New American West* (New York: G. P. Putnam's Sons, 1982), pp. 198–201.

[17]Skolnick, *House of Cards*, pp. 125–27.

[18]Edward A. Olsen, *My Careers as a Journalist in Oregon, Idaho, and Nevada; in Nevada Gaming Control; and at the University of Nevada* (Reno: University of Nevada Oral History Project, 1970), pp. 350–59; Skolnick, *House of Cards*, pp. 127–31.

releases and magazine stories citing evidence in Nevada casinos of so-called skimming, the practice of taking monies "off the top" before the totals were counted for tax purposes. For years there had been rumors that certain casinos, those reputedly controlled by the underworld, were involved in skimming. Of particular significance was an article in the *New York Daily News,* July 7, 1966, with a headline that left no doubt that the "Mob" was involved in skimming over $1 million a month from Las Vegas casinos. The article reported a secret federal investigation that revealed that Las Vegas casinos were pouring large sums of money each month into underworld treasuries in New York and across the nation. A little more than a year later an article in *Life* indicated much the same thing, noting that four casinos in Las Vegas—the Fremont, the Sands, the Flamingo and the Horseshoe—were involved in skimming. Las Vegas was described in the article as an "open city," a city open to all Cosa Nostra families.[19]

Nevada gambling officials vehemently denied the allegations and soon the issue intruded into the 1966 gubernatorial contest between the incumbent Sawyer and his challenger, Lieutenant Governor Paul Laxalt. Sawyer was extremely critical of the FBI and its director, while Laxalt, obviously aware of the strong support in Nevada for both, immediately came to Hoover's defense.

In spite of the protests and the campaign rhetoric, it soon became clear that the federal government had damaging information about Nevada gambling, which surfaced when federal indictments were brought against a number of Las Vegas gamblers. In January, 1973, Morris Lansburg and three others connected with the operation of the Flamingo Hotel-Casino pleaded guilty to concealing some $36 million from that casino. They were sentenced in April to varying prison terms and fines. Meyer Lansky, indicted at the same time, was scheduled to go on trial June 4, 1973, but his trial was postponed twice because of illness and finally dropped by Judge Foley in October, 1976. Lansky died in Florida January 15, 1983, nearly ten years after he was first ruled too sick to stand trial.[20]

Although the skimming convictions came in 1973, they covered

[19]*Life,* September 1, 1967, p. 51; ibid., September 8, 1967, pp. 91–102. Much of the same story was repeated in "The Mafia versus America," *Time,* August 22, 1969, pp. 18–27.

[20]*Nevada State Journal,* April 28, 1973, p. 1, col. 2; Skolnick, *House of Cards,* pp. 127–31; *Reno Gazette-Journal,* January 16, 1983, p. 1, col. 2.

criminal activities that had occurred from 1960 through 1967. The latter year marks the end of one era of gambling control in Nevada and the beginning of another, the year that Howard Hughes entered the Nevada gambling industry with the purchase of the Desert Inn Hotel-Casino. He entered the state when its gambling control machinery was facing a crisis of respectability and his reputation translated immediately to the gambling industry. Corporate investment in Nevada gambling, always potentially profitable, was made respectable by the presence of Hughes and encouraged to develop by the passage of the Corporate Gaming Act of 1969, which opened Nevada gambling to publicly traded corporations without the necessity of licensing all stockholders.

The Corporate Gaming Act of 1969 was a mixed blessing: although it encouraged conservative banking institutions to invest in gambling, it also created some problems of its own. According to one official it opened a "can of worms" by forcing control officials to distinguish between active and passive stockholders, in effect causing the state to lose control of the passive stockholder and making it more difficult to find hidden interests. In spite of potential control problems, there is little doubt that the 1969 act attracted a number of traditional financial institutions to the gambling industry. By fiscal 1980, the twenty largest publicly owned casino operations in Nevada generated nearly 50 percent of the state's gross gambling revenue and employed almost 50 percent of the individuals working in the industry.

The extent of the involvement of large public corporations in Nevada gambling led some to believe that the image and integrity of the casino gambling industry in Nevada had been restored. Credit for this was given to Nevada's control policy, which was summarized in one report, "Nevada has used its 45 years of experience in the gaming field to develop a regulatory system that is sophisticated, efficient, and on the whole, capable of maintaining the integrity of the gaming industry at an acceptable level."[21]

Nevada's gambling control machinery may be sophisticated, but a

---

[21]Eadington, "Evolution of Corporate Gambling," p. 20; "Gambling in America," Final Report of the Commission on the Review of the National Policy toward Gambling (Washington, D.C.: Government Printing Office, 1976), pp. 83–86. The quote is on p. 86.

number of cases of criminal involvement, revealed by the federal
government beginning in 1976 and continuing through 1983, place
its efficiency in real question. Involved in the illegal activities were a
number of important Las Vegas casinos, including the Aladdin,
Stardust, Fremont, Hacienda, Marina, and Tropicana. In each case,
federal investigators using wiretaps and government informants
produced evidence indicating that organized crime figures either
were hidden owners of the clubs or were involved in skimming.
Federal officials began their successful moves against organized
crime in Nevada gambling when a Detroit federal grand jury
indicted four persons on August 2, 1978, for concealing their
interests in the Aladdin. On March 12, 1979, the four were
convicted of conspiracy as was the Aladdin Hotel Corporation.[22]
Following the convictions, the Nevada Gaming Commission closed
the casino when its officers refused to comply with conditions set
down by the commission.[23]

Another significant victory came when the FBI announced that
Joe Agosto, a former Tropicana Hotel show producer and reputed
to be a mob associate, had turned government informant and would
plead guilty to charges that he had conspired to skim money from
the Tropicana's casino. Ten others indicted along with Agosto were
charged with skimming monies from the Tropicana from June,
1978, to February, 1979. Agosto and two others pleaded guilty, and
six of the others charged were convicted on July 1, 1983. Agosto's
testimony included a description of how he moved into virtual
control of the gambling activities at the Tropicana although he was
not a licensee.[24] Besides its immediate usefulness in fighting mob
activities in Nevada by revealing operating procedures of the mob,
Agosto's testimony showed the almost impossible control problem
faced by Nevada gambling authorities under the Corporate Gaming
Act of 1969.

The federal government's case against underworld activity in Las
Vegas was broadened when a federal grand jury in Kansas City,
Missouri, on October 11, 1983, issued indictments against fifteen
individuals, charging them with skimming casino funds and con-

[22]*Nevada State Journal*, August 3, 1978, p. 1, col. 4; March 17, 1979, p. 1, col. 1.
[23]Ibid., July 25, 1980, p. 24, col. 1.
[24]*Reno Gazette-Journal*, June 19, 1983, p. 3E, col. 1; *Nevada State Journal*, July 2,
1983, p. 2D, col. 2.

spiring to establish and maintain hidden interests in gambling casinos including the Stardust and Fremont hotel-casinos and the Hacienda and Marina casinos. On January 10, 1984, additional indictments were issued by a Las Vegas federal grand jury against five employees of the Stardust, charging them with skimming and conspiracy.[25]

Nevada gaming officials were not inactive during these events. Instead of aggressively trying to control illegal activities, however, they appeared to be simply reacting to federal charges. Thus, they missed an opportunity to act against the Stardust and other units of the Argent Corporation when a 1976 audit showed skimming from those clubs. And Nevada authorities acted to close the Aladdin and force Allen Glick, president of the Argent Corporation, out of Nevada gambling only after the convictions in the Aladdin case. Unfortunately, control authorities then licensed individuals in the Stardust who were soon in trouble with both state and federal officials.

It should be clear that legalized gambling in Nevada, particularly in Las Vegas, is tainted with the association of mobsters and that the record of federal convictions since 1973 contrasts sharply with the record of Nevada.[26] It should be clear, too, that cooperation between the federal authorities and those in Nevada must improve in order to successfully fight underworld organizations with strong interstate connections. Actions by Nevada gaming officials appointed by Governor Bryan indicate that the new administration understands those problems and is ready to move aggressively to solve them. Examples of measures taken by gaming officials illustrate the new policy. The Cal-Neva Club at Lake Tahoe was closed for a number of alleged gaming violations. Gaming authorities took control of the Stardust, fined the club and its owners some $3 million, revoked the gaming licenses of the owners, and demanded the sale of the Stardust and other operations controlled by the owners.

[25] *Salt Lake Tribune*, October 12, 1983, p. 2A, col. 1; *Reno Gazette-Journal*, October 12, 1983, p. 1A, col. 2, and January 11, 1984, p. 1A, col. 2.
[26] A series of fifteen articles in the *Reno Gazette-Journal*, July 14, 1985, through July 28, 1985, by Ken Miller, "The Other Nevada: Gaming, Politics and the Mob," followed by six editorials by Ev Landers July 28 through August 2, 1985, covers the problem of mob infiltration in Nevada gambling and should dispel any doubts that the problem still exists. See also the *Reno Gazette-Journal*, Oct. 1, 1983, p. 1C, col. 2.

Gambling has become so dominant in Nevada's economy that it is easy to lose sight of the important roles played by other activities such as mining, agriculture, federal interests, and warehousing and manufacturing.

MINING

Nevada's mineral production since 1950 has varied widely, demonstrating again the bonanza-borrasca (boom-to-bust) nature of the mining industry. Nevertheless, production has moved from $38.5 million in 1950 to almost $671.3 million in 1984.[27] Mining has declined only in its relative importance in Nevada's economy.

The Korean War had a marked effect on Nevada mining during the 1950s, stimulating record productions. That was particularly true of copper, which remained the top mineral producer, accounting for approximately 50 percent of the total state output during the years from 1950 until the late 1970s. The demands of the war for copper also stimulated the development in 1953 of a second major open-pit mine near Yerington and a new company town, Weed Heights, under the management of the Anaconda Copper Company. The Korean War also created a market for mercury, tungsten, and iron ore.

The 1950s marked the entrance of Nevada into the rank of oil-producing states, when an oil well began operation in 1954 in the Eagle Springs field in Railroad Valley, some fifty miles southwest of Ely. The Eagle Springs production has been consistent but of minor importance.

Nevada's mineral production fell as the demands of the Korean War ended. It began to rise again in the middle 1960s as U.S. involvement in Vietnam increased. Again, copper production rose sharply as a third copper-producing area, the so-called Copper Canyon district south of Battle Mountain, owned by the Duval Corporation, began production in 1969.

More important to the long range development of mining in Nevada was the opening in 1965 of the first open-pit gold mine in the United States, near Carlin. In 1969 a second mine opened sixty miles southwest of Carlin in the Cortez mining district. The produc-

[27]See Appendix, table 2, pp. 406–7.

tion of "invisible gold" from these low-grade deposits placed Nevada once again in the forefront of gold-producing states.[28]

Perhaps the outstanding event of the 1970s in Nevada mining was the virtual end of copper production in the state. Copper had remained Nevada's number one producer in the early and mid-1970s. By 1976, however, it was clear that Nevada's copper industry was in trouble. Kennecott, the state's largest producer, had started cutting its operations in 1975 and closed its mines at Ruth and part of its reduction plant at McGill on May 1, 1978. Kennecott continued to retrench until by 1983 it had ceased production of copper. Anaconda closed its Victoria mine in 1977, just two years after it was opened. It also closed its Weed Heights operations in 1978. The Duval Corporation closed its copper operations near Battle Mountain the same year. 1977 was the last year that copper was the number one mineral producer in Nevada. Copper production declined so rapidly in Nevada that by 1980 it was no longer classified separately, ending over sixty years of domination of the state's mining industry.[29]

Another important feature of Nevada's mineral output in the 1970s was the rather substantial production of certain industrial minerals such as gypsum, from deposits near Arden and Apex in Clark County and near Gerlach in Washoe County, and barite, from mines in Lander, Elko, and Nye counties. Barite production increased enough after 1978 to make that mineral second only to gold in Nevada's total production. Other industrial minerals that have been produced in commercial quantities in Nevada since 1950 include sand and gravel, diatomite, borax, limestone, silica, perlite and fluorspar.

Buoyed by increasing world metal prices, Nevada mineral production increased after 1978, leading a number of companies to expand their Nevada operations. By the end of 1980, Nevada mining was so active that mining experts predicted the development of a third major mining boom to rival the earlier ones on the Comstock, and at Tonopah, Goldfield, and Ely. Particularly exciting were three areas: a huge molybdenum operation northwest of

[28]Samuel W. Matthews, "Nevada's Mountain of Invisible Gold," *National Geographic* 133 (May 1968):688–79, offers a fascinating picture of the development that has made possible Nevada's resurgence as a gold producer.
[29]See Appendix, table 2, pp. 406–7.

Tonopah, developed by the Anaconda Copper Company at a cost of over $200 million; Freeport Gold's Jerritt Canyon project north of Elko, developed at a cost of $115 million; and the extensive new barite deposits near Battle Mountain. The total investment in major new mines in the state by 1981 was estimated to be over $700 million. Mineral production followed the new activity, jumping from $238 million in 1979 to $525.9 million in 1982. The future seemed bright, yet within a year declining metal prices marked the beginning of another borrasca. Eight major mines, representing hundreds of millions of dollars of investment, had stopped operations by the end of 1982.

Mine closures and declining employment after 1981 led many observers to proclaim that Nevada's mining industry was in its worst slump in forty years. Yet the production figures for 1983 of $640.1 million mirror no depression.[30] This mixed picture of an outward depression in the face of a consistent rise in total production continued in 1984 and 1985. The explanation seems simple enough: three of Nevada's traditional mineral producers, copper, barite and molybdenum, continued their downward spiral while gold production expanded, more than making up for the decline in the other minerals. Another hopeful sign for mining in Nevada came from the oil industry. New wells in eastern Nevada and the expanding output of older ones led to a predicted production of over three million barrels of oil for 1985.[31]

Nevada should figure more prominently in the development of another alternate energy source, geothermal energy. Whatever the prospects for its development, Nevada should be able to take advantage of any growth since nearly one-half of all the geothermal leases in the entire United States are in Nevada. Nearly two million acres have been leased for development, almost as much as for the other ten western states combined. Nevada has forty-two known geothermal resource areas and thirty-two production wells have been sunk in recent years.[32]

[30]See the *Minerals Yearbooks* and the Nevada Bureau of Mines yearly bulletins on the *Nevada Mineral Industry* for the years from 1973 to the present. See also the *Reno Gazette-Journal*, July 31, 1982, p. 2B, col. 3; March 15, 1983, p. 2, col. 4; February 3, 1984, p. 8B, col. 2.

[31]*Reno Gazette-Journal*, September 8, 1985, p. 1D, col. 2; September 15, p. 1F, cols. 2–4.

[32]Ibid., August 1, 1982, p. 3A, col. 1.

AGRICULTURE

Agricultural production in Nevada since 1950, in spite of occasional setbacks, has shown a steady increase from a low of $38.9 million in 1955 to a high of $233.1 million in 1980. Livestock continue to make up the largest share of the total agricultural output. Sheep production has never completely recovered from the decline of the 1930s when the total number of sheep in Nevada dropped from over one million head to about half that number by 1945 and to a little more than 100,000 in the early 1980s. The number of cattle in Nevada increased from 320,000 in 1930 to approximately 660,000 at the end of 1983.[33]

The future of Nevada's agricultural development, as it has always been, is tied to the problem of adequate water. Nevada's supply is as limited as the possible solutions to the problem. Suggestions to bring water to Nevada from the Columbia River basin or to obtain a large share from the Colorado River have not received any real support. Better usage and conservation of existing water supplies have been proposed; particularly, covering the canals used to transport water for the Newlands Project has been suggested. An important development in insuring a better supply for southern Nevada came in 1982 with the completion of the southern Nevada Water Project from the Colorado River to Las Vegas.[34] Another possible source lies in the further development of subsurface water. A few areas, like the Moapa Valley in Clark County, appear to have reached nearly the maximum use of such water sources. There are regions of the state, however, where more effective goundwater development might increase the agricultural potential. Another possible source of subsurface water is in the deep levels of carbonate rocks, so-called aquifers, under the surface of Nevada's southern and eastern counties. That possibility apparently was at the center of the plan to base the MX missiles in southern and eastern Nevada. Although the MX deployment system was discarded by President Reagan in October, 1981, a test well at Coyote Springs in southern Nevada produced a flow of water from such carbonate rock.[35]

[33]Ibid., February 19, 1984, p. 8F, col. 2.
[34]Florence Lee Jones and John Cahlan, *Water: A History of Las Vegas,* 2 vols. (Las Vegas: Las Vegas Valley Water District, 1975).
[35]*Nevada State Journal,* August 4, 1983, p. 1, col. 1. See the *Reno Gazette-Journal,* February 26, 1984, p. 1A, col. 2, for an article on aquifers in Nevada.

Defense measures aside, the demands for additional water for Nevada, as elsewhere, are urban rather than rural. That is true particularly of Nevada's two major urban areas, Las Vegas and Reno. The former is a community built to some degree on the use of subsurface water. In addition to underground water, Las Vegas receives water from the Colorado River via the Southern Nevada Water Project. The farsighted water policies of Las Vegas officials made possible the rise of a metropolitan area numbering nearly 500,000 people in 1980, with another half million people projected by the year 2000.

In contrast, the city of Reno has made little use of subsurface water, relying basically on the Truckee River for its supply. Reno, however, has to compete with a number of other users for a share of that supply, including Lake Tahoe property owners, Truckee Meadows ranchers and farmers, the Truckee-Carson Irrigation District, and particularly the Pyramid Lake Indians.[36] To date, in the Reno area, there has been rather strong reaction against unlimited growth and consequently no major efforts to develop additional water supplies.

A movement initiated in 1979 with the passage of a law claiming that the public domain in Nevada was the property of the state of Nevada gained immediate and widespread support of Nevada agriculturists as well as those in other western states. Under the act the attorney-general was directed to bring suit in federal court to possess those lands, which make up some 86 percent of the total acreage of Nevada.[37] The Sagebrush Rebellion, as the movement was called, lost its impetus as many opponents, including sportsmen, environmentalists, and others, concluded that the movement was a quick way of placing the public acreage in the hands of real estate agents, and the Reagan administration, theoretically in favor of states' rights, indicated it had no intention of giving up control of the public lands. The federal government's program of "privatization," to sell thirty-five million acres of public land within five years, no doubt helped push the Sagebrush Rebellion into the background.[38]

[36]*Reno Gazette-Journal,* June 25, 1983, p. 1A, col. 2.
[37]*Statues of Nevada* (1979), chapter 633, pp. 1362–67.
[38]Reno Gazette-Journal, November 21, 1982, p. 1A, col. 2; April 21, 1983, p. 1C, col. 2.

FEDERAL INTERESTS

Although not a revenue producer in the usual sense of the word, the Federal government's economic assistance to Nevada has meant the expenditure of hundreds of million dollars annually and accounted for the employment of over ten thousand individuals within the state. Although federal aid is not new to Nevada, it reached new dimensions when the U.S. Atomic Energy Commission (AEC) in December, 1950, designated the Frenchmen's Flat area in southern Nevada as the Nevada Proving Grounds. The first atomic bomb was detonated there on January 27, 1951, and for the next ten years, most of the nuclear devices exploded there were above ground. Underground testing became a fixed policy of the AEC in 1962, although it wasn't until the next year that the United States signed a treaty with Russia and Great Britain to ban atmospheric testing of nuclear weapons. Underground testing did not eliminate objections to nuclear explosions because although the dangers from radioactive fallout were lessened, many believed that underground testing increased the threat of earthquakes and risked the contamination of water supplies. Most Nevadans have accepted the tests because the economic advantages of the AEC operations to the state have tended to obscure possible dangers. Those economic advantages received a boost in 1956 when the Nevada Test Site was selected for the development of nuclear reactor engines for spacecraft and for rocket propellants. The Nevada Test Site was at the height of its activity during the period when projects of the National Aeronautics and Space Administration (NASA) were being tested there. The closing of most of its activities in the 1970s created sharp but temporary dislocations in the economy of southern Nevada.

The center of activity within the test site is a most unusual boom camp, whose inhabitants are trained workmen, engineers, and scientists, working with the most sophisticated equipment yet produced, a remarkable contrast to the heterogeneous fraternity of an earlier era that opened Nevada to settlement with pick and shovel. The test site town of Mercury was given semipermanent status with the establishment of a post office in 1964.[39] The federal government has listed the Nevada Test Site as one of three possible

[39]*Nevada State Journal*, April 28, 1983, p. 1A, col. 4.

sites for a major nuclear waste storage area, a prospect that has not received strong support, particularly in view of the difficulties with the Beatty nuclear waste dump during its operation.

All in all, the expenditures connected with the test site, and the impetus the site has given to the development of local industry, constitute an important element in the state's economy. Although the AEC property is not on state tax rolls, the agency does provide significant sums of money to support local schools.

WAREHOUSING AND MANUFACTURING

A new element was added to Nevada's economic development when the 1949 legislature made the first provision for a tax-free area for warehousing merchandise in interstate commerce. The so-called free-port privilege exempted from the state's personal property tax merchandise originating outside Nevada and consigned to a warehouse in the state for storage but destined for reentry into interstate commerce. In 1954 the tax exemption was extended to merchandise assembled, processed, disassembled, broken in bulk, relabeled, or repackaged in the state and also to property moving in interstate commerce through the state. The free-port privilege was written into the Nevada constitution by an amendment in 1960. In 1969 the legislature added the word "manufactured" to the list of operations through which personal property in interstate transit retains its *no situs* tax exemption. It also defined "processed" to include feeding, watering, and caring for livestock and the slaughtering of livestock. Thus feed lot and packinghouse operations have become part of the free-port policy.

A reversal of the free-port policy in Nevada is unlikely since it would require an amendment to the constitution. More importantly, the policy has been of definite economic benefit. In addition to the money spent in constructing the warehouses, an estimated 7.5 persons are employed for each 10,000 square feet of space. In 1979 the estimated total square feet of space in the Reno-Sparks area was 16,300,000, which represents 12,200 workers. Estimates indicate that warehousing in the Reno-Sparks region will increase approximately 1.5 million square feet per year in the foreseeable future, thus accounting for a yearly labor increase of 1,100 workers.[40] The

[40]*Reno Gazette-Journal*, August 7, 1983, p. 1F, col. 2.

Las Vegas area has also become a significant distribution site for the West Coast, and a few smaller communities with good rail and road connections, such as Elko and Winnemucca, have made contributions to Nevada's warehousing industry.

Manufacturing has not been a major factor in Nevada's economic growth. The state has not been in a position to compete effectively in manufacturing since it lacks sufficient water to satisfy certain industries and lacks fuel resources for even its own heavy industries. In addition, Nevada is too far from sources of many necessary raw materials, and its labor supply, although often sufficient numerically, cannot fill the needs of high-tech industries for qualified personnel. On the other hand, a number of light industries have been attracted to the state because of its geographic position, good transportation, heavy population growth, advantageous tax structure, and the favorable attitude of its business and political leaders.

Manufacturing in Nevada is centered in the Las Vegas and Reno metropolitan areas and is mainly confined to light industries such as food processing, printing and publishing, cosmetics, chemicals, telephone and microwave communications equipment, and electronic products. Las Vegas has benefited because of its association with the Nevada test site and the prime contractors of the AEC. One of the most important industrial areas in the state is the old Basic Magnesium plant at Henderson, which was converted to private industrial use after World War II. The availability of low-cost hydroelectric power and important raw materials and the proximity of markets in the heavily populated southern California area make it a desirable site for manufacturing. The recent allotment of additional Hoover Dam power to Nevada should increase the potential for the development of manufacturing in southern Nevada.[41]

A major push toward the increased development of manufacturing in Nevada resulted when the national economic recession of the early 1980s demonstrated that Nevada's gambling industry was not recession proof. That realization sent Nevada's leaders into a search to find ways to diversify the state's economy and move it away from the almost complete dominance by the gambling industry. Increased manufacturing, particularly high-tech industry, appeared to be a workable solution to the problem.

[41]Ibid., May 15, 1983, p. 9C, col. 1.

A report authorized by the 1983 state legislature, however, indicated Nevada was not in a favorable position to compete with other states because of three factors: Nevada did not have a trained labor force; utility bills in the state were high; and the state had a less-than-satisfactory image.[42] The untrained labor force was seen as the major limiting factor, and the report suggested that legislators and others recognize the need to upgrade faculty research and graduate programs on the university level. The University of Nevada Board of Regents, in the latter part of February, 1984, tried to meet part of that challenge by authorizing a College of Engineering and Computer Science for the University of Nevada, Las Vegas. The 1985 legislature followed that action by appropriating some $15 million for the construction of a major engineering building for the Las Vegas campus.

In spite of the problems, a number of small high-tech industries had entered Nevada and were operating successfully at the time of the 1983 report. Particularly interesting is Bently of Nevada, which moved into the Minden area of Carson Valley some years ago. The firm manufactures precision instruments and employs approximately one thousand persons. In 1983 the company announced a plan to establish a large industrial park in the area to attract other small industries. Other firms that have located in Carson Valley or the Carson City–Reno–Sparks metropolitan district manufacture X-ray machines, computers, industrial microsystems, computer disc drive control systems, and similar high-tech devices. The move to bring new industrial development to northern Nevada has been aided substantially since 1983 when the Economic Development Authority of Western Nevada (EDAWN) was formed. Since its inception EDAWN has worked not only to promote new manufacturing firms but to encourage the location of distribution centers for manufactured items. It was a partner with local businesses and the state economic authority in the successful bid to have the Porsche automobile distribution center located in Reno. It is presently engaged in a campaign to bring Far East goods to western Nevada, an attempt to make warehousing a part of high-tech industry.

Even more successful than the achievements in northern Nevada have been those in Clark County. With the encouragement of the

---

[42]*Nevada State Journal,* June 3, 1983, p. 8A, col. 2.

Nevada Development Authority, founded in the 1950s as the Southern Nevada Industrial Foundation, 58 new businesses located in the Las Vegas area bringing 4,858 new jobs from 1980 through 1984. The estimated financial impact of those developments exceeded one-half billion dollars. The NDA presently consists of nearly 700 business-oriented individuals representing over 600 businesses.[43] The aggressiveness of the authority and its excellent promotional plans no doubt will continue to have a major part in bringing new industry and wealth to southern Nevada.

The development authorities in Clark and Washoe were not alone in their efforts to bring new industries to Nevada. State political leaders, particularly Governor Bryan, made strong commitments to such programs, including the establishment of a state economic authority at Governor Bryan's suggestion. There were problems to face in any effort to lure industry to Nevada. A major obstacle was spotlighted in a study released late in 1982 that placed Nevada eighth among eleven western states in favorableness of business climate.[44]

The extent Nevada officials were willing to go in overcoming that statistic was shown when Governor Bryan called a special session of the legislature March 29, 1984, to pass legislation to enable Citicorp of New York to open a regional credit card center in Las Vegas. The measure passed the legislature without difficulty and was signed into law almost immediately by Governor Bryan, who called the legislation an economic milestone in moving Nevada from near total reliance on gambling. Citicorp plans for the Las Vegas center included building a 120,000 square-foot center at a cost of $8.5 million and employing a minimum of 1,000 workers.[45] The center was in operation by the summer of 1985.

There is little doubt that such efforts to attract industry have had and will continue to have a definite impact on the economy of Nevada. Whether or not that impact will be sufficient to seriously change the relative position of gambling in the economy is open to question.

[43]*Las Vegas Review-Journal,* June 2, 1985, p. 3J, cols. 1–6.

[44]*Reno Gazette-Journal,* November 14, 1982, p. 1F, col. 2; Sam E. White, "Nevada's Business Climate 1980 to 1982: A Comparison of Economic Diversification Factors among Western States," *Nevada Review of Business & Economics* 7 (Summer 1983):8–14; "The Comprehensive Economic Development Plan, vol. 1, pt. 4, State of Nevada. Governor's Office of Planning Coordination, January, 1978, Carson City, Nevada, pp. 2, 40.

[45]*Reno Gazette-Journal,* March 31, 1984, p. 1A, col. 4.

In the first place, any increase of jobs and people, from whatever cause, helps to feed the gambling industry. Secondly, gambling interests have shown great ingenuity in maintaining the allure of gambling where it already exists and in seeking new marketing areas. Of particular interest in that respect are the border towns of Jackpot, near the Idaho border; Wendover, on the Nevada–Utah border; and Laughlin, near the southern tip of Nevada. In all of those areas large casinos have been built and undoubtedly they will continue to bring additional gambling revenues to the state.

The Role of Clark County

Southern Nevada dominates the state's economic and political life. It controls the major part of the gambling industry: the defense and space industries in Nevada are centered there; the area has great power and water potential for industrial expansion; it is favorably located for increased warehousing and manufacturing development and has more than half of the total population of the state. Large on the list of attractions in southern Nevada is the city of Las Vegas itself. Aided by a mild climate, the large metropolitan area of southern California from which to draw tourists, and a most unusual chamber of commerce, which has continuously and effectively extolled the virtues of constant growth, Las Vegas grew from a small community of 24,624 people in 1950 to 442,464 in 1980. It is estimated that the metropolitan area will be over one million people by the year 2000. In the process, the desert city with huge, glittering hotel-casinos with lavish floor shows and flashing neon signs became the entertainment capital of the world. Although that entertainment has centered on important names in music and show business, it has not been confined to them, for Las Vegas has also hosted most of the major prize fights in the past decade and is the site for auto races, tennis matches and golf tournaments. Such activities have made Las Vegas an exciting place, one of the most popular tourist attractions in the United States, attracting 12 million people annually.[46]

[46]For a variety of interesting views of Las Vegas see the following: C. Gregory Crampton, *The Complete Las Vegas* (Salt Lake City: Peregrine Smith, 1976); Peter Wiley and Robert Gottlieb, *Empires in the Sun: The Rise of the New American West* (New York: G. P. Putnam's Sons, 1982); Perry Bruce Kaufman, "The Best City of Them All: A History of Las Vegas, 1930–1960" (Ph.D. diss., University of California–Santa Barbara, 1974); Tom Wolfe, *The kandy-kolored, tangerine-flake streamline baby* (New York: Farrar, Straus & Giroux, 1965).

CHAPTER 16

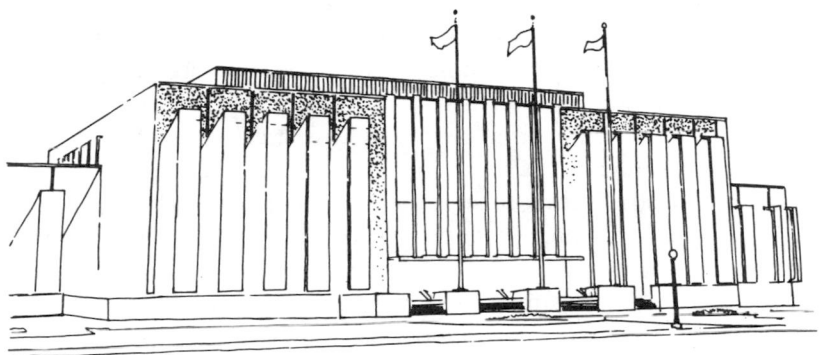

The Political Scene since 1950

NEVADA POLITICS SINCE 1950 has displayed a number of characteristics that have become familiar patterns to Nevada voters. Until recently the Democratic party held a majority of registrations, which enabled it to dominate elective offices in the state. The elections of 1982 and 1984 showed a strong Republican challenge to that dominance. In the years of the preeminence of the Democratic party, the Republican party was able to maintain a solid state organization by virtue of its showing in the gubernatorial and presidential races. In nine elections for governor since 1950, the Democrats have been successful five times and the Republicans four. In presidential campaigns, Nevada voters have supported the Republican nominee in 1952, 1956, 1968, 1972, 1980, and 1984, and the Democratic nominee only in 1960 and 1964. Nevada's record of supporting the successful presidential candidate since 1912 was broken when voters supported Gerald Ford in 1976.

Another characteristic of Nevada politics, a strong conservative bias, persisted through the 1984 election and into the 1985 legislature. With few exceptions successful candidates for office in Nevada regardless of party ran and were elected on conservative platforms. Thus a consistent campaign strategy is to try to pin the label "liberal" on opponents.

That conservatism has been mirrored in legislative enactments and executive actions. In spite of liberal divorce and gambling laws, which have definite economic origins, Nevada legislators have generally followed conservative patterns; both legislators and governors since 1950 have shown a strong fiscal conservatism that crosses party lines.

To date there is little to suggest that the growing dominance of Clark County will alter that conservative bias, particularly in fiscal matters.

Nevada political campaigns were particularly fascinating in the early 1950s, when Nevada Democrats seemed bent on proving how a two-to-one voter registration in their favor could be turned into defeat at the polls. The first instance came in 1950 in the gubernatorial race, which pitted the incumbent Democrat, Vail Pittman, against Charles Russell, a Republican former state senator and one-term U.S. congressman. Both listed Ely as their home and both were newspaper publishers. Neither was an exciting candidate, although both were well known and well liked throughout the state. Pittman began with two big advantages, a nearly two-to-one voter registration in his favor and the support of organized labor.

As the campaign proceeded it became apparent that factionalism within the Democratic party, nurtured by decades of animosity between the Pittman and McCarran forces, threatened to nullify those advantages. Rumors of a tie-in between the Russell and the McCarran forces to defeat Pittman appeared in some state newspapers.[1] The election results seemed to verify the existence of such a coalition. Russell, the Republican nominee for governor, received a statewide percentage of 57.6 percent of the vote and

---

[1] *Elko Independent*, October 12, 1950; *Reno Evening Gazette*, October 21, 1950.

McCarran, the Democratic nominee for the U.S. Senate, received 58 percent in his victory over George Marshall, an attorney from Las Vegas.[2]

A second Democratic bloodletting took place during the 1952 election for U.S. senator. George Malone, the incumbent, had only token opposition in the Republican primary. The Democratic primary, however, produced one of the most unusual political upsets in Nevada history. Alan Bible, a McCarran protégé serving a second term as state attorney-general, was defeated by Thomas Mechling, a recent arrival in Nevada and virtually without political experience. Although his victory over Bible was by a slim margin of 475 votes, Mechling no doubt would have beaten Malone in the general election had he been content to wage an aggressive campaign against him. Instead he opened his campaign for the general election with a frontal attack on the McCarran machine and thus presented Malone with the miracle he needed to stay in the Senate. The strategy backfired when just before the election McCarran made a dramatic announcement that he would not support Mechling and hoped that his friends would not support him either. Malone won by 2,722 votes, the second time in six years he had been handed the senate seat by factionalism within the Democratic party.

In the other national races, Eisenhower and Nixon electors won a sweeping victory over those of Adlai Stevenson and John Sparkman. The Eisenhower landslide no doubt was important in the victory of Cliff Young, a Reno attorney, over Walter Baring, the incumbent Democrat, in the race for the house seat.

The factionalism within the Democratic party that had cost them important elections in 1950 and 1952 seemed to be pushed aside in 1954 when Senator McCarran announced shortly after the primary elections that he would support the entire Democratic ticket, which included his old enemy Vail Pittman, the nominee for governor. His action, a turnabout from his lone wolf image, appeared to be a

[2]Jerome Edwards, *Pat McCarran: Political Boss of Nevada* (Reno: University of Nevada Press, 1982), pp. 142–43; Mary Ellen Glass, *Nevada's Turbulent '50s: Decade of Political and Economic Change* (Reno: University of Nevada Press, 1981), p. 8. Correspondence in the Charles H. Russell and Vail Pittman papers, both in the Getchell Library, University of Nevada, Reno, supports the conclusion that McCarran supported Russell for governor.

means of ensuring a united party behind him should he run for reelection in 1956. Highlighting the new unity was a series of speeches by McCarran supporting all of the Democratic nominees. During the tour, on September 28 at Hawthorne, the senator died of a heart attack. Although Governor Russell appointed Ernest Brown, a Republican, to the post, the Nevada Supreme Court ruled that McCarran's unexpired term would have to be filled by election, which Alan Bible won in 1954.

The Democratic unity heralded by McCarran before his death received a heavy blow from a series of articles in the *Las Vegas Sun* that alleged gangsters had infiltrated Las Vegas gambling. Not only did the articles implicate certain local and state officials including former Democratic lieutenant governor Cliff Jones, but they seemed to imply that gambling controls would be eased if Pittman were elected Governor.[3] Although he was never tied directly to the practices alleged in the articles, Pittman was unable to dispel suspicion and he was defeated by Russell in a close race.[4]

Russell, the first Republican to hold the governorship since 1934, was faced with a myriad of problems, most of which were attributable to the heavy influx of population and the tremendous growth of the gambling industry. He met those problems with courage, intelligence, and honesty, with the result that his eight years in office brought needed reforms in a number of areas: gambling control, the support of public and higher education, the civil service, and personnel management.[5] His administration was certainly one of the most important in Nevada history.

Republicans looked forward to the 1956 election in Nevada, confidant that Eisenhower would be reelected and buoyed by the announcement that Alan Bible would not run for reelection to the U.S. Senate. Republican Congressman Cliff Young appeared to be a real threat when Bible, strongly pressured by national and state Democrats, reconsidered and decided to enter the Democratic

[3]See chapter 15.

[4]Vail Pittman was convinced that the Thunderbird case, which involved Cliff Jones, and the related articles in the *Sun* caused his defeat. In a letter of December 11, 1954, to Frank H. Bartholomew, president of the United Press Association, Pittman wrote, "Had the election been held before the Jones debacle, I would have won by an overwhelming vote, is the consensus throughout the state." Vail Pittman Papers, no. 54, Getchell Library.

[5]Glass, *Nevada's Turbulent '50s*, pp. 7–73.

primary. The resulting Bible-Young race brought the only excitement to a rather lackluster campaign. Bible won in a close race.

Developing more local interest than any of the candidate races was the third attempt by labor in four years to eliminate the right-to-work law, which had been passed in 1952. This time labor initiated two petitions, an initiative petition to repeal the statute, and an initiative constitutional amendment to prohibit right-to-work laws in Nevada. Both measures were defeated, the initiative statute by 53.9 percent of the total vote and the initiative amendment by a 56.9 percent margin.[6]

The 1958 election brought the Democratic party a near sweep of the national and state offices, demonstrating the effectiveness of a newfound unity. Among the Republican casualties was incumbent Senator George Malone, who had been handed two successive terms in the U.S. Senate by factionalism within the Democratic party. This time he was not so lucky, going down to defeat by Howard Cannon, a Las Vegas attorney. In the house contest, Walter Baring overwhelmed his Republican opponent, Robert Horton, and Governor Russell, seeking an unprecedented third term, was unable to stop the successful challenge of his Democratic opponent, Grant Sawyer, a youthful, politically appealing former chairman of the Democratic party and a member of the university board of regents. Rex Bell was the only Republican to win a state office in 1958, defeating the unknown Phil Cummings for the lieutenant governorship.

Governor Sawyer began his administration with a dynamism seldom seen in Nevada's executive office. His message to the 1959 legislature outlined an extensive program of reform, but before the session was over he had found tradition and a Republican-dominated senate obstacles to legislative leadership. Nevertheless, his achievements include a much needed reform of the gambling control machinery, the establishment of a human rights commission, and limited administrative reorganization. Sawyer's liberal political and social views were counter-balanced by a strong fiscal conservatism and during his eight years in office, the governor played a more positive role in legislative leadership than had

[6]A careful analysis of the three right-to-work elections can be found in Elmer Rusco, *Voting Behavior in Nevada* (Reno: University of Nevada Press, 1966), pp. 20–32.

previous office holders. Sawyer was effective in keeping the spotlight of public attention on the executive office, and his activities outside Nevada made him an important figure in western Democratic politics.

The 1960 election was dominated by the presidential race, and the Democrats, after some threats of internal strife, came together sufficiently after John F. Kennedy's nomination to bring a narrow state victory for him in November. The only other major contest saw Walter Baring defeat former U.S. Senator George Malone for the House seat by a sizeable margin.

The unity of the Democratic party continued through the 1962 election, enabling the big three of the Democrats, Bible, Sawyer, and Baring, to win sweeping victories. The only office lost to the Democrats was that of lieutenant governor, which since 1954 had somehow come to represent the private domain of the Republican party. Rex Bell had won the office in 1954 and again in 1958 but had died in office in 1962. The Democrats might also have won that race had not the name of their candidate, Berkeley Bunker, evoked unfavorable memories among Democrats for the part he played in defeating Governor Carville in the 1946 Democratic primary. As it was, Paul Laxalt, a personable young Carson City attorney, was able to draw large numbers of Democrats to his side for a clear victory.

In the 1964 election, Nevada voters again demonstrated their disregard for party lines, but that time it was more because of the personalities involved than party factionalism. In the major contest that year, the incumbent U.S. senator, Howard Cannon, with registration two to one in his favor nearly lost to lieutenant governor Paul Laxalt. The latter proved to be an excellent speaker, able to communicate easily with voters and with a loyal and aggressive statewide organization. Although he campaigned vigorously, Cannon on the other hand created little enthusiasm, even within his own party. The visit of President Lyndon Johnson to Nevada may well have provided Cannon with his narrow, forty-eight-vote victory. A recount, demanded by Laxalt, raised the margin of Cannon's victory to eighty-four votes.[7]

Between the 1964 and 1966 elections there occurred in Nevada,

[7]This was the first statewide recount in the history of Nevada, although in two earlier statewide elections the state supreme court had reviewed ballots. In neither of those cases was the appeal to the court preceded by a recount: the first involved the

as in a number of other states, reapportionment of the state legislature. The action was the result of a series of events initiated by a U.S. Supreme Court decision in 1964, which declared unconstitutional the so-called little federal plan, that is where one house represents population and one house represents territory. Since Nevada had been operating on such a plan since 1915, the court decision was strongly denounced throughout the state by Republican and Democrat alike.

When the Nevada legislature met in January 1965 it faced the prospect of mandatory reapportionment, for the federal district court at Las Vegas had called for a three-judge panel to reapportion the legislature in June if it had not been done by legislative action by April 15. Although the court warning was clear, the legislators failed to act on a reapportionment plan during the regular session. That failure brought the federal court into the picture again. The three-judge panel ruled that both houses of the Nevada legislature were malapportioned and ordered the governor to convene a special session of the legislature by October 30, 1965, to reapportion it in accordance with the principles of representation set forth in the court's opinion. If such a plan was not submitted by November 20, the court itself would reapportion the legislature or call for at-large elections of legislators in 1966. The special session was called, the legislators adopted a plan to increase each house by three seats and apportion each essentially by population, and the federal court reluctantly accepted the reapportionment.[8]

Since the initial reapportionment, the Nevada legislature has been reapportioned after each decennial census. Those actions, reflecting the heavy population movement into southern Nevada, brought Clark County into a numerical majority control of both houses of the legislature. To date, that control has not changed the basic conservatism of the state, although it has led to a gradual but persistent shift of power in favor of Clark County.

In 1966, Nevada voters were offered what many writers described

election of Reinhold Sadler as governor in 1898 and the second the election of Joe Josephs as clerk of the supreme court in 1910.

[8]*Dungan* v. *Sawyer,* 253 F. Supp. 352 (1966). See Eleanore Bushnell, *The Nevada Constitution: Origin and Growth,* 5th ed. (Reno: University of Nevada Press, 1980), pp. 81–86.

as a dream contest—between two young and capable political leaders, the incumbent governor, Grant Sawyer, and the incumbent lieutenant governor, Paul Laxalt. Sawyer's administration had been marked by conscientious and capable leadership but was facing the same two-term tradition he had fought in defeating Charles Russell in 1958. Laxalt had another advantage in the fact that he had had no primary contest, while Sawyer experienced a very bitter primary against him by Reno attorney Charles Springer, a former supporter who had been alienated by Sawyer's refusal to step down. Although Sawyer easily won the primary, it may have been a costly victory since it apparently rekindled old party feuds among the Democrats. In any event, Laxalt scored a clearcut victory over his opponent.

Laxalt's popularity was no doubt responsible for bringing the Republican party two other victories in 1966, those of Ed Fike as lieutenant governor and Wilson McGowan as state controller. Congressman Baring easily defeated his Republican opponent, Ralph Kraemer. The Democrats won control of both houses of the state legislature, which for the first time in Nevada history included a woman elected to the senate and a black man to the assembly.

Governor Laxalt continued the pattern of strong executive leadership and fiscal conservatism followed by his two predecessors in office. He showed real political astuteness in keying his recommendations to the moods and needs of the electorate and skillfully working with a divided legislature to gain most of the program he suggested.[9] From an economic standpoint, the most important measure passed during the Laxalt administration was a corporate gambling law to further encourage big corporations to enter Nevada gambling. Probably the most important measure recommended but not passed by the legislature was a fair housing bill.

The 1968 election in Nevada created little excitement among the voters. In the two major contests the Democratic incumbents easily defeated their opponents, with Alan Bible winning his fourth election to the U.S. Senate by defeating Ed Fike, the Republican lieutenant governor, and Walter Baring gaining the House seat for an unprecedented ninth time.

In 1970 Nevada lost one of its most glamorous political figures

---

[9]In an analysis of the governor's program, Cy Ryan of the Associated Press wrote, "Democrats, with a touch of envy, complained that Laxalt interfered with the lawmakers more than any governor in the past." *Nevada State Journal*, April 26, 1969.

when Governor Paul Laxalt indicated that he would not be a candidate for office. The decision was received joyously by the Democrats and unhappily by the Republicans, for Laxalt was considered a sure winner for a second term, or had he chosen to run for the Senate, a formidable threat to the incumbent Democrat, Howard Cannon. Ed Fike then became the Republican party choice for the governorship, and William Raggio, a Reno attorney, was named to challenge Cannon.

Fike was an early favorite in his campaign against the Democratic nominee Mike O'Callaghan, a former high school teacher and welfare administrator, and although his campaign was well organized and well financed, he was unable to overcome the heavy Democratic registration in the state and a surprisingly hard-driving campaign by O'Callaghan. In the other contest for national office, Walter Baring won his tenth term as Nevada's lone member in the House of Representatives.

For the Republicans the only bright spot in the 1970 election was the victory of a young attorney, Robert List, who defeated the three-term Democratic incumbent attorney general, Harvey Dickerson, proving once again that an attractive Republican candidate with ample expense money could overcome the heavy Democratic registration in the state.

Even more than his three predecessors, Governor O'Callaghan took an active role in the legislative process, offering an ambitious program and lobbying aggressively for his proposals in the 1971 legislature. From the beginning of his eight years in office, O'Callaghan demonstrated that he would be a people-oriented governor. Many of the achievements of the first session demonstrated that attitude, including Nevada's first fair-housing act and a number of antipollution and environmental measures.

The legislature, reapportioned itself in 1971, making an important change by the establishment of single-member districts in the assembly. The reapportionment gave assembly candidates a manageable constituency, greatly reducing the cost of campaigning and increasing the possibility of direct contact with each potential voter. The idea did not win support in the state senate where adoption of such a rule would have cost some incumbent senators their seats.[10]

[10]For additional details about the 1970 election see Don W. Driggs, *The 1970 Election in Nevada, Governmental Research Newsletter,* Bureau of Governmental

The 1972 campaign in Nevada brought the Democrats control of both houses of the legislature, initiating a pattern that has continued through the 1982 election. The numerical superiority of that party, however, has been of little significance since most political issues in the legislature are dealt with along conservative lines regardless of party affiliation.

The 1972 election also brought an end to the long political career of Walter Baring. The primary campaign was his undoing. Baring's differences with Democratic party leaders, increasing strongly as he turned from moderate liberalism to ultraconservatism, had caused problems in earlier primaries. Somehow he had managed to survive them and to run strong races in the general elections, aided by the support of conservative Republicans. The accumulation of years of animosity within his party and the strong favorable voter association with the name of his opponent, James Bilbray, finally brought defeat. Bilbray, however, was unable to translate his primary triumph into a general election victory, partly because Baring threw his support to the Republican candidate, David Towell.

Governor O'Callaghan's second state of State message echoed again his strong interest in social issues and programs, showing particular concern for dependent and emotionally disturbed children, for the elderly, the handicapped, consumers, and working people. His message called for a 41 percent increase for higher education generally and a 300 percent increase for the three community colleges then existing. As had been the case in 1971, O'Callaghan gained most of what he had requested, leading one legislator to declare flatly that the session had been a rubber stamp for the governor. About the only major area of disagreement between the executive and legislative branches came over the Equal Rights Amendment, which the governor recommended but the legislature voted down.[11]

The highlight of the 1974 Nevada election was the contest for the Senate seat left vacant by Alan Bible, who was retiring. Bible was the

Research (Reno: University of Nevada, March 1971). A brief analysis of the work of the 1971 legislature can be found in Eleanore Bushnell, *Commentary on the Legislature—1971, Governmental Research Newsletter,* Bureau of Governmental Research (Reno: University of Nevada, May–June, 1971).

[11] *Journal of the Assembly (Nevada),* 57th sess. (1973), pp. 35–47; *Las Vegas Sun,* April 27, 1973, p. 1, cols. 3–5; *Nevada State Journal,* April 27, 1973, p. 1, cols. 4–7.

first U.S. senator from Nevada since the beginning of the direct election of senators to vacate his position voluntarily. His withdrawal meant that for the first time in Nevada history a popular election for a regular six-year Senate term would be held without an incumbent as a candidate. Either the incumbent governor, Mike O'Callaghan, or the former governor, Grant Sawyer, both Democrats, were expected to seek the post. Neither entered the race but former Republican governor Paul Laxalt did. His opponent in the general election was Lieutenant Governor Harry Reid, who had won a hotly contested primary over the liberal Maya Miller. In spite of Laxalt's proven vote-getting ability, an October poll showed Reid ahead. At that point Reid made a political mistake when he impugned the honesty of his opponent's financial dealings in constructing the Ormsby House in Carson City. He even went so far as to demand a full financial disclosure from each member of Laxalt's family. The strategy backfired in northern Nevada where the Laxalt family was quite popular. An additional factor in Reid's defeat (he lost by only 624 votes) was his failure to get out the vote in Clark County, where he was strongest; voter turnout in that county was 69.6 percent compared to 75.9 percent outside.

The governor's race in 1974 was no-contest, with the very popular O'Callaghan receiving 91 percent of the vote in the primary and 67.4 percent in the general election, the highest ever in a Nevada gubernatorial contest. Two other contests in 1974 were also of some importance. The incumbent congressman, Republican David Towell, was defeated by newcomer James Santini, a Democrat, who emphasized in his campaign the ties between Towell and President Nixon, who had recently resigned. The only bright spot for the Republicans was the victory of the incumbent attorney-general, Robert List, over state senator Richard Bryan, a Democrat. Bryan lost by just 701 votes, the victim also of a failure to get Clark County voters to the polls.

Governor O'Callaghan's third state of the State message to the legislature in January, 1975, while continuing to emphasize social programs called for restricted spending, the result of a slower percentage increase in revenues from the sales and gasoline taxes. The 1975 legislature had difficulty dealing with the myriad problems that faced it, setting a record of 122 days in session before adjourning on May 20. The usual confusion over adjournment was

compounded by the inability of the legislative bill-drafting process
to keep up with the continuous demands of legislators. Some
observers labeled the session the worst in Nevada history, a criticism
justified by the procedures and length of the session rather than by
its accomplishments. Governor O'Callaghan received most of what
he had asked for in his message, including an increase in welfare
grants, the broadening of tax exemptions for the elderly, and the
appropriation of $7.4 million for a prison for youthful offenders.
Again the legislature refused approval of the ERA.[12]

The 1976 presidential race in Nevada was noteworthy in two
ways: it was the first time in sixty-four years that Nevada voters did
not favor the winning candidate, and it was the first election to use
the state's new presidential primary law, enacted in 1973. In that
primary President Ford made only one appearance in the state, a
brief visit to Las Vegas on election eve. On the other hand, his
primary opponent, Ronald Reagan, toured the state, making the
most of his close personal ties to Senator Laxalt. Reagan's victory on
May 4 was substantial. He received 66.25 percent of the vote,
compared to 28.8 percent for Ford. The Democratic hopefuls, Jerry
Brown, Jimmy Carter, and Frank Church, all campaigned. The
victor was Brown with 52.7 percent of the votes cast. The first
presidential primary in Nevada was hailed as a success since it
brought the leading candidates into the state. The voter turnout as a
result was a respectable 62.7 percent.

The most interesting characteristic about the party primaries held
in September, 1976, was the extensive voter use of a category
provided by Nevada law allowing voters to cast their ballots for
"none of the above." Thus in the Democratic primary for the U.S.
Senate, the incumbent, Cannon, received 86 percent of the vote, but
the "none of the above" category received more than either of his
opponents. The Republican party could find no well-known candidate to run against the incumbent, James Santini, for Congress, and
as a result the "none of these candidates" category received 47.2
percent of the vote. In the 1976 general election Nevada voters
supported President Ford, but in other contests the Democrats

---

[12]*Journal of the Assembly (Nevada)*, 58th sess. (1975), pp. 25–33; *Las Vegas Sun*, May
22, 1975, p. 3, cols. 2–7; *Nevada State Journal*, May 22, 1975, p. 1A, col. 6.

swept the state, choosing Cannon for the Senate and Santini for the House.

As in earlier messages, O'Callaghan's fourth and last state of the State speech emphasized people-oriented social issues and a conservative fiscal policy. As in previous sessions, the governor received most of what he had asked for in his message. The gambling laws were rewritten, a four-year medical school was approved, elaborate ground rules were established for tenant-landlord relationships in a new fair-housing bill, the open-meeting concept was strengthened, the Tahoe Regional Planning Agency was reorganized, a full-time parole board was established, a bill limiting the growth of casinos at Lake Tahoe was passed, and the legislature eliminated seventy-three boards and commissions. Once more the session failed to approve the ERA.[13]

The 1978 Nevada election centered on the gubernatorial race and on two major issues, the ERA and cutting taxes. Once O'Callaghan made it clear that he had no desire for a third term, the race for governor developed into a contest between Attorney-General Robert List, Republican, and Robert Rose, the Democratic lieutenant governor. List had a number of factors in his favor: no primary opposition, a sizeable campaign chest, the backing of the state's four leading newspapers, and an adroit use of his friendship and past favorable working relations with the outgoing O'Callaghan. Rose, on the other hand, although supported by a heavy Democratic voter registration was hurt by a divisive primary, brought about when former state senator John Foley decided at the last minute to enter the race. Besides acting as a spoiler in the primary, Foley refused to support Rose in the general election. In addition, during the campaign List was able, with the support of a friendly press, to give Rose a liberal image, a potent label in conservative Nevada. List won the general election with 58.6 percent of the vote.

Rose was the only major Democratic candidate to lose in the 1978 election. Myron Leavitt was elected lieutenant governor and the other state offices except state controller went to Democrats. Particularly impressive was the 74 percent vote garnered by Richard

[13]*Journal of the Assembly (Nevada)*, 59th sess. (1977), pp. 33–39; *Nevada State Journal*, May 10, 1977, p. 1, cols. 5–6; *Las Vegas Review-Journal*, May 9, 1977, p. 1, cols. 2–6.

Bryan for attorney-general. The Republicans did make gains in the legislature, winning nine additional seats in the assembly and two in the senate. Two ballot measures were of particular importance: a nonbinding referendum on the ERA, which showed a substantial majority opposed to the idea; and a tax-reducing measure that if repassed in 1980 would limit the real property tax to 1 percent of market value. It was obvious from the votes on those two measures that both issues would figure prominently in future legislative deliberations.

Governor List in his first message to the legislature in January, 1979, attacked the problem of a tax cut by suggesting a 30 percent reduction in property taxes, a repeal of the sales tax on food, and a tax deferment for the elderly. The recommendations were obviously an effort to forestall voter approval of the 1 percent property tax question in 1980. Generally, List followed the philosophy of all recent Nevada governors in promoting fiscal conservatism. His suggested budget called for retrenchment in some areas such as the University of Nevada system and a no-growth proposal for most other agencies. Major measures suggested in his message were passed simply because most Democrats in the legislature supported his financial program. The most important legislation was a $244 million tax reform bill calling for a 27 percent property tax reduction. Besides the tax measure, the session also passed a measure labeled immediately the "Sagebrush Rebellion," which sought to gain state control of some fifty million acres of federally controlled public lands in Nevada. Once more the ERA was defeated and a new record was established when the legislature adjourned after 133 days in session.[14]

The 1980 election in Nevada brought few surprises with voters again demonstrating their conservatism. In the presidential race, Ronald Reagan won by a decisive 62 percent margin; Jimmy Carter's 27 percent total vote was the lowest since the defeat of John W. Davis in 1924. It was the fourth consecutive election in which Nevada voters supported the more conservative Republican nominee for the presidency. The Nevada presidential preference primary was a victim of the 1980 campaign since neither Reagan nor

---

[14]*Journal of the Assembly (Nevada)*, 60th sess. (1979), pp. 49–59; *Nevada State Journal*, May 29, 1979, p. 1, cols. 1–4; *Las Vegas Review-Journal*, May 29, 1979, p. 3A, cols. 1–9.

Carter gave it any attention; both had sufficient numbers of pledged delegates to insure nomination by the time the May 27 primary was scheduled. The 1981 legislature, recognizing the uselessness of the primary, abolished it.

Laxalt's victory in the Senate race was almost as impressive as Reagan's for the presidency. Although a heavy favorite to win the race, he agreed to debate his Democratic opponent, Mary Gojack. The debates gave Nevada voters an unusual opportunity to see and hear two candidates for a major office who disagreed upon just about every issue involved in the campaign: ERA, abortion, the Salt II Treaty, capital punishment, the Panama Canal Treaty, Gay rights, national health insurance, affirmative action, forced busing, and bilingual education. At their conclusion, it was clear that Laxalt had succeeded in demonstrating not only his own conservatism but Gojack's very liberal stance. Laxalt's personal charm and his close association with Ronald Reagan also were important in his easy victory; he carried every Nevada county and ended with a 58.5 percent margin of the state vote.

While Reagan and Laxalt were demonstrating that Republicans could win in Democratic Nevada, James Santini and the legislative candidates were proving that the state was still basically Democratic in its voting habits. Santini was returned to the House in an easy victory, 67.5 percent of the votes cast. In the legislature, the Democrats survived the election with the same party alignment as in 1978, a 15–5 margin in the senate and a 26–14 edge in the assembly.

Two interesting results emerged from the nine ballot propositions. Question no. 6, reducing the property tax, which passed by a large majority in 1978, was defeated by a combination of diverse groups and strong bipartisan opposition. At the same time an advisory referendum in eight counties to determine voter preference on whether the MX missile system should be placed in Nevada resulted in a resounding forty-one thousand against and just nineteen thousand for.[15]

[15]Eleanore Bushnell and Don W. Driggs, "Nevada: Business as Usual," *The Social Science Journal* 18 (October 1981): 65–76. The 1976 election in Nevada is summarized in the *Nevada Public Affairs Report,* Bureau of Government Research, vol. 15 (Reno: University of Nevada, February 1977), pp. 1–11. The 1978 Nevada election is covered in B. Oliver Walter, ed., *Politics in the West: The 1978 Elections* (Laramie, Wyo.: Institute for Policy Research, University of Wyoming, 1979), pp. 90–102.

Governor List's second biennial message, January 19, 1981, called for a tight budget and austerity programs for most institutions in reaction to the marked depressive effects the economic recession in the United States was having on Nevada's gambling industry. On June 4 the legislature ended its longest (137 days) and most costly ($2.8 million) session. It was an unusually conservative session with setbacks for women (the ERA was again defeated), minorities, and environmentalists. Its main achievement was passage of the governor's tax package, which cut an average 50 percent from the property tax and increased the sales tax from 3.5 percent to 5.75 percent. There was little opposition to the measure since legislators were well aware that some kind of property tax relief was necessary to keep Question no. 6 from resurfacing. Yet some outside opinion noted that the tax package posed certain risks since it shifted the revenue burden from the property tax to the sales tax and such a shift was predicated to some extent on the idea that Nevada's economy was recession proof and thus tourism, continuing strong, would bear the burden of the change. By the time the legislative session ended, however, the nation was obviously in a major recession and there were many signs that Nevada would not escape its effects.[16]

The 1982 election in Nevada was marked by substantial gains by the Republican party. They won two of the three national races contested and made inroads into state offices usually dominated by the Democrats. Although they lost the governorship, Republicans were elected attorney-general, treasurer, and controller, the largest number of state offices controlled by that party since 1930.

The most unusual outcome in the election was the upset victory of Chic Hecht, a Las Vegas businessman, over Howard Cannon, a veteran senator of twenty-four years. A lackadaisical campaign by Cannon and a closing media blitz by Hecht that emphasized the negative aspects of his opponent's senatorial record brought about Cannon's defeat. The victory of Republican Barbara Vucanovich over Mary Gojack for Nevada's new congressional seat, while not a major upset, was surprising because of its magnitude. Vucanovich like Hecht emphasized close ties with President Reagan and

[16]*Nevada State Journal,* January 23, 1981, p. 1, cols. 2–4; June 5, 1981, p. 1, col. 4; June 7, 1981, p. 1, cols. 1–4 and page 8A, cols. 1–4.

indicated she would support his policies. Her close ties with Senator Paul Laxalt also contributed to her landslide victory.

In the governor's contest, Attorney-General Richard Bryan's victory over the incumbent Republican, Robert List, was more substantial than expected. Although the tax question received major attention during the campaign, the key to List's defeat appears to have centered around the question of his leadership, particularly incidents that suggested the governor's office politicized the Gaming Control Board and the Gaming Commission. A bright spot for the Republicans on the state level was the substantial victory of Brian McKay over Democrat Mahlon Brown for the office of attorney-general.[17]

When the 1983 legislature adjourned on May 22, it could mark some solid if not spectacular achievements. The most difficult problem was the issue of taxes. There was general agreement that the state had to have additional revenue because the windfall from the sales tax became a victim of the recession. Yet there was little agreement as to how to obtain such increases. Governor Bryan's proposal appeared to be too complex, and in its place two tax versions emerged: an assembly bill that called for a 35 percent increase in property taxes, and a senate draft that would increase property taxes by 30 percent and include a 5 percent wholesale soft drink tax. It was estimated that the assembly measure would bring $8.4 million more than the senate bill, all of which would be earmarked for education. In spite of strong support from Bryan, what appeared to be an adamant stand by assembly leaders wilted under the stronger more mature leadership of the senate, and the senate bill was passed into law.

Although Governor Bryan was more successful in pushing other parts of his program in the legislature, he was handicapped somewhat by the fact that a number of important Senate leaders had not supported him in the primary election and continued to challenge his control of the Democratic party. Another challenge to his leadership came from Lieutenant Governor Robert Cashell, also a Democrat but soon to leave that party to join the Republicans. Bryan's greatest legislative success came with the establishment of two separate commissions, one to handle economic development

[17]*Reno Gazette-Journal*, November 4, 1982, p. 10C, cols. 1–4.

and the other to promote tourism. Even that victory was tempered by the fact that Cashell, obviously ambitious for the governor's job, was appointed chairman of each of the two new commissions.

The 1983 legislative session left no doubt that gambling interests were in control of the legislature. Their powerful lobbies brought them everything they wanted. They killed a lottery bill; prevented any significant increase in gambling taxes; severely limited tip earner's benefits, which would have added greatly to their overhead costs; obtained a law making gambling debts legally collectible; secured a measure that allowed offtrack, parimutual wagering and still another that allowed live telecasts of horse racing at sports books. Gambling interests also supported a broad-based property tax increase in order to take pressure from the passage of a possible gambling tax increase.[18]

A major event in Nevada in the early 1980s, certain to influence the Nevada political scene for years to come, was a wide-ranging investigation announced by the FBI on May 3, 1982. The investigation was in reality a sting operation into suspected high-level political corruption in the silver state. Evidence collected in this 18-month so-called YOBO investigation was placed before a federal grand jury, which began handing down indictments in October, 1982. By the end of 1983 two of those indicted, Joe McClelland, a Reno city councilman, and Floyd Lamb, state senator from Clark County, had been tried. McClelland was convicted in the summer of 1983 for accepting $3,750 in an alleged plot to win the approval of the city council of Reno for a new bank.[19] Lamb was tried on the first of two indictments against him in September, 1983, and found guilty of trying to extort $20,000 from former FBI undercover

[18]Ibid., May 29, 1983, p. 1C, cols. 2–4; *Nevada State Journal,* June 20, 1983, p. 1C, cols. 2–4.

[19]*Nevada State Journal,* March 30, 1983, p. 1A, cols. 2–4. The beginnings of the FBI operation are detailed in the *Nevada State Journal,* the *Las Vegas Sun,* and the *Las Vegas Review-Journal* from May 4, 1982, through most of the remainder of that month. Ultimately five defendants were convicted and sentenced as a result of the YOBO investigation. Besides Lamb and McClelland, Jack Petitti, a former Clark County commissioner was convicted March 13, 1984, sentenced to a six-month term and fined $15,000. Two other defendants, former state senator Gene Echols and former Clark County commissioner Woodrow Wilson, pleaded guilty to charges against them and were sentenced on August 3, 1984, to two-year suspended sentences. See the *Reno Gazette-Journal,* August 4, 1984, p. 2B, cols. 1–5, and August 7, 1984, p. 2B, col. 1.

agent Steve Rybar. Two weeks after his conviction, Lamb resigned from the Nevada State Senate, where he had served for twenty-six years.[20]

It was clear as the 1984 election approached that the Nevada Republican party was in a stronger position than it had been for decades. The 1982 election gave the party three of Nevada's four voices in Congress, three of the six major state offices (increased to four when Lieutenant Governor Cashell switched parties), and brought the party enough seats in the Nevada Assembly to mount a challenge to the Democratic leadership of that house.

Just as important to the prestige of the Republican party in Nevada was the restoration of the state's strong voice in the nation's capital under the leadership of the Republican senator, Paul Laxalt, lost since the death of Senator McCarran in 1954. Laxalt's powerful position in national affairs is not based—as was McCarran's, Pittman's, and Stewart's—on committee assignments or sponsorship of important national legislation. Instead it depends upon a remarkable bond of friendship between Laxalt and President Reagan, which has enabled the Nevada senator to assume a unique role as one of the presidential advisors and as general chairman of the president's 1984 reelection campaign. That development has brought some unique benefits to Nevada, not the least of which are the appointment of a number of Nevadans to important national posts in government and in the Republican party. Examples are Frank Fahrenkopf as chairman of the Republican Party National Committee, Robert Broadbent as an assistant secretary of the Interior, and Robert Horton as director of the Bureau of Mines. Laxalt's friendship with Reagan, his basic conservatism, and his own ability no doubt will continue to play an important role for Nevada in national politics.

Nevada generally agreed with the rest of the nation in the 1984 election by giving overwhelming support to President Reagan by a vote of 188,797 to 91,655 votes for Mondale. In addition, Nevada Republicans, although outnumbered in voter registration by the Democrats, gained major victories in important areas, insuring that the state's traditional conservatism would continue. The official

[20]*Nevada State Journal,* September 14, 1983, p. 1A, col. 5; *Las Vegas Sun,* September 27, 1983, p. 1, cols. 2–4.

voter turnout of 82.6 percent of those registered appeared to indicate a healthy interest by Nevadans in the political process. In actual fact, however, it represents only 47.8 percent of those eligible to vote.[21]

The contests for the two congressional seats created little excitement. Barbara Vucanovich, a strong Reagan supporter, was re-elected to represent congressional district no. 2, defeating her Democratic opponent, Andrew Barbano, by a nearly three-to-one margin (99,775 to 36,130). Democrat Harry Reid's victory over his Republican rival, Peggy Cavnar, was also impressive (73,242 to 55,391).

The only statewide contest was an interesting race for justice of the Nevada Supreme Court between the incumbent, Noel Manoukian, and Cliff Young, a former U.S. congressman and state senator. Young's campaign, based almost entirely on his allegation that Manoukian was a divisive influence on the court, apparently struck a responsive chord among Nevada voters. He won by a vote of 135,318 to 123,111, the first victory over an incumbent supreme court justice since 1950. Lilly Fong, the first person of Chinese background ever elected to a state office in Nevada, was defeated in her bid for a third term on the University of Nevada System Board of Regents.

More important to the immediate future of the state was the capture of the Nevada assembly by the Republican party. It marked the first time since 1971 that the Republicans had controlled that body, emerging from a 23–19 minority in 1983 to a 25–17 majority for the 1985 session. The Republican victory assured a conservative assembly and made almost impossible the passage of any meaningful tax increase. The Republicans also strengthened their position in the state senate by reducing the 17–4 Democratic majority to 13–8. A key characteristic of the Republican surge in the Nevada legislature came from the great gains in Clark County, the traditional stronghold of Nevada Democrats.[22]

The new leadership in the assembly assured gaming interests a powerful role in the 1985 legislature since all of the power positions

[21]*Reno Gazette-Journal,* November 29, 1984, p. 1C, col. 3; November 15, 1984, p. 4C, col. 1; November 8, 1984, p. 1A, col. 1.

[22]Ibid., November 8, 1984, p. 1A, col. 2; p. 22A, col. 3; p. 1C, cols. 1–4; p. 2C, col. 1; November 29, 1984, p. 1C, cols. 1–3; November 11, 1984, p. 23A, col. 4.

in that body, speaker, majority leader, and chairmanships of the important committees, went to Republican members of the assembly who had received the top or "Green" rating on a chart that had surfaced months earlier. The chart, prepared by gaming lobbyists, reflected the position of Nevada legislators in relation to their voting records on gaming-oriented legislation, "Green" indicating the most favorable rating.[23]

The 1985 Nevada legislative session came to a close June 4, 1985, after the most expensive, the second longest, and one of the most bitter meetings in its history. Any accomplishments of the session were clouded in its closing days by the action of the Republican-dominated assembly in voting retroactive pay to state employees and university personnel but refusing it to public school teachers. One news article labeled the action "mean-spirited" and a punishment of the teachers for not endorsing Republicans in the 1984 election. The assembly vote refusing the bonus to public school teachers appeared even more repulsive when the legislature at the same time voted elected officials a 19 percent increase in salary.[24] Although senate Republicans repudiated the action of their assembly counterparts and the senate restored the bonus for teachers, the episode was not likely to be forgotten and the Republican party appeared the certain victim of the ill-advised action.

The teacher-bonus quarrel was only one of a number of actions that led some observers to label the 1985 session the worst in recent history and one of the most politicized. Yet it was almost inevitable that politics would be involved in nearly every legislative action, given the ingredients present at the time: a Democratic governor, obviously hoping for a second term; an ambitious Republican lieutenant governor waiting in the wings; a Democratic senate and a Republican-dominated assembly.[25] In spite of the political atmosphere, Governor Bryan's program was generally approved because it was conservative, modest, and realistic. The changes in his budget made by the legislature were minor. His biggest disappointment was the reduction of special education funding by $5.3 million. In

---

[23] Ibid., November 11, 1984, p. 23A, col. 1.

[24] Ibid., June 4, 1985, p. 9A, col. 1 (editorial); June 5, 1985, p. 1A, cols. 2–5; *Las Vegas Sun*, June 9, 1985, p. 1A, cols. 2–5 (editorial).

[25] *Reno Gazette-Journal*, June 5, 1985, p. 1C, cols. 2–5.

addition his suggested one-year "cooling-off" law for former gaming authorities was shelved, the "sunset" law on soft drinks was allowed to expire, and his attempt to get a gaming fee to fund additional gaming agents failed.[26]

Again, the gaming industry was the big winner. Like mining and railroad interests before it, gaming dominated the state's economy and also dominated the 1985 legislature. It showed its legislative muscle by getting most of its legislative program passed into law and by stopping those measures it opposed. Thus the industry was able not only to block Senator Mello's attempt to raise gaming taxes and the governor's plan to fund new control agents from an assessment against casinos but to reduce its own taxes. It accomplished the latter by laws that made it possible to deduct the value of cars, mink coats, or other giveaways from taxable gross revenues and by the exemption of certain gratuities, service charges, and entertainment from the casinos entertainment tax. The industry once again was able to help block a proposal for a lottery.[27]

If gaming was the major winner, labor was a big loser. Although it successfully fought off the so-called fire-at-will proposal, it could not prevent the passage of laws providing for lie detector tests, for three-way insurance, and worst of all, a measure that limited picketing during a strike.

Legislators succeeded in holding off any major tax increase, but reality forced them to approve a number of laws that raised fees and taxes. The largest increase tied together a one-cent-per-gallon fuel tax, a three-dollar increase in vehicle registration, and various trucking fees, to provide an estimated $13.8 million annually for highway repairs. The state property tax was increased three cents to cover medical bills for the poor.[28]

Although it was a session where special interests dominated and the legislators appeared indifferent to the general public, the 1985 legislature may be remembered more positively for its actions in trying to improve education, to protect children, and to halt spiraling health costs.[29] Like most of its predecessors, however, it was a catch-up legislature, and many of the so-called accomplish-

[26]Ibid., June 5, 1985, p. 1C, cols. 2–5.
[27]Ibid., June 3, 1985, p. 2C, cols. 1–5; June 6, 1985, p. 21A, col. 1.
[28]Ibid., June 5, 1985, p. 1C, col. 4.
[29]Ibid., June 9, 1985, p. 2C, col. 1 (opinion); June 10, 1985, p. 1C, cols. 2–5.

ments of the session, for example in education, came because legislators had failed to take action earlier. Opinion polls taken after the session showed that Governor Bryan had gained strength but his potential opponent in 1986, Bob Cashell, lost some political support during the session.

The growing political power of the gaming industry, so clearly in evidence in the 1983 and 1985 legislative sessions, poses fundamental problems to the state of Nevada and its people, and in a different way, to the gambling industry itself. Unlike agriculture and mining, for example, legal gambling in Nevada is not a basic industry but a priviledged one, existing because the people through their state legislature voted it into existence. Its pressure on legislators and other elected officials has increased proportionately with the increased dominance of the industry in the state's economy. Today that power is so great that it brings into question the ability of the state of Nevada to control it. The problem also imposes obligations on the gambling industry to police itself in the interest of the state and its people.

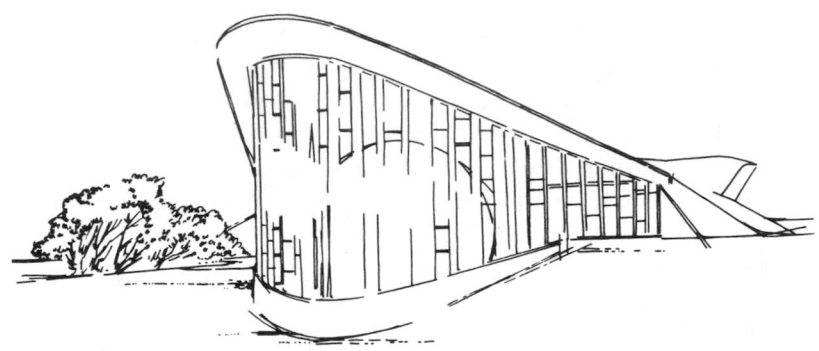

CHAPTER 17

A Social and Cultural Appraisal

CONGRESS CREATED NEVADA with little foreknowledge of the resource base necessary to sustain economic growth, cultural life, and a political society enjoying the privileges of sovereignty. Technological innovation in the form of mining and processing techniques enabled the quick exploitation of the Comstock lode and the extension of railroad transportation through the state. Both of those events held out the promise that Nevada could sustain itself as a mining society and as an exporter of stock on the hoof to faraway markets.

Although the mining technology of the nineteenth century provided the dynamism of early Nevada, the technology alone without a continuing rich ore base could not sustain Nevada life after the Comstock ore body played out. Again at the beginning of the twentieth century, new discoveries of gold and silver brightened the state's fortunes, along with copper mines in White Pine County. Although the copper endured long after the Tonopah and Gold-field mines, the state still awaited newer technologies to tap resources yet unpredictable for Nevada's future prosperity. Those came in the form of automobiles, vast interstate highway systems, the construction of Hoover Dam, air-conditioning for desert casinos, sophisticated air transportation, and extensive media advertising to build new industries based upon tourism and gambling in the far reaches of Nevada's deserts. They provided Nevada the wherewithal to build a population base within its impoverished borders.

From the beginning the Great Basin provided its people with a marginal economic life. Congress further complicated the picture by dividing the basin into two states, leaving the rugged mountains and playas to the west of the Salt Lake mostly to Nevada. The aversion of Congress and the mining population to Mormonism at midcentury promoted Congress's determination to create another state to share the lands of the Great Basin, splitting the western portion of the Great Basin from the Mormon territory. That was a geographic absurdity (although a political necessity) that most Nevadans have long celebrated for social and religious reasons. At the same time, Nevada eventually paid dearly for that division by a transient society, the uncertainties of the boom and bust mining economy, and the lack of a cultural cohesion other than the quick pursuit of wealth. The unapologetic pursuit of wealth and the quest for lady luck at the gambling tables ultimately provided Nevada with its twentieth-century bonanza and some would say also confirmed the wisdom of detaching the western lands of the Great Basin from the Mormon commonwealth.

Although Nevada's society has undergone vast changes since the days of the Comstock, a certain continuity is evident between its original mining frontier and the gambling-based society of the late twentieth century. The two eras on the surface, however, appear quite different. Mining developed in isolated desert areas spawning rude, dusty towns that soon collapsed into ghostly ruins. Not a single town based on mining went on to develop the stability and prosperity of Reno or Las Vegas. Those two urban centers of Nevada originally drew their prosperity from transcontinental transportation—serving as supply towns to distant mining areas and as centers for local stock raising. Las Vegas and Reno finally tapped a source of commercial wealth quite undreamed of when the state legalized casino gambling during the decade of the Great Depression.

In the two decades between the world wars Nevada chose to open itself on an official and public basis to types of naughty fun that were banned for social reasons in other states. Nevada laid the foundations for a society and economy that were not just a continuation of the past tradition of frontier permissiveness. Rather Nevada developed commercially, on an urban (and some would even say industrial) basis, what had once been considered vices characteristic of an isolated male frontier society. That industrialization process can be typically seen in the modern press's treatment of what Nevadans now commonly call the gaming industry in the state.

What have been the social and cultural accomplishments of a society that has existed under admittedly strained circumstances, from the mining frontier to the gambling mecca of the late twentieth century? The glamor associated with modern Nevada hides a society with the worst alcoholism rate in the nation and a suicide rate double the national average; a society first in violent crime, first in divorce, and attractive to hoodlums of all kinds, particularly underworld figures.[1]

As early as the 1920s Anne Martin, the state's progressive crusader for women's rights, deplored the deterioration of Nevada's society. Since statehood in 1864 it had become "the ugly duckling" and "weak sister" in the family of states. By the 1920s, except for the copper towns, most of Nevada's mining prosperity had come and gone, leaving only a doubtful future in the hands of the state's rangelands agriculture. Unfortunately, contended Martin, the monopolization of water resources by large stock operators prevented the growth of a democracy of small farmers in Nevada, further condemning it to political bosses and the rotten borough image of the previous century. Nevada's mining, ranch hand, and railroad worker society was made of men living without benefit of

---

[1] Neal R. Peirce and Jerry Hagstrom, *The Book of America: Inside 50 States Today* (New York: W. W. Norton, 1983), pp. 703–13; *Reno Gazette-Journal*, November 6, 1983.

home and family. Here the saloon and the brothel became the main symbols of popular entertainment and social discourse. Assessing the progress of the state for *The Nation* magazine in 1922, Martin concluded that the state's population remained small, mostly male, poor, and transient.[2] Such a population was hardly a viable base upon which to build a livable society concerned with good government, the arts, literature, and the values of family life. Nevada's poverty and declining population (down from 81,874 in 1910 to 77,407 in 1920) reflected the poverty of resources that its desert and sagebrush expanses had come to represent after the failure of the mining camps.

Still most agreed that Nevada offered great potential if the state could find a stable economic base. Other western states had similar problems, but Nevada's were more urgent. During the enthusiasm for irrigation and the reclamation of arid lands at the beginning of the century in western America, many people, including Francis G. Newlands of Nevada, felt that the answer to Nevada's instability was the growth of agriculture based on irrigation to replace the economy based on mining. In part, Martin was complaining over the failure of that dream by the 1920s and what that failure meant in terms of education, democratic politics, and the general health and quality of life in Nevada.

Ironically, growth and stability ultimately came to Nevada in the form of some of the very vices that Martin and other reformers abhorred. What kind of society has been built upon the urbanization and industrialization of what had once been seen as the not very admirable pastimes of a mining and rural ranching society? How have the press, education, churches, fraternal organizations, and human rights fared in such a society from the nineteenth-century mining frontier to the gambling frontier of the late twentieth century? Those are legitimate questions to ask of a modern state that has taken a road to economic growth that most states have shunned to protect themselves from the excesses of gambling, drinking, divorce, and even legalized prostitution.

[2]Anne Martin, "Nevada: Beautiful Desert of Buried Hopes," *The Nation* 115 (July 26, 1922): 89–92.

THE MEDIA AND EDUCATION

The journalistic tradition in the territory and early statehood period was rich with the names of the *Territorial Enterprise:* Mark Twain, Wells Drury, and Dan DeQuille. Gold Hill, situated next to Virginia City on the Comstock, boasted of the *Gold Hill News* and an editor, Alf Doten, who left a careful diary of late-nineteenth-century Nevada life that is a valuable source for theater and social history. The press in other mining communities thrived and died with the fleeting fortunes of mining life. Some of the more prominent newspapers in those communities in the nineteenth century were the *Eureka Sentinel,* the *Daily Inland Empire* of Hamilton, the *Pioche Record,* and after the turn of the century, the *Tonopah Bonanza,* the *Goldfield News,* and the *White Pine News.* The large number of newspapers in Nevada, upward of five hundred, in comparison to its small population reflects the high hopes of the state's communities, the relatively small amount of capital needed for small presses, and the importance attached to newspapers in the decades before radio and television communication.

By the late twentieth century, the principal newspapers of Las Vegas and Reno dominated journalism in the state. The huge nationally owned Gannett Company bought the two Reno newspapers and consolidated the morning and evening papers into the *Gazette-Journal* in 1983. The paper's new style of publication emulated in format Gannett's nationally circulated newspaper *U.S.A. Today.* In the south the *Las Vegas Sun* and the *Las Vegas Review Journal* served the most populous area of the state. Las Vegas became one of the most competitive newspaper towns in the nation, with the editor, Herman (Hank) Greenspun, imprinting his personality on the *Sun* to an extent unusual in an age of increasingly indistinguishable papers.

One newspaper outside of the state has played an important role in Nevada affairs from its home base in Sacramento. The *Sacramento Bee* in the 1930s investigated the failure of the Wingfield banks at a time when it would have been difficult for the Nevada press to reveal inadequacies in the state's supervision of Wingfield's banking practices. In the 1980s a dispute occurred with Nevada's powerful senator Paul Laxalt, when the *Bee* accused a casino once under the ownership of the Laxalt family of skimming winnings to avoid taxation.

Commercial radio arrived in Nevada in 1928, but it was not until the 1970s that public FM radio established itself in Las Vegas and Reno. Las Vegas led the way in educational public television in the early 1970s and Reno followed in 1983 with a public channel operated from the University of Nevada–Reno campus. Although the public programs do not reach beyond the Reno and Las Vegas areas, they do serve the 85 percent of the state's population concentrated in those two urban centers.

In the nineteenth century the establishment of stable educational institutions in the shifting mining communities of Nevada was difficult. Nevada's frontier did not attract families who began communities but rather large numbers of single males. The transient nature of the population and the small number of children make education a minor theme in the state's history. From the beginning, the state constitution provided for the establishment of a system of public schools supported entirely by local property taxes. Except in the Comstock communities, that tax base was illusive. Private education attempted to fill some of the shortcomings of the public schools and sometimes asked for public aid to private schools. The Sierra Seminary in Carson City; St. Mary's and St. Joseph's on the Comstock, started by Father Patrick Manogue; and Bishop Whitaker's four-year Episcopal preparatory school for girls, in Reno, were all examples of early private educational efforts.

As the mining depression after 1880 eroded Nevada's economy and already sparse population, education also declined. In 1887 district attorneys were designated ex-officio county school officers, but their performance of their duties was lax. Not until after the turn of the century and the return of prosperity during the Progressive era were public school systems reformed, in the Reorganization Act of 1907. The act gave the state board of education more power, raised the standards for teachers, and provided an improved curriculum and better central supervision of rural schools. The increased population brought by World War II and the emergence of a more normal pattern of family life in the state brought an increase in the number of school-aged children. By 1955, through the means of a new sales tax, the state committed more resources to education. In addition, a study by the Peabody Foundation recommended that Nevada consolidate its over one hundred school districts into seventeen, along the boundary lines of existing counties. The implementation of that reform gave Nevada a consolidated modern school system financed from both state and local sources. By 1983–84, the average SAT scores for high school students in Nevada stood above the national average, with Washoe County schools leading the way, compensating for the below-average scores in Clark County, which suffered from many of the problems of inner city schools.[3]

After the state university was moved from Elko to Reno in 1885, higher education in the state was the sole province of the land grant school in Reno until the establishment of Nevada Southern University in 1959. Eventually renamed the University of Nevada–Las Vegas, the new university signaled a shift of population to the south. By 1969 the legislature along with help from Nevada's new resident, Howard Hughes, began funding a medical school in Reno and an extensive state-wide two-year community college system that eventually opened schools in Reno, Carson City, Elko, and Las Vegas. The Desert Research Institute, founded in 1960 "to promote all the research objectives of both campuses of the University of Nevada," became the fourth division of the university system by action of the board of regents in 1971. Private institutions of higher learning have not flourished in Nevada. The establishment of Old College in Reno in 1980 and an accompanying law school in 1982 sought to tap the new sources of private support for higher education in the state. Public monies for higher education remained scarce. For 1985–86 Nevada ranked forty-second among the states in its per capita support of higher education and forty-fifth in per capita ability to pay. Nevada ranked lowest among the thirteen western states in the percentage of population completing four years of college. The figures ranged from the low of 14.4 percent (Nevada) to a high of 23 percent (Colorado) of the population with a college degree. These figures present a continuing challenge to higher education in Nevada.[4]

---

[3]William R. Eadington, Glendell W. Atkinson, and James H. Frey, *Observations on the Quality of Life in Nevada: A Comparison of Recent Ranking Studies as They Relate to Nevada and Its Metropolitan Areas* (Reno: University of Nevada, 1984), p. 15.

[4]*Chronicle of Higher Education*, October 30, 1985; *Nevada Statistical Abstract, 1983–84* (Carson City: Governor's Office of Community Service, 1984), p. 145.

CHURCHES AND FRATERNAL ORGANIZATIONS

The churches were also bearers of culture in the state. Before the lure of gold and mineral riches, the Mormons came to the remote western and southern reaches of the Great Basin to trade with the overland migration and to secure those lands for the Mormons. But the return of the Mormons to Salt Lake City in 1857 for the Defense of Zion during the Mormon war, and the subsequent discovery of the Comstock lode, ended Mormon influence in the western portions of the Great Basin. With the arrival of a new mining population came the clergy of more mainstream religious denominations. The Catholics and Methodists established pastorates in the Carson Valley in 1858 and 1859. Those two denominations along with Episcopalians were the major religious groups on the Comstock. Baptists and Presbyterians were not numerous until the post-1900 mining boom in precious metals and copper. A black congregation maintained a Baptist church at Virginia City from 1863 to 1866. Congregationalists and Lutherans established churches in the state before 1900. The Chinese established joss houses, or temples of worship, and a Jewish Protective Society was formed in Reno, with a permanent Hebrew congregation in Eureka, Nevada, by 1876.[5] Church membership, never great in the raucous mining camps, reflected the patterns of ethnic immigration to the state.

The censuses of 1870 and 1880 show Nevada to have a greater percentage of foreign born inhabitants than any other state. In his innovative work on Nevada immigrants, Professor Wilbur S. Shepperson believes European immigrants found in Nevada an unstable, fluid society.[6] The lack of an established societal structure made it easy for immigrants to improve their economic level. With no dominant social group to compete with or break into, the Nevada immigrants, be they Irish, Italian, Slav, Greek, or Basque, found avenues to opportunity fairly uncomplicated by the established social structures that prevailed in more settled areas. The Chinese found a different situation, for they met with the persistent racial

[5]John P. Marschall, "Jews in Nevada: 1850–1900," *Journal of the West* 23 (January 1984): 62–72.
[6]Wilbur S. Shepperson, *Restless Strangers: Nevada's Immigrants and Their Interpreters* (Reno: University of Nevada Press, 1970).

discrimination that was widespread on the Pacific Coast. European immigrant cultures were not directly under attack in the indifferent atmosphere of frontier Nevada and therefore their reaction did not display the defensiveness apparent in the fanatical devotion to the institutions and culture of their homeland that are apparent elsewhere. Consequently no extensive parochial school systems emerged. In any event this would have been difficult to maintain in the transient community life. Although a society constantly on the move offered an openness to the newcomer, it also offered no substance, no values or structure other than the harried quest for fortune. Questions of religion, ethnic background, even personal morality could not be the vital issues in such a culture because there was no solid, enduring society to make those judgments.

Newcomers to Nevada found little social structure, but they did find a situation open to their own creation. If that happened to be the building of personal wealth and loyalty to family traditions, there were few nay sayers to question those goals or suggest they might not be compatible with the welfare of the community. For the immigrant that meant little turmoil involved in the Americanization process. Divorce, boxing contests, prostitution, and ultimately gambling and mafioso influence, all seem to reflect the easy relationships in Nevada life. All might have conflicted at one time with good societal values, but when there was no influential "good society," there could be little conflict or restraint upon practices frowned upon in other states.

The compatibility of Nevada's Catholic immigrant population and homegrown Protestants can be seen in the appeal of Masonry to Protestants and Catholics alike in the state. Many times Italian immigrants brought with them an anticlericalism that placed them in the ranks of American Masonry for a time. It was not unusual to see Nevada's Irish Catholic politician, Pat McCarran, joining in Masonic festivities as he won votes across all ethnic lines.[7]

In 1926 the total church membership in Nevada was 19,769 in a

---

[7]James S. Olson, "Pioneer Catholicism in Eastern and Southern Nevada, 1864–1931," *Nevada Historical Society Quarterly* 26 (Fall 1983): 159–71; Alice Frances Trout, "Religious Development in Nevada," *Nevada Historical Society Papers* (1917): 149; Albin J. Cofone, "Themes in the Italian Settlement of Nevada," *Nevada Historical Society Quarterly* 25 (Summer 1983): 120; Jerome E. Edwards, *Pat McCarran: Political Boss of Nevada* (Reno: University of Nevada Press, 1982), p. 194.

population of approximately 85,000, or less than 25 percent. That was substantially less than the 40 percent national average. The four largest denominations in Nevada according to those figures were the Roman Catholics (8,477), Latter-Day Saints (4,889), Episcopalians (2,933), and Methodists (1,084). Both the Catholics and the Mormons have continued to be the dominant religious groups in Nevada. By 1985 Mormons in Nevada numbered 66,964, mostly concentrated in Clark County and southern Nevada. Catholics continued as the largest denomination with 164,000 members in a state whose population would reach one million by 1986.

Male fraternal organizations offered camaraderie, community service, and even life insurance for members. The Masons, the Odd Fellows, and the Knights of Pythias provided their members with insurance policies, death benefits to orphaned children and the widowed who might be left penniless after a disaster in the industrializing and accident-prone mines of the state. Often the fraternal and benevolent organizations reflected the needs of a particular ethnic group, such as the German Turnverein of Virginia City, the Ancient Order of Hibernians, the Irish American Benevolent Association, the Italian Benevolent Association, and the Jewish Benevolent Association. Some organizations grew out of a particular common experience, such as the Grand Army of the Republic, for those who fought in the Civil War.

The development of religious, fraternal, and educational institutions on the Comstock set the pattern for their development in the many other boom camps of that era and even for those that followed in the twentieth century, since the state, from the standpoint of population, communication, and transportation was still a frontier area when Tonopah was discovered in 1900. A number of fraternal organizations that had been comparatively unknown on the Comstock, such as the Benevolent and Protective Order of Elks, the Fraternal Order of Eagles, the Knights of Columbus, the United Ancient Order of Druids, and the Brotherhood of American Yeomen, became quite active during the Tonopah-Goldfield and Ely booms. Reflective of the changing immigrant pattern in Nevada were the many Greek and Serbian societies formed in the boom camps that developed after 1900.

LIBRARIES

In the isolated mining camps of Nevada access to information from the outside world was essential. Newspapers alone could not fill the demand in the age before instant electronic communication. Libraries and reading rooms sponsored by fraternal organizations, churches, or labor unions served the appetites for reading matter on the Comstock and in other mining communities. The Oddfellows and Masonic lodges had established libraries on the Comstock by 1866, and by 1877 the Miners' Union provided the largest library facility in Virginia City. Although by 1895 the legislature officially encouraged public libraries in Nevada, it provided no support during the years of depression. The Reno Library Association formed shortly thereafter, but not until 1903, with the support of the Carnegie Foundation, did Reno have regular library service. After the turn of the century in the new mining camps to the south in Tonopah and Goldfield and east in the Ely copper mining district new reading clubs came into existence but no publicly supported library system. The University of Nevada Library, the state library at Carson City, and the Nevada Historical Society organized in 1904 in Reno held the major collections in the years between the Comstock boom and the 1920s.

The legislature did not move into the business of encouraging counties to support libraries until 1927 when it authorized county commissions to set aside fifteen hundred dollars annually for the support of county libraries. Some county libraries appeared and in 1931 the Andrew Carnegie Library in Reno became the Washoe County Library. Increased local, state, and federal aid to libraries after the Great Depression and World War II brought public libraries to all but four of Nevada's seventeen counties by 1970. The contributions of the Max C. Fleischmann Foundation in the 1960s and the 1970s brought libraries to all counties and replaced others by 1980. The Nevada Library Association was officially incorporated in 1963 to promote library service in the state. On occasion it cooperated with the state's America Civil Liberty Union in fighting attempts at censorship by various groups and legislative actions.

CREATIVITY IN THE ARTS

Nevada in the late twentieth century moved toward a population of nearly a million people, away from a pattern of sparse population divided by immense distances of basin and range. It also became one of the most urban states in the nation. Nearly 87 percent of its population lived in the urban areas of Reno–Sparks–Carson City and especially Las Vegas, which were themselves separated by over four hundred miles of sage, sand, and mountains. The stability of this new population growth in both the north and the south grew in part from the migration to the sunny West and from the success of gaming-tourism. The state was finally reaching a population that could sustain the institutions associated with the creative arts. In the palmy days of the Comstock, Virginia City could boast of literary, dramatic, and musical performances equal to any comparable western city. But beyond that brief twenty-year period, the scattered small towns of Nevada provided few opportunities for the development of artistic achievement except the entertainment found in the saloons, dance halls, and red-light districts.

Before World War II, literary efforts were the state's most prominent contributions to the arts. Most often the literary figures were not Nevadans but commentators making observations as they traveled into the country of mines, desert mountains, and endless sage and sun. Probably the earliest literary work about the area that became Nevada was Henry deGroot's seventeen-page pamphlet, *Sketches of the Washoe Silver Mines,* published in San Franciso in 1860. The literary quality of magazine writer J. Ross Browne is much better. Browne visited the Comstock in 1860 and wrote a series of articles that were first published in *Harper's Monthly* magazine (January, 1861) as "A Peep at Washoe." He enlarged upon that story in *Crusoe's Island* (1864) and reported on a second trip in 1863 in *Adventures in the Apache Country* (1868). The two accounts constitute a remarkable record of the early Comstock period, offering an unusual opportunity to contrast a major mining boom at its inception with the later development of an urban setting.

Mark Twain attracts the most attention as a literary figure of early Nevada. His brief stay in Nevada from 1861 to 1864 provided the material for *Roughing It* (1872). It has been called the best literary work of the period, but some consider it tedious and burdened with humor that does not always have a universal appeal. Twain also comments on his Nevada experiences in his *Autobiography,* published posthumously in 1913.

Much of the enduring literature of the Comstock was historical and descriptive. William Wright (under the pseudonym of Dan De Quille) produced the *Big Bonanza* (1876), and Eliot Lord's *Comstock Mining and Miners* appeared in 1883. The first history of the state was a subscription, or "mug" volume, *History of Nevada* (1881), edited by Myron Angel. Several other mug histories were published between 1900 and the 1930s, but the state's small population made books about Nevada history unprofitable. That did not prevent Herbert H. Bancroft from including a history of Nevada in his multivolume state histories in 1890. Effie Mona Mack's *Nevada: A History of the State from the Earliest Times through the Civil War* (1936) was the first to be written by a professionally trained academic historian. Treatments of the wider scope of the state's history, however, did not draw a good deal of interest even after World War II. More narrow facets of the state's history attracted historians and adventure writers.

Apart from the journalists, only a handful of Nevada authors gained national or even regional prominence during the Comstock era. Women authors were among the best known. Sarah Winnemucca Hopkins, daughter of the Paiute chief Winnemucca, wrote *Life among the Piutes: Their Wrongs and Claims* (1883), which appealed to the Indian reform movement of the decade. Ella Clark Mighels produced works on Nevada-California themes, including *The Little Mountain Princess* (1880) and *Story of the Files* (1893). Mary McNair Mathews in *Ten Years in Nevada; or, Life on the Pacific Coast* brought a narrow and judgmental eye to Comstock life. John Franklin Swift contributed a long, subtly critical novel *Robert Greathouse* (1878), set in the fashionable society of Virginia City. Charles C. Goodwin emerges as another Comstock writer in his novels *The Comstock Club* (1892) and the *Wedge of Gold* (1893), and his uncritical reminiscence, *As I Remember Them* (1913).

Poetry was a popular genre in the Comstock period. Feelings about the mountains, the loneliness of the desert, the Indians, and the mining boom found their way into verse in books, pamphlets, and newspapers. Rollin Daggett, who became editor of the *Territorial Enterprise* in 1874 and served one term as congressman

(1870–81) was one of the better-known Comstock poets. His most famous work, "My New Year's Guests," honored the builders of the West. Another journalist, Sam P. Davis, who began his career on the Comstock and ended it after the turn of the century in Carson City, received regional acclaim for his poem "The Lure of the Sage-brush."

In the first two decades of the new century several Nevada writers produced locally notable work in fiction. Miriam Michelson wrote *The Madigans* (1904); the most successful novel of Philip Verill Mighels was *The Furnace of Gold* (1909); the most important woman writer of the decade was Ada Meacham Strobridge, *In Miner's Mirage Land* (1904), *Loom of the Desert* (1907), and *Land of Purple Shadows* (1909). Sam P. Davis gained nationwide recognition for his short story "The First Piano in Camp" (1919). The next decades saw the emergence of the Reno divorce novel and casino novels centered in Las Vegas.[8]

Nevada themes have been used by a number of nationally prominent authors: by B. M. Bower in nine books published between 1929 and 1939; by Harry Sinclair Drago, a sometime Nevadan who wrote several works between 1922 and 1940 on Nevada subjects, particularly sheep and the Basque sheepherders (one of his better-known novels is *Following the Grass*, 1924); by James M. Cain in *Past All Dishonor* (1946); Octavus Roy Cohen in *Borrasca* (1953); Vardis Fisher in *City of Illusion* (1941); Zola Ross in *Bonanza Queen* (1949), *Tonopah Lady* (1950), and *Reno Crescent* (1941); George Stewart in *Sheep Rock* (1951), and popular writer Louis L'Amour in *Comstock* (1980).

Undoubtedly the most important Nevada writers since 1940 are Walter Van Tilburg Clark and Robert Laxalt. Critics have ranked Clark's *The Ox-Bow Incident* (1940) among the best western novels ever written. Two other novels, *The City of Trembling Leaves* (1945) and *The Track of the Cat* (1949), and a collection of short stories, *The Watchful Gods and Other Stories* (1951), assured Clark an important place among twentieth-century American fiction writers. Robert Laxalt won national attention with the publication in 1957 of *Sweet Promised Land*, a tribute to his Basque immigrant father. His second

[8]Ann Ronald, "Reno: Myth, Mystique, or Madness?" *Halcyon: A Journal of the Humanities* (1979): pp. 87–101.

work, *Man in a Wheatfield* (1964), was also well received and his more recent *In a Hundred Graves* (1973) returned to Basque immigrant themes.

Other midcentury authors writing on Nevada subjects include Nora L. Bowman, in *Only the Mountains Remain* (1958); Robert Lloyd Pruett, *Scarf Cloud* (1947); Charles O. Ryan, *Nine Miles from Dead Horse Wells* (1959); Walter C. Wilson, *Oneness Trail* (1959); and Sessions Wheeler, *Pauite* (1965). Modern cowboy themes have been addressed by Owen Ulph in the *Fiddleback* (1983) and *The Leather Throne* (1985). Ulph's contributions can be seen as part of a regional acceleration of writing on state, folk, and environmental themes. New York–based writer John McPhee addressed the unusual geological and environmental heritage of the state in *Basin and Range* (1981). Great Basin Indian themes were treated in Feral Egan's *Sand in the Whirlwind* (1973); Gae Whitney Canfield's biography of Sarah Winnemucca, *Sarah Winnemucca of the Northern Paiutes* (1983); and Thomas Sanchez's, *Rabbit Boss* (1973).

In the performing arts, local literary and dramatic societies in many towns offered entertainment and an outlet for artistic expression. Both theater and opera groups regularly appeared in Virginia City's Piper's Opera House during the Comstock's heyday. Productions of Shakespeare by touring companies from the East and San Francisco also drew large crowds in the mining frontier.

Most of the indigenous art of the boom camps was of the "saloon" variety, and collectors have removed much of it from the state, although a few primitive landscapes painted during the state's early years are held by the Nevada State Historical Society. More typical of the period are the intricate wood engravings, wrought-iron work, and stained glass windows of the Comstock mansions and churches, and the elaborate wood, granite, and marble memorials in the old cemeteries found in many abandoned mining towns.

The landscape itself in Nevada, with its subtle colors of sagebrush and desert and its opaque mountains, offered challenging subjects for artistic interpretation and description. As early as 1881, C. B. McClellum depicted the beginning of Reno as a mere bridge across the Truckee River. Beyond this pioneer art little can be said of such endeavors in Nevada. The University of Nevada, with few students and a constant lack of funds, did little to encourage artistic development. An instructor in freehand drawing was employed in

1905, but a separate art department was not formed until after World War I and it remained a one-person department until World War II. Only with the expansion of the department under the chairmanship of Craig Sheppard in the 1950s and the establishment of the Las Vegas campus was the university in a position to draw in artistic talent and offer it opportunities for expression and development.

Under New Deal programs in the 1930s the Works Progress Administration (WPA) employed artists to paint pictures and murals for public buildings, usually on historical and economic themes. Under the same program Robert Caples did a series of charcoal sketches of the Paiute Indians that have been celebrated for their sensitivity. He was perhaps the first Nevada artist of more than local stature. German immigrant Hans Meyer-Kassel also falls into the ranks of Nevada artists, but he came to the state in the 1930s with an already established reputation.

Since the 1950s the increasing numbers of professional and amateur artists in the state have organized cooperatives to market their works. Many new galleries have been opened, especially in Las Vegas and Reno. It has become increasingly fashionable for artists to exhibit their work in libraries, department stores, banks, professional offices, and even in hotels and casinos. The work of the Nevada Art League in the 1960s eventually led to the establishment of the Sierra Nevada Arts Foundation in Reno. In the early 1960s the Allied Arts Council of Las Vegas was formed to strengthen communication between the media and the arts. In addition the council has sponsored a number of special projects such as Dance Week, James Joyce week, choreographers workshops, Artists and Business workshops, a series of Art-A-Fairs, Jazz Month, and art festivals. Its very attractive magazine *Arts Alive* enjoys wide circulation. The city of Las Vegas employs a cultural affairs administrator and spent an estimated $600,000 in 1984 for the direct support of the arts. Although the activities in both Las Vegas and Reno have not made the cities into national cultural centers, they have improved the quantity and quality of cultural events available to the citizens of Nevada's two urban areas. Those cultural events are often well-hidden secrets to most outsiders, who see and hear little about Nevada except through the eyes of highly charged and superficial entertainment publicists.

The history of music in Nevada is as uneven as that of art and drama. The peculiar entertainment facilities of modern Las Vegas and Reno have created a lively fund of specialized musical and sometimes theatrical talent that generally expands the cultural fare of both cities. In the nineteenth century the sparse population on the mining frontier made the barroom piano rather than the formal concert the chief form of musical entertainment. But professional musical troupes did visit the larger and richer mining communities. The churches and especially the public school programs provided the music productions that entertained Nevadans. The Comstock era did produce two well-known musicians who spent part of their lives in the state and have been eagerly claimed by Nevadans as their own: Emma Wixom, known professionally as Emma Nevada, and Richard Jose, a native of Cornwall. The depression following the decline of the Comstock stopped the flow of musical entertainers to Nevada towns, and although a revival took place during the Tonopah-Goldfield boom, it lasted only as long as those camps were at their height. An amusing incident involving musicians is told by Mrs. Hugh Brown in her reminiscence *Lady in Boomtown* (1968). Mrs. Brown, who grew up in San Francisco society, decided to hold a formal tea in her home in the rough mining camp of Tonopah. She found that the only musicians she could hire were those from the red-light district.

In modern Las Vegas considerable strides have been made in encouraging musical dance productions. The formation of the Nevada Dance Theatre began in the 1970s under the direction of Vassilli Sulich. Drawing dancers from the Las Vegas strip, it developed in a few years into one of the ten leading ballet groups in the United States. The talented composer, pianist, and conductor Virko Baley founded the Las Vegas Symphony Orchestra and the Las Vegas Chamber Players. On the opera scene, Baley also began the Opera Theatre of Nevada, which aspires to become a full-fledged opera company. The Children's Theatre Association in 1980 named the Rainbow Company children's theater group the best new children's theater in the United States.

In Reno, the Nevada Opera Guild productions under the direction of Ted Puffer have attracted regional and national attention since 1967. The Community Concert series began in Reno in 1935 as did the Reno Little Theater. By the 1980s the Nevada

Repertory Company, the Space Theater and the Proscenium Players of Carson City offered live theater to northern Nevadans. The Reno Philharmonic Orchestra, Ron Daniels conductor, was organized in 1969 by Gregory Stone with musicians from the university, the clubs, and the community. Other musical efforts in Reno include the Reno Chamber Orchestra, conducted by Vahe Kochayan, the University of Nevada–Reno Symphonic Choir and the Concert Choir, conducted by Perry Jones, the Sierra Nevada Chorale, and the UNR Symphony Orchestra.

State government generally has not taken an active role in the promotion of Nevada's cultural development. In 1967 on the recommendation of Governor Laxalt the legislature established the Nevada State Council on the Arts to seek federal support from the National Endowment for the Arts for a variety of local programs. The first federal appropriations came in 1968 with a grant of $25,000 to the state council. Although Nevada ranked almost last among the states in its per capita support of the arts from state funding, the Nevada State Council on the Arts received $123,549 in 1985 for the year to underwrite artistic and dramatic events. This represents a considerable increase in state support, which began in 1974 with a $15,000 appropriation. The director of the Nevada State Council of the Arts, William L. Fox, estimated that combined annual state and federal appropriations for the arts could reach $1,000,000 by 1990.[9]

Similarly the Nevada State Humanities Committee began functioning in 1971 with grants from the National Endowment for the Humanities created by Congress in 1965 under the same act that created the Arts Endowment. The committee has funded programs of humanistic and social concern including a series of annual cowboy poetry conferences in Elko beginning in 1985. Nevada's small population made it a high per capita recipient of federal funds from this program. Since 1979 the committee has sponsored the annual publication of *Halcyon: A Journal of the Humanities,* which addresses questions of international, national, and state interest.

The state and county governments have been active in establishing museums with the help of the humanities committee and the

[9]William L. Fox to W. D. Rowley, October 25, 1985; *Neon: Newsletter for the Nevada State Council on the Arts* (Fall 1985).

federally supported State Historical Preservation Office. In 1979 the state legislature combined the Nevada State Museum and the Nevada Historical Society into the Department of Museums and History. By 1986 the department supervised the Nevada State Museum and the Nevada Railroad Museum, both in Carson City; the Nevada Historical Society and its museum in Reno; the Lost City Museum in Overton; and the Southern Nevada Museum and Historical Society in Las Vegas.

THE ENVIRONMENT

Clearly the state's interest in museums sprang partly from a desire to provide attractions beyond casinos for the state's all-important tourist industry. Outside of the artificial environments of museums and casinos exist the vast expanses of Nevada that have long offered recreation to the minds and bodies of residents and tourists alike. Hunters, fishermen, skiers, outdoor enthusiasts of all types have found in Nevada compelling opportunities for a variety of wilderness experiences that provide escape from the stress of urban life. Once dismissed as a barren and alien landscape, Nevada's sage deserts divided by rugged mountain ranges present a grandeur that overshadows the glitter of a Las Vegas or Reno.

State congressional representatives have shown increased attention to that aspect of Nevada's environment through their support of bills in the 1985 Congress to create hundreds of thousands of acres of wilderness areas in the state and even Nevada's first national park, in the Mt. Wheeler area of White Pine County. The proposals have come in spite of opposition from Nevada's powerful mining and livestock interests. The changing attitude toward Nevada's environment, from exploitation to preservation, can also be seen in the strident opposition from Nevada political leaders and especially Governor Richard Bryan in 1985 to the location of a permanent nuclear waste site in Nevada, despite the state's long acceptance of the nuclear testing site at Yucca Flat, Nevada. The governor argued that nuclear waste storage and tourism were incompatible and that Nevada had already done its fair share in shouldering the burdens imposed on the nation by the nuclear arms race and the development of nuclear power with its associated waste products.

DIVERSITY OF PEOPLES

Nevada's statehood and the development of its mineral resources in the late nineteenth century coincided with waves of new immigrants coming to the United States. By 1870 Nevada had the largest proportion of immigrants in its population than any other state. As late as 1910 nearly one-fourth of the state's population was foreign-born and it was not until 1950 that the percentage of foreign-born in the United States as a whole exceeded that of Nevada.[10] It is difficult to assess the social and cultural impact of this immigration, but it clearly left a mark on the state's educational, religious, and fraternal institutions. The languages and customs of the immigrant groups became an integral part of the state's heritage in place names, literature, music, dances, and festivals.

Although new immigrants generally found comfortable niches in Nevada life, some incidents show the rejection and difficult times experienced by many. In the so-called Charcoal Burners' War of 1879 in Eureka County, striking Italian charcoal suppliers were attacked, resulting in the death of five workers. Sometimes dismissed as a labor dispute, the event can be accurately described as an incident of violence against foreigners. In the White Pine copper mines in 1908 an attempt was made to deport a group of Greek workers from McGill in sealed railroad boxcars. They were released at Ely, but it was many years before Greeks and other East Europeans found acceptance.

By the end of World War II most prejudice against the new immigrants from Europe had disappeared, but where color was part of the issue of minorities acceptance was slower. During the Comstock era the Chinese suffered innumerable indignities and were the target of anti-Chinese riots. The decline in the Chinese population in the state after 1900 and the small numbers of Japanese immigrants coming into Nevada after the turn of the century virtually eliminated problems concerning Chinese and Japanese minority groups in the state. By 1963 the Nevada Equal Rights Commission noted that it could find no solid evidence of prejudice against either of the two Oriental groups.

The problems of the black minority in Nevada have persisted from the earliest days of statehood. The fur trade and overland trail

[10]See Appendix, table 1, pp. 404–5.

era brought some blacks into the Great Basin. Among them was Jim Beckwourth, a black mountain man, who settled temporarily in California. In 1851 he explored a cutoff from the Truckee River route that avoided the difficult Donner Pass and instead used a pass farther to the north that was named for him. The road through Beckwourth Pass became an important alternate route to California between 1851 and 1861.

Although blacks were not participants in the events leading to the formation of the territory and then the state, the Civil War period, when Nevada emerged as a political entity, was critical in setting forces in motion that would change the status of blacks in the states and the nation. Both the territory and the new state constitution of Nevada in 1864 reflected the dominant midnineteenth-century intention to exclude blacks from politics by designating only white men as suffrage holders. The territory prohibited nonwhites from giving evidence in criminal cases against whites and outlawed the cohabitation and intermarriage of the races. One of the few political leaders to oppose the discriminatory legislation was Territorial Governor James W. Nye, who argued, unsuccessfully, that such laws were "behind the Spirit of the Age." Yet blacks had to pay the poll tax required of all male residents (uncivilized Indians excepted). The 1865 legislature stipulated that separate public schools must be maintained for Mongolians, Indians, and Negroes. According to the report of the superintendent of instruction, a public school with twenty-nine nonwhite children operated in Storey County in 1866. Evidently maintaining separate schools proved too costly and the law was ignored between 1866 and 1872, when it was declared unconstitutional by the state supreme court.

Nevada's strong loyalty to the Republican party during the Reconstruction years forced it to modify many of the antiminority provisions in its laws and constitution by 1870. It stood in the forefront of states supporting the new Civil Rights Act of 1866 and the Fourteenth and Fifteenth amendments. But although the Nevada legislature supported the national Republican party in extending rights to blacks, it was reluctant to see those rights enforced locally. The legislature rejected a bill that would have repealed all state laws in conflict with the Civil Rights Act. Blacks did begin enjoying voting rights in Nevada in 1870 after Nevada in 1869 became the first state to ratify the Fifteenth Amendment. The white clause, however, was not removed from the state constitution until 1880, but by that time laws preventing blacks from serving on juries and testifying in court cases involving white persons had been repealed.

Blacks were only a handful of the total population in the state until after World War II. There were just 44 blacks in a population of 6,857 in 1860 and 134 in a population of 42,335 in 1900. More blacks entered Nevada during the booms of Tonopah, Goldfield, and Ely after 1900, but still the numbers were small compared to those of immigrant groups from Europe. During those years Nevada's Progressive senator, Francis G. Newlands, declared that the Fifteenth Amendment had been a mistake and should be repealed to remove blacks from the political process.[11] Since World War II the black population has increased at a much faster rate than the white. The 1960 census showed 13,484 blacks in a total population of 284,276, representing 4.7 percent compared to .3 percent in 1900. As significant as the increased total numbers was the concentration of blacks in Las Vegas, where they constituted 8.7 percent of the total population in 1960. The census figures for 1970 and 1980 show the continuation of that trend. In 1980 the state population grew to 800,493 with blacks numbering 51,203. Of that total 46,238 resided in Clark County, mainly in Las Vegas, North Las Vegas, and Henderson.

The struggle against discrimination took the form of a search for legislation to prevent individual businesses and realtors from practicing discrimination against blacks. In this difficult road, Nevada generally responded to national events rather than becoming a leader in abolishing discrimination in accommodations, employment, and housing. Restaurants and casinos often displayed signs "No colored trade solicited." Because of that and the actions of Nevada congressmen in defending states' rights against federal intervention because of their fear of interference with the gambling industry, Nevada had become known as the "Mississippi of the West" by the 1950s.[12] State civil rights legislation came before the

[11]William D. Rowley, "Francis G. Newlands: A Westerner's Search for a Progressive and White America," *Nevada Historical Society Quarterly* 17 (Summer 1974): 69–79.

[12]Elmer R. Rusco, "Good Time Coming?" *Black Nevadans in the Nineteenth Century* (Westport, Conn.: Greenwood Press, 1975), p. 211.

legislature in the 1959, 1961, and 1963 sessions with no results. But a Commission on the Equal Rights of Citizens with the power of subpoena was established to investigate civil rights in Hawthorne, Reno, and Las Vegas.

National and state political events in 1964 paved the way for successful civil rights action in the 1965 legislature. The assassination of President John F. Kennedy and dramatic actions by his successor, Lyndon B. Johnson, brought a sweeping national Civil Rights Act in July, 1964, which enlarged federal power to protect voting rights, opened access to public facilities to all races on an equal basis, made it possible for the federal government to speed up school desegregation, and ensured equal opportunities in unions and in businesses that employed over twenty-five people. Besides the favorable atmosphere created by the 1964 national legislation, a lobbying effort by Eddie Scott, Clyde Mathews, and Jim Anderson in the legislature helped the passage of state civil rights legislation in 1965. Also, Lieutenant Governor Paul Laxalt's close defeat by incumbent Senator Howard Cannon was attributed particularly to his poor showing among the black voters in Las Vegas. When the legislature met in January, 1965, Laxalt came out in favor of civil rights legislation, swinging many conservative Republican and Democratic legislators to its support. Attempts to gain a fair housing law were blocked in the 1969 legislature, but determined effort by Clark County's assemblyman and Nevada's first black legislator, Woodrow Wilson, and encouragement by Governor Mike O'Callaghan brought success in the 1971 legislature. A serious racial incident erupted in West Las Vegas on October 5, 1969, resulting in two deaths, many injuries, and some property damage. Blacks interviewed by reporters during and after the riot expressed strong dissatisfaction with housing, the lack of job opportunities, poor recreational facilities, police harassment, and the slow progress of integration in Las Vegas schools.

The latest waves of immigration into Nevada have come from Mexico and southeast Asia. In the 1980s people of Hispanic origin became the largest single minority in the state as the population explosion in Mexico spurred an illegal migration to the United States. They provided a ready labor source for the gaming-tourist industry as well as the ranches of rural Nevada. By 1985 it was clear that Hispanics had become increasingly dissatisfied with their role in

Nevada society and through their League of United Latin American Citizens (LULAC) Councils, a number of which had been established in the state, were seeking better educational programs, more opportunities for better paying jobs, and a wider representation politically. At the same time, Hispanics actively sought to keep their culture alive through Spanish-language newspapers, Spanish radio and television programs, and heritage celebrations. Increased health and educational expenditures by local governments to serve the new population caused some concern in the state, but generally employers enjoyed the new labor source and did little to cooperate with authorities in enforcing immigration laws.

On the other hand, Asian immigration was legal, growing largely out of a U.S. commitment to accept the dispossessed of Viet Nam after the American involvement in that country. Those refugees have found jobs in the tourist economy of Nevada—in casinos, hotels, and restaurants. Their children along with Hispanic children have made up the largest number enrolled in special English language classes offered by the public schools in federally backed programs.

Although present when Euro-Americans arrived in Nevada, the Indians of Nevada have often found themselves strangers in their own land. That has been particularly true after the urbanization of Nevada that occurred as a result of both the mining frontier and the growth of the later casino tourist industry. The Indians of Nevada lost a way of life that had evolved through centuries of adaptation to the hostile desert environment. The broader outline of this story repeated the pattern set by Euro-Americans from colonial times, and the solutions applied by the federal government were no more successful in Nevada than they were elsewhere.

The relationship of Nevada Indians to white society has been the dominant theme in state Indian history. Establishing Indian reservations, white encroachments on Indian lands, water rights, and finally the question of state or federal sovereignty on reservations have from time to time been major issues in Indian-white relations. Urban colonies have also been a feature of Nevada Indian life. These small urban reservations, dating from 1917, had hoped to break the isolation of Indian life in the state and promote assimilation. The federal government first recognized Indian reservations in the state when Frederick Dodge, the Indian agent for the western part of Utah Territory, recommended that two reservations be established for the northern Paiutes. In 1859 Dodge marked the boundaries for the Pyramid Lake and the Walker Lake (River) reservations. Over the years the federal government established additional reservations in northeastern White Pine County (Goshute), in Clark County (Moapa), in northeastern Humboldt County (Fort McDermit), in western Humboldt County (Summit Lake), in northern Elko County (Duck Valley and South Fork), in Nye County (Duckwater), in Churchill County (Fallon), in Lyon County (Yerington), and in Douglas County (Washoe).

With the establishment of ranches, mining communities, and commercial towns along the route of the transcontinental railroad, Nevada Indians worked as farm and ranch laborers, domestics, and unskilled laborers in the cities and on the railroads. Some tried ranching both on and outside of the reservation lands, but for the most part they lived on the periphery of white settlements. Although earlier most Indians did not live on reservations, that situation had changed by the late twentieth century. Of Nevada's 13,205 Indians (1.6 percent of the state's total population and the smallest minority group in the state), by 1982 7,799 lived on reservations or in urban Indian colonies.

The disruption of Indian life by the arrival of fur traders, travelers, and miners in the nineteenth century caused serious economic, social, and psychological dislocation for Great Basin Indians. In most instances their response was to survive by eking out a living on the edges of white society. Some sought solace in spiritual explanations of their fate and in the hope for better times to come. In the nineteenth century one such person was a northern Paiute by the name of Jack Wilson, the son of a Paiute medicine man, who grew up in a white family and community. Wilson drew upon Christian ideas and Paiute views of a spiritual world to revive the ghost dance ritual that promised union with the Indian ancestors of the recent past and a triumphant future for the Indian, overcoming the oppressions of white society. Wilson became known as the prophet Wovoka in the 1880s, and his teachings drew great attention among the Great Plains Indians, particularly the Sioux. The Sioux's determination to practice the ghose dance and the U.S. government's ban on the ceremonies eventually led to the infamous massacre at Wounded Knee, South Dakota, in 1890. The Wovoka and ghost dance phenomenon never reached such proportions among the Great Basin Indians, but Jack Wilson remains an important figure in Nevada Indian history because of his role in shaping a spiritual response to the disintegration of Indian life before the final onslaught of white society in the late nineteenth century.

Attempts by the federal government to solve the problems of the Indian were plagued by many of the same problems in Nevada as elsewhere in the nation. Reservation lands never provided an adequate economic base for Indian life nor did reservation Indians have the capital or skills required to move away from the self-defeating paternalism of the Bureau of Indian Affairs. Efforts at educating the Indians lacked direction and adequate funding for supplies and qualified instructors. A nonreservation boarding school was established south of Carson City in 1890. First called Clear Creek Indian School and then the Stewart Indian School, it provided instruction through the tenth grade with a mainly vocational curriculum. Not until 1932 did public school education become a possibility for reservation Indian children. The 1934 Indian Reorganization Act (IRA) placed the responsibility for the education of Indian children with the states. In Nevada the transferral was completed in 1947, when the Indian Education Division (Nevada) of the Bureau of Indian Affairs became part of the Nevada State Department of Education. By 1956 all Indian day schools became public schools.

Although Indians were granted full citizenship in 1924, ten years passed before Nevada tribes, under the IRA, began a slow but not always steady progress toward the assumption of a more active role in determining their own destiny. The Pyramid Lake Paiute Tribe, the Reno-Sparks Indian Colony, and the Washo Tribe of Nevada and California were legally incorporated in December, 1935, thenceforth to be governed by elected tribal councils. Other Indian groups in the state soon followed their lead.

Events since that time indicate that Nevada tribal groups have made some progress toward unity of action. A Students' Cooperative Trading Post, later known as Wa-Pai-Shone, Inc., was established to encourage Indian arts and crafts and market the products. In 1939 the first annual intertribal fairs were begun at Walker River Reservation, and the first Great Basin Indian Conference was held at Stewart in 1940. The organization of the United Paiutes and the Western Shoshone Nation, the establishment of the Inter-Tribal Indian Council of Nevada, the holding of the first Nevada Inter-Tribal Indian Conference at the University of Nevada in 1964, and the publication of numerous newsletters and the monthly newspaper the *Native Nevadan* testify to a growing desire among Nevada Indians to organize and apply political pressure to solve their problems. With their incorporation, the tribal councils also gained the ability to hire lawyers and bring suits in the courts, a giant step toward addressing many of their problems in the state.

Those problems continue to be considerable. Substandard housing has been attacked by government programs with some success, but for many years Indian colonies near Nevada towns were examples of some of the poorest housing facilities in the state. Poor land and the lack of water made agriculture virtually impossible on Nevada Indian reservations. With one of the most beautiful desert lakes in the world, the Pyramid Lake Indians found themselves in a losing battle against the Newlands irrigation project and the growth of the Reno-Sparks urban area for the precious waters of the Truckee River that feeds the lake. A series of court decisions in the 1970s defeated a concerted effort by the Department of the Interior on behalf of the Pyramid Lake Indians to redivide the waters of the Truckee in favor of the tribe. In 1985 Senator Laxalt introduced a bill in Congress that sought to effect a permanent solution to the Truckee River water controversy by granting the Pyramid Lake Paiutes certain financial advantages and a guaranteed lake level in return for opening the Stampede Reservoir waters for municipal and industrial use in Reno and Sparks. The measure seemed assured of passage when the Pyramid Lake Tribal Council gave its support. That action was nullified, however, by a later majority vote of tribal members opposing the bill and it seems unlikely that Congress will act on the measure in face of that opposition.[13]

Although the future of sport fishing at the lake remains questionable, plans continually emerge to develop casino gambling on the shores of the lake similar to Lake Tahoe's resorts. The question of gambling on Indian reservations has come to the fore with the beginning of bingo games on the Moapa Reservation in 1984. The

[13]*Reno Gazette-Journal*, September 1, 23, 24, and October 4, 1985.

Nevada Gaming Control Board wished to control the operations, but it cannot interfere with federal sovereignty over the reservations. The board's position is that such operations should be prohibited on Indian reservations especially in Nevada, where gambling is legalized and under the regulatory control of the state. If those enterprises continue on Indian reservations, contends the state, there will be no adequate supervision to prevent abuses. On the other hand, Indian leaders in Nevada and elsewhere oppose interference by state government. They believe that federal regulation of gambling, other than bingo, is the only alternative to prevent abuses that would arise from state regulation and at the same time allow the Indians the economic benefits that would come from casino gambling.[14]

Nevada Indians in recent years made another intrusion into the realm of federal-state relations when a number of so-called smoke shops were established on Indian lands. These outlets, usually with easy access to major highways, sell cigarettes free from heavy state taxes and as a result have proved quite successful.

Bingo-type gambling and smoke shops are the latest in the many efforts by Nevada Indians to develop a self-help philosophy and thus overcome the legacy of paternalism imposed by the Bureau of Indian Affairs. Many efforts in the 1950s and 1970s to develop economic programs, using Economic Development grants, attempted to establish arts and crafts distribution centers, motels, restaurants, and ranches. Not all have been successful since they faced the sometimes hostile inertia of traditional Indian communities and the everpresent stinginess of the Nevada environment. The option of gambling represents a triumph over environment: it does not rest upon the exploitation of a specific natural resource but rather upon the whims and foibles of humanity.

The struggle of Nevada's Indian peoples to live in the land of their fathers suggests that there is throughout the history of this strange land a haunting feeling of promises unfulfilled, aptly expressed by Walter Van Tilburg Clark in his faintly ironic poem "Sweet Promised Land of Nevada." Clark tells how the Lord labored five and one-half days to complete the rest of the world, leaving Nevada

[14]*Reno Gazette-Journal,* October 17, 1985, p. 4C, col. 1.

until the last because he wanted to make it the best of his creation. Unfortunately, he could not finish Nevada before his day of rest:

> So the hills are in rows and they're piled up too high;
> They are colder than death and they trouble the sky
> Though at night you may freeze, yet at noon you will fry
> In the unfinished land of Nevada.
>
> So the lakes are all dry and the rivers all flow
> Underground and no green thing will venture to grow,
> And all the sweet breezes that come there to blow
> Will tear off your hair in Nevada.
>
> So, with rivers and lakes that forever run dry,
> The Lord's only creatures that can multiply
> Are the rattler, the jack and the little bar-fly,
> The little bar-fly of Nevada.
>
> So, this is the land that old Moses shall see;
> So, this is the land of the vine and the trees;
> So, this is the land for My children and Me
> The sweet promised land of Nevada. O-o-o-oh—The sweet
>   promised land of Nevada.[15]

[15]Walter Van Tilburg Clark, *City of Trembling Leaves* (New York: Random House, 1945), pp. 552–65. Used by permission.

Appendix

GOVERNORS OF NEVADA

Territory

James W. Nye	1861–64

State

H. G. Blasdel, Republican	1864–70
L. R. Bradley, Democrat	1871–78
John H. Kinkead, Republican	1879–82
Jewett W. Adams, Democrat	1883–86
C. C. Stevenson, Republican	1887–90
Frank Bell, Republican, acting governor	1890
R. K. Colcord, Republican	1891–94
John E. Jones, Silver	1895–96
Reinhold Sadler, Silver, acting governor	1896–98
governor	1899–1902
John Sparks, Silver-Democrat	1903–1908
Denver S. Dickerson, Silver-Democrat, acting governor	1908–10
Tasker L. Oddie, Republican	1911–14
Emmet D. Boyle, Democrat	1915–22
James G. Scrugham, Democrat	1923–26
Fred B. Balzar, Republican	1927–34
Morley Griswold, Republican, acting governor	1934
Richard Kirman, Sr., Democrat	1935–38
E. P. Carville, Democrat	1939–45
Vail M. Pittman, Democrat	1945–50
Charles H. Russell, Republican	1951–58
Grant Sawyer, Democrat	1959–66
Paul Laxalt, Republican	1967–70
Mike O'Callaghan, Democrat	1971–78
Robert List, Republican	1979–82
Richard Bryan, Democrat	1983–

UNITED STATES SENATORS AND REPRESENTATIVES FROM NEVADA

Senators

James W. Nye, Republican, 1865–73
William M. Stewart, Republican, 1865–75
John P. Jones, Republican and Silver, 1873–1903
William Sharon, Republican, 1875–81
James G. Fair, Democrat, 1881–87
William M. Stewart, Republican and Silver, 1887–1905
Francis G. Newlands, Democrat, 1903–17
George S. Nixon, Republican, 1905–12
W. A. Massey, Republican, 1912–13
Key Pittman, Democrat, 1913–40
Charles B. Henderson, Democrat, 1918–21
Tasker L. Oddie, Republican, 1921–33
Patrick A. McCarran, Democrat, 1933–54
Berkeley L. Bunker, Democrat, 1940–43
James G. Scrugham, Democrat, 1943–45
E. P. Carville, Democrat, 1945–47
George W. Malone, Republican, 1947–59
Ernest S. Brown, Republican, 1954
Alan Bible, Democrat, 1954–74
Howard W. Cannon, Democrat, 1959–82
Paul Laxalt, Republican, 1975–
Chic Hecht, Republican, 1983–

Representatives

H. C. Worthington, Republican, 1864–65
Delos R. Ashley, Republican, 1865–69
Thomas Fitch, Republican, 1869–71
Charles W. Kendall, Democrat, 1871–75
William Woodburn, Republican, 1875–77
Thomas Wren, Republican, 1877–79
Rollin Daggett, Republican, 1879–81
George W. Cassidy, Democrat, 1881–85
William Woodburn, Republican, 1885–89
Horace F. Bartine, Republican, 1889–93
Francis G. Newlands, Silver and Silver-Democrat, 1893–1903
Clarence Van Duzer, Silver-Democrat, 1903–07
George A. Bartlett, Silver-Democrat and Democrat, 1907–11
E. E. Roberts, Republican, 1911–19

Charles R. Evans, Democrat, 1919–21
Samuel S. Arentz, Republican, 1921–23
Charles L. Richards, Democrat, 1923–25
Samuel S. Arentz, Republican, 1925–33
James G. Scrugham, Democrat, 1933–42
Maurice J. Sullivan, Democrat, 1943–44
Berkeley L. Bunker, Democrat, 1945–46
Charles H. Russell, Republican, 1947–48
Walter S. Baring, Democrat, 1949–52
Clifton Young, Republican, 1953–56
Walter S. Baring, Democrat, 1957–72
David Towell, Republican, 1973–74
James Santini, Democrat, 1975–82
Harry Reid, Democrat, 1982–
Barbara Vucanovich, Republican, 1982–

TABLE 1

Comparative Population Statistics, 1860–1980

	1860[a]	1861[b]	1870	1880	1890	1900	1910	1920	1930	1940	1950	1960	1970	1980[e]
Total Nevada Population	6,857	16,347	42,491	62,266	47,355	42,335	81,875	77,407	91,058	110,247	160,083	285,278	488,738	800,493
% Increase from Previous Census, Nevada			519.7	46.5	−23.9	−10.6	93.4	−5.5	17.6	21.1	45.2	78.2	71.3	63.8
% Increase from Previous Census, U.S.			22.6	30.2	25.5	21.0	21.0	15.0	16.2	7.3	14.5	18.5	13.3	11.4
Virginia City	2,345	2,704	7,048	10,917	8,511	2,695	2,244	1,200	590	1,009	603	515		
Goldfield							4,838[c]	1,558	692	554	336	184		
Reno			1,035	1,302	3,563	4,500	10,867	12,016	18,529	21,317	32,497	51,470	72,863	100,756
% Increase from Previous Census, Reno				22.7	173.6	26.3	141.5	10.5	54.2	15.0	52.4	58.4	41.6	38.3
Las Vegas							945	2,304	5,165	8,422	24,624	64,405	125,787	164,674
% Increase from Previous Census, Las Vegas								143.8	124.2	63.1	192.4	161.6	95.3	30.9
% Rural Population, Nevada	100		83.4	68.9	66.2	83.0	83.7	80.3	62.2	60.7	47.5	35.1	19.1	14.7

TABLE 1—*Continued*

	1860	1861	1870	1880	1890	1900	1910	1920	1930	1940	1950	1960	1970	1980
% Urban Population, Nevada			16.6	31.1	33.8	17.0	16.3	19.7	37.8	39.3	52.5	64.9	80.9	85.3
Total Foreign-born Population, Nevada	2,064		18,801	25,653	14,706	10,093	19,691	16,003	15,095	11,041	11,413	13,133		
% Foreign-born, Nevada	30.1		44.5	41.2	31.0	23.8	24.1	20.7	16.6	10.0	6.6	4.6		
% Foreign-born, West						19.6	19.8	17.4	15.1	10.6	8.0	6.7		
% Foreign-born, U.S.						15.3	16.3	14.5	12.7	9.6	7.5	5.9		
Total White Population, Nevada	6,812		38,959	53,556	39,121	35,405	74,276	70,699	84,515	104,030	149,908	263,443	448,177	703,345
Total Non-white Population, Nevada	45		3,532	8,710	8,234	6,930	7,599	6,708	6,543	6,217	10,175	21,835	40,561	97,440
Black	45		357	488	242	134	513	346	516	664	4,302	13,484	27,762	51,203
Indian			23[d]	2,803	5,156	5,216	5,240	4,907	4,871	4,747	5,025	6,681	7,933	13,205
Chinese			3,143	5,416	2,833	1,352	927	689	483	286	281	572	955	2,979
Japanese				3	3	228	864	754	608	470	382	544	1,087	2,315
Filipino									47			280	817	4,064
Korean														2,055
Vietnam														1,124
Other							55	12	18	50	185	268	2,007	23,674

[a]The 1860 census covered Carson, Humboldt, and St. Mary's counties, Utah Territory.

[b]The 1861 special census covered the newly organized Nevada Territory. The 1870 increase for Nevada is based on the 1860 census.

[c]Conservative estimates indicated that Goldfield had a population well over 15,000 people in 1907 and 1908, making it Nevada's largest city in those years.

[d]Before the 1890 census no account was taken in the federal enumeration of Indians not taxed. Those taxed were reported as "civilized" Indians.

[e]The 1980 census reflects a rapid growth, also, of the Standard Metropolitan Statistical Areas (SMSA) for both Las Vegas (Clark County) and Reno (Washoe County). The Las Vegas SMSA in 1980 showed a total of 463,087 people and a percentage change of 69.5 from 1970. The Reno SMSA in 1980 showed a total of 193,623 people and a percentage change of 59.9 from 1970. Projections from various sources, including the U.S. Census Bureau, indicate a continued rapid growth of population, ranging from 1 million to 1,733,000 by the year 2000.

TABLE 2

MINERAL PRODUCTION, 1859–1984

Year	Gross Yield	Year	Gross Yield
1859	$ 257,000	1908	14,647,265
1860	1,000,000	1909	25,817,389
1861	2,500,000	1910	31,428,336
1862	6,000,000	1911	33,386,031
1863	12,500,000	1912	35,546,873
1864	16,000,000	1913	32,428,352
1865	16,507,728	1914	26,801,456
1866	13,454,831	1915	31,820,525
1867	15,742,464	1916	47,539,367
1868	13,056,906	1917	45,016,273
1869	39,272,687	1918	48,635,168
1870	17,087,752	1919	27,847,151
1871	20,111,671	1920	21,474,997
1872	23,896,402	1921	11,772,633
1873	32,640,677	1922	13,018,953
1874	30,321,705	1923	20,920,599
1875	35,290,308	1924	21,764,291
1876	45,272,839	1925	20,434,576
1877	46,671,870	1926	20,597,970
1878	30,919,653	1927	23,640,630
1879	16,943,257	1928	31,349,454
1880	11,882,786	1929	31,493,646
1881	8,681,223	1930	16,275,086
1882	7,718,015	1931	9,407,836
1883	7,617,173	1932	4,283,635
1884	6,832,607	1933	4,612,585
1885	7,324,062	1934	9,035,285
1886	6,944,965	1936	25,778,266
1887	7,187,895	1937	34,039,068
1888	8,828,010	1938	24,945,376
1889	8,095,123	1939	31,379,445
1890	6,895,512	1940	43,864,107
1891	5,559,469	1941	46,341,000
1892	3,464,502	1942	46,313,000
1893	3,001,678	1943	56,525,000
1894	1,995,830	1944	51,800,000
1895	2,104,550	1945	31,307,000
1896	3,480,102	1946	35,454,000
1897	3,628,190	1947	42,639,000
1898	3,141,090	1948	42,503,000
1899	2,716,096	1949	37,373,000
1900	2,632,923	1950	38,499,000
1901	2,754,736	1951	57,074,000
1902	3,366,607	1952	64,231,000
1903	2,832,821	1953	73,523,000
1904	4,489,960	1954	89,138,000
1905	6,412,825	1955	113,220,000
1906	13,276,269	1956	126,681,000
1907	16,328,232	1957	86,023,000

Year	Gross Yield	Year	Gross Yield
1958	68,854,000	1972	181,000,000
1959	66,093,000	1973	201,813,000
1960	80,335,000	1974	257,876,000
1961	81,533,000	1975	258,390,000
1962	83,074,000	1976	233,683,000
1963	85,441,000	1977	263,816,000
1964	85,137,000	1978	250,408,000
1965	99,966,000	1979	252,497,000
1966	112,637,000	1980	390,798,000
1967	90,883,000	1981	522,549,000
1968	114,034,000	1982	543,800,000[a]
1969	168,295,000	1983	640,119,000
1970	186,349,000	1984	671,273,000[b]
1971	160,143,000		

Sources: Mackay School of Mines, University of Nevada–Reno, and the Nevada Bureau of Mines and Geology, Reno, Nevada.

[a] The production figures for 1982 do not mirror the depression in Nevada's mining industry, which saw the closing of dozens of properties, mainly because gold production dominated the industry and continued its steady rise.

[b] The 1984 figure is an estimate based on the 1984 preliminary yield.

TABLE 3

Gambling Revenues, 1946–85

	Statewide Total	% Change	Clark County	% Change	Douglas County	% Change	Washoe County	% Change
1946	$21,575,472							
1947	30,988,497	43.6						
1948	35,880,854	12.2						
1949	38,973,744	8.6						
1950	39,489,703	1.3						
1951	48,237,930	22.1						
1952	55,235,560	14.5						
1953	73,935,930	33.8						
1954	84,354,058	14.0						
1955	94,368,588	11.8						
1956	115,643,000	22.5						
1957	131,910,000	14.1						
1958	145,037,000	10.0						
1959	172,184,000	18.7						
1960	197,358,000	14.6						
1961	209,382,000	6.1						
1962	229,615,000	9.7						
1963	252,045,000	9.8						
1964	286,329,000	13.6						
1965	301,245,000	5.2						
1966	336,828,000	11.8						
1967	362,584,000	7.6						
1968	406,013,000	12.0						
1969	477,114,000	17.5						
1970	550,058,000	15.3						

TABLE 3—*Continued*

	Statewide Total	% Change	Clark County	% Change	Douglas County	% Change	Washoe County	% Change
1971	608,047,000	10.5	$388,814,000		$75,365,000		$124,989,000	
1972	678,326,000	11.6	433,651,000	11.5	86,655,000	15.0	135,564,000	8.5
1973	804,287,000	18.6	534,005,000	23.1	94,563,000	9.1	147,122,000	8.5
1974	936,283,000	16.4	636,274,000	19.2	103,271,000	9.2	162,660,000	10.6
1975	1,065,392,000	13.8	729,956,000	14.7	116,684,000	13.0	180,053,000	10.7
1976	1,186,211,000	11.3	799,913,000	9.58	131,134,000	12.4	211,669,000	17.6
1977	1,380,565,000	16.4	927,184,000	15.9	147,760,000	12.7	251,819,000	19.0
1978	1,670,313,000	21.0	1,125,559,000	21.4	172,840,000	17.0	311,323,000	23.6
1979	1,979,067,000	18.5	1,325,916,000	17.8	191,516,000	10.8	400,069,000	28.5
1980	2,274,067,000	14.9	1,534,225,000	15.7	204,647,000	6.9	446,405,000	11.6
1981	2,463,184,000	8.3	1,646,355,000	7.3	231,351,000	13.0	483,320,000	8.3
1982	2,599,694,000	5.5	1,737,346,000	5.5	237,035,000	2.5	517,631,000	7.1
1983	2,683,592,000	3.2	1,786,425,000	2.8	232,642,000	-1.9	547,376,000	5.7
1984	2,990,000,000	11.5	1,950,000,000	9.1	279,000,000	20.3	628,000,000	14.6
1985	3,200,000,000	7.9	2,100,000,000	10.4	288,600,000	3.5	642,600,000	2.3

NOTE: Figures are for gross revenue for fiscal years ending June 30. Years from 1946 through 1955 are from the reports of the Nevada Gaming Commission. Those from 1956 through 1984 are furnished courtesy of Stuart E. Curtis, economic research analyst for the Nevada Gaming Control Board. Although gross revenues, statewide, have never declined, the rate of growth reflects state and national political and economic policies and actions. Particularly revealing are the percentage changes from 18.5 in fiscal 1979 to 3.2 in fiscal 1983, mirroring the national recession of those years. It is quite obvious Nevada's gambling industry is not recession proof as believed by some. The 1984–85 statistics reveal the dramatic effect of the end of the national depression. The -1.9 percentage change in 1983 for Douglas County reflects the closure of Highway 50 from Placerville, and the 1984 percentage increase of 20.3, the effect of its reopening.

Sources

GENERAL

Materials for study and writing of Nevada history are scattered widely. This is of no particular significance, except in the case of manuscripts, where travel to the individual depository is necessary. In recent years a number of interested institutions have made efforts to keep Nevada documents in the state and make it the center of historical research on Nevada. Some success has been achieved: within a radius of 30 miles from Reno, researchers have access to four important depositories whose combined resources provide many of the basic sources necessary for the study of Nevada history. These are the Nevada State Historical Society and the Special Collections Division of the University of Nevada Library, both at Reno, and Nevada Archives and the Nevada State Library, both at Carson City.

The Nevada State Historical Society includes in its collection a substantial number of emigrant diaries, old newspapers, and manuscript sources, of which the most important is the William Morris Stewart collection of letters and other papers. Another potentially important collection is the George A. Wingfield Papers, whose use is restricted for fifty years, and the Tasker L. Oddie Papers, which have not yet been cataloged.

The Special Collections Division of the University of Nevada Library under the direction of Robert D. Armstrong has become in recent years a major source for Nevada history. Besides the good holdings of secondary materials on Nevada and the West, it now has an excellent collection of newspapers on microfilm and has as its ultimate objective the microfilming of all extant Nevada newspapers. The basic collection of microfilm was made possible through a cooperative effort of the Nevada State Library, the University of Nevada libraries at Reno and Las Vegas, and the Desert Research Institute, located in Reno. Besides the secondary works and its newspaper collection, the Special Collections Division also has many important manuscript collections. The Alf Doten collection, which includes a diary by this important Comstock journalist with continuous entries from 1849 to 1903, edited by Walter Von Tilburg Clark, is scheduled for publication in 1972. Mammoth collections, mainly business records, of the Virginia and Truckee Railroad and of the Consolidated-Virginia Mining Company and a small collection of Grant Smith Papers are also available in this depository. The papers of many state politicians have been added in recent years, including Vail Pittman, Charles Russell, George A. Bartlett, and others. The Oral History Project, under the direction of Mary E. Glass, has added a number of important memoirs to the collection including, among others, those of Colonel Thomas W. Miller, former governor Charles A. Russell, and the multimillionaire Norman Biltz. Some of the oral histories are presently under restricted usage. An attempt is also being made to obtain copies for the university library of all theses and dissertations written at other universities on Nevada subjects. The Nevada State Library has the basic secondary work and the best collection of newspapers, including those microfilmed under the direction of the Desert Research Institute. The state library is also the depository for all published official documents of the state government.

The Nevada Archives has been in operation for only a few years but has established an important manuscript collection. Theoretically, all the official letters and papers of all state officials are to be housed here, as well as all manuscript sources of Nevada government. Selected papers of the late Senator Patrick McCarran are also located here. Unfortunately, many papers of early officials have been lost or misplaced. Consequently, the more important collections are those of the governors since 1900.

Outside Nevada, the best collection of sources on the history of the state are located in the Bancroft Library at Berkeley, for some of the best manuscript sources from Nevada and many other western states found their way to that depository. Some of the more important Nevada collections in the Bancroft are the H. M. Yerington Papers, part of the Grant H. Smith Papers, and the Anne Martin Papers, besides literally hundreds of smaller manuscript items dealing with Nevada's early history. There is also an extensive collection of Goldfield mining records. The Bancroft Library has more manuscript items about Nevada than all of the Nevada repositories combined.

Another important California repository is the Henry E. Huntington Library at San Marino, housing the John W. North Papers, the Tasker L. Oddie Papers, and a sizable collection of the John P. Jones Papers. Other California repositories that should not be neglected are the California State Library, the California Historical Society, the Society of California Pioneers, the Federal Records Center at San Francisco, and the University of California at Los Angeles.

A number of Utah repositories, such as the Utah State Archives, the Utah State Historical Society, Brigham Young University, and the Office of the Church Historian in Salt Lake City, are important, particularly for the history of Carson County, Utah Territory, and for the Nevada territorial period and the early years of statehood.

Outside the West, the most important repositories are: Yale University Library, where numerous Nevada manuscript collections are located, particularly the Francis G. Newlands collection; the Library of Congress, which has the very important Key Pittman collection; and the National Archives. The latter two repositories no doubt have many more Nevada items than have been used by scholars, since their Nevada material has not been completely cataloged.

Unfortunately, many manuscript collections are divided, with parts in two or even three repositories. Good examples are the John P. Jones materials, with sizable collections at the Henry E. Huntington Library and the University of California at Los Angeles Library and a smaller collection at the Society of California Pioneers; the Tasker L. Oddie Papers, split between the Huntington Library and the Nevada State Historical Society; and the records of the Virginia and Truckee Railroad, which for some reason were divided between the Bancroft Library and the University of Nevada Library at Reno.

The University of Nevada at Las Vegas is developing a collection of materials on southern Nevada, with particular emphasis on gambling in the state. The library there, as a participant in the newspaper microfilming project mentioned above, has microfilm copies of most Nevada newspapers.

In 1967 the University of Nevada distributed mimeographed copies of *A Preliminary Union Catalog of Nevada Manuscripts*, compiled and edited by Robert D. Armstrong. This guide, long overdue, is indispensable in the search for Nevada materials. Also useful are two other guides: John G. Folkes, *Nevada Newspapers, a Bibliography: A Compilation of Nevada History, 1854–1964*, Nevada Studies in History and Political Science, no 6 (Carson City: University of Nevada Press, 1964); and Russell R. Elliott and Helen Poulton, *Writings on Nevada: A Selected Bibliography*, Nevada Studies in History and Political Science no 5 (Carson City: University of Nevada Press, 1963). The first catalogs Nevada newspapers and the second includes secondary works and important magazine articles. An excellent summary of sources for the study of Nevada history will be found in Robert D. Armstrong, "Sources for Nevada History: A Survey of Institutional Collections Outside the State," *Nevada Historical Society Quarterly* 14 (Fall 1971): 33–38.

Other than two junior high school texts, there is not a single history treating the state from its beginning to the present era. Certain phases of Nevada history have been covered very well, others satisfactorily, and many others, not at all. The so-called general histories of Nevada are, for the most part, "mug," or subscription, volumes, where basic publishing costs were met by those willing to pay for the privilege of having their pictures and/or biographical entries in the volumes. These histories are of uneven merit, from poor to excellent. By far the most useful is Myron Angel, editor, *History of Nevada, with Illustrations and Biographical Sketches of its Prominent Men and Pioneers* (Oakland, Calif.: Thompson & West, 1881). A reproduction with an introduction by David Myrick was published by Howell-North in 1958. The mass of detail and general accuracy make this volume indispensable for the early history of the state. One of its major weaknesses, the lack of an index, was corrected with the publication of Helen J. Poulton's *Index to Thompson and West's History of Nevada*, Bibliographical Series, no. 6 (Carson City: University of Nevada Press, 1966).

A second general history which covers the same basic material as Angel is Hubert Howe Bancroft, *History of Nevada, Colorado and Wyoming, 1540–1888* (San Francisco: The History Company, 1890). Published nine years after the Angel work, this volume is poorly organized and filled with minor errors, but it cannot be ignored as a source.

An example of mug history at its worst is the volume by Thomas Wren, editor, *A History of the State of Nevada, its Resources and People* (New York: Lewis Publishing Co., 1904). The book is a rehash of Angel to 1881, and little of importance was added for the period from that date to the date of publication.

Another subscription history of uneven merit which brings the story of Nevada to 1913 was edited by Sam Davis, *The History of Nevada*, 2 vols. (Reno, Nev.: Elms Publishing Co., 1913). Since the chapters were written by different authors, the quality is uneven; some are good, but others are inaccurate, badly organized, and nearly worthless for research purposes.

The latest of the mug histories is the work by James Scrugham, ed., *Nevada: A Narrative of the Conquest of a Frontier Land . . .* , 3 vols. (Chicago: American Historical Society, 1935), which gives the longest continuous coverage of any of the general histories. The emphasis is almost exclusively political for the period since the Comstock.

Effie Mona Mack's *Nevada: A History of the State from Earliest Times through the Civil War* (Glendale, Calif.: Arthur H. Clark, 1936), is the first general history of Nevada written by a professional historian and is the first to include an adequate bibliography. Unfortunately, it covers Nevada history only to 1878.

A readable, interpretative study of Nevada is Richard G. Lillard's *Desert Challenge: An Interpretation of Nevada* (New York: Knopf, 1942; paperback edition, Lincoln: University of Nebraska Press, Bison Books, 1965). The chronological coverage includes 1940, and although it treats many topics not found elsewhere it makes no pretense of being a comprehensive history of the state.

A recent work by Gilman M. Ostrander, *Nevada: the Great Rotten Borough, 1859–1964* (New York: Knopf, 1966), as the title suggests, is a political history of the state. It is not a comprehensive political history but a monograph to prove a thesis. As a result, the story is fairly full where sources were found to support the thesis. Where they were not available, great gaps occur in the historical background. Nevertheless, this is an important contribution since Professor Ostrander used a number of hitherto unused primary sources and succeeded in making some acute observations concerning the background of Nevada politics.

Two junior high school texts deserve mention. The first, *The Nevada Adventure,* by James W. Hulse, rev. ed. (Reno: University of Nevada Press, 1969), is a superbly written summary based on careful research. Although written for junior high school students and necessarily abbreviated, adult readers will find it the best available single-volume history of the state. The text by Effie Mona Mack and Byrd Sawyer, *Here is Nevada: A History of the State* (Sparks, Nev.: Western Printing & Publishing Co., 1965), is a new edition of their earlier volume, *Our State, Nevada.* This work, though not as well organized nor as readable as the Hulse volume, does include a mass of information about the state not included elsewhere.

Two works which are not, strictly speaking, historical works, are: *Nevada: A Guide to the Silver State* (Portland, Ore.: Binsford & Mart, 1940); and *Political History of Nevada,* 5th ed. (Carson City, Nev.: State Printing Office, 1965). The first, part of the Nevada Writer's Program, was under the general sponsorship of Jeanne E. Wier and edited by Sheila Rast. It is an invaluable tool particularly for the study of Nevada local history. The second is not a comprehensive history, although it does have an excellent account of the political development of the area from the period when it was part of Mexican territory to statehood, with excellent maps denoting the geographical changes. Its greatest contribution is its summary of each state general election since 1864 and each primary since 1910, and its convenient listings of state officials, including the composition of each legislature since 1864. The book is issued by the secretary of state, John Koontz; the research for the past few issues has been done by Art Palmer.

A number of unpublished M.A. theses directed by members of the University of Nevada history department and dealing with Nevada history are in the University of Nevada Library and constitute an important source. Of particular importance are: Dana Evans Balibrera, "Virginia City and the Immigrant" (1965); Lucile R. Berg, "A History of the Tonopah Area and Adjacent Region of Central Nevada, 1827–1941" (1942); Gary P. BeDunnah, "A History of the Chinese in Nevada, 1855–1904" (1966); Mary E. Glass, "The Deutschen of Douglas: The German Foundations of Douglas County, Nevada, 1856–1930" (1965); Gloria Griffen, "Early Exploration, Routes, and Trails in Nevāda" (1951); Nellie Shaw Harnar, "History of the Pyramid Lake Indians, 1852–1959" (1965); Orville Holderman, "Jewett W. Adams and W. N. McGill: Their Lives and Ranching Empire" (1963); James W. Hulse, "A History of Lincoln County, Nevada, 1864–1909" (1958); Buster L. King, "The History of Lander County" (1954); Jack L. Millinger, "Political History of Nevada, 1891–1900" (1959); Patricia Fee Olmstead, "The Nevada-California-Oregon Border Triangle: A Study in Sectional History" (1958); Frederick W. Reichman, "Early History of Eureka County, Nevada, 1863–1890" (1967); Allura Nason, "The Basques—Sheepmen of the West" (1964); John L. Schramel, "Honey Lake Valley, California, and Western Nevada: A Study in Sectional Development, 1850–1864" (1966); Shelton H. Short, "A History of the Nevada Livestock Industry Prior to 1900" (1965); Richard C. Sieber, "Nevada Politics during the Comstock Era" (1950); Philip D. Smith, Jr., "Nevada Volunteers in the Civil War" (1959); Rodney Smith, "Austin, Nevada, 1862–1881" (1963); Velva C. Trulove, "City Government in Nevada" (1950); George W. Umbenhaur, "Nevada County Government" (1951); Leon H. Van Doren, "Tasker L. Oddie in Nevada Politics, 1900–1914" (1960).

Documents from each level of government—national, state, and local—have been used extensively in the preparation of this book. United States government publications such as the reports of the Interstate Commerce Commission, the reports of the U.S. Bureau of the Mint, the U.S. Bureau of the Census, and the U.S. Office of Indian Affairs, bulletins and professional Papers of the U.S. Geological Survey, numerous congressional documents, and many miscellaneous publications were used.

Among the most important state of Nevada publications are the indispensable *Appendices to the Journals of Senate and Assembly* which incorporate the reports of all state officials, state commissions, and state boards. Publications of certain state agencies are of particular interest, such as the numerous research bulletins of the Nevada Legislative Counsel Bureau, the Papers and historical quarterlies issued by the Nevada State Historical Society, the papers (mostly anthropological) issued by the Nevada State Museum, and the *Nevada Highways and Parks* magazine, published quarterly by the Nevada State Department of Highways. In addition to the published national and state records, the unpublished records in a number of Nevada counties were used. These included such materials as mining locations, proceedings of the boards of county commissioners, proceedings of town boards, journals of births and deaths, and dozens of miscellaneous records from the offices of county clerk and county recorder. The county archives also include files of newspapers printed in the county.

Newspapers are some of the primary sources for local and state history. California and Nevada newspapers furnish the only guide to a continuous chronological record of Nevada's history, and this book could not have been written without them. Among other things they furnish the only guide to arguments for and against important legislation, since legislative debates are not officially recorded. Annual and historical editions often give us contemporary accounts of important events, thus filling in large gaps in the record. In addition, the newspapers, with their continuous coverage of local events, give the most direct social and cultural record available. Particularly on the mining frontier, the newspaper, with all its faults, is perhaps the most important social record available; because it is often the only record available, its political and economic coverage cannot be overlooked.

Sources used in the preparation of each chapter of the present study will be discussed in greater detail in the following pages.

CHAPTER 1

THE PHYSICAL ENVIRONMENT

The general geologic summary was taken mainly from two sources: Eliot Blackwelder, R. R. Miller, C. L. Hubbs, and Ernst Antevs, "The Great Basin, with Emphasis on Glacial and Postglacial Times," *University of Utah Bulletin* 38, no. 20 (1945); and Thomas B. Nolan, *The Basin and Range Province in Utah, Nevada and California*, U.S. Geological Survey Professional Papers, no. 197-D (Washington, D.C.: GPO, 1943). Still useful but somewhat dated are "Bibliography of Geologic Literature in Nevada," by Vincent P. Gianella, and "Bibliography of Geologic Maps of Nevada Areas," by Robert W. Prince, both contained in *University of Nevada Bulletin* 39, no. 6 (December 1945), Geology and Mining Series, no. 43. Readers interested in a more up-to-date and technical explanation of the geology of the basin range province should see John Keith Sales, "Structural Analysis of the Basin Range Province in Terms of Wrench Faulting" (Ph.D. diss., University of Nevada, Reno, 1966). For a more general summary of Pleistocene geology see Richard F. Flint, *Glacial and Pleistocene Geology* (New York: Wiley & Sons, 1957). A very readable and interesting chapter on Nevada's geologic past appears in Richard G. Lillard, *Desert Challenge: An Interpretation of Nevada* (New York: Knopf, 1942); paperback edition, Lincoln: University of Nebraska Press, Bison Books, 1966).

The geologic history of prehistoric Lake Lahontan has attracted attention widely from a variety of scientists including archeologists, geologists, and anthropologists, as well as from writers with less technical interests. The major problem over the years has been the dating of the origin, the high-level periods, and the disappearance of the lake. One of the earliest treatises on the geology of Lake Lahontan is still very useful and, according to present geologists, accurate in detail—the work by Israel Cook Russell, *Geological History of Lake Lahontan, a Quaternary Lake of Northwestern Nevada*, U.S. Geological Survey Monographs, vol. 11 (Washington, D.C.: GPO, 1885). Also useful but not as accurate is Arnold Hague and S. F. Emmons, "Descriptive Geology of the Fortieth Parallel," in *Report of the Geological Exploration of the Fortieth Parallel*, edited by Clarence King, 7 vols. (Washington, D.C.: GPO, 1870–80). Important work on the geology of Lake Lahontan was accomplished during the 1920s by Professor J. Claude Jones, but his dating of the lake has been generally discarded. His most important works are *The Geologic History of Lake Lahontan*, Carnegie Institution of Washington Publications, no. 352

(1925); and "Age of Lake Lahontan," *Geological Society of America Bulletin* 40 (September 30, 1929): 533–40. The best recent work on the geology of Lake Lahontan is Roger B. Morrison, *Lake Lahontan: Geology of Southern Carson Desert, Nevada*, U.S. Geological Survey Professional Paper no. 401 (Washington, D.C.: GPO, 1964). Challenging some of Morrison's results is the work by Wallace Broecker and Aaron Kaufman, "Radio-carbon Chronology of Lake Lahontan and Lake Bonneville II, Great Basin," *Geological Society of America Bulletin* 76 (1965): 537–66. A brief summary of the various datings can be found in H. M. Wormington and Dorothy Ellis, editors, *Pleistocene Studies in Southern Nevada*, Nevada State Museum Anthropological Papers, no. 13 (Carson City, 1967). Two recent popular articles on Nevada's ancient lakes are useful and well written: Samuel G. Houghton, "Pyramid Lake—An Ancient Remnant," *Nevada Highways and Parks* 27 (Winter 1967): 24–34; and Samuel G. Houghton, "Mono and Walker Lakes—A study in Contrasts," *Nevada Highways and Parks* 28 (Spring 1968): 8–16.

A great deal of research on earthquakes has been accomplished by staff members of the Mackay School of Mines. Their activity received a definite boost when a seismological laboratory was established by the school. The present director is Dr. Alan I. Ryall. A useful *Catalog of Nevada Earthquakes, 1852–1960*, prepared by David B. Slemmons, Austin E. Jones, and James I. Gimlett, was released recently in mimeograph form by the Mackay School of Mines. See also David B. Slemmons, "Pliocene and Quaternary Crustal Movements of the Basin-and-Range Province, USA," *Osaka City University Journal of Geoscience* 10 (March 1967): 91–103.

For Nevada's natural resources the following have proven useful: U.S. Geological Survey in collaboration with the Nevada Bureau of Mines, [Nevada's] *Mineral and Water Resources* (Washington, D.C.: GPO, 1964); and *Nevada: The Silver State* (Carson City, Nev.: State Department of Education, 1957); U.S., Department of the Interior, Office of Information, *Natural Resources of Nevada* (Washington, DC.: GPO, 1964).

Additional sources used for this chapter are William D. Billings, *Nevada Trees*, University of Nevada Agricultural Extension Service Bulletin no. 94, 2d ed. (March 1954); U.S., Department of Agriculture, *Yearbook of Agriculture, Soils, and Men* (Washington, D.C.: GPO, 1938); U.S., Weather Bureau, *Climates of the States: Nevada*, Soil Survery Staff (Washington, D.C.: GPO, 1960); U.S., Department of Agriculture, *Soil Classification: A Comprehensive System*, 7th Approximation, Soil Survey Staff, Soil Conservation Service (Washington, D.C.: GPO, 1960); U.S., Department of Agriculture, *Supplement to Soil Classification System*, Soil Conservation Service (Washington, D.C.; GPO, 1968):

CHAPTER 2

BEFORE THE WHITE MAN

Useful in obtaining background for this chapter were three works: Jesse Jennings and Edward Norbeck, eds., *Pre-historic Man in the New World* (Chicago: University of Chicago Press, 1964); Richard R. Pourade, editor, *Ancient Hunters of the Far West* (San Diego, Calif.: Union-Tribune Publishing Co., 1966); and H. M. Wormington, *Ancient Man in North America*, 4th ed., Denver Museum of Natural History, Popular Series no. 4 (Denver, 1957).

Archeological-anthropological activities in Nevada received major emphasis with the formation and development of the Nevada State Museum. In the 1950s the museum began publication of an Archeological-anthropological series and later issued a popular series. Additional impetus to such studies came with the organization of a separate department of anthropology at the University of Nevada in the 1960s and the establishment of the Center for Western American Studies under the University of Nevada's Desert Research Institute. The activities of these groups along with a number of expeditions under the leadership of Dr. Robert F. Heizer of the University of California, Berkeley, have resulted in a number of archeological surveys in Nevada which have added immeasurably to the knowledge of the state's prehistoric background.

A good place to begin the study of Nevada's prehistory is Gordon L. Grosscup's *Bibliography of Nevada Archaeology*, University of California Archaeological Survey Report no. 36 (February 15, 1957). A useful and interesting summary of Nevada sites is Donald R. Tuohy, *Nevada's Prehistoric Heritage*, Nevada State Museum Popular Series, no. 1 (January 1965). The most recent work on the Tule Springs site in southern Nevada is the comprehensive report edited by H. M. Wormington and Dorothy Ellis, *Pleistocene Studies in Southern Nevada*, Nevada State Museum Anthropological Papers, no. 13 (1967). This work disagrees substantially with earlier findings by Harrington and Simpson. For the latter evaluation, see Mark R. Harrington and Ruth D. Simpson, *Tule Springs, Nevada: With Other Evidences of Pleistocene Man in North America*, Southwest Museum Papers, no. 18 (1961).

The most extensive exploration of the Gypsum Cave site was done by Mark Harrington, who wrote dozens of articles on expeditions he supervised there. His most important work on the subject is *Gypsum Cave, Report of the Second Session Expedition*, Southwest Museum Papers, no. 8 (1933). It is evident today that Harrington was in error regarding his dating of artifacts at Gypsum Cave. See particularly Richard Shutler's articles in Wormington and Ellis, *Pleistocene Studies in Southern Nevada*, noted above.

Lovelock Cave, the first archeological site in Nevada to be explored scientifically, was reported in Llewellyn L. Loud and Mark R. Harrington, "Lovelock Cave," *University of California Publications in American Archaeology and Ethnology* 25 (February 1929). See also Gordon L. Grosscup, *The Culture History of Lovelock Cave, Nevada*, University of California Archaeological Survey Reports, no. 52 (1960). Later studies, as recently as 1969, have been conducted in the Lovelock Cave area by University of California teams under the supervision of Dr. Robert F. Heizer. A late report of this work appears in Robert F. Heizer and Lewis K. Napton, "Biological and Cultural Evidence from Prehistoric Human Coprolites," *Science* 165 (August 8, 1969).

In addition to the archeological work involved directly at Lovelock Cave, a number of surveys and excavations under the supervision of Donald Tuohy of the Nevada State Museum have been conducted in recent years at Pyramid Lake. Although no official results have been published, preliminary investigations reported in the newspapers show that the Lovelock culture extended throughout the Pyramid Lake area and lasted in point of time to about 1500 A.D. See the *Nevada State Journal*, October 13, 1966, p. 41.

The most recent summary of the Lost City site is that by Richard Shutler, Jr., *Lost City, Pueblo Grande de Nevada*, Nevada State Museum Anthropological Papers, no. 5 (1961). The pioneer work at this archeological site, as in so many others in Nevada, was done by Mark Harrington, who wrote a number of articles about his explorations. See, particularly, Mark R. Harrington, "Excavations of Pueblo Grande de Nevada," *Texas Archaeological and Paleontology Society Bulletin* 9 (1937): 130–45.

Other important archeological sites in Nevada have been summarized in the following items: Robert Fleming Heizer, "Preliminary Report on the Leonard Rockshelter site, Pershing County, Nevada," *American Antiquity* 17 (October 1951): 88–98; Robert F. Heizer and Alex D. Krieger, "The Archaeology of Humboldt Cave, Churchill County, Nevada," *University of California Publications in American Archaeology and Ethnology* 47 (November 1, 1956); Phil C. Orr, *Pleistocene Man in Fishbone Cave, Pershing County, Nevada*, Nevada State Museum Department of Archaeology Bulletin no. 2 (February 1956); Richard Shutler, Jr., Mary E. Shutler, and James S. Griffith, *Stuart Rockshelter, A Stratified Site in Southern Nevada*, Nevada State Museum Anthropological Papers, no. 3 (1960); S. M. Wheeler, *Archaeology of Etna Cave, Lincoln County, Nevada* (Carson City: Nevada State Park Commission, 1942).

The fascinating story of Nevada petroglyphs is told in Robert F. Heizer and Martin A. Baumhoff, *Prehistoric Rock Art of Nevada and Eastern California* (Berkeley: University of California Press, 1962).

For a useful but general discussion of the Indians of Nevada, see Charles H. Poehlman, editor, *Know Your Nevada Indians*, State of Nevada Department of Education (Carson City, Nev.: State Printing Office, 1966). The Poehlman volume somewhat supercedes an earlier State Department of Education publication edited by E. A. Haglund, *The Washoe, Paiute, and Shoshone Indians of Nevada* (Carson City, Nev.: State Printing Office, 1961).

Other general works on Nevada Indians which were useful are: Warren d'Azevedo, Don D. Fowler, Wilbur A. Davis, and Wayne Suttles, *The Current Status of Anthropological Research in the Great Basin: 1964* (Reno: Publications Division, Desert Research Institute, University of Nevada, 1964); Jack D. Forbes, *The Nevada Indian Speaks* (Reno: University of Nevada Press, 1967); Effie M. Mack, *Nevada: A History of the State from the Earliest Times through the Civil War* (Glendale, Calif.: Arthur H. Clark, 1936); Jesse D. Jennings and Edward Norbeck, eds., *Prehistoric Man in the New World* (Chicago: University of Chicago Press, 1964); Willard L. Part et al., "Tribal Distribution in the Great Basin," *American Anthropologist* 40 (October–December 1938): pp. 622–38 Donald R. Tuohy, *Nevada's Prehistoric Heritage*, Nevada State Museum Popular Series, no. 1 (January 1965).

For the general reader, a good place to begin the study of the Washo Indians is James F. Downs, *The Two Worlds of the Washo* (New York: Holt, Rinehart, & Winston, 1966). See the following in addition: S. A. Barrett, "Washoe Indians," *Bulletin of the Public Museum of Milwaukee* 2 (May 10, 1917): 1–52; Grace M. Dangberg, "The Washo Language," *Nevada Historical Society Papers* 3 (1921–22): 145–52; Grace M. Dangberg, "Washoe Texts," *University of California Publications in American Archaeology and Ethnology* 22 (March 15, 1927): 393–443; Warren d'Azevedo, editor, *The Washoe Indians of California and Nevada*, Anthropological Papers, no. 67 (Salt Lake City: University of Utah Press, 1963); Jane G. Hickson, *Dat-So-La-Le*, . . . Nevada State Museum Popular Series, no. 3 (December 1967); John A. Price, *Washo Economy*, Nevada State Museum Anthropological Papers, no. 6 (June 1962).

The following works on the Northern Paiutes were consulted: Nellie Shaw Harnar, "History of the Pyramid Lake Indians, 1842–1959" M.A. thesis, University of Nevada, 1965); Omer C. Stewart, "Culture Element Distributions:

14. Northern Paiute," *University of California Anthropological Records* 4 (April 3, 1941): 361–446; Omer C. Stewart, "The Northern Paiute Bands," *University of California Anthropological Records* 2 (1939); Ruth Underhill, *The Northern Paiute Indian of California and Nevada*, U.S. Office of Education, Office of Indian Affairs Publication (Lawrence, Kans.: Haskell Institute Printing Department, 1941); and Margaret Wheat, *Survival Arts of the Primitive Paiutes* (Reno: University of Nevada Press, 1968). The latter is a fascinating result of years spent researching the life and culture of the Paiutes. Another book on the Northern Paiutes, by a member of that tribe, is interesting but not always accurate, and expectedly biased toward the Indians—Sarah Winnemucca Hopkins, *Life Among the Paiutes* . . . (Boston: Putnams, 1883). An interesting novel about the Pyramid Lake Indians, which focuses on the 1860 war, is Sessions S. Wheeler's *Paiute* (Caldwell, Idaho: Caxton Printers, 1965).

For studies of the Southern Paiutes see the following: Robert C. Euler, *Southern Paiute Ethnology*, with a section entitled "Environmental Setting and Natural Resources," by Catherine S. Fowler, Anthropological Papers, no. 78 (Salt Lake City: University of Utah Press, 1966); Isabel T. Kelly, "Southern Paiute Bands," *American Anthropologist* 36 (October–December 1934): 548–61; Isabel T. Kelly, "Southern Paiute Shamanism," *University of California Anthropological Records* 4 (1939): 151–67.

The Nevada Shoshones have not received as much special attention as have the Washos and the Northern Paiutes. A standard reference on the Shoshones is Julian H. Steward, "Cultural Element Distributions: 13. Nevada Shoshone," *University of California Anthropological Records* 4 (1941). A more general work is Virginia Cole Trenholm and Maurine Carley, *The Shoshonis: Sentinels of the Rockies* (Norman: University of Oklahoma Press, 1964); it includes a number of references to the western Shoshones of Nevada. A recently published book by Edna B. Patterson, Louise A. Ulph, and Victor Goodwin, *Nevada's Northeast Frontier* (Sparks, Nev.: Western Printing & Publishing Co., 1969), has an excellent chapter on the western Shoshones of northeastern Nevada.

Some attention has been given to peyotism among Nevada Indians; see particularly Omer C. Stewart, "Washoe-Northern Paiute Peyotism: A Study in Acculturation," *University of California Publications in American Archaeology and Ethnology* 40 (January 25, 1944): 63–140.

The religious phenomenon of the ghost dance, which originated with a Nevada Indian, Wovoka (Jack Wilson), has received much attention, some of it less than scholarly. See, for example, Paul D. Bailey, *Wovoka, the Indian Messiah* (Los Angeles: Western Lore Press, 1957). Also, see Chester W. Cheel, "The Ghost Dance," *Nevada Magazine* 1 (December 1945): 14–15; Grace Dangberg, "Wovoka," *Nevada Historical Society Quarterly* 11 (Summer 1968): 1–53; John Greenway, "The Ghost Dance," *American West* 6 (July 1969): 42–48; and David H. Muller, *Ghost Dance* (New York: Duell, Sloan & Pearce, 1959).

CHAPTER 3

THE TRAILBLAZERS

For Spanish explorations in the Great Basin the best accounts are Herbert E. Bolton's two books, *Outposts of Empire* (New York: Knopf, 1939), and *Pageant in the Wilderness: The Story of the Escalante Expedition of the Interior Basin, 1776* (Salt Lake City: Utah Historical Society, 1950). The latter work cites substantial evidence to indicate that the Escalante expedition did not enter present Nevada. For the Garcés expedition see Father Francisco Garcés, *A Record of Travels in Arizona and California, 1775–1776*, edited by John Galvin (San Francisco: John Howell Books, 1965). For an earlier translation see Elliott Coues, ed., *On the Trail of a Spanish Pioneer: The Diary and Itinerary of Francisco Garcés*, 2 vols. (New York: Francis P. Harpson, 1900). The best overall summary of the exploration of the Great Basin is Gloria Griffen Cline, *Exploring the Great Basin* (Norman: University of Oklahoma Press, 1963). A still useful summary of exploration in Nevada is Fred N. Fletcher, *Early Nevada: The Period of Exploration, 1776–1848* (Reno, Nev.: A. Carlisle & Co., [1929]). This volume is also printed as part of volume 1 of James Scrugham's *Nevada: A Narrative of the Conquest of a Frontier Land . . .* , 3 vols. (Chicago: American Historical Society, 1935). For the southern part of the basin see LeRoy and Ann Hafen, *The Old Spanish Trail: Santa Fe to Los Angeles* (Glendale, Calif.: Arthur H. Clark Co., 1954).

The summary of the fur trade in the Far West by LeRoy Hafen in the first volume of *The Mountain Men and the Fur Trade of the Far West* (Glendale, Calif.: Arthur H. Clark Co., 1965) is excellent, and the biographies of various fur traders which already have appeared in this series, edited by Hafen, are useful.

The importance of Jedediah Smith in the opening of the Great Basin was ignored for over a century. The pioneer in resurrecting Smith was Maurice Sullivan, and his two volumes on Smith are still useful: *The Travels of Jedediah Smith* (Santa Ana, Calif.: Fine Arts Press, 1934), and *Jedediah Smith, Trader and Trail Breaker* (New York: Press of the Pioneers, 1936). Two more recent works have further enhanced Smith's reputation: Dale L. Morgan, *Jedediah Smith and the Opening of the West* (Indianapolis: Bobbs-Merrill, 1953), and Dale L. Morgan and Carl I. Wheat, *Jedediah Smith and his Maps of the American West* (San Francisco: California Historical Society, 1954). See also Harrison Clifford Dale, *The Ashley-Smith Explorations and the Discovery of a Central Route to the Pacific, 1822–1829, with Original Journals*, rev. ed. (Cleveland: Arthur H. Clark Co., 1941). Francis Farquhar, in his well-researched article "Jedediah Smith and the First Crossing of the Sierra," *Sierra Club Bulletin* 28 (June 1943): 36–53, establishes Smith's route from California in 1827 as over Ebbetts Pass. See also his book, *History of the Sierra Nevada* (Berkeley: University of California Press, 1965).

The best work on Peter Skene Ogden's activities in Nevada has been done by Gloria Griffen Cline. Her work, *Exploring the Great Basin*, already cited, should be supplemented by her article in the *Nevada Historical Society Quarterly* 3 (July–September 1960): 3–11, titled "Peter Skene Ogden's Nevada Explorations." Joseph R. Walker's trapping expedition through the Great Basin in 1833–34 is best told in Zenas Leonard, *Adventure of Zenas Leonard, Fur Trader*, edited by John G. Ewers (Norman: University of Oklahoma Press, 1958). The story also appears in Washington Irving's *The Adventures of Captain Bonneville, U.S.A., in the Rocky Mountains and the Far West*. This volume has been printed in many editions, but by far the best is that edited by Edgely W. Todd and published by the University of Oklahoma Press in 1961.

The activities of John Frémont in Nevada have been given a great deal of attention in a variety of sources. The standard biography is that by Allan Nevins, *Frémont, Pathmaker of the West*, new ed. (New York: Longmans, Green, 1955). An earlier but longer life of Frémont by Nevins is *Frémont, The West's*

Greatest Adventurer . . . , 2 vols. (New York: Harper & Brothers, 1928). Another biography considered by some scholars as better balanced than the Nevins's works is that by Cardinal L. Goodwin, *John Charles Frémont: An Exploration of His Career* (Stanford, Calif.: Stanford University Press, 1930). A briefer, but excellent, summary of Frémont's activity in the Far West is included in William H. Goetzmann's *Army Explorations in the American West, 1803–1863* (New Haven: Yale University Press, 1959). The official report of his first two expeditions appear in U.S., Congress, Senate, *Report of the Exploring Expedition to the Rocky Mountains in the Year 1842, and to Oregon and North California in the Years 1843–44*, by John Charles Frémont, 28th Cong., 2d sess., March 1, 1843, S. Report 174 (Washington, D.C.: Gales & Seaton, 1845). For Frémont's own version of his expeditions, see John Charles Frémont, *Memoirs of My Life . . . Including in the Narrative Five Journeys of Western Exploration during the Years 1842, 1843, 1845–6–7, 1848–9, 1853–4* (Chicago: Belford, Clarke & Co., 1887). Much more usable is John Charles Frémont, *Narratives of Exploration and Adventure*, edited by Allan Nevins (New York: Longmans, 1956). For a sometimes not too complimentary picture of Frémont, see Charles Preuss, *Exploring with Frémont: The Private Diaries of Charles Preuss, Cartographer for John C. Frémont on His First, Second and Fourth Expeditions to the Far West*, translated and edited by Erwin G. and Elizabeth K. Gudde (Norman: University of Oklahoma Press, 1958). For Professor Vincent P. Gianella's view of Frémont's crossing of the Sierra in 1844, see his article "Where Frémont Crossed the Sierra in 1844," *Sierra Club Bulletin* 44 (October 1959): 54–63. A new addition to the many materials on the Frémont expeditions is presently being published by the University of Illinois Press as *The Expeditions of John Charles Frémont*, Donald Jackson and Mary Lee Spence, editors. Only the first volume, *Travels from 1838 to 1844*, has been published to date (1970).

The story of the passage of the emigrants through the Great Basin has brought forth a rich and varied mass of materials. The following selections are those which have been of most help in writing this chapter. For the general story, in addition to the Fletcher and Cline books on the exploration of the Great Basin, the following are all well written and well researched: Robert G. Cleland, *Pathfinders* (Los Angeles: Powell Publishing Co., 1929); Owen G. Coy, *The Great Trek* (Los Angeles: Powell Publishing Co., 1931); Dale L. Morgan, *The Humboldt, Highroad of the West* (New York: Farrar & Rinehart, 1943); Irene Paden, *The Wake of the Prairie Schooner* (New York: Macmillan, 1943); George R. Stewart, *The California Trail* (New York: McGraw-Hill, Inc., 1962). The latter is a fascinating summary of the emigrant movement to California beginning with the Bidwell-Bartleson party in 1841 and continuing year by year through 1858. In addition, the stories told in emigrant diaries, contemporary travel accounts, and emigrant guide books are indispensable for a balanced account of the emigrant movement through Nevada.

The first emigrant party, the Bidwell-Bartleson, comes to life in John Bidwell's *Echoes of the Past: An Account of the First Emigrant Train to California* . . . (Chico, Calif.: Chico Advertiser, n.d.). Another edition of Bidwell's *Echoes of the Past* was edited by Milo M. Quaife and published in Chicago by R. R. Donnelley and Sons in 1928. The best biography of Bidwell is that by Rockwell D. Hunt, *John Bidwell: Prince of California Pioneers* (Caldwell, Idaho: Caxton Printers, 1942). See also Marcus Benjamin, *John Bidwell, Pioneer: A Sketch of His Career* (Washington, D.C., 1907).

Although dozens of books have been written about the Donner party,

George Stewart's *Ordeal by Hunger: The Story of the Donner Party* (Boston: Houghton Mifflin, 1960) is still considered to be the best secondary account. For an account of the Hastings cutoff, see Charles Kelly, *Salt Desert Trails: A History of the Hastings Cut-off and Other Early Trails Which Crossed the Great Salt Lake Desert Seeking a Shorter Road to California* (Salt Lake City: Western Printing Co., 1930). An interesting article by Thomas F. Andrews, "The Controversial Hastings Overland Guide: A Reassessment," *Pacific His- torical Review* 37 (February 1968): 21–35, points out that the Hastings guide did have some redeeming features. A more recent article by the same author defends Hastings, "The Ambitions of Lansford W. Hastings: A Study in Western Myth-making," *Pacific Historical Review* 39 (November 1970): 473–93.

Other works about the emigrants, trappers, and explorers which were found particularly interesting and useful are: James P. Beckwourth, *The Life and Adventures of James P. Beckwourth,* edited by T. D. Bonner (New York: Knopf, 1931); Edwin Bryant, *What I Saw in California . . . ,* notes, index, and bibliography by Marguerite E. Wilbur (Santa Ana, Calif.: Fine Arts Press, 1936); Charles Kelly and Dale L. Morgan, *Old Greenwood* (Georgetown, Calif.: Talisman Press, 1965). An indispensable source, mainly because of the docu- mentation which has been added in the footnotes by the editor, is James Clyman's *James Clyman, Frontiersman . . . As Told in His Own Reminiscences and Diaries,* edited by Charles L. Camp (Portland, Oreg.: Champoeg Press, 1960). J. Goldsborough Bruff's *Gold Rush . . .* edited by Georgia W. Read and Ruth Gaines (New York: Columbia University Press, 1949), is one of the classic journals of trail. *Nevada's Northeast Frontier* (previously cited) has a very useful chapter by Victor Goodwin on the early explorations of north- eastern Nevada which incorporates years of painstaking field research. A much more detailed and important work is the same author's *The Humboldt: Nevada's Desert River and Thoroughfare of the American West* in a limited edition of twenty-five copies, U.S. Department of Agriculture, Nevada Humboldt River Basin Survey, 1966.

Two other volumes which are useful for the Sierra crossings, particularly the 1833–34 Walker expedition, are: Earl W. Kersten, Jr., "Settlements and Economic Life in the Walker River Country of Nevada and California" (Ph.D. diss., University of Nebraska, 1961); and W. W. Maule, *A Contribution to the Geographic and Economic History of the Carson, Walker, and Mono Basins in Nevada and California* (San Francisco: U.S. Forest Service, California Region, 1938).

CHAPTER 4

THE FIRST SETTLEMENTS

For the period beginning with the settlement of western Utah Territory, the newspaper becomes an important source for the history of Nevada. Partic- ularly useful in the preparation of this chapter was the *Daily Alta California,* a San Francisco newspaper which began publishing in 1849 and has a number of important entries concerning the early settlements in what was then the western part of Utah Territory.

The best summary of the settlement of the Mormons in present western Nevada is that by Juanita Brooks, "The Mormons in Carson County, Utah Territory," *Nevada Historical Society Quarterly* 8 (Spring 1965): 7–24. Mrs.

Brooks's research places an entirely different light on the chronological sequence in the settlement of Nevada. In addition to the Brooks article, the *History of Nevada*, edited by Myron Angel, and Bancroft's *History of Nevada, Colorado and Wyoming* (both previously cited) are excellent for the Mormon settlement in Carson County. The chapter on anarchy and confusion in Mack, *Nevada*, pp. 173–93, is not only a good summary, but adds new information taken from early California newspapers. For the first settlements see also John Reese, "Mormon Station," *Nevada Historical Society Papers* 1 (1913–16): 186–90, and Effie Mona Mack, "Nevada's First House," *Nevada Magazine* 1 (July 1945): 8–11, 21. The memoir of Hampden S. Beatie, "The First in Nevada," *Nevada Historical Society Papers* 1 (1913–16): 168–71, was written many years after the narrated events occurred and therefore should be used with caution. A recent article attempts to correct the chronology of the first settlement: Russell R. Elliott, "Nevada's First Trading Post: A Study in Historiography," *Nevada Historical Society Quarterly* 4 (Winter 1970): 3–12.

For the early Mormon settlements in what later became southern Nevada, the following works have been useful: Elbert Edwards, "Early Mormon Settlements in Southern Nevada," *Nevada Historical Society Quarterly* 8 (Spring 1965): 29–43; Andrew Jensen, "History of Las Vegas Mission," *Nevada Historical Society Papers* 5 (1925–26): 115–284; and Francis H. Leavitt, "The Influence of the Mormon People in the Settlement of Clark County," (M.A. thesis, University of Nevada, 1934).

In addition to the works cited above, a most useful publication is the *Political History of Nevada*, issued by the secretary of state's office. The last edition, 1965, was researched and written by Art Palmer and is particularly good for the beginnings of political activities in Carson County, Utah Territory, including brief remarks about the Mexican occupation of the area and a detailed report of the activities of the Utah territorial government from 1850 to 1861. An excellent series of maps showing the political and geographical changes during these years is included. Since much of the political activity between 1850 and 1855 came from so-called squatter governments which operated effectively but without legal authority, the "First Records of Carson Valley—1851" are of particular importance. These records, made readily available to the the researcher by publication in the *Nevada Historical Society Quarterly* 9 (Summer–Fall 1966), cover the activities of the squatter government from November 12, 1851, to March 5, 1855. The official records of Carson County, Utah Territory, are in the state archives in Carson City, Nevada.

A useful recent summary of the preterritorial period is contained in an article by Kent D. Richards, "Washoe Territory: Rudimentary Government in Nevada," *Arizona and the West* 11 (Autumn 1969): 213–33.

For the discovery of gold in Carson County, the best works are Eliot Lord *Comstock Mining and Miners*, U.S. Geological Survey Mongraphs, vol. 4 (Washington, D.C.: GPO, 1883); Grant H. Smith, *The History of the Comstock Lode, 1850–1920*, University of Nevada Geology and Mining Series, no. 37 (1943); and William Wright [Dan De Quille], *The Big Bonanza* (New York: A. A. Knopf, 1947). There is a difference of opinion among historians concerning the date of the original gold discoveries in present Nevada. The argument stems from the more basic disagreement as to whether the DeMont-Beatie party arrived in 1849 or in 1850. The Smith version, that gold was first discovered in Gold Canyon in the spring of 1850, seems the most reasonable and fits the chronological sequence established by Mrs. Juanita Brooks. See also the *San Francisco Daily Alta California* for August 23, 1850, for an article on the activities of the miners of Gold Canyon in 1850.

CHAPTER 5

TERRITORY TO STATEHOOD, 1861–1864

The Bancroft and Angel histories, cited earlier, are primary reference works for this period. Also useful is the *Political History of Nevada*, 1965 edition, and the first volume of Scrugham's history of Nevada. The best summary of the territorial period from a political-constitutional standpoint is Eleanore Bushnell's *The Nevada Constitution: Origin and Growth*, rev. ed. (Reno: University of Nevada Press, 1968). Particularly useful is Dr. Bushnell's discussion of the debates in the 1864 constitutional convention. The debates are found in the *Official Report of the Debates and Proceedings in the Constitutional Convention of the State of Nevada . . . July 4, 1864 . . .*, by Andrew J. Marsh, official reporter (San Francisco: F. Eastman, 1866). The debates in the constitutional convention of 1863 supposedly were published; if so, the records continue to elude researchers. The territorial records, including the Correspondence of Orion Clemens, Secretary of the Territory, April 1, 1861– November 10, 1864, are available in the Nevada Archives, Secretary of State, Carson City, Nevada. The records of the First Legislative Assembly of the Territory of Nevada are found in William M. Gillespie, *Journals of the Legislative Assembly of the Territory of Nevada* (San Francisco: Valentine & Co., 1862).

Newspapers continue to be of primary value, but unfortunately, many important issues are missing. The *Virginia Evening Bulletin* is available for much of 1863 and 1864, and California newspapers such as the *San Francisco Alta California* and the *Placerville Mountain Democrat* often have important comment on events in Nevada territory. The *Humboldt Register* (Unionville, Nevada) is excellent for comments against the statehood movement.

The activities of John Wesley North during the Nevada territorial period are easily followed in the John Wesley North Papers, located in the Henry E. Huntington Library at San Marino, California. A biography of North by Merlin Stonehouse, *John Wesley North and the Reform Frontier* (Minneapolis: University of Minnesota Press, 1965), adds useful information about this controversial figure. William Morris Stewart's activities in the 1863 constitutional convention and during the territorial period in Nevada have been defended strongly and consistently by the late Effie Mona Mack. See particularly "William Morris Stewart, 1827–1909," *Nevada Historical Society Quarterly* 7 (Centennial Issue, 1964), and "Life and Letters of William Morris Stewart, 1827–1909: A History of His Influence on State and National Legislation" (Ph.D. diss., University of California, Berkeley, 1930). The William Morris Stewart Papers are in the Nevada State Historical Society Library in Reno. Unfortunately, the papers covering the territorial and early statehood aspects of the senator's career have been lost. William Morris Stewart, *The Reminiscences of Senator William M. Stewart*, edited by George Rothwell Brown (New York: Neal Publishing Co., 1908), is useful but inaccurate in a number of instances. Territorial Governor James W. Nye has not received much scholarly attention. A short biography by Effie Mona Mack, "James Warren Nye, A Biography," *Nevada*

Historical Society Quarterly 4 (July–December 1961): 8–59, is the only printed biography presently available to scholars.

In addition to the works cited above, the two following works are useful for the background of Nevada's entrance into the Union: Frederic Lauriston Bullard, "Abraham Lincoln and the Statehood of Nevada," *American Bar Association Journal* 26 (March and April, 1940): 210, 213; and Edward S. Dodson, "A History of Nevada during the Civil War" (M. A. thesis, University of Oregon, 1947).

The question of the Nevada boundaries is summarized very ably in Mack's *History of Nevada.* A more detailed study of the same question is Beulah Hershiser, "The Adjustment of the Boundaries of Nevada" (M.A. thesis, University of Nevada, 1911). This thesis was printed in the *Nevada Historical Society First Biennial Report* 1 (1907–08): 121–34. The so-called Sagebrush War is covered by most of the secondary works already cited. For additional material, see Asa M. Fairfield, *Fairfield's Pioneer History of Lassen County, California* (San Francisco: H. S. Crocker, 1916), and Maude S. Taylor, "The Sagebrush Rebellion," *Nevada Magazine* 2 (January 1947). The relationship of the Honey Lake region of California to Nevada's territorial development is covered in John Schramel's "Honey Lake Valley, California, and Western Nevada: A Study in Sectional Development, 1850–1864" (M.A. thesis, University of Nevada, 1966).

Other sources which have been used for this chapter include J. Wells Kelly, compiler, *First Directory of Nevada Territory* (San Francisco: Commercial Steam Presses, Valentine Co., 1862; a new edition of this work with an introduction by Richard Lingenfelter was published in 1962 by the Talisman Press of Los Gatos, California); Earl Pomeroy, *The Territories and the United States, 1861–1890* (Philadelphia: University of Pennsylvania Press, 1947); Ralph Friedman, "Nevada's Telegram," *Nevada Highways and Parks* 29 (Summer 1969): 54–61. A recent and very useful article on the background of the events leading to territorial status by Kent D. Richards was cited in the previous chapter. Another article by the same author, continuing the story during Nevada's early territorial period, may be found in the *Nevada Historical Society Quarterly* (Spring 1970): 29–39, titled, "The American Colonial System in Nevada." A new and interesting approach to the Nevada constitutional convention of 1864 is Gordon M. Bakken, "Taxation of Mineral Wealth and the Nevada Constitutional Convention of 1864," *Nevada Historical Society Quarterly* 12 (Winter 1969): 5–15.

CHAPTER 6

EARLY STATEHOOD: THE ECONOMIC FOUNDATIONS

The Paiute Indian War of 1860, or more accurately, the Pyramid Lake Indian War, is covered in a number of works already cited, including those by Angel, Bancroft, Davis, Lord, Mack, and Wright [De Quille]. Of these, the best account is found in Wright's *Big Bonanza.* An excellent summary, told from telegraphic dispatches, letters, and newspaper accounts is that by William C. Miller, "The Pyramid Lake Indian War of 1860," *Nevada Historical Society Quarterly* 1 (September 1957): 37–53; and ibid. (November, 1957), 98–113. For an account by a latter-day Paiute, see Nellie Harnar, "History of the Pyramid Lake Indians, 1842–1959" (M.A. thesis, University of Nevada,

1965). Another earlier account is David E. W. Williamson, "When Major Ormsby was Killed: A Review of the Most Important Engagement with Indians Recorded in the Annals of Nevada," *Nevada Historical Society Papers* 4 (1923–24): 1–28. For a useful summary of the military posts established in Nevada to protect against the threat of Indian attacks, see George Ruhlen, "Early Nevada Forts," *Nevada Historical Society Quarterly* 7 (Centennial of Statehood, 1964). Although fictionalized, the account of the battle which appears in the novel *Paiute* (Caldwell, Idaho: Caxton Printers, 1965), by Sessions Wheeler, is based on a good deal of field research. A more scholarly account by the same author appears in *The Desert Lake: The Story of Nevada's Pyramid Lake* (Caldwell, Idaho: Caxton Printers, 1968).

The first major geological report on the Comstock was that by Ferdinand P. W. Richthofen, *The Comstock Lode: Its Character, and the Probable Mode of Its Continuance in Depth* (San Francisco: Sutro Tunnel Company, 1866). Many other summaries have been made since, but the standard work is still George F. Becker, *Geology of the Comstock Lode and the Washoe District,* U.S. Geological Survey Monographs, vol. 3, (Washington, D.C.: GPO, 1882).

Effie Mona Mack's *History of Nevada* has an excellent chapter on the building of the Central Pacific through Nevada, and David Myrick's *Railroads of Nevada and Eastern California* (Berkeley, Calif.: Howell-North Books, 1962) is indispensable for the story of Nevada railroads.

The best short summary of the mining booms of this period is the chapter in Rodman Paul's *Mining Frontiers of the Far West, 1848–1880* (New York: Holt, Rinehart and Winston, 1964) titled "A Study in Contrasts: California and Nevada, 1859–1880." Essential for statistics of mineral production from each of these districts is Bertrand F. Couch and Jay A. Carpenter, *Nevada's Metal and Mineral Production (1859–1940, Inclusive),* University of Nevada Geology and Mining Series, no. 38 (November 1, 1943). An earlier work, Francis Church Lincoln, *Mining Districts and Mineral Resources of Nevada* (Reno: Nevada Newsletter Publishing Co., 1923), contains excellent summaries of each important mining development in Nevada to that time. An extremely useful guide, although outdated, is the Writers' Program's *Nevada: A Guide to the Silver State* (Portland Ore.: Binfords & Mort, 1940). A much more recent summary of Nevada ghost towns and mining camps with good maps and numerous pictures is Stanley Paher, *Nevada Ghost Towns and Mining Camps* (Berkeley, Calif.: Howell-North Books, 1970).

For romanticized, interesting, but not always accurate accounts of the dozens of mining camps discovered in Nevada during the Comstock era and after, see the following works: Don Ashbaugh, *Nevada's Turbulent Yesterday . . . A Study in Ghost Towns* (Los Angeles: Westernlore Press, 1963); Nell Murbarger, *Ghosts of the Glory Trail* (Palm Desert, Calif.: Desert Magazine Press, 1956); *Pioneer Nevada,* prepared by the Thomas C. Wilson Advertising Agency for Harold's Club (Reno, Nev.: Harold's Club, 1951). A fine photographic coverage of many Nevada mining booms of this period is Lambert Florin's *Western Ghost Town Shadows* (Seattle: Superior Publishing Co., 1964).

Of the booms outside the Comstock, some have been given attention by brief articles, some by master's theses, and one or two by full-length books. In the case of the more important mineral discoveries, the Professional Papers of the United States Geological Survey are important as are the more up-to-date studies of the geology of these booms published by the Mackay School of Mines of the University of Nevada.

For Aurora, Angel's *History of Nevada* is particularly useful, as is "Sketches of the Washoe Silver Mines," by Henry De Groot, found in J. Wells Kelly's *First Directory of Nevada Territory*. In addition, the following works are of some importance: J. Ross Browne, *Resources of the Pacific Slope* (San Francisco: H. H. Bancroft, 1869); Carl P. Russell, *Early Mining Excitements East of Yosemite* (San Francisco, 1928); W. W. Maule, *A Contribution to the Geographic and Economic History of the Carson, Walker and Mono Basin in Nevada and California* (San Francisco: U.S. Forest Service, California Region, 1938); and Joseph Wasson, *Bodie and Esmeralda* . . . (San Francisco: Spaulding, Barto, & Co., 1878). A very interesting diary, or excerpt thereof, has Aurora as a setting, although the setting could just as well be any of a dozen other Nevada mining boom regions. Nevertheless, it adds to the picture of the housewife and family in the early boom period. See Richard G. Lillard, editor, "A Literate Woman in the Mines: The Diary of Rachel Haskell," *Mississippi Valley Historical Review* 31 (June 1944): 81–98. Another interesting view of Aurora is presented by Mark Twain in *Roughing It*.

The town of Austin has been the subject of a number of historical items, many of them romanticized. A story of the town taken from its famous newspaper, the *Reese River Reveille*, is found in Oscar Lewis's *The Town That Died Laughing* (Boston: Little, Brown, 1955). A more solid summary of the boom is that by Rodney Smith, "Austin, Nevada, 1862–1881" (M.A. thesis, University of Nevada, 1963). A collection of interesting stories with Austin as a setting is Fred H. Hart's *The Sazerac Lying Club: A Nevada Book* (San Francisco: Henry Keller, 1878). Another M.A. thesis which adds some detail about Austin is Buster L. King's "The History of Lander County" (M.A. thesis, University of Nevada, 1954). For a discussion of the development of the Reese River silver process, see Ernest Oberbillig, "Development of Washoe and Reese River Silver Processes," *Nevada Historical Society Quarterly* 10 (Summer 1967).

Although the Eureka boom was much more productive than the one at Austin, it has not attracted as much attention from historians. Two master's theses treat various phases of the boom: Franklin Grazeola, "The Charcoal Burners War of 1879: A Study of the Italian Immigrant in Nevada" (M.A. thesis, University of Nevada, 1969); Fred Reichman, "History of Eureka County" (M.A. thesis, University of Nevada, 1967). An article by Phillip I. Earl, "Nevada's Italian War," *Nevada Historical Society Quarterly* 12 (Summer 1969): 47–87, adds some information on the Charcoal Burners War. A very scarce and important item is Lambert Molinelli & Company's *Eureka and Its Resources: A Complete History of Eureka County, Nevada* . . . (San Francisco: H. Keller & Co., 1879). Because of its complex geological history, the U.S. Geological Survey has given particular attention to Eureka. See Arnold Hague, *Geology of the Eureka District, Nevada, with an Atlas*, U.S. Geological Survey Monograph, vol. 20 (Washington, D.C.: GPO, 1892), and Thomas R. Nolan, *The Eureka Mining District, Nevada*, U.S. Geological Survey Professional Papers, no. 406 (Washington, D.C.: GPO, 1962).

The Hamilton boom has been given more scholarly attention than most of the lesser Nevada mining discoveries, although from the standpoint of production it was of minor importance. The best work is the excellent study by W. Turrentine Jackson, *Treasure Hill* (Tucson: University of Arizona Press, 1963). See also Russell R. Elliott, "The Early History of White Pine County, Nevada, 1865–1887," *Pacific Northwest Quarterly* 30 (April 1939): 145–68. An excellent early description is Albert I. Evans, *White Pine: Its Geographical Location, Topography, Geological Formation, Mining Laws* . . . (San Francisco: Alta California Printing House, 1869). Some interesting sidelights on life in a declining boom town (Hamilton) are found in "Letters from a Nevada Doctor to His Daughter in Connecticut (1881–1891)," *Nevada Historical Society Quarterly* 1 (September 1957): 15–31, and ibid. (November, 1957): 81–97, edited by Russell R. Elliott. See also Samuel F. Hunt, *Mining Resources and History of White Pine Mining District, Nevada* [*Ely, Nev.*: Ely Mining Record print, 1910], and B. F. Miller, "Nevada in the Making . . . ," *Nevada Historical Society Papers* 4 (1923–24): 255–474.

An excellent account of the Pioche boom can be found in James W. Hulse's *Lincoln County, Nevada, 1864–1909: History of a Mining Region*, Nevada Studies in History and Political Science, no. 9 (Reno: University of Nevada Press, 1971). Franklin A. Buck's *A Yankee Traveler in the Gold Rush* . . . , compiled by Katherine A. White (Boston: Houghton, Mifflin, 1930), has interesting contemporary accounts of Pioche during its boom period.

Unfortunately there is no good history of agriculture in Nevada. Some of the general histories, particularly Angel, are of some help. A brief history, not well organized, is that by Cecil Creel, *History of Agriculture in Nevada* (Carson City: Max C. Fleischmann College of Agriculture, University of Nevada, 1964). A summary which is useful but hard to follow is Cruz Venstrom and Howard Mason, compilers, *Agricultural History of Nevada*. It includes the 10th Census of Agriculture of the United States for Nevada, 1880. (A typed and handwritten copy, dated 1944, is in the Getchell Library, University of Nevada, Reno.) The recently published volume on *Nevada's Northeast Frontier* (previously cited) has three excellent chapters on the cattle and sheep industries of northeast Nevada by Mrs. Edna Patterson and Mrs. Louise Ulph. Additional material on Nevada's livestock development can be found in the following items: Velma A. Truett, *On the Hoof in Nevada* (Los Angeles: Gehrett-Truett-Hall, 1950); Clel Georgetta, "Sheep in Nevada," *Nevada Historical Society Quarterly* 8 (Summer 1965): 14–38; Mrs. John Patterson, "Early Cattle in Elko County." *Nevada Historical Society Quarterly* 8 (Summer 1965): 1–13; Sheldon Short, "A History of the Livestock Industry Prior to 1900" (M.A. thesis, University of Nevada, 1965); Byrd Wall Sawyer, *Nevada Nomads: A Story of the Sheep Industry* (San Jose: Harlan-Young Press, 1971).

CHAPTERS 7 AND 8

THE COMSTOCK
and
COMSTOCK ERA POLITICS

Three works are essential to the study of the Comstock era. The earliest of these, and in many respects the most important because of the comprehensiveness and accuracy of its coverage, is William Wright [Dan De Quille], *History of the Big Bonanza* . . . (San Franciso: A. L. Bancroft & Co., [1876]). This work was reissued in 1947 by Alfred A. Knopf as *The Big Bonanza*. A second important contemporary account and more useful than De Quille on some subjects such as labor, the immigrant, and technological developments, is Eliot Lord, *Comstock Mining and Miners*, U.S. Geological Survey Monographs, vol. 4.

(Washington, D.C.: GPO, 1883). The Lord work was reprinted by Howell-North (Berkeley, Calif., 1959). A more recent work which has become a standard reference of the Comstock Lode because of its accuracy is Grant H. Smith, *The History of The Comstock Lode, 1850–1920,* University of Nevada Geology and Mining Series, no. 37, (July 1, 1943). Another older work and still useful although it repeats much of the Lord material is Charles H. Shinn, *The Story of the Mine, As Illustrated by the Great Comstock Lode* (New York: D. Appleton, 1896). Two somewhat romanticized but interesting accounts are: George D. Lyman, *Saga of the Comstock Lode: Boom Days in Virginia City* (New York: G. Scribners, 1934); and Carl B. Glasscock, *The Big Bonanza: The Story of The Comstock Lode* (Indianapolis: Bobbs Merrill, 1931). The best short summary is the superb chapter on the Comstock Lode found in Rodman W. Paul, *Mining Frontiers of the Far West, 1848–1880* (New York: Holt, Rinehart & Winston, 1964). Another good summary can be found in William S. Greever, *The Bonanza West: The Story of the Western Mining Rushes, 1848–1900* (Norman: University of Oklahoma Press, 1963). A number of the general histories cited earlier have useful summaries of the Comstock. The better accounts will be found in Angel, Bancroft, Mack, and Scrugham.

The most useful account of the Virginia and Truckee Railroad is that which appears in David Myrick, *Railroads of Nevada and Eastern California,* vol. 1 (Berkeley, Calif.: Howell-North Books, 1962). A more dramatic account is found in the works by Lucius M. Beebe and Charles M. Clegg. See particularly *Virginia and Truckee: A Story of Virginia City and Comstock Times* (Oakland, Calif.: G. H. Hardy, 1949); and *Steamcars to the Comstock: The Virginia and Truckee Railroad, the Carson and Colorado Railroad* (Berkeley, Calif.: Howell-North, 1957). A short but useful account is that in Gilbert Kneiss, *Bonanza Railroads,* 4th rev. ed. (Stanford, Calif.: Stanford University Press, 1954).

The best accounts of the water system and the V-flume are found in Wright's *Big Bonanza;* Lord's *Comstock Mining and Miners;* and Edward B. Scott, *Saga of Lake Tahoe . . .* (Crystal Bay, Nev.: Sierra-Tahoe Publishing Co., 1957); and John D. Galloway's *Early Engineering Works Contributory to the Comstock,* University of Nevada Geology and Mining Series, no. 45 (June 1947). A rather hilarious account of Fair and Flood's journey down the V-flume is told by Bert Goldrath in "River in a Box," *Argosy* 352 (March 1961): 34–39, 104–5.

For the story of Adolph Sutro and the building of the Sutro Tunnel, the best work is Robert E. Stewart and Mary Stewart, *Adolph Sutro* (San Francisco: Howell-North, 1962). An earlier biography by Eugenia Holmes, *Adolph Sutro: A Brief Story of a Brilliant Life* (San Francisco: Photo-Engraving Co., 1895) is much too laudatory and should be used with care.

For the story of the financial control of the Comstock, the following works are useful: Cecil G. Tilton, *William Chapman Ralston, Courageous Builder* (Boston: Christopher Publishing House, 1935); George D. Lyman, *Ralston's Ring: California Plunders the Comstock Lode* (New York: Charles Scribner's Sons, 1947); Oscar Lewis, *Silver Kings: The Lives and Times of Mackay, Fair, Flood, and O'Brien, Lords of the Nevada Comstock Lode* (New York: Knopf, 1947); Ethel Manter, *Rocket of the Comstock: The Story of John William Mackay* (Caldwell, Idaho: Caxton Printers, 1950). The Grant H. Smith Papers located in the Bancroft Library at Berkeley include a book-length manuscript on the life of John Mackay.

The best descriptions of early Virginia City are found in Mark Twain,

Roughing It (Hartford, Conn.: American Publishing Co., 1872), and J. Ross Browne, *A Peep at Washoe and Washoe Revisited* (Balboa Island, Calif.: Paisano Press, 1959). Browne's descriptions are particularly useful since the single work cited above combines two impressions of the Comstock boom, one noted in 1860 and the other in 1863. A recent publication adds a young boy's impressions of Virginia City during its maturity: John Taylor Waldorf, *Kid on the Comstock* (Berkeley, Calif.: University of California Press for Friends of the Bancroft Library, 1968). A rather bitter picture of Virginia City is drawn by Mary M. Mathews in *Ten Years in Nevada; or, Life on the Pacific Coast* (Buffalo: Baker, Jones & Co., 1880). A better balanced story by a woman is Louise M. Palmer, "How We Live in Nevada," *Overland Monthly* 2 (May 1869): 457–62. A brief glimpse of a miner's family life comes from the excerpts of the diary of James Galloway, found in J. D. Galloway, *Early Engineering Works* (previously cited). The long diary of Alf Doten, 1849–1903, edited by Walter Van Tilburg Clark, is scheduled for publication in 1972. A dramatic account of the great 1875 fire can be found in Lewis Atherton, editor, "Fire on the Comstock," *American West* 2 (Winter 1965): 24–34. Among dozens of other works which add color to the Comstock story, the following are recommended: Lucius Beebe and Charles Clegg, *Legends of the Comstock Lode* (Stanford, Calif.: Stanford University Press, 1954); Helen S. Carlson, "Names of Mines on the Comstock," (M.A. thesis, University of Nevada, 1955); Duncan Emrich, editor, *Comstock Bonanza . . .* (New York: Vanguard Press, 1950); Marvin Lewis, editor, *Mining Frontier: Contemporary Accounts from the American West in the 19th Century* (Norman: University of Oklahoma Press, 1967); Miriam Michelson, *The Wonderlode of Silver and Gold* (Boston: Stratford, 1934).

Very useful for the story of the theater on the Comstock is Margaret Watson, *Silver Theater: Amusements of the Mining Frontier in Early Nevada, 1850–1864* (Glendale, Calif.: Arthur H. Clark, 1964). Additional detail about the Virginia City theater, particularly after 1864, can be found in William Charles Miller's "An Historical Study of Theatrical Entertainment in Virginia City: . . . 1860–1875" (Ph.D. diss., University of Southern California, 1947). For the history of music on the Comstock, see Felton Hickman, "A History of Music on the Comstock, 1860–1875" (M.A. thesis, Brigham Young University, 1954).

The importance of immigrants to the development of the Comstock was first hinted at in Eliot Lord's *Comstock Mining and Miners* (previously cited). Since that time, writers like Charles Shinn and, more recently, Rodman Paul have pointed again to this neglected area. A recent master's thesis touches some aspects of the immigrants' contribution: see Dana Balibrera, "Virginia City and the Immigrant" (M.A. thesis, University of Nevada, 1965). An important contribution to the literature on immigrants in Nevada is Wilbur S. Shepperson's *Restless Strangers: Nevada's Immigrants and Their Interpreters* (Reno: University of Nevada Press, 1970). See also Arthur C. Todd, *The Cornish Miner in America* (Glendale, Calif.: Arthur H. Clark Co., 1967). The Chinese question is given consideration in Gary BeDunnah's "History of the Chinese in Nevada, 1855–1904" (M.A. thesis, University of Nevada, 1966). An interesting attempt to analyze the effect of the industrial boom on the frontier is Robert B. Merrifield's "Nevada, 1859–1881: The Impact of an Advanced Technological Society upon a Frontier Area" (Ph.D. diss., University of Chicago, 1957).

Manuscript sources are very important for the political history of the

Comstock. Particularly useful are the following: the Henry M. Yerington
Papers at the Bancroft Library, Berkeley, California; the William M. Stewart
Papers at the Nevada State Historical Society, Reno, Nevada; the John Wesley
North Papers and the John P. Jones Papers at the Huntington Library in
San Marino, California; and the Grant H. Smith Papers, also at the Bancroft
Library.

Also important for the political summary in this chapter are the *Appendices
to the Journals of the Senate and Assembly* of the Nevada legislature. In
these volumes are the annual and biennial reports of all state officers, all commissions and boards, and many miscellaneous reports ordered by the legislature
or by the governor. The *Journals of the Senate and the Assembly* are essential
for following the political record of this period. See also Richard C. Sieber,
"Nevada Politics during the Comstock Era" (M.A. thesis, University of Nevada,
1950). The following political biographies were found useful: Effie Mona Mack,
"William Morris Stewart, 1827–1909," *Nevada Historical Society Quarterly* 7
(Centennnal Issue, 1964). William M. Stewart's *Reminiscences of Senator William
M. Stewart of Nevada*, edited by George R. Brown (New York: Neal Publishing
Co., 1908), is interesting but unreliable. The other side of the Stewart-North
feud is well told in Merlin Stonehouse, *John Wesley North and the Reform
Frontier* (Minneapolis: University of Minnesota Press, 1965). Another recent
biography, Francis R. Weisenburger, *Idol of the West: The Fabulous Career of
Rollin Mallory Daggett* (Syracuse, N.Y.: Syracuse University Press, 1965) is a
good account of a minor Comstock political figure. There is no biography of
John P. Jones, but in addition to other general works on the Comstock, the
work by Harry M. Gorham, *My Memories of the Comstock* (Los Angeles: Sut-
ton House, 1939), adds some information. There is an excellent chapter on
Jones in Allen Weinstein's *Prelude to Populism: Origins of the Silver Issue,
1867–1878* (New Haven: Yale University Press, 1970); interesting items on
Jones and Stewart appear in David Rothman's *Politics and Power: The United
States Senate, 1869–1901* (Cambridge: Harvard University Press, 1966). The
only available biography of James W. Nye is that by Effie Mona Mack, "James
W. Nye, 1814–1876," *Nevada Historical Society Quarterly* 4 (July–December
1961): 1–59.

An interesting recent work on Nevada's political history which has good
material on the Comstock period is Gilman M. Ostrander, *Nevada: The Great
Rotten Borough, 1859–1964* (New York: Knopf, 1966). Also of interest on the
political conflict between Jones and Sharon is David Toll, "Collision on the
Comstock," *Nevada Highways and Parks* 26 (Winter 1966): 32–40.

Newspapers, particularly the *Territorial Enterprise*, the *Virginia Evening Bul-
letin*, and the *Gold Hill News*, are an essential source for the Comstock era.
A number of works relating to the newspapers and the men who worked on
them have been written. The story of Samuel Clemens [Mark Twain] on the
Comstock starts with his own works, *Roughing It* and his *Autobiography*. In
addition see Henry Smith, editor, *Mark Twain of the Enterprise* (Berkeley:
University of California Press, 1957). Also useful is Effie Mona Mack, *Mark
Twain in Nevada* (New York: Charles Scribner's Sons, 1947). An excellent article
is that by Dixon Wecter, "Mark Twain and the West," *Huntington Library
Quarterly* 8 (August 1945): 359–78. The observations of another Comstock
editor are told in Wells Drury, *An Editor on the Comstock Lode* (Palo Alto,
Calif.: Pacific Books, 1948). Also see Charles C. Goodwin's *As I Remember
Them . . .* (Salt Lake City, 1913). An interesting summary of the history of the

Territorial Enterprise is Lucius Beebe and Charles Clegg, *Comstock Commotion: The Story of the "Territorial Enterprise" and "Virginia City News"* (Stanford, Calif.: Stanford University Press, 1954). For a summary and listing of newspapers published on the Comstock, see John G. Folkes, *Nevada's Newspapers: A Bibliography* . . . , Nevada Studies in History and Political Science, no. 6 (Carson City: University of Nevada Press, 1964).

CHAPTER 9

THE DEPRESSION PERIOD, 1880–1900

Two of the better general histories of Nevada, Angel and Mack (both previously cited), do not cover the period of depression, and a third, the very useful Bancroft summary, includes only the years before 1890. Consequently, for the history of Nevada during this period one must rely even more heavily than before on newspapers, reports, legislative journals, and short articles in various magazines. For a statistical indication of the decline in mining after 1880, see particularly Couch and Carpenter, previously cited, and for population figures, the United States census returns for 1880, 1890, and 1900. In addition to works previously cited, there are a few items which add to the information on agricultural development. The story of the Adams-McGill livestock development is told in Orville Holderman, "Jewett W. Adams and W. N. McGill: Their Lives and Ranching Empire" (M.A. thesis, University of Nevada, 1963). Particular emphasis is given to the livestock empire of John Sparks in Velma Truett, "From Longhorns to Herefords," *Nevada Highways and Parks* 24 (Centennial Issue, 1964): 30–31, 59. Also of importance for this chapter is Patterson, Ulph, and Goodwin, *Nevada's Northeastern Frontier*, mentioned in an earlier chapter. The reports of the surveyor general, which may be found in the *Appendices to the Journals of the Senate and Assembly* and the United States census summaries on agriculture are particularly useful for agricultural statistics. Now available at the University of Nevada, Reno, is the state office of the United States Department of Agriculture, Statistical Reporting Service.

For the story of the fight for reclamation and irrigation in Nevada, two good sources are available: Mary Ellen Glass, *Water For Nevada: The Reclamation Controversy, 1885–1902*, Nevada Studies in History and Political Science, no. 7 (Carson City: University of Nevada Press, 1964); and William Lilley III and Lewis L. Gould, "The Western Irrigation Movement, 1889–1902: A Reappraisal," in *American West: A Reorientation*, edited by Gene Gressley, University of Wyoming Publications, vol. 32 (Laramie, Wyo., 1966), pp. 57–77. Of some value for Newlands's role in the irrigation struggle is Francis G. Newlands, *The Public Papers of Francis G. Newlands*, edited and placed in historical setting by Arthur B. Darling, 2 vols. (Boston: Houghton Mifflin, 1932). See also William Lilley III, "The Early Career of Francis G. Newlands, 1848–1897" (Ph.D. diss., Yale University, 1965). Roy M. Robbins, *Our Landed Heritage: The Public Domain, 1776–1932* (Lincoln: University of Nebraska Press, Bison Books, 1962), is also useful for background information on the struggle to irrigate the arid west.

The story of the Newlands Project can be obtained only by reference to many minor items, since no complete history of the project has been written. In addition to the items on Newlands already cited, the following references are useful: F. B. Headley and Cruz Venstrom, *Economic History of the Newlands Irrigation Project*, University of Nevada Agricultural Experiment Station

Bulletin no. 120 (October 1930), and Meredith M. Miller, George Hardman, and Howard G. Mason, *Irrigated Waters of Nevada,* University of Nevada Agricultural Experiment Station Bulletin no. 187 (June 1953).

The silver issue in Nevada politics is covered best in a work by Mary Ellen Glass, *Silver and Politics in Nevada: 1892–1902* (Reno: University of Nevada Press, 1969). The book by Ostrander (previously cited) is particularly helpful for this period. An excellent work for a detailed summary of the whole silver question in national politics is Ellis Paxson Oberholtzer, *A History of the United States since the Civil War,* 5 vols. (New York: Macmillian Co., 1917–1937). A better summary of the silver question is Walter T. K. Nugent's *Money and American Society, 1865–1880* (New York: Free Press, 1968). Stewart's *Reminiscences* give a one-sided view of his activities. Another favorable view of Stewart's part in the silver fight is the biography by Effie Mona Mack, *William M. Stewart.* His own papers in the Nevada State Historical Society are more revealing. By far the best manuscript source available is the H. M. Yerington Papers at the Bancroft Library. The John P. Jones Papers at the Henry E. Huntington Library add some interesting items. Useful for the decade of the 1890s is Jack L. Millinger, "Political History of Nevada, 1891–1900" (M.A. thesis, University of Nevada, 1959). The Koontz *Political History of Nevada* is essential for details of each election held in the state. Samuel Davis, editor, *The History of Nevada,* 2 vols. (Reno, Nev.: Elms Publishing Co., 1913), is quite good for this particular subject. Scrugham's *Nevada* is also useful for the political history of Nevada in these years.

The *Congressional Record, U.S. Statutes,* and state records such as the *Journals of the Senate and Assembly* are essential for documentation. The newspapers, particularly the *Territorial Enterprise,* the *Carson Morning Appeal,* the *Reno Evening Gazette,* the *Nevada State Journal,* and the *Silver State* (Winnemucca), are filled with political items during these years.

CHAPTERS 10 AND 11

TWENTIETH-CENTURY BOOM: COPPER BECOMES KING

and

POLITICS OF THE PROGRESSIVE ERA

Most of the material on mining and labor developments in this chapter is a condensation of my book, *Nevada's 20th Century Mining Boom: Tonopah-Goldfield-Ely* (Carson City: University of Nevada Press, 1965).

Two recent books and one published in 1929 which was not cited in the above work add substantially to the social history of the period. Mrs. Hugh Brown's *Lady in Boom Town* (Palo Alto, Calif.: American West Publishing Co., 1968), is an interesting account of Tonopah during its boom and after. Herman W. Albert's *Odyssey of a Desert Prospector* (Norman: University of Oklahoma Press, 1967) is the account of a successful banker's early career spent as a prospector in Nevada toward the beginning of the twentieth century and as such gives an excellent picture of the role played by these individuals in the numerous mining booms which struck Nevada at this time. The older work, Anne Ellis, *The Life of an Ordinary Woman* (Boston: Houghton Mifflin, 1929) devotes some three chapters to life in Goldfield in the early 1900s.

The only general histories of the state to cover this period are: Scrugham, *History of Nevada,* 3 vols.; Davis, *History of Nevada,* 2 vols.; and Lillard,

Desert Challenge. All of these books have been previously cited but neither singly nor collectively are they adequate. The best political coverage is Ostrander's *Nevada: The Great Rotten Borough,* mentioned previously.

The only important political figure of the era who has received careful attention to date is Key Pittman. The biography of Pittman by Israel, previously cited, made extensive use of the Key Pittman Papers in the Library of Congress. Although somewhat unfriendly, the work is by far the best published biography of a Nevada political figure.

Unfortunately, no complete biography of Senator Newlands is available. However, his early career is very well covered in a doctoral dissertation, William Lilley III, "The Early Career of Francis G. Newlands, 1848–1897" (Ph.D. diss., Yale University, 1965). In addition, selected Newlands papers were published in *The Public Papers of Francis G. Newlands,* mentioned previously. A large collection of Newlands's papers are located in Yale University Library.

Little attention has been given to the career of Tasker L. Oddie. Leon Van Doren, "Tasker L. Oddie in Nevada Politics, 1900–1914" (M.A. thesis, University of Nevada, 1960) covers his career through the governorship. Much more important is the doctoral dissertation by Loren Briggs Chan, "Sagebrush Statesman: Tasker L. Oddie of Nevada" (Ph.D. diss., University of California at Los Angeles, 1971).

The Stewart Papers in the Nevada State Historical Society in Reno still are valuable for the early part of the twentieth century, as are the Yerington Papers in the Bancroft Library at Berkeley, California.

The George A. Bartlett papers were acquired recently by the Special Collections Division of the University of Nevada Library, Reno. Bartlett was Nevada's representatvie in Congress from 1907 to 1911 and a district court judge from 1927 to 1931 in Washoe County. The papers have not been cataloged, so their importance at this time can only be guessed. However, Bartlett was prominent in Silver-Democratic and then Democratic politics for many years, and his letters should provide an important source for this period.

The socialist colony near Fallon is given careful attention by Wilbur S. Shepperson in *Retreat to Nevada: A Socialist Colony of World War I* (Carson City: University of Nevada Press, 1966). The Socialist party in Nevada has received little attention from historians or political scientists. Unfortunately, the same thing is true of the Progressive era in Nevada.

The woman's suffrage drive in Nevada is covered briefly in Austin E. Hutcheson, editor, "The Story of the Nevada Equal Suffrage Campaign: Memoirs of Anne Martin," *University of Nevada Bulletin* 24 (August 1948). The Anne Martin Papers, including material on the Nevada suffragist movement and her two campaigns in 1918 and 1920 to capture a United States Senate seat, are located in the Bancroft Library, University of California, Berkeley.

CHAPTERS 12 AND 13

WORLD WAR I AND THE 1920s
and
THE DEPRESSION AND THE NEW DEAL

So little has been written about Nevada history since 1900 that newspapers are even more essential for any meaningful narrative of the twentieth century than for earlier periods.

The *Appendices to the Journals of the Senate and Assembly* contain the annual or biennial reports of state officials, some of which, such as the reports of the commissioner of labor, are essential for the story of Nevada during and after World War I. Other state records such as the *Statutes, Journals of the Senate and Assembly*, etc. were used extensively in the writing of this chapter.

There is no detailed history of Nevada during World War I. However, the official papers of Governor Boyle in the Nevada Archives include a variety of materials which should prove useful for such a study. The important postwar labor strikes are covered in Russell R. Elliott, *Radical Labor in the Nevada Mining Booms, 1900–1920*, Nevada Studies in History and Political Science, no. 2 (Carson City: University of Nevada Press, 1961).

Ostrander's *Nevada: The Great Rotten Borough* has many important leads for the political history of this era. Israel's *Nevada's Key Pittman* is fundamental to the study of Pittman's fight for silver, both in 1918 and during the New Deal. A master's thesis by Barbara Thornton, "George Wingfield in Nevada from 1896 to 1932" (M.A. thesis, University of Nevada, 1967), gives a detailed account of the events surrounding the Cole-Malley political crisis. The facts of that issue also can be followed in the newspapers, the *Appendices to the Journals*, the *Nevada Statutes* and the *Nevada Reports*. On occasion, Richard Lillard's *Desert Challenge* is useful for insights on the events of this period. The article by J. E. Wier, "The Mystery of Nevada," in *Rocky Mountain Politics*, edited by Thomas C. Donnelly (Albuquerque: University of New Mexico Press, 1940), is not very helpful.

A number of works have been written on the Boulder Canyon Project. See particularly William Gates, compiler, *Hoover Dam, Including the Story of the Turbulent Colorado River* (Los Angeles: Wetzel Publishing Co., 1938); Ralph B. Simmons, compiler, *Boulder Dam and the Great Southwest* (Los Angeles: Pacific Publishers, 1936); U.S. Bureau of Reclamation, *The Story of Hoover Dam*, U.S. Department of the Interior Bulletin no. 9 (Washington, D.C.: GPO, 1961); Malcolm T. Thompson, "To Tame a Giant," *Nevada Highways and Parks* 29 (Winter 1969): 9–16. For very interesting details about living conditions at the damsite during construction, see Erma Godbey, *Pioneering in Boulder City, Nevada*, Oral History Project, Center for Western North American Studies (Reno: Desert Research Institute, University of Nevada, 1967).

The story of the failure of the Wingfield banks in 1932 is based mainly on Reno newspapers, the series of articles on Wingfield by Arthur Waugh in the *Scaramento Bee*, the *Joint Legislative Commission Report* on the bank crisis, and the *George Wingfield Bankruptcy Hearings*.

Very little has been written about New Deal activities in Nevada. A few recent publications may indicate a move to correct this deficiency. Besides Harold T. Smith's doctoral dissertation on the New Deal in Nevada (in preparation), the following works are important: John A. Brennan, *Silver and the First New Deal* (Reno: University of Nevada Press, 1969); James T. Patterson, *The New Deal and the States: Federalism in Transition* (Princeton, N.J.: Princeton University Press, 1969); the entire issue of the *Pacific Historical Review* 38 (August 1969) is devoted to the New Deal in the West. It includes the following articles: T. A. Larson, "The New Deal in Wyoming," pp. 249–75; James T. Wickens, "The New Deal in Colorado," pp. 275–93; Michael P. Malone, "The New Deal in Idaho," pp. 293–311; Leonard Arrington, "The New Deal in the West: A Preliminary Statistical Inquiry," pp. 311–17; and James T. Patterson, "The New Deal in the West," pp. 317–29.

For specific information on the New Deal in Nevada the researcher must go to state and federal records for information on the dozens of agencies which functioned during the period. The Cecil Creel Papers, located in the Getchell Library, University of Nevada, Reno, have a number of useful items on the depression in Nevada. Creel was head of the Nevada Agricultural Relief Committee and continued in that capacity when it was absorbed into the Nevada Emergency Relief Administration. He was the first director of the federal relief program in Nevada. His brief volume on the *History of Agriculture in Nevada,* cited in chapter 8, has some useful information about Nevada agriculture during the 1930s. Alton E. Glass, *The Life of Alton Glass,* Oral History Project, Center for Western North American Studies (Reno: Desert Research Institute, University of Nevada, 1966), has a few important items on the Taylor Grazing Act in Nevada.

Besides the works already mentioned, a biography of Patrick Anthony McCarran by his daughter, Sister Margaret Patricia McCarran, appeared in two issues of the *Nevada Historical Society Quarterly* 11 (Fall–Winter 1968) and ibid. 12 (Spring 1969). As one should expect, the biography is prejudiced in favor of McCarran; nevertheless it is an important addition to the very limited historical material for this era, particularly so since the author had access to items not presently available to other researchers. McCarran attracted a great deal of attention in eastern newspapers and national magazines, and as a result there is a rather extensive bibliography of certain aspects of his career as a United States senator. Particularly illuminating is a series of articles by Abbot J. Liebling on McCarran's relations with the Pyramid Lake Indians which appeared in the *New Yorker,* January 1, 1955, pp. 25–30; January 8, 1955, pp. 33–36; January 15, 1955, pp. 32–36; January 22, 1955, pp. 37–38. The work by James T. Patterson, *Congressional Conservatism and the New Deal* (Lexington: University of Kentucky Press, 1967), places McCarran's New Deal record in proper focus. Most Nevada newspapers were friendly to McCarran during his later career, paticularly the *Nevada State Journal.* The *Las Vegas Sun* generally opposed him. A sizable collection of McCarran papers are available in the Nevada State Archives, but these for the most part add little to what is already known about the senator.

CHAPTERS 14, 15, AND 16

NEVADA AND WORLD WAR II,
ECONOMIC DEVELOPMENT, 1950–70
and
POLITICS, 1950–71

A most important source of interesting detail about Nevada's war effort is the *Nevada Defense News Letters,* 5 vols. (Carson City: Nevada State Council of Defense, 1941–45). Also important is Hugh A. Shamberger, *Memoirs of a Nevada Engineer and Conservationist,* Oral History Project, Center for Western North American Studies (Reno: Desert Research Institute, University of Nevada, 1967).

A scholarly history of Nevada's legalized gambling is yet to be written. Dozens of articles in magazines and many more in the newspapers, plus a great many books, have done little to present a factually accurate account. Perhaps the best of the popular accounts of Nevada gambling, although very much outdated, is Oscar Lewis, *Sagebrush Casinos: The Story of Legal Gambling in Nevada* (Garden City, N.Y.: Doubleday, 1953). More recent works which to some extent are exposés of gambling are: Edward Reid and Ovid Demaris, *The Green Felt Jungle* (New York: Trident Press, 1963), and Wallace Turner, *Gamblers' Money: A New Force in American Life* (Boston: Houghton Mifflin, 1965). Harold I. Smith, Sr., with John Wesley Noble, *I Want to Quit Winners* (Englewood Cliffs, N.J.: Prentice-Hall, 1961) is a disappointment in many ways, but still useful for a personalized account of Nevada gambling by one of its main innovators. For background material on gambling in the United States in addition to Turner's book, the following are useful: Ross Coggins, compiler, *The Gambling Menace* (Nashville, Tenn.: Broadman Press, 1966); Alex Rubner, *The Economics of Gambling* (New York: Macmillan, 1966. One of the most useful works on gambling in Nevada is Robert Lee Decker, *The Economics of the Legalized Gambling Industry in Nevada* (Ph.D. diss., University of Colorado, 1961). Also important for the economics of gambling in Nevada is Reuben A. Zubrow, *Financing State and Local Government in Nevada*, Nevada Legislative Counsel Bureau Bulletin no 44 (Carson City, Nev., 1960).

In addition, the following magazine articles are important: Joseph F. McDonald, "Gambling In Nevada," *Annals of the American Academy of Political and Social Science* 269 (May 1950): 30–34; Robert Laxalt, "What Has Wide-Open Gambling Done to Nevada," *Saturday Evening Post*, September 20, 1952, p. 44; Keith Monroe, "The New Gambling King and the Social Scientists," *Harper's*, January 1962, pp. 35–41; Fred J. Cook, "Las Vegas: Golden Paradise," *Nation*, October 22, 1960, pp. 297–302. An excellent article on the origin of Nevada's gambling law is Frank Johnson's, "The Man Who Brought Gambling to Nevada," *Nevada Centennial Magazine* (Las Vegas, Nev.: Charles R. Bell, 1964). The same magazine has a good summary, pp. 76–85, of the development of gambling in southern Nevada in an article by John Cahlan titled "Glamour Was Added." Essential for the history of gambling in Nevada are the annual reports, tabulations, and charts of the Nevada Gaming Commission. A short history of gambling in Nevada, written by Walter Wilson, is the preface to the 1963 gaming commission report.

An indispensable source for the economic development of Nevada since 1950 is Albin J. Dahl's, *Nevada's Economic Resources*, Bureau of Business and Economic Research Report no. 3 (Carson City: University of Nevada, 1964). A detailed coverage of Nevada's free port law can be found in Albin J. Dahl, *Nevada's Free Port Law*, Bureau of Business and Economic Research report no. 5 (Carson City: University of Nevada, 1966).

Industrial magazines are useful sources for recent developments in nuclear testing and mining development. Examples are: *NTS News*, published by Reynolds Electric Company; *EGG*, published by Edgerton, Geymerhausen, and Grier; and the *Kennevadan*, published by the Nevada Mines Division, Kennecott Copper Corporation.

A recent issue (Winter 1968) of the *Nevada Highways and Parks* is a special report on Nevada's business and industry. Although some of the articles are not as factual as one might like, they are useful in updating Nevada activities in gambling, mining, agriculture, transportation, recreation, and manufacturing.

Robert C. Horton, "An Outline of the Mining History of Nevada, 1924–1964," in *Outline of Nevada Mining History*, published in 1964 as Nevada Bureau of Mines report number 7, brings the story of Nevada mining nearly to the present. The newspapers are the basic source for new developments in mining as well as other areas. Recent mining statistics can be obtained from the *Minerals Yearbook,* published annually by the United States. These statistics are available from the Mackay School of Mines.

A good source for agricultural statistics from 1925 to 1959 is E. E. Wittwer's "Nevada Agriculture," *University of Nevada Bulletin* no. 210 (May 1960). The basic source for all agriculture statistics in the United States is the Agricultural Marketing Service (presently called the Statistical Reporting Service) of the U.S. Department of Agriculture. An office of the Statistical Reporting Service is located in the Max C. Fleischmann College of Agriculture, University of Nevada.

Since 1948, the *Western Political Quarterly* is of particular importance for Nevada politics because of its biennial coverage of the elections in each of the western states. The 1967, 1969 and 1971 sessions of the Nevada legislature have been analyzed in the *Governmental Research Newsletter,* distributed by the Bureau of Governmental Research, University of Nevada, Reno, adding one more dimension to the materials available for the study of Nevada's political history.

The *Memoirs* of Thomas W. Miller, cited previously, is an excellent source for recent political events in Nevada; it should be used with caution, since Miller sometimes tends to magnify his role in the events he narrates. The career of Norman Biltz is traced briefly in an article by Freeman Lincoln, "Norman Biltz, Duke of Nevada," *Fortune,* September 1954, pp. 140–44. Biltz, one of Nevada's most important political figures, completed an Oral History Project for the university, but unfortunately the manuscript is restricted. The Vail Pittman Papers and the Charles Russell Papers, both located in the Getchell Library in Reno, are important for this period, as are the official papers of Governors Carville, Pittman, Russell, and Sawyer, located in the Nevada State Archives, Carson City, Nevada. The Oral History completed by former governor Charles Russell is also restricted at the present time.

An excellent analysis is Elmer Rusco's *Voting Behavior in Nevada,* Nevada Studies in History and Political Science, no. 9 (Reno: University of Nevada Press, 1966).

CHAPTER 17

A SOCIAL AND CULTURAL APPRAISAL

References on the social and cultural development of Nevada are quite meager, particularly for the period after 1900. Separate histories of art, literature, religion, education, and fraternal organizations in Nevada remain to be written. There are some excellent sections on the early history of journalism, religion, education, and literature in the Angel and Davis volumes already cited. The Federal Writers' Program's *Nevada: A Guide to the Silver State* (Portland, Ore.: Binfords & Mort, 1940) has pertinent materials on social and cultural developments through the 1930s. In addition to the above references, there are useful items available for most of the subjects covered in this chapter.

For the story of Nevada newspapers, see John G. Folkes, *Nevada Newspapers: A Bibliography,* Nevada Studies in History and Political Science, no. 6 (Reno: University of Nevada Press, 1964); and Richard E. Lingenfelter, *The Newspapers of Nevada, 1858–1958: A History and Bibliography* (San Francisco: J. Howell, 1964). For Nevada education, see Harold N. Brown, "History of Elementary

Education in Nevada, 1861–1934" (Ed.D. diss., University of California, Berkeley, 1935); the *Nevada State Education Association Research Reports* (annual); Samuel B. Doten, *An Illustrated History of the University of Nevada* (Reno: University of Nevada, 1924); Dean E. McHenry, *The University of Nevada: An Appraisal*, Legislative Counsel Bureau Bulletin no. 28 (Reno, Nev., 1956); University of Nevada, *Self-Evaluation Report No. 1 to the Commission of Higher Schools of the Northwest Association of Secondary and Higher Schools, Jan. 1958*, (mimeographed). For religion in Nevada, see Thomas K. Gorman, *Seventy-five Years of Catholic Life in Nevada* (Reno, Nev.: Journal Press, 1935); Leonidas L. Loofbourow, *Steeples among the Sage: A Centennial Story of Nevada's Churches* (Oakland, Calif.: Lake Park Press, 1964); Alice F. Trout, "Religious Development in Nevada" (M.A. thesis, University of Nevada, 1916; this item is also published in the *Nevada Historical Society Papers* 1 [1913–16]: 143–67); Works Progress Administration (WPA), *Inventory of the Church Archives of Nevada: Protestant Episcopal Church* (Reno, Nev.: Historical Records Survey, 1941), and WPA, *Inventory of the Church Archives of Nevada: Roman Catholic Church* (Reno, Nev.: Historical Records Survey, 1939). For the story of fraternal organizations, besides the excellent chapter in Angel's *History of Nevada*, see Carl W. Torrence, *History of Masonry in Nevada* (Reno, Nev.: Carlisle Printers, 1944). For Nevada library development, see *Legislation toward Effective Library and Related Services for the People of Nevada,* Nevada Legislative Council Bureau Bulletin no. 25 Carson City, Nev., 1954); Linda Newman, "Early Public Libraries of Nevada" (research paper, University of Nevada, 1969). For the story of the literary development of the state, see *Nevada Historical Society Papers* 1 (1913–16) for a number of articles on literary developments in Nevada to that time. For the history of art in Nevada, see Jane and Howard Hickson, "Sage, Sand, and Paint," *Nevada Centennial Magazine* (1964): 40–42, 155–56. For minorities, see H. Clyde Mathews, Jr., *A Report of the Nevada Advisory Committee, March, 1963*, U.S. Commission on Civil Rights (Mimeographed); H. Clyde Mathews, Jr., *Oral Autobiography of a Modern-Day Baptist Minister . . .* (typescript, University of Nevada, 1969); Phillip J. Earl, "Nevada's Italian War," *Nevada Historical Society Quarterly* 12 (Summer 1969): 47–87; Wilbur Shepperson, "Immigrant Themes in Nevada Newspapers," *Nevada Historical Society Quarterly* 12 (Summer 1969): 3–47; Jack D. Forbes, *Nevada Indians Speak* (Reno: University of Nevada Press, 1967); C. H. Poehlman, editor, *Know Your Nevada Indians*, State Department of Education, Carson City, Nevada, 1966 (mimeographed); Helen McGinnis, "The Dutch Creek Boom," *Nevada Highways and Parks* 29 (Spring 1969): 42; Carole Wright, "Nevada Indians Quietly Press Self-Help," *Nevada State Journal*, March 8, 1970; Alvin M. Josephy, Jr., "Here in Nevada a Terrible Crime . . .," *American Heritage* 21 (June 1970): 93–101; James P. Beckwourth, *The Life and Adventures of James P. Beckwourth*, edited by T. D. Bonner (New York: Knopf, 1931); William Hanchett, "Yankee Law and the Negro in Nevada, 1861–1869," *Western Humanities Review* (Summer 1965): 241–50; Arthur G. Pettit, "Mark Twain's Attitude toward the Negro in the West," *Western Historical Quarterly* 1 (January 1970): 51–63; Elmer Rusco, *Voices of Black Nevada, Governmental Research Newsletter,* Bureau of Governmental Research (Reno: University of Nevada, 1971).

Much of the material on the current status of the arts in Nevada and of the problems of minorities has been obtained from newspapers, interviews, and correspondence with interested individuals.

Addendum to the Sources

Documentary sources for the study and writing of Nevada history have increased substantially since publication of the first edition of this work in 1973, not only because of increased interest in the state's history but also because of the aggressive and cooperative efforts of Nevada officials and others to obtain Nevada records and keep them in Nevada depositories. Thus, the collections of major political figures in Nevada in recent years are housed in Nevada. The very important Senator Patrick McCarran papers, the collection of longtime member of the U.S. House of Representatives Walter Baring, and the papers of single-term House member David Towell are located at the Nevada Historical Society in Reno. The significant collections of U.S. senators Alan Bible and Paul Laxalt; the papers of Jim Santini, a four-term U.S. representative; and the records of Eva Adams, who was an administrative assistant to senators McCarran and Bible for a long time and at one time director of the U.S. Mint are all housed in the Special Collections department of the Getchell Library at the University of Nevada–Reno. The papers of Howard Cannon, a four-term U.S. senator from Nevada, are located in the Special Collections department of the James Dickinson Library at the University of Nevada–Las Vegas. The private papers of recent Nevada governors—Grant Sawyer, Mike O'Callaghan, and Robert List—have not been committed to any depository as yet. Hopefully, they will be housed in the Nevada Archives along with the governors' executive records, which must remain there by law.

Political collections are only a part of the collection activities of these agencies. A wide range of materials have been added by these depositories. For example, the Getchell Library, UNR, added the large Lorenzo D. Creel collection on the history and Indian culture of Pyramid Lake; the architectural collections of Frederick DeLongchamps and Edward Parsons; the collection of James E. Church, founder of the Snow Survey; the papers of Walter Van Tilburg Clark; the professional papers and maps of Robert Allen, longtime state engineer; the papers of Jay Carpenter, former director of the Mackay School of Mines, and the papers of Joseph F. McDonald, Reno newspaperman. Similarly, the Nevada Historical Society has added a variety of collections, including the large John T. Reid group of records of anthropological and historic Indian relations; medical records (the Hood collection); burial records (Ross-Burke and Knobel Mortuary materials); labor records (Carpenters' Union, Local no. 971); records of fraternal groups (Knights of Pythias);

gambling records (Silver Spur Casino, Reno); records of women's clubs (Nevada Federation of Business and Professional Women's Clubs, 1920–80, the American Association of University Women collection, and the records of the Reno Soroptimist Club).

The Special Collections department of the James R. Dickinson Library on the University of Nevada–Las Vegas campus has added dozens of important manuscript collections and hundreds of photograph collections in the past few years. A particular effort has been made to obtain collections that relate to the history of southern Nevada, such as the Charles P. "Pop" Squires collection on the history of southern Nevada, and those that concern the gambling industry. Research facilities in southern Nevada were enhanced when the Nevada State Museum and Historical Society opened its Las Vegas building. With the opening of that unit, the Nevada State Historical Society began transferring manuscript collections relating to southern Nevada, such as the Helen Stewart collection and the Frank Buol papers.

The Nevada State Archives during the past few years has strengthened its position as the primary depository for state agency records by purifying its archival records in line with the legislative mandate to house the records that emanate from all state agencies. Thus manuscript collections previously held by the archives that were not directly related to state government, such as the McCarran and Baring papers, were transferred to other depositories, and state and territorial agency records that had been scattered earlier to various repositories are being transferred to the state archives at Carson City. It should be noted that the minutes of the Gaming Control Board and those of the Gaming Commission, invaluable sources for the study of the Nevada Gaming industry, and the executive records of the governors are also housed in the state archives.

An important development in the continuing efforts to improve the study and teaching of Nevada history in the schools was the publication by the Nevada Historical Society of a pamphlet series of teaching aids to supplement textbook material. Seven units in the projected series have been published to date: *Nevada Symbols: Reflections of the Past; Nevada's Water: Lifeline for a Thirsty Land; Clark County: The Changing Face of Southern Nevada; Native Americans of Nevada; The Mountain Men: Early Explorers of Nevada; The Pioneering Experience of Nevada;* and *The Comstock.* The pamphlets are furnished free to schools throughout Nevada.

Also directed to pupils in the elementary and secondary schools of the state, supported by the Grace Dangberg Foundation, is the projected series titled *Nevada: Its Land and Communities.* The first volume, by Marie E. Freeman and Jeffrey Kintop, *What Time is This Place?* (Reno, Nev.: Research and Educational Planning Center, College of Education, University of Nevada–Reno, 1982), is an outstanding publication. In a unique approach the book introduces the student to techniques to be used "to unlock the meaning of historical evidence which is available to everyone." The unit is a wonderful beginning for researchers, young and old alike. A teacher's guide is available. The second volume in the series, by Marie E. Freeman and Maria H. Davis, *Alpine to Alkali* (Reno: Grace Dangberg Foundation, 1983), is also an outstanding contribution to the study of Nevada history in the public schools. Its main purpose "is to explore the natural characteristics of Nevada and the Great Basin so that the events of Nevada history can be understood in their geographical setting."

A number of other important research aids have been published in recent years. The most important is the compilation by Stanley Paher, *Nevada: An Annotated Bibliography* (Las Vegas: Nevada Publications, 1980). The volume includes over 2,500 annotated entries. Other references include James L. Higgins, *A Guide to the Manuscript Collections at the Nevada Historical Society* (Reno: Nevada Historical Society,

1975); Eric Moody, *An Index to the Publications of the Nevada Historical Society, 1907–1971* (Reno: Nevada Historical Society, 1977); Robert D. Armstrong, *Nevada Printing History: A Bibliography of Imprints and Publications* (Reno: University of Nevada Press, 1981); Richard E. Lingenfelter and Karen Rix Gash, *The Newspapers of Nevada: A History and Bibliography, 1854–1979* (Reno: University of Nevada Press, 1984); Alvin R. McLane, *Pyramid Lake. A Bibliography* (Reno: Camp Nevada, Monograph no. 1, 1975); Mary B. Ansari, *Bibliography of Nevada Mining and Geology, 1966–1970* (Reno: Mackay School of Mines and Nevada Bureau of Mines and Geology Report no. 24, 1975); and Mary B. Ansari, *Nevada Collections of Maps and Aerial Photographs* (Reno: Camp Nevada, Monograph no. 2, 1976).

Two histories of Nevada were published in this period: a single volume by Russell R. Elliott, *History of Nevada* (Lincoln: University of Nebraska Press, 1973), and an interesting interpretive study by Robert Laxalt, *Nevada: A Bicentennial History* (New York: W. W. Norton, 1977). A heterogeneous collection of stories on Nevada of unequal importance by various authors was published as *Nevada Official Bicentennial Book* (Las Vegas: Nevada Publications, 1976), under the editorship of Stanley M. Paher.

The following books cover general Nevada materials not readily available elsewhere: Helen S. Carlson, *Nevada Place Names: A Geographical Dictionary* (Reno: University of Nevada Press, 1974); Myrtle T. Myles, *Nevada's Governors from Territorial Days to the Present* (Sparks, Nev.: Western Printing and Publishing Co., 1972); and Robert P. Harris, Nevada Postal History (Santa Cruz, Calif.: Bonanza Press, 1973). A guidebook by David Toll, *The Compleat Nevada Traveler* (Reno: University of Nevada Press, 1976), does not supplant the still useful W.P.A. guide published in the 1930s but does update it. A revision of the Toll Book was published in 1981 by the Goldhill Publishing Company. A guide by Mary Ellen and Al Glass, *Touring Nevada* (Reno: University of Nevada Press, 1983), is a much more structured approach for tourists visiting Nevada, suggesting day or longer trips to specific locations.

The sixth edition of Eleanore Bushnell and Don W. Driggs, *The Nevada Constitution: Origin and Growth* (Reno: University of Nevada Press, 1984), updates the work in line with the latest research and new interpretations.

CHAPTER 1

THE PHYSICAL ENVIRONMENT

Richard A. Bartlett, ed., *Rolling Rivers: An Encyclopedia of America's Rivers* (New York: McGraw Hill, 1984), includes four Nevada rivers, the Carson, the Walker, the Truckee, and the Humboldt. Another river study is Phillip L. Fradkin, *A River No More: The Colorado River and the West* (New York: Knopf, 1981). See also John G. Houghton, Clarence M. Sakamoto, and Richard O. Gifford, *Nevada's Weather and Climate* (Reno: University of Nevada, Nevada Bureau of Mines and Mackay School of Mines, 1975), and Samuel G. Houghton, *A Trace of Desert Waters: The Great Basin Story* (Glendale, Calif.: Arthur H. Clark, 1976). John A. McPhee, *Basin and Range* (New York: Farrar, Strauss, Giroux, 1981), is a provocative and readable explanation of the Great Basin, emphasizing the theory of plate tectonics and its relationship to the geologic history of the Basin-Range Province. The basic work first attracted attention when part of it was published in two installments in the *New Yorker* magazine, October 20 and 27, 1980. The very useful work by Israel Russell, *Present and Extinct Lakes of Nevada*, first published in 1885, was reprinted in 1976 by Camp Nevada, Reno, Nevada. For an account of the Black Rock Desert in northwestern Nevada, see Sessions Wheeler, *The Black Rock Desert* (Caldwell, Idaho: Caxton Printers, 1978).

Coverage of the natural history of the Great Basin received new impetus with the establishment of the Max C. Fleischmann series in Great Basin Natural History. The most recent publication in that series is Fred A. Ryser, Jr., *Birds of the Great Basin: A Natural History* (Reno: University of Nevada Press, 1985). Although the word definitive is overworked, it seems safe to use it to describe that excellent work. An earlier publication in the series is Ronald M. Lanner, *Trees of the Great Basin: A Natural History* (Reno: University of Nevada Press, 1984). See also the same author's *The Piñon Pine: A Natural and Cultural History* (Reno: University of Nevada Press, 1981).

Chapter 2

BEFORE THE WHITE MAN

On Indian archeology see Robert G. Elston, *A Contribution to Washo Archeology*, Nevada Archeological Survey Research Paper no. 2, December 1971, University of Nevada, Reno. A number of works on Nevada Indians from the Indian viewpoint were published in the 1970s. These include: *Newe: A Western Shoshone History* (Reno: Inter-tribal Council of Nevada, 1976); *Numa: A Northern Paiute History* (Reno: Inter-Tribal Council of Nevada, 1976); *Nuwuvi: A Southern Paiute History* (Reno: Inter-Tribal Council of Nevada, 1976); *Wa She Shu: A Washo Tribal History* (Salt Lake City: University of Utah Printing Service, 1976); *Personal Reflections of the Shoshone-Paiute-Washo* (Reno: Inter-Tribal Council of Nevada, 1974). A moving fictionalized account of Washo life can be found in Thomas Sanchez, *Rabbit Boss* (New York: Ballantine Books, 1973). A very important work on the Pyramid Lake Indians is Martha C. Knack and Omer C. Stewart, *As Long as the River Shall Run: An Ethnology of Pyramid Lake Indian Reservation* (Berkeley: University of California Press, 1984). The basic account of the ghost dance was inadvertently omitted from the first edition of this work: see James Mooney, "The Ghost Dance Religion and the Sioux Outbreak of 1890," *14th Annual Report of the Bureau of American Ethnology*, vol. 14 (Washington, D.C.: Government Printing Office, 1896). An interesting addition to the literature on the ghost dance is L. G. Moses, "James Mooney and Wovoka: An Ethnologist's Visit with the Ghost Dance Prophet," *Nevada Historical Society Quarterly* 22 (Summer 1980): 71–86. David Miller's *Ghost Dance*, originally published in 1959, was reprinted by the University of Nebraska Press in 1985.

The following references report important archeological surveys in various parts of Nevada in the 1980s. For the interesting find of a thirteen-thousand-year-old mammoth in the Black Rock Desert of northwestern Nevada, see the *Reno Gazette-Journal*, August 22, 1982, p. 1B, col. 1. For the story of an Indian summer home on Mt. Jefferson in the Toquima range six thousand years ago, see the *Nevada State Journal*, September 5, 1981, p. 1, col. 2. The 1985 discovery of an Indian burial ground near Fallon is considered by some scientists to be one of the most important archaeological discoveries ever made in Nevada; see the *Reno Gazette-Journal*, October and November 1985. See also David Hurst Thomas, "The Secrets of Hidden Cave," *Nevada Magazine* 40 (July-August 1980): 42–45. It should be remembered that newspaper and magazine reports are preliminary and that the real significance of those and other archeological sites that are presently being surveyed will not be known until the formal reports are available.

CHAPTER 3

The Trailblazers

A number of important works on explorations in Nevada were published in the 1970s. George R. Brooks, *The Southwest Expedition of Jedediah Smith: His Personal Account of the Journey to California, 1826–27.* (Glendale, Calif.: Arthur H. Clark, 1977), prints the long-lost part of Smith's journal, bringing together the basic documentation for Smith's important place in the exploration of the Great Basin. Other important additions are Bil Gilbert, *Westering Man: The Life of Joseph Walker* (New York: Atheneum, 1983); Gloria Griffen Cline, *Peter Skene Ogden and the Hudson's Bay Company* (Norman: University of Oklahoma Press, 1974); and Glyndiver Williams, ed., *Peter Skene Ogden's Snake Country Journals, 1827–28 and 1828–29* (London: Hudson's Bay Record Society, 1971). Additional works on John Frémont include Ferol Egan, *Frémont: Explorer for a Restless Nation* (Garden City, N.Y.: Doubleday, 1977), reprinted by the University of Nevada Press in 1985; and Mary Lee Spence and Donald Jackson, *The Expeditions of John Charles Frémont,* 2 vols. (Urbana: University of Illinois Press, 1973–74). The third volume of that very significant series, edited by Mary Lee Spence, was published by the University of Illinois Press in 1984. Two other works on the explorers are worth noting: Fray Angelico Chavez, translator, *The Domínguez-Escalante Journal: Their Expedition through Colorado, Utah, Arizona, and New Mexico in 1776* (Provo, Utah: Brigham Young University Press, 1976); and Elinor Wilson, *Jim Beckwourth: Black Mountain Man and War Chief of the Crows* (Norman: University of Oklahoma Press, 1972). Probably the best work on the emigrants yet published is John D. Unruh, Jr., *The Plains Across: The Overland Emigrants and the Trans-Mississippi West, 1840–1860* (Urbana: University of Illinois Press, 1979). A very interesting account of the trails to California, with excellent illustrations, is Thomas H. Hunt, *Ghost Trails to California* (Palo Alto, Calif.: American West Publishing Company, 1974). A detailed and interesting account of the latter part of the emigrant journey to California is Harold Curran, *Fearful Crossing* (Reno: Great Basin Press, 1982).

CHAPTER 4

THE FIRST SETTLEMENTS

A detailed study of the first settlements in Nevada has yet to be written. A few items of interest published during the past decade follow: Leonard Arrington, *The Mormons in Nevada* (Las Vegas: *Las Vegas Sun,* 1979); Richard H. Jackson, ed., *The Mormon Role in the Settlement of the West,* Charles Redd Monographs in Western History no. 9 (Provo, Utah: Brigham Young University Press, 1978); Leonard Arrington, *Brigham Young: American Moses* (New York: Knopf, 1985); Grace Dangberg, *Carson Valley,* "Historical Sketches of Nevada's First Settlement" (Minden, Nev.: Carson Valley Historical Society, 1972); Richard E. Lingenfelter, *Steamboats on the Colorado River, 1852–1916* (Tucson: University of Arizona Press, 1978).

CHAPTER 5

TERRITORY TO STATEHOOD

This period of Nevada history has been the subject of some of the most important studies published in the past decade. A research guide is Robert D. Armstrong, *Territorial Nevada: A Guide to the Records* (Reno: A National Historical Publications Project, Nevada Historical Society, [1978]). James W. Hulse's article "The California-

446

Nevada Boundary: The History of a Conflict," *Nevada Historical Society Quarterly* 23 (Summer 1980): 87–109 continues in Fall 1980, pp. 157–78. Two significant works were published under the auspices of the Nevada Legislative Counsel Bureau. The first is an excellent contemporary account of the debates during the first two sessions of Nevada's Territorial legislature, Andrew J. Marsh, *Letters from Nevada Territory, 1861–1862,* edited by William C. Miller, Russell W. McDonald, and Ann Rollins (Carson City, Nev.: Legislative Counsel Bureau, State of Nevada, 1972). The second is a record of the debates on the 1863 constitution, Andrew Marsh, Samuel L. Clemens, and Amos Bowman, *Reports of the 1863 Constitutional Convention of the Territory of Nevada,* edited by William C. Miller and Eleanore Bushnell (Carson City, Nev.: Legislative Counsel Bureau, State of Nevada, 1972). Since the defeated 1863 document was the basis for the 1864 constitution, these records are essential to the study of Nevada constitutional history.

Three excellent articles by David A. Johnson reveal the need for a new interpretation of Nevada's territorial and constitutional periods. The first, "A Case of Mistaken Identity: William M. Stewart and the Rejection of Nevada's First Constitution," *Nevada Historical Society Quarterly* 22 (Fall 1979): 186–98, reverses the role usually assigned to Stewart in the ratification of the 1863 constitution. The second, "Industry and the Individual on the Far Western Frontier: A Case Study of Politics and Social Change in Early Nevada," *Pacific Historical Review* 51 (August 1982):243–65, reassesses the ratification of the 1864 constitution along economic lines. The third article, "The Courts and the Comstock Lode: The Travail of John Wesley North," *Pacific Historian* 27 (Summer 1983): 31–47, although not dealing directly with the constitutional issues, uses North's judicial career to show the effects of the movement from individual to corporate ownership of the mines on legal and political issues.

CHAPTER 6

EARLY STATEHOOD: THE ECONOMIC FOUNDATIONS

The temporary pause in the Comstock rush occasioned by the Paiute War is covered in Ferol Egan, *Sand in a Whirlwind: The Paiute Indian War of 1860* (Garden City, N.Y.: Doubleday, 1972), reprinted by the University of Nevada Press in 1985. The use of fictional dialogue detracts from this sympathetic treatment of the Indians. Nellie Shaw Harnar, *Indians of Coo-yu-ee-Pah (Pyramid Lake)* (Sparks, Nev.: Dave's Printing and Publishing Co., 1974), among other items, covers the Pyramid Lake War of 1860 from an Indian point of view.

For a well-researched, detailed, and interesting account of Reno's early history, see John M. Townley, *Tough Little Town on the Truckee,* History of Reno Series, vol. 1 (Reno, Nev.: Great Basin Studies Center, 1983), the first of a projected three-volume series. A shorter, excellent account of the same city is William D. Rowley, *Reno: Hub of the Washoe County . . .* (Woodland Hills, Calif.: Windsor Publication, 1984). For additional information on Reno see Guy Louis Rocha, "Reno's First Robber Baron," *Nevada Magazine* 40 (March–April 1980): 28–29, and Doris Cerveri, *Reno: A Pictorial History* (Reno: The Nevada Self-Help Foundation, 1981).

For less-known areas of Nevada during this period see Donald Abbe, *Austin and the Reese River Mining District: Nevada's Forgotten Frontier* (Reno: University of Nevada Press, 1985), and Marvin Lewis, *Martha and the Doctor: A Frontier Family in Central Nevada* (Reno: University of Nevada Press, 1977). The account by Roger D. McGrath, *Gunfighters, Highwaymen, and Vigilantes* (Berkeley: University of California Press, 1984), focuses on Bodie, California, and Aurora, Nevada. See also John M. Townley,

Conquered Provinces: Nevada Moves Southeast, 1864–1871 (Provo, Utah: Brigham Young University Press, 1973).

Although there is still no detailed history of agriculture in Nevada available, a number of items published in the past decade add details to the story, including John M. Townley, *Alfalfa Country: Nevada Land, Water, and Politics in the Nineteenth Century* (Reno: Agricultural Experiment Station/Max C. Fleischmann College of Agriculture, University of Nevada, [1981]). Clel Georgetta, *Golden Fleece in Nevada* (Reno, Nev.: Venture Publishing Co., 1972), is an overly detailed history of the sheep industry in Nevada. Molly Flagg Knudtsen, *Here is our Valley* (Reno, Nev.: Helen Marye Thomas Memorial Series no. 1, College of Agriculture, University of Nevada, 1975), is an interesting account of the Grass Valley Ranch in Central Nevada. By the same author, *Under the Mountain* (Reno: University of Nevada Press, 1982), gives additional views of ranching in central Nevada.

CHAPTERS 7 AND 8

THE COMSTOCK AND COMSTOCK ERA POLITICS

Three works published within a few years of each other add substantially to the story of organized labor on the Comstock and the American West: Ronald C. Brown, *Hard Rock Miners: The Intermountain West, 1860–1920* (College Station, Texas: Texas A&M University Press, 1979); Richard E. Lingenfelter, *The Hardrock Miners: A History of the Mining Labor Movement in the American West, 1863–1893* (Berkeley: University of California Press, 1974); and Mark Wyman, *Hard Rock Epic: Western Miners and the Industrial Revolution, 1860–1910* (Berkeley: University of California Press, 1979). A valuable addition to the history of the V & T Railroad is Ted Wurm and Harre W. Demoro, *The Silver Short Line: A History of the Virginia and Truckee Railroad* (Glendale, Calif.: Trans-Anglo Books, 1983).

A number of works published during this period add important material to the social history of the Comstock era. The most important is the three-volume *The Journals of Alfred Doten, 1849*–1902, edited by Walter Van Tilburg Clark (Reno: University of Nevada Press, 1973). An interesting and provocative study of prostitution is the volume by Marion S. Goldman, *Gold Diggers and Silver Miners: Prostitution and Social Life on the Comstock Lode* (Ann Arbor: University of Michigan Press, 1981). For another aspect of Comstock social life see Steve Frady, *Red Shirts and Leather Helmets: Volunteer Fire Fighting on the Comstock Lode* (Reno: University of Nevada Press, 1984). A good illustration of the value of historical archeology is Eugene M. Hattori, *Northern Paiutes on the Comstock: Archeology and Ethnohistory of an American Indian Population in Virginia City, Nevada* (Carson City: Nevada State Museum, Occasional Papers no. 2, 1975). The Chinese on the Comstock are treated in Russell M. Magnaghi, "Virginia City's Chinese Community, 1860–1880," *Nevada Historical Society Quarterly* 24 (Summer 1981): 130–57. Three works on the Comstock have appeared recently as reprints: Wells Drury, *An Editor on the Comstock Lode* (Reno: University of Nevada Press, 1985), first published in 1936; Charles Shinn, *The Story of the Mine* (Reno: University of Nevada Press, 1980), first published in 1896; and Mary M. Mathews, *Ten Years in Nevada; or, Life on the Pacific Coast* (Lincoln: University of Nebraska Press, 1985).

Of varying importance to the history of the Comstock are: Warren Hinckle and Frederick Hobbs, *The Richest Place on Earth: The Story of Virginia City, Nevada, and the Heyday of the Comstock Lode* (Boston: Houghton Mifflin, 1978)—a popular history that adds little to the story of the Comstock era; and Myra Sauer Ratay, *Pioneers of the*

Ponderosa: How Washoe Valley Rescued the Comstock (Sparks, Nev.: Western Printing and Publishing Co., 1973). Two important works that add technical information on mining during the Comstock era are Clark C. Spence, *Mining Engineers and the American West: The Lace-Boot Brigade, 1849–1933* (New Haven, Conn.: Yale University Press, 1970), and Otis E. Young, Jr., *Black Powder and Hard Steel: Miners and Machines on the old Western Frontier* (Norman: University of Oklahoma Press, 1976).

The conflict between California and Nevada over water rights is treated in Grace Dangberg, *Conflict on the Carson* (Minden, Nev.: Carson Valley Historical Society, 1975); and W. Turrentine Jackson and Donald J. Pisani, *A Case Study in Interstate Resource Management: The California-Nevada Water Controversy, 1865–1955* (Davis: University of California–Davis, 1973).

A number of biographical studies covering the Comstock era have been published since 1973: John T. Dwyer, *Condemned to the Mines: The Life of Eugene O'Connell, 1815–1891, Pioneer Bishop of Northern California and Nevada* (New York: Vantage Press, 1976); Russell R. Elliott, *Servant of Power: A Political Biography of Senator William M. Stewart* (Reno: University of Nevada Press, 1983); Ruth Hermann, *Gold and Silver Colossus: William Morris Stewart and His Southern Bride* (Sparks, Nev.: Dave's Press, 1975); David Lavender, *Nothing Seemed Impossible: William C. Ralston and Early San Francisco* (Palo Alto, Calif.: American West Publishing Co., 1975); Eric N. Moody, *Western Carpetbagger: The Extraordinary Memoirs of "Senator" Thomas Fitch* (Reno: University of Nevada Press, 1978); and Richard H. Peterson, *The Bonanza Kings: The Social Origins and Business Behavior of Western Mining Entrepreneurs, 1870–1900* (Lincoln: University of Nebraska Press, 1977).

CHAPTER 9

THE DEPRESSION PERIOD, 1880–1900

For the water question during these years see the previously mentioned work by Jackson and Pisani, *A Cast Study in Interstate Resource Management*, and John W. Bird, "A History of Water Rights in Nevada," *Nevada Historical Society Quarterly* 18 (Spring 1975): 27–32, and 19 (Spring 1976): 27–34. Also useful is Michael C. Robinson, *Water of the West . . .* (Chicago: Public Works Historical Society, [1979]). See also Douglas H. Strong, *Tahoe: An Environmental History* (Lincoln: University of Nebraska Press, 1983).

Jerry M. Cooper, *The Army of Civil Disorder: A Federal Military Intervention in Labor Disputes, 1877–1900* (Westport, Conn.: Greenwood Press, 1980), is important for its coverage of its federal intervention in Nevada during the 1894 Pullman strike. An excellent analysis may be found in Joseph A. Fry, "Silver and Sentiment: The Nevada Press and the Coming of the Spanish-American War," *Nevada Historial Society Quarterly* 20 (Winter 1977): 223–40. Hugh Shamberger, *Candelaria and Its Neighbors* (Carson City: Nevada Historical Press, 1978), is the story of a mining camp that had a short revival during the depression period.

CHAPTERS 10 AND 11

TWENTIETH CENTURY MINING BOOM: COPPER BECOMES KING
AND
POLITICS OF THE PROGRESSIVE ERA

Emmett L. Arnold, *Gold Camp Drifter, 1906–1910* (Reno: University of Nevada Press, 1973), offers interesting glimpses of the life of a miner at Goldfield, Tonopah, and Rawhide. Biographical studies include Loren B. Chan, *Sagebrush Statesman:*

Tasker L. Oddie (Reno: University of Nevada Press, 1973), and George Hildebrand, *Borax Pioneer: Frances Marion Smith* (San Diego, Calif.: Howell-North Books, 1982). Lorena Edwards Meadows, *A Sagebrush Heritage* (San Jose, Calif.: Harlan-Young Press, 1972), tells the story of Ben Edwards, an important merchant in the boom mining camps of Candelaria, Aurora, and Tonopah. Nancy B. Schreier, *Highgrade: The Story of National, Nevada* (Glendale, Calif.: Arthur H. Clark, 1981), is an excellent study of one of the lesser-known mining booms. A number of monographs by Hugh Shamberger are important for this period: *The Story of Fairview* (Carson City: Nevada Historical Press, 1974); *The Story of Rochester* (Carson City: Nevada Historical Press, 1973); *Silver Peak* (Carson City: Nevada Historical Press, 1976); *The Story of Wonder, Churchill County, Nevada* (Carson City: Nevada Historical Press, 1974); and the latest and one of the most significant of these important volumes, *Goldfield* (Sparks: Nev.: Western Printing and Publishing Co., 1982).

See also Donald J. Pisani, "Western Nevada's Water Crisis, 1915–1935," *Nevada Historical Society Quarterly* 22 (Spring 1979): 3–20; and John M. Townley, *Turn This Water into Gold: The Story of the Newlands Project* (Reno: Nevada Historical Society, 1977). Guy Louis Rocha, "Radical Labor Struggles in the Tonopah-Goldfield Mining District, 1901–1922," *Nevada Historical Society Quarterly* 20 (Spring 1977): 3–45, adds significant new material to the story of labor in these boom camps. Another aspect of the Goldfield labor troubles is told in the forthcoming (1986) publication by Sally Zanjani and Guy L. Rocha, *The Ignoble Conspiracy* (Reno: University of Nevada Press), a detailed account of the Smith-Preston trial during the bitter labor struggles at Goldfield. Other studies include Eric N. Moody, "Nevada's Bull Moose Progressives: The Formation and Function of a State Political Party in 1912," *Nevada Historical Society Quarterly* 16 (Fall 1973): 157–80; William Rowley, "Francis G. Newlands: A Westerner's Search for a Progressive and White America," *Nevada Historical Society Quarterly* 17 (Summer 1974): 69–79, and William Rowley, "Senator Newlands and the Modernization of the Democratic Party," *Nevada Historical Society Quarterly* 15 (Summer 1972): 25–36. Sally Springmeyer Zanjani, *The Unspiked Rail: Memoir of a Nevada Rebel* (Reno: University of Nevada Press, 1981), offers a superb biography of George Springmeyer, one of Nevada's most important political figures in the first three decades of the twentieth century. Anne Howard, *The Long Campaign: A Biography of Anne Martin* (Reno: University of Nevada Press, 1985), provides an excellent biography of a major leader in Nevada's suffrage movement and the first woman to run for United States senator.

CHAPTERS 12 AND 13

WORLD WAR I AND THE 1920s
AND
THE DEPRESSION AND THE NEW DEAL

A variety of studies covering the period from World War I through the New Deal include: Phillip I. Earl, "By the Seats of Their Pants: Aviation's Beginnings in Nevada," *Nevada Historical Society Quarterly* 23 (Summer 1980): 110–24; Jerome E. Edwards, *Pat McCarran: Political Boss of Nevada* (Reno: University of Nevada Press, 1982)—an excellent study, detailing the rise to power of one of Nevada's most important political figures; Norris J. Hundley, *Water and the West: The Colorado Water Compact and the Politics of Water in the American West* (Berkeley: University of California Press, 1975); Eugene P. Moehring, "Public Works and the New Deal in Las Vegas," *Nevada Historical Society Quarterly* 24 (Summer 1981): 107–29; Beverly Bowen Moeller, *Phil Swing and Boulder Dam* (Berkeley: University of California Press, 1971);

James S. Olson, "Rehearsal for Disaster: Hoover and the Banking Crisis in Nevada, 1932–1933," *Western Historical Quarterly* 6 (April 1975): 149–61, and Guy Louis Rocha, "The I.W.W. and the Boulder Canyon Project: The Final Death Throes of American Syndicalism," *Nevada Historical Society Quarterly* 21 (Spring 1978):3–24.

CHAPTERS 14, 15, AND 16

NEVADA AND WORLD WAR II,
ECONOMIC DEVELOPMENT, 1950–1984
and
POLITICS, 1950–1984

A good starting point for material covered in these chapters is Mary Ellen Glass, *Nevada's Turbulent '50s: Decade of Political and Economic Change* (Reno: University of Nevada Press, 1981). Very useful for economic development are various publications of the Bureau of Business and Economic Research of UNR's College of Business Administration. The following are particularly important: Thomas F. Cargill, *Is the Nevada Economy Recession Proof?* Paper no. 79–4, Bureau of Business and Economic Research, College of Business Administration [1979]; Albin J. Dahl, *Nevada's Economic Development: An Overview,* Bureau of Business and Economic Research, Paper 77-6 (February 1977), College of Business Administration, Reno, Nevada; and Sam E. White, "Nevada's Business Climate, 1980 to 1982: A Comparison of Economic Factors among Western States," *Nevada Review of Business and Economics* 7 (Summer 1983): 8–14. This quarterly publication of the Bureau of Business and Economic Research carries a section on Nevada's economic indicators, enabling the reader to keep current with economic trends in the state. See also State of Nevada, "The Comprehensive Economic Development Plan," Governor's Office of Planning Coordination (Carson City, Nev., January 1978); State of Nevada, Department of Conservation and Natural Resources, "Truckee River," Water Supply Report no. 1 (Carson City, Nev., September 1978); and State of Nevada, Department of Conservation and Natural Resources, "Water Conservation in Nevada," Water Planning Report no. 1 (Carson City, Nev., August 1979).

A large number of important sources on gambling have become available since publication of the first edition of this book. Of particular interest are a number of oral histories of individuals connected with the gambling industry in Nevada: Robbins E. Cahill, *Recollections of Work in State Politics, Government, Taxation, Gaming Control, Clark County Administration, and the Nevada Resort Administration* (Reno: University of Nevada Oral History Project, 1976); William F. Harrah, *My Recollections of the Hotel-Casino Industry and as an Auto Collecting Enthusiast* (Reno: University of Nevada Oral History Project, [1980]); Leslie S. Kofoed, *Kofoed's Meanderings in Lovelock Business, Nevada Government, the U.S. Marshall's Office, and the Gaming Industry* (Reno: University of Nevada Oral History Project, 1972); and Edward A. Olsen, *My Career as a Journalist in Oregon, Idaho, and Nevada; in Nevada Gaming Control; and at the University of Nevada* (Reno: University of Nevada Oral History Project, 1972). Biographical studies include Donald L. Barlett and James B. Steele, *Empire: The Life, Legend, and Madness of Howard Hughes* (New York: W. W. Norton, 1979); Dennis Eisenberg et al., *Meyer Lansky: Mogul of the Mob* (New York: Paddington Press, 1979); and Leon Mandel, *William Fisk Harrah: The Life and Times of a Gambling Magnate* (Garden City, N.Y.: Doubleday, 1982).

For the gambling industry see Susan Anderl, *A Gambling Catalog: A List from the Research Collection at the University of Nevada, Las Vegas* (Las Vegas: James R. Dickinson Library, UNLV, 1978), and Stephen A. Powell, *A Gambling Bibliography Based on the*

Collection, University of Nevada, Las Vegas (Las Vegas: James R. Dickinson Library, UNLV, 1972). See William R. Eadington, ed., *Gambling and Society: Inter-disciplinary Studies on the Subject of Gambling* (Springfield, Ill.: Charles C. Thomas, Publisher, 1976). Also by Eadington are *The Economics of Gambling Behavior: A Qualitative Study of Nevada's Gambling Industry,* Bureau of Business and Economic Research paper no. 11 (Reno: University of Nevada, 1973); "Fifty Years of Gaming," *Nevada Magazine,* special issue 41 (March–April 1981); and "Gambling in America," Final Report of the Commission on the Review of the National Policy toward Gambling (Washington, D.C.: Government Printing Office, 1976). A well-researched volume by Jerome H. Skolnick is the best overall view of the gambling industry: *House of Cards: The Legalization and Control of Casino Gambling* (Boston: Little, Brown, 1978). A more recent and more detailed story of gambling and gambling control in Nevada is Ken Miller, "The Other Nevada: Gaming, Politics, and the Mob," a series of fifteen articles on the problem of gambling control in Nevada appearing in the *Reno Gazette-Journal,* July 14–July 28, 1985. The articles by Miller were followed by a series of six editorials by Ev Landers on the same subject, also in the Reno Gazette-Journal, July 28–August 2, 1985. The articles and the editorials should dispel any doubts as to the illegal activities of underworld figures in the Nevada gambling industry.

The city of Las Vegas has received a good deal of attention as the nation's gambling mecca. For various views of the city see the following: C. Gregory Crampton, *The Complete Las Vegas* (Salt Lake City: Peregrine Smith, 1976); Florence Lee Jones and John Francis Cahlan, *Water: A History of Las Vegas,* 2 vols. (Las Vegas: Las Vegas Water District, 1975); and Perry Bruce Kaufman, "The Best City of them All: A History of Las Vegas, 1930–1960," (Ph.D. Diss., University of California, Santa Barbara, 1974). George Lewis, "The Man Who Created Las Vegas," *Nevada Magazine* 40 (July–August 1980): 46–47, tells the story of "Pop" Squires and the development of Las Vegas. See also Stanley Paher, *Las Vegas: As It Began, as It Grew* (Las Vegas: Nevada Publications, 1971). The chapter "Nevada: Gomorrah on the Desert," in Neil R. Peirce and Jerry Hagstrom, *The Book of America: Inside 50 States Today* (New York: W. W. Norton, 1983), emphasizes the part played by Las Vegas in the state's history. Guy Louis Rocha, "Gable vs. Gable," *Nevada Magazine* 41 (November–December 1981): 29–31, shows the importance of the Gable divorce in stimulating the divorce business in Las Vegas. A biographical study is found in Carrie M. Townley, "Helen J. Stewart: First Lady of Las Vegas," *Nevada Historical Society Quarterly* 16 (Winter 1973): 215–44, and continued in 17 (Spring 1974): 3–32. Peter Wiley and Robert Gottlieb, *Empires in the Sun: The Rise of the New American West* (New York: G. P. Putnam's Sons, 1982), provides a provocative study of Las Vegas as one of the important new cities in the southwestern United States. Tom Wolfe, *The kandy-kolored tangerine-flake streamline baby* (New York: Farrar, Straus, & Giroux, 1965), is a fascinating appraisal of the architectural innovations in the growth of the Las Vegas strip.

As noted in chapter 15, the Nevada Test Site has played an important role in the economic development of southern Nevada. The problems associated with atomic testing at the site are explored in a very important work by A. Constandina Titus, *Bomb in the Backyard: A Difficult Stewardship* (Reno: University of Nevada Press, 1986). An excellent source for articles on various aspects of the Nevada economy is the *Nevada Review of Business and Economics,* published by the Bureau of Business and Economic Research, College of Business Administration, University of Nevada, Reno.

For brief but valuable comments on recent Nevada elections, see Eleanore Bushnell and Don W. Driggs, *The Nevada Constitution: Origin and Growth,* 6th ed. (Reno: University of Nevada Press, 1984), pp. 79–83. The 1974 and 1976 elections are covered in *Nevada Public Affairs,* Bureau of Governmental Research, University of Nevada, Reno: "The 1974 Election in Nevada," by Don W. Driggs, vol. 14 (April 1976), and "The 1976 Election in Nevada," by Don W. Driggs, vol. 15 (February 1977). For the 1978 election see "Nevada," by Eleanore Bushnell and Don W. Driggs, in B. Oliver Walter, ed., *Politics in the West: The 1978 Elections* (Laramie, Wyo.: Institute for Policy Research, 1979), pp. 90–102. For the 1980 elections see Eleanore Bushnell and Don W. Driggs, "Nevada: Business as Usual," *Social Science Journal* 18 (October 1981): 65–75.

Newspapers are particularly important for the recent political history of Nevada since few analyses are available. Also important are the articles in the *Nevada Public Affairs Review,* published by the Senator Alan Bible Center for Applied Research, University of Nevada, Reno. For other aspects of Nevada politics see Eleanore Bushnell, *Sagebrush and Neon: Studies in Nevada Politics* (Reno: Bureau of Government Research, University of Nevada, Reno, 1973), Eric N. Moody, *Southern Gentleman of Nevada Politics: Vail M. Pittman* (Reno: University of Nevada Press, 1974), and Peter C. Petersen, *Reminiscence of My Work in Nevada Labor, Politics, Post Office, and Gaming Control* (Reno: University of Nevada Oral History Project, 1970). For a critical and provocative view of the Nevada political and economic scene since 1940 see James Hulse, *Forty Years in the Wilderness: Impressions of Nevada, 1940–1980* (Reno: University of Nevada Press, 1986).

Chapter 17

A SOCIAL AND CULTURAL APPRAISAL

For a 1920s appraisal of Nevada see Anne Martin, "Nevada: Beautiful Desert of Buried Hopes," *The Nation* 115 (July 26, 1922): 89–92. See also William R. Eadington, Glendell W. Atkinson, and James H. Frey, *Observations on the Quality of Life in Nevada: A Comparison of Recent Ranking Studies as They Relate to Nevada and Its Metropolitan Areas* (Reno: University of Nevada, 1984). For additional information on education in Nevada see *Chronicle of Higher Education,* October 30, 1985, and *Nevada Statistical Abstract, 1983–1984* (Carson City, Nev.: Governor's Office of Community Service, 1984). The story of Nevada newspapers is brought up to date in Richard E. Lingenfelter and Karen Rix Gash, *The Newspapers of Nevada: A History and Bibliography, 1854–1979* (Reno: University of Nevada Press, 1984).

In the past decade a number of works have been published on religious groups in Nevada. See, for example, Leonard Arrington, *Brigham Young: American Moses* (New York: Knopf, 1985). Juanita Brooks, *Quicksand and Cactus: A Memoir of the Southern Mormon Frontier* (Salt Lake City: Howe Brothers, 1982), is a very readable story about Mormon society in the Bunkerville area of southern Nevada. Robert Gottlieb and Peter Wiley, *America's Saints: The Rise of Mormon Power* (New York: G. P. Putnam's Sons, 1982), contains interesting material about the Mormons in southern Nevada. See also John P. Marschall, "Jews in Nevada: 1850–1900," *Journal of the West* 23 (January 1984): 62–72, and James S. Olson, "Pioneer Catholicism in Eastern and Southern Nevada, 1864–1931," *Nevada Historical Society Quarterly* 26 (Fall 1983): 159–71.

A recent biography that deals briefly with the work of the Fleischmann Foundation in funding the Nevada State Museum and building and funding a number of county libraries in Nevada is Sessions Wheeler, *Gentleman in the Outdoors: A Portrait of Max C. Fleischmann* (Reno: University of Nevada Press, 1985). A new interest in the arts and humanities in Nevada is evident in the following publications. *Arts Alive,* published by the Allied Arts Council in Las Vegas is a rather sophisticated little magazine that not only acts as a calendar of events for artistic programs and events for southern Nevada but also, from time to time, focuses on specific art forms, such as the dance. *Encore,* a Sierra Arts Foundation publication in Reno, performs much the same function for northern Nevada. *Halcyon: A Journal of the Humanities* is published annually by the Nevada Humanities Committee, Reno, Nevada, edited by Wilbur S. Shepperson. This excellent periodical, which began in 1979, acts as a visible record of humanistic activity in the state. Its issues attest to its success in stimulating "thoughtful research and commentary in the humanistic disciplines." The most important work on higher education in Nevada published during these years is James W. Hulse, *The University of Nevada: A Centennial History* (Reno: University of Nevada Press, 1974).

A valuable appraisal of Nevada's most important author appears in Charlton Laird, *Walter Van Tilburg Clark: Critiques* (Reno: University of Nevada Press, 1984). The works of two other Nevada authors published in the 1970s and 1980s should be mentioned: first, two books by Anthony Amaral, *Mustang: Life and Legends of Nevada's Wild Horses* (Reno: University of Nevada Press, 1977), and *Will James: The Last Cowboy Legend* (Reno: University of Nevada Press, 1980). Two works by Owen Ulph defy easy description: *The Fiddleback: Lore of the Line Camp* (Salt Lake City: Dream Garden Press, 1981), and *The Leather Throne: A Novel Account* (Salt Lake City: Dream Garden Press, 1984). Both works reflect Ulph's attempt to rescue the cowboy from admirers and detractors alike.

A number of works on minorities in Nevada should be mentioned: Michael S. Coray, "'Democracy' on the Frontier: A Case Study of Nevada Editorial Attitudes on the Issue of Nonwhite Equality," *Nevada Historical Society Quarterly* 21 (Fall 1978): 189–204; Roosevelt Fitzgerald, "Blacks and the Boulder Dam Project," *Nevada Historical Society Quarterly* 24 (Fall 1981): 255–61; Elmer Rusco, *"Good Times Coming?": Black Nevadans in the Nineteenth Century* (Westport, Conn.: Greenwood Press, 1975); Adam S. Eterovich, *Yugoslavs in Nevada, 1859–1900* (San Francisco: R. and E. Research Associates, 1973); William A. Douglass and Jon Bilbao, *Amerikanuak: Basques in the New World* (Reno: University of Nevada Press, 1975); and William Douglass, ed., *Beltran: Basque Sheepman of the American West* (Reno: University of Nevada Press, 1979). Gae Whitney Canfield, *Sarah Winnemucca of the Northern Paiutes* (Norman: University of Oklahoma Press, 1983), is the best biography of Sarah to date. Katherine Gehm, *Sarah Winnemucca: Most Extraordinary Woman of the Paiute Nation* (Phoenix: O'Sullivan Woodside & Co., 1975), is a popularized account. See also Nellie Shaw Harner, *Indians of Coo-Yu-Ee-Pah: The History of the Pyramid Lake Indians and Early Tribal History, 1825–1834* (Sparks, Nev.: Dave's Printing and Publishing, 1974); and Edward C. Johnson, *Walker River Paiutes: A Tribal History* (Salt Lake City: University of Utah Printing Service, 1975). Mary K. Rusco, "Chinese in Lovelock, Nevada: History and Archaeology," *Halcyon* (1981): 141–52, is an interesting study of an ethnic minority in a white farming community as revealed from an interdisciplinary archaeological and historical research project. See also, Eugene M. Hattori, Mary K. Rusco, and Donald Tuohy, *Archaelogical and Historical Studies at Ninth and Amherst, Lovelock, Nevada* (Carson City, Nev.: Nevada State Museum, 1979), and Gregg Lee Carter, "Social Demography of the Chinese in Nevada," *Nevada Historical Society Quarterly* 18 (Summer 1975): 73–90. Very little has been published to date on Nevada's largest minority, the Hispanic Americans. See, however, Robert Rivas, "Report: The Condition of Education for Hispanic Americans in the Clark County School District" (Las Vegas: Hispanic Committee for Quality Education, August 5, 1982).

Index

Index